Event Studies

Event Studies is the only book devoted to developing knowledge and theory about planned events. It focuses on event planning and management, outcomes, the experience of events and the meanings attached to them, the dynamic processes shaping events and why people attend them.

This title draws from a large number of foundation disciplines and closely related professional fields, to foster interdisciplinary theory focused on planned events. It brings together important discourses on events including event management, event tourism and the study of events within various disciplines that are able to shed light on the roles, importance and impacts of events in society and culture.

New to this edition:

- New sections on social and intangible influences, consumer psychology and legal environment, planning and policy framework to reflect recent developments in the field.
- Extended coverage of philosophy and research methods and how they can best be used in event studies, social media as a marketing tool and the class and cultural influences of events.
- New and additional research notes, expert opinions and examples throughout the book from a wide range of international events and scholars.
- An updated companion website to include PowerPoint slides and an updated Instructor's Manual including suggested lecture outlines and sequence, quizzes per chapter and essay questions.

Donald Getz is Professor Emeritus, the University of Calgary. He works as a management consultant and also holds guest positions at several universities. In addition to event studies, areas of expertise include wine and food tourism, evaluation and impact assessment, consumer research and special-interest travel. Professor Getz co-founded and was Editor-in-Chief of *Event Management: An International Journal*.

Stephen J. Page is Professor and Deputy Dean (Research and Professional Practice) in the Faculty of Management, Bournemouth University. He holds an Honorary Doctorate from the University of West London and is an Honorary Professor at Cardiff Metropolitan University. He has worked as a tourism consultant with different organizations, including the United Nations World Tourism Organization, VisitScotland, Scottish Enterprise, Highlands and Islands Enterprise, Harrah's Casinos and Sky Tower, Auckland, New Zealand among many other clients. He is the author and editor of 39 books on tourism, leisure and events and is Reviews Editor of the leading tourism journal, *Tourism Management*.

Books in the Events Management Series
Edited by Glenn Bowdin, Leeds Metropolitan University, UK
Don Getz, University of Calgary, Canada
Conrad Lashley, Nottingham Trent University, UK

Event Studies

Theory, research and policy for planned events

Third edition

Donald Getz and Stephen J. Page

Routledge
Taylor & Francis Group

LONDON AND NEW YORK

Third edition published 2016
by Routledge
2 Park Square, Milton Park, Abingdon, Oxon OX14 4RN

and by Routledge
711 Third Avenue, New York, NY 10017

Routledge is an imprint of the Taylor & Francis Group, an informa business

First edition published by Butterworth-Heinemann 2007
Second edition published by Routledge 2012

British Library Cataloguing in Publication Data
A catalogue record for this book is available from the British Library

Library of Congress Cataloging in Publication Data
A catalog record for this book has been requested

ISBN: 978-1-138-89916-2 (hbk)
ISBN: 978-1-138-89915-5 (pbk)
ISBN: 978-1-315-70802-7 (ebk)

Typeset in Iowan Old Style
by Sunrise Setting Ltd, Paignton, UK
Printed in Great Britain by Ashford Colour Press Ltd.

Contents

Plates

Figures

Tables

Events in focus

Research notes

Expert opinions

Series preface

The events industry, including festivals, meetings, conferences, exhibitions, incentives, sports and a range of other events, is rapidly developing and makes a significant contribution to business and leisure-related tourism. With increased regulation and the growth of government and corporate involvement in events, the environment has become much more complex. Event managers are now required to identify and service a wide range of stakeholders and to balance their needs and objectives. Though mainly operating at national levels, there has been a significant growth of academic provision to meet the needs of events and related industries and the organizations that comprise them. The English-speaking nations, together with key Northern European countries, have developed programmes of study leading to the award of diploma, undergraduate and postgraduate awards. These courses focus on providing education and training for future event professionals, and cover areas such as event planning and management, marketing, finance, human resource management and operations. Modules in events management are also included in many tourism, leisure, recreation and hospitality qualifications in universities and colleges.

The rapid growth of such courses has meant that there is a vast gap in the available literature on this topic for lecturers, students and professionals alike. To this end, the *Routledge Events Management Series* has been created to meet these needs and to create a planned and targeted set of publications in this area.

Aimed at academic and management development in events management and related studies, the *Events Management Series*:

- provides a portfolio of titles which match management development needs through various stages;
- prioritizes publication of texts where there are current gaps in the market, or where current provision is unsatisfactory;
- develops a portfolio of both practical and stimulating texts;
- provides a basis for theory and research underpinning programmes of study;
- is recognized as being of consistent high quality; and
- will quickly become the series of first choice for both authors and users.

Preface to the third edition

Edition three of *Event Studies* brings Professor Stephen J. Page to the book, as co-author.

Stephen J. Page is well known for his contributions to tourism and event studies, in particular as co-editor of the *Routledge Handbook of Events*.

While all the fundamentals of the book remain the same, periodic updates are desirable for several reasons. First, the literature on planned events keeps expanding at a rapid pace, particularly with the publication of many new special-topic books and journal articles as the new synthesis by Getz and Page (2015) documents for event tourism. These add new insights and expand our thinking about event studies. Second, the world keeps changing. Some new trends are emerging, and others identified in the past have become mainstream. Finally, each new edition provides the opportunity for authors to expand on certain topics of great interest and especially to take advantage of research we have undertaken. We hope that readers benefit from the changes made, and in particular direct your attention to the following:

- new and enhanced research notes that add breadth to the originals
- new and revised expert opinions
- new photos
- new figures
- references to many new articles and books to provide a much greater synthesis and roadmap of the literature on events
- an expanded discussion of curriculum and pedagogy for event studies, event management and event tourism
- expansion of the ontological and theoretical discussion related to events.

Acknowledgements

The following have made a direct contribution to this third edition and we are especially thankful for their help. Their affiliations are in the pertinent Expert Opinion sections: Steve Brown, Matt Frew, Joe Jeff Goldblatt, Phil Long, William O'Toole, Ian Patterson, Martin Robertson and Ully Wuensch.

We would also like to thank Emma Travis and Pippa Mullins at Routledge and Stephen would like to thank Jo, Rosie and Toby Page for keeping him entertained whilst writing.

A number of organizations and bodies have provided the authors with permission to reproduce material in the book and we wish to express our thanks to them. Figure 1.6 has been reproduced from Page and Connell's *Visitor Attractions and Events: Responding to Seasonality* (2015) and Figure 10.1 from Tommy D. Andersson, Erik Lundberg's *Commensurability and sustainability: Triple impact assessments of a tourism event* (2013) both published in the journal *Tourism Management*, with the kind permission of Elsevier; Figure 2.2 from Page and Connell's *Leisure: An Introduction* (2010), with the kind permission of Pearson Education Ltd.; Figure 6.8 from *A Modern History of International Meetings 1963–2012* (2013), with the kind permission of ICCA; Figure 6.9 from A. Coughlan's *Tourism and health: using positive psychology principles to maximise participants' wellbeing outcomes* (2015) published in *The Journal of Sustainable Tourism* and Figure 8.5 from Jackson, Crawford and Godbey's *Negotiation of Leisure Constraints* (1993) published in the journal *Leisure Sciences*, both with the permission of Taylor and Francis; Figure 9.3 from Getz, D., Andersson, T., and Larson, M.'s *Festival stakeholder roles: Concepts and case studies* (2007) published in the *Event Management* journal, with the permission of Cognizant Communication Corporation; Figures 3.2 and 6.1 from Page's *Tourism Management* 5th Edition (2015), Figures 3.3, 4.1, 6.4 and Table 6.2 from Page and Connell's *Routledge Handbook of Events* (2014), Figure 5.2 from Pigram and Jenkin's *Outdoor Recreation Management* (1983), Figures 5.3 and 12.2 from Hall and Page's *Geography of Tourism and Recreation* (2014), all with the permission of Routledge.

Chapter **1**

Introduction and overview of event studies

LEARNING OBJECTIVES

Upon completion of this chapter students should know the following:

- the definition and characteristics of event studies as an academic field, and specifically its core phenomenon and major themes or components;
- why students and academics study planned events;
- different perspectives on the study of planned events – foundation disciplines and closely related professional fields;
- three major subdivisions (or discourses) within event studies: the discipline-based or classical, event tourism and events management;
- emerging interdisciplinary theories of planned events;
- major forces shaping planned events, and important trends and issues.

What is event studies?

Event studies is the academic field devoted to creating knowledge and theory about planned events; the scope of events spans individual celebrations and community festivals, sports, business meetings and exhibitions; it also includes mega events, which have largely become the realm of professionals, corporations and entrepreneurs. Within the study of events, an academic field of knowledge requires a unique core phenomenon as the principal focus for academic inquiry. It is the study of all planned events that is the main focus of this book within the field that is known broadly as 'event studies'. As a recent area of growth, event studies encompasses the planning and management, outcomes, experience of events and meanings attached to them, and all the dynamic processes shaping events and the reasons why people attend them.

Event studies draws from a large number of foundation disciplines and closely related professional fields, and the interconnections between these areas of study should foster interdisciplinary theory focused on planned events to better understand why they exist, and how we can manage them better to derive positive outcomes as well as minimizing undesirable and unforeseen consequences of hosting planned events. As a relatively new field of study, event studies brings an exciting and unique set of perspectives to bear on three important discourses on events, including event management, event tourism and the 'classical' study of events within various disciplines that consider the roles, importance and impacts of events in society and culture.

Event studies as a field of study is defined by its holistic approach towards events as a phenomenon, including all the issues surrounding planned events, in addition to their management, design and production. In this respect, event studies can exist without event management, and in fact it already does. When an economics researcher or sociologist examines the impacts of an event, regardless of any interest in its planning or production, that is one approach to event studies. When a newspaper writes about the pros and cons of bidding for an event in its particular community, that too is an element of event studies. In short, events have policy implications that cannot be ignored, and they are not the sole domain of event producers and managers. This begins to illustrate why the study of planned events is both a fascinating and essential feature of many post-modern societies with the growth in consumption of events by people as part of everyday leisure time as participants, as spectators and as consumers of fun and entertainment (Page and Connell 2010). So, why should we study events?

Why study planned events?

Many readers of this book will be students interested in a professional or business career related to planned events. The careers potential and entrepreneurship opportunities associated with planned events have grown dramatically, in tune with general trends in the experience economy (see Events in Focus 1.1 for a discussion of the experience economy).

EVENTS IN FOCUS

1.1 The experience economy and events

Pine and Gilmore's (1999) *The Experience Economy* makes an interesting contribution to the study of events because it argues that the experience economy is the next stage in the evolution of society from a service economy. The initial work by Pine and Gilmore suggested that businesses need to create experiences that are memorable, given the increased levels of education of many consumers and their pursuit of value-added elements within the experience they purchase. The essence of the Pine and Gilmore (1999) study was that the production of experiences, such as those which are associated with events, will need to focus on a number of aspects of consumption, including:

- the need to create a sensation
- the need to personalize the experience; to develop trust and a bond with the consumer which has been embodied in the use of brands.

The experience economy concept suggests that we need to focus on four areas of experience:

- entertainment
- education

- aesthetic (i.e. an ability to immerse oneself in something)
- escapism in what is consumed.

Consequently, events will need to be designed to allow participants and audiences to engage in discrete ways ranging from absorption through to immersion. Such experiences need to be able to accommodate different modes of participation, from passive through to very active forms of involvement. They also need to engage all of our senses (i.e. hearing, sight, touch, smell and taste).

Source: Adapted and developed from Page and Connell (2010).

In addition, many professionals entering public service, or the not-for-profit sector, will encounter events and related issues at some point; they need to know how to relate to events as businesses or as policy instruments.

There are more general, educational reasons for studying planned events. Within the 'experience economy', planned events are a very important and expanding social and cultural phenomenon, which is of considerable interest to students and practitioners in many fields. Events reflect changes in popular culture and continue to make high culture accessible. Whatever one's cultural interests, from entertainment to opera, planned events are an enduring delivery vehicle.

The diversity of perspectives being adopted on planned events is amazing, and the literature continues to grow and expand accordingly. The numerous citations in this book show just how important events have become to all kinds of professions and policy-makers, having grown exponentially in line with the rapid growth in the subject as a field of study since the 1990s. However, as this book will demonstrate, the study of events has a long and rich tradition within many disciplines, especially within the social sciences where many of the underpinning concepts and approaches we examine can be traced back to the early twentieth century. Therefore, this book provides a major contribution to our understanding of event studies on two dimensions:

- *horizontally* by looking at the depth and richness of its study within specific areas and disciplines
- *vertically* by embracing the scope and breadth of the subjects and topics now being studied within event studies, within disciplines and subject areas.

Education for planned events

In the first edition, a pyramid-shaped model with event studies at the top, resting on a foundation of event management degree and diploma programmes was developed, which in turn existed primarily because of the large 'industry' and career opportunities in the events sector. The principal argument was that event studies would not exist without this foundation, and that it mostly relied on teachers and researchers within the event management field. This is no longer the case, as there are now instructors teaching event studies using this book in the first year of event programmes, reflecting the maturing of the subject. The study of events can also occur outside event management and tourism-related programmes, as outlined by Barron and Leask (2012), and in due course it will become an accepted interdisciplinary field. Accordingly a new education model is presented here, building on the current thinking around the issues highlighted by Barron and Leask (2012). In this framework (see Figure 1.1), event studies is all-encompassing and interdisciplinary, while the other discourses or fields are applied in nature. It is not necessarily linked to, nor dependent upon, the closely related applied fields, but in practice is closely associated with them through educational programmes where the researchers are situated.

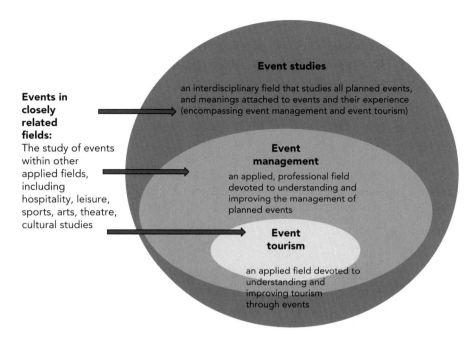

Figure 1.1 Event studies, event management and event tourism

There is an ongoing debate within many vocationally oriented subjects that the focus of study does not necessarily mean it is a distinct discipline. These types of debates have affected many subjects that have grown from the 1960s such as marketing, which has a number of founding disciplines that contribute to its study (e.g. psychology and sociology). Similar debates have been reiterated in more recent times around the growth of areas like tourism, which have a great deal of synergy with the subsequent growth of event studies.

John Tribe (2004, 2006) argued that tourism is not a discipline, but a field of study drawing on a number of disciplines. The same can be said of event studies: the things that are to be studied about events require theories and methodologies from a number of disciplines. And just like tourism, the preoccupation so far has been with event management or business studies, rather than all the other perspectives which can be taken on tourism or events.

Accepting that event studies will be a 'social and political construct' (Tribe 2004: 47), it is reasonable to conclude that one's perspective on, or object of interest in, events will determine which disciplines are drawn upon. An interest in the impacts of mega events on housing, for example, could draw upon sociology, urban planning and political science. An interest in the nature of festival sustainability will use management theory, social psychology and other sources that contribute understanding. To create event-related knowledge, the contributions of theory and methodologies from multiple disciplines are required. Where a number of disciplines are drawn upon, we can say that the new field of study is multi-disciplinary in nature. With time, the interactions might establish a field of knowledge with its own theories and methodologies, and this can be said to be interdisciplinary in nature. That should be the goal. Ultimately, if the field builds a strong body of knowledge with its own theories and approaches to the study of knowledge, it may also grow into a distinct subject area that could be deemed a discipline such as marketing has in more recent years, although this remains hotly debated.

Tribe (2002) tackled the subject of what a higher-level curriculum for tourism should embody and this has relevance to the study of events. Tribe (2002: 338) argues that most tourism studies are vocational and business oriented (just as event management is), but there is a need to produce 'philosophic practitioners' who can deliver 'efficient and effective services while at the same time discharging the role of stewardship for the development of the wider tourism world in which these services are delivered'. Stewardship, in this context, can mean sustainable development.

In a recent book entitled *The Routledge Handbook of Tourism and Hospitality Education* (2014), Tribe re-examined the notion of philosophical practitioners, while Dredge *et al.* (2014) provided some perspectives on what curriculum for tourism, hospitality and events should provide at the core. Tribe (2014: 17–29) referred to the thoughts of Barnett (1990: 202–203) who advocated six basic requirements for any advanced education, each of these being important to students, and they are incorporated in various ways into this book (our thoughts related to this book are parenthesized for each point):

1. a deep understanding of some knowledge claims (this brings ontology into the picture, that is, what we collectively claim to know about planned events);

2. a radical critique of knowledge claims (do not take all claims as given, but challenge them);

3. competence to develop critique in the company of others (being able to engage in various discourses, such as that concerning the meaning and importance of events);

4. self-direction and independent inquiry (knowing where you want to go and how to get there with regard to learning and professionalism; develop lifelong learning capability);

5. self-reflection (intellectuals and professionals always think carefully about what they are doing, why they are doing it, and potential outcomes; do we have enough information or theory? what can we learn from evaluation?)

6. open dialogue and cooperation (being part of a free, professional community and a responsible citizen).

In considering the sometimes divergent directions taken by liberal education versus vocational training in these largely applied fields, Dredge *et al.* (2014) argued that each teaching institution engages in a dynamic process of curriculum design that results in differences, including the potential for innovation. Those teaching event studies or applied event tourism/management should not only combine some elements of training with more theoretical and philosophical subjects, but also develop the student's capability for life-long learning. Starting with some basic skills and simple concepts, educational programmes can add more complex knowledge and expert practices as appropriate and for competitive advantage.

The professional event manager or event-tourism planner has to have more than skills. Professionals must have a broad base of knowledge, together with the ability to reflect upon how it will shape both specific managerial or business decisions and the wider implications of events in society and the environment. They also have to posses a well-developed sense of ethics and professional responsibility, which should be based on a solid foundation that includes philosophy and comparative cultural studies.

However, there are fundamental differences between the paths that tourism studies and event studies have trodden in establishing themselves as fields of study. The growth of tourism education can be traced back as far as the 1930s, and its major boom was in the 1980s. Event studies, in contrast, has had a more recent and compressed, even meteoric growth, and some of the drivers of that growth are shown in Figure 1.2. As Getz (2014) argued, there are two distinct and potentially complementary approaches to events education:

- an interdisciplinary approach, which is based upon the theoretical and intellectual basis of higher education, with a philosophical approach underpinned by traditional disciplines and new subject areas;

- the professional bodies approach, which is based on competencies and skills, with factual knowledge and problem-solving at the heart of the curriculum.

Drivers
1. Industry demand
2. Student demand
3. Professionalizing the field by industry bodies
4. Commericialization of events globally
5. Increased use of events as a means of place development, sponsorship and branding
6. Global growth in events as a form of consumption by visitors and residents
7. Increasing instrumentalism of events whereby they are considered appropriate means for realizing many public-sector and private goals

Figure 1.2 Key drivers of the growth in event education

What this shows is a more refined and industry-focused growth in event education, and to a lesser degree research has characterized this expansion to meet the rising demand for events professionals. The industry bodies' ultimate objective was to professionalize a field of study in much the same way as nurse education in many countries, which shifted from colleges to universities. In the case of event studies, the subject arose from many of the collaborations of stakeholders (professional bodies, employers, public-sector agencies and universities and higher education institutions) to capitalize on the main drivers of growth outlined in Figure 1.2. These drivers range from more macro and global processes around place branding and using planned events to reposition destinations, through to more micro and localized demands for a professional workforce to service the demand for planned events along with meetings, conventions and other events (often called MICE). This has been a second phase of growth for many countries that had expanded their tourism economies and then regarded planned events as the next natural stage of development in the 1980s and 1990s, to expand their economies around the concept of the growing experience economy as a dimension of increased consumer demand for entertainment and leisure experiences.

These trends have certainly meant that there is and will continue to be a growing need for planners and policy analysts who must deal with complex issues related to events from many different perspectives (e.g. social, cultural, economic, environmental), for whom event studies provides a necessary foundation. Linked to this will be a rising need for higher education and life-long learning in the profession of event management (i.e. continuing professional development), and educators must ask that anyone with a higher degree, or a professional with advanced standing, should be well versed in theories and methods of this dynamic and fast-changing area. They will be the mentors of the next generation of professionals, and we always expect more of the next generation.

According to Leiper (1981, 1990), if we are to adopt a multidisciplinary approach, it involves studying a topic (for us, planned events) by including information from other disciplines, whereas an interdisciplinary approach blends various philosophies and techniques to create a synthesis. This has to be an ideal, future development. For now, we are drawing on many disciplines and fields and attempting to lay the foundation for the growth of event studies as it is still at a pivotal stage of development across a much wider range of subject areas than tourism has embraced. It should also be stressed that some researchers are already applying interdisciplinary approaches to the study of planned events, and this book should facilitate that approach by demonstrating core themes that require new concepts and methods.

Echtner and Jamal (1997: 879) also supported this developmental approach, arguing that there needs to be 'liberalism with regard to methodological approach and, concurrently, greater attention to clearly explicated theory and methodology'. Event studies should therefore embody 'holistic, integrated research; the generation of a theoretical body of knowledge; an interdisciplinary focus; clearly explicated theory and methodology; and the application of qualitative and quantitative methods, positivist and non-positivist traditions'. This raises the question: are we entering a stage of development where eventology exists?

Eventology

In the English language, 'ology' added to a noun indicates 'the study or science of', so 'eventology' would mean (and you will not find it in the dictionary) the study or science of events. It's an awkward term (imagine 'festivalology' or 'meetingsology' and you get the point), and those in established disciplines like biology do not like newcomers, especially in fields of applied study, taking on the veneer of pure science.

However, Professor Joe Goldblatt (2011) uses the term in a specific way, related to his model of how events foster cultural progression through innovation, and this is a very useful conceptualization. Goldblatt (2011: xii) argued that: 'Eventology is the study of planned events to promote positive societal benefits.' Bringing together people through planned events is said to make societies healthier, smarter, wealthier and fairer, greener, safer and stronger. These can be considered a worthwhile (or normative) agenda, with events as instruments of policy. Professor Goldblatt's expert opinion, later in this chapter, also introduces a mathematical notion of eventology as a subset of probability theory, and this idea has only recently been introduced to planned events.

The challenge of science is to establish cause and effect. Consider this problem when we examine the desirability of developing a philosophical approach to 'event services', again under the heading of epistemology and ontology, and finally when we look at outcomes and impact assessment.

A framework for understanding and creating knowledge about planned events

The core phenomenon

What defines a field of study is the 'core phenomenon' – phenomenon means a state or process known through the senses, in other words something that can be 'experienced'. We are studying a universal phenomenon that has importance around the world, in every culture and society. Incidentally, the alternative, more popular definition of 'phenomenon' is that of a 'remarkable occurrence', which can be a synonym for 'special event'!

A three-part core is depicted in Figure 1.3, consisting of:

1. the study of all planned events, and no other discipline or field attempts to do that;
2. the experience of events (by all the stakeholders, even the public at large);
3. meanings attached to events (for example, as institutions or entertainment) and to the experience of events.

This definition of the core of event studies broadens the field considerably, and imposes a substantial theoretical and philosophical component.

What do all planned events have in common that justifies their own field of study? They have the following characteristics:

- *timelessness*: events are inherent in all societies and integral to civilization itself;
- *global importance* in terms of public policy, industry and corporate strategy;

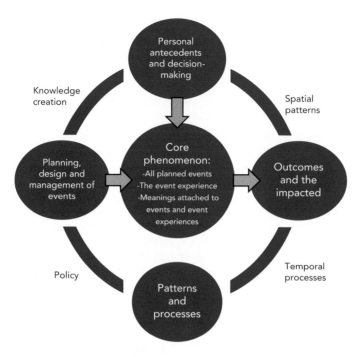

Figure 1.3 A framework for understanding and creating knowledge about planned events

- recent and rapidly *expanding professional practice* of event management and also event tourism and event policy careers; business opportunities abound;
- recognition that events are *fundamental to the experience economy*, indeed are essential to the evolving nature of leisure and culture;
- a high level of *student demand*, leading to a proliferation of event management programmes globally, many with specializations, which in turn fosters further academic research and publication to advance knowledge in the field.

The essence of the planned event is that of *an experience that has been designed* (or at least the experience is facilitated), which would not otherwise occur. There are many styles of planned events, produced for many purposes, but in every case there is intent to create, or at least shape, the individual and collective experiences of the audience or participants. New forms are always being created, and this in itself is of considerable interest.

Multiple perspectives on experiences and meaning have to be included in designing events. Obviously there are paying customers or invited guests at planned events, but we also need to recognize the organizers including staff, sponsors and other facilitators (providing resources and support), regulators (e.g. city officials), co-producers, participants (as in athletics events), exhibitors and suppliers. A further dimension is the pivotal role of volunteers, as numerous events cannot exist without them. Consequently this raises a number of fundamental questions around the experience and meaning of events:

- What motivates all these stakeholders and what different experiences do they have?
- How do all these stakeholders react to the designed experience or at least to the setting and programme of events?

To address these questions, we need to examine a number of key concepts around the experience and meaning of events associated with the study of semiotics and meaning.

Semiotics and the meaning of 'meanings'

A key proposition we need to start with in the discussion of the meaning of events is – *do all events and event experiences have hidden or profound meanings?* Not necessarily, because an experience can be purely hedonistic, which means it gives pleasure without significance or symbolic meaning. In fact, many people would describe such experiences as 'fun' or 'diversions'. Conversely, many experiences, and therefore events as facilitators and packagers of experiences, are *significant* in social, cultural, economic and environmental terms because they generate impacts that are either valued and desired, or are negative and unwanted. Event experiences may also have *symbolic meaning* for participants, host communities and entire nations. To assist in understanding these issues in more depth, we can turn to the field of linguistics and the concept of semiotics.

Semiotics is the study of signs and symbols, and therefore of how meaning is conveyed and interpreted. The symbols can be language, icons (that is, symbols like a logo or brand) or objects, including people. Meaning can also be conveyed through actions, and institutions also hold meanings. The very idea of 'leisure' holds meanings for individuals and groups that are in part socially and culturally determined (Page and Connell 2010). To some, leisure has negative connotations and is to be avoided, and to others it is their reason for being. Therefore, understanding events as part of societal attitudes towards leisure and entertainment, fun and hedonism, is only a partial understanding. Wider studies of the social psychology of events as a leisure experience or business phenomenon are required in order to fully appreciate the individualized nature of meaning and what events convey to individuals and groups (i.e. families and kinship groups and friends). An important step is to consider the symbolic meanings associated with events.

Symbolic meaning refers to *mediated* experiences where an object, sign, word or action means something else, or conveys ideas and feelings beyond itself (Levy 1959). For example, the event is not merely interpreted as entertainment, but it is understood by some or all of the audience that it may be an expression of nationalism, or community identity. Within the study of symbolic meaning, we also need to be cognizant of the growing importance of how marketing has utilized these mediated experiences to communicate the value of an experience using the notion of branding. Marketing is defined as: 'a social and managerial process by which individuals and groups obtain what they need through creating and exchanging products and value with others' (Kotler *et al.* 1999: 12). To help simplify and create recognizable signs and symbols, marketing as a profession uses the concept of branding which is about communicating with intended customers using a name, logo, symbol or word to simplify and create awareness or to attract an audience and a perception of quality or value in the intended experience or event.

Therefore, in an event setting, how symbols are used will affect how they are perceived and interpreted. Sometimes organizers will be completely unaware of symbolic meanings attached to their events and actions. But some events deliberately seek to convey meaning, which is the essence of theming. Cities and destinations use events to convey positive images and meanings, so the event itself becomes a symbol and branding is applied to create the value or quality message. This is the essence of hallmark events. Sponsors at events believe that the goodwill generated by the event will attach itself to their brands, and the brand itself is a symbol of quality or value. To illustrate these principles in action, a study by Wooten and Norman (2008a) reported that visitors to a coastal shrimp festival placed more importance on the coastal location (the event setting) than the shrimp (the theme or 'object' of the event) when explaining their satisfaction. People attending or participating in an event can attach their own meanings to the experiences, regardless of what others want them to experience. The Research Note 1.1, concerning meanings, illustrates a variety of applications and methods.

> **1.1 RESEARCH NOTES ON MEANINGS**
>
> 1. Crespi-Vallbona, M. and Richards, G. (2007). The meaning of cultural festivals: Stakeholder perspectives in Catalunya. *International Journal of Cultural Policy*, 13(1): 103–122.
>
>   Traditional and popular culture events in Catalunya, Spain, were examined as to the aims of various stakeholders in the events. Researchers found there was generally a high level of agreement regarding the importance of cultural events in underpinning Catalan identity; however, stakeholders differed in the meanings they attached to identity. Policy-makers placed greater emphasis on economic and political issues, whereas cultural producers were more concerned with social aspects of identity.
>
> 2. Wooten, M. and Norman, W. (2008). Interpreting and managing special events and festivals. In A. Woodside and D. Martin (eds), *Managing Tourism: Analysis, Behaviour and Strategy*, pp. 197–217. Wallingford: CABI.
>
>   Objects and settings at the Kentucky Arts Festival (Kentucky, USA) were examined for their symbolic meaning, to determine if the audience experiences matched what organizers claimed was unique about the event. Results demonstrated a fair degree of congruence, but not on all measures. In other words, the audience might not be getting the full symbolic meaning of the festival that the organizers intended.
>
> 3. Kaplanidou, K. and Vogt, C. (2010). The meaning and measurement of a sport event experience among active sport tourists. *Journal of Sport Management*, 24(5): 544–566.
>
>   Researchers aimed to understand how active sport tourists perceive the meaning of a sport event experience, and to develop a scale for that meaning. Results from focus groups suggested that participants attribute meanings related to organizational, environmental, physical, social and emotional aspects of the experience.

Event studies is also concerned about how meanings are attached to planned events by individuals, groups and society. For example, is the event perceived to be a shared cultural experience or personally self-fulfilling? And we also have to examine meanings from different perspectives. Each stakeholder in the process wants, expects and receives potentially different experiences and attaches potentially different meanings to the event. Do they receive the experiences that were planned for them?

Theory on experience and meanings

In social science, which is where event studies are largely located, as we shall show in later chapters, the subject areas seek to develop our knowledge and understanding by building theories which are broadly defined as propositions derived from empirical observations. The resulting theories help us to explain the complexity of the real world and to help guide further research activity. Although there are many debates within social science over what theory is, how you develop it and its purpose, in event studies the interdisciplinary development of the subject means that theories from cognate areas are often used and adapted to the event context to explain how event phenomena occur and develop. In the context of events as experiences, this means we tend to borrow and rely upon theory that has been developed in social psychology and leisure studies so as to begin to understand what event experiences are and how they are constructed.

Therefore a useful starting point in seeking to understand event experiences, and meanings attached to them, is through the use of 'personal and social constructs' (Kelly 1955) based on the study of psychology. The basic argument from Kelly's work is that personal constructs enable an individual to develop an understanding of their own psychology by the constructs they use. These constructs are created by an individual's experiences and their own ideas about reality, based on observations of the real world. For example, when people attend concerts their expectation is to be entertained, and probably also to have fun with like-minded fans in a dynamic social setting. Going to a conference requires that we think in terms of having a learning experience. We are supposed to be happy when we go to festivals, and sad when we attend funerals.

Consumption of all kinds is the social norm, leading to enormous expenditure on entertainment events. So we need theory on both personal antecedents to attending events (including needs, motives, preferences, constraints) and the social constructs that give events broader meanings and importance within societies and cultures.

To a degree, expectations are shaped purposefully by advertising, branding and the media. 'Event experiences' are the hot topic in branding and marketing, so corporations know how to create the experiences necessary to foster positive brand attitudes and increased consumption. This leads us into the world of the psychology of branding (e.g. Evans 2013) and its use to shape expectations and the desire to consume. However, we also need to be aware of whether some event experiences are exploitive and deceiving. Even where the event experience is created by not-for-profits or government agencies, there is the possibility that the meanings we are to attach to the experience are part of some propaganda or social marketing scheme and several Olympic Games have been accused of such behaviour, none more explicitly than the 1936 Games hosted in Nazi Germany.

To help develop our understanding of event studies and the role of events as experiences, the book is structured thus: Chapter 2 introduces each form of event and talks about the experiences associated with them. Pertinent theory is introduced in the discussion of foundation disciplines and closely related professional fields in Chapters 3–5. Chapter 6 applies and develops theory pertaining to event experiences and meanings, specifically the theory of liminality, drawing from anthropology and the study of rituals. The planned event experience is then modelled as a particular kind of liminal/liminoid zone – a special space and time, a different realm of existence, that has to be symbolically or ritualistically marked for its special purposes. In this liminal/liminoid zone, event-goers are aware of the contrasts with everyday life, and this is an important part of the experience. The concepts of 'flow' and 'peak experiences', drawing from social psychology and leisure studies, which describe how some people feel and act when 'in the zone' – how they get totally involved and lose track of time – are also introduced.

To understand event experiences we also need to look at communication, learning and interpretation theory (i.e. how do we motivate attendance, shape expectations and create the best learning environments?). Theories on 'serious leisure', 'ego involvement' and 'commitment' help us understand event motives, experiences and meanings for those participants who seek out specific event opportunities and the personal benefits they provide.

Chapter 7 examines event design, commencing with a discussion of the meaning of design as both a creative and technical problem-solving process, its theoretical foundations and how design is applied to planned events. The theme, programme, setting, services and consumables are all subjects of design. One major conclusion we wish to stress is that *every event experience will be unique to the individual*, because experiences are internal psychological states. We also interpret our experiences from different frames of reference. Related to that conclusion is the assertion that event planning and design cannot create experiences, but only suggest, facilitate or constrain them. The ability to influence the event, audience demand, is conditioned by antecedents and decision-making by consumers.

Antecedents and decision-making

'Antecedents' include all those factors shaping individual and collective needs or demands for events, and how choices and decisions are made. Theory from a variety of disciplines is useful, particularly from marketing and psychology, and in turn that theory has been adapted by consumer behaviour researchers in leisure and tourism studies (Hall and Page 2014; Page and Connell 2010). In Chapter 8, a framework is provided for organizing the discussion, starting with the personal dimension: personality; needs and motives; personal and interpersonal factors; expectations; and event careers. Both 'intrinsic' (related to free choice and leisure) and 'extrinsic' (related to work and obligation) motives are important in shaping what impacts on the demand for events. Juxtaposed with demand are structural, personal and interpersonal constraints acting against our desires to participate in, or attend, events, which has a long tradition of study within leisure studies as the contributing field (Page and Connell 2010).

The decision-making process starts with how people negotiate through constraints, as some people manage better than others to realize their personal goals by overcoming barriers to participation in events, whilst others may have multiple layers of constraints that coalesce to prevent participation (e.g. a lack of income, inadequate access and knowledge of how to overcome such barriers). Attention is also given to information searching and use, event attractiveness (the pull factors), substitution, loyalty and novelty seeking as key elements affecting the demand for events.

Following event experiences we have to consider satisfaction with the event, the meanings attached to experiences, and the possibility of personal development and transformation. These factors and ongoing recollection (if indeed the experience was memorable) shape future intentions. Some people clearly become highly 'involved' or engaged in sports, the arts and other lifestyle or leisure interests and are therefore more committed to events. Commitment and resulting 'event careers' can also be work or business related, which moves into the area of serious leisure we will examine later. Identifying and catering to the 'highly involved' is of particular interest to event designers and marketers and is a focus of marketing strategies, including the increased use of social media.

Planning, design and management

Planned events happen by conscious human design; they are created by organizations with many stakeholders, usually with specific goals in mind. This is largely the event management or business domain, focusing as it does on mobilizing resources, transforming processes, management systems and professionalism. Yet as events are means towards an end (e.g. profit, celebration, branding, political benefits, place marketing), we always must carefully assess goals and take a multi-stakeholder approach, meaning we need to be cognizant of the wider range of objectives and needs of hosting associated with a specific event. This leads us into the realm of event tourism (Getz and Page 2015), wherein events have specific roles to play in attracting tourists, fostering a positive destination image and acting as animators and catalysts within a specific location, region or country. It is also the 'urban imaging' question (part of place marketing) in which, according to Hall (2005: 198), events play a prominent role as places increasingly compete with each other for visitors' attention and event spending.

Chapter 7 is specifically devoted to event design, as it needs to follow directly from the discussion of planned event experiences and meanings to illustrate how to create events that match with expectations and visitor preferences, while the remaining planning and management topics are covered in Chapter 9. Each of the key management 'functions' is discussed in turn, not in a 'how-to' style, but to stress the main topics within each function, their disciplinary foundations and unique issues or applications for events. Examples of event-specific research are provided to illustrate the application of theory in practice.

Outcomes and the impacted

'Outcomes' are a dominant area of growth in event studies research and whilst they appear to follow logically from many of the other themes, they can also be a starting point in their own right for the analysis of events as a phenomenon that affects people and environments. Many events are created or assisted by authorities and sponsors, with intended outcomes clearly expressed. Tourism organizations work backwards from the goals of putting bums on seats or beds, then decide what events to bid on, create or market. Sponsors determine which target segments to build relationships with, or to sell to, then decide on their event-marketing strategies. Government agencies routinely formulate social and cultural policies, then assist the event sector in implementing those policies. Impacts can also be unintended and unmeasured, giving rise to evaluation and accountability problems which make the assessment of impacts an interesting pursuit but intensely political, as different factions seek to interpret the findings for their own political purposes.

In Chapter 10 we discuss personal, social, cultural, economic and environmental outcomes. For each of these outcome categories a conceptual framework is presented, encompassing 'stressors or causal factors' (in theory, how can events cause impacts?). Potential outcomes (major consequences, based on what the literature has revealed and theory suggests) and possible responses (policy, planning and management of the system to achieve desired outcomes and prevent or ameliorate the unexpected and negative) are both considered.

Patterns and processes

The theme 'patterns and processes' represents the broader environmental influences and the dynamic aspects of our event studies 'system': temporal processes; geographical (spatial) patterns; policy; and creating knowledge. Chapter 4 presents the three disciplines of history, human geography and future studies. Together they help us answer questions like 'where do events come from and how do they evolve over time? How are they distributed in time and space, and why? What cultural and political, technological and economic forces shape events?'

Policy is a theme running throughout the book, with Chapter 11 devoted to events and public policy. Policy is a force that both reacts to and shapes the planned event system. Events are increasingly influenced by formal government policy, including funding and regulations. Numerous events are created and marketed for strategic policy reasons, usually economic, but also cultural and social. And as events become larger and generate more substantial impacts, they cannot be ignored by policy-makers and political parties. Specific attention is given to what event-related policy should consist of, in an integrated approach, and how it should be formulated.

Creating knowledge about events is the remaining theme of importance, which is discussed in Chapter 12. The greater the volume of research, theory and management knowledge that is generated, the better we will be at creating meaningful experiences, formulating effective policy, achieving goals, marketing events and preventing or managing outcomes. To accomplish this requires knowledge about knowledge-creation! What is the nature of knowledge and theory, what are the appropriate methodologies and techniques we can use, and how should events-related research be done? Chapter 12 also provides a research agenda for advancing event studies and some specific suggestions for research projects. In Chapter 12 the book's conclusions are presented, emphasizing the big ideas discussed throughout.

A theory of planned events?

It is unlikely that a single, grand theory can be advanced to cover all important aspects of planned events, but a set of interrelated theories that deal with the key elements is within reach. These constructs, assembled in an interdisciplinary fashion from available theories adapted to events, provide substantial explanatory power regarding all the important elements of the framework. This is how many areas of leisure and tourism studies have developed through time, and events seem to be following a similar pathway to harnessing the interdisciplinarity of event studies. We need integrative theory that accomplishes the following:

- explains the roles and importance of planned events in human society and culture (this covers antecedents and meanings, spatial and temporal patterns), addressing a key challenge of how event spaces are transformed through a temporary activity that redefines how people view and enjoy everyday spaces;
- provides deep insight into the evolution of events, including indications of how various forms of events and their functions are developing (this covers policy, strategy and environmental forces);
- explains how event experiences are influenced, and how meanings – at the levels of personal, group and society – are attached to event experiences (this covers the core phenomenon and also planning, management and design, antecedents and consequences);
- suggests ways in which the outcomes of planned events can be predicted and controlled, as in establishment of cause-and-effect-relationships (this covers planning, policy and outcomes).

Throughout this book we will examine many theories and ideas that can help build the integrative sets of theory for planned events and these are brought together in the concluding chapter. Exchange theory provides fundamental insights on why civilization needs and creates events, both in an economic and cultural frame. A 'convergence model' is presented (see the final chapter), which pertains to the tendency for form and function to merge over time, particularly for larger events and when they serve political purposes. 'Serious leisure' combined with 'social world' theory shows us the connections between our leisure interests and events, while the 'event travel career trajectory' extends that line of reasoning to event tourism.

How the literature has evolved

Where do ideas come from, what are the seminal works in our field, and where do we go to get information and ideas? The creation of the first peer-reviewed journal for event studies in 1993 marked a major turning point, not only providing an outlet for researchers but also helping to legitimize the field of studies. At first this and other applied fields were multidisciplinary in nature, drawing from the theories and methodologies of various established disciplines. With the creation of a number of publishing outlets for event-related research, the era of interdisciplinary research began – that is, developing new theories and methods designed explicitly for event studies. All this has greatly hastened the number of researchers and publications, and, more recently, has led to an explosion in specialized book topics.

Figure 1.4 shows selected publications prior to 1980 and for the period 1981–1992. The early period included a number of one-off studies, especially from sociological and anthropological perspectives. After 1981 we see an acceleration of event-specific research in the tourism periodicals, then in event-specific journals. Along the way are notable books that helped shape the field.

Several reviews of the research literature have been published and for a historical overview, consult the works of Formica (1998), Getz (2000b) and Harris et al. (2001). Hede et al. (2003) reviewed special events research for the period 1990–2002. Sherwood's doctoral dissertation (2007) also entailed a large-scale review of pertinent literature and specifically examined 85 event economic impact studies prepared in Australia. A more recent review by Mair and Whitford (2013) concluded that the majority of research had focused on economic impacts, yet even more work on this topic is needed. Mair and Whitford (2013) acknowledged that the most important topics for future research were socio-cultural and community impacts, then environmental impacts and sustainability issues, as well as the policy dimensions of event tourism.

Also important is the major Routledge four-volume collection of key studies in the field, *Event Tourism* (Connell and Page 2010). That compendium traced the evolution of key studies back to the 1920s with

1922–1980

- Allix, A. (1922). The geography of fairs. *Geographical Review,* 12(4), 532–569.
- Naik, T. (1948). Aboriginal festivals in Gujarat. *Easter Anthropologist,* 2(1), 16–21.
- Boorstin, D. (1961). *The image: A guide to pseudo-events in America.* New York: Harper & Row.
- Turner, V. (1969). *The ritual process: Structure and anti-structure.* New York: Aldine de Gruyter.
- Greenwood, D. (1972). Tourism as an agent of change: A Spanish Basque case study. *Ethnology,* 11, 89–91.
- Ritchie, J. R. B. and Beliveau, D. (1974). Hallmark events: An evaluation of a strategic response to seasonality in the travel market. *Journal of Travel Research,* 14, 14–20.
- Turner, V. (1974). Liminal to liminoid, in play, flow and ritual: An essay in comparative symbology. In E. Norbeck (ed.), *The Anthropological Study of Human Play,* Vol. 60, pp. 53–92. Rice University Studies.
- Duvignaud, J. (1976). Festivals – sociological approach. *Cultures,* 3(1), 14–25.
- Della Bitta, A., Loudon, D., Booth, G. and Weeks, R. (1978). Estimating the economic impact of a short-term tourist event. *Journal of Travel Research,* 16, 10–15.
- Vaughan, R. (1979). *Does a Festival Pay? A Case Study of the Edinburgh Festival in 1976.* Tourism Recreation Research Unit, Working paper 5, University of Edinburgh.
- Davidson, L. and Schaffer, W. (1980). A discussion of methods employed in analyzing the impact of short-term entertainment events. *Journal of Travel Research,* 28(3), 12–16.
- Lavenda, R. H. (1980). The festival of progress: The globalizing world-system and the transformation of the Caracas carnival. *Journal of Popular Culture,* 14(3), 465–475.

1981–1992

- Turner, V. (ed.). (1982). *Celebration: Studies in Festivity and Ritual.* Washington: Smithsonian Institution Press.
- Gartner, W. and Holocek, D. (1983). Economic impact of an annual tourism industry exposition. *Annals of Tourism Research,* 10(2), 199–212.
- Ritchie, J. R. B. (1984). Assessing the impacts of hallmark events: Conceptual and research issues. *Journal of Travel Research,* 23(1), 2–11.
- Olds, K. and Ley, D. (1988). Landscape as spectacle: World's fairs and the culture of heroic consumption. *Environment and Planning D: Society and Space,* 6, 191–212.
- Syme, G., Shaw, B., Fenton, D. and Mueller, W. (eds). (1989). *The Planning and Evaluation of Hallmark Events.* Aldershot: Gower.
- Getz, D. (1989). Special events: Defining the product. *Tourism Management,* 10(2), 135–137.
- Hall, C. M. (1989). The definition and analysis of hallmark tourist events. *GeoJournal,* 19(3), 263–268.
- Handelman, D. (1990). *Models and Mirrors: Towards an Anthropology of Public Events.* Oxford: Berghahn Books.
- Goldblatt, J. (1990). *Special Events: The Art and Science of Celebration.* New York: Van Nostrand Rheinhold.
- Getz, D. (1991). *Festivals, Special Events, and Tourism.* New York: Van Nostrand Rheinhold.
- Ritchie, J. R. B. and Smith, B. (1991). The impact of a mega-event on host region awareness: A longitudinal study. *Journal of Travel Research,* 30(1), 3–10.
- Hall, C. M. (1992). *Hallmark Tourist Events: Impacts, Management and Planning.* London: Belhaven.

Figure 1.4 Selected early event studies, 1922–1992

the Allix (1922) publication on fairs. One might also argue that the professional field of event management pre-dates the academic study of this phenomenon, as the first convention and visitors bureau (CVB) was established in the USA at Detroit in 1896 (Ford and Peeper 2007). Interestingly, as Ford and Peeper (2007) found, there were also examples, pre-dating Detroit, of attracting meetings and convention business to towns and cities, facilitated by the spread of the railroad in the USA. Therefore, the academic study of the professional events sector has taken several hundreds of years to reach fruition, and if sporting events such as the Olympiad are included, then their management and organization – as opposed to their philosophical rationale – can be dated back to early civilization.

As Formica (1998) observed, there were few articles related to events management or tourism published in the 1970s – he found only four in *Annals of Tourism Research* and the *Journal of Travel Research* (*JTR*). Events were not yet 'attractions' within the tourism system of Gunn's landmark book, *Tourism Planning* (1979), although in passing he did mention 'places for festivals and conventions'. In the 1960s and 1970s the events sector was not recognized as an area of separate study within leisure, tourism or recreation, all of which were rapidly growing in the academic community and in professional practice.

Ritchie and Beliveau published the first article specifically about event tourism in 1974, the topic being how 'hallmark events' could combat the seasonality of tourism demand. They examined the Quebec Winter Carnival and included the citation of an unpublished study of the economic impacts of this event, dated in 1962. Most of the pioneering published studies were event economic impact assessments, notably Della Bitta *et al.* (1977), who reported on a Tall Ships event. Another early study of the economic impacts of event tourism was conducted by Vaughan in Edinburgh in 1979, where the Tourism Recreation Research Unit at the University of Edinburgh had recently been established.

Event tourism expanded dramatically as a research topic in the 1980s. Two notable research articles from early in this decade were those by Gartner and Holecek (1983), on the economic impact of an annual tourism industry exposition, and Ritchie (1984), on the nature of impacts from hallmark events, which remains a classic in terms of citations and influence. A major study of festival visitors and the economic impacts of multiple festivals in Canada's National Capital Region was conducted in the latter part of this decade (Coopers and Lybrand Consulting Group 1989), followed by a similar major study in Edinburgh (Scotinform Ltd 1991). These remain landmarks in terms of their scope and cross-event comparisons. However, the most recent update of the Edinburgh Festivals Impact Study (2011) expands the scope of this important research through a triple-bottom-line approach.

Mill and Morrison's (1985) USA-based text *The Tourism System* explicitly recognized the power of events. The 1985 TTRA Canada Chapter conference was themed 'International Events: The Real Tourism Impact' (Travel and Tourism Research Association and Canada Chapter (TTRA) 1986), with the impetus coming from the planned 1986 Vancouver World's Fair and the 1988 Calgary Winter Olympics. Internationally, the AIEST (1987) conference produced a notable collection of material on the general subject of mega events.

Australian scholars were involved with event tourism very early and their influence has continued, especially with substantial research funding (now terminated) from the Cooperative Research Centre programme in Sustainable Tourism. Prior to the America's Cup Defence in Perth in 1988, the People and Physical Environment Research Conference (1987) was held under the theme of the Effects of Hallmark Events on Cities. Soutar and McLeod (1993) later published research on residents' perceptions of that major event.

One of the most influential research projects of that period was the comprehensive assessment of impacts from the first Adelaide Grand Prix (Burns *et al.* 1986). At the end of the 1980s, Syme *et al.* (1989) published a book entitled *The Planning and Evaluation of Hallmark Events*, and Hall (1989) wrote an article on the definition and analysis of hallmark tourist events which noted the need for greater attention to social and cultural impacts.

In 1990, a landmark year in the event management literature, as Goldblatt's book *Special Events: The Art and Science of Celebration* was published, followed by *Festivals, Special Events and Tourism* (Getz 1991) and a year later *Hallmark Tourist Events* by C. M. Hall (1992). In the early 1990s, academics were clearly leading the way, as at that time there were few if any degree programmes and few courses available anywhere that featured event management or tourism. In the USA George Washington University pioneered event management education, leading Hawkins and Goldblatt (1995), in a journal article, to address the need for event management education. Interestingly, their article also asked how events should be treated within a tourism curriculum.

The mid- to late 1990s were the 'take-off' years for the academic institutionalization of event management, and with it a more legitimized advancement of scholarship on event tourism and event studies. This process has been roughly 25–30 years behind the equivalent for tourism, hospitality and leisure. There is also no doubt that leisure, tourism and hospitality provided a large part of the foundation, having adapted discipline-based theory and methodology, supporting event-specific courses, and spinning off event management degree programmes.

The journal *Festival Management and Event Tourism* (later renamed *Event Management*) was founded by Don Getz and Bruce Wicks in 1993, with vital support from Bob Miranda, President of Cognizant Communications Corp. Uysal *et al.* (1993), in the very first issue, began an enduring research theme on why people attend and travel to festivals and events, while Wicks and Fesenmaier (1993) looked at service quality at events and Getz (1993a) examined organizational culture. In the next year Bos (1994) examined the importance of mega events in generating tourism demand, and Crompton and McKay's (1994) article on measuring the economic impacts of events set the stage for many subsequent impact studies. John Crompton's many contributions also include his research-based book, published by the National Parks and Recreation Association in 1999 and entitled *Measuring the Economic Impact of Visitors to Sport Tournaments and Special Events*. In 1997, the *Journal of Convention & Exhibition Management* was launched (renamed the *Journal of Convention & Event Tourism* in 2004), with a broad focus on the convention and exhibition world in contrast to *Event Management*.

A very large number of research projects were commenced in Australia in preparation for the Sydney 2000 Summer Olympic Games. Faulkner *et al.* (2000) reported on this impressive initiative and many papers were subsequently published. As the twentieth century closed, the world celebrated with numerous special events. No doubt this gave a boost to the events sector and its tourism value. Several noteworthy articles were published right at the turn of the century, including state-of-the-art commentary and methodology for conducting event impact assessments by Dwyer *et al.* (2000a, 2000b). These more or less laid to rest any debate on what needed to be done, and how to do it validly, although the Cooperative Research Centre for Sustainable Tourism in Australia continued (through to 2009) to release impact studies and models (notably Jago and Dwyer 2006).

With so much attention having been given previously to the economic dimensions of event tourism, it was to be expected that scholars would seek more balance. Although research on social and cultural impacts of events goes back to occasional anthropological studies like Greenwood (1972), the conceptual overview provided by J. R. B. Ritchie (1984) and a noteworthy piece of sociological research by Cunneen and Lynch (1988), who studied ritualized rioting at a sport event, suggest that the decade beginning in 2000 really ushered in a systematic and theoretically grounded line of comprehensive event impact research. This has led to important discussions on sustainability.

The literature on events has now grown beyond anyone's capability of reading it all, with a number of distinct specializations having emerged. In very practical terms, this probably defines 'maturity' or at least the path towards impending maturity. The longstanding divisions based on types of events remain (especially sports events, business events and festivals), the Olympics will always attract its own scholarship, while world's fairs and other mega events retain an allure, much of which can be dated to major events such as the 1851 Great Exhibition in London that continue to attract scholarly attention from the social science community for the wider impact on society and economy.

The field has evolved to the point where the emphasis is now on specific aspects of event management/tourism, specific types of events and event-related research and discourses. A summary of recent specialized books, mostly since 2010 (see Table 1.1), illustrates the growing diversity and depth of event studies and provides a handy starting point for students and researchers interested in particular topics or broader themes. Also see the Further Reading lists suggested at the end of each chapter.

Table 1.1 A summary of recent specialized books

Book themes	Selected book titles and authors
Arts and culture	Yeoman *et al.* 2004; Du Cros and Joliffe 2014
Audiences and their expectations	MacKellar 2013a
Battlefield events	Reeves *et al.* 2015
Careers	Columbus 2011
Commemorative events	Frost and Laing 2013
Community festivals and events	Jepson and Clarke 2014
Coordination	Silvers 2004
Design	Monroe and Kates 2005; Berridge 2007; Malouf 2011; Richards *et al.* 2014
Enduring festivals	Derrett 2015
Entertainment	Sonder 2003
Ethics and social responsibility	Henderson and McIlwraith 2013
Fashion events	Williams *et al.* 2013
Feasibility	O'Toole 2011
Food/beverage events	Hall and Sharples 2008; Cavicchi and Santini 2014
Future of events	Yeoman *et al.* 2014
Handbook of events	Page and Connell 2011
Human resources	Van der Wagen 2006; Van der Wagen and White 2014; Baum *et al.* 2009
Marketing and communications	Hoyle 2002; Masterman and Wood 2006; Preston 2012
Meetings, conventions, exhibitions	Davidson and Cope 2003; Davidson and Rogers 2006; Fenich 2005; Allen 2008; Krugman and Wright 2006; Mair 2013; Rogers 2013
Music	Gibson and Connell, 2012
Olympics	Preuss 2004; Roche 2006; Theodoraki 2007; Toohey and Veal 2007; Poynter and MacRury 2009; Gold and Gold 2010; Hiller 2012; Weed 2012
Operations management	Tum *et al.* 2006
Policy	Foley *et al.* 2011
Portfolio management	Ziakis 2013
Power and politics	Merkel 2013
Project management and logistics	O'Toole and Mikolaitis 2002
Risk	Tarlow 2002; Silvers 2008
Rituals and traditional events	Laing and Frost 2014
Social change	Picard and Robinson 2006
Social impacts	Richards *et al.* 2013
Sponsorship	Skinner and Rukavina 2003
Sport and events	Solomon 2002; Masterman 2004; Funk 2012; Shipway and Fyall 2012; Preuss 2013; Dashper *et al.* 2014
Sustainability, the environment and green operations	Raj and Musgrave 2009; Jones 2010; Goldblatt and Goldblatt 2011; Pernecky and Luck 2013; Case 2013
Tourism	Getz 2013
Urban events	Richards and Palmer 2010; A. Smith 2012, 2015
Visitor attractions and events	Weidenfeld *et al.* 2015
Volunteering	Smith *et al.* 2014
World's fairs (expos)	Findling and Pelle 2008

Major subdivisions (discourses) within event studies

It is clear that there are three predominant subdivisions (or discourses) concerning planned events. While they tend to run in separate directions, it is essential for event studies to integrate them more fully. An online article by Getz (2010) concerning festivals provides a substantive basis for this interpretation of the literature, with over 400 citations along with more recent syntheses such as the *Routledge Handbook of Events* (Page and Connell 2010), with its wider social science reach.

Discipline-based approaches

Many disciplines contribute to an understanding of the roles, meanings, importance and effects of planned events in society and culture. These disciplines employ their own methodologies and theories, reflecting different research paradigms (i.e. a distinctive approach with its own methodologies, concepts and view of the world), and they all contribute something of value to event studies. The key point is that in each discipline (and in many closely related fields) the focus is not on events – events are one of many phenomena being studied. And the object is not to develop theory about events.

Later in this book, each of the foundation disciplines and related fields are examined for their contributions. The best established lines of pertinent research are from cultural anthropology and sociology, which might be labelled 'classical' discourse, in which some of the important topics are rites, rituals, symbolism and celebration. In particular, these concepts, along with liminality and communitas, play a key part in the model of the planned event experience developed in this book.

Event tourism

'Event tourism' is an applied area within event studies, as it takes an instrumentalist approach. An ontological mapping of the literature (see Figure 1.5) clearly reveals the dominant themes to be the production, attraction and marketing of festivals and events for tourism and other forms of development, with a heavy methodological emphasis on marketing and economic impact assessment. A thorough review of the literature within this discourse has been published in an article by Getz (2008) as well as the book *Event Tourism* (Getz 2013a), and is the subject of a four-volume set by Connell and Page (2010).

The roles of events in tourism and development constitute the core propositions that created and delimit this sub-field. They are: (1) events attract tourists (to specific places, and to overcome seasonality); (2) events contribute to place marketing (including image formation and destination branding); (3) events animate attractions and places, which essentially means that anyone with a park or facility is almost automatically in the events business; and (4) events can act as catalysts for other forms of development or improved capacity to attract tourists through infrastructure gains and more effective marketing. These 'propositions' are not theories because it is not possible to use the experience of others or the findings of available research to explain or predict the precise impacts of event-tourism policies, strategies or actions. Rather, the collective wisdom that propels event tourism is the belief, based on experience and analysis, that desired outcomes can be obtained through development and marketing efforts. Accordingly, each 'proposition' must be understood as containing an inherent element of uncertain outcomes.

Ontological mapping is concerned with claims to knowledge within fields of study, and therefore terminology is important. The key terms unique to event tourism include descriptors that explicitly reflect the tourism-related roles of events, namely hallmark, signature, iconic, mega, regional or media. These types of event have a role to play in the planning and management of event portfolios, as assets for destinations to value.

Dominating this discourse has been three themes, each embodying key terminology and concepts that set it somewhat apart from the others. The first theme is that of outcomes, with the emphasis placed on assessment of economic impacts of events and event tourism. Figure 1.5 mentions a number of lines of research, with key topics being event-tourist expenditure and yield, seasonality effects, estimation of

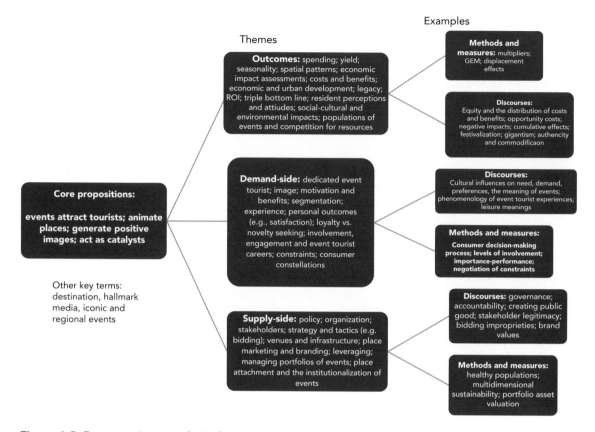

Figure 1.5 Event tourism: ontological mapping

gross and net economic impacts, occasionally more comprehensive studies of costs and benefits, return on investment and an interest in leveraging events and planning for long-term legacies such as urban renewal or re-positioning in a place-branding context. The general acceptance of a sustainability paradigm by academics has led to a more triple-bottom-line approach encompassing environmental and socio-cultural impacts, so that resident perceptions and attitudes are now a very important topic, and this has expanded into a multi-stakeholder approach to evaluating outcomes. Moreover, the dominant positivistic emphasis on measuring impacts in monetary terms is giving way to a more interpretive, and sometimes critical, evaluation of the roles, costs and benefits of events, including the matter of exactly who gains or loses. As this matures we can expect to see more research and practical applications of portfolio management (i.e. cumulative and long-term value from events as assets) on the dynamics of populations of events, within which competition for resources and markets is a dominant consideration.

Figure 1.5 also indicates some methods and measures being employed in each theme, some of which are unique to event tourism. Displacement effects are in this category – as an event has the potential to displace other tourists (especially if held in peak seasons) – as is time displacement, which occurs when people alter their planned or necessary travel in order to take in an event. The term 'casual event tourist' refers to those non-residents who attend an event but do not travel because of its attraction. Also indicated in the diagram are various discourses found in the literature, and sometimes they occur politically, with the dominant one being economic or financial justification of public-sector intervention in the events and tourism marketplaces. To justify venues, bidding, marketing and hosting events governments generally require economic impact assessments and measures of public attitudes and support. Academics and certain interest groups like to ask more difficult questions, including those pertaining to the ideal of requiring full cost and benefit disclosure and attention to the distribution of impacts (especially: which elite groups benefit? and which disadvantaged segments pay the price?). Often hidden in event accounts are externalities like security costs and inflation, crime and pollution, giving rise to debates over measurement and disclosure. Opportunity costs are a related concern, as events and tourism are not necessarily the only or best way to achieve policy aims. As events have become standard tools in development, more and more attention and debate can be expected regarding long-term and cumulative impacts (which relates to the concepts of event portfolios and populations).

Theme two is analysis and development of demand. Event-tourism markets can be generally separated into business events, sports, entertainment, festivals and other cultural celebrations. Within each of these markets the emphasis is placed on dedicated event tourists, which are those individuals who travel principally because of an event. Key research topics have included studies of motivation and the benefits sought, the image of events and their venues and host destinations, satisfaction, the overall event-tourist experience and effects on future behaviour including event or destination loyalty.

When it comes to the supply side of the development equation, there are many actors involved within the public, private and not-for-profit sectors. Not all events are produced with tourism in mind, but they might nevertheless attract tourists or entertain casual visitors to a city. Organizers might want tourists as one segment, even if they emphasize appealing to residents. On the other hand are event development corporations that have the explicit mandate of bidding on events, creating them, and marketing destinations through the appeal and imagery of events. Business events – and sports in particular – are capital intensive, generally requiring major facilities; they are often developed by separate organizations such as convention bureaus and sport (tourism) commissions. Cultural celebrations, and especially festivals, are favoured by communities all around the world in part because they are not necessarily capital intensive, can be created anywhere, and tap into both community and tourist desires for authentic social and cultural experiences.

MICE is an acronym for meetings, incentives, conventions and exhibitions (Schlentrich, 2008). Often described as an 'industry', it is better thought of as a collection of primarily business events that depend on specific types of facilities called convention and/or exhibition centres. Smaller MICE venues can be described as meeting or assembly venues and are often within hotels, resorts and other facilities. Incentive travel does not quite fit into planned events, although it is possible that a tour arranged as a reward for star employees or leading salespeople can be considered a special event from their perspective. Such a tour might also include small events like parties, seminars and exhibitions.

It is worth noting that theory development in event tourism borrows heavily from economics and consumer behaviour. Much of the knowledge base of this discourse is, however, purely 'factual' (what you need to know in order to develop event tourism) and of the problem-solving kind (how to attract tourists). In looking for event-specific theory, we need to refine the concept of 'attractiveness' as it applies to various events (that is, their drawing power for specific segments) and in the context of combating seasonality of demand and the over-concentration of tourism. Seasonality refers to the way in which destinations see a rise and fall in demand as visitors peak at certain points in time and decline at others.

Connell *et al.* (2015: 285) suggested that:

> *As Getz (2010) argues, the strategic development of events and festivals at a destination level has an important role to play in attracting visitors, contributing to place marketing and expanding the economic impact of tourism. Within this positive frame, events are widely positioned as a strategic tool to assist in combating seasonality, a premise established in an early study by Ritchie and Beliveau (1974).*

Connell *et al.* (2015) describe how one sector of the visitor economy (i.e. Scottish visitor attractions) sought to harness events to address seasonality, particularly the very concentrated patterns of tourism visitation in Scotland. As Figures 1.6 and 1.7 show, the conceptual framework used by Connell *et al.* (2015) demonstrates how the analysis of event tourism has to span various disciplines (i.e. geography, economics, politics and policy analysis and management) to understand the nuances of event activity and its use in specific business contexts.

This study also highlights the wider need to understand how substitution of demand from tourism markets can be adapted to include residents and the school markets in terms of building the business opportunities which off-peak events (see Table 1.2) can provide as businesses understand what event themes

Figure 1.6 Simplified conceptual framework

Source: Connell *et al.* (2015: 285). Reprinted from *Tourism Management*, 46, Connell, J. Page, S. J. and Meyer, D., Visitor attractions and events: Responding to seasonality, 283–298, Copyright (2015), with permission from Elsevier.

- Hartman (1986) argued that the complexity of seasonality is created by the interplay of factors in both origin and destination areas where flows of tourism are conditioned by a wide range of social and cultural factors (e.g. imagery), economic factors (e.g. price) and physical factors (e.g. the availability of skiing in winter periods).
- Seasonality has both a distinct time-based element and a more neglected spatial component. Hartman (1986: 12) defined tourism seasonality as 'temporal variance in the phenomenon of tourism activities' and acknowledged the existence of a spatial element.
- Butler (2001: 5) argued that 'little research has addressed the problem of whether seasonality varies in nature and intensity on a spatial basis either within or between destination areas'. The point is further reaffirmed by Baum and Lundtorp (2001), who argue that there is no concept or theory of tourism seasonality.
- Butler and Mao (1997) recognize that urban tourism is often the least seasonally affected form of tourism; seasonal spatial patterns within destinations are not readily charted and understood.
- Seasonal variations in destination characteristics can act as a magnet for visitors seeking ephemeral experiences linked with climate or nature, such as the autumn market (Spencer and Holecek 2007), as well as economic-driven destination experiences such as Christmas markets (see Haid *et al.* 2006).

Figure 1.7 Perspectives on tourism and seasonality that inform events research

Source: Connell *et al.* (2015: 285).

Table 1.2 Off-peak seasonal theming of visitor attractions

- Harvest theme, with a focus on harvest produce, local foods and traditional celebrations of food production and rural life, such as Apple Day (September/October).
- Hallowe'en, with a clear focus on attracting families with children for low-scare experiences (e.g. dressing-up, pumpkin carving, storytelling), and for adults/adult groups with moderate scare experiences (e.g. ghost tours, theatrical events and other entertainment) (late October, and corresponding with the half-term school holiday in the UK).
- Christmas preparations/celebrations, often with a primary focus on shopping, where attractions offer a significant retail operation, and special menus in restaurants/cafés. This can help to keep a shop and café open even if the main attraction remains closed (December). Attractions may also offer limited opening for special Christmas events, e.g. in England and Wales, National Trust houses traditionally close in winter for conservation purposes but now offer limited opening with a Christmas theme such as 'dressing the house for Christmas'.

Source: Connell *et al.* (2015: 286).

appeal to visitors. Such research also indicates the notion of an event travel career trajectory for people who become more and more involved in serious leisure pursuits, building an increasing engagement with events as part of holiday and weekly leisure experiences.

Olympic and mega event tourism

Mega events have a special appeal, so a great deal of attention is always focused on major sporting events and particularly the Olympic Games. While the basic tourism-related issues are often the same, mega events are quite different in terms of policy, funding and urban impacts. Tourism flows are altered (both positively in the immediate period of the event and often negatively in the lagged effect post-event), but it must be remembered that there are always finite limits to the number of tickets that can be sold to visitors. World's fairs have much more potential to attract large numbers of tourists because of their scale and length. All mega events are viewed as promotional tools, so that image-enhancing effects are potentially much greater than direct tourism impacts.

The Economics of Staging the Olympics by Preuss (2004) includes an assessment of tourism impacts, while the book *Olympic Tourism* by Weed (2008) pays special attention to the nature of tourism related to the Olympics and how the Games can be leveraged for broader and longer-term benefits.

Education and careers in event tourism

Once the preserve of marketing professionals, now numerous DMOs (Destination Marketing Organizations) and special-purpose event development agencies are employing event-tourism professionals who understand the roles events can play in destination development and marketing. A background in tourism, events and marketing is ideal, but increasingly there will be specializations within event development agencies and DMOs. Table 1.3 presents a number of positions and key associated tasks.

Event management

The first major textbook on this subject was Professor Goldblatt's *Special Events: The Art and Science of Celebration* (first published in 1990, with the seventh edition in 2014), and Goldblatt has remained at the forefront of event management studies and professional development through multiple books. This was followed closely by Getz (1991) with the book *Festivals, Special Events and Tourism*, and a year later came M. Hall's book, *Hallmark Tourist Events* (1992). Raj *et al.* (2008), Allen *et al.* (2011), Bowdin *et al.* (2011) and

Table 1.3 Careers in event tourism

Typical functions	Major tasks
Event facilitator/coordinator	Work with events in the destination to help realize their tourism potential (funding, advice, marketing)
	Liaison with convention/exhibition centres and other venues
	Liaison with sport and other organizations that produce events
Event tourism producer	Create and produce events specifically for their tourism value
	Stakeholder management (with numerous event partners)
Event tourism planner	Develop a strategy for the destination
	Integrate events with product development and image making/branding
Event tourism policy analyst and researcher	Work with policy-makers to facilitate event tourism
	Conduct research (e.g. feasibility studies, demand forecasting, impact assessments and performance evaluations)
Event bidding	Bid on events
	Develop relationships leading to winning events for the destination
	Conduct risk assessments and feasibility studies for each potential bid
Event services	Provide essential and special services to events (e.g. travel and logistics; accommodation and venue bookings; supplier contacts)

1.1 EXPERT OPINION

The many contributions of Professor Goldblatt to the development of professionalism and education in event management are recognized around the world.

A future for planned events in education

Professor Joe Goldblatt, FRSA, Executive Director, International Centre for the Study of Planned Events, Queen Margaret University, Edinburgh, Scotland

Having spent nearly 30 years in the classroom as a teacher of event management and, most recently, event studies, I am convinced that events are a strong curricular current or stream that must flow throughout the entire curriculum in the future. The strong current that represents event studies is one that impacts every human life both personally and professionally throughout every lifetime.

Recently, the producer of the 2004 Olympic Games Opening Ceremony in Athens, Greece, asked me about the types of students we were producing to ensure a sustainable future for the field of planned events. I answered by describing how my curricular ambitions and outcomes had changed during the past quarter of a century in higher education.

When I first entered the classroom my goal was to produce the next producer of the Super Bowl Half-Time Spectacular or other mega or hallmark event. However, over time, I have realized that it is far more important to return to the original goal of public education and that is to produce well-rounded citizens who are motivated and prepared to contribute to society. Part of this well-roundedness is the ability to appreciate and support planned events at the local, regional and national level. The legendary original producer of Disneyland's Main Street Electric Parade (Robert Jani, 1934–1989) once told me that 'The size of the event does not matter. What matters most is the integrity of the outcome.'

One example of this phenomenon was exemplified in a meeting I had with a third-year event studies student: 'I want to become a paediatric nurse,' she confided to me. When I asked why she was going to make this career change she answered, 'I have always loved children and everything I have learned in event studies will make me a better nurse.' This type of change of career is not uncommon for the millennial generation and therefore event studies is, I believe, excellent preparation for a lifetime of many different career pursuits. The skills one will learn in organization, time management, establishing aims and objectives, team work and other key workplace tasks will serve every student well, not just for their first job but their last one as well.

Throughout one's lifetime there are innumerable opportunities to attend, fund, support, participate in and even produce planned events. Whether you become a member of a local government council, a corporate officer or an event planner, you will have many opportunities to encourage the development and sustainability of planned events. Within higher education, the very best institutions will recognize this fact and provide you with opportunities to explore event studies as a stream that runs throughout the entire general studies curriculum.

We know now that event studies is the emerging field, as was tourism many years ago. It is based upon many different classic theorems from established disciplines, including, but not limited to, anthropology, psychology, sociology and others. Recently I have even explored and written an article in the field of eventology, with Professor Oleg Vorab of Russia, which is a subset of probability theory within mathematics. Perhaps one day you will be able, through a future scientific model, to help to better forecast or predict the outcome of a planned event and, through manipulation of some independent variables, actually improve the sustainability of the event itself.

Indeed, planned events and event studies have great potential throughout the entire curricular structure of a great modern institution of higher education. By recognizing the importance of events and their impact on everyday life, we may use planned events to incrementally or in some cases actually dramatically change the world within which we live now and in the future.

One day, public bodies and private sponsors may even link their future support to the planned events to positively impact not only the economy but also health, social cohesion, education and, of course, environmental sustainability. Therefore, it is important for institutions of higher education, and the faculty and students who populate these institutions, to recognize that event studies is an opportunity for significant social change.

The Scottish author Robert Louis Stevenson wrote, when describing my adopted city of Edinburgh, 'An *event* strikes root and grows into legend when it finds congenial surroundings.' Through a growing awareness of event studies and the potential planned events within human society the world may indeed be greatly changed for the better, as you provide through event studies the congenial surroundings to create the stronger roots that indeed will one day grow into even more legendary events. Therefore, as you advance the field of event management to a much greater level in higher education through event studies you must recognize that it is not as important to produce the next mega event as it is to help extend the roots that will grow our field of study and profession to achieve even greater heights in the future.

Shone and Parry (2004) have also produced notable texts. In addition, there are many more practical books from the event practitioners' point of view, such as the series written by Judy Allen (e.g. Allen 2008, 2014).

EMBOK, the event management body of knowledge (Silvers *et al.* 2006), has been created by practitioners and academics to codify the skills and knowledge required by professional event managers. There are five main knowledge domains: administration; design; marketing; operations; and risk, each with numerous subdivisions. Much of this knowledge base has to come from business or managerial literature. For example, 'marketing mix' and 'stakeholder management' are generic. The managerial and problem-solving skills needed by professionals are stressed, whereas theory is not addressed. EMBOK also has implications for licensing and cross-border job mobility. It tells academics what a full degree programme in event management should cover, but the means of acquiring all the pertinent skills and knowledge has to include on-the-job experience which underpins why the curriculum needs to be almost focused on employability and the link to work. This is even more the case than with predecessor vocation subjects such as sport, leisure and tourism that have contributed to the growth of event education. With the emphasis on organizing, managing, people interaction and operational issues, many curricula are underpinned by substantive placement elements and industry involvement in the delivery and production of degree programmes.

Event management and event studies interrelationships

Against this background of the growth of event education and research the philosophy embodied in this book is unambiguous: teaching event management requires a blend of management fundamentals (easily obtained from business schools, but usually taught within event management or tourism/hospitality degree programmes) and the specific study of planned events. In this approach, specializations are taught after the fundamentals have been acquired, although we realize there will probably be continuing demand by students and professional bodies for a quick introduction to specialized career paths serviced by conversion Masters programmes, continuing professional development (CPD) and event MBA programmes in due course. The argument presented here is that event management is generic, and the knowledge can be applied to all types of events. But we need to understand the fundamentals of events as planned activities before we can begin to look at managing them.

Traditionally the specializations within events education have been aligned with professional bodies, including those devoted to meetings and conventions, exhibitions, festivals and sports. *We argue that this is now very antiquated thinking*, and it will not survive the rapid growth in event-related career paths that now include policy and analysis positions, private enterprise, new forms of events and the amazing possibilities opened up by global communications and social media for the co-creation of events. In the experience economy, increasingly diverse market segments (that is, social worlds or communities of interest) are generating their own events and event-travel careers. Specialization also occurs by the type of employer, namely venues and corporations, government departments and non-profit associations, all of which have unique perspectives on the roles of events. With generic event management as the foundation, all these possible specializations are open and available – as is the expanding boundaries of events into specialist fields such as facilities management.

In Table 1.4, major career paths in event management are illustrated, with sample job titles and pertinent professional associations. Many countries have their own national-level associations, and there are many certifications offered by educational institutions as well. The book *The Complete Guide to Careers in Special Events* by Gene Columbus (2011) provides practical advice, and plenty of information, for the aspiring professional. See Chapter 9 for a discussion of theory and research on careers in the events sector.

Forces, trends and issues

What explains the rapid growth and expansion of planned events in the modern world? No one who has studied the events sector could conclude anything else, but will this trend continue? The sector has seen

Table 1.4 Careers in event management

Event types and settings	Sample job titles	Sample related professional associations and certifications
Festivals and special events		
Public, private and non-profit sectors Social and private entrepreneurship	Producer (overall responsibility for the festival) Designer (artistic, usually) Manager (general, or functional area) Coordinator (usually at city level)	IFEA (International Festivals and Events Association): Certified Festival and Event Executive (CFEE) International Special Events Society (ISES): Certified Special Events Professional (CSEP)
Meetings and conventions		
Private consulting companies Corporations Associations Government agencies Venues with meeting services and facilities	Meeting planner Event coordinator (at a convention or exhibition facility)	Convention Industry Council (CIC): Certified Meeting Professional (CMP) Meeting Professionals International (MPI): Certificate in Meeting Management (CMP; CMM) Professional Convention Management Association (PCMA): CMP
Exhibitions (trade and consumer shows)		
Companies producing and designing exhibitions Employees of exhibition venues	Exhibition producer/exhibition designer	International Association of Exhibitions and Events (IAEE): Certified in Exhibition Management (CEM)
Sports		
Employee of professional team Employee of amateur league Private company producing events Employee of venue	Sport event manager Sport coordinator	The Certified Sports Event Executive (CSEE) Programme, open only to National Association of Sport Commissions members *www. sportscommissions.org*
Corporate events		
Employee of corporation Private consultant	Public relations manager Event producer	Generic event or meeting management
Venues		
Employee of facilities Consultant	Facility manager Event coordinator	International Association of Venue Managers (IAVM): Certified Facilities Executive (CFE)
Fairs		
	Fair manager, producer	International Association of Fairs and Expositions (IAFE): Certified Fair Executive (CFE)

an unprecedented growth in the demand for event activity as well as a rise in the supply of event venues and activities since 1945. Ford and Peeper (2007) point to the early nineteenth-century willingness of Americans for association as one factor behind the growth of meetings and conventions. They also point to the willingness to share knowledge in the industrial age (compared to a secrecy culture in Europe) along with the need for people spread out over a wide geographic area to gather in order to share new ideas and knowledge. Added to this was the need for boosterism by cities to overcome the impact of the 1890s' depression in the USA. This can best be summarized as the need for innovation in a fast-changing society, where industrialization was the powerhouse of the economy. Many of these general trends still remain important today: the desire for people to share ideas and knowledge in face-to-face meetings, with the added elements of consumer consumption and entertainment. What these evolutionary factors illustrate are the implications for the growth of individual events and the entire events sector. If we understand the underlying forces, document the trends and discuss the issues that arise, then surely we will be better able to plan for the future.

Table 1.5 summarizes the ensuing discussion, beginning with an overview of major forces.

Forces

For convenience, force-field analysis often follows the acronym PEST – which can be interpreted broadly to mean Population (including demographics) and Politics (with law), Economy and Environment, Society and culture (including values), and Technology. While it is fairly easy to suggest powerful forces, these are usually interrelated and often compounding. And there is always tension between those forces propelling growth and those constraining it. So far, the forces that have propelled growth of the events sector are outstripping any resistance factors (also see the section on future studies for a related discussion).

Population

The world's rapidly growing population not only fuels growth in the demand and need for planned events, it is also a constant pressure on all of the planet's resources, recently giving rise to fears about food and water shortages, and the end of cheap (fossil-fuel) energy. Sustainability issues also arise from global climate change, which is projected to result in the serious displacement of populations and crises for the global economy. These are the main worries, or limiting factors. Eventually they will profoundly influence the world in many ways.

Several aspects of population and demographics deserve special attention in the context of planned events. The first is large-scale migration, or diaspora, and the resulting changes in social life and culture. Many once homogeneous societies are now multicultural, and the mix is changing. This often imposes serious strains on the fabric of society, but also potentially enriches life. Most of the world's population, especially migrants, live in cities that are getting larger and more complex. Urban life is a source of many stressors on the environment and on human health. In many places rural areas continue to depopulate, while in others the divisions between rural and urban life have blurred because of lifestyle migrants, tourism and second homes. Events that bring people together and provide identity for persons, groups and places have taken on much greater significance.

Intergenerational differences, and the process of changing values and preferences over time, have not been studied to any extent in the context of events. We will have to borrow extensively from leisure and tourism studies to provide insights, but there is no doubt that younger generations are going to have to deal with many more serious challenges, compared with the post-war baby-boomers, and many different opportunities. Technology, in particular, has moved so fast that it is difficult to comprehend all the ways it is influencing habits and preferences in social life, work and leisure. Another generational issue of importance is the

Table 1.5 Forces, trends and issues related to planned events

Forces	Trends	Issues
Population		
Migration and diaspora	Rising demand for events of all kinds	Can events relieve urban stresses? Bring diverse groups together?
Urbanization; urban stress	Events for urban and rural identity, social integration	Are there limits to festivalization?
Generational changes	Events reflecting changes in demography, diaspora	What does the next generation want in planned events?
Politics and law		
Country/global/civic (in)stability; protests, riots	Events increasingly viewed as instruments of public policy; as foundations of civil society	Education and training; certification of event professionals
War, terror	Increasing regulation and professionalism in the events sector	Danger of events being exploited for reasons of propaganda and ideology
Policies affecting travel, culture, leisure and events		Danger zones (for tourists and residents)
Economics		
Wealth and disparity rising together	Events increasingly viewed as instruments of corporate strategy	Commodification vs. authenticity
Globalization	Event tourism on the rise	Exclusion of the disadvantaged and dispossessed
Financial crises as a threat	More events for profit	Elitism (owing to politics, pricing)
Environment		
Climate change	Threats to leisure and travel	Need for events that are sustainable; events as social-marketing tools (for environmental change)
Peak oil; renewable energy	Threats to prosperity and peace	Will event tourism become impossible?
Water and food shortages		
Society and culture		
Values (favouring change or status quo?)	Experiences drive leisure and travel	Proving that events solve problems and make things better
Multiculturalism vs. exclusion	Diversity in event forms and cultural functions	Supporting sustainable event populations and portfolios
	Social integration as a policy objective favouring new events; events and civil society	
Technology		
Global communications	Media events on the rise	Threat of spectacle replacing participation
Social media	Social media affecting event	Virtual vs. live event experiences
Potential to create and solve problems	Technology of marketing, logistics, producing events	

continuing decline in exercise and outdoor activity and the resulting contribution towards unhealthy life-styles, with predictions of obesity epidemics in many developed countries.

Politics and law

There always seem to be factors such as conflicts, terrorism, disease or civic unrest that impact on tourism – and on event tourism in particular – affecting the perception and stability of environments in which to host events. It is easy to cancel conventions, competitions and festivals, and governments seeking to restore order or prevent unrest will often see public gatherings as a threat. But whatever the source of disruption, be it political or a new global pandemic (like swine flu), the effects are usually regionalized, and long-term trends show that global tourism growth has always rebounded. More specifically relevant are the many policies and regulations enacted by governments affecting travel, culture, leisure and events, and these vary from country to country. During the past five decades such policies have given a major boost to leisure, consumerism, tourism and event development. On the other hand, pressure to deal with climate change results in carbon taxes and, potentially, other measures that could increasingly act to slow growth or impose specific barriers to travel and events.

Increasing regulation and professionalism in the events sector also means that advanced education is becoming more and more essential, and inevitably professionals and companies will have to be licensed in order for events to get approvals and insurance. The education, life-long learning and ever more detailed training of event professionals is necessary both for safety and health reasons and to ensure that companies and governments realize their goals.

Economics and the propelling force of globalization

We know that economic recessions kill demand for many events, and while this is a periodic phenomenon, it has not slowed the long-term growth in travel or planned events. Despite being defined in many ways, globalization is in general a collection of forces resulting in greater integration of economies and cultures. Global communications, transportation advances, capital flows, migration and freer trade are major contributing factors. The world is shrinking in real and perceived terms as people and their lives seem to draw closer; this is described as time–space compression (Warf 2008), as transport and communications have made the world a much easier place in which to communicate and travel. We are all interconnected and global events, even the broadcast of minor events, reinforce these perceptions.

In examining globalization and sport tourism, Higham and Hinch (2009: 18) argued that 'The first general characteristic of globalization is the accelerated compression of time and space.' This is followed by growing interdependence, but with marked inequalities of its costs and benefits. These forces are reflected in the 'spec-tacularization' of sport mega events like the World Cup and the Olympics. Fans can travel easily to numerous international events, while favouring highly developed economies with modern transport. Both teams and fans are more mobile than ever. Higham and Hinch continued to argue that (2009: 26): 'Sport is ubiquitous as a form of popular culture while maintaining its significance as a form of place-based local culture.'

Globalization has many potential consequences for planned events. Mass global communications make it possible to reach out to everyone, and instant communications encourage people to meet virtually and in person. The democratization of tourism makes it possible for increasingly large numbers of people to attend festivals and events. But there is a concomitant tendency for standardization (as 'global parties' produced for tourism or as the 'live communications' of corporations) that threatens local control and authenticity. The mass movement of people, both migration and business tourism, encourages the spread of ideas. Diaspora (people moving away from their homes in large numbers) leads to a desire to retain or reinvent root cultures through festivals and events.

Globalization is accepted by many as good, or at least inevitable, and is rejected and countered by others. Invariably, anti-globalization protestors show up at international political meetings, concerned over the tendency for wealth to concentrate in rich countries, and the obvious failure of international efforts to eliminate poverty. The term 'glocalization' has been coined to describe a process in which the local culture is preserved (this applies to events) within global systems, but is this mostly wishful thinking? How can it be implemented?

Overall, globalization helps explain rapid growth in the planned events sector, as a consequence of more trade and travel, easier communications and mass migrations. Ideas spread quickly. Everywhere we go, cities and nations are competing, corporations are pushing their brands, everything is for sale. This notion leads to a very serious issue: the commodification of experiences and the services we consume.

Environment

Everyone now talks about global climate change, and we know this process carries many threats, including coastal inundation, more severe weather, water and food shortages, political turmoil and resultant mass population displacements. And although oil supply increased and prices dropped into 2015, the threat of diminishing supplies framed around the notion of peak oil production has been reached (see Becken 2015); it is easy to become pessimistic about the future of the planet, not to mention the implications for tourism and events. This is because much of the economy and society in developed nations is dependent upon oil (and also the by-products of oil) for its functioning. Against those negative prospects are the possibilities that technology, especially through renewable energy sources, can prevent or mitigate the effect of oil dependence and its contribution to climate change. But the effects of climate change are already evident, and governments and industry have been very slow to react. These factors all have to be considered when we look at sustainability and the future of planned events.

Society and culture

Values are constantly shifting, and this is reflected in consumer patterns and political upheavals. Some of this is predictable, based on changing demographics (what does Generation 'next' want?), migration (e.g. from Asia to Western nations) and more pluralistic, better-educated and more connected societies. Ideally these shifts will result in an integrated, healthier and creative new society. But we can also expect major public and political reactions to racial and religious mixing, to economic downturn, to food or water shortages, and to environmental problems. How these forces will translate into political and economic action is more difficult to predict and can be country- and city-specific. Keep scanning the media and news for evidence of dominant trends.

Probably the biggest challenges to peace and prosperity are increasing forced migration (i.e. refugees from conflict, poverty, environmental catastrophes or disease) and the widening gap between rich and poor countries (and also between the wealthy class and all others, even within developed nations). These forces will influence many aspects of politics, society and economics.

Technology

Scanning the pages of *The Futurist* through 2014, it becomes clear that technological changes are at the forefront of thinking about the future and monitoring trends. In a year-end summary called Outlook 2015 (www.wfs.org) the World Future Society points to the fact that the revolution in IT (information technology) is still in its infancy! More controversial is talk about AI (artificial intelligence) and what that prospect might do to technology and society. Some particularly relevant forecasts relate to the impact that technology is having on jobs, with many entire categories set to disappear and be replaced by others that are either nascent or not yet invented! The age of specialization is leading to many more careers in which mastery of both knowledge and IT are prerequisite. Advances in technology also bring new opportunities for cultural exchanges and development, and this certainly has implications for the event sector.

The availability of instant, global communications has numerous potential consequences for planned events, and we will consider social media trends in detail. There now exists the potential for solving many difficult problems through technological advances, for example in terms of health, safety, food and water supplies, and carbon storage. One relevant area in which progress is accelerating is that of wearable technology, and this can make physiological monitoring of audience biometrics a practical form of consumer feedback, not to mention having implications for health and safety.

Major trends

Big trends are easy to spot, and there are many 'trend-spotters' on the Internet, publishing books and advising corporations and governments. Because consumer trends are the most closely watched, as they directly impact businesses of all kinds including events and tourism, a new section has been added on top consumer trends that might influence the events sector.

Real value comes from spotting trends early on, so as to prevent something from happening or to capitalize on new opportunities. The following trends are already well established, but within each there are many possible sub-trends that need to be identified and monitored. Consider how each trend reflects the major underlying forces.

Consumer trends

Trend-spotters can see what is happening around them, but they cannot predict the future. Related to event studies, practitioners and researchers should be aware of the trends but not assume they will continue, especially in the realm of consumerism where conditions change very fast. Here are some consumer trends and forecasts coming from trend-spotters that might have a real impact on the events sector.

- sampling: consumers increasingly want to try something first and pay later (especially true for games, but maybe this applies to co-creating event experiences as well);
- crowd sourcing: working with unknown others can be an innovation driver in the events and venues design world; this seems to connect to the whole co-creation of experiences concept;
- visualization is replacing text and discussion (why are there so many photo and video sites online? Learn to communicate experiences with pictures and video);
- wearable tech (use it to monitor visitor experiences, including heartbeat reactions to stimuli on sites);
- female values becoming established (there is no doubt abut the consumer power held by females in the Western world – how is it expressed in event design?);
- bargain hunting: various apps make it possible to find bargains and consumers always seem to want the best price – what does this do for event ticket prices?;
- instant sharing: social networking means that everyone connects quickly, so that consumer dissatisfaction can quickly translate into a backlash or even a protest or boycott; by the same means, happy eventgoers can immediately convince others to share in the experience.

The continued growth of festivals and events

The continued growth and expansion of events around the globe has been commented upon frequently, although it is impossible to quantify on a global scale. Indeed, in most countries there are no statistics on festival/event numbers and growth trends. Long *et al.* (2004: 1) noted that: 'In recent years there has been a clear increase in the number of festivals and events taking place across the world, though it is problematic to put an exact figure to this.' These researchers, all attached to the Centre for Tourism and Cultural Change at Leeds Metropolitan University, provide a number of reasons for the growth and spread of festivals. They (2004: 1) claimed that:

> *international tourism, as an important dimension of the wider concept of globalisation, has in many cases, shifted festivals from being relatively parochial and stable concerns with more or less localised audiences, to events that can attract global audiences, either as tourists, or via other forms of communicative media.*

And growth

> *can be explained in part by an increasing, if not necessarily articulated, desire to re-assert local/ community identities as part of an effort to combat a sense of cultural dislocation associated with processes of globalisation (Manning 1983; Boissevain 1996; De Bres and Davis 2001; Quinn 2003). For others, and in contrast, a number of festivals, such as carnivals and melas, are themselves expressions of globalised and diasporic cultures and identities and are becoming more visible beyond the confines of their 'host' communities as a consequence of their external promotion by festival organizers, the media and tourism marketing agencies, contributing to the building of 'global festival themes'.*

See Research Note 1.2.

1.2 RESEARCH NOTES ON THE GROWTH OF FESTIVALS

1. Janiskee, R. (1994). Some macroscale growth trends in America's community festival industry. *Festival Management and Event Tourism*, 2(1), 10–14.

   Robert Janiskee, geographer, was a pioneer in event studies. His landmark analysis in the USA led to the conclusion (1994: 13) that: 'It appears that recurring community festivals increased in number at an average annual rate of approximately 4.6 per cent between 1930 and 1991, with the number of festivals doubling about every 15 years.' His research examined types, locations and timing, and he believed that the observed rate of growth could not be sustained everywhere.

2. Yolal *et al.* (2009). An examination of festival motivation and perceived benefits relationship: Eskisehir International Festival. *Journal of Convention and Event Tourism*, 10(4), 276–291.

   Growth in festival numbers, size and frequency has been observed in many countries. The paper by Yolal *et al.* (2009: 276) noted how 'small towns and cities across Turkey are increasingly being encouraged to develop and organize festivals and events to improve their images; stimulate urban development; foster economic, cultural, and social life; and attract visitors and investment'. The authors concluded there are more than 1,350 festivals and events held annually in Turkey.

3. Lashua *et al.* (2014). Introduction to the special issue: Music and Tourism. *Tourist Studies*, 14(1), 3–9.

   A special issue of *Tourist Studies* on music and tourism points to the rapid growth of music festivals and concerts as cultural and touristic phenomena. Topics covered by contributors include the festival experience, fandom, authenticity versus commercialization, self-identity and place marketing.

Sport events and participation trends

Sport participation and events continue to expand. Dan Jones, partner in the Sports Business Group at Deloitte, commented that:

> *2014 proved to be another hugely successful year for sport in the UK. Glasgow's Commonwealth Games was a highlight, with 1.3m tickets sold for the 11 days of sporting competition, making it Scotland's biggest-ever sporting event. Across all professional sports events, the total number of spectators exceeded 67m in 2014, which demonstrates the UK public's huge appetite for watching live sport.*

> *(www2.deloitte.com)*

One of the fastest-growing segments has been that of participation sports – those events that are mostly for amateurs, and are often non-competitive in nature. Rapid growth has been observed in running and multi-sport events, for example. British Triathlon reports steady rises in both participation numbers and events for the period 2009–2014 (britishtriathlonmedia.org).

The 2014 State of the Sport (Part I: Non-Traditional Running Events) by the organization Running USA (www.runningusa.org) reported,

> *In just five years, the number of estimated finishers in US non-traditional events has grown from low six figures in 2009 to a staggering 4 million in 2013, a nearly hard-to-believe 40-fold increase. In addition, a handful of mass participation adventure series in 2009 has rapidly expanded to more than 35 non-traditional or themed running series that included mud, color, foam, electric, zombie and even ugly sweater runs by 2013. Across the country, themed races and obstacle events have attracted a loyal audience of fitness-minded people who want to be active, but not necessarily competitive; many just want to have fun, enjoy the camaraderie of others and focus more on the social, team-building aspect rather than serious competition. This proliferation of themed races appeals to nearly everyone and offers a unique twist to the straight-laced classic road races of the First Running Boom by providing participants a less-competitive atmosphere where they can focus on fitness, fun and the experience that they can and do share with friends and family; in addition to possibly contributing to a charitable cause.*

Not all sports are growing, and the trend watcher must never assume that growth will continue or that growth in one area applies across the board. Golf has been in decline for some time, in terms of numbers of North American participants and rounds played, although there has been a small gain in female golfers and it is growing in Asia! If participation declines you can expect fewer events (and golf courses).

Continued expansion of the entertainment industry

Stein and Evans (2009: 11), discussing the entertainment industry, commented that 'Americans have become obsessed with entertainment and celebrities.' This appears to be the case globally, facilitated by all forms of media. One consequence is that the marketplace is crowded: 'We are saturated with entertainment options. So, for one segment of the entertainment market to grow, another segment must decline' (2009: 1). Thus, 'Event planning is a lucrative business within the entertainment industry and can be an ideal career for those who thrive on details' (2009: 279).

One obvious area of growth has been the number of award shows, as it seems the celebration of entertainers has never been more popular. Providing fans with the opportunity to vote on something is always popular and has never been easier.

Entrepreneurship and a festival 'industry'

The existence of private festival-producing companies, and a professional class of event managers, makes it possible to 'order' an event to specification. Festivals and other celebrations can now be assembled from various inputs, if the money is available. This makes festivals retail commodities to be created or purchased as needed; successful event producers can go on to produce more events. More experienced customers are demanding ever-higher standards and quality, not to mention more unique experiences. Festivals have been able to provide these, although there must be limits to how much variety can be provided, and there are likely limits within a life-cycle model to how long any given festival can remain fresh. In addition to a private festivals sector, many festivals have been established by 'social entrepreneurs' who create non-profit festivals for a cause (and interesting jobs for themselves). Little is known about these people and their work, but they are vital in the festivals sector. Presumably social entrepreneurs have the option of being profit-oriented, although the scant evidence available suggests that profit-seeking entrepreneurs have to stay in well-defined niches with minimal public-sector and non-profit competition. Such entrepreneurs are particularly at a disadvantage in attracting government grants or subsidies, although not – it appears – in terms of attracting volunteers.

The experience economy and co-creation of experiences

Advances in the experience economy are relentless, with general recognition now that sophisticated, post-modern consumers want unique, personalized and memorable experiences. This applies especially in the sectors of entertainment, tourism, hospitality and events. Furthermore, many highly involved people, engaged as they are in various 'serious' lifestyle and leisure pursuits, invest heavily in travel and events and they want them to contribute to experiences, participating themselves in experience creation. Event producers therefore must become experience designers and co-creators.

Prahalad and Ramaswamy (2004) called for a strategic approach to experience creation drawing on shared values, allowing customers to co-create in the search for personal growth. Co-creation means that a company (event) and customer (or potential audience) share in the creation of value by allowing customers to shape experiences to suit their needs and desires. This is in stark contrast to the idea of consuming a single product, with experiences shaped entirely by the event producers. It recognizes that personal experiences are always different, and the customer increasingly does not want what everybody else is getting. Therefore, personalization is a key trend.

Is this new ideal possible for planned events? In some cases the design of events can be modified to permit co-creation, and this is a 'liberating' or 'enabling' approach. In others, the format of an event is fixed and consumers are tightly constrained – as in a theatrical performance with everyone in ticketed seats. Outside the event, however, other related experiences can be created, employing social media for discussion and extended dialogue about what should go into an event. At the leading edge of event management, designers are conceiving entirely new forms of events that will enable the liberation of experiences. But more importantly, members of social worlds and the unlimited number of communities of interest are creating their own events.

Gigantism and mega events

Horne (2006) suggested three main reasons for the expansion and growth in attraction of mega events: global audiences generated through satellite and other communications technologies; growth in corporate sponsorship; and place marketing, to showcase cities and countries. Preuss (2009) concluded that mega sport events are now too expensive for host cities, requiring senior government commitments, and argued that 'Increasing event gigantism clearly creates trouble for host cities by demanding infrastructure that is oversized and/or not sustainable for a city in the long term' (2009: 132). The increasing size of events in itself reflects a number of forces including globalization through media coverage and global sponsorship, increasing demand for event attendance and justification of the costs in terms of place marketing, and economic and urban development. The events themselves could and should be operated at a smaller scale, but they are no longer simply sport events.

Policy instrumentalism and festivalization

The creation and exploitation of events by public policy-makers can be divided into two general areas: civil society and social/cultural policy on the one hand, and tourism and place marketing on the other. Planned events play an important role in the 'civil society'. This term has multiple, interrelated connotations, so its usage is somewhat confusing. Definitions include the following:

- The totality of voluntary civic and social organizations and institutions that form the basis of a functioning society as opposed to the force-backed structures of a state (regardless of that state's political system) and commercial institutions of the market (from Wikipedia).
- Civil society refers to the arena of uncoerced collective action around shared interests, purposes and values (www.traditionalknowledge.info/glossary).
- A society where individuals cooperate with other individuals and with public authority in tackling their individual and social problems. The civil society also ensures representation of those interest groups which cannot represent themselves by using economic and political means of influence (www. mk.gov.lv).

With these three definitions in mind, we can posit that planned events are both institutions of civil society (at least the public and non-profit ones) and instruments of civil society. Governments wanting to strengthen civil society (either because they believe in this form of democracy, or to devolve responsibility for certain 'public goods') create and support events that reflect or promote certain values (this is social marketing), foster voluntarism and, in a number of ways, boost community development. Numerous groups with shared values employ events to promote their own interests, and for the most part this is a positive phenomenon.

So pervasive are festivals and events as instruments of public policy that some authors have described the process as 'festivalization'. There are several connotations, however, that need to be explored. According to Richards (2007a) this term has recently entered the literature. It appears to have arrived through translation from the writing of two Germans, Häussermann and Siebel (1993). The dominant usage refers to the festivalization of urban policy or politics, presumably following Häussermann and Siebel, who argued that cities competing for cultural consumers create or support festivals for different target markets, and consequently the cities become festivalized (in German the term used was *Festivalisierung*).

Richards (2007a: 282), in a book chapter entitled 'The festivalization of society or the socialization of festivals? The case of Catalunya', stated that:

> *The concept of festivalization is a fairly widely accepted phenomenon among analysts of urban policy and cultural trends (Häussermann and Siebel 1993). In this chapter it refers to the increasing use of flagship festivals and large cultural events as a means to market major cities. Furthermore, I will argue that festivalization is not just limited to city marketing objectives but is becoming a new policy paradigm in the field of urban culture.*

Frank and Roth (2000: 237) discussed events and the media, concentrating on forces shaping public discourse surrounding major events. The dominating influences were politics and the cultural sector, leading these authors to conclude that 'non-state actors gain importance in the process of the festivalization of city politics'. Long *et al.* (2004: 8) referred to the festivalization of urban policy as 'it may also be the case that urban development policies themselves are becoming "festivalized" with cultural festival spaces being conceived as a contribution to an urban aesthetic streetscape as part of wider planning, architectural and design processes'. Apparently anything can be festivalized, as intimated by Long *et al.* (2004: 3) who discussed the festivalization of advertising and product branding. In a paper entitled 'Festivalization of urban space in Morocco', Belghazi (2006) discussed the festivalization of spaces and whole cities as part of event tourism and place-marketing strategies.

There appears to be a general negativity associated with the term 'festivalization', as if it was an undesirable process, or at least that it carries risks. In this way it connects to the terms 'commodification' and 'commoditization', which are frequently employed in a derogatory sense to describe the process of festivals losing their cultural authenticity when exploited for tourism or other commercial purposes. This line of criticism specific to festivals seems to have started with ethnographic studies by Greenwood (1972, 1989).

To Richards (2007a), festivalization implies commodification and a removal of control from local to national and global, arguing that, increasingly, festivals are aimed at the socialization of communities, rather than tourists and economic development.

Social media and social networking

Although progress in the technology of communications and entertainment is rapid, it is the use of social media that has caught everyone's attention – whether in the context of public uprisings, their role in spawning or facilitating new events (both planned and 'spontaneous') or as social networking tools connected to serious leisure, social worlds, subcultures and related niche events. We have now gone past the age of both broadcasting (i.e. mass media like television, radio, newspapers and magazines with content aimed at a generic 'audience') and narrowcasting (employing the same media for diverse and fragmenting niche markets). Users are now able to create and utilize their own global networks, with no one in charge and everyone a content producer.

The basic ingredients are the digital communications devices and networks (i.e. mobile devices plus commercial networks, or at least access to the Internet) and self-forming groups. The groups can share information, and persons in the groups can interact. The evolution of social media and networks is rather difficult to predict, as they are changing and growing at astounding speed. Their exploitation for marketing events has already been well established. How the events sector uses them in the future is still an open question.

What can social media do? Consider the power of these characteristics individually and in any combination:

- instant global communications including virtual events (like a meeting) and live 'netcasting' of events (watching sports in real time);
- marketing events to target communities online (you need your own database or access to various networks of potential users);
- facilitating easy and cheap publication (e.g. event advertising and content);
- tools that make everyone a journalist, such as reporting on event experiences;
- sharing at an enormous scale (articles, ideas, photos, profiles, music, videos at or about events);
- real-time collaboration among researchers, events managers, public agencies, institutions and corporations (for the purpose of getting embedded in a support network);
- discussion and public discourse, everywhere and all the time (planning and evaluating events, co-producing the experiences, reporting the 'news' about events);

- social networking or group formation around events or leading to event-related travel; connecting to others with similar interests; virtually experiencing social events;
- amusement (will gaming take the place of live event experiences?);
- shopping (buying tickets and travel packages).

The implications of social media are manifold. Organizations and governments can no longer control information and discourse, not even news reporting. Corporations have found that brands are not theirs to exclusively create and manage, as everyone has an opinion and a potential audience. And the event experience can be augmented by pre-, during and post-event interactions to foster engagement and increase satisfaction. New niche markets are being created all the time, reflecting real and virtual social worlds; they offer the opportunity to co-create events interactively with online communities (see Research Note 1.3).

1.3 RESEARCH NOTE ON SOCIAL MEDIA

Hudson, S., Roth, M., Madden, T. and Hudson, R. (2015). The effects of social media on emotions, brand relationship quality, and word of mouth: An empirical study of music festival attendees. *Tourism Management*, 47, 68–76.

Hudson and fellow researchers studied the influence of social media on customer relationships regarding music festivals. Results show that social media had a significant influence on emotions and attachments to festival brands, and that social media-based relationships led to desired outcomes, such as positive word of mouth.

Major issues

Commodification

Has everything been commodified, that is, turned into commercialized, profit-making business? Have people disengaged from authentic experiences and resorted to entertainment and spectacle, as suggested by Debord (1983)? It often appears this way, and it is a worrying trend. The French philosopher, building on Marxist traditions, argued that culture had become 'an immense accumulation of images', a sequence of commercial fragments detached from original experience. In this pessimistic interpretation of the modern world people are denied authentic, live experiences such as festivity or celebration and instead are fed a steady barrage of spectacle – things we passively watch instead of experiences we live.

The potential dominance of spectacle

Spectacle exists within the realm of the visual as something viewed (by 'spectators', obviously); but it is larger than life, colourful, exciting and novel, otherwise we would perceive it to be ordinary and unremarkable. We are easily seduced by spectacle, otherwise people would tire of fireworks and lasers, parades and outlandish costumes, and it is a substantial part of entertainment in general and events programming in particular.

Gotham (2005a) wrote about spectacle in the context of urban festivals in New Orleans, using Guy Debord's theory of the spectacle and the writings of Henri Lefebvre (e.g. his book *The Production of Space*, 1991) to examine conflicting meanings assigned to the celebrations. Different stakeholders employed festivals to attract tourists, empower communities or sow dissent. Viewed as spectacle, in the tradition of Debord, a festival is merely one manifestation of everything becoming a commodity as opposed to festivals or carnivals as participatory experiences. According to anthropologist John MacAloon (1984), a festival is a joyous celebration of unity, cooperation, accomplishment and excellence, while a spectacle is a grandiloquent display of imagery evoking a diffuse sense of wonderment and awe.

Regarding the Olympic Games, MacAloon (1984: 242) argued that of the genres of cultural performance, spectacle and games appeared first, followed by festival and ritual. Spectacles are not only things to be seen, he argued in his 'theory of spectacle', but also possess symbolic codes. Spectacles must be grand, dramatic or huge. There is no spectacle without actors and audience, or performers and spectators. Spectators must be excited by the spectacle, or otherwise emotionally moved. The Olympics, said MacAloon (1984: 245), 'must be seen, and seen in person, to be believed'. Host cities are transformed, animated. The scale and intensity of the overall experience cannot be captured on television.

Ritual is a duty, but spectacle is by choice. Outsiders, or uninformed audiences, might mistake ritual for spectacle or not care about the embedded cultural meanings. While 'festival' requires a certain style of celebratory mood, and internal 'special observances', spectacle does not. MacAloon was suspicious of spectacles, as they tend to be 'tasteless' and become a 'moral cacophony'.

Although the Olympic Games are proclaimed to be a festival, MacAloon (1984: 250) said that festival and spectacle are in opposition. Nevertheless, both share one feature – they erect frames of cultural performances around a variety of genres; they both make 'differentiated forms of symbolic action into new wholes by means of a common spatiotemporal location, expressive theme, affective style, ideological intention, or social function'.

In this way the Olympics embodies a ritual organized around the classic rites of passage (that is, opening and closing ceremonies) which introduce liminality, intensification (i.e. victory and medal awards), closure and reaggregation. Using the concepts of van Gennep and Turner, MacAloon (1984: 253) noted that at the Olympic Games 'the assembled thousands and the space that they occupied are released into an extraordinary expression of spontaneous communitas'.

MacAloon concluded (1984: 268) by saying that spectacle has destructive effects on ritual, festival and games. These genres of cultural performance bring people together – a 'communitas' – whereas spectacle is just about watching. On the other hand, in societies favouring individualism, spectacle can act to bring people into a festival or ritualistic environment that they would otherwise be suspicious of.

Rockwell and Mau (2006) gave historical examples of the power and misuse of spectacle by the Nazis at Nuremberg and the Fascist Mussolini, through his revival of traditional games-festivals to manipulate nationalism. Do contemporary events also seek to manipulate people for political purposes or profits?

The high costs of bidding and hosting major events

Many issues are raised by this trend, not the least of which are the opportunity costs associated with such a vast commitment of resources. Particularly when austerity cuts in many European public-sector organizations reduce public spending per se. The opportunity cost of bidding may have very unpalatable local consequences politically. This is because bidding requires significant resources which are 'consumed' by mega events with seldom any consideration of what else society could do with the money and labour. Usually we get only vague promises of benefits in the bidding process, including tourism gains and future events that can be held, or development of sport and housing as a legacy. Post-event accountability is generally lacking, or unconvincing, with benefits not demonstrable and costs rising.

Virtual events and augmented reality

What people usually mean by 'virtual event' is really a form of online and remote communications. This includes teleconferences and online streaming of sports or entertainment. There has been a fear for many years that people will stay at home or in their offices rather than attend meetings, conventions, exhibitions or any entertainment offering.

Sadd (2014) argued that the transformational power of technology will impact upon the design of events, and that blended technology fusing the virtual and the real is the way forward, but she also maintained that gatherings of people still need interaction for the co-creation of experiences. Sadd discussed how augmented reality (AR) changes perceptions of reality and permits interaction, and this is a different concept from replacing real events.

Planned events are social by nature, and many people will only resort to 'virtuality' when the real thing is not available: this is not necessarily a replacement. It is great to augment events with live streaming and online interconnectivity, and many meetings should be conducted remotely rather than waste energy through travel, but these are not the planned events we want to participate in for social reasons. Event business is better done in person, otherwise exhibitions would have died out long ago, but traditional trade shows have found that they need to add substantial educational and social components to attract exhibitors and customers.

Having made the case, however, there are exceptions. Consider the choice between watching sports on television (or your personal communications device) and going to the live event. Some people will prefer the remote experience, as it is cheaper, often easier to see the details, and comes with additional commentary and information.

1.4 RESEARCH NOTE ON TECHNOLOGY

Locke, M. (2010). A framework for conducting a situational analysis of the meetings, incentives, conventions, and exhibitions sector. *Journal of Convention and Event Tourism*, 11(3), 209–233.

Locke (2010) argued that technological advances in information and communication technology 'have had a significant impact on the MICE sector in all parts of the world. Virtual meetings, webcasts, podcasts, teleconferencing, video conferences, distance learning, blogs, and interactive multimedia are becoming increasingly common tools in the corporate world.' Her literature review revealed that the lead time for planning events has decreased, in part owing to communications and information processing software (e.g. for online registration). Venues must provide a high standard of technology. Technology is also employed to improve the experience, as in assisted speaker–audience interaction. Locke also discusses virtual conferencing, noting that some observers believe that technology is changing the ways in which people meet, while others see these as supplementing traditional in-person events.

1.5 RESEARCH NOTE ON VIRTUAL EVENTS

Pearlman, D. and Gates, N. (2010). Hosting business meetings and special events in virtual worlds: A fad or the future? *Journal of Convention and Event Tourism*, 11(4), 247–265.

Pearlman and Gates (2010) discussed trends impacting on events, including economic recession, that have led to increasing interest in technological solutions to business-information challenges. Their research investigated the awareness, acceptance and adoption of virtual reality applications. They found that 'virtual meetings and special events are innovative and viable methods to effectively and efficiently achieve organizational objectives. Still, in the early stages of development, the use of virtual reality within the meetings, incentive, convention and exhibition industry looks promising; however, widespread adoption may be years away.'

Sustainability

Underlying forces continue to generate growth and diversity in the events sector, and this is likely to continue in the foreseeable future. But there are limiting factors, or threats, that will eventually check growth – especially in event tourism. When and how this will happen is still uncertain. In the concluding chapter a future scenario based on the end of tourism is presented, enabling some speculation about how events will be affected if dramatic and permanent changes occur to our global environment and economy.

Sustainability is a broad concept, and various threads of this discourse run throughout this book: green operations; ecological footprint and carbon loadings; the future of event tourism; institutionalization; economic viability; managerial competence; population ecology and portfolio management; costs and legacies. Bringing them all together to formulate a clear and integrated measure of sustainability is all but impossible, if for no other reason than multiple stakeholder perspectives on event goals and impacts.

It is probably wise to think of sustainable tourism and events as a process of continuous striving for improvement; setting and attaining goals for green operations is likely the starting point for most events, and should not be the end. Through a continuous process of evaluation and strategic planning, all events can pursue a more sustainable path.

Martin Robertson has been looking at the trends as well, and his views are summarized below.

1.2 EXPERT OPINION

Trends and the future of events

Martin Robertson, School of Tourism, Bournemouth University, UK

The future of events is more certain than many would think. There will continue to be a demand for events and an increase in supply opportunities. Professionalization and accreditation are already viewed as vital to ensure events provision is at a level that is comparable with other developed industries. In an increasingly competitive world for events (for hosts, providers, managers and services), and one in which the avoidance of risk and an awareness of legal liability are likely to emerge more strongly than they have so far, a streamlining of the number of providers and the variables that influence event performance and evaluation is inevitable. There is, thus, a likelihood (if not complete certainty) that two forms of events will dominate the market. One of these will be an increasingly infrequent but far more spectacular (and costly) event designed to attract a larger number of markets. The other will be a smaller, very much more precisely targeted event. Another important influence is the internationalization of the event industry as fluctuations in the economy take place, and the growth of the professional middle classes in previously less active parts of the world. This has a strong link to our need to understand and provide for new event markets.

Ethics and internationalism

As the consumption and provision of managed events emerge in new international markets, so too a new range of ethics and international social and cultural values will enter into the mind-set of event managers (and the stakeholders who influence their action). While the BRIC countries (Brazil, Russia, India and China) will dominate in these changing times, there are a great number of other countries (particularly from Asia and the Asia-Pacific market) that will enter the event marketplace. Each may have marked varieties of cultural value. As such, the needs of each market are likely to be different. It is important that the service delivery and product design of events respond to these differences.

However, it is not just an awareness of cross-cultural and cross-national values that will be required. As the economic strength of each of the BRIC (and economically related) countries grows, so too the numbers of the professional middle classes and a demand for new levels of quality will also develop. This brings with it both a challenge and opportunities for success.

Ethics and international social and cultural values will enter into the mind-set of more event managers (and the stakeholders who influence their actions). The Asia and Asia-Pacific market expands as the numbers who form the professional middle classes grows ever larger. For both event providers and event tourism this elicits a conundrum of market forces and producer requirements. There is evident a marked variety of cultural values. There is a great number of countries and a marked variety of cultural value. The needs of each market are therefore different. It is important that the service delivery and product design of events responds to this.

Technology

The use of technology will animate both event experience and the format of its management in ways not thought of previously. Assisting group and individual interaction and participation in events technology (whether in the form of social media, or networking and collaboration software and hardware) will certainly be of benefit to new event users (audiences, delegates or participants). New video-conference, virtual and augmented immersive technologies will increasingly allow events to assist participation that responds to the needs of time-poor market groups, as well as offering responses to the potential negative environment and social impacts caused by large space- and resource-'hungry' events. Virtual event, real-time video streaming and distribution through multiple personal handheld media will supplement rather than replace attendance at events but they will become more crucial to success as their provision becomes an anticipated norm in the mind of the event attendee.

This rapid rise in the technologies available to both managers and consumers of events will add costs that many in the sector will find hard to bear. This may determine a growth of and reliance on the resources of existing venues (such as a convention centre) or the action of specialist services. Audio-visual specialists have always been significant components of event planning, management and provision, but an accelerating change in technical specifications and capacity in both this area and for other technologies is likely to increase the costs of their services.

Curation, augmentation and the strategic design of events

Not looking very far into the future it is possible to see that the success of many organized events will be determined by skills more recently associated with the great changes in the curation of museums. This is to say that the brilliance and precision that is already required of managing events will become more exacting. The inspirational spectacle that makes the exhibitions that travel the museums of the world so attractive has ignited in the minds of viewers (and prospective event attendees) a quality that is difficult to authenticate in the smaller and less well-funded event. Budgets, funding sources, other stakeholder interests, and a demand for defined and measurable levels of quality will have a more profound influence than they already do. As such there is a strong possibility that the creative flair often associated with the running of events will be required to be more readily auditable and, correspondingly, the creative process – from initial draft idea to the event performance – will require greater efficiencies. As such the design of an event will become more clearly linked to the event's strategic function (as well as the more immediate satisfaction of all those involved). Translating design to function will exercise new skills.

Technology will assist in the translation of design and will be relied upon more and more in the bidding process for events. Detail, clarity and strict affirmation of costs in the bidding process will be expected. Free open-source software, such as Google Sketchup8, and a rise in easily accessible animation tools will make this detail more readily available – and potentially reduce the cost of a bid as more flamboyant elements can be eradicated with digital and mobile visual representation.

'Festivalization' and political will

Both readily accepted meanings of 'festivalization' have significant and real overtures for the future of events. In the first meaning – that there is an oversupply of festivals – and in the second – that festivals are an accepted part of our social fabric – there is clear evidence that events and festivals are becoming an increasingly normalized occurrence. As such, the unique nature of events that makes them special is under threat. In cities well known for hosting events, such as Melbourne and Edinburgh, the pressures of maintaining uniqueness means that events become increasingly expensive. For the public and private organizations with responsibility for governing event pro-grammes in any one destination this brings with it an increasing range of challenges which short-term partnerships are not best suited for. It is thus more likely that the multifarious strategic associations and purposes of events that already exist will become more pronounced, not less. As political power must be exercised through networks of associations, the significance of a broker or 'champion' to negotiate these relations will increase markedly.

STUDY GUIDE

In this first chapter the student should gain understanding of how and why event studies is defined and justified as a field of academic inquiry. Consideration has been given to why anyone should study planned events, including the obvious relationship to event management and event tourism professional educa-tion, but also the importance of events within many other disciplines, fields of enquiry and policy domains.

Study the framework for understanding and creating knowledge about planned events, as this has been important in structuring the book. Each of the components is considered later, in detail, in one or more chapters. Be comfortable in explaining the three major subdivisions of event studies and how they inter-relate: disciplinary perspectives (including the 'classical' social and cultural perspective rooted in soci-ology and anthropology), event management and event tourism. The last two subdivisions are applied, leading to distinct career paths, whereas the disciplinary perspective is much more theoretical. All three have policy implications for governments concerned with events and their impacts. They are also called 'discourses': each has its own tradition in the literature, in terms of epistemology (underlying theory and methodology) and ontology (bodies of knowledge). Those topics are considered later in the book.

Start to consider the major challenges and issues facing event management and event tourism, as well as the big policy issues for governments at all levels. There are many specific points throughout the book. Careers are introduced here, and there is some theory and research on careers later in the book when we look at human resources. Also relevant is the later discussion on ethics and professionalism.

Be able to answer, in full sentences and paragraphs, the study questions – all are potential exam questions based on this chapter.

STUDY QUESTIONS

- Define event studies and explain why it is, or is not, an academic discipline.
- What is the core phenomenon of event studies, and whose experiences are we interested in?
- How are meanings attached to events and event experiences?
- Explain each component of the framework for understanding and creating knowledge about planned events, and be able to illustrate each of them with specific research examples.
- Outline the three main subdivisions within event studies and how they relate to policy and careers.
- What are the various specializations open to event management and event tourism professionals, and how are the necessary knowledge and skills obtained?
- Discuss major forces shaping planned events and resulting trends and issues.
- How do you think social media are shaping the demand for events, and the event experience?

FURTHER READING

See the References section for all references cited in the book. At the end of each chapter is a short list of books recommended for additional reading that elaborate upon key topics.

Bowdin, G., Allen, J., O'Toole, W., Harris, R. and McDonnell, I. (2011). *Events Management* (3rd edn). Oxford: Butterworth-Heinemann.

Getz, D. (2013a). *Event Tourism: Concepts, International Case Studies, and Research*. New York: Cognizant.

Goldblatt, J. (2014) *Special Events* (7th edn). New York, NY: John Wiley & Sons.

Page, S. J. and Connell, J. (2014). *Routledge Handbook of Events*. London: Routledge (student paperback edition).

Chapter **2**

The world of planned events

LEARNING OBJECTIVES

Upon completion of this chapter students should know the following:

- definitions and the nature of events and planned events;
- meanings attached to time and how they make events special;
- the critical importance of place and setting;
- how size, length, frequency and periodicity of events are important variables;
- classifications of events in terms of their form, function and experiential dimensions;
- how and why event forms and functions converge;
- differences between planned and unplanned events.

Describing and classifying events

The world of planned events is diverse and exciting, with almost unlimited scope for variety in form, function and event experiences. The meanings we attach to these events, and the importance they have always held in our personal and collective lives, make them fundamental components of culture, business and lifestyles. This chapter starts with basic definitions of 'event' and 'planned events', including a discussion of differences between planned and unplanned, and the question of scale (small versus large events). The inherent temporal and spatial dimensions of events are discussed, as this is fundamental to understanding much of the related theory.

Many adjectives are used in conjunction with the term 'event' and we need to understand how they arise from consideration of either the form or function of planned events. Terms like 'hallmark', 'mega' or 'iconic' refer to the function of events (e.g. for image making and place marketing, their size and significance, and their unique appeal). The comprehensive event typology illustrated in Figure 2.1 is largely based on their form. When we associate specific form, setting and programming with event types like 'festival', 'convention' or 'sport competition', we are really creating and reflecting 'social constructs' that are based on tradition and common, societal expectations. Concluding this chapter is a profile of each of the main types and key subtypes of planned events.

What is an event?

Common dictionary definitions of 'event' stress three points:

> *Event: an occurrence at a given place and time; a special set of circumstances; a noteworthy occurrence.*

Events, by definition, have a beginning and an end. They are temporal phenomena, and with planned events the event programme or schedule is generally planned in detail and well publicized in advance. Planned events are also usually confined to particular places, although the space involved might be a specific facility, a very large open space, or many locations simultaneously or in sequence. As will be argued, what we call planned or special events are a matter of perspective and are social constructs.

When you search 'event' on the Internet you will encounter its use in many other fields, for example in finance (events that disrupt the markets or change a business), physics (e.g. 'event horizons'), biology (e.g. 'extinction events'), philosophy (e.g. 'mental events'), climatology (e.g. 'weather events'), medicine (e.g. 'adverse events'), probability theory (e.g. events as 'outcomes of experiments') and computer science (e.g. 'event-driven programming'). In many cases, the temporal dimension is more important than the spatial (i.e. geographical) in most of these usages.

No matter how hard one tries, it is literally impossible to replicate an event; by definition they only occur once, creating a unique experience for the audience or participants. Although planned events might be similar in form, some aspect of setting, people and programme will ensure that the event is always tangibly or experientially different. The expectations, moods and attitudes of guests and participants will always be new, so their experiences will differ regardless of the programme and setting. This uniqueness of events makes them attractive, even compelling, so that cultivating a 'once in a lifetime' image for an event is the marketer's goal. However, these goals have also become very commonplace in other areas of consumer behaviour, as businesses and organizations seek to create unique selling propositions in marketing terms, to delight their customers consuming services and more experientially focused products. All the planned events we talk about in this book are social events: they are for people, and not merely events in our own, personal lives.

Virtual events

All planned events are social in nature, and that is because people have a need to be together – to socialize, celebrate and do business. While online or teleconferenced events have their place, they are not replacements. In this book we talk about virtual events in several places, but they are not the object of, or at the core of, event studies although there is growing interest in the rise of technology and its potential impact on the conventional notion of the event. The Expert Opinion by Dr Matt Frew examines some of the trends and issues related to technology and virtuality.

2.1 EXPERT OPINION

Future events and technology culture: dreamscapes or dark fantasy?

Dr Matt Frew, Ph.D., Senior Lecturer in Event Management, School of Tourism, University of West of Scotland.

Glance over the shoulder of history and you will see a trajectory of technological transformations in the world of work, life and leisure. The impact of technology has always generated patterns of reaction, from Luddite fears and mass fascination, to dismissive fad. Interestingly, events occupy a pioneering place in the discourse of technology. From the conspicuous consumption of industrial innovation in the Great Exhibition of 1851 (Hall 2006) and the Nazi TV propaganda of the 1936 Berlin Olympics to the 2014 Brazilian World Cup, a 'sporting event that has generated bigger TV audiences and more social network chatter than any in history' (Watt 2014), technology and events have a symbiotic relationship.

Today we are in an age of acceleration where, I argue, a globally evolving techno-capitalism (Suarez-Villa 2009) and techno-culture (Dijck 2013) is changing not only events but the structuring relations of life, society and the self. Consider for a moment the *last century* and the impact of innovations such as the silent then talking pictures, radio or the masses mesmerized by the magic box of early TV. Now, consider the *past decade* – the explosion of digital and social media, smart technologies, holographics, haptics, brain-to-computer interface, augmented reality and the rebirth of virtual reality (Kaku 2012). The Internet of Things and era of big data has just begun and given that, from the 'dawn of civilisation until 2003, human kind generated five exabytes of data. Now we produce five exabytes every two days' (Schmidt, cited in Booch 2014: 21), the speed and scale of technological transformation is unprecedented. A paradigm shift is at play, where we are swamped by a technological tsunami that is moving so fast and is networked in a daily convergent conversation of billions, that it has become a given. So in this age of accelerating techno-culture what does the future hold for events?

Currently, most events are stuck grappling with techno-cultures of convergence (Flinn and Frew 2014) where the digital lifestyles of consumers represent a new mode of social commerce (Solis 2013) to be mined. The problem is, that while modern events demand a digital heartbeat that engages with and feeds the desire for digital, as much as experiential, distinction, this is only the tip of the technological iceberg. Today's trajectory of technology reveals a shift from an external functionality to the internalization, embodiment and immersion of technologies. This is reflected in the lift and leave of traditional computing, to our constant smartphone companions, to the integrated wearables such as Google Glass and on to the digital layering and animation of the inanimate world through the augmented reality of iOptik. What we are witnessing is a transhuman e-volution, a digital disruption of desire, whereby technologies are, increasingly, challenging the structuring relations of our world, in particular, time, space and subjectivity. Our techno-future is one directed at overcoming those physical laws and, most importantly, frustrations with the embodied state.

Although social, digital, smart-technologies, wearables and augmented reality demonstrate a globally accelerating techno-culture, developments in virtual reality (VR) represent a game-changing future for events. While VR has been around for a few decades, primarily the bastion of gamers, engineering, processor and software advances have catapulted it into the limelight as a pioneering future technology. Currently, while the likes of the University of Southern California's Project

Holodeck and major corporations, such as Sony's Project Morpheus and Google's augmented reality project Magic Leap, jostle for position, Oculus Rife is leading the way in immersive VR. Oculus, recently purchased by Facebook's Mark Zuckerberg for $2 billion, produces spectacular off-world constructs where the depth of immersive experiences is designed to achieve 'presence': that feeling of actually being there. With VR and the likes of Oculus the 'end game' is where 'people will spend part of their days virtually teleported if you will, place shifted' (Christensen 2014). Moreover, when integrated with the sensory, force-feedback of haptics and holography the visions of VR promise new dreamscapes where the 'warm embrace; the view, sounds, breeze, and smells of the beach' (Schybergson 2014) are possible. The constructing of such dreamscape 'realities', where you will feel 'truly present . . . share unbounded spaces . . . not just moments with your friends online, but entire experiences and adventures' (Zuckerberg, cited in Dredge 2014), is of critical importance for future events, if not for life.

Accelerating techno-culture and its VR dreamscapes promise much for the future of events. Time, space and subjectivity are blurred, re-written if not erased. Go anywhere, anyplace, anytime; live and relive past memories; be young, old or assume a new self, a new performativity, and be whoever you want to be. As Schmidt and Cohen of Google put it:

> If you're feeling bored and want to take an hour-long holiday, why not turn on your holograph box and visit Carnival in Rio? Stressed? Go spend some time on a beach in the Maldives . . . Through virtual-reality interfaces and holographic projection capabilities, you'll be able to 'join' these activities as they happen and experience them as if you were truly there.
>
> (2013: 24)

Of course academic enquiry will always hit the pause button for critical reflection. For one thing, technology is far from neutral; there is always a dark side for, as history shows, while we shape technology, technology always shapes us and that leads to critical questions if not resistance (Dijck 2013; Frew 2014). Indeed the ability to 'place shift' us to magical dreamscapes, where we can visit the Pyramids of Giza, enjoy an Olympics or World Cup in real time, rewind and be up front at a Beatles gig or adopt a new performative persona and take a walk on the festive or sexual wild side, has a magnetic appeal. In an instant, issues of events, tourism or sports such as capacity are overcome, sustainability and environmental impacts radically reduced, inequity and inclusivity claimed, physical disability or age eliminated and, of course, new modes of commerce created (Kaku 2012). However, while future dreamscapes offer promise, they also herald a dark fantasy.

Already concerns are being raised about escapism, exploitation and the possible dystopian nightmare that future techno-culture may produce (Gumbel 2014). After all, if we can achieve immersive 'presence', that feeling of being 'truly there', or, better, recreate self, relive and reboot life itself, why would we ever leave the dreamscape? Moreover, when you do leave, are you faced with a life and self that is fundamentally disappointing, being ever reminded of that new, younger, adventurous performative self of the dreamscape? Undoubtedly, many will shake their heads and dismiss such notions as folly, arguing for a truly human event experience and how the virtual will never replace or be as authentic as lived, embodied reality. I would argue that this is a deflective if not dying debate. Forget privileging the present over the past, real over the virtual experience. While we do not know the detail of the future, what we do know is that these transformational technologies are here. The drive and direction of techno-culture is accelerating and with VR dreamscapes the very notion of the 'real' and the 'self' is up for grabs.

Interestingly, the leaders of techno-culture and eminent futurists tend to reference movie culture as the template of imagination and inspiration but also as a critical counterpoint to those who insist on a universal notion of the 'real', essentialist or embodied 'self' (Kaku 2012; Kurzweil 2008). Whether *Star Trek*, *Total Recall*, *Minority Report*, *The Matrix* or *Transcendence*, they point out how we are turning 'popular science fiction concepts into science facts' (Schmidt and Cohen 2013: 5). More importantly, they recognize the problem of how the 'physical and virtual worlds' need to 'coexist, collide and complement each other' and how this accelerating techno-culture 'will greatly affect how citizens and states behave' (Schmidt and Cohen 2013: 31). It is safe to assume that future events will play a central role in the discourse of accelerating techno-culture, as sites offering dreamscape promise or dark fantasy events will become cultural battlegrounds where the moral, embodied and socio-political tensions of the day, as much as notions of the 'real' and the 'self', will be fought out. Future events in future techno-culture will, increasingly, reflect the dissolution of the structuring relations of time, space and subjectivity. To dismiss such ideas as 'fantastical' would, ironically, be correct for the future is, indeed, now.

No such thing as events!

Having made the case for 'events' as discrete phenomena, it is worth noting that in a Buddhist interpretation, everything is interdependent and all events arise from previous events, and in a more general philosophical context 'events' might not actually exist (for elaboration, and perhaps confusion, see the online article by Mansfield 1998).

This line of argument posits that events cannot be separated completely from their context, from the flow of what is happening in the world and in our daily lives. What we call a planned event is in reality an integral part of many people's lives and many stakeholders' actions, with various environmental forces acting upon us. Events, therefore, are merely the perceived intersection (in time and/or places) of different people and the consequences of various flows of activity. This makes perfect sense philosophically, and certainly event managers and policy-makers must be experts at assessing environmental forces, but for pragmatic reasons it does not affect our perception that planned events exist, and that event studies is a vital subject. One need only refer to common language (i.e. the vernacular) to know that discrete events are central to most people's understanding of the world and their own lives. We measure time and events, even if it is arguably an illusion, and therefore we need and recognize events to mark important occasions and define periods of activity.

Event-history analysis

This method within social science focuses on socially significant events in the lives of people, such as the various rites of passage. But these events could also be episodes, such as education and unemployment, jobs and relationships as part of the notion of the life cycle. Rapoport *et al.* (1975) in *Leisure and the Family*, building on the classic studies of family life and leisure of Rowntree and Lavers (1951), identified the notion of a family life-cycle model and the interrelationship between stages in the life cycle, work and leisure. This has an important bearing on the stages in an individual's and family's life where events will have specific meaning. Rapoport *et al.* (1975) identified four stages: Youth, Young Adulthood, Establishment and Later Years, although we also need to include childhood in these stages. The period of establishment, which is the largest in the family life cycle, is where the majority of social events occur (marriage, childbirth and child rearing and maintaining friendships) and work careers. The concept of stages helps to explain how people engage with events and the type of events they will consume in their work and leisure time, including the increasing blurring of work and leisure. This led Stebbins (1982) to observe that 'serious leisure' was evolving, where leisure and work activities overlap. To explain this emergence of 'serious leisure', Stebbins argued that:

> *Leisure in post-industrial society is no longer seen as chiefly a means of recuperating from the travail of the job . . . if leisure is to become, for many, an improvement over work as a way of finding personal fulfilment, identity enhancement, self-expression, and the like, then people must be careful to adopt those forms with the greatest payoff. The theme here is that we reach this goal through engaging in serious rather than casual or unserious leisure.*
>
> (Stebbins 1982: 253)

This has an important bearing on the patronage of events during the establishment stage of the family life cycle if people become engaged with others in various communities of interest (e.g. as event volunteers) or through serious leisure pursuits. And it is worth asking, what the planned events are that we have attended that hold special meaning in our lives, some possibly even being transforming experiences, and how these have evolved through time.

Time is of the essence

Time is not a simple concept, and we use expressions of time in many ways – some of which are highly relevant to event studies. First, time is often conceptualized as being 'cyclical', as with the annual calendar. Seasonal changes are important in terms of climate, food production and the very rhythms of social life, and this helps explain the evolution of many rituals and festivals as discussed in Chapter 1 (Connell *et al.* 2015). We tend to mark the 'passage of time' by annual holidays and celebrations, and we particularly look forward to them coming around next year. However, our modern conception of time and how it is defined through the working week, and the distinction between work time and non-work (leisure) time (see Page and Connell 2010), is fundamental to the analysis of events. This distinction between work and leisure is very much a construction of the capitalist period, particularly the Victorian period, and, as recognized by Billinge (1996), time was used geographically to channel leisure activities such as attending events (e.g. football matches) to appropriate times and places outside of formal work time. This created a social necessity for recreation as freedom from work: a non-work activity to recreate body and soul, to be refreshed for the capitalist economic system, with its regulated time discipline of a place for everything, and everything in its place (Billinge 1996). As the capitalist system of production developed and leisure became more defined in non-work time, the working day developed into a more standardized eight-hour phenomenon (Rybczynski 1991; Cross 1986) and a consumer culture also developed alongside leisure (Cross 1993). For time to be available for participation in events, we need to understand the evolution of the modern working week and the rise of the weekend as a leisure setting.

As Page and Connell (2010) illustrated, the five-day working week that has dominated industrial society is now changing in 'post-modern' society, with more blurring of work and leisure time. This is reflected in the reduction in working time from six days, to five and a half, then to a five-day working week. In some societies working on a Saturday is still a routine activity, but the notion of work time and leisure has very important impacts on when events are scheduled and who will attend.

Likewise, time also has an important influence when looking at 'biological' time and the individual and family life cycle: the maturing of one's body and mind marks the passage of a life, relative to others going through the same 'life-stage' changes. These various stages are marked by events we celebrate. Events mark life's changes (*rites de passage*, like birthdays and anniversaries), its triumphs (graduation and other formal ceremonies), its fun and joy (festivals, leisure pursuits, family reunions) and even its temporary pains (goodbyes and funerals). Time and its use in contemporary society therefore have a very significant bearing on the nature of events we celebrate and their impact on our work and non-work time.

'SOCIAL AND CULTURAL CONSTRUCTS' OF TIME

As will be seen later, the conceptualization of the liminal/liminoid zone for the planned event experience is a social construct, and will vary from culture to culture. In most Western societies the meanings and values attached to escapism, free time, leisure pursuits, having a good time (e.g. hedonism) and being entertained, reflect the growth of the public and private consumption of leisure time (Page and Connell 2010). Events as leisure pursuits can be traced back through history and so they are not necessarily new. What is new is the way in which our post-modern lives and the globalized nature of leisure consumption have impacted upon the production and enjoyment of so many planned events. Indeed such events are not only accepted but expected. As discussed above, the construction of time through a capitalist society has led to the social and cultural construction of time outside of work and the perceived 'need' for annual holidays, numerous special days for commemorations (of just about everything) and time for ourselves where we engage in events. Historical analyses of the way the state has legislated to create leisure time over the past 120 years, to create the conditions in which events as experiences can be enjoyed by more people, have democratized the process of event participation as a mass form of consumption. This is especially the case in time–space compression (see Warf 2008), making attending global and mega events more accessible. This reflects the abundance of leisure choices that digitally connected societies now take for granted, and where events allow people to be co-present in a specific time and place.

TIME AS A 'COMMODITY'

Time is precious in our society; therefore it has become a commodity with high value. We gladly pay for 'quality time' with our friends and families, and this often involves event experiences. We will sacrifice more money to have more 'free time'. We hate 'having our time wasted'. We all know that we cannot 'buy time', but we can certainly 'lose time'. These values and attitudes are all shaped by our culture, and perhaps it would be healthier if our cultural perceptions of time changed.

How we use, perceive and value time are important considerations in event studies. Events are temporal phenomena, with start and end points, yet the experience of them begins before and possibly never ends! Clawson and Knetsch (1966) conceptualized recreational travel as a multiphase experience, consisting of five major phases: anticipation, travel-to, on-site, travel-back and recollection. Anticipation and recollection can be just as important as the experience itself. In this way, the packaging of events, a key to effective event tourism development and marketing, should be much more focused on the overall experience than on the technical aspects of travel, accommodation and event tickets.

The value of time varies a great deal among people, at various stages in their lives, and among cultures. 'Time is money', sure, and people want value for their 'investment' of time, but how does this apply to planned events? On one hand a short, intense event experience can be just what is needed, but people are also willing to give up large blocks of time to travel to events. Can we measure the value of events by reference to the time various people invest in them? Is it possible that people value time differently, and therefore the identical event experience can be much more satisfying to some? This illustrates an important role for research in positive psychology (see Filep and Pearce 2013) with its focus on how individuals and groups can make their normal life more fulfilling through experiences such as events, especially the event participant valuation and meaning of time.

In *Faster: The Acceleration of Just About Everything*, Gleick (2000) argued that everybody now expects that everything can and should be done immediately, giving rise to time pressures in our 24-hour society. In fact Cornish (2004) contextualized this, arguing that the pace of change had accelerated to the point that we now live in an age of hyperchange in society. Cornish argued that this hyperchange combines with the range of super trends which affect society (i.e. technological progress, deculturation, the loss of local culture through globalization, environmental decline and deterioration, increased mobility and economic progress leading to increased prosperity).

We need to think of planned events as a respite from this rapidity, a way to escape these time pressures and if not to slow down, at least to savour the moment. The value of time in the event may therefore be escapism from the routines and rigours of everyday life in much the same way that the annual holiday has been evaluated by researchers for many years with a diversity of views and attitudes. This is why understanding the social psychology of event participants, as discussed in Chapter 3, has such an important role to play in revealing how events fit into our complex modern-day lives and the meaning we attach to events.

A time and a place

Planned events occupy and temporarily transform spaces (or venues), and for the duration of the event one's experience of that place is altered. In turn, many events are intrinsically linked to their setting and community. As Hall and Page (2014: 150) concluded, 'Event Studies has been characterised by a comparative neglect of the way in which events and festivals transform places and spaces from what are everyday environments', whereby the event transforms locations 'into temporary environments that contribute to the production, processing and consumption of culture, concentrated in time and space' (Waterman 1998: 54). Hence, place and culture combine within a set timeframe to produce a temporary experience that is bound by place, with patterns and flows of mobility (see Batty *et al.* 2003).

Culture varies geographically, so the influence of place and culture on events is reinforcing. Cross-cultural comparisons are necessary to fully appreciate the differences in how events are created, valued, managed and experienced. In turn, events influence the places and cultures in which they occur, especially when mega events are imposed on a culture that has not experienced such investment and media attention.

Attachment to places, and place identity, can be influenced by planned events (De Bres and Davis 2001; Brennan-Horley *et al.* 2007). This is the community-building role of events, and it is of considerable interest to social policy-makers and politicians in general. Every nation and community needs its celebrations, events that generate pride and a sense of belonging, and which build development capacity through volunteering, capital investments and improved marketing. Similarly, communities of interest and subcultures express themselves through events, and they need events and event places to identify with, as

> *the cultural facets of festivals cannot be divorced from the commercial interests of tourism, regional and local economy and place promotion. Selling the place to the wider world or selling the festival as an inseparable part of the place rapidly becomes a significant facet of most festivals.*
>
> *(Waterman 1998: 60–61)*

Festivals and events are increasingly used strategically to help define and brand places. Hallmark events give identity and a positive image to their host community, while venues and resorts can also have their hallmark events. The exploitation of festivals in place marketing and tourism is a worry to many observers fearing commodification, loss of cultural authenticity and over-production of events.

Some events achieve 'iconic' status so they can occur anywhere and still be successful, but they always require specific venues and leave some kind of tangible legacy in terms of urban renewal, tourism and transport infrastructure, and social and environmental change. Mega events, including world's fairs, Olympic Games, other major exhibitions and sport events, have all been studied from many points of view, but there has been little attention paid to the question of whether other events can permanently transform a place.

Planned events

We need a specially constructed definition for this book, and for what we are calling event studies. The events we are considering are planned for one or more purposes, they do not just happen, and they are all unique. We have three components to the definitions around the notion of a planned event. Planning an event and the experience of the event are interconnected:

1. 'Planned events' are live, social events created to achieve specific outcomes, including those related to business, the economy, culture, society and the environment.
2. Event planning involves the design and implementation of themes, settings, consumables, services and programmes that suggest, facilitate or constrain experiences for participants, guests, spectators and other stakeholders.
3. Every event experience is personal and unique, arising from the interactions of setting, programme and people.

All planned events get 'labelled': as festivals, conferences, fairs, sports or another formal title. These are really social constructs, because when we use descriptive terms like 'festival' or 'convention', most people have an idea of what they mean. To the individual, these events look and feel different, with different intentions, meanings and programmes. The typology illustrated in Figure 2.1 is based primarily on the *form* of the event (i.e. what it looks like and how it is programmed, which means how it is scheduled or scripted for the audience). Even so, any event can fulfil multiple functions, facilitate similar experiences and have many meanings attached to it. To illustrate the complexity in event typologies, du Cros and Jolliffe (2014: 46) use the following categories of events: inspirational events (to build creative capital), affirming events (for encouraging events that link to cultural identity), pleasurable events that offer tourism, leisure and recreational experiences, enriching events that facilitate personal growth and celebratory events that can celebrate issues such as cultural diversity (e.g. the Opening Ceremony of the Olympic Games for London 2012).

Figure 2.1 Typology of planned events

'Form' derives from the combination of various 'programmed elements of style' (discussed in Chapter 7) that make event types different. For example, the hallmark of a sport event is athletic competition, of a conference it is various interactive learning mechanisms, of a festival it is celebration manifested in theme, symbolism and emotional stimulation. Form is therefore a primary concern of event planners and designers, or at least their usual starting point. The basic and generally accepted forms of meetings, sport events, fairs and festivals can be taught, although in each culture there are going to be differences in their style and meaning.

Historically, 'form' has shaped professionalization and led to the establishment of many professional associations around each specific event form (e.g. meetings). In this tradition, meeting professionals have become the most organized globally, community festivals and arts festival producers have separate associations, and sport event managers attend their own conferences.

Form is equally applicable to unplanned events. Every event has some form that leads us to call it a celebration, protest, riot or party. What exactly are the 'cues'? First of all, the way people behave, because people assembling for protests obviously behave differently to those getting together to party. A casual meeting of friends or workmates looks and feels quite different from a spontaneous crowd celebrating the home team's victory.

Second, we can ask the people involved what they are doing and why they got together, and this should easily reveal whether the event is a spontaneous discussion or a party. That, of course, leads us to consider experience and meanings. The programme elements of style are not always applicable to unplanned events because they are the tools of event planners and designers. If a celebrating crowd breaks into song and dance, we cannot call that programmed, but it is an activity virtually identical to what happens in many designed event experiences. In other words, the spontaneity and randomness of celebrations and experiences are what make planned events unique and difficult to replicate.

Convergence of forms and functions

It is readily apparent that forms and functions of planned events often overlap, and it appears that they are universally tending to converge. Some of this occurs naturally as cultures change and people experiment, but some of it is quite intentional. For example, the Olympics is ostensibly a celebration of amateur sport (the amateurs are long gone, unfortunately), but they are also mandated by the International Olympic Committee to include an arts festival. Host cities add conventions, exhibitions and many other functions designed to leverage these and other mega events. Television turns the whole thing into entertainment and spectacle, packaged in such a way as to maximize advertising revenue. In the case of London 2012, preceding the Games were four years of Cultural Olympiad, called:

> the largest cultural celebration in the history of the modern Olympic and Paralympic Games . . . a chance for everyone to celebrate London 2012 through dance, music, theatre, the visual arts, film and digital innovation and leave a lasting legacy for the arts in the UK.
>
> *(www.london2012.com)*

This culminated in the London 2012 Festival:

> At the heart of the festival will be a programme of commissions by some of the finest artists in the world in events ranging from pop to film, from visual arts and fashion to theatre, from circus to carnival, from opera to digital innovation . . . In total, the festival will feature more than 1,000 events, with an estimated audience of more than three million people. Some of the events will be ticketed, some will be free to attend.
>
> *(www.london2012.com)*

Another good example of convergence is the annual Kentucky Derby Festival in Louisville, Kentucky. This city was the winner of the IFEA award as the top North American Festival City, population over 1 million, in 2010. What was once a simple horse race (now iconic in the world of thoroughbred racing) is now something much more, as the following demonstrates from the event's website (http://derbyfestival.org):

> *Mission: Bringing the community together in celebration. The Derby Festival represents the spirit and pride of the community and showcases Louisville at its best. To provide creative and unique entertainment and community service for the people of Greater Louisville, that directly contributes to the aesthetic, cultural, educational, charitable and economic development of the area.*
>
> *The Kentucky Derby Festival's schedule includes over 70 events – most of them occurring in the two weeks leading up to the Kentucky Derby horse race. The annual celebration is kicked off by a day-long air show and fireworks extravaganza – Derby Festival's Opening Ceremonies: Thunder Over Louisville – one of the nation's largest annual fireworks shows. The ensuing two weeks of excitement and entertainment promises something for everyone. For sports fans there is basketball, volleyball and golf. For music lovers the concerts are almost non-stop. With two-thirds of the Festival events free, families can enjoy numerous just-for-kids' activities without stretching their pocketbook. Other highlights include a half and full marathon, hot-air balloon events and live bed racing! The Great Steamboat Race pits historic paddle-wheelers on the mighty Ohio River. The event that started it all, the Republic Bank Pegasus Parade, marches down Broadway on the Thursday before The Run for the Roses.*

The Derby Festival is one of many 'community festivals' across North America that celebrate community itself. Their appeal is wide, and so their programme is diverse. They defy classification as a single-form event, so convergence is their hallmark. Convergence is also apparent in the nineteenth-century San Antonio fiesta event that has now evolved into a 200-event, ten-day phenomenon (Hernández-Ehrisman 2008); a fiesta-city product has been developed.

Convergence is a powerful argument for a generic approach to event management education. Professionals will have to be increasingly flexible and inventive, not restricted to just being a meeting planner or exhibition designer or festival coordinator. Also, working for venues means engaging with a diverse range of events.

The other important aspects of convergence relate to their meanings and impacts. When conceived as instruments of policy and strategy, events can achieve wider appeal and greater impact by combining elements of style and form. To achieve greater economic benefits, larger and more diverse events are becoming the norm. To generate positive images, more television coverage is required, reaching different and fractured target audiences. To foster social integration, policy-makers have to ensure that events have relevance to many interests. Foley *et al.* (2012) also argue that many events are now decontextualized in time and space, meaning they are inherently portable and capable of being planned at different places. The Formula 1 Grand Prix is one such event – whilst its form remains clear, it exhibits the characteristics of convergence as wider commercial interests and sponsorship combine elements of style and form and it assumes mega-event status. In the final chapter a convergence model is illustrated (Figure 12.2), combined with exchange theory, in an effort to both summarize what is happening in the events sector and to theorize about underlying forces and evolutionary processes. This conceptual model is also fully discussed in the Getz chapter in the book *The Future of Events and Festivals* (Yeoman *et al.* 2014).

Functions of planned events

'Function' gets us into the world of public policy (see Foley *et al.* 2012) for business and professional event management. Why are events held? What is their intended outcome? This is also a key starting point for planned events, and it cannot be left to chance. What if a meeting planner merely assumed that the purpose of a large conference was to allow speakers to address the delegates, when the organizers and attendees really wanted a great social occasion?

Function comes in layers, like an onion. At the outside, superficially, the event might be planned as a community celebration, a festival to involve all residents. But are there also expectations that it will attract tourists? Promote a positive city image? Make money for local charities and businesses? Foster inter-organizational cooperation? The list is potentially endless. Historically, festivals and fairs performed important roles that were not discussed or planned, they just happened because they were needed. Markets and fairs were necessary for trade; parties and celebrations were fitted organically into everyday life; games were not professionalized as sport. But for the most part that era has passed and most events are planned to meet numerous specific economic, business, social, cultural and other policy aims.

The event planner and designer, therefore, seldom has a free hand. Potentially many stakeholders are involved in determining multiple event goals, and they often conflict. When the goals are made clear, perhaps prioritized, the real work of event design can begin. If the goals are not made explicit, problems are likely to occur. Nevertheless, the designer can at least assume certain things about the event's form as long as terms like 'festival', 'fair', 'tournament' or 'conference' are used – if the stakeholders all agree that the event should be a celebration or festival, specific goals are not absolutely needed to start planning. Again, this is because the types of planned events have become social constructs. Using the example of arts events, du Cros and Jolliffe (2014: 46) identified four specific focal points that may help to classify the function of such events: a commercial orientation, an industry focus, an individual artist focus and a public focus, although admitting that each type of event will still have to establish the specific focus within each category.

What follows are some common terms that pertain to the functions of events. Their definition is not fixed, and they are open to interpretation.

Hallmark events

'Hallmarks' are not only distinctive features, but also symbols of quality or authenticity. A significant debate occurred in the 1980s over the terminology of hallmark events following the landmark paper by J. R. B. Ritchie (1984: 2) who defined them as:

> *Major one-time or recurring events of limited duration, developed primarily to enhance the awareness, appeal and profitability of a tourism destination in the short and/or long term. Such events rely for their success on uniqueness, status, or timely significance to create interest and attract attention.*

Ritchie identified a number of different types of hallmark events: world's fairs and expositions, unique carnivals and festivals, major sporting events, significant cultural and religious events, historical milestones (e.g. the five hundredth anniversary of the European discovery of America in 1992), classical commercial and agricultural events, and major political personage events.

C. M. Hall (1989) expanded the debate on hallmark events, focusing on the issue of scale, defining them as events designed to attract national and international attention for a destination. However, as Hall (1989) also argued, confining the term 'hallmark' to large-scale events overlooks the community festivals and local celebrations (see Jepson and Clarke 2014 for numerous case studies of such events) which can be described as hallmark given their regional and local significance. Hall preferred to use the term mega events to describe major events such as world's fairs and the Olympic Games targeted at the international tourism market.

Further refinement of the definitional debate includes a focus on celebration as being the hallmark (or distinctive feature) of festivals. We might also like to consider a hallmark event as belonging to a very special class that represents the best event, one that is authentically embedded in a particular place or culture. These are recurring events that have become so closely associated with their host community or destination that the form is an important part of its image and branding. These events provide, and feed off, place identity. Rio de Janeiro and New Orleans have their Mardi Gras, Calgary has its Stampede, and Edinburgh its Tattoo, all permanent 'institutions' in their cities, full of tradition and generating competitive advantages from a tourism perspective. For this reason, our definition is more wide ranging and embraces this diversity:

> *Hallmark events are those that possess such significance, in terms of tradition, attractiveness, quality or publicity, that the event provides the host venue, community or destination with a competitive advantage. Over time, the event and destination images become inextricably linked. Hallmark events are, by definition, permanent 'institutions' in their communities or societies.*

If cities or resorts want to design a hallmark event, they need to meet multiple criteria, and should keep in mind the power of convergence in form and function. Hallmark events must attract tourists, generate positive images and be co-branded with the destination. Such events also have to be acceptable to the host community, preferably becoming traditional and institutionalized. The institutionalization of an event was demonstrated by Lavenda (1980) in the political analysis of the Carnival of Caracas, Venezuela, where the old carnival was transformed into a highly organized, European mass event. As Lavenda (1980) illustrated, the wild, rowdy behaviour and attitude of a barbaric event was pilloried in the media to justify the creation of the civilizing model based on the carnivals in Venice, Paris and Rome (i.e. masked and with floats) to create a directed and institutionalized event in which around 30 per cent of the population became involved.

To be a permanent institution requires the demonstration of benefits to the residents, including the way the media portrays the negative and positive elements. Finally, hallmark events have to be planned with long-term sustainability in mind. That requires taking a triple-bottom-line approach (see Chapter 10) to their intended outcomes, the involvement of residents at all stages and concern for how impacts are evaluated in a multi-stakeholder manner. A full discussion of the meanings and planning process for hallmark events is available online (see Getz *et al.* 2012).

2.1 RESEARCH NOTE ON RESIDENT RESPONSES TO MEGA EVENTS

Chien, P. M., Ritchie, B. W., Shipway, R. and Henderson, H. (2012). I am having a dilemma: Factors affecting resident support of event development in the community. *Journal of Travel Research*, 51(4), 451–463.

The authors suggest that residents' intention to give or withhold support of hosting an event in the community can be viewed as a social dilemma. They examined the effects of event publicity, perceived fairness of event portrayal and residents' commitment to 2012 Olympic and Paralympic sailing events on residents at Weymouth and Portland in the UK. They concluded that event publicity is linked to residents' supporting behaviours indirectly through commitment. Perceived fairness of event portrayal was identified as a moderator of the event publicity effect; when media reports of the event are considered biased or unfair, the effect of both positive and negative event publicity is attenuated.

Iconic events

Sometimes 'iconic' is used to describe a community's best-known event, but there has to be more than just fame or reputation involved. An 'icon' is a graphic representation of something, in other words a symbol. The correct use would therefore be: Mardi Gras stands for Rio or New Orleans, it is the city's iconic event. This is similar to saying that the Eiffel Tower is a symbol standing for Paris. The other use of 'iconic event' described earlier is one that has strong appeal all on its own and can be held successfully anywhere. It symbolizes something of potentially global significance. For example, the FIFA World Cup or the Olympics are loaded with symbolic meaning, so that many people want to attend because of what they represent, not where they are. And what they represent (i.e. their meanings) is, of course, of great interest in event studies.

A further illustration is offered by Scotland's Homecoming Celebrations in 2009, a ten-month pro-gramme of events to celebrate Scotland's contributions to the world. The underlying rationale was to inspire people with Scottish ancestry to visit Scotland to join in the celebrations. These were themed around the following: Burns, Whisky, Golf, Great Scottish Minds, Ancestry, Culture and Heritage. However, for the purpose of illustrating the significance of iconic events, three such events formed the core of the celebrations (i.e. the Burns Supper, the Clan Gathering and the Highland Homecoming) sup-ported by a further 400 directly funded and partner events. This was repeated in 2014 in a year in which Scotland also hosted the Commonwealth Games.

In Research Note 2.2 by Getz and McConnell, participants in two 'destination events' are compared. The events are 'iconic' for the target segments, runners and mountain bikers, because of their unique locations in the mountains and their high level of difficulty.

2.2 RESEARCH NOTE ON INVOLVEMENT AND ICONIC EVENTS

Getz, D. and McConnell, A. (2014). Comparing trail runners and mountain bikers: Motivation, involvement, portfolios, and event-tourist careers. *Journal of Convention and Event Tourism*, 15(1), 69–100.

'Amateur trail runners and endurance mountain bikers are compared with regard to motivation, involvement in their sport, competitive-event portfolios and event-travel careers. Because the dominant motivation for both samples, and for both men and women, was personal challenge, it is concluded that for many respondents involvement is directed more towards physically demanding sport than towards a particular kind of sport or event. This involvement has led a majority to devel-op an event-travel career. Implications are drawn for sport-event management and event-tourism marketing. Recommendations are made for further research to explore the relevance of brand communities and consumption constellations in event tourism.'

Premier or prestige events

These events are defined within specific categories, so that the World Cup is football's 'premier' event; its prestige is unrivalled. All sports and special interests tend to have prestige and premier events, and while some are located in permanent places or venues, many of them move around. Some, like the Boston Marathon, combine elements of iconic and hallmark status, given the media coverage and attention which the prestigious event brings to the location or nation. The bidding process to host these 'premier' events has now become a highly developed activity. In fact Austin, Texas, USA has branded itself as the live music capital of the world and it has a major impact upon visitation, generating around $800 million a year in music tourism spending. Similarly, Nashville has branded itself as the Home of Country and Western and New Orleans as the Home of Jazz, making it a major platform for music-related events.

Mega events

'Mega' refers to the largest and most significant of events as highlighted under the discussion of hallmark events. The definition and implications of these events were examined in the AIEST (1987) conference proceedings in which Marris (1987) said that mega events should exceed one million visitors and be 'must-see' in nature, while Vanhove and Witt (1987) added that they should be able to attract worldwide publicity. If we equate 'mega' with large size, then they are usually the Olympics, world's fairs and other major sport events. But even a small music festival can have 'mega' impacts on a small town in terms of tourists, economic benefits or disruption as illustrated above in the discussion of hallmark events. The term can also refer to media coverage and impacts on image, as in 'the convention attracted worldwide publicity and put the city on the tourist map'. Therefore, we suggest that:

> *Mega events, by way of their size or significance, are those that yield extraordinarily high levels of tourism, media coverage, prestige or economic impact for the host community, venue or organization.*

The benefit of this definition is that it allows for 'mega events' to be situated within the context of a particular venue or organization rather than using a specific quantitative measure of scale. In other words, 'mega' is a relative term, not an absolute measure.

Media events

Media events are created primarily for broadcast audiences, such as the 2014 MTV music awards hosted in Glasgow, Scotland, an event which is directly related to the media and the power of television and the Internet to reach global audiences (see Reid 2006 for a review of a previous MTV event). Examples include surfing events that really need to be heavily edited and packaged to make for good viewing, and eco-challenges in remote places over long, arduous courses. However, any event can be packaged for the media, and that might be an essential part of its sponsorship appeal or subsidies from tourism and government agencies. In other words, any event can become a media event – it is a function, not a form.

Cause-related events

These are established to raise money, or to promote a cause, which makes them part of social marketing. While any form of event could perform this function, common types of fund-raisers are gala dinners, concerts, entertainment shows, endurance events (in which donors support participants financially), sponsored sport events (e.g. the UK's annual fun run Race for Life, which has 300 local races to raise money for Cancer Research UK) as well as celebrity sports and auctions.

Corporate events

Any event produced by or for a corporation fits this category, with common types being product launches, meetings, grand openings and publicity stunts. An alternative meaning is the trend for large sport events in particular, like the Super Bowl, to become so tied to corporate sponsors and related hospitality that they in effect become 'corporatized'. A further shift in the events world has been the emphasis on 'experiential marketing' to develop brands and sustain relationships with customers and other corporate stakeholders. The term 'live marketing' has crept into the language to describe the use of events for these purposes. A related concept is the 'brand land', or the creation of venues devoted to 'brand experiences', and of course these corporate monuments have to be animated with events. Ulrich Wuensch gives an expert opinion on corporate events later.

Publicity stunts

Any event designed to garner publicity falls into this broad category, but it is usually associated with politicians and movie stars. Publicity agents should be expert at contriving events or situations that appeal to the media, or to crowds, so that they become 'news'. But to the degree that they are obvious in their intent, or manipulative, they can easily backfire. See elsewhere our discussions of 'pseudo events' and authenticity.

Special events

Although this term is often used generically for the planned events field, and has been popularized by an important professional association (ISES), what is 'special' about any event is a subjective interpretation by either the producer or the guest. Jago and Shaw (1999) asked adults to describe important attributes of 'special events' and discovered that the number of attendees, international attention given to the event, perceived improvement to image and pride in the host region, and an exciting experience were the main factors explaining perceived specialness.

A long list of factors that can contribute to any event's specialness starts with its uniqueness as we emphasized earlier (see Getz 2005) and includes elements of style (like hospitality, symbolism, festive spirit, theming and authenticity), meeting multiple goals, and appealing to different stakeholders and audiences. Two perspectives on 'specialness' have to be taken: is it special to the organizers, or to the participants and customers? Therefore, a special event can comprise the following two features:

1. A special event is a one-time or infrequently occurring event outside the normal programme or activities of the sponsoring or organizing body.
2. To the customer or guest, a special event is an opportunity for an experience outside the normal range of choices or beyond everyday experience.

Spectator and interactive events

'Interactive' events embody person–setting or person–person interactivity, unlike 'spectator' events, which are inherently passive. Interactivity is thought to foster a higher level of involvement or engagement, making it a crucial element in 'experience design'. A study of mega screens in public places in Melbourne, Australia and Incheon, South Korea (Papastergiadis *et al.* 2013) for the presentation of a cultural event – to display public art – illustrates the changing boundaries between spectating and interaction.

Participant events

These are events that are held for people to be involved, not just to spectate. 'Participants' are more than customers or guests, they are necessary for the event to exist. Meetings and conventions do not exist without delegates; there are no marathons without runners; dance festivals need dancers. Exhibitions also require participants, namely the exhibitors. Such events provide 'targeted benefits' (i.e. they are customized experiences), they can be viewed as subcultural manifestations, and are highly sought after by competitive tourist destinations that can either create them or bid on them. For example, Coghlan and Filo (2013) examined participants' experiences and motivation at charity/sport events and the role of adventure philanthropy in such participation.

An events industry?

An industry, in conventional terms, means a sector of the economy that produces the same goods or services, such as the automobile industry. This definition is problematic for events because of their diversity of forms and purposes, as Leiper (2008) observed in relation to tourism. He said we need to use the plural 'tourism industries'. As well, different kinds of event producers and suppliers feel they are part of a tourism industry, an exhibition industry, even the cultural industry. This last term, cultural industry, is worthy of further discussion; see Events in Focus 2.1; also see Figure 2.2.

EVENTS IN FOCUS

2.1 The cultural industries and events, S. J. Page and J. Connell (of Exeter Business School)

The term 'culture industry' was popularized in the 1930s when the Frankfurt School emerged (the collective name for a group of critical theorists who worked at the Frankfurt Institute for Social Research in the 1920s). Within that paradigm were theorists such as Adorno and Horkheimer, whose work culminated in terms such as 'culture industry'. Within that term, the focus was on criticisms of the commoditization of art and its reproduction to create repetitive cultural products for mass consumption. The basis of their arguments was the contention that the culture industry was run by capitalism for profit, and so the experiences which the culture industry provided were for popular mass appeal. In stark contrast, such theorists were critical of popular culture. This is because it was interpreted as a form of social control, where popular entertainment socialized the mass population into passivity to make them compliant citizens.

As Page and Connell (2010) demonstrated, a notable transformation in post-modern society is the shift from tangible elements of culture such as the built heritage, museums and monuments to more intangible leisure resources such as image, identity, lifestyle, narratives of the city, creativity and the media. All of these elements enhance the consumer's experience of culture and its consumption in event experiences. For elaboration, see the book *The Arts and Events* by du Cros and Jolliffe (2014).

Hesmondhalgh (2007) is one of the most widely cited studies on the cultural industries and it highlights the context in which events operate as they draw upon the core industries and peripheral sectors (see Figure 2.2 on classifying the cultural industries), all of which coalesce in the formation of planned event experiences in differing degrees and ways. Therefore, one interesting approach to the interpretation of the growth and development of the event sector within a post-modern society is the commoditization, commercialization and creation of consumer experiences around culture (both high and low, with low representing popular culture). The event sector(s) are a clear outcome of the cultural industries' growth in which leisure, tourism and serious leisure have coalesced with work and pleasure to develop what many would label as the event phenomenon.

There are also wider political explanations of why people use the term 'industry' or 'industries' when they want to legitimize their activities and gain government support. Those in the arts seldom think of themselves as being part of an industry, because the word carries connotations of production for economic purposes rather than art for the sake of art. It is also common to talk about the service industry or industries, of which events are clearly a part, and increasingly to view events as being an integral part of the experience economy and creative industries. Numerous private-sector suppliers serve the events sector,

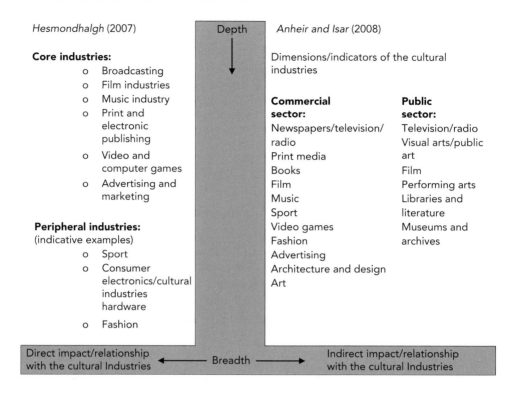

Figure 2.2 Classifying the cultural industries – their scale and scope

Source: Page and Connell (2010: 354). Reprinted from *Leisure: an introduction*, S. J. Page and J. Connell, Pearson Education Ltd (2010).

Developed from D. Hesmondhalgh (2007) *The Cultural Industries*. Sage: London; H. Anheir and Y. Isar (eds) (2008) *The Cultural Economy*. Sage: London; A. Pratt (2008). Locating the Cultural economy. In H. Anheir and Y. Isar (eds) *The Cultural Economy*. Sage: London, 42–51.

creating a kind of 'industry'. Raj *et al.* (2008: 5) said: 'If there is still a case for the existence of an, albeit diverse, events industry, then it is the industry's specialist support services that provide the best argument for it.' Ultimately, it is a matter of perspective and political purpose that leads one to call events of one type, or the entire events sector, an industry. It makes the most sense when speaking of economic goals and outcomes, and the least sense when referring to the social and cultural dimensions of events.

An experiential typology?

Function and form do not predetermine personal experiences, mainly because people create their own experiences within event settings, and will assign meanings to event experiences that can be independent or only loosely related to the event's purpose and programme. Great experiences can be obtained without planned events, but event designers want people to have a great experience at their event. To date, most event designers have had to operate in accordance with established norms (the social constructs again) for event production – such as how to produce an effective meeting, how to programme an arts festival or how to run a tournament. Alternatively, the designer has to work according to instinct, within a creative mentality, and rely on both subtle and overt feedback to determine if the event experience was both pleasant and as intended.

We cannot easily develop a typology of events based primarily on experience, because so many possible experiences can be had at events. Both festivals and sports events can facilitate joy, celebration, excitement, self-fulfilment or aesthetic appreciation. While their form and functions might be completely different, at the experiential level (and to some extent at the level of their meanings) they can be quite similar. That is why a phenomenological research methodology (see Chapter 3) offers considerable scope for a better understanding of event experiences, because it focuses on the individual's state of mind while experiencing the event (for an example, see Ziakas and Boukas's 2013 study of Limassol Carnival, Cyprus).

A full range of possible personal and social experiences tied to events is likely not possible, but certainly the major ones people talk about can be identified – as long as we keep in mind the limitations of language and how people express themselves. For example, the section on experiences, and in particular the cognitive, affective and behavioural (conative) dimensions of experiences, expands upon this theme as do the sections on social worlds, involvement and benefits.

Planned versus unplanned events

It might come as a surprise to realize how much of what we see and hear on broadcast media is really about planned events. Consider the attention given to entertainment and sport, both having numerous, dedicated television channels (at least where cable and satellite TV are found). Add the ample coverage given to political events (including news conferences), private events (e.g. famous weddings), food and beverage events, and so on, and it really adds up.

Now consider the range of 'unplanned' events that get media exposure, so much so that we wonder if they really are being planned. Indeed, in many cases they are clearly set in motion by people (maybe agitators, publicity agents or social activists) and they have a purpose, but they are categorically different from the events we are talking about when using the terms 'event management' or 'professional event manager'.

The distinctions sometimes get blurry, so it is necessary for event studies to encompass both. The only unplanned events we are not including are those that fall under the headings of accidents, forces of nature, wars and insurrections, and other completely unpredictable happenings that hit the news.

'Spontaneous mass celebrations' should be considered. For example, during the Calgary Flames' run for the Stanley Cup in 2003, the 'Red Mile' was created when thousands of fans frequenting bars along the city's 17th Avenue flooded on to the streets. They wore their team's red colours, had a party, attracted news media from all over North America, and were tolerated by the police and civic authorities. This kind of social phenomenon results in events that have a specific duration (as long as the series continues), require some measures and controls similar to planned festivals, yet take on a life of their own. Incidentally, merchants and civic officials decided afterwards that they would not tolerate such a spontaneous celebration in the future, as it posed many risks. Using traffic controls and police action, they prevented it from occurring in 2005. We can interpret this case as a triumph of regulation over spontaneity, which is a theme discussed again in the section on carnivals.

Table 2.1 is an attempt to classify the planned and unplanned events that event studies encompasses. It refers to their purpose or goals, programme or activities, type or degree of control and accountability. Note that these are not always mutually exclusive, as some events demonstrate elements of both planning and spontaneity.

The question of scale

Probably the vast majority of planned events are small and occur in the private or corporate spheres. But most attention focuses on the larger events that are open to the public, covered by the media and generate substantial impacts. So there is a continuum of planned events along the dimension of scale, and the extremes can also be associated with impacts and policy implications (see Table 2.2).

Table 2.1 Planned versus unplanned events

	Planned events (The realm of professional event designers and managers)	Unplanned events (The realm of spontaneity and unpredictability)
Purpose	Goals or outcomes are specified by producers of the event, and are influenced by key stakeholders	Purpose is self-defined; intentions of participants might be unclear, diverse, even contradictory
Programme	Planned and scheduled, usually in detail; designers seek to create 'experiences' for guests, participants and spectators	Spontaneous activities; or, once set in motion by agents, actions become rather unpredictable
Control	Controls are imposed by managers and other formal stakeholders, including governments	No management systems in place, only a degree of normal civic control; sometimes a police response is required
Accountability	Producers and managers are formally held accountable	No organization or legal entity is accountable over all; individuals can be held accountable for their actions, under law

Table 2.2 A question of scale

	Small events	Large events
Form and function	Tend to be single-form events (e.g. a meeting, competition, private function)	Tend to combine elements of style, such as sports becoming festivals, meetings adding exhibitions, or community festivals combining multiple events of all kinds (i.e. convergence)
	Less likely to be planned with tourists or media in mind	More likely to be planned to generate major economic and place-marketing benefits
The event experience	Mostly in the private and corporate spheres of interest	Mostly in the public sphere of interest
		Crowd dynamics can dominate
	The experience might be intensely private or shared with an affinity group	The event can affect entire communities through media coverage and shared attitudes
Impacts	Collectively they are significant (e.g. weddings, meetings, parties, most sport meets)	Each large event has substantial impacts (e.g. festivals, major sport events, fairs and exhibitions)
Media coverage	Individual, small events seldom attract media attention	The event itself is of interest to the media, or created primarily as a media event
Policy implications	Policies related to venues, and to events in general (e.g. health standards, green operations, permits required)	Policy decisions required for specific events (e.g. decision to bid; infrastructure investments; feasibility studies and impact assessments commissioned)

Frequency and periodicity

Does it matter how often an event is produced? In sports, teams play many games during a season and in the arts and entertainment sector concerts or shows are also regularly held. What if a fan or patron goes to many of these events? They can become routine for participants, producers and some of the audience. But we need to remember that every event is still somewhat unique. In fact, many people love sports because the action is infinitely variable and the outcome always unpredictable, making them an 'authentic' experience when compared with other forms of entertainment like TV and the movies. Also, no actors, musicians or performers can exactly reproduce their efforts from one show to the next so that the audience can return with some expectation of differences. Even frequently attended events can be 'special' to the audience depending on their expectations, mood and experiences. The timing (or periodicity) can also make the event special as in the case of winter festivals, occurring around the festive period.

As Dewar *et al.* (2001: 523) indicated:

> *At low latitudes (northern and southern) winter is a time of suspension. Life slows or stops, days grow shorter, warmth is a warm fire, snow and ice lock the land in a quiet world of white. Winter has been seen as a time of death, famine and fear by many cultures. At the same time it is celebrated as a time of friendship, relaxation, good cheer and festival, a time when the fields are fallow and there is time for play. This paradox is expressed in the ubiquitous winter festival. Christmas, solstice, or whatever the festival is, is a time to hold back the cold and dark with the light of celebration.*

This quotation illustrates not only the special attraction of the festive season but the emotion and surrounding ambience of the season of 'goodwill to all' that makes the Christmas period special; it is often marked in northern climates with Christmas lights, which in many towns and cities have become attractions in their own right.

The answer, therefore, is that frequency is not a defining criterion for inclusion in event studies. We are as interested in scheduled, routine theatre and sports as we are in festivals held only every ten years, as well as what makes the timing 'special'. Periodicity is a key issue, however, as one-time events are usually bid on, are expected to meet very specific objectives (such as attract tourists or generate profit) and might never be seen in an area again. One-time mega events have the greatest impact. Hallmark events by definition should be annual and permanent, as they are co-branded with the destination or community.

Activity or event?

Events contain many activities, but activities are not, by strict definition, events. 'Activity' is defined as the 'state of being active', 'energetic action or movement', 'liveliness' or 'a specified pursuit in which a person partakes'. A leisure or recreation activity is one that is pursued for its own, intrinsic rewards, and a business activity is pursued for its value-creating benefits or out of administrative necessity. Activities within planned events are mostly related to the theme (such as performances at a concert, matches in a competitive sport event or assemblies during a conference). Individual participants and guests at events engage in their own activities, often unscripted and personal (e.g. talking, eating, bodily functions, singing along, cheering, viewing, contemplating) and these also contribute to the overall event experience. Activities at events are influenced by interactions among the setting, the programme and other people.

Even so, the boundaries between activity and event are not really absolute. From the individual's perspective, engaging in a mountain climb, or any other adventure pursuit, might be a planned 'event' with a purpose, design (lots of preparations including a route to the summit), tight schedule, specific setting and the company of others. In this sense the activity of mountain climbing embodies specific events for the participants, but they are highly personal and not open to the public. Many people presumably reflect on their lives and careers as a series of events, and among them will be planned *rites de passage* such as anniversaries.

Length or duration

How long can a single event be? Remembering our earlier discussion about the fact that all events are really part of a continuum of experiences for individuals and a congruence of multi-stakeholder activity, this question of event length is somewhat pointless. If we call it an 'event', then for all practical purposes it is. We frequently see lengthy events, such as the one described by Liburd (2008) with reference to the year-long celebration in Denmark of Hans Christian Andersen's Bicentenary in 2005. The Cultural Capitals movement, which has been spreading globally, is usually a year-long 'event' (see Richards and Palmer 2010). Most of these are promotions, with multiple events packaged within, but they are certainly designed to be perceived as a single, noteworthy event.

Olympic and mega-event studies

People are fascinated by mega events, those that by definition are the largest or most publicized. And so too are researchers, who continue to examine the Olympics, world's fairs and major international sport tournaments from every conceivable angle. For example, social science publishers have developed entire lists of books focused just on the Olympics – in 2014, Routledge had 59 Olympic-titled books on its list reflecting the growing research interest in this field. A similar growth is apparent from searching 'Olympics' on Scopus, the academic search engine. In 1976, 12 articles were indexed, rising to 512 in 2012 and dropping to 243 for the year to October 2014, with over 3,600 articles indexed. Therefore, the Olympics as an event phenomenon has developed its own scholarly sub-area within events and sport research. A number of universities have established Olympic research centres in cooperation with the International Olympic Committee and there are always new articles and books coming out on the Olympics, largely because every winter and summer Olympic Games generate a flurry of interest in host countries (see, for example, Toohey and Veal (2007), who took a social science perspective on the Olympic Games).

While the discourse on the Olympics and other mega events stands out in terms of public interest and policy debates, most of the issues are the same as for lesser events. We can separate planned events by types, size, length, periodicity, impacts or whatever, but event studies seeks to unify rather than subdivide. Theory, in particular, should cross all subdivisions, although practical applications will naturally be different.

Description and examples of the major event forms

In this section each of the main forms of planned events is defined and described, with examples.

Cultural celebrations

'Celebration' has several connotations:

- a joyful occasion; special festivities to mark some happy event; a joyous diversion; to observe a day or event with ceremonies of respect, festivity or rejoicing (such as Thanksgiving celebrations);
- solemnization (the public performance of a sacrament or solemn ceremony with all appropriate ritual, such as to celebrate mass or a marriage);
- to extol, praise or acclaim;
- to make widely known.

Synonyms include: to commemorate, honour or distinguish.

We define 'culture' later, in the section on cultural anthropology, but at this point we can say that 'cultural celebrations' are solemn or joyous events that have cultural meaning. They may include many other types of planned event, but are separated from entertainment by the cultural values being expressed. Consisting of festivals, carnivals, heritage commemorations, parades, and religious rites and rituals, the study of cultural celebrations draws heavily from cultural anthropology. This is one of the oldest and best established approaches to event studies, focusing on the roles and meanings of festivity and celebration in, and across, cultures.

Festival

Although it does not do justice to the richness and diversity of meanings attached to 'festival', we propose the following simple definition:

Festivals are themed, public celebrations.

Falassi's (1987: 2) *Time Out of Time: Essays on the Festival* suggested that festivals were a social phenomenon found in virtually all human cultures, and in modern English the term has several meanings:

- a sacred or profane time of celebration, marked by special observances;
- the annual celebration of a notable person or event, or (of) the harvest of an important product;
- a cultural event consisting of a series of performances of works in the fine arts, often devoted to a single artist or genre;
- a fair;
- generic gaiety, conviviality, cheerfulness.

Falassi (1987: 2) continued to argue that in the social sciences, 'festival' means:

> *a periodically recurrent, social occasion in which, through a multiplicity of forms and a series of coordinated events, participate directly or indirectly and to various degrees, all members of a whole community, united by ethnic, linguistic, religious, historical bonds, and sharing a world- view. Both the social function and the symbolic meaning of the festival are closely related to a series of overt values that the community recognizes as essential to its ideology and worldview, to its social identity, its historical continuity, and to its physical survival, which is ultimately what festivals celebrate.*

The term 'festival' is much overused and misused. Some so-called festivals are nothing more than commercial promotions or parties. Indeed, 'festivity' is often used in the same way as 'having a good time'. Many community or broadly programmed festivals seem to forget what they are celebrating, or at least they do not interpret the meaning. However, Jepson and Clarke (2014: 3) propose the following definition for community festivals as:

> *Themed and inclusive community event or series of events which have been created as the result of an inclusive community planning process to celebrate the particular way of life of people and groups in the local community with emphasis on particular space and time.*

In this sense, 'festival' has often been reduced to a public entertainment programme, or a special time for fun and activities, rather than a celebration. Even arts festivals are guilty of using the term without paying attention to the meanings and how they are interpreted as we highlighted earlier. Is it a festival if there is nothing more than a series of musical performances?

The reason sociologists and anthropologists have spent so much effort studying festivals is that they reveal much about culture (i.e. the outcome of the socialization process, or learned behaviour, or a way of life that is shaped by religion, mores, traditions and roles) and the functioning of societies. Turner (1982) recognized that people have a need to set aside times and places for celebration where they are co-present, the theory which suggests that other actors may shape individual human behaviour which is rooted in notions of sociality and the company of others, or 'being with'. Eagleton (1981), Hughes (1999) and Ravenscroft and Mateucci (2002) thought festival and carnival provide a socially sanctioned forum for unleashing social tensions that would otherwise prove destructive. Ekman (1999), Farber (1983) and Geertz (1993) saw festivals as socially sustaining devices through which people express identities, connect with their place and communicate with the outside world.

Manning (1983: 4) saw festivals as providing a rich 'text', the reading of which provides much knowledge about local culture and community life. His view on 'celebration' was that it is 'performance' entailing the 'dramatic presentation of cultural symbols'. Celebration is also 'public, with no social exclusion', and is therefore 'participatory' entertainment.

The festival experience has been studied in depth, but as Falassi argues.

> *At festival times, people do something they normally do not; they abstain from something they normally do; they carry to the extreme behaviours that are usually regulated by measure; they invert patterns of daily social life. Reversal, intensification, trespassing, and abstinence are the four cardinal points of festive behaviour.*
>
> *(Falassi 1987: 3)*

This description, however, sounds more like 'carnival' than most contemporary 'festivals'.

The 'building blocks' of festivals can all be considered ritual acts, or 'rites', since they happen within an exceptional frame of time and space, and their meaning is considered to go beyond their literal and specific aspects:

> *The framing ritual that opens the festival is one of valorization (which for religious events has been called sacralization) that modifies the usual and daily function and meaning of time and space. To serve as the theatre of the festive events an area is reclaimed, cleared, delimited, blessed, adorned, forbidden to normal activities. Similarly, daily time is modified by a gradual or sudden interruption that introduces 'time out of time', a special temporal dimension devoted to special activities.*
>
> *(Falassi 1987: 4)*

Geographical research on festivals has viewed them as contested spaces where symbolic practices (a parade, for example) are used to consolidate or resist prevailing norms and values such as Sydney's Mardi Gras parade, which reveals 'the different ways bodies, emotions, sexuality and spatiality become entwined within the annual rhythms of this mega-event' (Waitt and Stapel 2011: 197).

As Hall and Page (2012) argue, 'this [contestation] is especially the case in spatial settings where events characterise the out-of-home forms of leisure (as opposed to the in-home forms except for where they are televised and consumed within the home). What characterises the event and its significance is the way it transforms everyday living and also serves as a means to reinterpret and represent locality and identity' (also see Cudny 2014 for a recent review of the field). In the case of festivals, Waterman (1998: 56) succinctly conveyed these points, arguing that:

> *a conventional approach to festivals in human geography in which the arts festival was little more than a transient cultural event with a measurable impact on the landscape, environment and economy might simply have been mapped or modelled . . . But festivals are cultural artefacts which are not simply bought and consumed but which are also accorded meaning through their active incorporation into people's lives . . . They epitomise the representation of contemporary accumulation through spectacle.*

Waterman (1998) highlights the significant role of place in the spectacle of events and their meaning (Olds and Ley 1988), building on the work of Jackson (1988), and the Notting Hill Carnival in London acts as a vehicle for expression of underlying political tensions as one of Europe's largest street festivals. In contrast, Richards (1996) argued that in the 1970s, festivals were recognized as being catalysts for arts development at the local level. Quinn (2006: 291) concluded that in Ireland, festivals over the past 35 years have expanded venue infrastructure, advanced community animation, developed local resources, expanded business in arts and related areas and developed tourist audiences. 'Festivalization', discussed in Chapter 1, is a term used in references to the strategic employment of festivals in place marketing and tourism promotion, as in the 'festivalization' of many historic cities (see, for example, Richards 2007a). Not all observers see this as a positive process.

Robinson *et al.* (2004) discussed how festivals, supposedly reflecting local and ethnic culture, have become part of cultural tourism. However, many are 'placeless' and created just for tourism, giving rise to questions about authenticity and appropriateness. The social meanings of festivals in contemporary economic and cultural life are therefore deserving of more attention. This discourse has been gaining momentum, as indicated in the books *Festivals, Tourism and Social Change* (Picard and Robinson 2006b) and *Festival Places: Revitalising Rural Australia* (Gibson and Connell 2011).

The British Arts Festivals Association provides a typology: music, dance, visual, theatre, film, comedy and street arts, and of course it is possible to subdivide these themes. Other popular festivals pertain to science, food and beverages, literature and arts for children and the family. Festivals with heritage and religious themes are widespread. In North America 'community festivals' are very popular (see Jepson and Clarke 2014 for some examples). These combine many elements of celebration, entertainment, spectacle and sports, often becoming hallmark events and tourist attractions. In essence they celebrate the community itself, provide a sense of identity and hopefully foster social cohesion. Referring to a festival's explicit theme is not always the best indicator of its meanings.

2.3 RESEARCH NOTES ON FESTIVALS

Grunwell, S. and Inhyuck, S. (2008). Film festivals: An empirical study of factors for success. *Event Management*, 11(4), 201–210.

This article reports on a study of film festival attendees that was undertaken to evaluate the success of a regional film festival and assist film festival managers and sponsors in future planning. Attendee characteristics and festival experience were evaluated, as well as the festival's economic impact on the local community. It also includes an overview of what makes film festivals unique as an 'industry', particularly their value in generating economic benefits as well as cultural opportunities for host communities.

Lee, J. (2014). Visitors' emotional responses to the festival environment. *Journal of Travel and Tourism Marketing*, 31(1), 114–131.

The researcher examined how emotions in three Texas-based, agricultural-themed festivals affected post-visit behaviour. 'Results revealed that festival atmospherics had a positive indirect effect on loyalty via positive emotions, satisfaction, and psychological commitment.'

Festivals are evolving

Although the organic forces giving rise to festivals remain intact, springing from a community's need to celebrate, they are evolving quickly in both form and function. It is readily observable that the term itself has been corrupted and commodified, along with the variations 'fest', 'festivity' and 'festive'. They have become commonplace, even trite, and no longer refer exclusively to a cultural celebration – and certainly not to sacred rituals. We can partake in regular 'lobster-fests' at the local seafood restaurant, or become 'festive' for the entire Holiday Season (involving over-consumption of food and drink).

Second, more and more so-called festivals are really entertainment productions, so much so that we argue that many young people only know festivals as outdoor music concerts. The behaviour of attendees is more like carnival, with revelry being the object. There are still festival-like elements to the experience, however, as generators of social communitas. Third, many festivals have been created for their instrumentalist values, such that they are no longer authentic reflections of community or culture, but of policy. O'Sullivan *et al.* (2009) observed that in Wales local/community events are driven by socio-cultural and also economic purposes, when it comes to government involvement. The vast majority are local, and oriented towards residents. Economic impact assessments are the dominant form of evaluation, so there is an evident mismatch between stated purpose and impacts measured.

Pop music festivals

Stone (2008) identified the origins of the modern era of outdoor pop music festivals, beginning in the USA in the 1960s with Monterey (1967) and Woodstock (1969). In Britain the earliest were the 1968–1970 Isle of Wight festivals and Glastonbury (1970). The number continues to grow each year in the UK. Stone defines these as recurring performance events with two or more live performances over one or more days, and packaged 'as a coherent whole'. Some are indoors, and some are even free. 'Pop' covers all popular musical genres. They can be competitive (e.g. battle of the bands), for-profit or not, single or multi-venue. The programme might include traditional festive elements like comedy and theatre, dance and merchandizing. Summer is the festival season, and success often depends upon good weather. Stone asserts that the audience has been growing and widening, it's not just young people or ageing hippies. And they are increasingly expensive entertainment options. Those who identify with sub- and counter-cultures are unhappy with the increasing cost, commercialism, professionalism and regulations imposed by governments.

Various experiences are associated with pop music festivals, including camping and communitas. Stone (2008: 223) argued that: 'Uniquely, many festivals serve as adult playgrounds, representing marginal, liminal zones devoted to hedonism and largely uninhibited play and fun.' People are also motivated to attend by the need for identity-building and affirmation, linked to the accumulation of 'popular culture capital'. In other words, it's the thing to do.

Stone lists recent trends in the form and themes of pop music festivals, and Events in Focus 2.2 provides the example of UK music tourism and the role of such festivals. This is a reflection of diversity, targeted live communications and the power of social media to attract audiences. These festivals include religious, urban, holiday-destination, premium, secret, teen's, deliberately constrained, boutique, women's, green, family, dual-location, economy, political, no-camping and virtual festivals.

EVENTS IN FOCUS

2.2 UK music festivals – scale and impact

In 2013, UK Music produced its report *Music Tourism: Contribution to the UK Economy*, in which it outlined the impact of the music tourism industry on the UK. Music festivals play a major role in this industry, where:

- music tourism contributed £2.2 billion to the UK economy in 2012;
- £1.3 billion was spent by music tourists, of which £6.5 million was from overseas tourists visiting the UK;
- 41 per cent of the market for music tourism was based around live events;
- music visitors attended a diversity of music venues such as arenas, festivals, live performances in parks and stadia; London alone has 349 live music venues.

> ### 2.4 RESEARCH NOTE ON MOTIVATION TO ATTEND MUSIC FESTIVALS
>
> Tkaczynski, A. and Rundle-Thiele, S. (2013). Understanding what really motivates attendance: A music festival segmentation study. *Journal of Travel and Tourism Marketing*, 30(6), 610–623.
>
> Attendees at an Australian Christian music festival were studied and segmented using TwoStep cluster analysis. Religion was a dominant motivator and while religious music was the main attraction, additional motivations were also important including the opportunity to *socialize with others* and *to spend time with friends*. While *headline artists* and *feature artists* were both essential, other activities such as *shopping* were also relevant. Most respondents purchased the *three-day pass*, which implies that the visitors came to the festival for the whole experience rather than seeing only one performer on a particular day.

Carnival

Carnival is a celebration preceding Lent and is associated with feasting, costumes, parades and revelry. Mardi Gras, or Fat Tuesday, is the last day within carnival season. People go to carnivals and Mardi Gras events for fun, play and revelry (even debauchery), enhanced or manifested through role reversal in masquerading, parades and costume balls. People love to dress up (or down), have a party, and suspend the social norms and even laws that govern everyday life.

Turner (1974) and other anthropologists and sociologists have paid considerable attention to carnivals, often distinguishing between the 'sacred' elements of traditional, religiously grounded festivals, and the 'profane' side of carnivals. Carnival remains a popular subject for academic researchers, including books by Riggio (2004) on carnival in Trinidad, and by Harris (2003) on folk theology and performance associated with carnivals. Nurse (2004) reported on the Trinidad Carnival from the points of view of tourism and the 'cultural industry'.

Carnival is the 'profane' side of festival. It is an integral part of civilization, embodying revelry, masquerading (and masks), role reversal, social licence and spectacle. To some it is a sanctioned form of mild civil disobedience, to others it is something to forbid or repress. Ritual, festivity, revelry and ecstasy perform a variety of roles, some say as safety valves, and might actually counter depression and lead to social health.

In Europe, carnival remains a strong tradition in many countries, especially where Roman Catholic populations are large, and the Federation of European Carnival Cities (www.carnivalcities.com) is the related professional association. According to FECC, there are at least nine types of European carnival, among them the Samba or Caribbean form that is popular in the New World, including Rio de Janeiro.

Carnivals have a very long history. They can have distinctive styles, but tend to feature masquerade or costume balls, parades, theatrical productions, feasting and partying. From the Carnival of Venice website (www. carnivalofvenice.com) comes this reminder:

> *The Carnival in Venice is no 'goof', no 'consumerist ceremony' as some people complain, but sincere, wonderful heartfelt tradition that goes back in time almost a millennium, and despite its age, still shows its vitality to whom participates to it in person or in spirit.*
>
> *Carnival in Venice is believed to have become official in 1296, lasted six weeks or longer, and built on an already established tradition of mask wearing. By the 18th Century it was a famous event embodying balls, spectacles, masks and theatre.*
>
> *(For the detailed programme visit the official website www.carnevale.venezia.it)*

Carnival continues to evolve. In cold climates 'winter carnivals' are flourishing, such as Quebec's Winter Carnival, which has become the city's hallmark event. 'Midsumma Carnival' in Melbourne, Australia, is an example of the numerous gay and lesbian Mardi Gras or carnivals held around the world, many of which have become major tourist attractions (Pitts 1999). As the following quote from the 'Midsumma' website explains:

> *Carnival transforms Treasury Gardens into the queerest park in Australia. Carnival is wearing her brand new Treasury frock so come and tell her she's beautiful and experience a spectacular hub of queer games, hot music, bump-your-booty dancing and sporting prowess as we celebrate the closing of Midsumma.*
>
> *(www.midsumma.org.au)*

According to Ehrenreich (2006) 'collective ecstasy', a part of carnival and akin to dancing in the streets, has been a part of human civilization from the very beginning. There is an age-old conflict between control exerted by social hierarchies and the desire for freedom of expression and behaviour. Religion and politics conspire to suppress natural tendencies. Ehrenreich points to the carnivalization of sports, and says that protest movements constantly reinvent the carnival. Turner's notion of 'communitas' in *The Ritual Process* (1969) and Durkheim's (1965) notion of 'collective effervescence' are related concepts.

To Bakhtin (1993), carnival is something people create for themselves (i.e. it is a liberating force) in contrast to the spectacles that those in power prefer. Debord (1983) in *Society of the Spectacle* argued that it occurs in 'an epic without festivals'. In other words, spectacle (in which audiences are passive spectators and consumers, rather than participants in experiences) is associated with power and control, while carnival or festivity fosters 'inclusiveness'. Gotham (2005a), in a review of urban spectacles associated with carnivals, highlighted the conflict and struggles over the meaning in such celebrations, while Addo's (2009) anthropological review examined the way in which spectacle had become ritualized by festival practices.

In the book *Rituals and Traditional Events in the Modern World* (Laing and Frost 2014), the editors and contributors examine how 'traditional events and the identities they support are increasingly being challenged and rituals may be lost'. Reacting against the homogenizing effects of globalization, many communities and events are recreating or inventing rituals, sometimes borrowing from others, in the pursuit of uniqueness and authenticity. Mardi Gras in New Orleans is one of the events examined in this context. It has been studied by many authors, including the work of Gotham (2005a, b; see Research Note 2.5).

2.5 RESEARCH NOTE ON MARDI GRAS

Gotham, K. F. (2005b). Tourism from above and below: Globalization, localization and New Orleans's Mardi Gras. *International Journal of Urban and Regional Research*, 29(2), 309–326.

'This article uses a case study of the Mardi Gras celebration in New Orleans to explain the connections between global forces and local actions in the development of urban tourism. It argues that the globalization and localization of Mardi Gras are occurring simultaneously with the result being a mix of homogenizing and particularizing influences in New Orleans. It develops this argument by distinguishing between "tourism from above" and "tourism from below", a distinction that helps to explain how tourism can help undermine as well as promote local differences. "Tourism from above" refers to the global-level forces of commodification, standardization and rationalization that affect all cities. "Tourism from below" refers to the ways in which local groups and individuals resist the homogenizing effects of globalized tourism and use tourism to anchor Mardi Gras in place and create new carnival traditions.'

Heritage commemoration

These are memorial services, specific ceremonies or broader events (even festivals) designed to honour the memory of someone or something. Most commonly they are marked in the context of national days, birthdays of kings and queens, battles or wars (through Remembrance Days and varying national emphases according to Van der Auwera and Schramme 2014). Programmes must include something symbolic and interpretive about the event or persons being remembered.

Frost and Laing (2013), in the book *Commemorative Events: Memories, Identities, Conflicts* emphasized that they are all about remembering and are held on the anniversaries of significant past events, either annually or after significant time periods. Such events provide fascinating insight into how societies see themselves, their heritage and their identity. These events, however, carry high propensity for controversy as memory and identity are highly subjective and other stakeholders hold different views of what should be commemorated and why.

'Heritage' is open to interpretation, often being a politically charged term. It means more than historic, and implies a value judgement as to what is important. McCarthy (2012) examined the 1916 Easter Rising in Dublin – which sparked off a series of events culminating in 1922 with the creation of the Irish Free State – and traces the historiography of the celebration of the event that challenged the British government whilst it was fighting the Great War. A further addition to the events literature is by Frost *et al.* (2008) in Research Note 2.6.

2.6 RESEARCH NOTE ON COMMEMORATIONS

Frost, W., Wheeler, F. and Harvey, M. (2008). Commemorative events: Sacrifice, identity and dissonance. In J. Ali-Knight, M. Robertson, A. Fyall and A. Ladkin (eds), *International Perspectives of Festivals and Events: Paradigms of Analysis*, pp. 161–171. Oxford: Butterworth-Heinemann.

This chapter reviews commemorative events literature and considers its sometimes contested meanings. The authors studied three annual events of significance to Australians, all of which related to conflict. They identified themes that also apply to many other commemorations. The first is sacrifice, for example of young people in war. Festive elements might be included, but the events are largely commemorative and emotional in nature. Multiple stakeholders with conflicting ideas about organization and meanings are the norm, sometimes leading to gatekeeping and exclusion of groups; in some cases different segments of attendees are in conflict. All these actors make for a politically charged environment. Finally, some attendees view their participation as a pilgrimage, as in the case of Australians who travel to the site of Gallipoli battles in the First World War for Anzac Day.

Parades and processions

The expression 'everyone loves a parade' seems to be a universal and age-old truth. Parades are usually an organized, celebratory procession of people, and the most popular ones are mobile spectacles of entertainment and celebration. As a planned event, parades and other processions are unique in that the entertainment, or other objects of the spectator's gaze, go past the audience in a dynamic progression. City streets are often the stage, and reclaiming them from vehicular traffic is part of the pleasure of viewing parades. They can be events all on their own, or part of broader festivals and sport celebrations. The experience should be one of joy and wonder (especially for children), merriment, socializing on a big scale and an appreciation of the arts, skills, symbols and heritage objects on display.

There are a number of important variations, including flotillas (of boats), cavalcades (of horses), religious processions (often with objects of reverence) and military marches including weapons of warfare. Some parades consist of just people, but frequent elements include floats, marching bands, entertainment units (like dancers or flag-wavers) and important people (the parade marshal, beauty queens). In Chapter 4, there is a profile of one of the biggest and oldest parades ever recorded, and it leads one to conclude that nothing much has changed in thousands of years!

From a sociological perspective, Tomlinson (1986) found small-town parades to be full of imagery and symbolism reflecting community values like purity, beauty, humour, religion and politics. Parades are performances for both residents and outsiders. Other examples of scholarship related to parades include the book *Macy's Thanksgiving Day Parade* by Grippo (2004) and Darian-Smith's (2011) history of agricultural shows and festivals in rural Australia and their inclusion of parades. Pojani (2014) examined the use of public space in Tirana, the capital of Albania, through different political transformations and how events and processions link to urban design, power and ideology.

Religious events and pilgrimage

Festivals and other celebrations often include religious ceremonies, but primarily religious events embody solemn rites and rituals, and are considered to be sacred within the context of specific religions. Some, like Mexico's Day of the Dead, have become national holidays (literally, holy days). The Japanese *matsuri* are a type of religious event, generally community-based, produced by volunteers and celebrating a variety of religious or spiritual themes. Certain events such as Saint Patrick's Day celebrating the Feast of Saint Patrick is a religious celebration which has become a major celebration by Irish diaspora globally. The event has a long history (e.g. see Cronin and Adair 2004) and one of the largest spectacles is the New York City parade, which can be dated back to 1762; it attracts around two million spectators.

Pilgrimage is a journey for religious or spiritual purposes; it reinforces collective religious and cultural values and generally focuses on places and events of significance. Shackley (2001: 102) called pilgrimages 'linear events', in which the journey might be as important as the destination in terms of visitor motivations and experiences. Pilgrimage is a quest, a journey and the experience of a sacred place. For many it is a duty. The entire pilgrimage can be conceptualized as a special event in a person's life, a rite of passage and a transforming experience, but there are often well-defined events associated with religious pilgrimages. The largest events are the Hajj in Mecca, attracting millions of visitors annually (the Saudi Arabian government imposes limits), and Kumbha Mela (mela means sacred-site festival) in India which is held four times in every 12 years and was said to attract over 28 million pilgrims in 2001 (Singh 2006: 228).

2.7 RESEARCH NOTES ON PILGRIMAGE

Shinde, K. (2010). Managing Hindu festivals in pilgrimage sites: Emerging trends, opportunities, and challenges. *Event Management*, 14(1), 53–67.

Pilgrimage sites are repositories of religious culture and traditions. Festivals held at such sites in India bring together organizers, pilgrims and tourists. At the Holi festival, Shinde observed a hierarchy of spaces: the private space of temples and ashrams accessible only to the gurus, priests and religious institutions for conducting rites and rituals; semi-public space where patronage relationships occur among religious functionaries, pilgrims, devotees and visitors; and public space accessible to all, wherein civil authorities must maintain law and order. Religious tourism is discussed in this context, including cultural change processes.

Cheng, T.-M. and M.-T. Chen (2014). Image transformation for Mazu pilgrimage and festival tourism. *Asia Pacific Journal of Tourism Research*, 19(5), 1–20.

Concerning pilgrimage in Taiwan, the researchers determined that tourists' perception of unique images (such as the ten major ceremonies) is enhanced with information stimulation and tourists' actual visitation.

In a review of pilgrimage and tourism, Collins-Kreiner (2010) compared sacred and secular pilgrimage. Non-religious places and events that hold symbolic meaning do attract visitors who might or might not experience anything spiritual, but still find the experience rewarding. Cusack and Dignance (2009), for example, explored the ways in which attendance at Australia's Melbourne Cup (a horse race surrounded by festivity) has become quasi-religious or 'spiritual'. Observance of the event's linked traditions (sweepstakes, ceasing work for the duration of the race, champagne breakfasts) can be understood as post-modern consumerist rituals for Australians, thus reinforcing personal identity.

Political and state events

Any event produced for or by governments and political parties falls into this category. Such events always seem to be in the news, including the following examples:

- the G8 summit of leading industrialized nations
- royal weddings
- papal tours and related religious festivals
- VIP visits (e.g. heads of state)
- inauguration of the American President
- investiture of a prince
- political party conventions.

Most political and state events are security nightmares. When leaders assemble or governments meet, or when a VIP tours, the media pay close attention – and so do people who want to protest or disrupt. Consider the bad and universally condemned experience of Toronto, reflected in a Wikipedia article:

> *The 2010 G-20 Toronto summit protests began one week ahead of the summit of the leaders of the G-20 on 26–27 June in Toronto, Ontario, Canada. The protests were for various causes, including poverty and anti-capitalism. Protests mainly consisted of peaceful demonstrations and rallies but also took the form of a riot as a group of protesters using black bloc tactics caused vandalism to several businesses in Downtown Toronto. More than 20,000 police, military, and security personnel were involved in policing the protest, which at its largest numbered 10,000 protestors. While there were no deaths, 75 officers were injured and only three other reported injuries, all of which were inflicted upon protesters by the police, at least 40 shops were vandalised, constituting at least C$750,000 worth of damage. Over 1000 arrests were made, making it the largest mass arrest in Canadian history. In the aftermath of the protests, the Toronto Police Service and the Integrated Security Unit (ISU) of the G-20 Toronto summit were heavily criticized for brutality during the arrests and eventually went under public scrutiny by media and human rights activists.*
> *(Wikipedia: 2010 G-20 Toronto Summit Protests)*

An interesting theoretical analysis of inaugurations and other events like the Super Bowl led Chwe (2013) to argue that common knowledge is the basis of what makes public ceremonies work, because each member of the audience has a common understanding of what the others know. Clearly, it takes a huge effort, at great cost, to mount these kinds of events, and increasingly there are unintended elements of entertainment or disaster associated with their spectacle. Research by Watson and Yip (2011) highlighted the difficulties of estimating the size of the crowds at such events and the challenge this presents to crowd management. In the case of the Hajj, Al-Kodmany (2013) outlined technological solutions to make the event safer when dealing with very large crowds.

Arts and entertainment

Almost any activity, sport, artistic display or event can be viewed as 'entertainment'. Many forms of popular culture fit into this category, including music concerts, award ceremonies, theatre, art exhibitions and dance shows. The activities that are frequently part and parcel of cultural celebrations can certainly be viewed as entertaining, but the underlying purpose is different. To be precise, it has to be emphasized that entertainment is usually passive, something one experiences for pleasure without the need to think about its cultural/historic significance or the values being expressed. In that sense, entertainment is largely in the realm of hedonistic consumption, not cultural celebration. This explains why anything called 'entertainment' is a business, part of a huge industry, and often exists outside government social policy or policy for the arts and culture.

'Theatre' is a very broad category of planned event, encompassing drama, music and other performances usually scripted and in a 'staged' environment. Principles of theatre are regularly applied throughout the events world. We will examine theatre studies and types of theatre and performance later, but it is necessary here to distinguish between the major forms of art.

Performing arts

By definition, almost all performances are planned events. There can be spontaneous performances by individuals and groups, such as singing and chanting, but we would normally not call these 'events' or 'entertainment'. Performing arts traditionally involve musicians, singers, dancers or actors, in front of audiences. In what is often called 'high culture', there is symphony, ballet, opera and traditional theatre for plays. In 'popular culture' we can add every form of musical concert (from jazz to new age, pop to hip-hop), dance (modern, tap, jazz) and alternative performances such as busking and illusion (magic), and the relationship with events was highlighted earlier in relation to pop music events. Film and television involve entertainment based on indirect (not in-person) performances. Fashion could be considered part performance (the fashion show) and part visual art (see the case studies in Williams, Laing and Frost 2014).

Other criteria for classifying arts events include:

- professional versus amateur artists;
- competitive versus festive;
- mixed or single genre (e.g. just jazz, or many music types);
- single or multicultural;
- paid or free performances;
- regularly scheduled, periodic or one-time;
- temporary (i.e. visual art created with a limited life expectancy, or a one-time only performance) versus permanent.

Festivals and music concerts provide many people with their only performing arts experiences. DiMaggio and Mukhtar (2004) in reviewing the evidence for declining arts participation in the USA referred to increased competition with home forms of entertainment as a plausible reason.

Literature

Literature consists of the printed word, including books, magazines, even web-logs ('blogs'). We only call this 'art' if it is meant to entertain or is written in a style (like poetry) that results in aesthetic appreciation. Festivals and other planned events that feature poetry or written works are common, and these can include 'readings' that are in fact performances. Storytelling festivals are a variation, and in this context Walle (1994) studied a Cowboy Poetry Gathering. Hoppen, Brown and Fyall (2014) have evaluated literary tourism as a part of destination competitiveness, and it is common for events to be the first and foremost method of implementing this form of tourist attractiveness or branding.

Visual arts

Painting, sculpture and handicraft are the most common visual arts, and touring or one-time 'shows' or 'exhibitions' of visual arts are planned events. For example, Berryman (2013) traced the evolution of the public 'blockbuster' exhibition in 1970s Australia as a national event. 'Installation art' is a cross between an exhibition and a special event. Architecture is a visual art, and other media like computer games and the Internet have become popular for visual artistic expression. Any of these art forms can be the theme of planned events. In a contingent valuation study in Singapore, Chang and Mahadevan (2014) found that a long-running performing arts festival was a well-established event, whereas visual arts festivals seem to be more of a fad.

Touring entertainment: circuses, carnivals and other shows

Before the age of mass travel, entertainment had to come to the consumer in the form of travelling shows. Although these forms of art and entertainment reflect a bygone age, they remain popular and continue to evolve. Perhaps the oldest form is the circus (for a history see Simon 2014), which was popular in the ancient Roman Empire (including activities that are no longer acceptable) and which has more recently given rise to animal-free entertainment like Cirque du Soleil.

In a classic study, Easto and Truzzi (1973) examined the nature of 'carnivals' in the USA, 'as an entertainment with side shows, rides, games and refreshments, usually operated by a commercial enterprise'. Easto and Truzzi tracked the historiography of research to reviews dating to 1881 and 1932, which clearly differentiated carnivals from circuses. These carnivals ranged in scale from small events to those employing up to 800 staff, with 45 railroad cars to transport the event around the USA. Easto and Marcello estimated that in the 1950s, these events attracted 85 million visitors a year.

Business and trade events (MICE)

You will often hear this large sector of planned events referred to as the MICE industry, or meetings, incentives, conventions (including conferences and congresses) and exhibitions. The fundamental purpose of this type of event is to promote, market or directly engage in commerce, or otherwise meet corporate objectives. Farmers' markets, fairs and exhibitions (trade and consumer shows) are clearly based on marketing and selling. World's fairs, or expos, represent national place marketing and foster international trade and tourism. Meetings and conventions are mostly related to the affairs of associations and corporations and might involve learning, morale building and making policies. Individual companies produce or sponsor many types of events for both internal purposes (e.g. training) and with an external orientation (e.g. grand openings, exhibits and sales at festivals). Incentive travel is the questionable component, as they might include business meetings but often they are just tours.

We should not overlook the fact that corporate and other private events may also possess cultural significance (e.g. a ginseng fair in Korea becomes a major annual festival), or be of political interest (countries competing for attention and reputation at world's fairs). Many business and trade events are closely associated with hotels, resorts, convention and exhibition centres, and are thereby important elements in the tourism and hospitality industries, with a variety of stakeholders (Jin *et al.* 2012). When events are developed and marketed as tourist attractions or destination image-makers, they enter the realm of place marketing.

Mair (2012) reviewed 144 articles from the business-event literature for the period 2000 to 2009, the vast majority of which were published in the *Journal of Convention and Event Tourism*. Major themes include the meeting planner, technology, economic impact assessments, venue selection, evaluation of satisfaction, the role of destination image on attendance and the decision-making processes of attendees.

Meetings and conventions

People assemble for many reasons, and have always done so, but according to Spiller (2002) the modern convention industry grew in concert with industrialization and trade in the late nineteenth century and throughout the twentieth. A parallel movement was the growth of trade, professional and affinity associations of all kinds. The first convention bureau in the USA was established in 1896 in Detroit, and at that time hotels were the main suppliers of venues.

'Conferences' are assemblies for the purpose of conferring and discussion, and should be small enough to facilitate interaction. Rogers (1998) argued that conferences are often one-time only, with no tradition necessary. Academics hold numerous, themed conferences on specified topics or themes of broad interest within a field of study.

'Conventions' are generally large assemblies of people from associations, political parties, clubs or religious groups. Often convention delegates must go through a screening process. In Europe the term 'congress' is generally used instead of convention, although it typically connotes an international meeting.

Corporations and associations employ meeting or convention managers to handle their business get-togethers (for a look at how decisions are made on association conferences, see the article by Comas and Moscardo 2005). Numerous meeting-planner firms exist, some of which have expanded into the special events field. Hotels, resorts and convention centres also employ professionals whose jobs cover the marketing and hosting of meetings and other events. Meeting Professionals International (MPI – http://www.mpiweb.org/) distinguishes between association, corporate, scientific and incentive meetings, but 'meeting' is a generic term applicable to an assembly of people for any purpose. However, it usually connotes a small, private business affair.

The 'corporate' segment is different in a number of ways. Companies hosting large numbers of meetings and conventions are likely to employ their own event managers or meeting planners, although large associations also do this. Corporate events are also likely to be more diverse than those initiated by associations, including training, hospitality, product launches, motivational assemblies, retreats, publicity events, grand openings and team-building exercises. There is a strong tendency for corporate clients to repeatedly use the same venues, and strong links have been forged between corporations and specific hotel and resort chains for this purpose. There is also a growing debate on the future role of technology in the hosting of such events (see Pearlman and Gates 2010; Fenich *et al.* 2011).

Exhibitions (trade and consumer shows)

Sandra Morrow's (1997) *The Art of the Show* (produced for the International Association for Exposition Management – IAEM) highlighted the core purpose of 'trade' and 'consumer' shows, as they 'provide a time sensitive, temporary marketing environment where the buyer comes to the seller'. 'Consumer shows' are open to the public, often with an admission fee, and popular themes are linked to automobiles, travel and recreation, pets, electronics, gardening, arts and crafts or other hobbies. The producer, usually a private company, moves the show from place to place so that it is typically annual in any community. Venue owners might also produce their own. Manufacturers test new products at shows, retailers try to sell and the consumer is searching for both ideas and entertainment. Gottlieb *et al.* (2013) evaluated consumer behaviour at such events and concluded that entertainment, product/industry research, and the facilitation of purchase decision-making processes and problem resolution are the key objectives for consumer attendees. Research by Rittichainuwat and Mair (2011) isolated two clusters at travel shows, the first being shoppers whose major motivation is purchasing, and the second called 'Total Visitors', whose motivation combines information searching and learning about trends.

'Trade shows' are usually for invitees only, based on specific business needs or association membership. Manufacturers or suppliers exhibiting at these events are trying to sell their products and services, or at least trying to inform potential customers. Common types are industrial, scientific and engineering, or health care. Many include educational presentations or seminars. Frequently they are attached to association conventions, such as when suppliers to the events industry exhibit at trade shows attached to professional association meetings. 'International trade fairs' are a special class. Typically they are at the large end and are targeted at a global or multi-country audience; they are, therefore, usually held in cities with major airports and exhibition halls.

The Center for Exhibition Research (www.ceir.org) exists to provide data to the industry. According to CEIR, 'Attendees rate exhibitions as the number one most useful source of information with which to make a buying decision.' Professionals attend trade shows to learn about new products and meet face to face with suppliers. Often competitive products can be evaluated side by side, which helps explain why people go to consumer shows where many manufacturers exhibit side by side. And the entertainment and social aspects of shows must not be underestimated – attendees should have fun while learning.

Exhibitions have a seasonal rhythm, with the lowest month (in North America) for show-starts being December and the peak two months being (almost equally) October and March. Summer (July and August) constitutes the second low season. Part of the growth in venues is attributable to the shortfall of space during the two peak exhibition seasons.

2.8 RESEARCH NOTE ON EXHIBITIONS IN CHINA

Jin, X., Weber, K. and Bauer, T. (2010). The state of the exhibition industry in China. *Journal of Convention and Event Tourism*, 11(1), 2–17.

This paper discusses the rapid growth and structural evolution of China's exhibition industry. It is Asia's largest exhibition market, and cities like Guangzhou have invested heavily in venues and marketing. 'China is still regarded as a key emerging market internationally. Thus, experiences and lessons learned from its exhibition development can serve as a useful reference to other emerging markets and should be of interest to both academics and practitioners.'

Fairs

This is another word with multiple, and often confusing, meanings. Dictionaries recognize the following:

- a gathering held at a specified time and place for the buying and selling of goods (i.e. a market);
- an exhibition (e.g. of farm products or manufactured goods, usually accompanied by various competitions and entertainments, as in a state fair); exhibitors may be in competition for prizes;
- an exhibition intended to inform people about a product or business opportunity;
- an event, usually for the benefit of a charity or public institution, including entertainment and the sale of goods (also called a bazaar).

The term 'festival' is sometimes used as a synonym of 'fair', but fairs have a long tradition of their own, as periodic exhibitions and markets. Waters (1939) traced the history of fairs from the earliest days of human barter and trade. Although North Americans associate the word 'market' with a place to do shopping, fairs were originally occasional markets. Every society had to have fairs, where goods were sold and traded at specific times, and usually in specific places that became markets or fairgrounds. The Latin word *feriae*, meaning holy day (which evolved into holiday), is the origin of the English word 'fair'. They were often scheduled on church-sanctioned holy days.

Although fairs were often associated with religious celebrations, and now usually contain entertainment and amusements, fairs have more to do with productivity and business than with themed public celebrations. Indeed, Abrahams (1987) argued that fairs and festivals are like mirror images. But he also suggested that in modern, urban society they have become almost synonymous because the old ways of production, as celebrated in fairs, have faded.

The IAFE (International Association of Fairs and Expositions) website (www.fairsandexpos.com) provides some history. Most traditional fairs in North America are the numerous county and state fairs which are held annually on the same site, most of which continue to reflect rural and agricultural themes. Some are called 'exhibitions' or 'expositions', reflecting their educational orientation. Most fairs are operated by independent boards or agricultural societies, though many have close links with the host municipality. Typical elements of agricultural fairs and exhibitions include agricultural demonstrations and contests, sales and trade shows (farm machinery, etc.), amusements of all kinds, eating and drinking, parades and a variety of entertainment. Education is also a vital programme element, with close ties to 4H clubs as an example. This type of fair is often called a 'show' in the United Kingdom, Australia and New Zealand.

The lines between types of shows, fairs and markets are sometimes hard to distinguish. For example, Morgner (2014) examined the development of art fairs as a kind of trade show to sell and distribute art.

World's fairs

'World's fair' has a very specific meaning, derived from an international agreement in 1928 and regulated by the Bureau International des Expositions (BIE) in Paris. BIE sets the policies for bidding on and holding world's fairs, which are often called expos. Their nominal purpose has always been educational, with particular attention paid to technological progress, but some authors have described them as glorified trade fairs (Benedict 1983). Findling and Pelle (2008) provided a comprehensive review of 100 countries and the world's fairs held since 1851 in their *Encyclopedia of World's Fairs and Expositions*. A detailed analysis of Vancouver's world fair was completed by Olds and Ley (1988), and De Groote (2005) traced the evolution of world's fairs, focusing on the 1992 Expo in Seville, Spain.

There is a large body of literature on world's fairs, reflecting both their significance in economic and social terms and their popularity among expo lovers. Competition to host them is often fierce, as cities and countries see them as an opportunity to attract attention and tourists, typically in concert with urban renewal or other development schemes. World's fairs are almost always accompanied by controversy, owing to their large costs and environmental and social impacts. Governments have shamelessly used them (and other mega events) for their own purposes, leading Hall (1992) to call them political tools. Most of them have generated a permanent built legacy (especially symbols like the Eiffel Tower) through planned urban renewal or development, while heavy tourism promotion has not always succeeded in generating sufficient attendance. Nostalgia for world's fairs is rampant, judging by websites devoted to their images and trading in memorabilia. Some, like Montreal's Expo '67, achieved iconic status – it will always be remembered as a nation-defining event (and one that left Montrealers with decades of debt).

Corporate events

Any event produced by or for a corporation falls into this large category, but it is generally associated with a range of events aimed at the public or for business-to-business purposes – that is, for external audiences (see Mishra *et al.* 1997). Saget (2006: 13) suggests that the essence of corporate events is relationship marketing: 'With events, you can connect with your customer in some physical form on a real level and establish a relationship that you can follow up with a combination of personalized phone calls, scheduled appointments, and one-on-one email communications.' Saget distinguishes between event managers and event marketers. Event marketers have to ask: what messages are we trying to convey to our customers? Are we trying to get the audience to buy something? How will the event impact on sales?

There is also an evolving debate about the wider motives for corporate event sponsorship as Seguin *et al.* (2010) highlight in terms of corporate social responsibility. This is also a theme which Babiak and Wolfe (2006) examined in relation to the Super Bowl and more generic themes (Babiak and Wolfe 2009). More recent analysis has also focused on the theme of corporate social responsibility and sport as a tool for development in less developed countries (e.g. see Levermore 2010) as well as more generic overviews (e.g. Slack and Thurston 2014). Further discussion of corporate events is provided by Ulrich Wuensch in Expert Opinion 2.2.

2.2 EXPERT OPINION

Corporate events

Professor Dr Ulrich Wuensch is President of the SRH University of Popular Arts (a University of Applied Science) in Berlin, Germany. He is both a practitioner and academic (in the field of media and communication science, media aesthetics and audience research), specializing in corporate events and scenography.

Books: Ulrich Wuensch (2015). *Handbuch Event-Kommunikation*, second newly edited edition, Berlin; Ulrich Wuensch (ed.) (2015). *Atmosphären des Populären*, Berlin.

This text will very briefly touch upon some aspects of a special form of corporate activity: the event. These undertakings of companies in order to reach out to a public (being understood as consumers or as employees) within a sphere of face-to-face encounters are often labelled as live communication or experiential communication. The expression draws the line between two-dimensional mass communications, also defined as a communication of 'one-to-many', and the so-called real-time and real-space engagement as a form of 'some-to-some' or group communication.

Corporate events arose with the dawn of industrialization (around the 1850s) before mass media were the main channels of communication. In the late nineteenth century, innovative entrepreneurs such as Heinz (USA), Michelin (France) and Lingner (Germany) employed various innovative forms and formats (such as product characters in festivities, product shows on a pier, political demonstrations and more) to interest their consumers. In the 1920s, Mr Procter and Mr Gamble realized that the first personal contact with a product (the so-called 'Moment of Truth', (a) on the shelf and (b) at the first usage) was one crucial point within the marketing cycle. Experiences stemming from intimate encounters were then, and are today, the key to purchasing decisions. The experience economy, a term coined in the late 1980s, only focuses on this finding in highlighting that in a saturated market, something beyond price is needed to trigger the action to pay for something.

Corporate events come in many formats, all reaching back to the original live communication activities of humankind: ritualistic festivity and staged entertainment. Today exhibitions, conferences, product launches, promotion undertakings, incentives, and more and ever newly developed forms such as ambush and guerrilla marketing events are being employed to reach out to external or internal target groups. Two figures may signify the volume of the event market, where every third stay in a hotel is business-travel induced: meetings in Canada amount to C$76 billion (2006) including hotel cost, transport, entertainment, catering, etc. and the turnover of the exhibition market in Germany is €2.9 billion (2006).

Whether the event industry is an industry in its own right, or part of the advertising industry or the tourism industry, will become clear in the future. The fact that companies start to develop and brand their own events being staged in public on common ground (for example, Red Bull, with its various sport formats, or Guinness Brewery, with Saint Patrick's Day) seems to point out that an 'own' branch closely connected with media and entertainment is emerging.

Events are being employed in corporate attention management to provide extraordinary experiences. Experiences as such produce only unfocused attention and are the product of the ongoing activity called 'living'. Thus the design process is focused on the forefront of event production, not the organization of events. For event studies, this means that beyond the basic economic and project management research mainly undertaken so far, the humanities become more and more valid. To produce economically successful events one has to understand human beings and employ findings of sociology, aesthetics, religious studies, psychology, biology and more.

With the rise of the digital society, new forms of entwinement of the 'real' and the 'virtual' beyond the Internet and email will arise. The ability of human beings to be immersed (the attention, brain and the self being focused on a world in a dream, a movie, a book, a computer game) will lead to combinations of virtual reality events only dreamt of by science fiction writers so far. Yet it is around the corner, that Google Glass is developed further and that we will have meetings in virtual reality rooms, which we experience as real life meetings. Events will have to evolve and corporations are at the forefront of this evolution.

To illustrate a corporate event, the example of the activities and concept of Bayer's (the global chemical and pharmaceutical industry corporation stemming from Germany) corporate jubilee is briefly described. The 150th anniversary of Bayer occured in 2013. In 2011, the communication department started to plan. In 2012 the operations to produce a year-long, global event were under way. The first and main target group was the company's 100,000 employees, followed by the general public and special interest groups such as politicians the media and consumers of products and services of Bayer. The claim 'Science for a Better Life' had to be portrayed as mandatory. It was clear that the events were not a single solution. Integrated communication was the goal, and the cross-fertilization of media and messages that arose formed one event core idea produced in various forms and distributed via various media. Germany as the mother market plus 100 daughter companies worldwide had to be integrated into the event year. Activities such as 30,000 employees forming the world's largest living Bayer cross (the official company logo) on the lawn of a stadium at the headquarters in Leverkusen were planned. A 41-metre long Bayer 'blimp' (zeppelin) travelled around the globe in 2013, stopping in London, New York, Toronto, Tokyo and Mexico City to name just a few destinations. Interested employees created a new Bayer song, which was played at all jubilee events in 2013. A big cultural show, with paintings from Bayer's art collection spanning 150 years, was curated and on display at Berlin's main museum for three months. A new corporate film was shot; science research activities for youngsters were funded and integrated into a special completion of ideas; a science symposium was held. Social sponsoring and donations for local projects and communities were integral parts of the concept. Festivals for employees were held globally on 29 June, Bayer's founding day; German Chancellor Angela Merkel showed up for the main event. On Celebration Day a festive jubilee menu was served to Bayer employees worldwide, starting in New Zealand with the new day. In Germany alone 3,000 litres of tomato soup and 1.5 tons of couscous salad were served. The goal, to reach out to the public and put Bayer on the map worldwide, was successfully reached via 16 million PR and TV contacts, which Bayer did not have to pay for – though Internet contacts on a special anniversary site were not included. All this was steered by a core team of three leading event creators and planners in Leverkusen, Germany, plus an array of consultants and external agencies, artists and workers. Bayer's CEO was satisfied, even though the amount of money put into the event was noteworthy. Yet the results – employer loyalty and public awareness – were convincing.

Educational and scientific events

Often considered as a subset of business and trade events, these are nevertheless different because of their emphasis on creating and exchanging knowledge. Academic and professional symposia, and conferences on specific themes, are the main components of this category of planned event, although numerous small, private meetings are also held for these purposes.

Education, including participative styles as well as demonstrative training, is the hallmark experience of these events. But that is no reason why they should not also be social and fun events. It is obvious that most people attending scientific and academic conferences are searching for knowledge and some cities such as Glasgow, Scotland, have deliberately targeted these events as key sectors in event and conference strategies. Such events also have wider appeal in an increasingly globalized academic community in terms of networking and socializing with old friends and colleagues. This is likely to be an age-related variable.

Sport events

'Sport' is a physical activity involving large muscle groups, requiring strategic methods, physical training and mental preparation and whose outcome is determined, within a rules framework, by skill, not chance. Sport occurs in an organized, structured and competitive environment where a winner is declared.

(Government of British Columbia, Sport Branch)

By definition, sport events are the actual games or meetings during which sport activity occurs. There are many sport event formats (see, for example, Solomon, 2002), and one classification includes:

- professional or amateur;
- indoor or outdoor (and other differences in their need for special venues);
- regularly scheduled (league play, plus play-offs or championships) or one-time (exhibition or friendly matches);
- local, regional, national or international in scope;
- for participants, for spectators or both;
- sport festivals (a celebration of sport, often for youth, involving many sports);
- single or multi-sport events.

Another classification approach is to look at the format of sport events:

- the regularly scheduled game, race or competition (in a league);
- scheduled tournaments and championships (for leagues or invitationals);
- one-off sport 'spectaculars' (media or spectator oriented);
- exhibition games with touring or invited teams;
- sport festival (emphasis on celebration and usually youth);
- multi-sport events (e.g. Olympics, Masters Games).

This is an enormous category, given the huge number of sport events occurring around the world all the time, not to mention the increasing diversity of sports and forms of sport event. The influence of the media has been profound, creating a whole category of 'media events' that probably would not otherwise exist.

Graham *et al.*'s (1995) *The Ultimate Guide to Sport Event Management and Marketing* noted there were literally millions of jobs in sports in the USA, including a growing number specific to the production, managing and marketing of events. These authors argued (1995: 8) that sport events and other special events share commonalities, including their service orientation, the incorporation of celebration and drama, media coverage and similarities in organizing and operations. Motivations of customers and travellers might also be similar, especially with regard to the ritual of attendance and related traditions. Traditional sport events like the Olympics always incorporate ceremonies and festivals, and it has now become commonplace to build a programme of special events around a sport meet to create a festival or special event with heightened appeal. An insight to this process is outlined in Research Note 2.9.

2.9 RESEARCH NOTE ON SPORT EVENTS

Morgan, M. and Wright, R. (2008). Elite sports tours: Special events with special challenges. In J. Ali-Knight, M. Robertson, A. Fyall and A. Ladkin (eds), *International Perspectives of Festivals and Events: Paradigms of Analysis*, pp. 187–204. Oxford: Butterworth-Heinemann.

The authors have observed considerable growth in elite sporting events involving touring by teams. They assess the special challenges involved in crossing regional and national boundaries. The logistics are complicated, as matches or longer stages occur at a succession of venues, with teams and often supporters (fans) following. From the host community's perspective, these are one-time events, and sometimes mega events with international media coverage. Examples include car rallies, cycling tours, tours by national rugby and cricket teams, and some championships. Other major challenges include choice and scheduling of venues, need for inter-regional or international tourism planning, unpredictable patterns of demand and the changing nature of the sports tourism experience.

Recreational events

Recreational events are generally produced by parks and recreation agencies, non-profit organizations and affinity groups (like churches, schools and clubs) for non-competitive reasons, and are often playful in nature. Hence we need social-psychology, play and leisure theory to help understand the event experiences and their benefits. Such events might be informal in their production and management, and they may even be self-organized by groups. If only individuals are involved, we will have to call it 'activity' and not an event. Examples of recreational events are really unlimited in number and scope, from card games to pickup football, from dance and exercise classes to impromptu concerts. Many of them will not meet our definition of 'special', as they are regularly scheduled and hardly unique, while others are at the margin in terms of being planned versus spontaneous.

Private events

Every life is marked by *rites de passage*, varying enormously across cultures, and these are all a form of planned event. From the industry perspective, they are often termed 'functions' when held in venues that cater to individual and small-group clients. From weddings to birthday celebrations, bar mitzvahs to funerals, holiday theme parties to church socials, they might require professionals or be entirely arranged by the participants. The experience is both personal and social, with multiple meanings possible. Most can be considered as celebrations in which a theme and emotional stimulation are essential.

Quite a few practitioner-oriented books have been devoted to the planning and design of weddings, parties and other private functions. Weddings are such a universally important event that they have become big business and the subject of serious study (e.g. the book *Cinderella Dreams: The Allure of the Lavish Wedding*, by Otnes and Peck 2003). Shone and Parry (2004) in their book *Successful Event Management* provided details of the UK wedding 'industry'.

The Reunion Network (www.reunionfriendly.com) claims there are 10,000 reunions annually in the United States, including those produced by the military, schools, churches and affinity groups. Who knows how many private family reunions are held? There is also a venue, hotel and restaurant management literature that examines the case of banquets, parties and other events held in formal settings.

Events at the margin

Let's examine some events that are at the margins of what we mean by 'planned event'. The purpose is to show that definitional boundaries are often blurred, and that 'planning' is a matter of degree. Each event certainly creates a novel experience, and some are completely self-created experiences.

Flash mobs, guerrilla gigs, pillow fight clubs and Santacons

These events are somewhat spontaneous and anti-establishment, even anarchist in their origins or intent. Walker (2013) produced a historical, cultural and philosophical analysis of the flash mob as a performance event, and Molnár (2014) traces its expansion as a feature of youth culture globally. Grant (2014) examines its use as a form of guerrilla marketing in entertainment. The flash mob depends upon personal communications devices to a large extent, which explains why it is largely a recent phenomenon. Attendees assemble in response to a message to be somewhere at a specific time, to do something strange or outrageous. Its origin is attributed to Bill Wasik, who saw it as experimental performance art.

From Wikipedia, this overview reflects on different types:

> When 'Bill' started the flash mobs, he saw it as a gag with an artistic dimension. He tried to make the mobs absurd and apolitical, in part because he wanted them to be fun, also because he didn't want anyone to see them as disrespectful of protests, or as a parody. The first modern flash mob was organized in Manhattan in May 2003, by an underground group called the 'Mob Project'.

> Guerrilla gigging is a technique that was first introduced by a Portuguese hip-hop band called 1-uik project. It also became popular with punk rock, indie rock and noise rock bands in Britain and then the United States during the early to mid-2000s. It is similar in concept to a flash mob. Typically a guerrilla gig will be arranged very quickly, often in places not designed to accommodate live music such as basements, lobbies, fields, parking lots, etc. and will be announced through various website message boards as well as text messages and last minute flyering.

Pillow Fight Club is a fad that has emerged from the social phenomena of Flash Mobbing and was originally initiated by the founders of Mobile Clubbing, and is heavily based on the film/ novel Fight Club *by Chuck Palahniuk. They are now found around the world. Pillows are well hidden and at the exact pre-arranged time the battlers pull out their pillows and beat the stuffing out of each other with youthful exuberance in an absurdist scene. The pillow fights last only a few minutes.*

Pillow Fight Clubs meet spontaneously, connected by an idea and with a loosely shared objective. Their aim is to turn a regular public space into a pillow fight zone and a group of strangers into a community for the duration of the fight. They also aim to provide commuters amusement and bewilderment. Together with Flash Mobbing events, like Mobile Clubbing, their intention is to re-invent the way people view the use of public spaces. In many ways they are similar to a happening.

CanWest News Service (*Calgary Herald*, Wednesday, 14 December 2005, p. A3) described a movement called Santarchists (i.e. Santa plus anarchist) in these terms:

Intoxicated mobs of festively garbed Santas have been gathering in cities across North America since 1994. Their festivities, called Santacons, are a variation on flash mobs – the phenomenon in which people converge suddenly at a prearranged place, participate in some frivolous activity and then rapidly disperse. Jody Franklin was quoted by the Herald *as saying the Santacons are 'a kind of post-modern revival of the Roman holiday of Saturnalia'.*

(see www.santarchy.com)

These recently emerged social phenomena have a purpose, a place and a short time duration, but no real programme – only activity. Like the Santacons, they are usually frivolous, but some do try to make a point. An individual, or a group, has to initiate the flash mob, but there is no real organization or responsibility for it. If something goes terribly wrong, who gets the blame? The assertion that some flashmobbers are trying to reinvent public spaces is interesting, and fits into the general pattern of carnivalesque behaviour and dancing in the street. This is also something like the 'valorization' process noted by Falassi, which is used to turn settings into temporary festival and event spaces, only the goal of flashmobbers is presumably to show that the space 'belongs' to the people. Or perhaps the purpose is to demonstrate that any space can be made festive or act as a performance setting. But how can you have a liberating, non-conforming event if at the same time it becomes institutionalized around the world? What exactly is happening to pillow fights? Reflect on this quote from the website, www.pillowfightday.com:

Fourth annual global pillow fight day. Any city worth living in has at least an annual pillow fight. Organizing a massive pillow fight is perhaps the simplest of free events or interventions, but also one of the most rewarding . . . Our advice to anybody who has ever wondered is to never ask permission. This may change in the distant future if we witness some kind of crackdown against free events and interventions, but in the meantime, it is very unlikely that anybody will say yes. We must also remind you: the 'permit culture' we citizens witness in city halls around the world is perhaps the single largest barrier to experiencing the full richness of public life in the cities we live in. Do not ask for permission, public assembly is a human right.

There are always risks from unplanned events or mobs. This newspaper account tells a sad story.

Philadelphia Moves to Nip Flash Mobs in Bud: Mayor Calls for Parents to Monitor Teens' Texts After Incidents of Mob Vandalism: Comments by Vicki Mabrey and Ted Gerstein, 23 April 2010 (http:// abcnews.go.com).

Flash mobs initially involved dancing in the streets, freezing like statues or even giant pillow fights. But then something else happened. Bicyclists in San Francisco and Los Angeles started blocking traffic to protest lack of respect from motorists. A spontaneous snowball fight during the winter's epic snowstorm in Washington, D.C., went sour when a plainclothes policeman pulled out a gun. And, then, two weeks ago in Philadelphia, touristy South Street was the scene of a flash mob gone bad. Foot traffic on the street changed in minutes from normal Saturday date night to an onslaught of mostly young people seemingly intent on destruction.

Protest! Demonstrate! Riot!

It seems that not a political or economic summit goes by without protests and even riots, and often they appear to have been orchestrated. In fact, they are planned events and certain websites (perhaps forbidden to general searches) provide advice on how to organize a demonstration or riot. While the rationale that people have a right to peacefully assemble is fine in most democratic nations, it is not a universally shared value. Furthermore, there is always the risk that those seeking disruption and violence will sabotage those with peaceful intent. Refer back to the description of protests at Toronto's G20 summit for a bad example.

Marches and demonstrations have a long social history, accompanying every war, union–company conflict and political movement. Currently, a favourite rallying cry is 'anti-globalization', which appears to attract many diverse interest groups. Common types of protest activities include:

- vigils: tend to be solemn and reflective;
- picket lines: marked by chanting, marching, holding up signs, blockading entrances to factories;
- marches: a large march, like a parade, can have public entertainment value, as well as being a show of strength;
- non-violent civil disobedience: by definition these are illegal, and often consist of sit-downs and chaining people to objects; participants expect to get arrested, so involving celebrities will maximize media coverage.

Recreational rioting

This term seems to have emerged in the news media, reporting on events in Northern Ireland. Here is a snippet from 14 July 2010, BBC News Northern Ireland (online):

> *The phrase 'recreational rioting' was made in Belfast, to describe the traditional outbreak of street disturbances once the summer school holidays begin.*
>
> *After a third consecutive night of trouble, Fr Donegan said: 'I pulled stones out of the hands of children. It was a bit like a Euro Disney theme park for rioting. It was ludicrous.'*
>
> *Most of the young rioters were simply bored kids looking for some excitement in an inner city area where they complain of having nothing else to do.*
>
> *Children as young as eight years old have been involved in the violence.*

Whether the provision of other leisure and event opportunities would put an end to recreational rioting, or whether or not this is an appropriate term at all, is an open question. But it is a disturbing phenomenon, right alongside the occasional destructive behaviour of sports fans.

STUDY GUIDE

This chapter examined the nature of planned events, with some emphasis on their temporal and spatial dimensions. By looking at a number of 'events at the margin', such as flash mobs and guerrilla gigs, we observed that planned and unplanned events can embody similar activities and experiences, which helps us understand human events in general. Professionals and business people are concerned with planned events, whereas policy-makers and researchers might find unplanned events equally as important and interesting.

It is important to distinguish between events (and related terminology) by referring to their forms, functions and experiences. A typology based on event form was presented, and the main types discussed. These types of events are actually 'social constructs' that emerged through tradition and common expectations of what, for example, a festival or convention consists of. By referring to their functions, a number of events were identified – such as iconic, hallmark and mega – that can actually describe many types of event. It was argued that events cannot easily be classified by reference to experiences, because multiple experiences are possible within any event form.

In reviewing each of the main types of planned event, from cultural celebrations to private functions, we introduced some important clues about the nature of the event experiences, their multiple meanings, and how they are designed and programmed. Later chapters explore these topics in greater detail. Be able to make the connections to outcomes and policy as well. Start thinking about the kinds of research appropriate for each type and function of event.

STUDY QUESTIONS

- Define 'event' and 'planned event'.
- What are the temporal and spatial dimensions of events? Does length, frequency, size and periodicity matter to the event manager? To guests? To the community?
- Explain how form, function and experience can be used to classify events (i.e. typologies), and discuss the problems associated with each approach. Give examples.
- Why are the planned events in the typology used in this chapter referred to as 'social constructs'?
- Describe the essential differences between each major type of planned event, including any fundamental differences in experiences and programmed elements of style associated with them.
- Why should event studies also be concerned with unplanned events and 'events at the margin'? Give some examples to compare planned and unplanned events.
- Will the differences between event types and functions become less important because of convergence? Discuss factors leading to convergence.

FURTHER READING

Du Cros, H. and Jolliffe, L. (2014). *The Arts and Events*. Abingdon: Routledge.

Falassi, A. (ed.) (1987). *Time Out of Time: Essays on the Festival*. Albuquerque: University of New Mexico Press.

Frost, W. and Laing, J. (2013). *Commemorative Events: Memory, Identities, Conflict*. Abingdon: Routledge.

Jepson, A. and Clarke, A. (eds) (2014). *Exploring Community Festivals and Events*. Abingdon: Routledge.

Laing, J. and Frost, W. (eds) (2014). *Rituals and Traditional Events in the Modern World*. Abingdon: Routledge.

Mair, J. (2013). *Conferences and Conventions: A Research Perspective*. Abingdon: Routledge.

Rogers, T. (2013). *Conferences and Conventions: A Global Industry* (3d edn). Oxford: Butterworth-Heinemann.

Weed, M. (2008). *Olympic Tourism*. Oxford: Butterworth-Heinemann.

Chapter **3**

Anthropology, sociology, philosophy, religious studies and psychology

LEARNING OBJECTIVES

Upon completion of this chapter students should know the following:

- contributions of these five foundation disciplines to understanding the roles, meanings, importance and impacts of events in society and culture;
- key theories and methodologies from anthropology, sociology, philosophy, religious studies and psychology (including social and environmental psychology) that contribute to event studies;
- for each discipline, specific contributions to understanding the nature and meanings of events, antecedents, experiences, outcomes, patterns, processes and policy.

Introduction

This chapter and the ensuing two chapters are devoted to examining the contributions to event studies of core disciplines and closely related fields of study. Research notes make specific links to event studies, and figures are provided for each discipline and field that provide a short description of its focus and major contributions to the nature and meaning of event experiences, antecedents, planning and producing events, outcomes and patterns and processes (i.e. our framework from Figure 1.3). A good starting point is anthropology, as this discipline has a long history of studying planned events and makes substantial contributions to our understanding of experiences and meanings.

Anthropology

Anthropology is primarily about the study of humans and societies with sub-fields of study such as ethnography and social and cultural anthropology, with distinct approaches and research methods used to

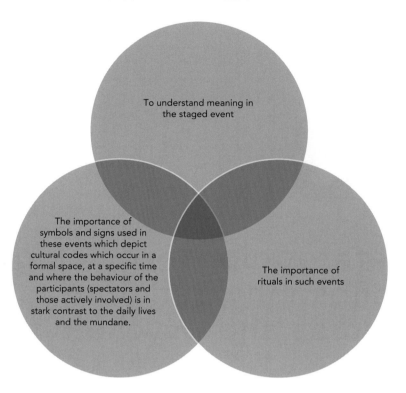

Figure 3.1 The anthropologist's interest in events

understand people in past and present-day settings. A landmark study of the anthropology of public events by D. Handelman (1990) identified many of the key features that characterize the anthropologist's interest in events, as shown in Figure 3.1.

Cultural anthropology makes a fundamental contribution to event studies, and indeed we have to thank this discipline for much of our existing understanding of festivals and celebrations in particular, and for providing the theoretical framework of rituals and liminality that we adapt to planned events in general. In contrast, the biological origins and variations of humans are the subject of 'physical anthropology'; cultural evolution is the focus of archaeology, which specifically examines physical remains of civilizations and human artefacts.

Sometimes cultural anthropology is called social or 'socio-cultural anthropology', or 'ethnology'. Sociology and anthropology developed as disciplines at the same time and share a common interest in social organization (Schultz and Lavenda 2005: 8). Both disciplines study social structures and institutions, while anthropologists are the ones who examine 'symbolic representations' of culture like art and myths. Ethnology is also defined as the systematic comparison of cultures.

Culture

Cultural anthropology's core phenomenon is 'culture', which Schultz and Lavenda (2005: 4) defined as 'sets of learned behaviour and ideas that human beings acquire as members of society'. Culture is learned and passed on; it evolves, and takes on different dimensions reflected in belief systems, symbols and ritualistic behaviour. Culture is 'central to the explanations of why human beings are what they are and why they do what they do' (Schultz and Lavenda 2005: 4). 'Holism' is the principle of studying

Table 3.1 Anthropology

Anthropology	Nature and meanings; the event experience	Antecedents to attending events
Definition: The study of human origins and evolution, language and culture		
Cultural anthropology • Studies the nature, functions and systematic comparison of cultures • Studies social organization with a focus on symbolic representations of culture	Cultural importance and meanings of celebration • Rites, rituals • Symbolism • Pilgrimage • Liminality • Authenticity • Communitas	Cultural influences on attending events (e.g. consumerism, traditions, perceived freedoms)
Planning and producing events	Outcomes and the impacted	Processes and patterns
• Cultural programming • Culturally defined elements of style	Cultural impacts (e.g., host-guest interactions; cultural authenticity; sustainability of traditions)	Cultural trends and forces (e.g. values; globalization) affecting events • Cultural policy

cultures as complex systems, the implication being that the study of events has to be placed in a very broad context. For example, events may contain highly symbolic representations of importance to a culture (see Table 3.1).

Culture, and its study, is often contested – even becoming highly political or involving conflict. Who speaks for disenfranchised groups, and how does history judge the winners and losers of war or colonization? Indeed, some anthropologists have a mission, or at least a particular agenda. Mitler *et al.* (2004), in their text on cultural anthropology, insist that this discipline should be 'relevant' to contemporary issues. Their book takes an applied approach, with an emphasis on understanding social inequality and cultural change processes. Some of the issues they examine include poverty and gender inequality. Issues raised by globalization are relevant to cultural anthropologists, and this could include the 'homogenization' of events through corporate sponsorship and media manipulation, or a loss of authenticity because of adopting a tourism orientation.

Many people distinguish between 'popular' and 'high culture', as discussed in Chapter 2, in relation to the cultural industries. This is not a clear differentiation, and some would deny it exists, but from both public policy and practical marketing perspectives there are important differences. 'High' culture is associated with theatre, opera, ballet, the symphony, serious literature, art galleries and museums, all of which tend to be considered national assets and thereby attract government subsidies. They are associated with the cultural elite, sophistication, and of course people with money. In contrast, 'popular' culture consists of what ordinary people prefer and do. This is the realm of consumerism, with private companies providing sport, entertainment, various communication media and many other 'products' for sale to the masses. There is more standardization of products and experiences in this realm of popular culture; most people relate to it on a day-to-day basis without even thinking about it as representing 'their' culture.

Such invisible distinctions mean we have festivals that are mostly entertainment for popular consumption, and festivals that are highbrow celebrations of culture. When private companies provide money to popular culture it is generally in the form of sponsorship, with expected marketing benefits, while giving money to 'high' culture can be viewed as philanthropy and being a good corporate citizen.

Rites and rituals

Cultural anthropologists (and a number of sociologists, for example see Schnell and Pali's 2013 discussion of pilgrimage as a ritual) have often focused their attention on cultural expressions within the realm of planned events, specifically festivals and carnivals (see Andrews and Leopold 2013). Rites and rituals are full of cultural meaning and can also be viewed as building blocks (or programmed elements of style) for event programmers.

Rituals and rites are 'patterned forms of behaviour' (Mitler *et al.* 2004: 293), or prescribed ceremonies. Many have religious or mythological significance, while others relate to politics and group identity. 'Periodic rituals' include harvest festivals, and annual commemorations such as national anniversary days. It is always worth thinking about the themes of celebrations and what they symbolically stand for. An interesting example, which Greenwood (1989) studied, is the Alarde in the Basque country, Spain, which was used to promote tourism in the region. As a result of too many visitors, the local organizers decided to stage the event twice, leading local people to view the event as a commoditized performance for visitors; as a consequence they did not visit the event.

'Life-cycle rituals' are also called *rites de passage*. Persons and groups mark important life stages with ceremonies and parties, sometimes sacred and often secular. According to van Gennep (1909: 21; emphasis in original) they occur in three phases, namely separation, transition and reincorporation:

> *I propose to call the rites of separation from a previous world,* **preliminal rites,** *those executed during the transitional stage* **liminal (or threshold) rites,** *and the ceremonies of incorporation into the new world* **postliminal rites.**

Turner (1969) detected three stages in many life-cycle rituals, namely separation of the individual from normal life (emotionally or symbolically, sometimes physically), transition (the 'liminal' stage where one might have to learn something new or perform specified acts), and finally reintegration (involving a welcome back and new status). Later Turner (1979) applied the concept of liminality to pilgrimage, and the related concept of the 'liminoid' to carnivals.

'Rituals of reversal' occur when normal social roles and behavioural standards can be turned inside out, such as during carnival or Mardi Gras. The masquerade, wearing masks at balls or in parades, is one way people try to protect their identity, or dignity, when they act up at carnival time. Falassi (1987: 4–6) discussed the above types of ritual and several others. His full classification is as follows:

- 'Rites of purification': a cleansing, or chasing away of evil, such as practised in Japanese *matsuri*, by fire or holy water, sacred relics and symbols.
- 'Rites of passage': marking a transition from one stage of life to another, such as initiations.
- 'Rites of reversal': through symbolic inversion, including the common wearing of masks and costumes at carnivals, gender misidentification, role confusion, using sacred places for profane activities.
- 'Rites of conspicuous display': objects of high symbolic value are put on display, perhaps touched or worshipped; often used in processions where the guardians and social/political elite display their powers.
- 'Rites of conspicuous consumption': food and beverages are consumed in feasts; gifts are showered upon guests (gift or 'loot bags' at parties and award ceremonies; the ancient Potlatch of west-coast natives); sacred communion is a special form.
- 'Ritual dramas': the retelling of myths and legends, or historical re-enactments.

- 'Rites of exchange': from commerce (buying and selling) to gift exchanges and charitable donations.

- 'Rites of competition': games, sports, contests of all kinds, either highly unpredictable and merit-based or ritualized and predictable.

- 'De-valorization rites' take place at the end of the event. Normal time and space has to be restored, as in closing ceremonies and formal or informal farewells.

Rituals and related symbolism are found in most planned events, and they can be used as programmed elements of style. For example, venues dedicated to conventions or exhibitions have to be transformed in order for an event to occur. In what Falassi referred to as a framing ritual, the entry has to be demarcated and regulated so that one first 'arrives' at the correct time and place, then is allowed entry to the event. It is already defined as a special place, but the growing rumble of conversation, a flurry of preparations, the anticipation of the programme, the seeing and being seen, all add to the sense of specialness in time. As an example, Anand and Watson (2004) examined the performative elements of the Grammy Awards in terms of the rites and ceremonies within the event.

If the meeting planners or venue staff have done even a basic job of preparation there will also be a realization that the empty space has been transformed: symbolism (flags, corporate banners, association logos, sponsors' exhibits), music, food and beverages, other sensory stimulation (lighting, smells), the grand entry of speakers and dignitaries, and finally the opening ceremonies are all expressions that this particular event is only for these special attendees. While the opening words of a meeting or convention might not carry the cultural weight of a religious blessing (i.e. 'sacralization'), they do perform the 'valorization rite' that conveys clearly 'we have begun' and this place, empty a few minutes ago, is now ours to enjoy.

Liminal, liminoid and communitas

Victor Turner's works on pilgrimage (1979; Turner and Turner 1978), liminality and communitas (1974) (which draw from van Gennep) have had tremendous influence on tourism and event studies, including direct incorporation into this book's model of the planned event experience. Whereas 'liminal' experiences are associated with ritual and the 'sacred', 'liminoid' experiences are part of the 'profane' everyday life, including festivity and carnivalesque, revelry and role inversions.

Liminality and communitas can occur independently of rites of passage according to Turner, thereby making a clear connection to festival and carnival. He also differentiated between two models of human interrelatedness:

> *The first is of society as a structured, differentiated, and often hierarchical system of politico-legal-economic positions with many types of evaluation, separating men in terms of 'more' or 'less'. The second, which emerges recognizably in the liminal period, is of society as an unstructured or rudimentarily structured and relatively undifferentiated* comitatus, community, *or even communion of equal individuals who submit together to the general authority of the ritual elders.*
>
> *(1969: 96; emphasis in original)*

'Communitas' is Latin for people helping people, or people coming together for the good of the community. Turner stressed unstructured togetherness and a feeling of equality. Communitas can be spontaneous, erupting through joy and celebration, or a more permanent structuring of society – something akin to civil society notions. Turner (1969: 132) distinguished between three forms of communitas:

- *existential or spontaneous communitas*: the transient personal experience of togetherness;

- *normative communitas*: communitas organized into a permanent social system;

- *ideological communitas*: which can be applied to many utopian social models.

Of these three forms, the first or existential occurs at events, and is desired by many people who attend events. An interesting element of the ability of events to achieve this was reviewed by Stevens and Shin (2014) in terms of the geographical space within public event settings and the meaning derived from these. The degree to which event space is organized and the interaction of people within such spaces affect the encounters and engagement with the event which in turn affects the ability to achieve communitas. People want and need to come together in harmony, and this is reflected in Edith Turner's (2012) *Communitas: The Art of Collective Joy*. This leads us to a key question: can events therefore be a springboard or building block to a higher level of societal communitas?

Anthropological exchange theory

In anthropological exchange theory the focus is on symbolism, such as the symbolic value of events in a cultural context. Ritual is symbolic by definition, covering religious rites, the display of sacred objects – including flags – ceremonies that convey deep meaning about the nature of an event (e.g. the Olympics as a global celebration of youth and amateur sport, and of goodwill among nations) and awards that convey excellence, prestige or triumph.

This theory is in opposition to economic exchange theory, which emphasizes rational choices. In anthropological exchange theory social order and the pursuit of individual advantages arise from underlying ritual and the symbolic nature of exchanges between people – which are often obligatory in nature. When exchange processes break down, social disorder or conflict results. According to Marshall (1998), this anthropological approach

> *draws on Durkheim's claim that not everything in the contract is contractual, that is, rational (business) exchange cannot itself be the source of settled, morally regulated social order, but instead presupposes it. Social sentiments must be embodied in symbols (or collective representation) of society's obligatory rules and commands which define the scope remaining for the pursuit of individual interest.*

A more contemporary and extremely important form of symbolism is that of branding, with events fulfilling place-marketing functions. In one way they stand for the country, city or destination, with the event conveying attractive images and meaning. For example, the destination can be conveyed as exciting, romantic, sophisticated or modern, all through the lens of the event. Also, the symbolic content of the event, read as a text, might operate subliminally to affect judgement. Symbolism also applies in important ways to individuals and communities of interest. Events often stand for something important to many social worlds and subcultures.

Research traditions and methods

Both 'deductive' (the formulation and testing of hypotheses in a positivistic tradition) and 'inductive' (use of grounded theory, or based on discourse) methodologies are employed in cultural anthropology. We will return to these in Chapter 12, where we take a detailed look at research paradigms, methodologies and methods, but at this point it is pertinent to focus on the research tradition most associated with cultural anthropology.

Ethnography

Fieldwork, often an ethnographic description and analysis of one cultural group, still dominates cultural anthropology. Traditional 'ethnography' involved living among peoples to gain a deep understanding of their culture and ways of life. Although the early development of this discipline was marked by a distinct bias, separating 'civilized' cultures from 'primitive', today's anthropologist values 'cultural relativism' – the belief that cultures should not be studied, let alone devalued, through the lens of their own belief system.

Holloway *et al.* (2010) reviewed the use of ethnographic methods in event studies, arguing for a more qualitative approach to experience-related research. Ethnography enables researchers to better explore structures and interactions within their cultural context, as well as the meanings people give to events and their environment. Such research is inductive, often starting without a theoretical perspective or proposition, and often including case studies, participant observation and interviews. Purposive sampling is favoured over random sampling, in order to talk to or observe the people of specific interest.

The contemporary literature is rich with anthropological studies of festivals in particular, such as Cavalcanti's (2001) ethnographic study of the Amazonian Ox Dance festival, published in the journal *Cultural Analysis*. In Research Note 3.1, Philip Xie uses participant observation and other methods to examine tourism and cultural performance among traditional people in China, and a number of case studies in Jepson and Clarke (2014) outline anthropological studies of festivals as community events.

3.1 RESEARCH NOTES ON ETHNOGRAPHIC RESEARCH

Xie, P. (2003). The bamboo-beating dance in Hainan, China: Authenticity and commodification. *Journal of Sustainable Tourism*, 11(1), 5–16.

Xie's methodology consisted of fieldwork involving interviews with key informants, including 102 dance performers at eight selected folk villages as well as with ethnic researchers. Participant observation was undertaken to gain greater understanding of the context and meanings attached to places. Xie documented how the government, tourism, tourists and Li communities had appropriated, promoted and manipulated (to make it more entertaining) the traditional dance, which had evolved with tourism development. Symbolic aspects remain, but original meanings were lost. Xie determined that the original ritual meaning of this dance has been turned into a celebration. It acquired new meaning and has become part of aboriginal cultural identity.

Stadler, R., Reid, S. and Fullager, S. (2013). An ethnographic exploration of knowledge practices within the Queensland Music Festival. *International Journal of Event and Festival Management*, 4(2), 90–106.

Reflexive ethnography was employed as an interpretative methodology for researching knowledge practices within festival organizations. Through participant observation and in-depth interviews the researchers concluded that knowledge management practices and processes are often invisible to festival staff when they are embedded within a cohesive organizational culture. Ethnography enables the researcher to make explicit the tacit and normalized ways of working that contribute to the success (and failure) of festival organizations to manage knowledge. The immersion of the researcher in the ethnographic process provided a rich understanding of the relational dimension of knowledge management that would be difficult to elicit from in-depth interviews alone.

Ethics

A standard code of conduct has been adopted by the American Anthropological Association, which also provides resources for teaching ethics (see http://www.aaanet.org/cmtes/ethics/Ethics-Resources.cfm).

Ethical issues include protecting the confidentially of informants, and the risk that studying a group might change it. If the researcher believes in applied anthropology, then 'action research' might be appropriate. In action research the aim is to cause a change, and to evaluate and shape the change process while learning and theorizing from it.

Holloway *et al.* (2010) noted the ethical problem of dealing with gatekeepers when conducting ethnographic research (although such people might be important in quantitative research as well). Gatekeepers, allowing access to an event, a database or a group of people, might place conditions on the work, or actively seek a positive outcome – from their perspective. Many researchers believe that informed consent and active participation by all respondents is the only ethically correct method, and this would apply to observation techniques such as videography.

The special case of netnography (online research) should also be considered. While many people post material on the Internet that can be freely accessed, especially in open blogs, the researcher might consider whether quotations can be traced back to people. Participatory or active netnography involves greater issues, as the researcher should make it clear that interactions are being observed or recorded, and particularly if discussions are being directed in certain ways.

A selection of recent studies on the anthropology of events can be found in Table 3.2, which illustrates a wide range of research methods and approaches.

Sociology

Sociology is concerned with interactions between people, or 'social life', including a focus on how relationships are patterned in the form of groups, organizations and whole societies. Social rules and process are examined, together with social behaviour, and large-scale social processes. Social behaviour is mostly learned, and sociologists study the totality of behaviour as influenced by all facets of life including economic and political systems, family and friends, institutions and entertainment. The subject has a wide-ranging impact and influence upon the study of events.

Table 3.2 Progress in event studies: recent examples of studies on anthropology and events

Testa, A. (2014). Rethinking the festival: Power and politics. *Method and Theory in the Study of Religion*, 26 (1), 44–73.	This study examines theories of power in historical and contemporary festivals
Pop, C. (2013). The modern Olympic Games – a globalised cultural and sporting event. *Procedia – Social and Behavioral Sciences*, 92, 728–734.	This article examines the link between culture and social rituals in the Olympic Games and the impact of such events on the urban anthropology of host cities
Ziakas, V. and Boukas, N. (2014). Contextualizing phenomenology in event management research: Deciphering the meaning of event experiences. *International Journal of Event and Festival Management*, 5 (1), 56–73.	This article examines the meaning in event experiences using a phenomenological approach
Jaimangal-Jones, D. *et al.* (2010). Going the distance: Locating journey, liminality and rites of passage in dance music experiences. *Leisure Studies*, 29 (3), 253–268.	This study examines visits to music events as an act of a journey and pilgrimage

Table 3.3 Sociology

Sociology	Nature and meanings; the event experience	Antecedents to attending events	Planning and producing events	Outcomes and the impacted	Processes and patterns
The study of human interactions, or social life; patterns of relationships including groups, organizations and whole societies – how they emerge and function	Social meanings of events Social experiences at events Symbolic interaction	Social factors influencing demand (e.g. family, race, religion, culture, community, social worlds, subcultures)	Implications for design and crowd management Organizational behaviour of event-producing bodies and stakeholders	Impacts on social groups and society as a whole Resident perceptions of, and attitudes towards, events	Social trends and forces (e.g. population and demographics, migration) that impact on the event sector Social development policy Diffusion of innovations

According to the online source www.sociology.org.uk, major themes in this discipline include the following (see Table 3.3):

- 'socialization process': learning how to become human and to behave in ways that accord with the general expectations of others (in short, to be socialized);
- the structure of 'social life': values, norms, roles and status (social controls);
- 'values' are beliefs that we have about what is important, both to us and to society as a whole;
- 'norms' are expected, socially acceptable, ways of behaving in any given social situation;
- 'role' – social roles we expect people to play;
- 'status' – earned or assigned;
- 'social groups': the nature of family, peers, institutions, nations, communities of interest; relationships within groups;
- 'culture and identity': influencing factors on cultural identity include age, gender, ethnicity and regionalism;
- 'subcultures': groups sharing a particular way of life.

Research traditions and methods

Sociologists use the scientific method and have a long tradition of 'positivistic' methodology. However, there has also been a long tradition of 'humanistic sociology', which stresses the understanding of cultural values, meanings, symbols and norms. Multicultural comparisons are important. Both quantitative and qualitative methods are used, as is ethnography – which is very much akin to cultural anthropology. There are several clear perspectives or theoretical approaches that shape both research methodology and what is studied by sociologists. Alternative, competing traditions of research are now widespread in sociology (Veal 2006).

Veal (2006) assessed the evolution of sociological research pertaining to leisure and tourism and concluded that the early modelling/prediction emphasis, based on large-scale social surveys and quantitative analysis (within the 'functionalist' tradition), had not worked well. More qualitative methods became fashionable in the 1970s and 1980s, with a shift towards learning more about why people did what they did, and what it meant to them, rather than just measuring and forecasting what they did. This era gave rise to research and theory development on leisure benefits and constraints.

Critical social theory

This approach starts with the premise that social 'reality' is historically constituted through social, cultural and political forces (Habermas 1973). The role of the critical researcher is therefore to reveal conflicts and contradictions and help eliminate the causes of alienation or domination. According to 'critical theory', the structure of capitalistic society marginalizes certain people and removes choices from them, which of course flies in the face of leisure being defined in terms of freely chosen, intrinsically motivated uses of time. 'Conflict theorists' emphasize conflicts in society, specifically between social classes, between men and women, and between different ethnic groups. The Marxist tradition has largely fallen out of favour, but it is obvious that many conflicts do remain.

One area of change which Richards *et al.* (2013: 219) acknowledge in the area of social theory is the work of Castells and the Network Society. Castells pointed to the growing global networks that co-exist alongside face-to-face communication in local communities, and events creating dispersed social networks. These networks create more opportunities for rituals of co-presence (see Chapter 2), where geographical proximity is not the only determinant of meeting and contact. Hence events do retain attributes as physical spaces for events, but virtual spaces also become important as nodes of and a focal point for virtual networks to meet. Castells (2010) also maintained that power resides in networks, and this idea connects to other important concepts like social media, social worlds and the co-creation of experiences.

Functionalism

From this perspective, everything in society has a purpose or function. The basic values of this perspective emphasize the idea of harmony and social consensus, based around shared values. Functionalists are likely to interpret everything in terms of large-scale social structures.

Symbolic interactionists

Within social psychology, 'symbolic interactionists' concentrate on the way people understand one another. They tend to focus on the individual, looking in particular at the way we create the social world through our behaviour (rather than looking at how society creates the individual). A key issue is the set of symbols and understandings that have emerged which give meanings to interactions.

Leisure and work take on meanings from social interactions, so that what we mean by work or leisure is in part determined by our social lives. Certain events might connote either work (say, a conference) and others leisure (a concert or festival). As well, the 'festival' for many people is symbolic of culture, while the trade show is symbolic of commerce. These are social constructs in the same way that we expect planned events to have a certain form and take place in certain settings.

Two books by Erving Goffman (*The Presentation of Self in Everyday Life*, 1959 and *Frame Analysis: An Essay on the Organization of Experience*, 1974) are of particular relevance to event studies. Goffman used the imagery of the theatre to show how people are social 'actors'. In any given social interaction there has to be an agreed-upon definition of what is happening, otherwise there is no congruence between the 'performers'. 'Actors' usually foster impressions that reflect well upon themselves. In communication theory and sociology, 'framing' is a process of selective control over media content or public communication. Framing defines how media content is packaged and presented so as to allow certain desirable interpretations and rule out others. However, there are also important differences to note in this type of framing and the framing rituals discussed by Falassi.

Social and cultural capital

Sociologist Pierre Bourdieu (1972, 1986) distinguished between economic, social, symbolic and cultural capital. Economic capital refers to a command of cash or other assets that can be invested for profit, while social capital consists of the possession of resources that derive from group membership, relationships, networks of influence and support. Cultural capital consists of knowledge, skills, education and other advantages possessed by a person that result in higher social status. Parents are said to transmit such advantages to their children. Symbolic capital accrues to individuals as resources on the basis of honour, prestige or recognition – that is, some people stand out as icons.

These concepts are in tune with a long tradition of philosophical thought and sociological theory on the value of networks, and the need to foster social cohesion through institutions and policy. There are clear conceptual links to notions of civil society and the power of communitas through celebration. In other words, social networking has value, and festivals and events can foster it – they also lead to the establishment of events for many social worlds and groups.

Reciprocity and trust are the foundations of 'social capital', and to some extent these qualities of social life are found in all communities and societies. Where social capital is high, people are more likely to be polite, talk to strangers, interact as equals and perform random acts of kindness. In other words, we 'invest' social capital in our community and expect others to do the same (this is similar to 'social exchange theory'). Voluntarism can be viewed as a form of social capital at the community level, as can community-based decision-making, informal business transactions and spontaneous celebrations.

Putnam (2004) placed more emphasis on benefits accruing to the community, while others (e.g. Bourdieu 1986; Coleman 1988, 1990) conceptualized social capital at the individual level. When a person develops a substantial 'social network' of friends, allies and collaborators, their social capital increases and when 'invested' or 'spent', it can result in a variety of economic, social, psychological and emotional benefits. Some people pursue the accumulation of social capital through deliberate networking, while others acquire it unconsciously. This is epitomized by the recent monograph by Richards *et al.* (2013) in which social capital is a dominant theme in many of the chapters, including case studies from the event spectrum from European Capital of Culture programmes to sport events.

3.2 RESEARCH NOTES ON SOCIAL CAPITAL

Finkel, R. (2011). Dancing around the ring of fire: Social capital, tourism resistance, and gender dichotomies at Up Helly Aa in Lerwick, Scotland. *Event Management*, 14(4), 275–285.

Finkel interprets this Shetland Islands traditional festival (Viking themed) in the light of community, tourism, traditions of the place and gender. Sacred places are created 'where the whole community can come together on a ritually repeated basis'. Over a thousand volunteers work on the festival each year, and it is a focal point for community cohesion – even though females are excluded from performing the Viking fire-drama. Some residents resist the commercial orientation promoted by tourism authorities, although others appreciate having an audience. In a world where top-down, instrumentalist policy towards festivals prevails, the author claims that this event is a good case of community initiative that generates social capital.

Williams, P. W. and Elkhashab, A. (2012). Leveraging tourism social capital: The case of the 2010 Olympic tourism consortium. *International Journal of Event and Festival Management*, 3(3), 317–334.

Researchers explored social capital emerging from the collective set of activities pursued by a network of stakeholders leveraging tourism benefits from the 2010 Vancouver Winter Olympic and Paralympic Games. Aspects of bonding, bridging and linking social capital creation were examined. Varying levels of confidence, trust, mutual respect, personal ties, shared values and human capacity were generated through the consortium's activities. This social capital was perceived as a valuable but fragile legacy capable of nurturing increased leadership and organizational capacity particularly when tackling issues confronting the industry's overall sustained prosperity.

Social worlds

Unruh (1980: 271) used the term 'social world' to describe 'the notion that actors, events, practices, and formal organizations can coalesce into a meaningful and interactional important unit of social organization for participants'. Involvement in social worlds is voluntary, even though 'guidelines, expectations, and rules certainly exist' (1980: 277). It can be partial, so that order within a social world is negotiated and its bounds are those of the 'universe of discourse'.

Total involvement in one social world is highly unlikely, given that leisure choices can lead to multiple affiliations. Interactions are mediated because of reliance on various channels of communication rather than spatial, kinship or other formal ties. Nevertheless, some meeting places are usually important (these can be events), and some places are associated with social worlds because of their concentration of actors, practices or events (a destination could become a mecca for runners, for example). Communication centres are vital, being the points where a great deal of the involvement is focused; communication sets limits on the extent of the discourse that defines a social world. Withdrawal from social worlds might carry a cost in terms of loss of one's interpersonal contacts.

Unruh provided a very useful framework for assessing social worlds. The analysis examines participants ('actors'), what they do ('practices'), important events in their social-world activities, and organizations involved in or influencing social worlds.

Actors

People can belong to a variety of social worlds in a fluid, evolving process that takes place over their lifetimes. Unruh (1980: 280) identified types of involvement. 'Strangers' are characterized by marginality, detachment and superficiality, but act as points of reference and comparison with other social worlds. 'Tourists' get involved out of curiosity but lack long-term commitment to a social world. These 'tourists' are not literally travellers; rather they are transitory members of social worlds and remain so as long as the community provides them with some rewards such as entertainment or profit. 'Regulars' (1980: 282) are 'habitual participants who are integrated in the social world's ongoing activities'. This represents a significant amount of commitment. Finally, 'insiders' are the most committed, have intimate knowledge of social-world activities, determine prestige, value and relationships, recruit new members, organize activities, and have the most to gain or lose from the success or failure of the social world.

Events

In Unruh's schema, 'events' are personal occurrences that are important to people involved in a social world, such as their first or most prestigious race. However, these can also be planned events that participants attend, including those events planned specifically to attract members of specific social worlds. It is likely, however, that many event organizers are not consciously appealing to communities of interest. However, it is also clear that events are produced by the insiders themselves; this was the case observed by Green and Chalip (1998) regarding the subcultural identity of female flag footballers.

PRACTICES

There is a behavioural dimension to 'practices' – specifically what members of the social world do. This can include travel to events, participating in clubs, buying and selling, and corresponding. There is also a symbolic and ritualistic dimension reflecting the values or ethos of the social world, including signs of membership and status, and prescribed or desired ways of speaking and doing things. Subcultures and other communities of interest tend to develop their own language.

FORMAL ORGANIZATIONS

Many organizations can play a role in shaping social worlds and facilitating networking among members: governing bodies and associations that are often hierarchical in nature; corporations intent on building brand communities for their own marketing purposes; clubs and teams; tourist organizations attempting to attract groups; events catering to special interests; and magazines and e-zines focused on special interests.

Unruh also developed levels of social-world analysis, from local to regional, dispersed, and social-world systems. A local or regional social world might have boundaries, but that is not what defines it – it only shapes that social world's scale and scope. Globally dispersed social worlds have grown enormously since Unruh's treatise, facilitated by travel, a proliferation of planned events (periodic and one-time), and the power of the Internet and other forms of interpersonal communication to bring together people with similar interests.

It is important to consider how social worlds link to the concepts of communitas, the power of networking, the formation and use of social capital, and special-interest tourism.

3.1 EXPERT OPINION

The mediating roles of social worlds on event tourism

Dr Ian Patterson is Associate Professor in the School of Tourism, the University of Queensland. The research he describes has been published: Getz, D. and Patterson, I. (2013). Social worlds as a framework for event and travel careers. *Tourism Analysis*, 18(5), 485–501.

We used Unruh's social-world framework to examine the pertinent events, travel behaviour and related preferences of those who engage in a variety of special interests. The idea was to compare various forms of serious leisure, namely amateur sports, arts, lifestyle pursuits and hobbies. Passive netnographic analysis has demonstrated the relevance of this approach, and substantial evidence has been found to support the notion of event-travel careers.

New understandings of how social worlds lead to, and mediate, participation in events and travel in general have been established. Evidence was clearly available on motivations, covering passion, self-identity, lifestyle, self-esteem and health. Evidence was also available on events, travel, networking and communications, portfolios of activities, specialization and beginning a career. Our searches yielded variable results that probably can be expanded upon in further research. To this end, a series of questions was created to analyse the netnographic evidence and these could be used or modified when conducting further interviews and larger-scale surveys, or through the use of interactive netnography.

Social worlds act to mediate the travel preferences and patterns of members in at least two major ways. Involved individuals can, of course, elect to make their own travel plans, either to special-interest events or for other social-world experiences. However, many organizations seek to influence these decisions, and peer-to-peer networking also has an impact. Understanding these processes will have profound marketing implications, but there are also other theoretical consequences.

Clear evidence has been found that these different leisure and sporting pursuits all generate and sustain interest in travel and lead to hierarchies of participatory, celebratory and competitive events, and other experiences involving social-world networking. It is also likely that some members of these social worlds were attracted in the first place by their interest in travel and the event dimension.

Many formal organizations are seeking to influence their members, some through their legitimate role as clubs, associations, governing or event organizing bodies, that makes them part of their social world. Others are employing advertising or other promotions, such as event and tour sponsorships, to increase memberships. Another possibility exists, and that is clandestine participation in social networking, which raises both legal and ethical questions.

To further advance research and theory on social worlds and event-tourist careers, a set of propositions has been developed. It is proposed that social worlds moderate travel patterns and references in the following ways:

1. Online and remote interaction among members stimulates interest in specific events and social opportunities (i.e. real-life sharing experiences) that creates travel demand.
2. Events present opportunities for personal and group development and identity-building, and reinforce social-world values.
3. Events can develop (or be assigned) symbolic/iconic appeal to members of social worlds.
4. To be effective, commercial organizations that market specific travel products and events to social worlds must reflect and enable the values and motivations of their members.
5. Events that are social as opposed to competitive in nature have quite a different appeal to various social worlds, and this can only be understood in the context of values and practices.

Subcultures

This is a somewhat vague and flexible term, with some scholars viewing them as deviants, and others associating them more with distinctive styles of dress and symbolic actions. In this book, emphasis is placed on social worlds and people involved in various leisure pursuits leading to interest in events and travel.

Social network theory

Analysing social networks (see Freeman *et al.* 1992; Scott 2000) is a very useful way to examine stakeholder relationships surrounding event policy and management. A 'social network' consists of individual 'actors' and the ties between them, either formal or informal. In one sense, it can be said that the more ties an actor has (e.g. the event organization), the more social capital it will accumulate. But, more importantly, the network itself gains capital and might assume a political life of its own, similar to the concept of a 'political market square' in which the actors negotiate to direct the future of a festival (see Larson and Wikstrom 2001; Larson 2002). Networks can be powerful determinants of policy and strategy. In the network society described by Castells, power resides in networks and in the modern world they are primarily electronic in nature.

Diffusion of innovation theory

Innovations, including both technology and ideas, are communicated through various formal channels and social networks (Rogers 1995). Individuals and organizations do not equally adapt innovation, rather there are the 'innovators', 'early adopters', 'early majority', 'late majority' and 'laggards'. When it comes to innovations that can provide competitive advantage or increased effectiveness, it can pay to be the innovator or the early adopter, but of course there are costs and risks associated with being first.

In the events sector we can observe innovation and diffusion in terms of new types of events and how they spread globally, usually through the influence of mass media. It is also clear that event producers copy ideas, which to a degree can be good, but without systematic benchmarking this can simply lead to standardization. And if every city and destination pursues the same event-tourism strategy, leading to 'festivalization', this has potentially negative consequences.

3.3 RESEARCH NOTES ON INNOVATION AND FESTIVALS

Hjalager, A.-M. (2009). Cultural tourism innovation systems – the Roskilde Festival. *Scandinavian Journal of Hospitality and Tourism*, 9(2–3), 266–287.

'Since 1971, Roskilde Festival (Denmark) has developed its role as a leading element in an emerging cultural innovation system. Festival organizers maintain long-term, dense and multifaceted relations. Funds from the (non-profit) festival are efficiently channelled into cultural and sports facilities, enhancing the attractiveness of the region. To keep ahead in the festival market, innovators in the field of managerial systems, technologies and services are deliberately invited to use the grounds as test benches for new ideas. . . . Since 2001 especially, wider-ranging organizational structures have been constructed and politically enforced with the aim of nurturing spin-offs, and including strong representation within the educational and research sectors.'

Jóhannesson, G. (2010). Emergent Vikings: The social ordering of tourism innovation. *Event Management*, 14(4), 261–274.

The author discusses how Iceland has experienced a rapid growth of tourism, which has increasingly been taken up as an option for economic development. Innovation in this field has been promoted by public actors. In one such tourism innovation project, the Gísla Saga project, in the small fishing village of Þingeyri, the local village festival, Dýrafjarðardagar, has been related to the innovation project. Using Actor-Network Theory, the researcher argues that it is important to follow the enactment of diverse styles of ordering for gaining insight into the emergent cultural economy of tourism. By tracing the practices through which the project is established, the article illustrates some of the ways in which tourism innovation relates to the social ordering of local communities.

Innovation and diffusion are not necessarily good or bad, but understanding how they work is important in terms of strategy and marketing. In particular, marketers want to learn who will be the first to adopt their products and services, then spread the word to other potential customers.

Social exchange theory

'Social exchange theory' (Hormans 1958) suggests that social action is different from straightforward economic actions within a marketplace (i.e. buying and selling), because social actors expect and receive rewarding reactions. Resource exchanges (as well as the bestowal of prestige or support) are, in this context, the result of free, personal choice based on the assessment of expected costs and benefits. People can feel pressure to give, but exchanges should balance out over time. The theory also embodies the concepts of power and dependency within relationships and social networks. In the context of event studies this theory has been used to explain variation in resident perceptions of, or attitudes towards, events. For example, people benefiting from event tourism will tend to be positive in their attitudes towards the event and its continuance, while people perceiving no benefit tend to be more critical and less supportive.

Contributions of sociology to event studies

It is highly relevant to note that Eric Cohen's (1988a) article entitled 'Traditions in the qualitative sociology of tourism' identified three principal traditions that all have importance for the study of festivals and events, namely those associated with the seminal works of Turner (see section on Anthropology, p. 89), Boorstin (see History, p. 163) and MacCannell.

Dean MacCannell's (1973, 1976) sociological thesis on the tourist mainstreamed the discussion of authenticity and the notion that it is sought out because of the inauthenticity of modern life. His work employed the notions of Erving Goffman (1959) on dramaturgy, and suggested that 'staged authenticity' was all that modern tourists could expect to find. This term gained enduring popularity, similar to 'pseudo events', and his work directly stimulated early articles on 'spurious' festivals (Papson 1981), as well as Buck's (1977) notion of using events for 'boundary maintenance' between tourists and sensitive cultural groups.

Within the tourism literature, commodification and authenticity have been important, festival-related themes. Greenwood (1972, 1989) first suggested that tourism commoditized culture, and particularly festivals, leading to the event's loss of meaning among residents. E. Cohen (1988b) defined commoditization as a process by which things become valued in monetary terms, or exchange value. Cohen's concept of 'emergent authenticity' applies to festivals; Cohen described how a re-created, tourist-oriented festival could become accepted as being authentic, over time. Thus, commoditization might lead to a festival acquiring new meanings for both tourists and residents.

Bernadette Quinn (2013: 2) discusses authenticity as one of the 'Key Concepts in Event Management'. Drawing from Olsen (2002), authenticity is viewed not as the quality of an object (e.g. asking the question 'is that an authentic performance or setting?' implies there is a correct, truthful interpretation), 'but as a cultural value constantly created and reinvented in social processes'. Festivals and other cultural celebrations both create and proclaim cultural meanings to themselves and outsiders. In this context, Richards (2007b) suggested that residents are more likely to emphasize a 'constructive authenticity' based on familiar cultural norms like traditions and language, whereas visitors tend towards 'existential authenticity' related to their own enjoyment and socializing. We return to this important authenticity theme later in the book.

Duvignaud's (1976) conceptual article on the sociology of festivals and festivity provides documentation of the ways in which these phenomena have been 'explained', including the dialectic between those, like

Durkheim (1965), who viewed festivity as an 'intensification of the collective being' and those who see festivals as being inherently subversive. Duvignaud also discussed festivity as play and commemoration, concluding there was no one correct interpretation.

Much of the pertinent sociological theory comes to event studies indirectly through leisure studies, and also through social psychology. Particular themes to explore in this discipline include:

- societal trends and forces shaping values and leisure;
- social change (e.g. globalization and homogenization);
- life-stage influences on event interests and attendance;
- population and demographic factors;
- human ecology (crowds, fads, trends);
- effects of family, gender, race, culture, community, and social class on demand and behaviour;
- social worlds, virtual communities or brand communities (of considerable interest to sponsors and corporations owning events);
- social behaviour at events; conflict theory;
- deviance (certain types of events, deviant behaviour at events);
- social costs and benefits (crime, prostitution, sport or art participation, civic pride, belonging and sharing, integration, cohesion);
- economic development and social inequality (power structures reflected in events).

More specific applications to event studies can be reviewed within the following sub-fields.

Sport sociology

Current research areas within sport sociology include: sport and socialization; sport and social stratification; sport subcultures; the political economy of sport; sport and deviance; sport and the media; sport, the body and the emotions; sport violence; sport politics and national identity; sport and globalization. In a special supplement to the *Sociological Review*, Horne and Manzenreiter (2006: 1) discussed the sociological study of sport as including 'ritualized, rationalized, commercial spectacles and bodily practices that create opportunities for expressive performances, disruptions of the everyday world and affirmations of social status and belonging'. Roche (2000) is quoted in reference to the Olympics, and it is argued that mega events have become much more central to urban modernity.

Environmental sociology

This is the study of societal–environmental interactions, including the causes of environmental problems and their impacts, ways to solve problems and even how conditions come to be viewed as problems. We could ask, for example, how the creation of social representations comes about, such as: 'mega events are environmentally destructive', or 'festivals are a means to change attitudes about the environment'.

Events and urban sociology

Mega events in particular can have profound impacts on urban forms and life, but the effects of many small events, individually and cumulatively, should not be overlooked. Consider the following research by Harry Hiller (see Research Note 3.4)

3.4 RESEARCH NOTE ON URBAN SOCIOLOGY

H. Hiller (2000a). Toward an urban sociology of mega-events. *Research in Urban Sociology*, 5, 181–205.

Hiller's contention is that 'from street festivals, parades, and pilgrimages to riots, marches of resistance and demonstrations, such expressive and instrumental activities have been among the most observable aspects of urban social life'. In defining mega events, Hiller (2000a: 183) says 'From the perspective of an urban analyst, any large-scale special event can be considered a mega-event if it has a significant and/or permanent urban effect – that is, if it is considered so significant that it reprioritizes the urban agenda in some way and leads to some modification or alteration of urban space which becomes its urban legacy.'

He assesses mega events as to their part in shaping urban processes – as change factors – and in that respect identifies and discusses roles: catalysts for change; land use changes; creativity in urban planning; mobilizing funds; supporting projects otherwise considered too expensive or ambitious; forcing an agenda by requiring completion at a set date; infrastructure improvements in select domains, like transport; producing signature structures which redefine urban space.'

Events and rural sociology

Robert Janiskee's studies (1980, 1985, 1991; Janiskee and Drews 1998) of rural festivals revealed their importance in social life and tourism, as well as their seasonal and geographic distribution. Rural communities are particularly vulnerable to social disruption caused by tourism, or large influxes of new residents seeking amenities. On the other hand, events and tourism can help to foster community development and self-reliance. Events are one of the few tourism 'products' that even the smallest of communities can produce, without large amounts of capital. However, the volunteer and leadership base might be inadequate for long-term sustainability.

In the book *Festival Places: Revitalising Rural Australia* (Gibson and Connell 2011), various authors explore themes relating to the roles of festivals and events in rural life, including economic development, place identity, tradition (and what it means to be living in the country), social integration (especially in an era where lifestyles and tourism bring newcomers to small towns) and community development. Davies, for example, argues that rural festivals are a catalyst for leadership development, social networking and capacity-building – all of which are essential to preserve or revitalize threatened rural communities.

Therefore, the social dimension of events has a major impact upon the development and direction event research follows; this is illustrated in Events in Focus 3.1, which sets out a number of emerging research agendas.

EVENTS IN FOCUS

3.1 Emerging research agendas in the social analysis of events

According to Richards *et al.* (2013) there are a number of emerging research agendas that coalesce into the following themes:

- events as generators of social capital to increase social identity and interaction for event participants and the local community;

- business models to support events, given the increasing demand from public authorities for a better justification of the social benefits accruing from hosting events;
- events as politics and policy, where events are used in the political arena in an emancipatory manner, in a dictatorial context or for economic reasons. Increasingly, the social outcomes from event hosting and political ambitions need to be better understood. For example, issues of social inclusion and exclusion are key areas for analysis (see Vanwynberghe, Surborg and Wyly 2013 and Tomlinson 2014 on Olympic legacies which often remain elusive). In fact, a recent study of the Glasgow Commonwealth Games by Gray and Porter (2014) illustrates how the use of compulsory purchase orders to create the athletes' village displaced working-class neighbourhoods based on a political mantra of 'necessity';
- management of event design issues to create a social dimension often called 'imagineering' (see Chapter 6 for more detail) along with the growing scale of events and their wide-ranging impacts on communities;
- co-creation, whereby both producers and consumers collaborate to develop events, which is changing the boundaries between producers, organizers and participants.

A number of key research challenges include:

1. problems of measurement in terms of accessing and using social indicators that measure concepts such as social capital;
2. a need for longitudinal research, to understand continuity and change induced by or related to events despite the difficulties of isolating causality in how events shape social phenomena;
3. the social dimension of events has largely been examined through community and local events and festivals where social consequences can be identified, and where the impact of business events has largely been focused on the corporate social responsibility objectives of sponsors and events hosts as opposed to the wider social effects of hosting different types of events;
4. collective as opposed to just individual experiences of events need greater attention, as much of the research effort has been directed towards understanding individual experiences of events rather than group experiences;
5. the use of social media to understand the networked society and the social implications in event research, including the development of Big Data approaches to capture and analyse event participation and satisfaction;
6. the changing role of different stakeholders and publics in shaping the social dimensions of events where research needs to be triangulated to capture the differing experiences of stakeholders rather than relying upon singular studies of one element of stakeholder experiences of events;
7. identifying the social dimension of events through the 'community' of networked and physically co-present people and stakeholders;
8. shifting event research from a focus predominantly on management, impacts and policy to more comparative and longitudinal studies of where the social impacts and benefits of events accrue.

Source: developed from Richards, de Brito and Wilks (2013)

Table 3.4 Philosophy

Philosophy	Nature and meanings; the event experience	Antecedents to attending events	Planning and producing events	Outcomes and the impacted	Processes and patterns
Critical thought on the nature of experience, the meaning of life and belief systems Aesthetics Ethics Phenomenology Hermeneutics	Aesthetic experiences Experiences that shape one's world-view How we give ethical meaning to experiences	The quest for the meaning of life as a motivator (self-discovery) Desire for aesthetic experiences as a motivator World-view as it shapes preferences	Values and ethics as a basis for producing and managing events (e.g. sustainability) A philosophy of event service	Evaluation of aesthetics Impacts on values and ethics at personal or social levels	Changing value systems affect event planning and policy

Philosophy

Philosophers use reasoning, not empirical research, to theorize about the meaning of life and belief systems. But the nature and scope of philosophy are subject to influence by changing societal values and scientific discoveries. People who contemplate the meaning of life generally fall into two categories: those who adopt religious or spiritual meanings, and those who search elsewhere, inside their own mind and value sets. Philosophy is concerned with the nature of religion and spiritualism, but does not embrace faith or divine revelation, only reasoning. However, philosophy provides a firm foundation in the analysis of event phenomena particularly around the themes in Table 3.4 and in the meaning of event experiences.

The nature of experience (phenomenology and hermeneutics)

What is experience, and how can we study it? These two key questions lead us to consider the critical role of 'phenomenology', being the method used to study people's consciousness and behaviour simultaneously. Applied to event experiences, we could ask people at various times before, during and after the event to describe and explain their actions and thoughts. How does the event appear to them? What meanings are they attaching to their experiences and behaviour? How does it affect them emotionally, intellectually, spiritually? There is great scope for advancing our understanding of the planned event experience through phenomenological methods, as demonstrated in Research Note 3.5.

3.5 RESEARCH NOTE ON PHENOMENOLOGY

Chen, P. (2006). The attributes, consequences, and values associated with event sport tourists' behaviour: A means–end chain approach. *Event Management*, 10(1), 1–22.

A phenomenological study of highly involved members of a fan club was conducted, in order to reveal important personal constructs of the meanings attached to their fan-related experiences. Means–end theory (see Olson and Reynolds 2001) provided the foundation for proceeding from an examination of the concrete (attributes of being a sport fan) to consequences of the event and travel experiences (functional and psychological outcomes) to the abstract (values or goals, like self-fulfilment). Means–end is designed to elicit non-verbal communications, hidden feeling and thoughts, and deeply held constructs and their interrelationships. Chen concluded that socialization was one of the most important, indeed essential aspects of the fans' experiences, consisting of developing one's sense of self-being through friendships, social support and identification with a group. This led to enjoyment, well-being and balance in life.

Hermeneutics

This is a Greek word for interpretation; it has become a branch of philosophy concerned with human understanding and the interpretation of 'texts'. All writing and symbolic communication (including performances and sports) can be viewed as 'text', and that text can be interpreted. What the researcher says about people or real-world phenomena is open to interpretation in two fundamental ways: has the researcher found the truth (if there is a single truth), and what does the analysis say about the researcher? If the researcher claims to have the truth, the researcher is likely a positivist schooled in certain traditions and making use of standard methods.

Aesthetics and art

Tastes and aesthetic appreciation are not absolutes, they are personal and vary a great deal. We can examine taste and aesthetic appreciation from a scientific perspective, considering cognition, sensory receptors and emotional responses, but this will never explain what we mean by 'art' or 'beauty'. While it is a philosophical issue at heart, aesthetics is also the realm of event designers. They learn what pleases and what does not, and how to solve practical problems with personal style.

Where exactly is the art in event design? Many festivals and exhibitions are within the domain of 'the arts' (see du Cros and Jolliffe 2014). That is, they are themed around a variety of arts, with most festivals featuring performing arts like music and dance and most exhibitions displaying visual arts like painting and sculpture. But are the events themselves a form of art? Where is the creativity in them? Is the aesthetic appreciation confined to the objects of the event (i.e. the arts on display, the performers) or do people gain aesthetic benefits from the form of the event itself?

Certainly party and wedding planners take pride in the art of the decorations (from flowers to table arrangements), while chefs generally present meals at least partially as art – not merely as something to eat. Art might be found in the lighting, sounds and smells of an event, or in the costumes and performances of the staff and volunteers (remembering Disney's dictum that staff are 'cast members'). But extending this aesthetic appreciation to the design of the whole event presents conceptual and practical problems. It is unclear whether most event planners and designers view their events, as a totality, as an art form. Certainly there is art in the design, but can we definitely state that a festival or event is a work of art in the same league as, say, a performance of a symphony orchestra?

3.2 EXPERT OPINION

Event as art

Dr Steve Brown is an event designer, and at Flinders University in Adelaide, South Australia, he is Head of Tourism, and Course Coordinator of the Festival and Event Design and Management programmes. This is his take on event as art:

> John Tribe writing about aesthetics and beauty argues that art 'attempts in different ways to capture the spirit of things freeing us from the conventional limitations of words and language and offering poetic, visual and musical representations that can engender deeper and different engagements with their subjects' (Tribe 2009: 11). In my role as an Event Designer my intent is to capture and engage the audience to provide experiences that free them from the conventional and offer 'poetic, visual and musical representations'. Event design is sometimes called an 'art' but it is more a philosophical approach that is audience-centric that, if applied correctly, *can* turn a simple event into a work of art.

Ethics

What is right or wrong, good or bad, and how do we judge behaviour or policy? This is the realm of ethics, and is also called 'moral philosophy'. Certainly political ideology and religious beliefs enter the picture, as both of these give people a moral code or set of values to live by. Others develop their own morality and ethics through philosophical means, but always with reference to other people and society in general. We cannot be ethical or moral in isolation.

Ethics applies to professional conduct, and no event management programme can be complete without instilling the need for ethical and legal behaviour. Students might ask, however, is 'legal' the same as 'ethical', and should the various professional codes of conduct govern us completely and without question? What place is there for personal and situational ethics, where you or I make the rules as we go?

Goldblatt (2011: 412) discusses ethics, noting that typical event-industry ethical issues include:

- breach of confidentiality (often covered in contracts, but sometimes implicit in professional dealings);
- gifts versus bribes (do gifts influence decisions? are bribes illegal?);
- sexual harassment (a legal issue in many countries with clear policies and training to address the issue);
- poaching clients (staff members who move take clients with them or go back and poach them);
- taking credit for others' work (i.e. not clearly identifying who is responsible for work produced);
- theft of ideas (which is the same as plagiarism, theft of intellectual property; secure copyright protection).

Henderson, and McIlwraith in their book *Ethics and Corporate Social Responsibility in the Meetings and Events Industry* (2013) take a broad view of ethics, suggesting that green practices, sustainability and corporate social responsibility are all interconnected. While many see the MICE sector as being simply about business, these authors want practitioners to always consider the harm or good that events can do both immediately (in the setting or community) and in the long term for the planet.

Is event tourism an ethical issue?

We know that tourism has a high carbon footprint, yet every city and country wants more of it! Is this simply a practical problem, with the solution lying in alternative energy sources? Or is it an enduring ethical issue? How much event tourism should we be encouraging or accepting? Page (2015) addresses a similar range of issues related to the growth of global tourism, in which travel related to events is a contributor. Page (2015) posits that some parts of the world with fragile environments should be free of tourism and this raises a whole range of issues, not least where travel to fragile environments becomes an 'event' in someone's life, with access to that opportunity available purely through being able to pay a premium price.

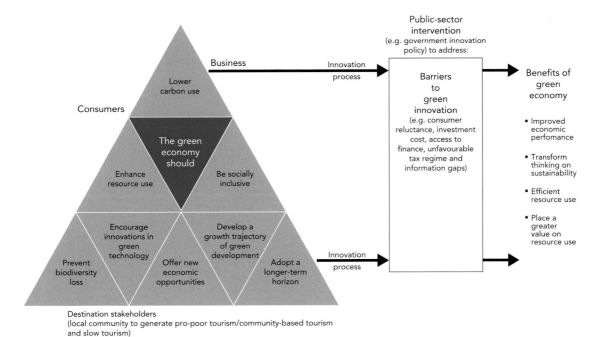

Figure 3.2 Principles of green economic growth

Source: Page (2015: 446), developed from OECD (2013) *Green Innovation in Tourism*, OECD. Paris. Reprinted from *Tourism Management, 5th Edition*, S. J. Page, Routledge (2015).

In the absence of clear-cut solutions to such problems, it is difficult to justify a particular ethical position. The problem with this particular dilemma is that there is no obvious solution, meaning that any point of view or political position will find some degree of support and legitimacy, plus there is a huge lobby for continued growth and development. Alternative energy might very well solve the problem – some day – but it is not yet within reach, despite new philosophical paradigms around notions such as the green economy, which aim to facilitate development while reducing carbon use and environmental impacts as illustrated in Figure 3.2 with reference to tourism. But this can equally be applied to events where the destination stakeholders are the local community and businesses who can potentially benefit from a new approach towards event development that adopts these principles.

Economic forces might also solve the pollution/global warming problem by making fossil fuels too expensive, but the resulting economic disruption could destroy countless jobs around the world, which is one of the attractions of the green economy paradigm since it builds economic growth around green principles. Taxing fuels and travel will similarly have an inevitable economic and social cost, probably with inequitable results that allow the rich to continue doing whatever they want and forcing the poor to stay at home. In short, taking an ethical position on event tourism will not solve the problem, and there is a need for such debates to establish workable solutions.

A philosophy of event service

Other applied professional fields incorporate philosophical positions, such as that found in 'leisure service'. If we view leisure and events as a public good, which was the basis for their provision in many Western countries from the mid-nineteenth century onwards (see Page and Connell 2010), then providing leisure, cultural and event services to people becomes a public-sector function. Certainly this philosophical position is embedded within many leisure and culture programmes that remain today, despite cuts in many public-sector budgets, although it is seldom made explicit regarding the events component.

The following questions must be addressed in developing any philosophical position about 'event service':

- Are all planned events fundamentally good?
- Under what conditions is public support justified?
- Must all events be environmentally sustainable in every possible way?
- Should all events contribute positively to individual and community health?
- What obligations to society and the environment do event professionals hold? (consider morality and ethics).
- What is the value of art events? What events are in bad taste? How should we judge beauty? (this is aesthetics).
- What can we learn about the event experience and the multiple meanings attached to events? (such as through hermeneutic phenomenology).

Religious studies

The study of religion includes attention to its origins and evolution, the comparison and analysis of belief systems, and the evaluation of impacts on society. The rites, rituals and celebrations of various religions are scrutinized, including the use of anthropological methods, and this has direct relevance in event studies (see Table 3.5).

'Theologians' hold religious belief systems and apply their specific beliefs and related values to interpreting or criticizing all aspects of human society. Since so many events are religious in origin or theme, or contain programmed elements that hold religious meaning (even something as common as an opening prayer or blessing), theology contributes to event studies. In some societies it is more a matter of spirituality, or even mysticism, that one finds reflected in modern events (see Events in Focus 3.2 on pilgrimages).

Table 3.5 Religious studies

Religious studies	Nature and meanings; the event experience	Antecedents to attending events	Planning and producing events	Outcomes and the impacted	Processes and patterns
The study of religions, emphasizing human society and behaviour Religious life and experience	Sacred experiences (religious rites, symbols, and celebrations) for believers Pilgrimage	Religious motivations for attending or rejecting events Quest for spiritual meaning as a motivator for belonging to religious groups	Ritual and symbolism incorporated into event programming	Religious trends and forces (e.g. the influence of religious lobbies)	Spiritual effects on the individual Impacts on religion Impacts on individual belief systems or faith

EVENTS IN FOCUS

3.2 Pilgrimages as events in early modern society

Pilgrimages can be dated to the ancient Greeks and travel to the Olympic City of Olympia. Pilgrimages became widely associated with Christianity at around the fourth century, initially with trips made on a voluntary basis or as a form of penitence. Trips were initially very localized in scale; they became more long distance during the First Crusade, when pilgrimages to Jerusalem took place. The period from the eleventh to the thirteenth century saw pilgrimages encouraged in Christian countries, with trips by nuns and priests permitted by their superiors; they were popularized in Geoffrey Chaucer's *The Canterbury Tales* and often involved visits to the shrine of Thomas Beckett, who had been murdered in Canterbury Cathedral. Other notable locations in Europe, such as Santiago de Compostela in Spain, were among a number of popular destinations for Italian pilgrims (see Schnell and Pali 2013, for an analysis of religious motives associated with modern-day pilgrimages on the same route). By the fourteenth century, changing attitudes towards pilgrimages begun to develop and by the fifteenth century, the spread of the Black Death and labour shortages saw a slowing down of pilgrim traffic in Europe. By the sixteenth century, pilgrimages were being challenged by thinking associated with the Protestant reformers of the Reformation – who opposed the cult of saints – driving much of the activity underground. The difficulties of early pilgrim travellers should not be underestimated; diary accounts outline the problems of travel on unmade roads, the threat to life posed by bandits, the limited availability of accommodation, disease and the time involved to make such perilous journeys – as outlined by Theilmann (1987).

Source: Theilmann, J. (1987). Medieval pilgrims and the origins of tourism. *Journal of Popular Culture*, 20(4), 93–102.

Festivals in many cultures are closely associated with religion. In Japan, annual *matsuri* are held at or in conjunction with Shinto shrines, on fixed dates. They symbolize a community's well-being and are particularly related to rice harvests. *Matsuri* in modern Japan often include large-scale, public celebrations like carnival, complete with masks, parades with traditional, iconic floats, sports and (to a Western eye) outrageously dangerous behaviour such as playing with fire. Plutschow (2013) in the book *Matsuri: Festivals of Japan* described and classified these local celebrations according to the deities being represented, and the related rituals.

3.6 RESEARCH NOTE ON RELIGION

Greenfield, G. (2010). Reveillon in Rio de Janeiro. *Event Management*, 14(4), 301–308.

'While Carnival remains the city's most popular event, *Reveillon*, the New Year's Eve celebration on Copacabana Beach in honour of the sea goddess, *Iemanjá*, has become a major tourist draw. A familiar personage in Brazilian popular culture, *Iemanjá* is a major deity in African-Brazilian religions. African and African-Brazilian beliefs, historically associated with lower-class and mixed-race people, were long scorned by Brazilian elites as the superstitious practices of ignorant people. The majority of practitioners of African-Brazilian religions in contemporary Brazil are lower class and visibly of mixed race. The *Reveillon* evokes and commodifies Brazil's preferred national image as a multicultural, multiracial democracy free of the Western stain of racism. As such, the celebration serves as a confirming ritual for Brazilians while, at the same time, packaging and presenting that image to tourists.'

Psychology

The study of the human mind, thought and behaviour constitutes psychology. There are many sub-fields and specialized applications, such as you will encounter in education and interpretation (the 'psychology of learning') and 'industrial psychology', applied to management. There are also divisions in psychology, notably 'humanistic psychology', represented by the works of Maslow, which takes a phenomenological approach that is in direct opposition to the scientific or positivistic paradigm that dominates the subject area. In this section we examine two mainstream branches, 'cognitive psychology' and the psychology of personality, then we turn to two blended sub-disciplines of particular relevance to event studies: environmental psychology and social psychology. Their significance in the wider debates on the contribution of psychology to event studies is demonstrated by Benckendorff and Pearce (2012: 165), who provide the most comprehensive review of the field and address the principal question facing psychologists:

> *What kinds of people seek to involve themselves in events and what motivates them to do so? The research in psychology which can assist in answering these questions derives from a combination of applied expertise in personality assessment and the study of social motivation.*

This illustrates the principal challenge for event research – the different ways people become involved in events and how we explain their motivation for that involvement (see Table 3.6). Whilst psychology remains a key discipline in understanding these issues, other interdisciplinary developments and new research agendas, such as experiencescapes (i.e. the on-site experience of events emanating from the work of Pine and Gilmore (1999) on the experience economy (see Chapter 1) and O'Dell's (2005) work on experiencescapes as fluid spaces in which people consume experiences (see Chapter 6 for more detail)), have a key role in contextualizing the application of psychology to event studies. This is because

> *The design of experiencescapes includes not only the setting but also the sensory, symbolic, temporal and meaningful aspects of experiences . . . An understanding of event experiencescapes therefore needs to consider cognitive, conative and affective responses to the setting, theme, programming, personal interactions and provision of services and tangible goods such as food, beverages and merchandise.*
>
> *(Benckendorff and Pearce 2012: 174)*

Therefore, what is discussed in this chapter should not be separated from the discussion of other themes shaping event research throughout the book, particularly the discussion of event experiences in Chapter 6.

Table 3.6 Psychology

Psychology	Nature and meanings; the event experience	Antecedents to attending events	Planning and producing events	Outcomes and the impacted	Processes and patterns
Explaining human personality and behaviour The study of perception, memory, feeling, knowing and thinking	Personal needs, motives, preferences Perceiving and experiencing events Abnormal behaviour	Effects of age, gender, education, life-stage, income, on demand Consumer behaviour Ego involvement	Design for personal experiences and transformation Implications for marketing and communications	Impacts on personality, values, attitudes Influence on future actions	Emergence of 'experience economics' as a major force

The contribution of psychology to event studies has been considerable and some of the most significant recent studies are outlined in Events in Focus 3.3, which demonstrates the richness of the contributions and themes they typically examine (see Table 3.6).

More specifically, Benckendorff and Pearce (2012) provide some key concepts related to how psychology can be applied to event participation by spectators and attendees, performers and participants, and elite participants in the pre-, on-site and post-event experience stages (see Figure 3.3). Approaches used to understand these human experiences are framed around personality, motivation, involvement, different theories associated with participation in events (e.g. role theory, identity, liminality, flow), satisfaction and self-actualization from different fields of psychology. The origin of different approaches to psychology and events and the use of such theories will be examined throughout this section.

EVENTS IN FOCUS

3.3 Recent studies on the psychology of events

The most significant synthesis of the field is in:

Benckendorff, P. and Pearce, P. (2014). The psychology of events. In S. J. Page and J. Connell (eds), *Routledge Handbook of Events*, pp. 165–185. London: Routledge.

Other more specialized studies that focus on specific areas of the psychological analysis of events include:

Ballantyne, J. *et al.* (2014). Designing and managing music festival experiences to enhance attendees' psychological and social benefits. *Musicae Scientiae*, 18(1), 65–83.

Gyimóthy, S. (2009). Casual observers, connoisseurs and experimentalists: A conceptual exploration of niche festival visitors. *Scandinavian Journal of Hospitality and Tourism*, 9(2–3), 177–205.

Kendrick, V., Haslam, R. and Waterson, P. (2012). Planning crowd events to achieve high participant satisfaction. *Work: A Journal of Prevention, Assessment and Rehabilitation*, 41(1), 3223–3226.

Lee, J. and Kyle, G. (2013). Segmenting festival visitors using psychological commitment. *Journal of Travel Research*, 53(5), 656–669.

Deng, Q. and Li, M. (2014). A model of event–destination image transfer. *Journal of Travel Research*, 53(1), 69–82.

	Pre-experience		On-site experience		Post-experience
Spectators and Attendees	Personality, motivation and involvement	+	Role theory, identity, liminality, experience analysis	→	Satisfaction, loyalty
Performers and Participants	Personality, motivation and involvement	+	Role theory, identity, liminality, experience analysis	→	Satisfaction, self-actualization, personal development, quality of life
Elite Participants	Personality and motivation	+	Flow, mindfulness, emotional and performative labour	→	Superior performance

Figure 3.3 Applying psychological ideas to event participation

Source: Benckendorff and Pearce (2012: 166). Reprinted from *The Routledge Handbook of Events*, S. J. Page and J. Connell, Routledge (2012).

Cognitive psychology

Mainstream psychology is largely positivistic and well known for using experimental research designs (both laboratory and field based). The dominant theoretical framework is 'cognitivism'. 'Cognition' involves the integration of memory, experience and judgement, derived from perception, to help us think about the world or about specific stimulants in the environment. Cognition therefore applies to how we perceive, think about and make sense of stimuli or whole events.

'Perception' is the process of acquiring, interpreting, selecting and organizing sensory information. How do sensory organs and the brain receive and interpret stimuli? People are not passive, they actively explore the environment and in many cases seek out specific forms of stimulation. People create 'mental models (or constructs)' to help with perception and knowledge creation. If we have no experience or 'mental map' as a frame of reference, we might not perceive a stimulus at all. Accordingly, the more experience we have with certain types of planned event experiences, the better we should become at perceiving and interpreting all their nuances.

'Experience' is more than perception – it requires exposure or involvement and has a transforming effect on the individual. The more we experience, presumably the better we should be at assimilating new knowledge (i.e. 'learning'). But experience can also change us holistically in terms of attitudes, values and personality, resulting in behavioural changes.

'Memory' entails encoding and storing, retaining and recalling information and experiences. We know that memories can be imperfectly formed, fade over time and be lost or hard to recall. So what makes for a memorable experience? And how do memories, pleasant or otherwise, shape future behaviour? We examine this further in Chapter 6 where the thoughts of Moscardo (2010) are elaborated upon.

'Thinking': the higher-order mental processes we tend to call thinking include 'reasoning' (making sense of things), 'creativity' (or imagination, innovation), 'judgement' (such as determining right from wrong, dangerous from risk-free) and 'problem-solving' (i.e. solving a puzzle, figuring out how to navigate a space). Thinking is based on how we use stored knowledge and how experience has shaped our processes and abilities. Knowledge and experience hopefully lead to 'wisdom' (being 'wise' is a relative term, or a self-perceived quality) and to greater effectiveness in whatever we choose to do.

Ego, identity, self-concept and ego involvement

Who do you think you are? Seriously, are you ordinary or special, smart or dull, an intellectual or a party-animal? And what ideally would you like to be? Something better or different than you are now, perhaps more like someone else that you admire? These are questions about your ego and alter ego.

Ego is a basic psychological concept, especially in Freudian theory, comprising that part of our personality that encompasses conscious awareness. It helps us make sense of the world, including separating reality from imagination. Our main interest is with personal identity, that is, who we think we are. As a 'loner', you might not connect with many people, but as a 'joiner' you likely belong to a number of social worlds and engage heavily in social networking. How we identify ourselves, say as a member of a particular sport or interest group, reflects our ego. We can seek and confirm identity through social arrangements and that very much includes social events.

Self-concept means the beliefs held about our self, including who we think we are in relation to how others view us and how we would like to be viewed. When we drive a certain kind of car we want it to reflect our self-concept, or the image we have of ourselves as 'sporty'. This also applies to being a sports fan, a runner, an artist or any other form of leisure that generates an interest in planned events. Marketers know how to aim their products and services at people holding specific self-concepts, and clearly these also relate to social-world involvement.

Dan Funk (2008) employs self-concept in his approach to studying consumer behaviour for sports and events, namely as an integral part of the 'psychological continuum model' (see also Funk and James 2001, 2006). Awareness, attraction, attachment or allegiance are the progressive steps open to consumers and participants. Self-concept connects specifically to identifying with a sport, event or team.

Ego involvement is another closely related psychological construct much used in leisure research, and it is an integral part of developing theory on the 'event travel career trajectory' (see Chapter 8). Obviously one does not get highly involved with a brand, leisure pursuit (see 'serious leisure', p. 187), event, sport or social world unless it reflects our self-construct. An interesting illustration of ego enhancement was observed by Lee *et al.* (2013) in their analysis of the motivational factors affecting volunteer intentions for involvement in local events in the United States. They found that ego enhancement was one of the principal motivations, along with altruism and concern for the community in volunteering.

Personality

Psychologists speak of the 'big five' personality characteristics or factors that are believed to 'differentiate individuals in a somewhat permanent way and across most if not all situations' (Mannell and Kleiber 1997: 156). Personality as it affects leisure has been scrutinized, but little has been done to connect personality to event-related behaviour.

'Extroversion': This factor includes traits such as assertiveness, gregariousness and excitement seeking, leading to the label 'high-energy people'. Extroverted people often pursue sports and take risks. 'Introverts', in contrast, have a low threshold of arousal and do not need as much stimulation. They are more likely to play computer fantasy games. Studies have found that travel preferences and styles correlate with extroversion or introversion (Plog 1972; Nickerson and Ellis 1991). Extroverts are also sensation seekers who are more likely to participate in adventurous, intense activities, and want greater variety (Zuckerman 1979).

'Agreeableness': Traits associated with this factor include trust, straightforwardness and altruism, and it is contrasted with hostility, indifference and self-centredness. 'Agreeable' people seek social settings, and are more likely to volunteer. Self-indulgence and escape are more associated with low levels of agreeableness.

'Conscientiousness': Order, dutifulness, achievement striving, self-discipline and deliberation are associated with this characteristic of personality. Managers might want staff who are high on this factor, as it is typically manifested in reliability, responsibility and being organized. Stebbins (1992) thought that conscientiousness was associated with a strong goal orientation and 'serious leisure'. However, being high on this factor might also result in lower levels of spontaneity and higher compulsiveness. If one is low on this factor, impulsiveness and seeking immediate gratification are likely to result.

'Neuroticism': A general tendency to experience distress is associated with neuroticism. Anxiety, hostility, depression and self-consciousness are likely to accompany this factor. Dislike of playful leisure experiences might result from being neurotic. People with this trait might get less pleasure and enjoyment from both individual and social experiences by reason of discounting the positive aspects of their own lives.

'Openness to experience': This is associated with aesthetic sensitivity, the need for variety, unconventional values, flexibility of thought, cultural interest and educational aptitude. Such people are likely to seek out sensory stimulation.

Personality traits have been studied in leisure, although some researchers have concluded that personality has more of an influence on the extent of participation than on the choice of sport or activity

(Mannell and Kleiber 1997: 163). There is yet no research evidence to show the connection to planned events, but readers will see the possibilities for examining event-related behaviour and experiences in the context of the following personality dimensions:

- 'Locus of control': How important is it to perceive that you are in control or have freedom to choose? Does this define your perception of what is leisure or enjoyable work?
- 'Attentional style': How do you typically process or deal with environmental and social stimuli? Can you easily get into the 'flow' of deep involvement in an activity or mental process?
- 'Type A behaviour': Some people are driven to compete and succeed, are always worried about getting things done; they feel they are running out of time and so they get impatient with others. How can they relax? How do you get them to pay attention?
- 'Playfulness': Are you a playful person, also curious, creative and joyful? Can males and females be playful together, or are there social constraints?
- 'The Autotelic personality': These people 'are able to find intrinsic interest and enjoyment in almost everything he or she does' (Mannell and Kleiber 1997: 174).
- 'Shyness': Shy people may feel the lack of control over their lives and have low social competence, therefore have a more difficult time finding satisfying experiences.

Leung and Law (2010) reviewed the literature on how personality theory has been applied to tourism and hospitality, and much of this relates to event studies. They concluded that four main areas of application were related to consumer behaviour, human resource management, leisure and education. Most researchers had examined one or more of seven dimensions of personality, grouped as follows:

- personality traits, most commonly the big five;
- biological factors that influence or are influenced by personality (extroverts and introverts, with extroverts being sensation seekers; can include compulsions or impulsive behaviour);
- factors within the mind that influence behaviour; includes needs and motivation;
- the cognitive domain: understanding of perceptions, thoughts, feelings, desires (underlying stable motives and other conscious experiences from an individual's point of view; includes locus of control and self-image);
- social and cultural domain: the public aspects of personality and relationships (social psychology);
- adjustment domain: related to mental health and how people cope; self-efficacy and pathological behaviour are included;
- brand personality (how brand values connect to self-constructs; involvement).

Applications of personality theory to planned events are less common. Certainly it is relevant to volunteer and employee selection and behaviour (stress, motives, relationships, conscientiousness). Event marketers will want to understand personality as it relates to information searching and buying behaviour, event and destination choice, and this encompasses psychographic segmentation such as that employed in ego-involvement scales. Other useful applications relate to perceptions of event quality, learning preferences at conferences or taking risks (as in many sports). Spirituality is increasingly considered as a motivator for travel and event participation, as is creativity. Personalities of leadership have been studied, but not for events. The personality of event brands related to consumer self-concept has not been examined.

Aggression and anti-social behaviour at events

All too often celebrations and sport competitions get out of control, resulting in fighting, riots or crime. Some protests are organized to achieve these results. Can events be designed and managed to prevent bad behaviour? Moyer (1968) identified seven forms of aggression, with the following pertaining to social behaviour:

1. Inter-male aggression: competition between males of the same species over access to females, dominance, status, etc. (watch particularly for males who get drunk at parties and carnivals).

2. Fear-induced aggression: aggression associated with attempts to flee from a threat (e.g. crowd reaction to a gunshot, fight or fire at an event).

3. Irritable aggression: aggression directed towards an available target induced by some sort of frustration (e.g. impatience and stress caused by waiting or discomfort, resulting in overt hostility towards event organizers).

4. Territorial aggression: defence of a fixed space against intruders (as when gangs interact, or incompatible market segments are forced to mix).

5. Instrumental aggression: aggression directed towards obtaining some goal, maybe a learned response to a situation (the example of institutionalized rioting at some events).

'Ritualized aggression' helps explain our fascination with competitive team sports, especially when cities and countries are playing against each other. This can be useful in reducing tensions, but it periodically gets out of control and results in fighting and rioting in the audience. A great deal of attention has been given to combating 'hooliganism' in soccer (see Stott *et al.* 2001). In fact Deery and Jago (2010) found that anti-social behaviour has the power to undermine the positive effects of events. This is because the media often focus on drunken, rowdy behaviour and vandalism, and the community might become opposed to events that tolerate or engender these negative social impacts. Community pride can easily be damaged in this way. For this reason, Events in Focus 3.4 focuses on a neglected area of research around the perception of crime and events.

EVENTS IN FOCUS

3.4 Crime and events: a neglected relationship?

Whilst anti-social behaviour may be a problem associated with events and, in some instances, may lead to crime, this raises important issues on wider debates about the perception of both residents and event participants related to the impact of events on community and visitor safety. As Barker *et al.* (2003) found, there are a few studies that have examined the perceived impact of crime on the community (e.g. Lankford 1996; Pizam 1978; Rothman 1978; Snaith and Haley 1999).

One consequence is that the influx of visitors associated with an event can lead to residents perceiving a decline in the level of safety. As Barker *et al.* (2002) indicated, concern for such impacts has generated a range of studies that examine residents' perceptions of special events in the host community, including the impact of crime (e.g. America's Cup Office 1987; Ritchie and Lyons 1990; Soutar and McLeod 1993), whilst visitor perceptions may also impact upon event attendance.

As Barker *et al.* (2003) suggest, there is a limited literature on the impact of crime on events, but the findings of such studies confirm that where events attract large numbers of people and generate hedonistic activities such as alcohol and drug consumption, this may lead to conditions which can exacerbate crime. An increase in criminal activity arising with tourism has been noted during the seasonal phenomenon of special events (Burns and Mules 1989; Hall *et al.* 1995) and holiday periods (Barker 2000; Rothman *et al.* 1979; Walmsley *et al.* 1983).

Studies of the America's Cup hosted in 1999–2000 by Barker *et al.* (2001) and Barker *et al.* (2002) highlighted the impact of improved visitor safety at events through environmental design as well as a displacement of crime due to an increased police presence during the duration of the America's Cup, which was intended to saturate the area and avoid crime hotspots developing. This illustrates what Barker *et al.* (2002) observed in relation to hotspot theory, which suggests that predatory crime is associated with certain types of geographical areas such that a relatively few locations, or 'hotspots', are associated with a high percentage of crimes. This means that during events, crimes will be directed to the areas where people attending are likely to congregate as participants and as an audience, potentially increasing an individual's risk of victimization from crime. For example, Hall and Selwood (1989) found an explicit relationship between the hosting of the 1987 America's Cup in Fremantle, Australia and an increase in petty crime. Personal crimes of sexual and common assault and robbery increased, combined with significant increases in minor offences (e.g. traffic infringements, drunkenness and disorderly behaviour) (Hall *et al.* 1995). Similarly, results were found by Barker *et al.* (2002, 2003) in their comparative study of the America's Cup in Auckland, and Getz (1997) also observed that social problems such as crime, anti-social behaviour or rioting can become institutionalized at events. Interestingly, a study by Baumann *et al.* (2012) examined the impact of sporting events and franchises on local crime rates in the USA, but found no evidence that these led to any major change in crime rates. However, they did observe that around a 10 per cent increase in property crimes occurred with hosting the Olympic Games, while hosting the Super Bowl actually saw a 2.5 per cent decrease in violent crime.

Therefore, in order to understand the wider experience of events it is important to recognize that external factors such as perception of and victimization through crime and anti-social behaviour can have a bearing when seeking to understand different dimensions of how people perceive their safety – which leads us to consider the contribution of environmental psychology.

Psychological research paradigms

Within the field of leisure and tourism, most psychological research is positivistic and deductive, and a great deal of it employs research methods that study small experimental groups, often students, and uses self-completion questionnaires (Veal 2006: 30). Consumer behaviour in general, and with regard to tourism in particular, is heavily dependent on theories from cognitive psychology within the wider field of environmental psychology.

Environmental psychology

Environmental psychology has considerable potential for enhancing event studies as it has tourism research (Fridgen 1984). It is an interdisciplinary field focusing on the perception and cognition of natural and built environments (see Moser and Uzzell 2003 for an explanation of its scope and application to leisure). Bell *et al.* (2001: 6) defined it as 'the study of molar relationships between behaviour and experience and the built and natural environments'. 'Molar' means the whole is greater than the parts, or a *gestalt* approach. 'Units' of environment and behaviour are studied, such as the festival place, sport arena, banquet hall or conference centre. Specific topics include arousal, stimulation, stress, adaptation, approach-avoidance behaviour, environmental design, wayfaring, work and leisure environments.

The environment is viewed as both the context for behaviour and a determinant of behaviour. Environmental psychologists also examine the consequences of human behaviour on the environment. Taking a festival place as an example, environmental psychologists would look at how people interact with the setting, how it can be designed or modified to reflect its purpose. Specific considerations would include capacity and crowding, personal space, noise and light, temperature and air flows. Would changing the lighting, for example, result in a more subdued audience? Would music enliven the place? Of course, event designers often know the answers from experience, but environmental psychology uses experimental and other research methods to develop both practical solutions and general theories. Although laboratory experiments are sometimes used, more popular methods are field experiments, descriptive and co-relational studies, and simulations (see Table 3.7).

De Young (1999) noted these important environmental psychology research themes:

- 'Attention': how people notice the environment; response to environmental stimuli;
- 'Perception' and 'cognitive maps': how people image the natural and built environment; formation of mental maps;
- 'Preferred environments': people tend to seek out places where they feel competent and confident, places where they can make sense of the environment, while also being engaged with it;
- 'Environmental stress' and 'coping': common environmental stressors include noise and climatic extremes; coping with stress can involve a change in physical or social settings, or seeking to interpret or make sense of a situation.

Table 3.7 Environmental psychology

Environmental psychology	Nature and meanings; the event experience	Antecedents to attending events	Planning and producing events	Outcomes and the impacted	Processes and patterns
Perception and cognition of natural and built environments Environmental design Wayfaring Behavioural settings and environmental stressors Personal space Crowding	How people perceive, make sense of, and value the event setting Environmental cues as to appropriate behaviour Feeling crowded or comfortable	Preferences for certain environments Fear of crowding and environmental risks	Implications for event setting design and management (e.g. legibility; facilitating interaction, setting the mood, flow)	Environmental factors directly impact on personal health, safety and satisfaction	Environmental preferences and fears are culturally shaped and evolve Event venue development, and use of places for events, constantly presents new opportunities and ideas about the environment

The 'Integrative Model of Environmental Psychology' from Bell *et al.* (2001: 21) can be adapted to event studies (see Figure 3.4). This model provides an overview of environmental psychology topics and their interrelationships. We start with environmental conditions, which for events means purpose-built venues or sometimes natural settings. Human–environment interactions are influenced by both biological (e.g. our need for occasional solitude, or the fear of heights) and learned factors (e.g. we are taught to respect nature or to show respect for others' property). Then we have to consider perceptions of the environment, or how we employ our senses to detect and give meaning to conditions in the setting (this is cognition).

'General effects of the environment' on behaviour include the study of sensory stimulation through noise, light, smell and colour, the effects of general environmental conditions (weather, pollution) and impacts of social interaction (personal space and crowding).

Closely linked to the general factors are the 'behavioural and experiential influences' of specific event settings. Their design, programming and management are explicitly intended to create, suggest or facilitate desired moods, behaviours and experiences. We need to examine all the common and unusual event settings, from sport arenas to parks, from convention centres to city squares. How does each factor alone and in combination with others affect, for example, the behaviour and mood of an audience at a concert? We need to be aware that event settings are often purpose-built, with their intended uses and appropriate behaviours known by convention, while some are unusual and have to be valorized for temporary event purposes. 'Setting affordances' and 'constraints' are those characteristics of the venue or place that suggest and/or allow for various activities and experiences, or which constrain them.

'Changing environmental cognitions' refers to learning from experience and the resultant changes in perceptions and motives. In terms of events this can encompass how people perceive and attach meaning to event settings and design elements. With education, event experiences can also lead to positive shifts in attitudes towards the environment, such as support for green operations and sustainable development. Finally, the interactions in this model include changes to cognition in general, or how we perceive our environment.

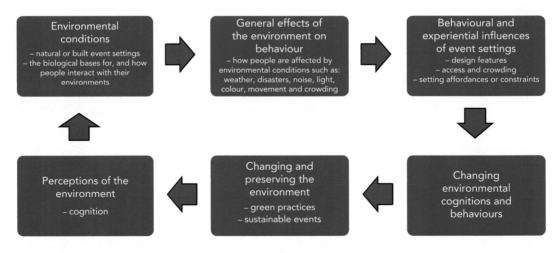

Figure 3.4 Environmental psychology and planned events

Note: Adapted from Bell *et al.* (2001).

Environmental preferences

According to Kaplan (1987), humans examine the contents and the spatial configuration of scenes. We have to process a lot of information gained by our senses, in a hurry. Kaplan showed that people prefer scenes or settings that are 'coherent', 'legible', 'complex' and contain some degree of 'mystery'. Legibility and mystery require more cognitive processing. Complexity and mystery together appear to stimulate involvement, or the desire to explore and comprehend the scene. Our responses to event settings and their design reflect certain predispositions, some of which are culturally influenced and some that are highly individual.

In Research Note 3.7 from Pettersson and Getz (2009) another kind of hotspot is featured, in contrast to cold spots at events, and these are related to experiences other than crime.

3.7 RESEARCH NOTE ON EVENT SETTINGS: HOT AND COLD SPOTS

Pettersson, R. and Getz, D. (2009). Event experiences in time and space: A study of visitors to the 2007 World Alpine Ski Championships in Åre, Sweden. *Scandinavian Journal of Hospitality and Tourism*, 9(2/3), 308–326.

'The spatial and temporal nature of event experiences was studied through interviews, participant observation and photography at a major sporting event. Results contribute to a better understanding of how visitors interact with the event setting and with each other, and help build theory on experiences, their design and management. Event tourists were observed spatially and temporally while enjoying various elements of the host village and four event arenas, while photographs and notes made by participant observers enabled a more focused evaluation of positive and negative experiences. Results identified the importance of social factors, as visitors wanted to be where the others were, revealed that surprise created positive experiences, and identified the existence of experiential "hotspots" defined in both time and space. It is concluded that positive experiences are more important than negative ones in terms of overall satisfaction. Implications are drawn regarding the nature of event experiences, their design and management, and on related methodological development.'

Hotspots and cold spots reflect event-goers' perceptions of the event or community environment related to both their expectation (e.g. the place should be exciting, animated, interesting) and the nature of the event (where will the entertainment be located, the races, the food?). These can be shaped by design, and can be changed as the event proceeds (if it is long enough). There is also the possibility that cold spots might be created or tolerated as a crowd management device – to keep people moving, or change their patterns, in order to avoid congestion and negative social or environmental impacts.

The behaviour setting

According to Barker (1968), places have culturally defined purposes and behavioural expectations. The setting and appropriate behaviour are perceived to be an integrated unit, or 'behavioural setting'. Outdoor settings are sometimes more ambiguous than indoor facilities, although this depends on many design and management factors. Certainly people attending a fair in an open area receive different 'cues' and exhibit different behaviour when compared with those attending an art exhibit indoors. Do guests intuitively understand the norms and limits? To be effective, we rely on conventions, or 'standing patterns of behaviour' in Barker's words, which in themselves are culturally determined. A study by Wickham and Kerstetter (2000: 167) argued that 'as individuals' attachment to their community increases so too do their positive feelings about crowds. These results challenge traditional notions about crowding and provide insight to festival managers interested in enhancing their relationship with the host community', since crowds have been associated with negative connotations of event experiences. This raises important issues about the behaviour and experience of individuals, which leads us to the area of social psychology.

Social psychology

Mannell and Kleiber (1997: 25) wrote that 'Social psychology is the scientific study of the behaviour and experience of individuals in social situations.' Its historical evolution is outlined by Allport (1937). Baron and Byrne (2000) defined social psychology as 'the field that seeks to understand the nature and causes of individual behaviour and thought in social settings'. For the purposes of event studies, social psychology helps us understand the nature and causes of behaviour at events, based on studying the relationship between the mind, groups and behaviours. Social psychology has a range of theories and concepts it uses to study these themes (see Table 3.8).

Self-determination theory

Self-determination theory (see Deci and Ryan 1985, 2000) is concerned with human motivation, specifically the development and functioning of personality within social situations. Within leisure, this approach asks if people really engage in actions with a full sense of choice. The social environment can either assist or hinder a person's striving for growth, development and a coherent sense of self through the satisfaction of basic human needs. When needs are unmet, or thwarted, people can suffer in terms of general well-being and psychological health.

Social cognition and social cognitive theory

Bandura (1977, 1986) provided a framework for understanding, predicting and even seeking to change human behaviour – individually and collectively. The theory states that behaviour is a result of the interaction

Table 3.8 Social psychology

Social psychology	Nature and meanings; the event experience	Antecedents to attending events	Planning and producing events	Outcomes and the impacted	Processes and patterns
Studies the behaviour and experience of individuals in social situations	Events as social experiences Social role schemas Subjective meanings attached to events through social interaction (i.e. events as social constructs)	The influence of social reference groups Social needs (seeking and escaping)	Design for environment–group interactions and dynamics Creating a social atmosphere; belonging and sharing	Satisfaction of social group needs	Changes in family, social groups and social norms affect events

of personal factors, behaviour and the environment. Social factors influence our beliefs and cognitive competencies. The environment modifies human behaviour, and in turn people seek to change it. The same set of stimuli might result in different behaviour because people construe the situation differently.

'Self-efficacy' is one of the key personal factors involved in Bandura's theory. It refers to a person's belief in their ability to perform a given behaviour successfully, which is different from a person's actual competency. Self-efficacy influences motivation and leisure behaviour. We are more likely to engage in activities that we think will produce desired outcomes, and this depends in part on our assessment of how well we can do the activity. Self-efficacy also affects how people respond to failure. In contrast, a person with high efficacy will attribute failure to external factors, where a person with low self-efficacy will attribute failure to low ability. People with high self-efficacy are generally of the opinion that they are in control of their own lives, while those with low self-efficacy see their lives as being shaped by others, or by destiny.

There are implications for education and training. Self-efficacy, or belief in one's own abilities, increases through mastery or success, and diminishes with failure. It can also be increased through example, by learning from others (especially peers and respected persons) how to accomplish a task. Positive encouragement is also important.

'Social cognition' is how we interpret, analyse, remember and use information about the social world. Baron and Byrne (2000: 80) said that we employ schema which are 'mental frameworks centring around a specific theme that help us to organize social information'. 'Social role schemas' apply to our expectations for the behaviour of ourselves or others in social situations, such as how lecturers act at a conference, how the master of ceremonies behaves at a gala dinner, or what a group of performers does at a concert. Schemas affect three basic processes of social cognition, as shown in Figure 3.5.

Schemas act as filters, saving us time and energy when we size up a social situation, and they are obviously based in part on experience and on cultural conventions. They have perseverance, generally lasting a long time. But they can also result in misconceptions and inappropriate behaviour if the cues we expect are not present or are misleading. They can have the effect of 'self-fulfilling prophecy' in that they can cause us to behave in ways that confirm them. We tend to notice only the cues consistent with our mental schemas, causing us to act in ways that confirm their validity.

Theory of planned behaviour

Originating with the work of Ajzen (1985, 1991), this very influential theory posits that behaviour is driven by 'behavioural intentions' (for example, 'I fully intend to go to that concert'). Intentions are

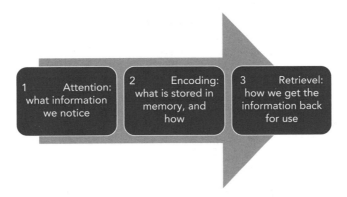

Figure 3.5 The process of social cognition

a function of the person's (a) attitudes towards the behaviour, (b) subjective norms and (c) perceived behavioural control. The theory states that a person's intention to do something is the most immediate determinant of behaviour.

'Attitude' towards the behaviour is defined as the person's feelings about the behaviour (positive or negative), and this stems from beliefs concerning the possible consequences of the behaviour and the desirability of those impacts (e.g. 'I think rock concerts are cool places to meet and be with friends, and that is top priority for me'). 'Subjective norms' are the individual's perception of what others will think, such as if one's peers will approve of the behaviour (e.g. 'all my friends think the X concert is going to be the best, and I want to be accepted by them').

'Perceived behavioural control' refers to feelings of choice (including having skills, resources and the opportunity to do something). As in leisure constraint theory, people who perceive they do not have the skills, resources or opportunities are unlikely to form strong intentions to go to events.

'Theory of planned behaviour' applies only to uncoerced, rational behaviour, but not all event attendance or participation will meet those criteria. As we know, extrinsic motives also apply to many events, such as work and social obligations. Irrationality might enter into the decision to attend events when, for example, people are in very strange circumstances (such as foreign cultures) or suffering from altered mental states due to such factors as alcohol, drugs, stress or illness. Research note 3.8, by Lee *et al.* (2014), examines the intention–behaviour gap associated with a mega event.

3.8 RESEARCH NOTE ON MEGA EVENT

Lee, C. K., Mjelde, J. W., Kim, T. K. and Lee, H. M. (2014). Estimating the intention–behaviour gap associated with a mega event: The case of the Expo 2012 Yeosu Korea. *Tourism Management*, 41, 168–177.

Demand (attendance) forecasts are often based on respondents' intentions to attend an event or purchase a product. People, however, do not always act on their intentions; an intention–behaviour gap exists. This study investigates the intention–behaviour gap based on a national survey using a quota sampling method ($N = 2015$) in the realm of visiting the 2012 Yeosu Expo. Results reveal that approximately 50 per cent of the respondents who had intentions to visit the Expo actually visited the Expo. The stronger the intentions are to visit the Expo, the larger the percentage of respondents who acted on their intentions. The researchers found that time and travel distance had a significant bearing on attendance, and that older, more educated respondents were more likely to follow through on intentions to visit.

Expectation-confirmation theory

Oliver (1977, 1980) reasoned that consumer satisfaction is determined by the interactions of expectations and perceived performance, mediated through positive or negative disconfirmation between expectations and perceived performance. In other words, if the guest expects a high level of service, but perceives it to be poor, it will lead to dissatisfaction. A dissatisfied customer is unlikely to be loyal or to say good things about the service providers.

This theory lies at the heart of SERVQUAL and other approaches to defining and measuring satisfaction, which have their origins in consumer behaviour research within marketing (Baron *et al.* in press).

Many researchers, however, believe that it is more practical and just as valid to measure 'post-hoc satisfaction', without a pre-measurement of expectations. Getz *et al.* (2001) used the 'post-hoc satisfaction approach' in evaluating a surfing event. One convincing argument is that many people show up at events without clear expectations of service or product quality, but they can always determine afterwards if they were satisfied or not. On the other hand, the more experienced the consumer, the more likely they are to hold firm expectations. We return to the quality issue in Chapter 7 when examining event design.

3.9 RESEARCH NOTE ON EVENT QUALITY

Tkaczynski, A. and Stokes, R. (2010). FESTPERF: A service quality measurement scale for festivals. *Event Management*, 14(1), 69–82.

The study addresses the question of what elements of performance-based research apply to event service quality. 'Results of this study at an Australian Jazz and Blues Festival led to the creation of FESTPERF, a three-factor solution that differed from the generic SERVPERF instrument and did not replicate the SERVQUAL factors. Two of these factors, Professionalism and Environment, predicted visitor satisfaction that may, in turn, lead to repurchase. The third factor, Core Service, did not predict intent by festival goers to revisit. A practical implication of this research is the availability of an event-specific model of service quality for further testing at other types of music festivals (e.g. rock, gospel, or pop, or at other special events).'

Audience and fan studies

One of the unifying topics in event studies, involving various theoretical perspectives covered in this and subsequent chapters, is that of the audience. Jo Mackellar in her book *Event Audiences and Expectations* (2013a) presents a spectrum of audience types that clearly connect to identity, involvement, serious leisure, subculture, communitas and values. She describes 'socializers', 'dabblers', 'enthusiasts' and 'fanatics' in terms of what benefits they seek in attending events or participating in other ways. Within the sport-related literature the fan is a topic of great interest, particularly in terms of determining motivations and styles of sport-event travel and behaviour. When the audience is a focus of research, many different perspectives can be taken to increase understanding and lead to improved design and management. These themes will be evident in the remainder of this book.

STUDY GUIDE

As a field of study, event studies must use and adapt theories, methodologies and research methods from many foundation disciplines, especially those in the social sciences. The potential for drawing on them to expand our knowledge base in event studies is almost unlimited, and it should result in interdisciplinary theory of and for planned events.

For each of the foundation disciplines in this and the next chapter, students should be able to summarize the main topics they cover, their core theories and methodologies, and types of research methods used. These can be illustrated by the research notes throughout this book. They also have direct bearing on the later discussions of experiences, outcomes and policy. Use the figures provided for each discipline as starting points for tracing various themes that run through the book. In particular, link the classical anthropology and sociology theories to the model of planned event experiences in Chapter 6.

STUDY QUESTIONS

- Are all planned events cultural phenomena? Are they all authentic?
- Explain ethnography and phenomenology in the context of research for events.
- What are social and cultural capital and how are these concepts useful in event studies?
- In what ways can we use social exchange theory in event studies?
- Connect social worlds and social network theory to the need for events.
- Where do ethics come from? (Link religion, philosophy and professionalism.)
- Are all pilgrimages religious in nature?
- Tie expectation–confirmation theory to event quality.
- Show how cognitive psychology supports our understanding of the planned event experience and why people attend events (be sure to include personal constructs).
- Describe the big five personality traits and explain why theory about personality is important for event marketing.
- Explain the Integrative Model of Environmental Psychology as adapted to event studies.
- Link the concept of behaviour settings to event design.
- Why are identity, self-cognition and self-efficacy theories important to understanding audiences and the planned event experience?

FURTHER READING

Ehrenreich, B. (2006). *Dancing in the Streets: A History of Collective Joy*. New York: Metropolitan Books.

Henderson, E. and McIlwraith, M. (2013). *Ethics and Corporate Social Responsibility in the Meetings and Events Industry*. Chichester: Wiley.

Mackellar, J. (2014). *Event Audiences and Expectations*. London: Routledge.

Picard, D. and Robinson. M. (eds) (2006). *Festivals, Tourism and Social Change: Remaking Worlds*. Clevedon: Channel View.

Quinn, B. (2013). *Key Concepts in Event Management*. London: Sage.

Turner, V. (ed.) (1982). *Celebration: Studies in Festivity and Ritual*. Washington, DC: Smithsonian Institution Press.

Chapter **4**

Economics, management, political science, law, history, human geography, future studies

LEARNING OBJECTIVES

Upon completion of this chapter students should know the following:

- contributions of these seven foundation disciplines to understanding the roles, meanings, importance and impacts of events in society and culture;
- key theories and methodologies from economics, management, political science, law, history, human geography and future studies;
- for each discipline, specific contributions to understanding the nature and meanings of events, antecedents, experiences, outcomes, patterns, processes and policy.

Economics

According to the *Encyclopaedia Britannica*, economics is a 'social science that seeks to analyse and describe the production, distribution, and consumption of wealth'. This is expanded by Craven (1990: 3), who argued that within economics the principal challenge is how we allocate resources given that many resources are scarce; therefore economists look at how these resources need to be allocated and the ways in which they are distributed. A key term in this debate is the term 'scarcity', meaning that most resources in society are finite and decisions have to be made on the best way to use and sustain them. Economists define resources in terms of:

- natural resources (e.g. the land)
- labour (e.g. human resources and entrepreneurship)
- capital (e.g. synthetic aids to assist in producing goods).

Collectively these resources constitute the factors of production that are used to produce commodities. These commodities can be divided into:

- goods (e.g. tangible products such as an aircraft)
- services (e.g. intangible items such as an event experience).

The total output of all commodities in a country over a period of time, normally a year, is known as the national product. As the production of goods and services can only satisfy a small fraction of consumers' needs and choices in society, we have to allocate resources to determine which goods and services to produce. The way in which goods and services are divided amongst people has been examined by economists in terms of the distribution of income and the degree of equality and efficiency in their distribution.

Macro- and microeconomics

Many of these issues are dealt with under the heading of 'microeconomics', which focuses on the firm, the consumer, production and selling, the demand for goods and the supply of goods. In contrast, macroeconomics examines:

> the entire economy and interactions within it, including the population, income, total unemployment, the average rate of price increases (the inflation rate), the extent of companies' capacities to produce goods and the total amount of money in use in the country.
>
> *(Craven 1990: 5)*

Meaning that a key focus within macroeconomics is how the national economy operates, employment and unemployment, inflation, national production and consumption, and the money supply in a country.

Macroeconomics has considerable importance for event studies, being concerned with the entire economic system (the study of which is sometimes referred to as 'political economy'). Governments and international agreements set the parameters within which economies operate, including the establishment of trading blocs (e.g. the European Union). Whilst most modern economies are more or less in the free-market mode, meaning that 'laws' of the marketplace are allowed to prevail, specific trading blocs do provide more favourable market conditions for members of that grouping; those outside blocs sometimes have to pay tariffs if they wish to trade with bloc members. Many governments intervene in the marketplace to some extent in order to achieve social, cultural and environmental goals. Investment in event tourism and grants for the arts represent two important policy interventions of concern in this book, and they have dominated much of the research literature (e.g. see Foley *et al.* 2012; Hall 2014).

One area of economics, 'welfare economics' (which is a branch of macroeconomics), has specific concerns with the evaluation of public policy in relation to its impact on the well-being of the population or specific groups within society. This concern in human geography (see p. 187) also created an interest in welfare geography, focused on who gets what, where and why. D. M. Smith (1977) has examined the concept of social well-being and welfare geography, arguing that concepts of territorial justice obscure the social and economic processes, whereby distributional justice by social groups is neglected and access to public goods is constrained. This is why most countries, for example, impose higher income taxes on the wealthy, and tax corporations, in effect enabling the transfer of wealth from the rich to the poor to address these social inequalities. How that government revenue from taxes is spent is a matter for party politics and public debate. 'Welfarist' political parties want government funds to be spent in ways that benefit the poor and disadvantaged, resulting in a high degree of government involvement in the economy. Conservative parties prefer to spend less, as their ideology suggests we should use resources to enable individuals rather than governments to make most economic choices. Accordingly, a welfarist government might justify direct production and subsidization of cultural festivals as a contributor to public good, while a conservative government might be more inclined to reduce income taxes in order to give consumers more choices (in other words, a 'supply-side' approach). Page and Connell (2010) review these policy choices in the context of the UK in relation to leisure and cultural policy, observing that in parallel with many other states, major shifts in policy occurred: the emphasis has shifted from state subsidy to a greater role for the private sector, with a corresponding growth in private-sector, profit-led events operated on a commercial basis.

These changes reflect the difficult decisions that governments have had to make in welfare economics. Is it possible to justify a policy that benefits some at the expense of others? Many people do support redistribution measures such as sliding tax scales, and modern governments like to take regular polls of voters to determine the popularity of various options, or to assess attitudes towards existing programmes. The difficulty is that, if a redistribution measure actually hurts some people to benefit others, is that justifiable? Of course these serious policy questions are not generally decided with planned events in mind (see Palma *et al.* 2013 and their discussion of cultural economics and events), but do get raised when public expenditures and subsidies for events are at issue, with events being the outcome of the policy decisions taken. Therefore, as Table 4.1 demonstrates, economics and the politics of how resources are allocated have a clear bearing on the event domain.

Below these macroeconomic issues, microeconomics affect individuals and their consumer behaviour, as well as specific business decisions and how supply and demand finds equilibrium in specific markets. In classical economics, 'laws of supply and demand' govern these processes. Important microeconomic questions regarding planned events are:

- What determines the price of an event and of the resources used to produce it?
- How are event buyers and sellers brought together in a functioning market? (This is crucial in the context of bidding on events: see Getz (2004) for an assessment of the marketplace and how it works both in theory, and in practice, for tourism agencies that bid on events.)
- How is the economic or financial feasibility of a proposed event assessed?
- What are the differences between types of event organizations in terms of how they operate (i.e. governmental, non-profit and for-profit)?

Table 4.1 Economics

Economics	Nature and meanings; the event experience	Antecedents to attending events	Planning and producing events	Outcomes and the impacted	Processes and patterns
Macroeconomics (or 'political economy'): the functioning of whole economic systems Microeconomics: the economics of consumers, and of doing business (by firms or other organizations)	The experience and meanings of consumption Perceived value for money, as it shapes the event experience	Economic incentives and barriers to consumption or participation Supply factors (e.g. cost of travel; alternatives)	The event's business model and economic feasibility Forecasting demand Economic development policy as it affects the event sector	Measuring economic impacts and externalities Costs and benefits evaluated (including their distribution)	Economic trends and forces (competition; globalization)

Economic exchanges: rational choice theory

This theory underpins microeconomics and consumer behaviour. People are assumed to act rationally and make rational choices when it comes to obtaining the benefits they want; they are acting as if they consciously and intelligently balance costs against benefits, even though we know that is often not true. If indeed people (and firms) are always able to maximize personal or corporate advantage – in every transaction – then the economic system is presumed to work most efficiently. Unfortunately, 'rational behaviour' in this context might include unethical or illegal behaviour, and so the system cannot be allowed to function without regulation. There are some obvious exceptions or complications that need to be discussed.

Theory of choice

Firms desiring to make a profit have difficult choices to make; they face a number of constraints regarding their necessary inputs (supplies, labour, rents paid). One combination of inputs will minimize costs, but will it permit the production of an attractive event? If profit is not the goal, a different set of inputs can be justified and in fact if a loss can be incurred (because of subsidies or debt forgiveness), the producers can afford to be rather careless in their use of resources. Little research has been done on how event producers make such choices, but some research employing stakeholder theory has addressed the issue of relative power between event organizers and their suppliers, and how this impacts on non-profit festival viability (see Andersson and Getz 2007).

Theory of allocation

When a business or institution has multiple goals for events, there has to be some kind of prioritization – it is generally not possible to commit resources to fulfil all goals equally. The necessary allocation of resources to meet each goal can be measured, then linked to its priority or 'weighting', and from that analysis an optimal strategy can be determined which will provide the company or agency with the best 'return' on its investment. In this context a key question becomes: how does one determine the relative value of committing resources to events versus other programmes, or one type of event compared with another?

Opportunity costs

Opportunity costs are also a key economic concept. Whatever resources a company or government devotes to events, they could be spent elsewhere. Are events worth the investment in terms of culture, health or tourism? This becomes a serious policy matter, because other opportunities always exist for meeting business and societal goals. So-called 'merit' goods and services are deemed by governments to require subsidies or direct government provision because of their importance and the inability or unwillingness of the private sector to fill the need. Thus, some governments justify the provision of festivals and sport events, or other forms of entertainment, for the 'public good'. Preuss (2009) found that economic analyses of mega sport events usually focus on the positive effects and legacies, while ignoring opportunity costs and the efficiency of using scarce resources. Preuss uses the measure 'efficiency' (i.e. the ratio: output/ input) of alternative investments, making it clear 'that the decision to stage a mega sport event cannot be taken in isolation and that there are many factors that need to be considered'. The argument put forward is based on a stakeholder's perspective and a spatial differentiation of interest groups.

Demand for goods and services

Demand, in economics, is a function of the relationship between price and the quantity 'demanded' for a good or service in specific circumstances. For each price, the demand relationship tells the quantity the buyers want to buy at that corresponding price. Consumers derive 'utility' (such as survival, pleasure, happiness, satisfaction) from spending their limited disposable incomes. Consumers always have choices, especially when it comes to entertainment and travel, and various economic methods of analysis exist in consumer behaviour to model these choices (e.g. see Louviere and Hensher 1983 and the use of multi-attribute choice behaviour modelling to identify how consumers make choices). A 'consumer surplus' can be created when the utility derived from an event exceeds the cost to an individual, or when a free or subsidized event is produced for an appreciative public (e.g. my expectations were exceeded; I would have gladly paid more for that experience; they should have charged an admission fee, it was so wonderful!).

The more one values an event the more one is willing to pay for it, up to a point. So demand rests on certain assumptions about consumer utility, choices and preferences embodied in economic methods of analysis such as willingness to pay (see Burgan and Mules 2001). The principle of 'diminishing marginal utility' says that consumers will eventually get less and less satisfaction from going to events, or any specific type of event, and therefore the benefits derived will at some level of consumption cease to justify the effort or cost required. In terms of supply and demand, there are two related 'elasticity' functions to consider.

Income elasticity: As incomes rise there is more for consumers to spend on goods and services, therefore overall demand for leisure, travel and events is directly linked to disposable incomes. But will events be 'preferred goods' that people want to spend more on? We know that as countries develop a middle class with rising incomes, more and more is spent on leisure and travel (in effect, there is high 'latent demand' for these goods).

Price elasticity: As price rises, overall demand should fall, so that when an event charges more, it can generally expect to attract fewer paying customers – or to attract different types of customer. Some events might be considered to be 'luxury goods' that attract customers who care little about rising prices, or are even attracted by the exclusivity that higher prices imply. In a free marketplace, supply and demand should eventually reach 'equilibrium', where no more events are produced than can be justified by what consumers are willing to spend. This does not happen, however, for reasons discussed below. In fact, the events sector is so oriented to government subsidies and non-profit values that it is difficult to apply any economic laws, except for the purpose of making comparisons to other sectors or revealing the extent of market distortions.

Economic demand for events

The normal assumptions made by economists regarding demand for goods and services often do not apply in the events sector. Consumers have multiple event choices, some of which are free or subsidized. All events that attract people for personal reasons (i.e. intrinsic motives) are in themselves substitutable with other forms of entertainment or activities. We should expect price elasticity, for example, to apply mostly to events that must be held (a wedding? an association meeting?) and for which supply alternatives abound. In a competitive environment, suppliers must always be wary of price increases.

Nevertheless, when setting the price for event admission, organizers do have to consider how it will affect potential demand. Price elasticity generally means that as price increases, demand will decrease – for the obvious reason that money is a scarce resource, but also because consumers have many alternative opportunities. Tribe (2005: 76–77) shows how elasticity is modified by the necessity of having the good or service, the number of substitutes, addictiveness of the good or service, consumer awareness and the time period (e.g. are tickets bought well in advance?). Furthermore, some goods and services are so useful and so cheap that increases in price will be too small to affect demand.

The income elasticity of demand also must be considered. Generally people spend more on leisure and travel as their disposable incomes rise, and corporations and governments also 'demand' more events as their profits or revenues increase. In part it is a matter of financial feasibility, but it is also a matter of preference.

Indeed, events (as leisure) can be considered preferred goods or services because people love to travel and be entertained. And civil servants as well as business people love to meet! Economics therefore provides a basis for demand forecasting, which, in the context of events, often means attendance forecasting. The inherent difficulty is that demand for, or interest in, many events is only partially influenced by the cost.

Willingness to pay

Willingness to pay is a useful economic concept to help determine event demand and to help set prices. Ask yourself how much you would be willing to pay for a choice ticket to a popular concert, then how much more or less you would be willing to pay for a ticket to a community festival. People are often unable to say exactly how much they would pay for any given opportunity, but they can at least compare it to other, normal purchases – we can call these 'value propositions'. For example, we often spend money to attend the cinema or rent a movie, so how much more is it worth to attend that concert? Twice as much? Three times? Market researchers use these value propositions to find a range within which most of their target segment would make a purchase.

A problem with willingness to pay is that some people will mislead you! Well, of course they will. Why volunteer that you would pay a lot of money for something that is currently free or cheap? Won't 'they' just use that information to raise the price? So researchers have to expect that expressed willingness to pay yields under-estimates of what people will actually pay. On the other hand, researchers have to recognize that if the price is raised, some people might indeed decide to stay away or be unable to afford the new price.

Tourists, it is often found, will pay more for events than locals. Studies of festivals in Canada's National Capital Region (Coopers and Lybrand 1989) found that those who travelled to the city especially for the events were willing to spend more than the residents. This happens because the event is the reason for their travel, and they are likely to attend just once. Residents have plenty of chances to attend (or go to other local events) and might want to attend more than once, so they are less willing to pay higher prices per visit. Tourists therefore often represent a higher-yield segment, but in smaller volumes. In one study, Barros (2006) employed willingness to pay (WTP) to examine demand for the EURO 2004 football event and determined there was a small proportion of the population who were prepared to pay for the event. Their WTP was positively related to the number of times that the individual attends a soccer game during the season and to the education level of the respondent, but negatively related to household income, being a fan of the team and to the perception that the event would be prestigious for the country. Barros concluded that Euro 2004 did not qualify as a 'Pareto improvement of the public good', since the aggregated willingness to pay was lower than the estimated total costs of the event. It should be kept in mind, however, that WTP is only one possible measure of 'public good'.

Pricing

Pricing strategies and tactics are a management and marketing function, but how people react to prices requires both economic and psychological theories. Only a few researchers have dealt with event-related pricing issues. Crompton and Love (1994) analysed the history of demand for a themed event (Dickens on the Strand in Galveston, Texas) as well as responses to questions about substitution opportunities, strength of reference price, distribution of trip costs, affluence of the target market and value for money. The researchers determined that attendance was mostly related to the life cycle of the event and its need to find new markets. Price could be raised without reducing demand, as each year 50 per cent were first-timers and regular residents could either get discounts in advance or free admission through dressing in period costumes. Demand was inelastic.

Examining many of the issues surrounding major-event ticketing, Happel and Jennings (2002) noted that few entertainment events, such as concerts, employed extensive price discrimination. It was common in the arts (e.g. symphony and opera), where there were often 25 or more ticket prices depending on event quality and seat location. At sport events, ticket prices usually remain the same across all games in a season, regardless of the quality of the teams playing. Happel and Jennings looked for reasons, and suggested that perhaps the arts institutions understood their customers better, or it was more important in the arts to be close to the performers. Sport might also employ a loss-leader strategy to get people into cheaper seats, then make a profit on merchandise and refreshments. Boyd and Boyd (1998: 169) challenged many of the conventional economic rules on pricing, arguing that:

> *the pricing of tickets to professional sporting events often appear to be inconsistent with traditional profit-maximising behaviour. For example, the existence of scalpers and 'ticket agents' who sell game tickets at prices significantly in excess of face value could suggest that teams set prices too low for profit maximisation.*

And it is known that some performers insist on keeping ticket prices as low as possible in order to be fair to their fans. Changing market conditions, and new technology, are likely to cause changes in event pricing. For example, being able to book and trade tickets online will alter consumer behaviour. In the context of leisure services, Crompton (2011) discussed the concept of the 'zone of tolerance', which is a price range in which consumer resistance might be minimized for new services or price increases. This has apparently not been tested for planned events, but relates closely to the WTP discussion.

Direct and induced demand

'Direct' demand for events consists of those people who pay to attend, or in other words the customers. As price goes up, normally direct demand will fall. If the event is free, direct economic demand cannot be measured, but 'willingness to pay' can be researched to get a 'value' for the event. Forecasting demand for an event is notoriously difficult (see, for example, Teigland 1996; Pyo *et al.* 1988; Spilling 1998; Mules and McDonald 1994), and so it is normal for many years of research on awareness, interest levels, market areas and segmentation, penetration rates and demand to precede mega events. The principal difficulty with forecasting event demand is in obtaining accurate and reliable data.

'Induced demand' is something quite different. It occurs when an event generates additional awareness for a destination, improves its image, and thereby attracts additional visitors. They might come before a major event to see the developing facilities, or simply because so much attention has been given to the area. Increased capacity is another factor to consider when explaining any tourist gains following an event, as new venues and hotels, better marketing, and heightened political support for tourism and other events are potential consequences.

Olympic cities have found that years before the big event they attract many more meetings and conventions than otherwise would select them. After the event there should also be a 'halo effect' attracting increased numbers, but it will fade over time. However, many external variables can interfere with induced demand, making it a risky proposition upon which to base forecasts of economic impacts. Kang and Perdue (1994) concluded that the 1988 Seoul Olympics did have a long-term, positive impact on tourist demand for Korea, and they believed this effect would be more pronounced for developing as opposed to established tourist destinations. A more long-run analysis of hosting mega events on tourism (including the Olympics) from 1950 to 2006, by Fourie and Santana-Gallego (2011), found that these events generally promote tourism but the periodicity (e.g. season in which they are held) affects the benefits.

Events and economic development

'Development' can mean economic growth, but it can just as easily refer to urban development and renewal, social and cultural development or sustainable development, with its heavy emphasis on environmental concerns. A number of paradigms, or schools of thought about development, have influenced government policies – including those pertaining to events.

'Modernization' refers to the process of becoming more like Western, industrialized societies through infrastructure development, industrialization and changing attitudes and patterns of work, a feature observed in the examples in Chapters 2 and 3. The all-too-eager development of tourism in many developing nations reflects a desire to be more modern, and tourism (generally requiring foreign investment and many economic concessions made to investors) has produced quick and obvious results. Mega events in particular fit into this approach because they are bold, globally communicated symbols of development. For example, Korea has effectively employed mega events in its modernization schemes (directed by central government) and China is following suit. China embarked on a very ambitious process of modernizing its industrial base, accompanied by airports, motorways, convention and exhibition centres and tourism resorts.

World's fairs were, right from the first, associated with modernization – both as a way for nations to show off their technological developments and to attract visitors to a special place that symbolized progress. Hosting international conventions and exhibitions is still viewed as a method for fostering trade and gaining valuable knowledge about economic development.

Dependency theorists stress the problems associated with development in developing countries, or poor regions within rich countries, typically by referring to 'core–periphery' models (for structural reasons, including foreign ownership, the core always dominates – see Page 1994 for a review of peripherality) and neocolonialism (economic power is exerted rather than direct military power, in order to keep developing areas subservient). In this approach, events can be viewed as the exploitation of host cultures, as part of the 'pleasure periphery' for rich foreigners, or as inappropriate users of precious local resources to further an unwanted development model where the former colonial powers are replaced by exploitative forms of development by these visitors (see Britton 1982 for a critical discussion of this concept).

Economic neoliberalism has been the dominant development paradigm since the 1970s, typified by less direct government involvement and an emphasis on freeing up market forces, as mentioned earlier with reference to leisure policy. The 'supply-side economics' of neoliberalism favours consumerism, free trade and private development, not government intervention or centralized planning. Taken to an extreme, the absence of government intervention will certainly result in inequities and problems, so what we see today is varying degrees of government involvement in the market. Critics of globalization argue that neoliberal policies result in the poor getting poorer and the rich getting richer, while local cultures and ways of life disappear.

In Canada and other countries neoliberal policies have resulted in less funding for the arts and events in general, a rise in corporate sponsorship and influence over the events sector, and quite possibly a decline in creativity because of the need for arts institutions and non-profits to stress commercially viable 'products'. An emphasis on tourism as industry, and events as new, competitive products, fits into the neoliberal way of thinking, so that any government funding is likely to be tied to specific Return on Investment (ROI) forecasts. The value of events in image development, place marketing and branding are aspects of neoliberal thinking.

Hall and Wilson (2011) point to the rise in neoliberalism in the public sector as a change to the relationship between the state and the private sector (i.e. the market). They argue that what constitutes the public good changes, whereby public-sector funding is used to benefit private-sector interests, with an expectation that this will have public benefits (e.g. in the subsidization of or support for major infrastructure projects such as stadia development).

Alternative development focuses on human needs and the human consequences of development, including concerns of gender equity, indigenous rights, physical, mental and social issues, and sustainable development.

Empowerment and local involvement, with an emphasis on the process of involving local people in development so they benefit, are hallmarks of this approach (Scheyvens 2002).

The 'triple-bottom-line' approach to event-tourism planning and impacts is a related concept. Hede (2007: 13) argued that 'the Triple Bottom Line (TBL) . . . borrowed from accounting and finance, amalgamates the social, economic, and environmental aspects of activities into one framework'. Within the context of special events, the TBL has been particularly linked to their evaluation. The considerable interest in developing 'green' events (Jones 2010) combined with the TBL fits within this paradigm.

A movement towards stressing the cultural and social value of events, and evaluations that treat these factors equally with economic impacts, may be one direction in which alternative thinking develops around state policy towards events in a post-modern society. For example, Whitford (2004a) argued that event policies in the Gold Coast and Brisbane, Australia, had city policies towards events which were predominantly underpinned by 'alternative', not classical economic development paradigms (namely modernization, dependency and neoliberalism). Whitford determined that these approaches were also becoming more widespread across Australia, using 'policy content analysis' to evaluate the internal and external factors influencing policy formation and contents, or the impacts of those policies. Indicators of an 'alternative' paradigm included the development of events not merely for tourism and branding, which is common in Australia and elsewhere, but for promoting cultural diversity, enhancing local ways of life and preserving heritage. Community development was another justification found in the Gold Coast and Brisbane for people's involvement in events. Whitford concluded that governments needed to be much more cognizant of the ideological focus within policies so that the goals and objectives of their event policies were better understood in terms of what they set out to achieve.

However, if an economic paradigm is as well established and accepted as neoliberalism has been in many countries, there is generally no such critical thinking. Rather, events, sports, the arts and business have all adapted to the new realities and compete on the basis of meeting the goals of neoliberalism or globalization. Paradigms change very slowly. Some very practical and valuable advice from Whitford is that researchers have to investigate the effectiveness of development-oriented policies that encompass events, so that policies are founded on fact, not dogma.

Claims made regarding the long-term, developmental benefits of mega events have to be treated with extreme caution. Research is seldom conducted longitudinally (see Chapter 3), and it is always going to be difficult to 'prove' that holding an event caused economic growth or social development. One thorough study, by Spilling (1998), concluded that the 1994 Winter Olympics in Lillehammer, Norway, had produced 'rather marginal' long-term impacts on the host region's economy. The benefits were largely confined to tourism, particularly for hosting new events! Spilling decided that the games could not be justified on economic grounds alone.

The economics of sustainability

There are substantial economic issues associated with any discussion of sustainability, or the related concepts of social responsibility, TBL and green events. In neoclassical economics, the world's natural resources are viewed as unlimited, or easily substituted through increased investment in capital or labour. We know this to be false, but it is extremely difficult to change the pro-growth paradigm that governs global economics. The most basic principle of sustainable economics is that natural resources (ie. the planet or global ecosystem and all things we call useful) should not be diminished. As articulated by Stallworth *et al*. (n.d.), 'The general consensus on sustainability among economists is based on the "constant capital rule" – the notion of living off interest or income and not consuming capital.' In so-called 'strong sustainability' there is no substitution for natural capital, it must be preserved. The 'precautionary principle' suggests that when in doubt, we act to conserve resources, not exploit them.

Hall (2012) scrutinized mega events from the perspectives of three frames of sustainability. In the economic approach, policy is narrowly focused on economic growth and image enhancement, with insufficient attention given to opportunity costs and long-term impacts. In the 'balanced' approach, Hall claims that little attention is given to equity issues and decisions to hold mega events are still largely based on purported economic gains. Third, in the 'steady-state' approach to sustainability, grounded in ecological considerations, more emphasis is given to natural capital and quality of life. In this paradigm, or world view, mega events are not justifiable. Hall concluded (2012: 129) that, 'Instead, sustainable events are more likely to be found in the smaller localized community based events that run over the longer-term or at least help maximize the use of existing infrastructure.'

Of course there are major impediments to implementing strong sustainability principles, not the least of which is the prevailing attitude that growth is necessary and good. However, also consider the case of energy and fossil fuels – can we continue to extract them until they are gone? If we do so, there will be a major cost relating to air quality and global warming, but (a) we continue to discover more oil and gas all the time (leading to a glut and cost reductions in 2014–2015) and (b) there will certainly be alternatives when they are gone – it's more a matter of cost than of a finite energy supply. There are very good reasons for events and tourism to strive for sustainability in all dimensions (the TBL), but exactly what is or is not sustainable will likely always be open to debate. The authors believe that 'sustainable events' is a matter of context, and that sustainable events or sustainable tourism is a process, not an end-state. We can always improve on the resource impacts associated with hosting events.

Justifying market intervention, or the subsidizing of events

Market economies are based on the premise that it is best to leave most decisions to independent firms and consumers, as government intervention usually results in distortions and often negative, unforeseen consequences. However, in the case of many policy fields – including social, environmental and cultural fields – intervention is frequently justified. In terms of economics, the following concepts are important in this context.

Market failure is a situation in which markets do not efficiently organize production or allocate goods and services to consumers, or where market forces do not serve the perceived public interest. It was frequently cited in Scotland by Scottish Enterprise as its justification for intervention around tourism, where perceived market failure existed and so state investment would help to address this imperfection, especially if it supported innovation (Franchetti and Page 2009). Mules and Dwyer (2006) noted that hospitality and travel firms cannot capture all of the benefits generated by events, so they will not fund them. Consequently, the tourism industry (through Destination Marketing Organizations – see Pike and Page 2014 for a detailed review) often funds events collectively, although this allows for 'free riders' who get benefits without paying. The free-rider problem is why the industry often asks for events to be publicly funded, because government tax revenue comes from every company.

If events of any type are deemed to be a 'public good', then free-market forces cannot be allowed to operate. These are goods from which everyone can simultaneously obtain benefits. Public goods retain the characteristics of 'non-rivalry' and 'non-excludability'. Non-rivalry means that one person's benefit does not reduce the benefit available to others, and non-excludability means that there is no effective way of excluding individuals from the benefit of the good, once it comes into existence (thereby creating the free-rider problem). Due to the free-rider problem, it is not profitable for a private firm to provide a public good.

Economic efficiency is a valid reason for bidding on and creating events, to the extent that they provide revenue or other tangible benefits for publicly owned and subsidized facilities and parks. To the extent that surplus capacity exists (i.e. resident use does not normally fill the venues) the marginal cost of producing events might be much less than the new income realized. Indeed, many facilities and parks are established with this tourist revenue in mind.

A related efficiency issue is that of attracting tourists to events. Andersson (2006) recommended creating surplus capacity in resident-oriented events in order to make it possible to attract tourists. This can often be done without imposing new costs on residents, and will likely generate tourist income that is of value to residents directly (through lower event charges for them) or indirectly (higher taxes for local authorities, and increased economic prosperity in the region).

Economic impacts of events

It is vital to distinguish between 'economic contribution', 'economic impacts' and 'net benefits' when evaluating events. As stressed by Dwyer *et al.* (2010: 11), 'It is widely acknowledged that both domestic and international tourism make an "economic contribution" to a destination, that tourism has positive and negative "economic impacts", and that it brings "benefits and costs" to a destination.' Event tourism can definitely bring new money into an area, but we must always ask at what cost, and who pays or benefits? Many studies have narrowly focused on the new money brought into a destination by tourism and have ignored the other crucial issues.

How is value created?

If we think in terms of an event 'industry', certain economic implications arise. First, economists will measure the economic value of the industry in such terms as jobs created, export earnings (i.e. through event tourism) or wealth created for residents. On the other hand, being an industry might suggest that government intervention is unwarranted and the private sector can take care of demand. Indeed, governments tend to want to meet basic needs, while industry aims to satisfy economic demands expressed through purchasing power. Governments are often big winners from events and tourism, depending upon what services and goods are taxed (e.g. hotels, restaurant meals and alcohol usually generate huge tax revenues) and which level of government gets the benefits.

Social and cultural value often require completely non-economic indicators of value, such as social integration and cultural development, although it is possible to employ the consumer surplus concept and willingness to pay method – or contingent valuation (see Andersson and Lundberg 2013; Armbrecht 2014) to estimate a monetary value for events or cultural institutions. Environmental value might be treated the same way, but in the context of events it is also possible to connect value to these efforts: awareness and education; recycling; energy and waste savings; reduced travel so as to generate a smaller carbon footprint; and positive monetary or labour efforts regarding conservation and restoration. The 'ecological footprint' method (see Collins and Flynn 2008; Collins *et al.* 2009) is a more complex method for estimating costs of events, but it can also be a value measure when applied to efforts to reduce an event's footprint.

Another important concept is that of 'externalities'. Normal, free-market economics often fails to take into account effects that are external to a specific business, exchange or event. For example, the air pollution, noise and accidents caused by traffic related to a tourist-oriented event are frequently excluded from an accounting of economic impact. They should, however, be included in a comprehensive evaluation of the costs and benefits of the event. The problems associated with assessing economic impacts of events are summarized in Events in Focus 4.1.

EVENTS IN FOCUS

4.1 Problems associated with the assessment of the economic impacts of events

Dwyer and Jago (2012: 130) identified three main types of criticisms associated with the assessment of the economic impacts of events:

In recent years, a growing number of researchers have been critical of the approach taken to assessing the economic contribution of special events. Three main types of criticism have been advanced:

1. Some argue that the economic contributions of events are often exaggerated. Many of the problems in event assessment arise due to exaggeration of event participant numbers and/ or their expenditure (Crompton and McKay 1994; Delpy and Li 1998). Only that proportion of expenditure which represents an injection of 'new money' into a destination is relevant to the calculation of the economic impacts. A number of critics (e.g. Porter 1999; Dwyer et al. 2000a, b; Matheson 2002; Matheson and Baade 2003; Crompton 2006) have highlighted inappropriate practices in event assessment (for example, inclusion of residents' expenditure as 'new money', exaggerating visitor numbers and expenditure, abuse of multipliers, inclusion of time switchers and casuals), as well as the tendency to ignore the various costs associated with special events, such as opportunity costs borne by the local community and displacement costs.

2. Other researchers have argued that the standard model used in event assessment needs a re-examination. Economic impact analysis involves estimating the additional expenditure generated by the event, and then using some form of economic model to estimate how this expenditure translates into increased income and employment in the destination. At issue is the relevance of Input-Output (I-O) modelling which, until recently, has been the standard technique for converting event expenditure data into economic impacts. These critics argue that the economic assessment models used for estimating the economic impacts of major events should reflect contemporary developments in economic analysis, particularly regarding the use of Computable General Equilibrium (CGE) modelling. They argue that in most cases, I-O modelling does not provide an accurate picture of the economic impacts of events and is thus incapable of informing event-funding agencies or governments of the 'return on investment' estimated from event funding (Dwyer et al. 2005, 2006a, b; Blake 2005; Madden 2006).

3. A third group of researchers argues that event assessment which focuses only on economic impacts is too narrow in scope to provide sufficient information to policy-makers and government funding agencies and that, where practical, a more comprehensive approach should be employed to embrace the importance of social and environmental impacts in addition to economic impacts. These critics highlight the potential importance of cost-benefit analysis (CBA) in event evaluation (Fleischer and Felsenstein 2002; Shaffer et al. 2003; Mules and Dwyer 2006; Jago and Dwyer 2006; Victorian Auditor General 2007; Dwyer and Forsyth 2009).

Source: Dwyer and Jago (2012: 130).

In Chapter 10 we return to many of the issues raised in this section related to the measurement of economic impacts and the question of benefits, costs and value; in Chapter 11 the related policy considerations are featured.

Management

Management is a very broad field of studies, with strong disciplinary connections to sociology, psychology and economics (Table 4.2). Four spheres of management that are applicable to events (profit, not-for-profit and governmental events, and the management of destinations which host events) have to be considered. Some will argue that management is a field of studies, not a discipline, because it is really the application of knowledge from a variety of disciplines. However, it is one of the crucial foundations of event studies and, unlike the other closely related professional fields that all have core phenomena, management applies to every field of human endeavour.

Business management

Many companies exist to produce or supply services to planned events, and they are profit-making businesses. We contend, however, that every event should be viewed as a business with the aim of making money. Money is needed to support the organization and improve the event, and it can be in the form of profit (to make individuals money) or 'surplus revenue' allocated to re-investment. If events are run as business propositions, it means that the owners/producers have to follow sound management principles and be focused on the long-term viability of the event. In other words, events need professional management to ensure their sustainability.

A business exists for several reasons, and if the event is seen as a business venture, the following factors apply:

- making money for those who invest in them (i.e. public or private 'enterprises');
- meeting needs or filling market gaps (i.e. consumers, sponsors and grant givers will pay for the event).

Table 4.2 Management

Management	Nature and meanings; the event experience	Antecedents to attending events	Planning and producing events	Outcomes and the impacted	Processes and patterns
Profit, not-for-profit, governmental and destination management	Consumerism (events as entertainment products)	Effectiveness of marketing	Project and strategic planning	The impacted as stakeholders	Evolution of management theory and practice
Theories of the firm	Commoditization of events	Image and branding	Management effectiveness and efficiency		Changes in factors that influence businesses and entrepreneurship (e.g. business development policy)
Institutional theory			Human resource management (managing people as resources and visitors)		
Management functions (leadership, organizing, leadership and planning)					Shifts in the competitive environment
Organizational ecology					

Neither of these criteria negates any social or cultural value attached to events. Indeed, many not-for-profit event organizations are established to create public goods or meet social needs, yet they still have to function as independent firms. Why do for-profit event-production companies exist, and why do not-for-profit event organizations occupy such an important place in the events sector? Each is a kind of firm, or independent organization that provides goods or services in exchange for money/resources.

Entrepreneurship can be explained in part by the following motivations, with examples specific to the events sector:

- independence (e.g. hands-on work; being one's own boss; escaping from the mundane; taking risks);
- creativity (e.g. pursuing an art or craft through events; the act of establishing something that has value and/or creates wealth; working with like-minded people);
- profit (getting rich, or just making a living).

Both private companies and not-for-profit event organizations are set up by 'entrepreneurs'. In either case they have to make a living. Many not-for-profit festival organizations, for example, are established by persons who want to create both an event and a career for themselves. In their case studies of Calgary festivals, for example, Getz *et al.* (2007) interviewed several festival creators who were clearly acting entrepreneurially, and without their initiative and leadership the events would not have existed.

Stokes (2014: 215) summarized the all-embracing role of the private sector in events:

> *At the macro-level, the vision and resources of corporate leaders impacts on both national and local portfolios of events. Sponsorship resources from the private sector and philanthropic contributions of business leaders provide a significant proportion of the funds needed to grow arts, sports and business events. Apart from the political and strategic leverage of corporate leaders and the provision of dollars through sponsorship and philanthropy, the private sector also brings entrepreneurial vision to the design and creation of events. Event organizers and promoters who are involved in staging, producing and marketing events make up a highly specialized industry globally that is gaining increased professionalism and credibility. At the micro-level, a complex network of businesses provide event-specific services (e.g. planners, promoters, venue owners/managers, entertainers, merchandise and licensing firms) while many others provide event-support services (travel and transport, tourist attractions, accommodation, retail and professional services). In effect, the private sector is both a recipient of revenue from events as well as the provider of direct and in-kind sponsorship.*

Figure 4.1 from Stokes (2014) illustrates the strategic and enabling role of the private sector in events, through destination-level inputs, event-specific inputs (e.g. event vision and concept creation), event planning, organization and management, the provision of event support services and event impact management and sustainability.

Tum (2014) adds to this, arguing that the main challenge of event management is in managing uncertainty. However, explaining the theoretical basis of the firm as an organizational structure for event management requires discussion of the key areas of management theory associated with how such organizations develop, function and can contribute to event development.

Resource-based theory of the firm

Firms and organizations should possess rare and valuable resources that give them sustainable competitive advantages by protecting against resource imitation, transfer, mobility or substitution (Penrose 1959; Barney 1991). Many events fall into the category of 'serial reproduction', where the same concept is replicated elsewhere. Applied to events, these rare and valuable resources could be intellectual capital

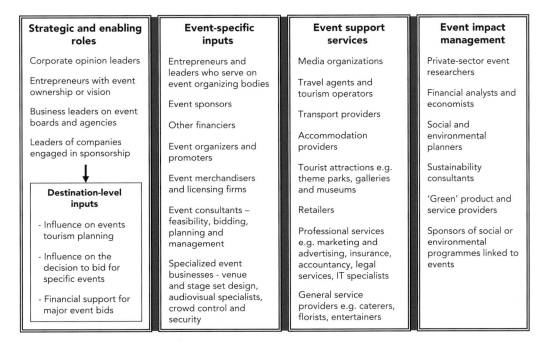

Figure 4.1 Roles and contributions of the private sector to events

Source: Stokes (2014: 219). Reprinted from *The Routledge Handbook of Events*, S. J. Page and J. Connell, Routledge (2014).

(creativity, knowledge), committed stakeholders (see 'stakeholder theory'), a special venue or an endowment, just as long as other events or organizations cannot do the same thing with their resources. Fostering innovation and maintaining authentic traditions are also vital in this context.

Knowledge-based theory of the firm

In this variation of the resource-based theory of the firm, organizations that possess, learn and retain valuable knowledge and capabilities, embedding them in their culture, management systems and stakeholder networks, can sustain competitive advantages and achieve superior performance (Barney 1991; Grant 1996). Information systems also provide advantages. Applied to events, managers should develop unique and inimitable knowledge or capabilities and make certain they are both retained and constantly developed. Consider, for example, the synergies to be gained through blending creative/artistic and business/management knowledge.

Stakeholder and network theory

'Stakeholder theory' (Freeman 1984; Donaldson and Preston 1995; Mitchell *et al.* 1997; Jawahar and McLaughlin 2001) helps explain the origins, operation and evolution of events, and provides direction to owners and managers on how to manage their internal and external stakeholder relationships (Izzo *et al.* 2012). Stakeholders are those persons or groups who can influence the organization, or are influenced by it. Core stakeholder attributes, according to Mitchell *et al.* (1997: 865–867), are:

- 'Power': 'The ability of a party that it has or can gain access to impose its will in the relationship.'
- 'Legitimacy': 'A generalized perception or assumption that the actions of an entity are desirable, proper, or appropriate within some socially constructed system of norms, values, beliefs, and definitions.'

- 'Urgency': 'The degree to which stakeholder claims call for immediate attention.'
- 'Stakeholder salience': is a function of possessing the other three stakeholder attributes: power, legitimacy and urgency.

There is also a moral aspect to stakeholder theory, which argues that managers should also work with all those affected by the organization, as in the case of events working with their community and special interest groups (Ziakis and Costa 2010b), regardless of their power to influence the organization.

Using the analogy of a 'political market square', Larson and Wikstrom (2001) and Larson (2002) examined several Swedish events. Stakeholders played 'power games' and negotiated from varying positions of power. They formed alliances to realize their goals for the event and the organization producing it. Critical roles identified among the stakeholders included those of 'gatekeeping' (deciding who gets in), negotiation, coalition-building, trust- or legitimacy-building, and identity-building for the event in general. Larson (2009b) later analysed event networks and concluded that they resulted in three different categories of Political Market Squares, which she labelled the jungle, the park and the garden; these represented tumultuous (i.e. jungle), dynamic and institutionalized event networks. The institutionalized network (i.e. the park) was often prescribed for stable event organizations. Larson called for more research on understanding tumultuous and dynamic event networks.

Merrilees *et al.* (2005) used stakeholder theory to analyse how the Goodwill Games were 'branded' in Brisbane, Australia. In this instance, building trust and legitimacy was crucial. Miffling and Taylor (2007) employed stakeholder theory in assessing the success of a youth-oriented event. To sustain itself in the long term, the organization has to manage its stakeholder relationships effectively, and if successful it might become a permanent 'institution' in its community. This means it has the support it needs to survive crises and to solve the social problems it exists for (Getz *et al.* 2007). In another application of stakeholder theory, Spiropoulos *et al.* (2006) examined the 20th Greek Festival of Sydney. The stakeholder environment of this event was closely tied to ethnicity, which suggests the value of examining social networks.

'Network theory' is closely related to stakeholder theory. 'Social networks' are often important for entrepreneurs, especially when obtaining the resources and support required to start an event. 'Social capital' in this sense means the network of people and organizations you can rely on to help you. Organizational networks obviously involve all the stakeholders, but there is an emphasis in network theory on 'centrality' as an attribute, their degree of 'connectedness' and 'bridging' organizations.

Prebensen (2010) examined value creation that arises from a result of stakeholders' participation, using network and co-creation frameworks. The study analysed seven stakeholder groups and their purposes for, and structures in, joining an event in the High North of Norway. In addition, the study examined the stakeholders' evaluation of values created through their own and others' participation in the event (i.e. value co-creation). The stakeholders include both organizations and individuals. The findings reveal that the various groups entail numerous reasons for participating in the event, classified as autotelic and instrumental value experiences.

4.1 RESEARCH NOTE ON STAKEHOLDERS AND NETWORKS

Izzo, F., Bonetti, E. and Masiello, B. (2012). Strong ties within cultural organization event networks and local development in a tale of three festivals. *Event Management*, 16(3), 223–244.

(This paper was recipient of the second biennial Donald Getz Award for Outstanding Research in Planned Events. The paper was selected from hundreds of submissions by a blue-ribbon panel of international scholars chaired by the editor-in-chief of *Event Management*, an international journal. The recipients received a financial award of $500.00 from the publisher of *Event Management*,

Mr Robert Miranda of Cognizant Communications Corp. The Getz Award was established in 2010 at Queen Margaret University by the International Centre for the Study of Planned Events, under the leadership of Professor Joe Jeff Goldblatt).

'In particular, this study addresses two research questions. First, how does network structure affect the success of the event and its outcomes on local development, other than in economic terms? Second, which main capabilities does the 'network orchestrator' need to promote the effectiveness of the event network? By analyzing three different Italian cultural festivals – 'Festivaletteratura' ('Festival of Literature' – Mantua), 'Festival della Scienza' ('Festival of Science' – Genoa), and 'Festivalfilosofia' ('Festival of Philosophy' – Modena, Carpi, Sassuolo) – this article sheds light on: (a) the features of successful event networks, (b) the dynamics linking network structure and the social outcomes generated, and (c) the typical bundle of relational capabilities that network orchestrators need. Then we draw some implications for management and offer some remarks to stimulate further research in the field of special events.'

Collaboration theory

Collaboration theory relates to how various stakeholders get together in partnerships, alliances or other joint efforts (see Wood and Gray 1991; Jamal and Getz 1995). In true collaborations each partner gives up some degree of control to work with others in achieving common goals. For example, events form professional associations which can be called alliances, but generally do not give up any independence in doing so. Events can partner with other events or with tourist organizations for joint marketing, again without giving up any real power. But if events agree to work closely with each other, perhaps sharing offices, staff and resources, this collaboration entails a loss of independence and poses some risks that must be balanced against the gains.

Most often collaborations work in 'policy domains' such as tourism and culture, or for major projects. Long (2000), for example, studied co-operation between tourism and the arts developed for the UK Year of Visual Arts. These were contractual and short-lived, as opposed to more permanent federations. Long concluded that lessons from this and other examples of collaboration and partnership can be applied to relationships with sponsors, reconciling goals, achieving economic efficiencies or dealing with political interests. Stokes (2004) examined inter-organizational relations of public-sector events organizations in Australia, where all states have events development companies or departments. She identified the relationships and knowledge used in event strategies, and identified the importance of shared knowledge as an incentive for participating in networks. Stakeholders include community representatives, public-sector managers such as events and tourism agencies, corporate leaders, events managers and tourism industry suppliers. Where stakeholders obtain and transfer knowledge about event tourism was mapped. Key elements in 'sociospatial knowledge networks' are activity spaces, place inventories and information nodes. A corporate orientation among stakeholders mostly applied at the state level, where emphasis was on tourism development such as bidding on major events. There was more of a community orientation at the regional level, as tourism-related outcomes were considered. For staging major events formal alliances and collaborations were created, but not for strategy in general.

Resource dependency theory

All firms require resources, but some are better at getting and holding them. Success is defined, in this context, as maximizing the organization's power (Pfeffer and Salancik 1978; Pfeffer 1981), which can come from reducing one's own dependency or making others dependent on you. Firms lacking essential resources will seek relationships that provide them, resulting in dependency. This is a form of 'social exchange theory' and it seems to work well for events faced with competition for scarce resources and uncertainty in resource availability.

Event failures might arise from a poor 'fit' with the environment, as in the case where a festival is not able to attract interest and support from its host community because of cultural differences, a lack of key contacts or internal management deficiencies. According to Donaldson (1996), 'fit' stems from how an organization adapts to accommodate environmental contingencies. Additional considerations relate to the scarcity of resources (what are the alternative sources?), the nature of the event's operational environment (competition or symbiotic relationships among resource users?), certainty versus fluctuations in resource availability (e.g. is long-term support guaranteed?) and variability in resource needs (are the same resources needed every year?).

To deal with these resource issues a number of strategies are available. Events can attempt to secure resources from many sources, store resources for hard times (i.e. a reserve fund) or switch to new resource suppliers. They can try to reduce their need (e.g. cost reductions), influence the resource providers (e.g. through policy lobbying) or decide to work with, or compete against, other organizations seeking resources.

This theory has been used together with stakeholder theory by Getz *et al.* (2007) to help explain both failure and the institutionalization of events. Other ecological and institutional theories of organizations also view the organization or firm in terms of its internal dynamics, environmental interdependencies and competing interests. Andersson and Getz (2007) examined the financial position of a tourism-oriented street festival in Sweden within the context of resource dependency and stakeholder management theory. Using data from a five-year period, they revealed how costs associated with the strongest stakeholders (that is, with the greatest bargaining power) greatly increased relative to costs associated with weak stakeholders. The festival was also more able to increase its revenues from weak stakeholders than from those in strong bargaining positions.

Competitive and comparative advantages

A 'comparative advantage' means that some events or event organizations have been endowed with better resources or appeal. This advantage could be in terms of support from their communities, which is a stakeholder issue, or in terms of their location. It could consist of 'tradition' or 'authenticity'. 'Competitive advantages' accrue from wise management of whatever you possess, such as by providing target segments with services (events) that they are willing to pay for, and doing it better than competitors. Adapting Porter's (1980) classic model of competitive forces, many events are revealed to be in a relatively weak position. An event has to first assess its competitive environment as to threats: it is generally easy to set up events so that competition is always likely to increase, and events are often substitutable by other events or other forms of entertainment and marketing. Both buyers (companies and customers) can go elsewhere unless there are few events or event-producing firms available. So how should events compete?

Porter's strategies for achieving and sustaining competitive advantage include a focus on costs (keeping costs low and passing savings on to the buyer), focusing on specific target markets, or on differentiation (being unique within the events sector). Competing on price is possible for events, even if their costs are high, when subsidies and sponsorship support are available to compensate. Competing through differentiation makes a lot of sense, but unfortunately numerous events exist for rather general purposes and many producers find it difficult to target in a narrow sense.

In event studies, little attention has been given to competitiveness among events or event companies, particularly how this manifests itself geographically where different regions host events that compete and may split market shares. Research on this important topic has to connect with stakeholder, institutional and population ecology theory, as well as with marketing and positioning strategy.

Agency theory

In 'agency theory' we consider how owners and managers/contractors interact. 'It is assumed that both parties are motivated by self-interest, and that these interests may diverge' (Scott 2001: 105). Sometimes managers know more about what is going on than owners; an example of this situation is when staff are intimately involved in an event and directors are remote. This results in 'information asymmetry' and the owners have to initiate inspections or incentives to ensure their policies are implemented. A central question raised by agency theory is: *do managers or subcontractors always act in the best interests of those who retained their services?* What if event managers ran their events to make more money, or preserve job security for themselves, rather than to meet the aims of the founders or key resource suppliers? This problem can arise in other situations, such as an event put out to tender by a government agency, or a charity hiring a production company to raise money through events.

There are other potential applications of agency theory in event studies. It relates to organizational culture and the role of founders and leaders (do they always get their way?). The processes of professionalization, bureaucratization and institutionalization might very well increase agency problems as more and more managers become involved and possibly begin to feel the event exists for their personal or collective benefits.

Organizational ecology theory

This theory, or interrelated group of theory fragments (Hannan *et al.* 2007), looks at whole 'populations' of organizations within their environment. While most management theory teaches that sound practice and adaptive strategies can ensure success, ecological models suggest that organizations are also likely to succeed or fail in response to environmental factors. The dynamics of populations of festivals and events must be considered, as well as the efforts of individual event organizations.

Seminal works in organizational ecology include: Hannan and Freeman (1977, 1984); Carroll (1984); Hannan and Carroll (1992); and Baum (1996). The original question posed by Hannan and Freeman (1977) was: why are there so many forms of organization? Looking back at the subsequent research efforts, Carroll and Hannan (2000) concluded that, clearly, organizational diversity has important consequences for individuals and social structures.

Ecological theory seeks to explain the rates of birth, growth and mortality of a 'population' of organizations in any given environment. Baum (1996) noted that all such theories begin with three observations. First, diversity is a property of aggregates of organizations, not of specific organizations. Second, organizations often have difficulty changing fast enough to adapt to uncertain environmental conditions. Third, organizations arise and disappear regularly, like the birth and death of animals.

Populations of events

In nature, a 'population' is defined by its 'species', as in the human population, but not so in organizational ecology. Baum and Oliver (1996) describe the concept of a population as follows:

> *A set of organizations engaged in similar activities and with similar patterns of resource utilization constitutes a population. Populations form as a result of processes that isolate or segregate one set of organizations from another, including technological incompatibilities and institutional actions such as government regulations.*

In other words, we should not assume that all festivals, or all periodic sport events, are alike, because they might have quite different activities (or services offered) and resource dependencies. The vast diversity of festival forms and styles (e.g. performing and visual arts, humour, spectacle, rituals, commemorations), variations arising from ownership (profit, non-profit, public) and differences attributable to size and location all make it very difficult to view them as a single 'species'. It might make more sense to consider performing arts festivals as a species, and other festivals as close cousins, but this analogy means little in practical terms.

There are two perspectives on events that make them resemble a single population, for both public policy and tourism-industry strategy. This is because the variations among festivals are not as important when considering what festivals can do for policy and strategy, from social marketing to place marketing. As instruments of policy, events are fit into 'portfolios' (see Getz 2005; Ziakis 2013) that must meet specified goals and account for their resources, especially if public money has been provided to them. Within a whole population of events in a given area it might not matter if single events fail or change in some dramatic way, but within a managed portfolio it might cause a serious problem.

Within ecological theory, individual organisms (i.e. events) share space and resources with other organizational populations and the dynamics of this 'community' affects all its members. For example, festivals might have to share venues and grants with other cultural institutions and tourist attractions. 'Communities' are those species sharing the same 'ecosystem', which can be defined as a city or nation. The ecosystem analogy could take on a number of interesting dimensions when applied to festivals or events. Many interactions with their environment can be analysed, not the least of which must be stakeholder relationships, marketing, ownership and decision-making.

Managed portfolios of events

In a tourism context, the idea of a managed portfolio of events is to develop and manage events as destination assets, although the same concept applies to a venue, company or agency. The key is to shift emphasis from single events (through bidding and the marketing of existing events) to multiple events managed strategically. According to Getz (2013a: 23), 'A full portfolio will consist of various types of events, for different target markets, held in different places, and at different times of the year, in pursuit of multiple goals.' Portfolio management enables longer-term strategies to prevail, thereby fostering sustainability of the events sector, and it facilitates synergies such as enhanced economic benefits and the fostering of social and cultural capital. 'In a portfolio approach the types of events, and their host or owners, will often be of less importance than the cumulative effects' (Getz 2013a: 23). Although it is likely that competition for events through bidding will remain intense, if portfolio thinking prevails there will be more attention paid to the long-term, sustainable values obtained by creating and supporting hallmark events that are co-branded with destinations, as well as a range of highly targeted, iconic events for special interest groups.

Ziakis (2013: 14), in *Event Portfolio Planning and Management: A Holistic Approach*, defined a managed portfolio in the following manner:

> *An event portfolio is the strategic patterning of disparate but interrelated events taking place during the course of a year in a host community that as a whole is intended to achieve multiple outcomes through the implementation of joint event strategies.*

This view on portfolios seeks to integrate tourism with other policy domains, and is therefore a broader conceptualization. Synergies can be fostered between economic, social and environmental policies through events.

Key concepts within organizational ecology

A basic step is to measure and keep track of 'vital statistics', that is, the demographics of the population. These data are seldom available, mainly because no agency keeps track of new events such as births, deaths, failure, growth rates and the overall health of the population (we will look at 'health' later). Unless there are policies and goals, the overall population and its health do not even become issues in most areas.

STRUCTURAL INERTIA

Organizational ecologists make a strong case that organizations tend towards 'structural inertia' – that is, they cannot adapt to changing conditions, and that is a major reason for failure. Change in the population therefore occurs through (in part) 'selection', a natural process of winnowing those organizations that do not hold a viable niche or which cannot adapt to change. Indeed, a case has been made that society imposes strong demands on organizations for accountability, and rewards reliability and predictability, thereby increasing the tendency towards inertia. The key concept here, in line with institutional theory, is that organizations must occupy a niche that ensures them resources and support.

COMPETITION VERSUS COOPERATION

Research supports the position that, in common with other non-profit sectors, most festivals and events would gain by pursuing a strategy of collaboration and sharing, however difficult this might be to implement. The barriers arise from the very nature of the sector, which is often dominated by small and volunteer-managed organizations. As an example of empirical support, Baum and Oliver (1996: 1421) found that the comparative success of the non-profit sector resulted in part because:

1. non-profits were more inclined to cooperate than compete, facilitating their expansion;
2. non-profits' greater social legitimacy made them more formidable competitors, impeding the expansion of for-profits; and
3. non-profits invested in institutional links that stimulated further non-profit growth.

Many event managers do not believe they compete directly with other events or institutions, but this is a fallacy. Within organizational ecology theory, the ecosystem has a finite resource base and the community or different organizations tend towards growth until limits are reached. The study of how events compete for resources, including audiences, sponsors, grants and audiences, is in its infancy, with evidence to date coming from research on festival management and stakeholders.

AGE DEPENDENCE

According to this theory, there is a greater risk of failure when an organization is either new or old. Older, more generalized organizations have a better chance of survival because the reliability of their performance encourages others to supply resources. The contrary position is that as periodic events age, there is an increased risk of obsolescence, in a competitive sense, and of senescence (or managerial failure), often due to complacency or a conservative culture that resists adaptation or resists compromise, which is needed to secure stakeholder support. New event organizations will often have a difficult time getting adequate resources and learning how to survive. When events can be set up in a free-market environment, as opposed to a heavily regulated setting, it seems likely that many will begin, without adequate resources, to survive a crisis. A key variable is the initial endowment or committed resources available to the event – how long can it last without becoming financially self-sufficient? Many festivals do expire, and failure is often linked directly to inadequate resources.

NICHE THEORY

Within an ecosystem, a 'niche' is occupied by a species that has evolved in such a way that it has a competitive advantage in securing particular resources. But in organizational ecology a single entity can also occupy a niche. The festival that occupies a 'narrow' niche is a 'specialist' organization that maximizes its exploitation of the environment by catering to a narrow audience or relying on one or a few key resources suppliers. They are often successful as institutions, but risk failure from unpredicted changes in the environment, such as new government policy. On the other hand, 'generalist' events work strategically to secure resources from many sources, to become financially self-sufficient and to avoid over-dependency. They usually prefer many small sponsors to one or a few big corporate supporters. They try to balance grants, sponsorships, ticket sales and other income. Generalist organizations accept a lower level of exploitation in return for greater security (Hannan and Freeman 1977: 948). If environmental forces are subject to frequent change, the sustainable event will want to become a generalist. 'Niche width' defines the resource or market space an organization could potentially occupy, if environmental conditions change. For example, do specialist organizations have any more resources to draw upon, or audiences to tap, if they face financial threats?

RESOURCE PARTITIONING

This concept relates to generalist versus specialist organizations. It makes predictions about founding and mortality rates among organizations as a function of market concentration, with generalist and specialist organizations sometimes being able to separate themselves – in effect partitioning the available resources. Carroll concluded that 'more available resources should translate into better chances of success for specialists when they operate in the more concentrated market' (Carroll 1985: 1272). Archibald (2007) found that for both commercial and non-commercial organizations, control of resource niches is important. A few large generalist organizations in a population tend to use all a sector's resources, but this leaves room for specialist organizations. In the context of events, both the human population and its economic prosperity must be considered, as cities should offer more opportunities for specialization.

DENSITY DEPENDENCE

This theory postulates that vital rates in the population are a function of the number of entities (i.e. events) in an area (Hannan and Freeman 1977). As density increases, there is likely to be an increase in both 'legitimation' (i.e. the process of festival/event creation is accepted as being natural) and competition for resources, which are opposing forces. At higher densities, the competition force is hypothesized to be stronger, thereby leading to reduced founding rates and higher mortality rates. This dynamic tension is suggested to result in an inverted U-shaped curve to describe founding rates (i.e. new, start-up events) and a normal U-shaped curve to describe mortality rates, over time. It also seems appropriate to consider how Butler's (1980) notion of 'critical limits to growth', from his destination life-cycle model, might apply in terms of whole populations of organizations. This has been added to Figure 4.2, providing a hypothetical model of event development within a given environment.

Alternatively, it can be hypothesized that in some environments (say, in a city with a proactive policy to grow the festival sector), resources available to festivals can be deliberately increased (e.g. more grant money) or competition decreased (through collaboration), thereby resulting in a temporal extension of the U-shaped curve and a larger event population. In that kind of facilitating, supportive environment, individual event organizations might also have a greater chance of both growth and institutionalization.

RELATIONAL DENSITY AND NETWORK THEORY

An additional element of organizational ecology theory is the concept of 'relational density' (Baum and Oliver 1992), which refers to the number of links tying organizations to institutions in the environment. This is also called 'embeddedness' in institutional theory, and is related to social network theory. An example of high relational density would be the city in which government policy seeks to grow and nurture the festival sector, resulting in more formal and stronger links between festival organizations, between the festival sector and politicians, and possibly between those key stakeholder groups and corporate sponsors and other grant givers. There has been little work undertaken on whole populations of events, and theory development utilizing organizational ecology as a framework for event studies is only beginning. In Research Notes 4.2 work from Norway on festival populations reveals a number of unique considerations, but also tends to support density dependence theory.

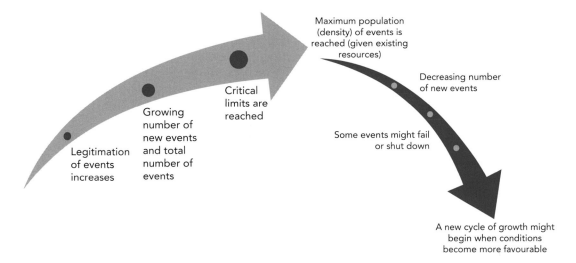

Figure 4.2 Organizational ecology – density dependence

Note: Adapted from Hannan and Freeman (1977) and Butler (1980).

4.2 RESEARCH NOTES ON THE STUDY OF A WHOLE POPULATION OF FESTIVALS

Jaeger, K. and Mykletun, R. (2009). The festivalscape of Finnmark. *Scandinavian Journal of Hospitality and Tourism*, 9(2/3), 327–348.

'The diversity of festivals in Finnmark, Norway, was researched with the aim of creating a festival map of the county's Festivalscape. Data were collected by questionnaires to the registered festival managers. It was concluded that Finnmark is a festive county where 72,000 people share close to 60 festivals arranged annually in 19 municipalities across the county. The festivals were categorized as either music, arts, sports or market festivals; however, the largest group were named thematic festivals, as they are each built around rather unique themes, thus representing a diverse example of festival variety and creativity. Even so, live music and food sales are found at most festivals, and all festivals have more than one main activity.'

Andersson, T., Getz, D. and Mykletun, R. (2013). Sustainable festival populations: An application of organizational ecology. *Tourism Analysis*, 18, 621–634.

'Data from whole populations of festivals in three Norwegian counties were examined. Analyses of festival start-ups demonstrated that the number of events in each county had risen faster than population growth before plateauing, and changes were correlated significantly with trends in the Norwegian gross domestic product. Data on festival age, theme and other variables were also considered in the light of whole population dynamics. It was concluded that the fundamental tenets of density dependence theory were empirically demonstrated insofar as rapid growth in the festival populations was not sustainable when resources diminished, but no data were available on festival failures. It appears that the hypothetical legitimation of festivals helps to explain rapid growth, as festivals became popular instruments of public policy.'

What is a healthy population of festivals?

The coming and going of festivals and events is often ignored, especially in countries where a free market is assumed and many players are at work in this sector – from diverse government agencies and non-profits to corporate sponsors and for-profit event companies. However, the growing exploitation of events for place marketing, tourism development and many social/cultural policy initiatives, means that festivals and events are coming under increased scrutiny, both individually and collectively. The question then arises, do we have a healthy population or portfolio of events in our area? Is there a need for strategy and/or intervention?

A population has to be able to sustain itself, given available resources. This might result in growth or decline as necessary, or as judged to be appropriate. In times of resource scarcity, adjustments to population size will have to be made consciously or through natural selection (i.e. the weak will be allowed to perish). A directed or coordinated open-system of organizations has to be able to adjust to its environment – or if possible influence external forces – in such a way as to sustain equilibrium, that is, the level of resource consumption that will keep it healthy. This might require planned adjustments to population size, or a reduction in resource consumption by all members.

However, festivals and other event-producing organizations are typically not able to achieve population equilibrium because they are not coordinated, nor is their sector directed by any agency. Owing to the special nature of festivals as manifestations of fundamental social, cultural and economic needs, and as instruments of policy and strategy, the health of festival populations requires additional and essentially goal-dependent considerations. Other periodic events, mainly sports in terms of numbers, can be given similar treatment insofar as they implement event-tourism policy and strategy or sport development and human health.

The International Festivals and Events Association (IFEA) (http://www.ifea.com/p/industryawards/worldfestivalandeventcityaward) annually awards 'festival city' status, and its evaluative criteria suggest what it takes to sustain a healthy population of events. Their main criteria are:

- Community overview: population; venues available and their capacity; infrastructure and parking availability; tourist numbers attributed to events.
- Community festivals and events: numbers, types and dates; budgets; sponsorship support; volunteer numbers and hours worked; attendance; target markets and numbers achieved; awards received; professionals with certification.
- City/governmental support of festivals and events: policies and support programmes; direct funding given; city roles and process in approval of events; coordination.
- Participation by city/politicians in events; regulations affecting events; training provided.
- Non-governmental community support of festivals and events: volunteer involvement in the event sector; total sponsorship provided; media support; support from DMO, Chamber of Commerce and other organizations; incentives to events from venues; access to local suppliers; direct industry involvement in the events sector.
- Leveraging 'community capital' created by festivals and events, such as: branding; tourism marketing; corporate recruiting; media coverage and public relations; enhancing exposure to the arts; encouraging social integration or celebration; better use of facilities or parks; long-term legacies of events.
- Extra credit for actions such as: skills development; availability of certificate or degree programmes in event management; sharing among festivals; efforts to recruit new events to the city.

Public administration

Our discussion of public policy and law in this book represents aspects of public administration. Governments do not have to obey the laws of the marketplace, such as supply and demand. They can create and subsidize events for a multitude of reasons, and not worry about profits or break-event points. Our discussion of 'public goods', 'equity' and 'failure of the marketplace' provides the justification.

Since many events are produced by, or subcontracted by, government departments and agencies, some attention to public administration is required in event studies. If the event functions as a programme within a governmental agency, then it is clearly an instrument of policy. Under some circumstances the event could be managed as an enterprise, either to make money or at least break even, in which case it has to operate like a business. This often means that a standalone event organization or division of a public-sector body is created to handle the event activity, with clear legal parameters of what it can do and its remit for event development and management.

Not-for-profit management

Festivals and sport events are often produced by not-for-profit organizations that are either in existence for other reasons, or are set up specifically to manage the event (see Ruperto and Kerr 2009; Edwards 2012). 'Not-for-profit' is a more accurate term than 'non-profit' to describe them, because they can make surplus revenue (and should aim to) but must use it to sustain and improve the organization and their events. Grant writing, fundraising, governance issues (especially with volunteer boards), service provision, needs assessments, volunteer recruitment and management and programme evaluation are topics of particular interest in this sector as well as not-for-profit marketing (see Taylor and Shanka 2008). Another relevant concept in terms of not-for-profit events is the notion of social entrepreneurship and population ecology (especially related to social movements). Social entrepreneurship has a focus on not-for-profit objectives where the wider issues of community and population well-being assume a greater role than a simple focus on profit.

Destination management

Destinations are really 'policy domains', defined for specific purposes of tourism marketing, and comprising the '4As' of attractions, accommodation, accessibility and ancillary services represented by the diverse range of stakeholders and organizations that coalesce to form the tourism sector. Events can be classified as attractions if they animate the destination as Connell *et al.* (2015) noted. There is a considerable debate about whether the organizations often created by public-sector bodies, collaborative public–private partnerships or private-sector organizations in fact 'manage' destinations as postulated by Pike and Page (2014), who argued that 'The term management implies control, and the authors here argue that very few DMOs have either the mandate or resources to effectively manage their destination even though stakeholders in the broader tourism industries.'

DMOs are usually limited in what they can achieve in terms of management, with many practical and logistical issues being controlled by local authorities (e.g. car parking, street cleaning, waste removal, control of crowds and visitors by the police during special events, and environmental issues) (Pike and Page 2014: 204). Consequently, these organizations predominantly market the destination and have a wider liaison role in 'management'.

Destination management is rather unique, because its exists for both public good (economic development) and private gain (members or partners such as hotels) to improve the competitiveness of the destination. As event tourism is now so well established, and globally competitive, how destinations plan, bid for, and in some cases produce and manage events is of considerable interest in event studies. The following Research Note 4.3 illustrates how destination marketing organizations view events.

4.3 RESEARCH NOTE ON LEVERAGING EVENTS

O'Brien, D. (2005). Event business leveraging: The Sydney 2000 Olympic Games. *Annals of Tourism Research*, 33(1), 240–261.

Business Club Australia was established to foster business networking and international trade development surrounding the 2000 Summer Olympic Games. O'Brien reported that accumulated knowledge was being institutionalized and applied in other event situations. The steps taken by the Club included generating public- and private-sector support for networking, and facilitation of networking between Australian businesses and visiting international business leaders (or politicians) before, during and after the event. Australians had to be convinced that the benefits of the event could be spread throughout the country.

Institutional theory and 'institutionalization'

Within organizations, 'institutional theory' refers to processes by which rules and norms become guidelines or controllers of behaviour. For example, how does an event's approach to stakeholder relationship management become 'institutionalized' over many years? This ties in with organizational culture and social network theory, with direct relevance to planning, decision-making, coordination and control systems. However, we are more interested here in what an 'institution' is, and how an event can become one.

Regarding the organization as an 'institution', Scott (2001) suggested that it is a social structure with a great deal of resilience; it provides meaning to social life, connotes stability and is taken for granted. Others believe an institution has to exist for a specific purpose, which is to achieve important societal goals or solve crucial societal problems.

The following criteria appear to be important factors determining event institutionalization, and should be tested through a variety of comparative research studies on different types of events:

- An event that is an 'institution' solves important social problems or meets important community goals.
- Society or the community cannot be without it – failure is unthinkable.
- Permanence is taken for granted.
- Support is assured – sponsors and agencies will always give it money.
- It is highly visible – everyone knows about it – the event has a strong, positive brand.
- It is expert in managing its stakeholder relationships.
- Key stakeholders have been internalized.

Fuller understanding of institutionalization also requires linkage with population ecology, resource theories of the firm and stakeholder theory. Chapter 9 explains the process in more detail.

Critical success factors for managing events

Is there a formula for event success, or at least a well-established list of critical success factors (CSFs)? Such a formula would be great, but experience is probably necessary to ensure the success of any venture, and researchers have not come up with a universal recipe. What works in one situation might not work in another, and over time conditions always change – a feature observed by Connell *et al.* (2015) in relation to visitor attractions and how they use events to extend the season in Scotland.

One attempt to develop CSFs through research was conducted by Jordan (2006), based on a study of planning for the Cricket World Cup of 2007, which was held in the West Indies. Her factors pertained to executive management (decision-making and project planning), collaboration and communication, community participation and involvement, and learning from past mistakes. Joliffe *et al.* (2008) also identified CSFs for a new event: community involvement; new partnerships and alliances in trade and tourism; branding of coffee and the destination; media coverage; new product (tours); and building business for local enterprises. A major goal of researchers is to aid managerial and planning decisions, in an effort to increase the likelihood of success. But this can never be assured by following a formula. That is why we have concepts and theories that can inform and guide, but cannot be employed deterministically.

Political science

Political science is the theory and practice of politics, political systems and political behaviour. Political scientists study government and its processes, public institutions, power and policy-making, politics, intergovernmental and international relations (see Table 4.3). 'Political philosophy', on the other hand, is more concerned with values and political ideas, such as the differences between Marxism and capitalism, or the meanings of rights and justice (from *Encyclopaedia Britannica Online*).

According to Hall (2014: 186–187),

> *politics is about power: who gets what, where, how and why . . . The conception of politics and the political is important because it shapes the questions that researchers do or do not consider as well as assumptions made when undertaking research . . . Some of the most widely used definitions of politics are:*
> - *Politics is the exercise of power.*
> - *Politics is the public allocation of things that are valued.*
> - *Politics is the resolution of conflict.*
> - *Politics is the competition among individuals and groups pursuing their own interests.*
> - *Politics is the determination of who gets what, when, and how.*

As Hall (2014) suggests, each of these different definitions revolves around the notion of actors (individuals, interest groups, and public and private organizations) each of whom are involved in a struggle for power. Hall (2014) points to the relative lack of research on the politics of events, aside from his seminal studies on politics and events (Hall 1989b, 1992) and the politics of tourism in which events also feature

Table 4.3 Political science

Political science	Nature and meanings; the event experience	Antecedents to attending events	Planning and producing events	Outcomes and the impacted	Processes and patterns
The study of governments, public policies and political behaviour	Events may take on political significance Attendance can be a political statement	Political motives to attend or stay away	Creating events as a political statement (e.g. protest; party loyalty; nationalism) Government policy and programmes re: events	Effects on politics, government, political parties and law	How politics and policies influence event development and attendance

(Hall 1994a). There are many political reasons for staging events, and politics often influences their management and marketing. Ideological reasons lie behind many mega events, wherein the dominant power in society seeks to demonstrate and reinforce its values, or to win support (Hall 1994a).

In many countries there are substantial, party-based differences in approaches to policy that impinge on the events sector. These are generally rooted in philosophy and traditional voting bases, such as Labour versus Conservative, but they also express the more mundane necessity of opposing the party in power. It is always worth asking if a 'party-political platform' reflects fundamental philosophical differences between parties, or if the opposition is simply trying to appear to be different. One might expect, for example, that a left-leaning party would stress equity issues and government interventions, such as making the arts accessible to everyone, while right-leaning parties would stress free-market economics and privatization.

Government intervention in the events industry is often justified, for reasons discussed previously (i.e. public goods and failure of the marketplace). But these arguments can disguise underlying political motivations, such as getting re-elected, spreading party-specific values (this is correctly termed 'propaganda') or catering to interest groups that support the party in question. As examples, Baker and Rowe (2014) focused on multiculturalism and the need for events to pay attention to this growing global trend, while Allen and Cochrane (2014) debated the corporatist politics surrounding London's hosting of the 2012 Olympic Games and the more place-specific politics manifested locally.

Interest groups and elites

Who supports public involvement with events, and why?, is a question too infrequently asked. Often the answer is disturbing, because getting the government to produce, subsidize or bid on events obviously benefits some more than others. The tourism industry benefits directly when major events are produced, but the arguments put forward in support of mega-event bids typically emphasize the public goods such as more jobs, economic development, new infrastructure and enhanced civic pride.

It is usually easy to identify the elite groups, or at least their interests with regard to events and particularly related to the decisions made concerning the bidding on and hosting of major events. For sports, elite athletes and the organizations representing them (e.g. Olympic committees) can gain tremendously from major events and new facilities for sport; they often frame major events as mechanisms for increasing participation, with imputed health benefits, without much or any proof being available. Those engaged in property development and the supply industry gain, hospitality and tourism usually benefit, and so do politicians who associate themselves with popular events. Of course one might argue that if so many benefit, surely society as a whole gains. That proposition requires a detailed cost and benefit evaluation whish is seldom conducted or made public.

Jennings (2013) argued that public events and big capital projects are 'an ideal vehicle for "high politics" and the predilection of policy-making elites for grand, iconic and schematic visions that offer high-profile policy successes and historic legacies'. The political rewards, however, should be set against the risks and especially the frequent failure of official economic forecasts to be realized.

Political attitudes and voting patterns

Political scientists often study elections and underlying voter attitudes and behaviour, including how political campaigns and specific messages affect the voter. When it comes to events, the most closely related approach has typically involved measures of resident or tourist perceptions of event impacts, and attitudes towards them. But such research has more of a sociological orientation than political science. More research is needed on how perceptions and attitudes translate into political action or voting patterns, and how interest groups lobby for and achieve their event-related goals. This is similar to stakeholder theory.

International relations

Events often involve international relations, both as a reflection of trade, power and cultural exchange. Consider the importance of hosting a mega event for national pride and the legitimacy of governments, the importance assigned to using events to foster trade and economic development, and the value of showcasing one's cultural and economic accomplishments in a global forum. Santos (2014) discussed how mega events were used to strengthen Brazil's position in global affairs, while Grix (2013) assessed how mega events use the promise of legacies to attract support.

Policy formulation

According to Page and Connell (2014: 226), 'the term "policy" is frequently used to denote the direction and objectives an organization wishes to pursue over a set period of time'. And in the view of Turner (1997), the policy process is a function of three interrelated issues:

- the intentions of political and other key actors;
- the way in which decisions and non-decisions are made;
- the implications of these decisions.

The policy context affecting events, and how events shape policy, has been receiving considerable attention. In their book *Event Policy: From Theory to Strategy*, Foley *et al.* (2011) argued that in the urban entrepreneurial policy environment of the previous decades, events were increasingly deemed unsupportable unless they achieved economic, social, cultural and environmental goals. Contemporary planned events have to fulfil multiple functions, which has changed the nature of events and their roles in society. With Scotland as their reference point, Foley *et al.* have evaluated how two quasi-, non-governmental bodies, EventScotland and Creative Scotland, have played a significant role in attracting event-based tourism visitation to the country.

The ways in which event-related policies are formulated and implemented are still deserving of greater study, especially in terms of cross-cultural comparisons. Certainly we are all aware of how many tragedies at events gave rise to health and safety regulations and policies are formulated post-hoc to prevent a reoccurrence as well as increasing concerns about public security at major events (e.g. see the special issue of *Urban Studies* (Giulianotti and Klauser 2011) which reviews security and surveillance at sport mega events). But what went into the decision of the Canadian government (and other nations) to ban tobacco sponsorship at events? Will the same happen to alcohol sponsorship? How did events lobby and why were they successful, or not? As the event management profession and industry become better established and more professional, it can be expected their lobbying efforts will increase and become more effective. But who sets and steers that agenda?

An interesting, events-related theme in policy-making is that of irrational decision-making. Elites, holding influence and power in society, tend to get what they want. It's a mutually reinforcing process! So when a mega event is desired, or perhaps a subsidy for certain types of event, rational decision-making can get in the way. Accordingly, various spurious arguments about tourism impacts or infrastructure gains are used to make it seem like a rational decision. Those who use rational arguments to oppose such decisions are then branded as being unpatriotic, irresponsible or stupid. This is how power gets abused.

A kinder explanation is that emotions get the better of people. Consider how emotional a country can get when it is bidding for the Olympics against a rival country (does London versus Paris 2012 come to mind?). In a highly charged, emotional context, irrational decisions are more likely to be made. How can that be prevented or ameliorated? Should it be?

Power and resources

Much of politics can be construed as a struggle for power, and power means control of resources. When elections are held, the balance of power shifts: lobbyists have more or less influence, funds are reallocated, and new policies become possible. Political science deals with how power and the economy are interdependent, and in the events context this requires studying how various parties (political or otherwise) exert influence to get what they want.

In his examination of *Tourism and Politics*, Hall (1994a) pointed out the negative side of using events to achieve political goals. Events not only can be used as an excuse for overriding normal planning and consultation processes, but can displace powerless groups – especially in the inner city – in the name of urban renewal and economic development. He rightly argued that mega events are almost always sought after by the community's elite who stand to benefit the most, whereas ordinary residents are seldom consulted. Hall noted that proponents of the successful Sydney, Australia bid for the 2000 Summer Olympic Games regarded opponents as 'unpatriotic' or 'unAustralian' and that the public was consulted only by means of polls.

In a recent edited book, *Power, Politics and International Events: Socio-cultural Analyses of Festivals and Spectacles*, Merkel (2013: 4) defines politics as being about social relations and decision-making processes that involve power and authority. Power is either of a collective nature, in which groups seek to achieve their common goals, or of a distributive nature, meaning who has power over whom, and what. This clearly relates to the resources issue, which is of singular importance regarding mega events and mega projects, being who gets what, and who pays. Merkel also notes how many events reflect or celebrate the four main sources of power: military, ideological, political and economic. This perspective on power links to the notion of events as 'texts' that can be read.

In the accompanying Research Note 4.4, Bonthuys analyses a very specific policy debate that often surrounds major events.

4.4 RESEARCH NOTE ON POLICY CONTROVERSY

Bonthuys, E. (2012). The 2010 Football World Cup and the regulation of sex work in South Africa. *Journal of Southern African Studies*, 38(1), 11–29.

'While the South African government expected the 2010 Football World Cup to stimulate economic growth and infrastructure development, and to foster a sense of national unity amongst its citizens, members of the public and the media anticipated an increased demand for commercial sex. The call, in 2007, by the National Commissioner of Police to legalize sex work for the duration of the tournament stimulated debates on the legal status of sex work. Media reports show how advocates for sex workers' rights used the publicity around the event to argue for the legalization of sex work and the protection of sex workers' human rights. However, these calls were persistently overshadowed by claims that up to 40,000 foreign women would be trafficked into the country for sex work, and that many children would be abducted or trafficked for the same purposes. Similar claims have been made in the past in relation to other large sporting events, especially the 2006 Football World Cup held in Germany. However, these fears have not materialized elsewhere, nor did they do so in 2010. Fears of sex trafficking represent a form of moral panic which, while purporting to focus on the well-being of trafficked sex workers, often instead provides justification for the harassment and punishment of sex workers. This happened at the German World Cup and such fears were used to similar effect in the Cape Town Metro. The preoccupation with trafficking and child sexual abuse distracts attention from more important issues in debates about sex work, such as the ways in which the state, global and local commercial interests, and beliefs about sexuality in the wider society, construct and uphold women's economic dependence on men and the routine exploitation of women's sexuality. These factors create and sustain the conditions which force women to resort to sex work, both in the formal sex work industry, and in "informal" sex work transactions.'

Do people have a right to hold and attend events?

In some countries the right to public assembly, and particularly for the purpose of protest or demonstration, is severely curtailed. The 'right' to attend an event might also be absent, given that in many societies there are barriers that cannot be surmounted, including cost, social status, or the availability of tickets that are rationed and channelled to the elite. The Olympic movement, and other elitist event owners, ensure that the best and often the most tickets go to those on the inside of the movement, to those politically connected, and of course to the top sponsors, leaving the public to enter lotteries for the 'privilege' of having a chance to win a ticket-purchase opportunity!

Veal (2010: 98) concluded that human rights are political in nature. If it can be said that people need leisure and sport, or travel, then it is more legitimate to claim a right to travel, to attend or hold events. Veal believes that statements about 'need' are value-based, not scientific, and that in this context need and rights are the same thing.

Research on the political science of events

Both humanistic and scientific methodologies are employed in political studies. Political scientists use methods and techniques that relate to the kinds of inquiries sought: primary sources such as historical documents and official records, secondary sources such as scholarly journal articles, survey research, statistical analysis and model-building.

Hall (1992: 99) argued that 'emphasis should be placed on the allocation of resources for events and the manner in which interests influence this process, particularly through the interaction of power, values, interests, place, and the processes of capital accumulation'. Research by Hiller (2000a) provided a look at the politics of event bidding, namely the people and organizations backing Cape Town's campaign to win the Olympics. Events, given their image-making potential, present attractive opportunities for propagandizing and blatant political messages. At its worst, this can lead to manipulation or control over media coverage – either to hide some elements or to highlight others. Event boycotts have occasionally been used as political tools, especially at the Olympics.

Law

Governments at all levels pass a multitude of laws, each of which is enforceable by the police or other formal action. Laws either forbid actions or mandate them. They govern how persons and organizations interact, and what happens in cases of violations and disputes. There is a vast legal system for law making and law enforcement, including layers of courts, the law profession and law enforcers (see Table 4.4). A central tenet of democratic societies is 'the rule of law', in which 'justice' is based on law and the courts rather than arbitrary decisions. This is all supposed to prevent abuses and protect 'fundamental rights', but of course all these concepts are value laden and change from one country to another as illustrated in Events in Focus 4.2.

Table 4.4 Law

Law	Nature and meanings; the event experience	Antecedents to attending events	Planning and producing events	Outcomes and the impacted	Processes and patterns
The legal system, including legislators, courts and police Specific laws and regulations	Events as real and implicit contracts Event experiences shaped by social/legal differences	Perception of legal implications as a factor in the decision to travel or attend events	Laws and regulations pertaining to event production Legal considerations for event management	Interpretations of justice Legal recourse for loss or injury at events	Changing laws and regulations; accountability

EVENTS IN FOCUS

4.2 The political impacts of the hosting of the 2010 Commonwealth Games, Delhi, India.

Stephen J. Page and Joanne Connell (2014)

In October 2010, Delhi in India hosted the Commonwealth Games (CWG) amidst a public focus on the poor state of the preparation of the infrastructure prior to hosting the event. A very insightful and detailed report by the organization Equations (2010) published in the lead up to the CWG identified the history of the Games approval process and the public policy environment associated with the event. It highlighted the major public subsidies which the event has required as costs spiralled out of control, and as media reports suggest it rose to over £3.8 billion (or may even rise higher as some estimates suggest) which is 114 times the original cost budgeted for in 2002. This is a huge cost for a country which has extremes of wealth and poverty. Up to 2007, Equations (2010) pointed to 300,000 people evicted and displaced to create the space for the Games, while it was predicted that demand for prostitution during the event would rise. The government restricted the number of street vendor licences available in 2010 to try and reduce the visual impact of street traders for visitors. Equations (2010) pointed to comparative data for other mega events where 720,000 people were forcibly evicted to make way for the 1988 Seoul Olympics, 1.25 million in Beijing and 30,000 in Atlanta due to the process of gentrification. Equations (2010) argued that the development of Games infrastructure and projects did not follow established environmental impact assessment guidelines, noting the huge impacts on natural resources of hosting the Games (i.e. in terms of demand for water and power, sewage discharge and solid waste management). These issues are not simply issues for developing countries, as subsequent studies of Olympic Games persistently highlight the displacement of poorer people to accommodate venues and development as illustrated most recently with Scotland hosting the Commonwealth Games discussed in Chapter 3.

Events operate within political and legal systems that at once facilitate, constrain and hold accountable the people and organizations producing them. What events can be held, and what activities allowed, is a legal matter. Every event producer understands the need for obeying laws, satisfying the regulatory agencies, involving the police in security matters and obtaining the advice of lawyers when it comes to contracts, risk assessment and many other technical matters. Event-producing organizations need to be legally sanctioned or incorporated. Taxes have to be paid and audits filed. One source is a book written and published by David Becker (2006) entitled *The Essential Legal Guide to Events*. However, the legal system and the laws it creates and enforces are different in every country.

Justice

'Distributive justice' is a principle that applies to economic development and impact assessment, raising the question of who benefits and who pays?, and within welfare geography it adds the additional concept of territorial justice whereby who benefits and pays has the added dimension of who is affected, where and why. The issue of distributive justice is illustrated in Events Focus 4.2, concerning the Commonwealth Games. 'Legal justice' is another concept altogether, and is tied closely to constitutions and the courts. If something goes wrong, can the aggrieved party find justice?

Legal considerations influencing demand, experiences and meanings

Do people assess legal liabilities and risks when making decisions to attend events? They should, given all the things that can and do go wrong, which are often followed by police action or lawsuits. As events exist within a legal environment, does this actually shape the experience or meanings attached to them? For example, attending a protest certainly carries with it some expectation of confrontation, possibly even civil disobedience. Going to a party and engaging in some form of elicit behaviour (drugs, drinking, sex) absolutely places the participant and others in a potentially dangerous situation. Even the most ordinary event experiences like attending a concert, convention or exhibition entail some form of risk, some degree of legal constraints on one's behaviour, and moral if not legal obligations in the case of emergencies. How do guests, consumers and participants feel about these issues?

Although advice is readily available on risk management and contracts for event management, little research has been undertaken on the legal side of events. There is a need to examine event organizations and the law, the marketing functions from a legal perspective, and the event experience as impacted by all the stakeholders' perceptions of liability. It has to be asked if the fear of litigation is seriously altering the practice of event management and the range of event experiences available. Certainly it can be observed that many forms of organizational and individual risk taking are declining.

History

Superficially history is about dates and chronologies, but historical facts are only the starting point. According to the American Historical Association (www.historians.org) history studies the human condition and social change. The ability to assess evidence, and to assess conflicting interpretations, is essential to what historians do. Because historians are usually researching a topic or theme, and often from a disciplinary perspective, it is common to speak of 'historical geography', 'historical sociology', etc. All of the disciplines we talk about in this book can be studied through the lens of historical fact-finding and interpretation (see Table 4.5).

Table 4.5 History

History	Nature and meanings; the event experience	Antecedents to attending events	Planning and producing events	Outcomes and the impacted	Processes and patterns
Documentation and analysis of human evolution and historic events Historiography evaluates historical evidence and interpretations	Importance of events through history Changing meanings attached to events Changes in how people experience events	Historical patterns and trends in demand for, and consumption of events Changes in why people attend and what they want from events	Evolution and life cycle of events Changes in the supply of events and event types Changes in planning and designing events	Historical evidence of impacts Analysis of long-term impacts	History of specific events and of event types Evolution of planned events in different cultures History reflected in, and commemorated through planned events

Historiography

Who chronicles the evolution and determines the importance of events through history, and on what evidence? Historical method is often focused on finding and understanding documents, determining their veracity, comparing the information with other sources and interpreting the meanings. There are standard issues concerning the accuracy of documents or witness testimony, the perceptual abilities of observers, the possibility of bias or outright lies. A search for the truth, or at least a consensus on what happened and why, is at the heart of much historical research. Many historians write about historical 'facts', whereas others are concerned with how history is researched and interpreted – these people are 'historiographers'.

To appreciate why events are a key area of research, we need to try to understand the different elements that combine to shape how people consume events – from a business activity through to their much wider use in leisure time. Cross (1993: 2) argued that:

> to understand when and why leisure behaviour took major changes of course . . . since the 16th century . . . Perhaps the greatest problem is that historians have seldom shown much interest in the question of explaining people's use of free time . . . In recent years, social history has frequently filled the gap left . . . social historians have explored those private sides of history, family, community, and work that had been so long neglected; and they have increasingly linked these social spheres to popular culture, much of which is leisure.

This quote highlights the importance of neglect by historians, as well as the link to popular culture, in which events are firmly anchored as they have played a key role in the evolution of society.

In any historical overview of events, two underlying themes are important: continuity and change. Continuity means that leisure has continued to be an important process, which remained influential in the pursuits of certain social classes. Change on the other hand characterizes the evolution of events through the ages, since events are a dynamic ever-changing phenomenon. Much of this change is based upon the interaction between the demand for, and supply of event opportunities through time.

In this sense we can speak of both the history of planned events and the historiography of writing about event history. Indeed, there has been much criticism about historical analysis. Post-modernists and critical theorists often argue that too much history has been written by and for elites, from a dominant positivistic perspective, often ignoring or devaluing minority groups, the exploited or losers of wars. If we get history wrong, then our contemporary values and attitudes might also be wrong. Consequently, there has been a shift in thinking within social history and its development as a field of inquiry so that the voices of minority or hidden groups get heard and documented where evidence exists. One important development from the mid-1970s was the emergence of oral history and the recording of historical experiences amongst such groups, so they were not lost.

A historical interpretation of events in America

In his book *The Image: A Guide to Pseudo-Events in America* (1961: 79), historian Daniel Boorstin opened a lasting debate about events and authenticity by claiming that life in America was full of 'pseudo events'. They are staged, scripted and counterfeit – just like many celebrities and tourism products:

> *The modern American tourist now fills his experience with pseudo-events. He has come to expect both more strangeness and more familiarity than the world naturally offers. He has come to believe that he can have a lifetime of adventure in two weeks and all the thrills of risking his life without any real risk at all.*

According to Boorstin, a pseudo event is:

- not spontaneous; it comes about because someone has planned or incited it;
- planned primarily, but not always exclusively, for the purpose of being reported or reproduced, and its occurrence is arranged for the convenience of the reporting or reproducing media;
- ambiguous in terms of its relation to the underlying reality of the situation; whether it is 'real' or not is less important than its newsworthiness and ability to gain favourable attention;
- usually intended to be a self-fulfilling prophecy (in terms of public relations, if we produce an event to show that something is good, we expect that the claim will be accepted).

And why are they so popular? Boorstin suggested the pseudo event is appealing because it is scripted and dramatic, includes a cast of interesting characters, and produces iconic images such as impassioned crowds, hugging families or rainstorms of patriotic balloons. It is designed to be reassuring, create the illusion that we who watch it are 'informed', and it leads to an endless number of other pseudo events.

Boorstin particularly criticized public relations professionals, and they remain sensitive to the issue of manipulation through pseudo events. Journalists are rightly concerned about pseudo events, fearing they are being manipulated and that their reporting of a staged event actually makes a falsehood appear to be true. Judith Clarke observed this problem in an article entitled 'How journalists judge the "reality" of an international "pseudo-event": A study of correspondents who covered the final withdrawal of Vietnamese troops from Cambodia in 1989' (Clarke 2003: 50). She said:

> *As proxy information-gatherers for their audiences, journalists often cover 'pseudo-events', whose purpose is to present to the world a version of reality set up by the organizers. These are usually people with links to wealth and power but they can also be out-groups trying to get their 'real' news noticed. For reporters the challenge is whether to cover these events at face value or delve deeper to find the truth.*

History through the lens of planned events

Many people remember history through the lens of events, both news and planned events. A history of the world (or any corner or aspect of it) has to include major planned and spontaneous events, particularly social history. Wars might or might not be planned, but victory celebrations and remembrance commemorations certainly are. A simple listing of dates and events is one way that people remember the flow of history. Some of those events just happened, others were planned. Increasingly, it seems that planned events are more central to our recollection and interpretation of history and geography.

Planned events now seem to occupy more space and time in the media, they enjoy a larger element of our attention, and they seem to have more impact on how we perceive ourselves and our place in the world. Whilst we do not want to discount the significance of wars and natural disasters, after a while – unless we were personally affected – they all seem to blur. But our memories of personal involvement in special events, of the big celebrations and shows we see on television, of the landmark meetings we went to – of the world getting together for 'The Games' or a Millennial party – those seem to endure.

There are good reasons why planned events mark and give meaning to history. First, we need to relate more to accomplishments and good times than to disasters and conflicts. Who really wants to remember death and destruction when it constantly repeats? We grow weary of it. Those desiring to keep alive the memory of dark parts of history have to go to great lengths to create historical places and events, even giving rise to what has been called 'dark tourism' (Lennon and Foley 2000).

And there is a diversity and creativity to planned events that signifies invention, rebirth, exploration, and other great triumphs of the human spirit. They help us to transcend our personal lives, to become fulfilled. Ordinary news hardly ever does that, and when we do feel satisfaction from a news story, how often is a story derived from or about a planned event? Think of sports, the arts, education, trade – all require events to generate news.

Several examples can be cited to show the range of historical interpretations that are being placed on events and their place in society and culture. Kachun's (2003) book *Festivals of Freedom, 1808–1915* examined the development of African-American freedom festivals following the abolition of slavery. This period of celebration marked an important process of adaptation and formation of an African-American consciousness. Johnsen (2009) focused on cultural heritage tourism in southern Norway, specifically maritime history, through the lens of two festivals. The researcher believed that recent growth in this form of tourism and celebration reflects the community's response to 'economic deprivation' (a relative term), population decrease and industrial decline.

Life-cycle research

The evolution and 'life cycle' of events is an important historical topic with management implications. Every consumer 'product', including events, has a life cycle. A life cycle is not fully predictable, nor is the model deterministic. Stages in the life cycle are not always clear, but events do have a birth, they grow and mature, and many die or require rejuvenation. This temporal aspect of events, and factors shaping the life cycle, have been studied by several researchers (Getz and Frisby 1988; Getz 1993a, 2000a; Frisby and Getz 1989; Walle 1994) (also see the discussion on organizational ecology).

Sofield and Li (1998) examined an 800-year-old festival in China from a historical perspective and showed how politics and tourism influenced its transformation in recent years. Despite the changes, the researchers believed it retained its cultural authenticity. Sofield and Sivan (2003) showed how Hong Kong's famous Dragon Boat Races had shifted from culture to sports tourism in their orientation, with tourism helping to preserve the tradition. For an account of the history of a category of event in its cultural context, see Brewster *et al.* (2009) on the Highland Games.

Beverland *et al.* (2001) compared the organization and evolution of several New Zealand wine festivals, concluding that all of them had changed in terms of organizational structure, programme, strategy or consumers, and indeed each stage had been marked by crises. In fact this seems to be an emerging theme, that sustainable events learn and adapt from crises, and that they have to rejuvenate themselves to avoid decline. In Chapter 9, more attention is given to sustainability and the institutionalization of events.

A *history of event producers and managers*

Many people share our fascination with reading about events in ancient history. What's more, many of the forms and styles of planned events have continued uninterrupted through thousands of years! But there is one question apparently few have asked: who planned and produced these ancient events? Were they revered and rich professionals? Did any historian record their stories? What can we learn from them?

The ancient Romans, although fond of their events, were contemptuous of slaves, prostitutes, actors and the procurers of gladiators. So perhaps the job of event producer was reviled, even while the rich sponsors were elevated in society by their largesse. Nevertheless they had a big job, and it must also have been dangerous. Consider the shows in which ferocious wild animals were turned loose on captives, or slaughtered; or the miniaturized sea battles requiring artificial lakes. Disasters were reported, such as crazed elephants rampaging through the crowd, and the collapse of temporary wooden seating. Standards were set for safety. And hooliganism was also known, with parochial rivalries among spectators resulting in riots; so much so that games had to be cancelled. It all sounds so familiar. (There are many websites devoted to ancient Roman and Greek games, such as www.roman-empire.net)

The greatest parade ever?

What is amazing about the Grand Procession of Ptolemy II Philadelphus is not just its scale, but the familiarity of many of its elements to modern observers of parades and festivals (Rice 1983). The historian/travel writer Athanaeus described the great tent decorated with elaborate care, then details of the parade which was full of religious symbolism and spectacle. Elements of modern parades were in evidence, including floats, numerous animals, soldiers and cavalry. One notable feature was the dispensation of free wine to the onlookers! Some historians believe the motivation for the grand procession was political, in order to legitimize the regime (http://ancientcelebration.blogspot.ca/2011/04/grand-procession-of-ptolemy.html)

There is an apt expression in French: *'plus ça change, plus c'est la même chose'* ('the more things change, the more they stay the same'). It certainly appears to apply to the world of events as highlighted above in terms of the twin points of focus on continuity and change in the history of events. Their forms, and many of their meanings, have endured in most civilizations for thousands of years. Their historical analysis has also been the focus of several seminal studies in human geography (e.g. Allix 1922 and the geography of fairs and Zelinsky's 1994 analysis of conventions in the USA and changes since the 1960s) to which our attention now turns.

Human geography

According to Hall and Page (2014: 149):

> The study of geography has a long and rich history in the social sciences and its hallmark features are its concern with place, space and the environment. Its distinctive contribution to these three elements (and geography of course does not have a monopoly on their analysis) is the way in which the synergies are examined focusing on the spatial elements (i.e. locational issues of where, why and more importantly who and what) exist in relation to human and physical phenomenon.

In the study of events, the predominant focus is from human geography with the focus on people and their activities (see Table 4.6) although there is also a role for physical geography, with the growing interest in environmental sustainability and the impact of hosting events on the natural environment and in resource use such as our carbon footprint and climate change.

Geographical analysis can be linked directly to any of the other social sciences, and what is particularly relevant to the study of events can be described as economic/developmental, cultural/social, historical, political or behavioural geography. Geographical analysis can also be applied to almost any form of human endeavour

Table 4.6 Human geography

Human geography	Nature and meanings; the event experience	Antecedents to attending events	Planning and producing events	Outcomes and the impacted	Processes and patterns
Studies human-resource interactions, especially spatial and temporal patterns of human activity and including impacts on the environment	Linking events to resources, culture and human activity (e.g. harvest festivals; seasonality factors) Interaction with the event environment and sense-making	Demand linked to distance and accessibility The influence of religion and culture across regions	Event settings Locational analysis	Environmental impacts analysed spatially	Spatial/temporal patterns (rural distribution; growth of events as part of urban renewal schemes)

or particular environment, so that we can also speak of urban and rural geography, or event geography. Links to physical geography, or the environmental sciences, are always present. And a feminist or welfarist/Marxist perspective can be taken on geographic studies, as epitomized in studies published in the journal *Antipode*.

Among the key event themes geographers analyse are:

- Events as spatial phenomena (i.e. they are not permanent landscape features and so they are a transient event, such as carnival).
- How places are transformed by events, particularly the role of scale in event analysis.
- Critical debates on event – place – space relationships such as who gets what, where? Why and when? Who can access? Who is excluded? As Hall and Page (2014: 149) observed, these critical debates' 'focus on consumption (as well as the production) of event related phenomena as a critical issue was already well established in the geographical analysis of tourism by the 1980s, especially with respect to the role of mega-events as spectacles of consumption'.

Behavioural geography draws mostly on psychology and focuses on the cognitive processes underlying spatial reasoning, decision-making and behaviour (see Table 4.6). Topics of relevance to events include 'wayfinding' (how people move around, including the development of new technologies such as GPS tracking research – see Pettersson and Zillinger 2011), the construction of 'cognitive maps' (our mental maps of places like event sites), 'place attachment' (our emotional connections to communities), the development of attitudes about space and place, and decisions and behaviour based on imperfect knowledge of one's environment. There is clearly a close connection to 'environmental psychology', as discussed in Chapter 3.

Historical geography studies geographical patterns through time, such as the evolving distribution of events in a region as well as their growing attraction in scale and time. How people interact with their environment creates 'cultural landscapes', and this can include a variety of resource-based, place-specific events given the growth in research within cultural geography informed by the cultural turn which connects the discipline to developments across other areas of social science. Similarly other developments such as the 'new economic geography', with its focus on globalization, have a key role to play in understanding how events have become global phenomena and part of the pursuit of cultural infrastructure as regions compete for inward investment to redevelop former industrial economies in a post-modern world.

Economic geography is the study of the location, distribution and spatial organization of economic activities. Questions asked might include: do economic 'laws' determine resource use, settlement patterns or the distribution and evolution of events? What unique, local or national political and cultural forces shape event formation, sustainability and density?

Development geography is a related field of inquiry, focusing on various factors that shape economic and social development, or population and demographics.

Welfare geography is also closely related, as highlighted in Chapter 3 and earlier in this chapter. Why are some people disadvantaged, and what does this have to do with resource use, urban form, or the distribution and nature of planned events? Welfare geographers tend to be 'critical' in their methodologies.

Cultural geography looks at the relationships between environment and culture. For example, it is clear that cultures are shaped by the places in which they developed, featuring climate and resources, and by trade and other external contacts, related to politics, accessibility and evolving communications. Cultural tourism is closely linked, especially in terms of assessing the distribution of cultural attractions or resources, consideration of cultural regions and place identity or distinctiveness.

Spatial and temporal patterns of events

The spatial and temporal distribution of events is clearly a topic for geographers with the focus on space, place and time. Event distribution patterns are at least partially dependent on the natural resource base, such as those themed or derived from agricultural products or other primary economic activities like mining. But the pattern of events in the landscape has been changing dramatically in response to powerful forces such as globalization and their use for political purposes. Specifically, the resource base of events has shifted away from natural resources and they are now created strategically.

Janiskee's many contributions to the geography of events deserve special recognition. For example, Janiskee (1980) examined the themes, locations, timing, programme of activities, reported attendance and benefits of rural festivals in South Carolina. In Janiskee's (1991) paper, he looked more carefully at festival history in the state, including when festivals were established, and their spatial distribution over time. Janiskee (1994) documented how his 'Fest List' database was compiled from various published sources and interviews and presented an analysis of growth in festival numbers. He saw clearly in graphical format an almost exponential growth rate, with exploding numbers of new events after 1970. In his (1996) study he examined the monthly and seasonal patterns of community festivals in the USA, making it clear that their numbers are relatively low in winter, late autumn and early spring. Although regional patterns are different, across the country a huge number occurs on the July 4 weekend. In the conclusions to this paper he raised the issue of saturation, and asked how many festivals can be held at any one time. It has been observed by other authors that growth in event numbers, and their concentration in certain areas or times of the year, could result in event failure (Jones 1993; Richards 1996).

Most contemporary festivals are held in summer or fair-weather months (also see Ryan *et al.* 1998, regarding New Zealand events), although it should be stressed that other types of events, like business meetings and conventions, peak in the spring and autumn and some sport events are most frequent in winter. Cultural factors and traditions help keep certain seasons dominant for specific types of events, but many are now being created specifically to overcome the traditional seasonality pattern of tourism. One study of event tourism seasonality was undertaken by Yoon *et al.* (2000), who examined the event market in Michigan. Wicks and Fesenmaier (1995) found summer to be the most popular for travelling to events in the US Midwest, with autumn being the next most popular.

Event tourism: the geographical perspective

Supply–demand interactions are fertile ground for event geographers and the most recent review of the field is provided by Hall and Page (2014), who review many of the themes we have discussed so far.

Analysis and forecasting of demand for a particular event or a region's events will in part depend on population distribution, competition and intervening opportunities.

Bohlin (2000) used a traditional tool of geographers, the 'distance-decay function', to examine festival-related travel in Sweden. He found that attendance decreased with distance, although recurring and well-established events have greater 'drawing power'. Getz (1991) illustrated several models of potential event tourism patterns in a region. One option is clustering events in service centres, as opposed to dispersing them over a large, rural area. These are related to the concept of 'attractiveness' and also have implications for the distribution of benefits and costs.

Analysis of the zones of influence of events has been undertaken by Teigland (1996) specific to the Lillehammer (Norway) Winter Olympics, and this method has implications for event planning, especially regarding mega events with multiple venues. The elements of these zones of influence are the gateways, venue locations, tourist flows, transport management and displacement of other activities.

Connell and Page (2005) modelled the spatial impacts of the World Medical Games hosted in Stirling, illustrating the spatial distribution of business impacts; as those researchers noted, the city centre locations benefited disproportionately compared with outlying districts, despite many of the venues being located outside of the city centre. This illustrates the importance of seeking to match demand with the available infrastructure and facilities when decisions are made to host events. In policy terms, two main outcomes were sought from this event: first, to showcase the ability of the city to host an event and thereby develop its role as an event location, and second, to assess the extent to which the wider Stirling region and its tourism sector could benefit from such activities led by the public sector. This theme of evaluating impacts in time and space was developed further by Tyrrell and Johnston (2014).

Event attractiveness

Arising from numerous event visitor studies, it can be concluded that most events rely on local and regional (day-trip) visitors, not long-distance tourists. Even world's fairs and Olympics must sell most of their tickets to residents. The concept of tourist 'attractiveness' must therefore be assessed for each event. How powerful an attraction is the event for various target segments? Who will travel and stay overnight?

Lee and Crompton (2003) assessed the drawing power of three events located in Ocean City, New Jersey. Three festivals in one city in one year (held in May, late September and November–January) were compared in terms of the number of tourists attracted specifically because of the event, and the distances travelled (i.e. the 'market areas'). All three proved to be valuable in drawing tourists (41–55 per cent of attendance) and generating economic benefits, although attendance was much higher at the September event. McKercher *et al.* (2006) considered the tourist attractiveness of festivals in Hong Kong, concluding that only a few people would travel for them, but they generated general image and cultural value.

Hierarchies of event places could be determined through analysis of existing events and event venues, leading to implications for place marketing. Improved measurement of the spatial distribution of event tourist activities and spending will aid in forecasting event impacts, as will studies of 'time switching' and 'displacement'. Analysis of event patterns in time and space is essential to gaining a better understanding of event trends and potential competition. One technique deserving wider application was used by Verhoven *et al.* (1998). Their 'demand mapping' enabled them to examine patterns of travel to festivals.

Time switching and displacement

There is no doubt that people alter their travel plans because of events. For example, they are going to a certain destination for business or pleasure anyway, but decide to time their visit with an event because it provides additional value to the trip. This 'time switching' is an important limitation in estimating the economic impact of events, because the spending of time-switchers cannot be attributed as a benefit of the event itself (Dwyer *et al.* 2000a, 2000b). Switching is more likely to occur in major cities and resorts that have considerable drawing power all year round, as opposed to small towns and rural areas where an event might be the only reason for people to make the trip. Accordingly, economic and image-related impacts of events can be expected to be greater in smaller population centres.

Another theoretical and methodological concern when conducting impact evaluations is the matter of 'displacement'. Regular tourists can be displaced when events take up available accommodation, and it is therefore often counter-productive to hold major events in the peak tourist season. For example, Hultkrantz (1998) was able to demonstrate that the World Championship of Athletics held in Gothenburg, Sweden in 1995, had the effect of displacing as many expected tourists as were attracted by the event, resulting in no gain in tourist volumes. Of course, it is possible that event tourists generate greater economic impact owing to their spending patterns, and there is also the publicity value to consider.

Major events also motivate people to travel to one place as opposed to another, so that during the World's Fair (Expo) in Vancouver, Canada (1986) normal travel patterns were disrupted – Vancouver and British Columbia gained, but the rest of Canada lost traffic (Lee 1987). The spatial distribution of costs and benefits is of particular interest in event geography, and so too are issues of social equity. Two very specific geographic questions are those of defining the region for which economic benefits are to be estimated, and measuring the spatial distribution of spending by visitors.

Economic geography and central place theory

This classic construct of economic geography – central place theory – has largely been ignored in the field of event studies. Basically it postulates that settlements emerge in a hierarchical pattern, with many small ones and few large ones. The larger settlements provide higher-order services. Modern reality, of course, is quite different from the original, rural-based model, but there remains some basic truth in the differentiation of settlements by their ability to host tourists. Daniels (2007) applied central place theory to a sport event, finding that the economic benefits were quite different in the two adjacent counties that were co-hosts. The larger population centre received most of the economic benefits because it was able to accommodate the service requirements of visitors. An important implication is that smaller towns have a tougher time generating economic benefits from events. They will have to co-brand and cooperate with nearby cities.

Event places

In terms of theory building, a crucial question is the extent to which certain types of events are resource dependent or rooted in specific environments. The matter of authenticity should be explored more from a geographic point of view, such as addressing the issue of how – for example – a food festival can both emerge from and reinforce a distinct sense of place. While economic and environmental impacts of events and event tourism have been explored by many, there is still a need for attention to the process by which events help shape and define urban environments, particularly in the context of urban renewal, mega events and event venues. More attention should also be paid to explaining, rather than mapping, spatial and temporal variations in events. What are the relative contributions of resources, culture, policy and economics in accounting for patterns?

All events require a venue (often specific facilities, but sometimes a street or open space), people to organize and manage them, customers to pay, and often sponsors to subsidize them. As communities and destinations become more competitive for tourism and investment, more economic resources are committed to events. So the nature and distribution of events is increasingly shaped by policy.

The study of event places has barely been addressed in the literature. Traditionally, many events have been associated with specific places that take on, at least temporarily, special cultural significance. Historically town squares and parks, even streets, have fulfilled this important civic function, but in recent decades the trend is to purpose-build festival and event places, including multipurpose sport and arts complexes, festival squares and parks, and waterfront facilities for community event programming. The results of these capital and social investments are special places that can be identified by their monuments, special-purpose buildings, attractive landscape and vistas, and frequent ceremonial use. They definitely attract visitors who view them as must-see, urban icons. Several authors have reported on the roles of events in urban renewal projects (Hughes 1993; Mules 1993), and it can be concluded that event programming and the creation of event places has become a necessary element in urban development.

What is the nature of an event place? Getz (2001) examined festival places, comparing a number in Europe and North America. A conceptual model was developed, but its testing and elaboration will require collaboration from the fields of environmental psychology, urban design, arts, event management and sociology. The model focuses on the interdependence of elements of setting (location and design), management systems (including the programme) and people. An important issue for researchers is to examine the interactions of event places with tourists and residents.

The capacity of sites or communities to host events is an important topic in need of further research. While crowds often add to the appeal of events, how much is too much? One study (Wickham and Kerstetter 2000) examined the relationship between place attachment and perceptions of crowding in an event setting. Abbott and Geddie (2000) argued that effective crowd management techniques can reduce management's legal liability. At the site level, attention is frequently given to the spatial component in estimating event attendance, such as through aerial mapping of crowds (Raybould *et al*. 2000) or spatial stratification in sampling (Denton and Furse 1993).

Event clusters

Certain locations have competitive advantages when it comes to developing new experiences for tourists, such being the case in food and wine clusters. As detailed in the book *Foodies and Food Tourism* (Getz *et al*. 2014), events play a critical role in branding clusters and in providing opportunities for direct visitor–supplier interaction. Cluster development involves the geographic concentration of attractions and services, and it can evolve naturally, based on unique terroir and pioneering entrepreneurship or through a concerted effort to establish more of them. Related to wine and food, this clustering process entails building the value chain to include tourist consumption and (hopefully) resulting exports. Even though seaports with fishing fleets and agricultural areas with unique produce have some advantages, from a demand-side point of view it can be said that there is much more potential within cities, resorts and other places where visitors naturally concentrate. That is why some cities hold successful food and wine events of international renown. These principles have been widely used in the design and development of visitor attraction complexes, where a major attractor will underpin destination development and the hosting of events adds further vitality and interest alongside the flagship attraction project that is designed to act as a draw card for visitation. This embodies many of the principles of human geography on achieving agglomerative benefits from the spatial concentration of visitors and events at key accessible locations.

Geographical methods applied to events

People often associate geography with mapping, but this is only one method of examining human interactions with their environments. Technological advances have made it possible to discover individual and micro-level interactions, as illustrated in Research Note 4.5.

4.5 RESEARCH NOTE ON GEOGRAPHICAL ANALYSIS OF EVENT VISITORS

Pettersson, R. and Zillinger, M. (2011). Time and space in event behaviour: Tracking visitors by GPS. *Tourism Geographies*, 13(1), 1–20.

'Research on tourist mobility in combination with the tourists' experiences has been rare to date. Previous studies focusing on the activities of tourists in time and space have most often used the method of time–space diaries. However, an important flaw in this method is that these recordings depend on the respondents' personal observations and notes. This disadvantage is avoided by using Global Positioning Systems (GPS) devices, which record their carriers' movements directly, thus replacing personal notes. This new method was used to study the time–space movements of visitors during the Biathlon World Championships 2008 in Ostersund, Sweden. In addition to the GPS devices, questionnaires were used to study the tourists' movements and experiences. In trying to combine methods to support the event analysis, the aim of the study is to evaluate the practicability of GPS devices during an outdoor sports event. Movements and experiences in time and space are studied. In order to answer questions regarding the visitors' movements on a macro-level, these methods were combined with bird's-eye view photographs taken of the race arena every minute.'

Future studies

Human fascination with the future is at least equal to our curiosity about the past. Visioning and goal-setting is totally future oriented. When we talk about planning events, we are actually seeking to shape the future. General research enables us to say more about probable future conditions, while marketing research gives us greater confidence that our plans will succeed. It is no wonder, then, that 'futurism' and 'future studies' have become so popular.

Future studies (Table 4.7) is not prophecy, as in predicting the future, nor is it science fiction in terms of letting one's imagination run wild. It is an interdisciplinary approach to gaining understanding of how today's conditions and trends will likely shape the future (in part, it is therefore impact forecasting), and how future conditions could be shaped by policies and actions taken (or not taken) today – as in how we need to reduce greenhouse emissions to avoid the worst effects of global warming. Trend analysis, forecasting, environmental and future scanning and scenario making are tools of future studies.

The future is a social construct

The future is by definition unknown, and somewhat unpredictable. Even the ways in which we think about it, and the language we use, is a social construct. To some, 'the future' is full of science-fiction images, to others it is the great unknown, and for entrepreneurs it is opportunity.

We incorporate the future into our daily lives when we say things like: 'it's a good investment' (i.e. I will be richer in a few years), or 'I will wait for the price to come down' (technological innovations are always expensive at first, then consumers see the price fall rapidly). Indeed, because technological progress is so fast, and most innovations have already been predicted (or pre-sold through exhibitions and TV programmes), we are no longer surprised by the next innovation – we are only surprised that it is not yet cheap to purchase! In other words, the future is already imagined and partially consumed.

Table 4.7 Future studies

Future studies	Nature and meanings; the event experience	Antecedents to attending events	Planning and producing events	Outcomes and the impacted	Processes and patterns
Future thinking (can we know or shape the future?) Trend analysis Environmental and future scanning Forecasting and scenario making	How we think about time affects our experiences and the meanings we attach to them	How do people plan for future events? Will virtual reality replace live event experiences?	Environmental and future scanning applied to the event sector	Predicting event impacts Future scenarios (likely and desired future states)	Changes in how we think about time and the future What do we envisage about the future of events?

The future is becoming an obsession, and this has direct policy implications. Politicians promise not just a better future, but actual deliverables. We begin to take for granted that it will get better, not worse, and that what has been promised will become reality. One of the key research methodologies employed in future research is scenario planning.

Futures Research Methodology

A generic source on future studies is Futures Research Methodology Version 3.0, edited by Jerome C. Glenn and Theodore J. Gordon (http://millennium-project.org/millennium/FRM-V3.html). A detailed review of such techniques and their use in tourism can be found in Page *et al.* (2010).

Trend analysis and extrapolation

A basic method is trend analysis and extrapolation, in order to demonstrate what will likely happen if current forces and trends continue. This is a useful starting point for discussions about the future. A related issue is to separate fast-paced, but short-lived fads adopted by specific groups from slow-growth but persistent trends that affect whole societies. According to the article on future studies in Wikipedia, there are three major types of trend. 'Mega trends' extend over many generations, consisting of complex interactions between many factors (e.g. major social trends such as the growth and globalization of event tourism). 'Potential trends' are possible new trends arising from innovations, projects, beliefs or actions that have the potential to grow and eventually go mainstream. Somebody has to identify these in the early stages, and they might get it wrong.

Once a mega trend is identified, many 'branching' or interrelated trends can be detected and evaluated. For example, the whole event tourism trend has many niche-market trends spinning off, including marathon running, food and wine events, etc. One can then look at trends in the market segments for each type of event, such as gender-based, linked to levels of involvement, or destination choices.

Delphi

This method has traditionally been a technique aimed at building consensus about an opinion or future conditions. Multiple rounds of surveying are typically required, both to identify trends and possible future consequences, and to assign probabilities and consider implications. As expert panels are usually recruited for Delphi, it is also a way to create new knowledge, or at least to synthesize the knowledge and opinions from many experts.

Ideally, through multiple rounds, the weight of evidence leads to a consensus or at least a dominant evaluation of what is likely to happen and its consequences. Enduring minority views are also of interest, as they describe alternative scenarios that might have to be taken into account by planners.

Its use in the events sector has been limited, but Carlsen *et al.* (2000) employed Delphi to examine event evaluation practice and needs, while Weber and Ladkin (2005) used the expert panel to identify and assess trends affecting the convention industry.

Scenario making

We can imagine the future in one of two ways. In the first we ask 'what might happen, and how can we prepare for it?' This approach includes the options of combating or opposing trends that lead to undesirable future states. It involves working backwards from a predicted or alternative future state. In the second approach, we ask 'how can we ensure the future that we desire?' This approach leads to strategies and actions intended to shape the future to our liking, such as policies and events that will achieve desired social or economic impacts. All future scenarios begin with an understanding of history, current forces and conditions, and trends. Scenarios emerge from understanding, not dreaming. The more you know about the world of events, the better you will be at scenario making and strategic planning.

According to Page *et al.* (2010: 123), 'scenario planning is a process that provides the organisation with the capability to think about the future and provides it with the skills needed to manoeuvre the organisation and, over time, to create change'. De Geus (1988) called this 'Adaptive Organisational Learning', where the organization 'creates a capability to understand, create and manage change that leads to competitive advantage'. As Chatterjee and Gordon (2006: 255) suggest:

> *In scenario planning the aim is to develop distinctive depictions of the future. Alternative scenarios are developed from the present situation for a desired time horizon. In a scenario planning exercise a number of driving forces will be identified. By making different assumptions about these driving forces or key influences, different 'stories' are formulated about how these interact. The scenarios are effectively those issues.*

As Page *et al.* (2010) suggest, scenario planning has a rich history dating to the 1960s. According to Ling (1998), within scenario planning there are a range of hard to soft techniques used in research, each having a variety of objectives ranging from intuitive and learning outcomes for the organization, focused on ambiguity, with softer techniques, through to more analytical techniques aiming for certainty. The softer techniques typically incorporate the following: informed fiction writing, behavioural simulation and scenarios (which are predominantly qualitative, embrace uncertainty, clarify risk, and enable organizational adaptive understanding). Harder techniques range from economic modelling and forecasting with a focus on certainty in the future, with quantitative precision and the use of single point projections.

Main themes in events-related futures

Specifically related to events, the book to consult is *The Future of Events and Festivals* (2014) edited by Ian Yeoman *et al.* The editors explain that some of the chapters are in the nature of predictions, and that making explanatory claims about the future must be based on knowledge and expertise (Yeoman *et al.* 2014: 4). Others are 'what-if' scenarios, which lead to questions on how to attain this future, or prevent it from happening. In the conclusions to the book. Yeoman *et al.* develop a set of cognitive maps to capture core concepts from the various authors' contributions. They conclude that three future views are predominant, focusing on consumer values and identity, political reasons and power, and the role of technology.

Figure 4.3 Themes associated with the analysis of event futures
Source: Developed from Yeoman *et al.* (2014).

Figure 4.3 is adapted from Yeoman *et al.* (2014) in order to illustrate the main themes and perhaps give ideas to students and researchers for futures research in event studies.

Global challenges

In the periodical *The Futurist* (May–June 2011) two futurists (Halal and Marien) provided four scenarios and two perspectives on what they called the Global MegaCrisis. A number of trends are depicted as leading to the crisis, including global climate change leading to food and water shortages, and a lack of political willpower to deal with the causes. They foresaw a general economic worsening, in part owing to institutional failures (i.e. the global financial crisis). Other threats include terrorism and cyber attacks and weapons of mass destruction. Making use of some expert input they evaluated the perceived severity of the threats and then developed four scenarios ranging from pessimistic to optimistic. While these futurists believed there would be severe challenges and problems facing the planet, eventually they thought a new order would emerge – one based on global information technology and artificial intelligence.

An influential futures perspective is the report *2013–14 State of the Future* by Jerome C. Glenn *et al.*, published by the Millennium Project (http://millennium-project.org/millennium/201314SOF.html). The '15 Global Challenges' as defined through a Delphi panel approach and tracked since 1997 by the Millennium Project are a springboard for thinking about event-specific challenges. For each of the following, readers are invited to develop at least one event-specific research topic:

1. *How can sustainable development be achieved for all while addressing global climate change?*

2. *How can everyone have sufficient clean water without conflict?*

3. *How can population growth and resources be brought into balance?*

4. *How can genuine democracy emerge from authoritarian regimes?*

5. *How can decisionmaking be enhanced by integrating improved global foresight during unprecedented accelerating change?*

6. *How can the global convergence of information and communications technologies work for everyone?*

7. *How can ethical market economies be encouraged to help reduce the gap between rich and poor?*

8. *How can the threat of new and re-emerging diseases and immune micro-organisms be reduced?*

9. *How can education make humanity more intelligent, knowledgeable, and wise enough to address its global challenges?*

10. *How can shared values and new security strategies reduce ethnic conflicts, terrorism, and the use of weapons of mass destruction?*

11. *How can the changing status of women help improve the human condition?*

12. *How can transnational organized crime networks be stopped from becoming more powerful and sophisticated global enterprises?*

13. *How can growing energy demands be met safely and efficiently?*

14. *How can scientific and technological breakthroughs be accelerated to improve the human condition?*

15. *How can ethical considerations become more routinely incorporated into global decisions?*
(http://millennium-project.org/millennium/challenges.html).

According to the Millennium Project, global challenges are interdependent and cannot be dealt with individually. Collaborative action is required, bringing together the efforts of governments, international organizations, corporations, universities, non-governmental bodies (NGOs) and creative individuals.

STUDY GUIDE

Each discipline has been discussed because of its existing and potential contributions to event studies, and students should be able to demonstrate applications from economics, management, political science, law, history, human geography and future studies. Find major themes running through this book that connect the discipline-based theory to management issues, event design, public policy-making and event tourism. For example, economic theory connects both to event pricing and justifications for governments to support and bid on events.

STUDY QUESTIONS

- What is meant by economic demand for events? How is it measured?
- Explain how rational choice theory fails to explain all decisions made regarding event demand.
- How does ideology shape event policy?
- What is power, and how does it affect decisions made about events?
- Why should policy-makers and tourism strategists be concerned with whole populations of events? What theory is applicable?
- Demonstrate how both stakeholder and network theory contribute to event management.

- How can an event become an institution? What are the implications?
- Discuss Boorstin's notions of 'pseudo events' and authenticity.
- What themes and issues are explored in 'event geography'?
- Define the 'attractiveness' of events in geographic terms. How can it be measured?
- What research methods are used in future studies? How can they be used in strategic planning and policy-making?

FURTHER READING

Becker, D. (2006). *The Essential Legal Guide to Events: A Practical Handbook for Event Professionals and Their Advisers*. Self-published.

Dwyer, L., Forsyth, P. and Dwyer, W. (2010). *Tourism Economics and Policy*. Bristol: Channel View.

Foley, M., McGillivray, D. and McPherson, G. (2011). *Event Policy: From Theory to Strategy*. London: Routledge.

Hall, C. M. and Page, S. J. (2014). *The Geography of Tourism and Recreation: Environment, Place and Space* (4th edn). Abingdon: Routledge.

Merkel, U. (ed.) (2013). *Power, Politics and International Events: Socio-cultural Analyses of Festivals and Spectacles*. Oxford: Routledge.

Page, S. J. (2015). *Tourism Management* (5th edn). Abingdon: Routledge.

Yeoman, I., Robertson, M., McMahon-Beattie, U., Backer, E. and Smith, K. (eds) (2014). *The Future of Events and Festivals*. Abingdon: Routledge.

Ziakas, V. (2013). *Event Portfolio Planning and Management: A Holistic Approach*. Oxford: Routledge.

Chapter **5**

Closely related professional fields

LEARNING OBJECTIVES

Upon completion of this chapter students should know the following:

- why and how events are important in closely related professional fields;
- the theoretical and methodological contributions from other fields to event studies;
- common interests in the nature and design of event experiences.

Introduction

There are a number of closely related professional fields that involve, contribute to and can benefit from event studies. Although professionals in these fields might not call themselves 'event managers', the coordination, production or marketing of events is sometimes an important part of their work. Leisure studies is the most advanced in terms of developing its own interdisciplinary theory, and possibly has the most to contribute to event studies. Similarly, tourism and hospitality are also very closely related, especially because of the importance of planned events as 'products' or 'attractions' and in view of the consumption of events in the leisure time of tourists. This chapter also reviews some new and emerging fields of relevance, including visitor studies, in which events are one part of their scope.

Leisure studies

The long history of leisure studies has been reviewed by Page and Connell (2010), with landmark studies identified in Page and Connell (2006). Its modern-day roots can be traced to the parks and recreation movement in North America in the mid-nineteenth century. Through the encouragement of Christian churches, wholesome and socially responsible activities such as outdoor recreation and camping, community sport and supervised children's play were encouraged in North America. This was achieved through the provision of public parks and open spaces, as well as recreation and sporting facilities to counteract idle activity, juvenile delinquency, drinking and gambling. It soon became apparent that the growth of parks and recreation services required professional training at the college and university level. In Europe, a different growth trajectory exists for leisure, which emerged from the early sociological investigations of the habits and behaviour of the population of urban industrial cities and their living conditions. The pursuit of different forms of leisure research informed by sociology continued from the early twentieth century into the growth of interest in the 1920s and 1930s as Page and Connell (2010) outlined. Subsequent development of the outdoor ethos towards recreation saw a significant boom in Europe in the early twentieth century, albeit constrained by the availability of leisure time.

In the USA, recreation and park management professionals are responsible for the provision and management of parks, recreation facilities, and leisure programmes and services. Their skill sets range from venue planning, management and marketing to community development and therapeutic recreation programming. Commercial recreation requires knowledge of business management and tourism. Hospitality services are often integrated in leisure facilities, and events are both users of these facilities and elements in leisure programming. Parks and recreation facilities and services are found within all levels of government, numerous not-for-profit organizations, educational and religious institutions, private clubs, the military and private corporations. Most towns and cities run sport facilities that host numerous events and parks that provide spaces for festivals and other public gatherings. Increasingly, they employ professional event managers to produce their own events, or event coordinators to oversee the events strategy and portfolio. Many are also explicitly involved in event tourism.

As Godbey and Shim noted (2008), and Page and Connell (2010), leisure studies emerged from European sociology departments, with concern focused on free time within industrial societies. Early leisure scholars paid attention to work/leisure patterns and time use, and later they examined leisure and social class, suburbanization, impacts of technology, community life and the effects of work arrangements on leisure; these remain key themes in the twenty-first century.

It was not long before academics from the newly emerging leisure and recreation field of study began to apply theory from the foundation disciplines to formulate and test possible theories within a social sciences framework. Indeed this theory building and testing continues apace as the example of Flinn and Frew (2014) illustrates, where they explore the interconnections between the experiential dimension of Glastonbury music festival, mystical and fantasy narratives and the political contestation of festivity, focusing on the narratives created through multi- and social media. Their theoretical analysis is underpinned by the theoretical developments around experience and the experience economy (see Chapter 6).

What is leisure?

Much debate occurs over how to define leisure (also reviewed in Page and Connell 2006, 2010). Figure 5.1 identifies some of the principal features to consider in seeking to understand what leisure is.

Therefore, leisure is often conceptualized as a component of lifestyle. To some it is activity, free time, meaningful and satisfying experience, or combinations of these. Certainly we take it for granted that leisure is based on free time and free choice, so attending events for their 'intrinsic worth' is leisure (this is a social construction of both leisure and many types of event). When people attend events for 'extrinsic' reasons (i.e. compulsion, the requirements of work or of social obligation) that is not necessarily leisure; although we still want them to have a memorable and rewarding experience. Some of the principal approaches to leisure and events are outlined in Table 5.1.

Stockdale (1985) listed three approaches to leisure:

- as a period of time, or focused on an activity or a 'state of mind' in which choice is the dominant feature; therefore, leisure may be a form of free time for an individual;
- in an objective sense, where leisure is perceived as the opposite of work and so leisure time is construed as non-work or residual time (i.e. that time left after all of the normal obligations have been fulfilled);
- in a subjective manner, where leisure is viewed as a qualitative notion, so that leisure activities only take on a meaning in relation to the perceptions and belief systems of individuals, but these activities can occur at any time and in any context rather than being bound by time and work issues.

Herbert (1988) extended these three perspectives, arguing that leisure is related to the time an individual exercises choices and is able to undertake activities in a voluntary manner, free from other constraints.

Glyptis's (1981) concept of leisure lifestyles highlighted the key role of individual perceptions of leisure.

Consequently a range of key issues need to be taken into account in defining leisure:

- the role of time;
- freedom from constraints or obligations;
- an individual's state of mind and perception of leisure;
- the significance of work and non-work (or for those with domestic responsibilities, the importance of the domestic routine) since Durant (1938: 31) recognized that the work ethic was the foundation of society, but 'Only when this division ceases, where leisure is complementary and not opposed to work' will the balance between leisure and work be better understood;
- the lifestyle of individuals.

Figure 5.1 Principles to consider in approaches to leisure

Source: Extracts from Page and Connell (2010: 11).

Neulinger's 'leisure paradigm' has been very influential in trying to identify the key elements of leisure. To Neulinger (1974), the defining criterion of leisure was 'perceived freedom'. That is, the individual must believe they have choice in whatever they are doing, and they want to do it for its own reward. Neulinger developed a model in the form of a diagram consisting of four cells labelled 'pure job' (constrained and extrinsically motivated), 'pure work' (constrained but intrinsically motivated), 'leisure job' (freely chosen but extrinsically motivated) and 'pure leisure' (intrinsically motivated and freely chosen).

We all recognize that various constraints (i.e. barriers to leisure) always apply to our choices and actions, and that none of us are completely 'free' to do whatever we want, whenever we want. As well, there are often combinations of intrinsic and extrinsic motivations for work and pleasure. So it is more appropriate to think of free versus constrained as a continuum, and intrinsic versus extrinsic motivation as not being diametrically opposed.

'Lifestyle' can be defined as a pattern of living, or as a set of values and actions reflecting personal preferences. There is no doubt that leisure and travel figure prominently in our lifestyle choices, to the point where we speak of the 'life of leisure' or say things like 'he is a globe trotter, a jet-setter'.

How do we define our lifestyles? By our material possessions, but also by reference to:

- where we live (coastal, mountain, suburban, urban) and what that means for recreation and event opportunities;
- what we do (hobbies, interests, travel – all connected to special-interest events);
- who we associate with (social networks, including events attended);
- our tastes and how we express them (art, music, food and wine, and the related events we attend).

Table 5.1 Parks and recreation management: leisure studies

	Nature and meanings; the event experience	Antecedents to attending events	Planning and producing events	Outcomes and the impacted	Processes and patterns
Parks management					
Parks managed for recreation, aesthetics and environmental protection	Communing with nature The outdoors experience as therapy	Parks are attractions and popular event settings Outdoor events have a special appeal	Planning for events as a park use Site planning	Impacts have to be evaluated across environmental, social and personal dimensions	Changing demand and political support for public parks Changes in resource availability and quality
Recreation management					
Public recreation Therapeutic (special needs) recreation	Events as fulfilling social and personal experiences Well-being and health from recreation	Recreation facilities are needed for certain types of events The facility as an attraction	Programming of recreation venues	Impacts on the person and society	Shifts in demand and political support for public recreation
Leisure studies					
Theories of play and leisure Intrinsic motivation Leisure constraints	Events yield leisure benefits Serious leisure Optimal arousal and flow Lifestyle meanings Leisure philosophy	Leisure motives for attending events Leisure constraints and negotiation Recreation specialization Ego involvement Commitment	Implication of theory for design and planning of programmes, venues and events	How to measure the benefits of leisure (e.g. health, self-fulfilment, social integration) Leisure careers	Leisure trends, fads

Two observations are important at this juncture because there has been a debate that in the post-war period, society in many Western countries changed and the transition to a consumer society led to the growth in leisure and consumptive lifestyles. The first major wave of growth in consumer spending in many Western countries after 1945 was in home ownership, then in car ownership, and then in accessing tourism and international travel. The impact of car ownership made people far more mobile and able to attend events and activities on a more spontaneous basis. As Page (2015) illustrates, many countries have also seen the amount of leisure time and paid holiday entitlement for their workers increase in the post-war period so that workers now have the opportunity to engage in the new forms of leisure consumption such as planned events. These changes have been described as being part of what has been termed the 'leisure society', a term coined in the 1970s by sociologists although long hours of work in many developed societies challenge whether this term ever really developed. One aspect of the leisure society marked by economies in developed countries has been a shift from a reliance upon manufacturing and production to new service-related employment, followed by an emphasis on experiences.

Page (2015) suggests that as society has passed from the stage of industrialization to one now described as post-industrial, where new technologies and ways of communicating and working have evolved, sociologists such as Baudrillard, in *The Consumer Society: Myths and Structures* (1998), have argued that we have moved to a society where work and production no longer dominate, having been replaced by leisure and consumption. Within wider notions of leisure, people are also seeking new forms of consumption that enable them to acquire cultural capital. As Page and Connell (2010) argue, the rise of technology, combined with the pursuit of cultural capital from visiting places and events, means that people are looking for more from their event experiences than simple enjoyment and entertainment at the point of consumption. They are looking for lasting memories and objects and tangible features, and these will be re-examined in Chapter 6 on issues around leisure experiences and the experience economy. Consequently, events have a more deep-meaning role in the consumptive activities of people than as passive spectators or participants. This marks a shift in the philosophical basis of leisure within society from the simple conception that it is non-work.

Leisure philosophy

Pieper (1952) and others were concerned that mere idleness should not be construed as leisure. In terms of Pieper's religion-grounded philosophy, true leisure consists of contemplative celebration, and festivals in his framework are of necessity spiritual in nature (that is, religious rituals). Some contemporaries stress that leisure exists as fun, pleasure or hedonism, including deviant and dangerous behaviour (Rojek 1995). More recently, Rojek (2005: 17) defined leisure as 'voluntary behaviour', with 'choice, freedom and voluntarism as the basic components in the narration of leisure'. Rojek's interpretation is based on how people speak of their voluntary behaviour, which can include work. Within a discourse on power and civil society, Rojek argued for leisure as a positive component in the life of 'active citizens'.

If one defines leisure as being more than just free time, or voluntary behaviour, then it tends to become a value-laden or ideological construct. Many people believe leisure has to be socially acceptable behaviour, that is, healthy and renewing of body and spirit. Others think that the very concept of leisure ties in to capitalist ideals and crass consumerism, reflecting who has power and money in society. Historically, as analysed by Veblen (1899), only certain social classes (being coercive or exploitive) had leisure, or could live a life of leisure, and they engaged in conspicuous consumption (materialism) and conspicuous leisure (wasting time). Critics rightly point out that who has leisure, and what they can do with it, is still highly differentiated within societies and between economies.

A prevailing philosophical position is that recreation and leisure are basic human needs (after Maslow 1968), thereby justifying public leisure services. Concomitantly, leisure generates numerous benefits for individuals that lead to broader societal benefits. The Academy of Leisure Sciences (White Paper No. 7) categorizes these benefits as: economic; physiological; environmental; psychological; and social. In recent years a great deal more attention has been given to the links between leisure, physical activity and health.

Associated with the work of Driver (see Driver *et al.* 1991) benefits-based management stresses the provision of services that deliver the benefits desired by consumers. Certainly benefits exist in marketing terms, as consumers are obviously willing to pay for many tangible and experiential benefits, but are there not also benefits that justify public investment and subsidies?

Is this philosophy transferable to event studies? Can we in fact talk legitimately about event services? Or is that merely another element in leisure? There is no doubt that in many jurisdictions events are viewed as legitimate 'public goods' in their own right, especially when it comes to cultural celebrations. Amateur sports are often assigned the same status, primarily for health reasons. Business events, however, tend to be viewed narrowly as part of economic development and tourism.

Ultimately it boils down to people with belief and commitment. First, ask yourself why you believe it is important to produce or support festivals and events. Is it something that should be debated in public and worked into public policy through political processes? Where will support come from – the business community, arts and cultural groups, neighbourhood committees, other social services? Do people have a right to public celebration and to a choice in attending events for business and pleasure? What is likely to happen, in line with leisure services, is that some events will be judged to be public goods and others will be considered private, that is, left to the free market. The balance will vary from place to place, and evolve over time (see Table 5.2).

Table 5.2 Meanings and philosophies of leisure applied to event studies

What is leisure?	Selected applications in event studies
Leisure as freedom from work, enabling contemplation and the arts without ulterior purpose; leisure as philosophy, the pursuit of understanding (de Grazia 1962)	Most planned events fall within a broad definition of leisure experiences; many events are in the business/economic realm but organizers still want attendees to have enjoyable experiences
Free time/non-work (Neulinger 1974)	Extrinsic motivators appear to apply to many events, yet attendees still usually retain the right to decline to attend
Freely chosen activity/intrinsically motivated pursuits (Kelly 1987)	Events directed at learning and aesthetic appreciation fit the Greek philosophy
Leisure as voluntary behaviour (Rojek 2005)	
Leisure as contemplation and spiritualism (Pieper 1952)	This philosophy applies to religious events and pilgrimages, and to sacred rites and rituals within many events
Play (Huizinga 1955; Ellis 1973)	Play and hedonism are essential in carnival and festivity
Hedonism, fun and pleasure (Rojek 1995)	Play is essential to events based on games and competition
	Playfulness as an expected state of mind at many events
	Numerous entertainment and consumption events (e.g. food and wine) cater to hedonism
Lifestyle 'Conspicuous leisure/ consumption', or a lifestyle of leisure by an exploitive social class (Veblen 1899)	Events can become central to serious leisure lifestyles (involvement; commitment; specialization) leading to event travel careers
	Attendance at events as a status symbol
	Prestigious events advocated and sponsored by the elite
Leisure as experience (pleasurable, satisfactory, memorable, transforming)	A phenomenological approach to understanding planned event experiences
	Experiential sampling and other methods to understand planned events and their meanings
	Events in the experience economy
	Experience design applied to events

Leisure experience

Experience is a fundamental concept in leisure. According to Mannell and Kleiber (1997: 11): 'Success is based on structuring the leisure environment in such a way as to create or encourage predictably satisfying experiences . . . it has become apparent that an understanding of the psychological or experiential nature of leisure must be developed.' What a person perceives, feels, learns or remembers – in a word, his or her experience – is often inferred from behaviour. Mannell and Kleiber also said we have to examine experience through the interplay of internal psychological dispositions (e.g. perceptions, feelings, emotions, beliefs, attitudes, needs, personality characteristics) and situational influences that are part of an individual's social environment (e.g. other people, group norms, human artefacts and media). As Kleiber (1999) argues, leisure can provide a basis for self-expression and potentially improve the human condition, particularly where the needs and barriers are addressed, and so it is potentially enabling for individuals.

To study leisure experiences, researchers have looked at what people are doing (the behavioural or 'conative' dimension), moods, emotions and feelings (the 'affective' or evaluative components), and thoughts and images (the 'cognitive' component). Also related are studies on concentration, focus of attention and absorption, self-consciousness, self-awareness and ego-loss, sense of competence, sense of freedom, arousal, activation and relaxation, intensity and duration. More work has been done on emotions than on cognition.

'Optimal experiences' are states of high psychological involvement or absorption in activities or settings. For example, Maslow's (1968) notion of the 'peak experience' ('moments of highest happiness and fulfilment') and Csikszentmihalyi's (1975) 'flow' ('the best moments of people's lives') occur 'when a person's body or mind is stretched to its limits in a voluntary effort to accomplish something difficult and worthwhile' (Csikszentmihalyi 1990: 3). Is this equivalent to the vernacular expression 'being in the zone'? Can it not apply equally to work or any other challenging or rewarding experience?

In fact much of the 1960s research in outdoor recreation still has a significant bearing on the notion of leisure and travel as experience. The Clawson and Knetsch (1966) model (Figure 5.2) suggests the leisure experience is a largely social psychological construct that involves the following elements: anticipation, the experience on site and value derived from the experience.

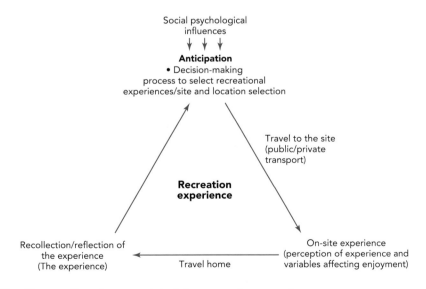

Figure 5.2 The Clawson five-phase model of the recreation experience

Source: Pigram (1983) in Page and Connell (2010: 175). Reprinted from *Outdoor Recreation Management*, J. Pigram and J. Jenkins, Routledge (1983).

This led Page and Connell (2010) to summarize the main focus of leisure researchers where the experience concept has generated the following three germane areas of study:

- *The form of the leisure experience, particularly the activity undertaken or where it is undertaken (the setting)*
- *The immediate experience of leisure at the place of consumption, which is evaluated at the time of experience and during the actual participation of leisure*
- *The experience of leisure after the event, to ask people to reflect on the experience.*

(Page and Connell 2010: 173)

More recently, researchers have begun to refer to the leisure experience as multidimensional in nature and characterized by the variety of experiences that can occur. For example, Lee *et al.* (1994) referred to the transitory, dynamic and complex nature of leisure experiences. To most people, leisure is seen as a mixture of pleasurable (sometimes unpleasurable) experiences that are generally characterized by feelings of fun, enjoyment and relaxation. As a result of the application of social psychological theory, leisure and event researchers are now more heavily focused on studying the feelings, attitudes and motivations of people's leisure and event behaviour, rather than concentrating purely on participation rates or future leisure or event trends. In other words, the variety, frequency and quality of the 'experience' has become more important to study as a measure of overall life satisfaction rather than the actual type of leisure or event that a person participates in (Smith and Godbey, 1991).

Applied to the study of planned events, there is an obvious first question to ask: do events provide leisure experiences? There is definitely an assumption made within event management and event tourism that most events exist to provide leisure experiences, in the form of entertainment, hedonism, celebration, games (including sport), cultural performances and self-development (including learning and aesthetic appreciation). These are believed by event designers to be in the leisure realm. Events that are primarily business related add the above-mentioned leisure elements to their programmes in order to make them more appealing or memorable. Working with tourism authorities, conventions and exhibitions often add tours and other add-on experiences to the event package to build in attractive leisure components to enhance the delegate experience.

Event researchers have increasingly focused on the experience of participants. Agrusa *et al.* (2008) studied runners in the Honolulu Marathon in 2006 and concluded that they valued the 'experience'; they also had a significant economic impact on the state of Hawaii's economy. First-time competitors placed a greater value 'on the experience' of participating and spent more than repeat runners; as well, the Honolulu Marathon satisfied their sensation-seeking personality trait. However, this declined with repeated exposure.

Atkinson (2008) examined how triathletes learned to physically manage, socially perform and individually reflect upon the endurance sport of triathlon as a leisure experience. They found that triathletes come together as a mutually recognized 'pain community' of like-minded actors, who learn to relish the physical and mental suffering from the sport. Atkinson (2008) discussed how they ritually punish their bodies in triathlon races which can induce a 'liminal' state for many participants. The triathlon as a planned event was described as physiologically exhilarating and novel for most competitors at first, and it became even more exciting when the triathletes started to push their body harder and longer. Group runs, rides and swims were seen as social occasions where these athletes could inflict further suffering on their bodies.

Leisure over one's life (the life-stage approach)

Overall, leisure participation decreases with age, and we can assume (in the absence of any specific evidence) that this also applies in general to attending and travelling to planned events as part of leisure.

There are bound to be exceptions, however, and these will be worth studying. Do retired people suddenly attend more social events? How does the life cycle relate to the concepts of 'involvement', 'serious leisure' and 'travel careers'? Leisure researchers have also noticed that people's interest in variety or change also varies over a lifetime, with experimentalism (novelty-seeking and trying things out) being strongest in youth. The social environment is changing rapidly as we mature, and young people are flexible in adapting to changes. Iso-Ahola *et al.* (1994) found that 'the tendency to seek novelty through new leisure activities declines with advancing life stages, whereas the tendency to maintain stability through old and familiar activities increases with life stages'.

Leisure careers and leisure socialization

Roberts (2006: 156) argued that 'The best predictor of any individual's future uses of leisure is the same person's last behaviour.' People are conservative, and become more so as they age. We tend to stick to routines, and we take fewer risks. It is therefore useful to longitudinally examine leisure careers, and this relates to other concepts like serious leisure, recreation specialization and involvement. Early involvement in the arts, particularly within the family socialization context, explains life-long involvement with 'high culture' (Roberts 2006: 157). It is unlikely that adults will show interest in opera or ballet if they were not socialized into these interests early in their lives. But early participation in sports does not necessarily lead to life-long sport careers. It is much easier for committed people to stay involved with sports than to restart after a lapse.

Self-determination theory

Deci and Ryan (1985) proposed this theory to explain how intrinsic motivation works. Intrinsically motivated behaviour occurs in the absence of any apparent external reward and when people have free choice. The activities, or events, are chosen out of interest in those events. The resulting experiences are optimally challenging and result in flow. Intrinsically motivated behaviour is based on the innate psychological need for competence, relatedness (love and meaningful social connections) and self-determination.

Self-construal (see also self-concept)

Self-construal refers to an individual's sense of self in relation to others (Markus and Kitayama, 1991). In collectivist cultures people tend to be more interdependent, whereas in more individualistic cultures they tend to be more independent. Self-construal is believed to affect cognition, emotion and motivation. Walker, Deng and Dieser (2005) argued that cultural differences must be taken into account when theorizing about intrinsic versus extrinsic motivation and the nature of free choice and leisure. Asian and other cultures with interdependent self-construals assign greater value to belonging and maintaining harmony, as opposed to individualism. Relatedness might be more important than autonomy and free choice, so that the basic assumption that leisure is based on free choice seems to be a 'Western' construct. These cultural differences should be considered when designing events, in communicating their benefits, and when considering event impacts on individuals and communities. Benefits to persons and groups have to be evaluated separately. In fact Gabrenya and Hwang (1996) observed that in Chinese culture, annual festivals and spectator sports facilitate social interaction outside normal social hierarchies and networks, thereby releasing people from usual constraints on behaviour.

Leisure constraints

Leisure researchers and theorists (e.g. Jackson *et al.* 1993; Jackson 2005) want to know why people participate, and what prevents them from doing what they want to do. Generic categories of constraints have been identified, including the intrapersonal (one's perceptions and attitudes), interpersonal (such as a lack of leisure partners) and structural (time, money, supply and accessibility). How people negotiate through constraints is an important issue. These are examined in more detail in the Antecedents chapter (Chapter 8) and have remained a major area of leisure research to date, as they can determine the level of involvement and engagement in leisure.

Leisure involvement

Based on psychological theory, Havitz and Dimanche (1999: 123) defined leisure involvement as 'an unobservable state of motivation, arousal or interest toward a recreational activity or associated product'. With regard to leisure, travel and lifestyle pursuits, it has been confirmed that people's preferences, behaviour and satisfaction are affected by their level of involvement with products and pursuits. How one actually becomes involved is another question, and is more difficult to answer. Many researchers utilize the Zaichkowsky uni-dimensional 'Personal Involvement Inventory Scale', but Kyle and Chick (2002) suggested that there is a general consensus that leisure involvement is best conceptualized as a multidimensional construct with the following dimensions being most important:

1. 'Attraction': perceived importance or interest in an activity or product, and the pleasure derived from doing or consuming it (for example, running offers certain benefits, but what is the additional pleasure derived from participating in a marathon?).

2. 'Sign': unspoken elements that the activity or product consumption conveys about the person (such as the prestige associated with certain events).

3. 'Centrality' to lifestyle: referring to both social contexts and the role of the activity or product in the person's lifestyle (people who are highly involved in the arts will demonstrate quite different levels of interest in certain art events, and will look for different benefits from their attendance).

Risk is sometimes included in involvement scales, such as those employed by Getz and McConnell (2011) to test participants' level of involvement with mountain biking. The risk element deals with the fact that highly involved event tourists place a higher value on well-run events because they invest so much of themselves (and their money and time) in making event and travel decisions. They really hate it when events are poorly run, and this presumably applies to the risks associated with any of their decisions. To someone less involved, the risk of a bad experience might be the same, but not the psychological consequences.

Kyle *et al.* (2007) later revised their scale to give much greater emphasis to the social aspects of 'enduring leisure involvement'; their new scale included dimensions of attraction, centrality, social bonding, identity expression and identity affirmation. Identifying with a social world is thereby linked to involvement, as well as finding one's identity, or re-affirming it through leisure and travel pursuits.

An application of involvement theory to travel and events can be found in Ryan and Trauer (2005). They studied a major participant-based, multi-sport event, for which they believe location was a secondary consideration for sport tourists. Masters Games attract a large core of sport 'enthusiasts' who invest heavily in their athletic pursuits – including travel – and also those who only participate at the local level. Ryan and Trauer talked about a 'career' that leads from local to international competitions. 'It can be hypothesized that participants form a degree of involvement with games participation that in part is a confirmation of self-identity as an exponent of a particular sport' (Ryan and Trauer 2005: 179). The highly involved participants who are willing to travel may be critical for the success of events.

Involvement was the core concept employed in a major study of 'foodies' and their food-tourism behaviour and preferences (Getz *et al.* 2014). That research demonstrated the critical importance of event attendance in defining the highly involved foodie, and thereby revealing the necessity for employing a range of events in attracting food tourists. The most highly involved, those whose personal and social identities were significantly linked to food, attended the most food-related events and preferred the most specialized, hands-on event experiences. While all foodies tend to enjoy food festivals, and food at other events like ethnic and multicultural festivals, it is the highly involved foodies who are most likely to seek out experiences that connect them to each other (i.e. communitas), to experts (the chefs are important) and to learning about food and its cultural heritage.

Recreation specialization

Bryan (1977: 175) described specialization as 'a continuum of behaviour from the general to the particular, reflected by equipment and skills used in the sport, and activity setting preferences'. As experience in an activity increases, it is theorized that people will progress from more general to specialized behaviour and related patterns of consumption. Their identification with the activity will also change. Characteristic styles of participation emerge, so that beginners can often be easily distinguished from the more experienced participants. The theory has been applied to many activities, and to comparison of participants in terms of their motivation, setting preferences, involvement, attitudes towards management and the use of information. It is clearly related to the concepts of ego-involvement, commitment and serious leisure. Burr and Scott (2004) argued that the recreational specialization framework could be applied to understanding visitors to the Great Salt Lake Bird Festival. They used a random visitor intercept and a mail-back survey, and site visits to observe the festival. Specialization (in 'birding') of those attending this festival was measured in terms of their behaviour, commitment and level of skill. Only a small fraction was found to be highly specialized or serious about bird watching, and these people were less satisfied with the event – which suggests the need for careful segmentation. Most visitors seemed to have an interest in birds, but they combined that interest with other leisure pursuits and enjoyed the general festival programming. To the organizers, this also helped them meet their aims of increasing awareness and improved conservation efforts. The authors suggested that specialization can be usefully applied to other types of events to increase understanding of motives and behaviour.

Commitment and serious leisure

'Commitment' is a social-psychological construct, used to explain consistent behaviour. In the context of leisure it has been defined by Kim *et al.* (1997: 323) as 'those personal and behavioural mechanisms that bind individuals to consistent patterns of leisure behaviour'. Those authors sought to explore commitment in terms of dedication, inner conviction, centrality, costs and social considerations. Becker (1960) used the term 'side bets' to describe what would be lost if an individual discontinued something he or she was committed to, such as loss of friendships, personal investments of time and money, as well as consideration of the absence of alternatives. Kim *et al.* (1997) determined that commitment (conceptualized as centrality to lifestyle) and social-psychological involvement scales were highly interrelated among a sample of birdwatchers, and that behavioural measures of involvement were more useful in predicting behaviour. According to these same researchers, involvement is likely an antecedent of commitment and might be at the root of 'serious leisure'.

Robert Stebbins's concept of 'serious leisure' (1982, 1992, 2001, 2006) appears to be closely related to commitment and involvement constructs. Serious leisure is (1992: 53)

> *the steady pursuit of an amateur, hobbyist, or career volunteer activity that captivates its participants with its complexity and many challenges. It is profound, long-lasting, and invariably based on substantial skill, knowledge, or experience, if not on a combination of these three.*

It is like pursuing a career, but without remuneration. Serious leisure participants 'typically become members of a vast social world, a complex mosaic of groups, events, networks, organizations, and social relationships'. The rewards of serious leisure include 'fulfilling one's human potential, expressing one's skills and knowledge, having cherished experiences, and developing a valued identity'. According to Stebbins, characteristics of serious leisure include:

- perseverance (learning to overcome constraints);
- developing a career (includes stages of achievement or reward; may be assisted by experts; may include a progression of events leading towards the highest level of participation);
- significant personal effort is required (acquiring knowledge and skills; travel);
- durable benefits as outcomes (e.g. self-fulfilment, enhancement of self-concept, self-esteem; social identity);
- an ethos associated with the social world (common interests and inter-communications related to the 'social object' of interest to the group, such as sport, art, wine);
- social identification with the activity (a subculture).

Shipway and Jones (2008) adopted an 'insider's' perspective on experiences at the 2007 Flora London Marathon (FLM) using the concepts of serious leisure and social identification to explore the experiences of 'serious' participants travelling to take part in this event. An ethnographic research design was utilized using a combination of interviews, observation and participant observation. Data collection commenced four months prior to the marathon and involved monitoring the experiences of participants, all of whom viewed their activity as a 'serious leisure' pursuit. This was followed up with a number of semi-structured interviews with participants in the two-week period after the event. The key finding was the strength of identification that participants had with the activity of running. The salience of this identity was heightened by the act of travel to, and residence in, London both before and after the marathon. A number of themes emerged from the data that were seen as consequences of this sense of identification, these being the unique ethos, language and behaviours of participants, the need for significant personal effort to complete the event, the perseverance of participants in the activity, both in terms of training and competing, the durable benefits obtained by the runners through participation, and the 'career structure' associated with distance running. Participants also followed behaviours prescribed by a particular prototype associated with the running subculture, resulting in homogeneity of dress, behaviour and values among the group.

Jo Mackellar's book *Event Audiences and Expectations* presents a model called the 'event audience spectrum' (Mackellar 2013a: 70), which is a form of benefit segmentation based on increasing levels of interest, commitment, knowledge and skills. This continuum owes its foundations to Stebbins and to the work of Brotherton and Himmetoğlu (1997); it starts with 'socializers' and progresses through 'dabblers' to 'enthusiasts' and 'fanatics'. Her SERPA model, for 'serious participation at events' (2013a: 77) combines elements of social-identity motivation with various psychological factors, including personal identity and commitment, that help explain serious participation in events and event-related travel. This model connects well with the foodies and food-tourism findings of Getz *et al.* (2014) and can form the basis of special-interest segmentation and the development and marketing of iconic events targeted at the highly involved.

Research methodologies and methods in leisure studies

The North American approach to the leisure studies field, in common with social psychology in general, has been largely positivist and quantitative, but there has been growing interest in values, beliefs, and the application of theory to practical social problems and policy issues (Mannell and Kleiber 1997: 27). This is in direct contrast to the European tradition that has been more theoretical and conceptual, and informed by sociology. Leisure researchers in North America have frequently used large-scale surveys, experiments and time diaries to observe and measure leisure quantitatively and to develop or test theories. More qualitative and interpretive methods include participant observation and unstructured interviews, case studies and introspection.

Researchers can observe experience by asking people what is on their minds. A full understanding of behaviour can only be obtained when we know what it means to the person – which is phenomenology. 'Experiential sampling' (Csikszentmihalyi and Csikszentmihalyi 1988) is the related method used in leisure studies, and we will revisit it later in this book.

At the nexus of leisure and event studies, Patterson and Getz (2013) conclude that leisure studies has a great influence on event studies, as both fields are focused on experience and related meanings from multiple perspectives, including personal and societal. Event managers might also do well to adapt the notion of leisure philosophy and leisure services to the planning and delivery of events, with an emphasis on benefits sought and realized. However, they argued that within leisure studies the planned event will undoubtedly remain a minor concern, one of many activities or 'experiencescapes' worthy of consideration by leisure policy-makers and parks/recreation practitioners.

Tourism studies

Tourism has evolved as a subset of leisure and it developed into a distinctive field of study in the 1970s and 1980s – initially in Europe and North America – but it is now emerging globally. Tourism is often studied as an industry, alongside hospitality, with related educational programmes stressing professional career preparation. But, like leisure and events, academics also want to study tourism as a social, cultural and economic phenomenon, and to consider all its potential impacts. Tourism, like leisure, has a major stake in planned events and has evolved along similar lines from a management orientation to a full-fledged field of studies with its own advanced degrees. When defining tourism, scholars tend to separate the industry-oriented approach from the broader 'tourism studies' approach that relies on multi- and interdisciplinarity. However, the blurring of boundaries is illustrated in Figure 5.3, which sets out the interconnections between leisure, tourism and recreation.

Leiper (1981) argued that a multidisciplinary approach was an impediment to tourism education, and that what is needed is an interdisciplinary approach that integrates concepts from other disciplines and fields (also see Hall and Page 2010 on the wider contribution of Leiper to this debate). Tribe (1997), on the other hand, recommended that there is nothing to be gained by disciplinary status, and that tourism studies does not qualify. Rojek and Urry (1997) asked, where does tourism begin and leisure studies end? What is clear aside from these tautological propositions on what tourism and leisure are (see for example, Hall and Page 2014 and Page and Connell 2010 on distinguishing between these areas) is that tourism has a clear role to play in event studies (Table 5.3).

Leisure and tourism studies clearly overlap if one views tourism as a social phenomenon taking place within leisure, and they overlap at the business and management level because numerous enterprises exist

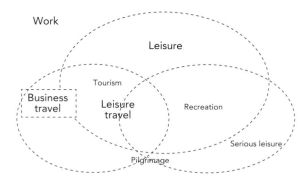

Figure 5.3 The relationships between leisure, recreation and tourism

Source: Hall and Page (2014). Reprinted from *The Geography of Tourism and Recreation*, 4th S. J. Page and C. M. Hall, Routledge (2014).

Table 5.3 Tourism studies and event tourism

	Nature and meanings; the event experience	Antecedents to attending events	Planning and producing events	Outcomes and the impacted	Processes and patterns
Tourism studies					
The study of travel and the touristic experience, and of the tourism industry					
Event tourism					
Travel related to planned events Destination development and marketing through events	The overall event travel experience Tourism roles of events: attractions; place marketing; image creation; animators Iconic events for various social worlds Event travel career trajectories	General travel demand affects event travel demand Specific motivators for event tourism Media coverage and media events influence demand Increasing supply of tourist-oriented events	Marketing for event tourists Packaging Events produced primarily for tourists or destination image enhancement Destination event portfolios	Event tourism impacts Economic impacts and EIAs Cost and benefit evaluations	Event tourism trends (e.g. changing demand for long- or short-haul event trips)

to deliver recreational/travel experiences; Figure 5.3 illustrates this interdependence. Event studies sits at the intersection (or nexus) of tourism, leisure and recreation, since it can occur within all of these areas, and some studies have lamented the decline of leisure studies as a subject, as event studies has taken centre stage (Spracklen 2014).

Events can be viewed as a subset of this leisure/tourism interdependence illustrated in Figure 5.3, but neither leisure nor tourism studies deals centrally with the planning, design, experience and management of events within these interdependent areas. Rather, in tourism and leisure, events are treated as attractions, activities, or aspects of some larger tourism/leisure construct such as business travel, pilgrimage or serious leisure.

Event tourism, the destination perspective

As with any niche market, or special-interest travel segment, we can define 'event tourism' from two perspectives – the consumer's and the destination's; a substantial review of the event-tourism field can be found in Getz (2008) and Getz and Page (2015). Here we look at event tourism as a destination strategy to develop and market events for their specific tourism and economic benefits. The five main roles played by events in tourism are discussed below.

Events as attractions

Although many tourism organizations stress international tourism, there is no doubt that most festivals and events are dependent on local and regional audiences. But whether events are true tourist attractions (i.e. motivating overnight or non-local travel), or a reason for visitors already in an area to stay longer, they can have tourism value. Events can also have the effect of keeping people and their money at home, rather than travelling outside the region. Event 'drawing power' or 'attractiveness' can be measured by how many tourists will be attracted, and how far or frequently they will travel. Important goals are to use events to overcome the seasonality problem, and to spread demand geographically throughout a country or region. Destinations often classify events according to their drawing power, scale or tourism potential. Bos (1994) reported on classification in the Netherlands, and the Economic Planning Group and Lord Cultural Resources (1992) developed a system for the Canadian province of Ontario. Often these are intended to assist in funding decisions, but it is a practice that entails some difficult decisions. Is it current or potential attractiveness that should be the main criterion for receiving assistance? How are events of different types to be compared? Should peripheral locations receive special consideration?

Resources for event tourism consist of more than just events. An inventory of resources has to include organizations capable of producing events, companies that sponsor them, agencies to assist, all possible resources (human, financial, natural, political) and themes. One issue to consider is that cultural and environmental 'resources' are often in the public domain and anyone can 'exploit' them without compensation or regard to impacts. The 'law of the commons' applies here, as a community and its resources could become damaged by too many events, too much event tourism or by poorly managed events. This is a strong argument for public policy and regulation of events, encompassing the principles of resource stewardship and sustainability.

The goal should not be to maximize event tourism volumes, but to develop a manageable and balanced portfolio of events that meet multiple goals and generate many benefits (see Chapter 12 for details). An emphasis on event tourist quality, that is, attracting high-yield, dedicated event tourists, is preferred. Strategies employed in event tourism have not generally been evaluated for effectiveness. A substantial part of the event tourism business is bidding on events. This process has been described as a special-purpose marketplace by Getz (2004), who studied the event bidding goals, methods and attributed success factors of Canadian DMOs. Bidding has also been studied by Emery (2001), Persson (2002), Westerbeek *et al.* (2002), Berridge (2010) and Foley *et al.* (2012). Lockstone-Binney *et al.* (2014) have extended this rather neglected line of research by focusing on the roles of ambassadors in the bidding process.

Other destination development strategies include starting (and sometimes owning) new events for tourism purposes, using events in theme years, cultivating and improving many local and regional events, developing one or more events into 'hallmark' status, and hosting the occasional mega event. An interesting example of developing events as attractions was studied by Brown (2010), examining the visiting friends and relatives (VFR) market in Cape Breton, Canada. The study examined how VFR tourists attended local festivals and events, with Brown concluding that it was an important tourist and event segment, and that marketing directly to residents (i.e. the local hosts) is the key.

Events as animators

Resorts, museums, historic districts, heritage sites, archaeological sites, markets and shopping centres, sports stadia, convention centres and theme parks all develop programmes of special events. Built attractions and facilities have everywhere realized the advantages of 'animation' – the process of programming interpretive features and/or special events which make the place come alive with sensory stimulation and appealing atmosphere.

The potential benefits of animation through events are of major importance to facility and attraction managers:

- to attract people who might otherwise not make a visit because they perceive the facility or attraction itself to be uninteresting;
- to encourage repeat visits by people who might otherwise think that one visit is enough;
- to attract publicity for the site or facility, including the highlighting of historical events associated with the site;
- to encourage longer stays and greater spending;
- to target groups for special functions.

Venues are almost automatically in the events business, out of necessity. Pearce (1998) examined how attractions in different countries were adding events and integrating with festivals and events in their marketing. Whitfield (2009) documented the rise of meetings and conventions seeking unusual venues, and how various attractions were adapting their facilities and marketing to cater to this planned-event market.

Events and place marketing: co-branding

Kotler *et al.* (1993) in *Marketing Places* identified the value of events in enhancing the image of communities and attracting tourists. They demonstrated how places compete for investments, quality people and tourists, all in pursuit of more liveable and prosperous communities. 'Place marketing' provides a framework within which events and event tourism find multiple roles, as image-makers, quality-of-life enhancers and tourist attractions. More traditional approaches to economic development stressed industrialization and the provision of physical rather than cultural infrastructure, and downplayed the economic value of tourism.

'Co-branding' between events and destinations is one strategy gaining popularity (Brown *et al.* 2001; Chalip and Costa 2006). Jago *et al.* (2002, 2003) argued that there was substantial potential for events to be used in destination branding but that neither event nor destination managers do a good job in harnessing that potential. The intent is to reinforce the destination's brand with compatible events, a transferral of positive images, with a classic case being surfing competitions in Surfers Paradise. This is because most destinations contain an array of events, largely beyond the control of the state, and for that reason it might be wise to focus on one or a few well-imaged 'hallmark events' to achieve place-marketing and branding goals.

Gibson and Davidson (2004) examined the application of place marketing through events, and related political debates, in the context of how Tamworth became Australia's self-proclaimed country music capital. Andersson and Niedomysl (2010) focused on how, why and what Swedish cities hope to achieve by engaging themselves in hosting the try-outs to the Eurovision Song Contest (ESC). The study relied on stakeholder interviews and found that local authorities did more collaboration than competition for the events. Various motives for bidding applied, including demonstrating that the town or city was interested in hosting events. The try-out itself was viewed by locals as little more than a good party.

Events as image makers

It is apparent that major events can have the effect of shaping an image of the host community or country, leading to its favourable perception as a potential travel destination. With global media attention focused on the host city, even for a relatively short duration, the publicity value is enormous, and some destinations will use this fact alone to justify great expenditures on attracting events. For example, Wang and Gitelson (1988: 5) observed that the annual Spoleto Festival in Charleston, South Carolina does not appear to be economically justifiable, 'but the city holds it every year to maintain a desirable image'. Cameron (1989) noted the role of festivals and events, and cultural tourism in general, in altering the image of the Lehigh Valley in Pennsylvania.

Hede and Jago (2005) placed the discussion in the context of theory about planned and reasoned action (Ajzen and Fishbein 1973; Fishbein and Azjen 1975; Fishbein 1980; Ajzen 1985, 1991) in which positive perceptions created by the publicity surrounding events (or viewing the events, or reading about them) leads to positive attitudes, intentions to travel there, and eventual travel. This theory, or belief, underlies a great deal of destination promotion. Hudson *et al.* (2004), however, in conceptualizing (with a graphic model) the process by which events might influence travel choices, concluded that there were many intervening factors separating perception from travel behaviour, and that watching events – especially sport events – might lead to travel elsewhere to participate in the sport. Indeed, many sport event broadcasts do not provide much in the way of destination imagery or information.

Longitudinal studies of the impact of hosting the 1988 Winter Olympic Games in Calgary (Ritchie and Smith 1991) showed how a definite positive image boost grew, peaked and started to decline afterwards. This life cycle of image enhancement related to one-time events has also been noted by Mackellar and Nisbet (2014). But additional gains in tourism infrastructure and the legacy of enhanced tourism marketing and organization can potentially sustain the effect.

Pertinent research has been mostly on how events might change destination image (e.g. Chalip *et al.* 2003; Hede 2005; Li and Vogelsong 2005; Mossberg 2000b; Shibli and the Sport Industry Research Centre 2002; Ritchie *et al.* 2006; Smith 2005; Ferreira and Donaldson 2013; Kim *et al.* 2012, 2014). Results have been mixed.

The somewhat limited research on media impacts suggests that enhanced image is difficult to obtain, let alone prove (Mossberg 2000). A study by Boo and Busser (2006) concluded that the festival under study did not contribute to a positive destination image among participants. Indeed, it appeared to have a negative impact owing to poor marketing and quality. The researchers pointed out the necessity for further research on the imputed connections between events and image enhancement. Hede (2005), however, concluded that Australians who viewed telecasts of the Athens 2004 Olympics did change their overall attitude toward Greece as a destination. Ritchie *et al.* (2006) concluded that media broadcast of events helped change images of Canberra, and they recommended that events be part of any promotional strategy for national capitals.

Chalip *et al.* (2003) examined the effects of different media (destination and event advertising, and event telecasts) on nine dimensions of destination image and intention to travel to the host destination (Gold Coast, Australia) from New Zealand and the USA. They found that different media had different impacts in foreign countries, not all of which were positive, and that different media could do more or less to attract tourists. For example, some media exposure convinced respondents that the event might have negative impacts on the Australian natural environment.

Gripsrud *et al.* (2010) demonstrated the interrelationships between hosting an international mega-sport event, country image, product image and purchase intentions for the Winter Olympics in Turin, Italy in 2006. A quasi-experimental design was employed, based upon two samples of undergraduate students in Norway. Data were gathered both before and after the Olympic Games took place. The study indicates that dimensions of country image for those who are very interested in sports may be changed by hosting a mega-sport event. However, there is no guarantee that the image of the host country will improve. It may actually deteriorate. This finding underscores the importance of managing international sport events properly.

Proactive media management is generally necessary to secure desired media coverage and communication of the desired image for events and destinations (Getz and Fairley 2004). For example, Andrew Smith (2008, 2009) examined the use of major events to promote peripheral urban areas and concluded that it is very difficult to intervene with the media to secure desired outcomes for places. Jutbring (2014) analysed exactly how brand values of the destination can be encoded in media coverage of events. Chen (2012) examined how the hosting of major international events provided the government with opportunities to boost its image among the Chinese population. Xue, Chen and Yu (2012) indicate that hosting events can be both a positive enhancement to a country's image as well as a useful public relations tool (see Research Note 5.1).

5.1 RESEARCH NOTE ON HOSTING EVENTS

Xue, K., Chen, X. and Yu, M. (2012). Can the World Expo change a city's image through foreign media reports? *Public Relations Review*, 38(5), 746–754.

'Hosting global events like the World Expo is a new form of public relations for cities, but few studies have been conducted to explore the extent to which they can change the content of media reports and media attitudes toward city image. We conducted a content analysis of all Shanghai-related news reports from November 2009 to April 2011 in 30 English newspapers in 10 countries. We found a few interesting discoveries. First, the Shanghai Expo 2010 did affect newspapers' agenda-building, with the Expo being the topic of most reports and the most important news before and during the Expo. Second, the Expo brought changes to the news frames of newspapers, but the changes were still constrained by media practices. Third, the Expo improved newspapers' attitudes towards Shanghai's city image, particularly towards the city's potential. Finally and most importantly, global events such as the Expo do have a significant impact on the content and attitudes of newspaper reports, but a single event cannot produce long-lasting effects. Therefore improving city image requires "better actions than just better words".'

What happens when negative publicity strikes a destination? To a degree, bad news events can be managed: both to minimize the negative impact and to fight back. Ahmed (1991) argued that negative images can be turned into positive ones by organizing festivals and commemorations of the event, although this is restricted mostly to natural disasters and entails the risk of stirring up unhappy or controversial memories.

Although it can be concluded from the evidence that events can potentially have an image-change effect, the measurement of media effects remains a difficult problem for evaluators. Advertising-equivalence measures are predominant, with the major shortcoming of only considering quantity and content, not impact. Alternatives include more reliance on expert opinion from target market areas and a fuller analysis of social media. The power of social media to empower citizens to create alternative narratives to the official media responses to events has become a new area for research on events (see McGillivray 2014).

Events as catalysts: leveraging and the legacy

Mega events, such as world's fairs and Olympic Games, have been supported by host governments in large part because of their role as catalysts in major redevelopment schemes. The Knoxville World's Fair was conceived as a catalyst for urban renewal through image enhancement and physical redevelopment, and left a legacy of infrastructure, a convention centre, private investments, a better tax base and new jobs for the Tennessee city (Mendell *et al.* 1983). Dungan (1984) gave a number of examples of the indirect and direct physical legacies of major events. Atlanta's 1996 Summer Olympic Games generated two billion dollars in construction projects in Georgia, including sport facilities, an urban park in central Atlanta, housing improvements and educational facilities (Mihalik 1994). Major events tend to attract investment into the hospitality sector, especially hotels and restaurants. Sometimes these additions have been brought forward in time, while others represent new infrastructure related to expected longer-term increases in demand. Sport events generally lead to new or improved facilities which can be used to attract events in the future, and improvements to convention or arts centres can have a similar effect. In this way a community can use the event to realize a 'quantum leap' in its tourism development, accelerating growth or jumping into a higher competitive category.

'Leveraging' events is a related concept. The idea is to exploit or 'leverage' events for broader business benefits, through enhancing event tourist spending at the event and elsewhere in the destination, and through building new relationships (Faulkner *et al*. 2000). Chalip and Leyns (2002) showed how events can be leveraged for enhanced local benefits by working with businesses, and Chalip (2006) expanded this concept with regard to the social leveraging of events – that is, tying events to social and educational causes.

The 'legacy' of events is also part of the 'catalyst' role, to the extent that it is planned. Ritchie (2000) deduced ten lessons from two Winter Olympics for getting the most out of the investment in the long term. See Chapter 10 on 'Outcomes' for more discussion on these topics.

Ziakas's (2014) review of mega-event leveraging derived a list of ten key research themes for further study, namely:

- *Equity and sustainability*, so that distributional justice is achieved and through triple bottom line accounting, the outcomes might be better distributed.
- *Social capital and diversity*, so that mega events can be used to transfer social capital to more civic gatherings and bridge the gaps within communities around diversity.
- An ability to accommodate a *diversity of meanings* associated with the event and to transcend divisions across borders.
- *Localization of leveraging benefits and capacity building*, to grow the collaboration and ability of the area to host such events by harnessing the latent potential through collaboration and coordination.
- *Inclusiveness and co-creation*, especially through a participative planning process and the wider engagement of publics in the process.
- *Authenticity* in the event, avoiding over-commercialization and protection from politics.
- *Cultural revitalization*, with local communities being empowered with the opportunity to devise their own leveraging plans.
- *Accountability and evaluation*, with a holistic overview of the leveraging plans.
- *Holistic strategy development*, with a cross-leveraging strategy to encompass event portfolios.
- *Ideology and marginalization*, understanding the processes which lead to people being marginalized through event leveraging strategies.

Whilst this list of areas for research is laudable for readers, it is somewhat devoid of the reality of how leveraging works in practice – especially the highly politicized nature of decision-making in the real world – and detached from the mechanisms that shape mega-event development. Such a socially inclusive agenda for mega-event development is probably very idealistic and fails to acknowledge the dynamics of the bidding and implementation process where costs and benefits are not reviewed against a social checklist to enhance the public good. Typically the prime purpose is for area development within an economic setting, whereby the investment from the public sector has an overriding focus on employment growth and cultural strategy to elevate the image and commercial appeal of a destination. The social outcomes tend to be by-products of the wider economic strategies to replace lost employment in areas that have been transformed through the loss of local industries in global economic restructuring. This has been expressed in some critiques as the entrepreneurial city or location, seeking to engage in new economic opportunities, sometimes at a major cost.

Cities competing as event capitals

Any city can call itself an event capital, but what does it mean? In a highly competitive international marketplace, cities will inevitably want to brand themselves in such a way as to attract attention and respect. Gothenburg, Sweden has often referred to itself as a European event capital, and Edmonton, Canada has identified itself as a festival capital. Singapore wants to be the events and entertainment capital of Asia (see Foley *et al.* 2008). Increasingly there are awards to be won! Edinburgh won IFEA's World Festival and Event City award for 2010 and was declared the 'most outstanding global entry' (www.ifea.com). IFEA said: 'There is a real sense of magic in the transforming power that a truly great festival brings to a city. The intensity of that magic in Edinburgh is not from one festival, but twelve.' Melbourne, Australia won the 'Ultimate Sports City' award from *Sport Business* magazine (www.sportbusiness.com), competing against 24 other cities, for the third time in a row. Criteria included the number of annual sports events held, major events held or hosting rights secured between 2006 and 2014, numbers of federations hosted, facilities/venues, transport, accommodation, government support, security, legacy, public sports interest and quality of life.

Hospitality studies

This professional field is focused on hotels, resorts and food and beverage services (e.g. catering, restaurants and bars) and often encompasses elements of the travel and tourism industry. Some diploma and degree programmes specialize in clubs, business and industry dining, leisure services, campus dining, convention facilities, transportation, theme parks, state and national park operations, and casino operations. Increasingly convention and event management is included within hospitality curricula. Frequently hospitality and tourism programmes are integrated within business schools, and in some cases with sport and leisure as well.

Hotel, club, convention-centre and restaurant managers are responsible for the events or 'functions' markets in their properties, while many resorts specialize in festivals and sport events suited to their recreational amenities and beautiful settings. The most common 'functions' held in hotels, restaurants and other hospitality venues are:

- weddings with banquets
- private parties (graduations, bar and bat mitzvahs)
- meetings and conventions
- consumer and trade shows
- entertainment events
- corporate functions like product launches.

For hospitality establishments to enter the conventions or exhibitions market they must have special-purpose facilities, equipment and services above and beyond the usual catering competencies. An important trend is the use of unique, non-traditional venues for meetings and conventions, such as museums, historic houses or even zoos. Most hospitality programmes are applied in nature, usually requiring hands-on training and job experience. At the university level there is increasing emphasis on hospitality studies, or the academic bases for a professional career in hospitality. This foundation has to include general business management, services management and marketing, the special management challenges of hospitality venues, and events or functions – often tied to catering (see Table 5.4).

Table 5.4 Hospitality management and hospitality studies

	Nature and meanings; the event experience	Antecedents to attending events	Planning and producing events	Outcomes and the impacted	Processes and patterns
Hospitality management					
Hotel, resort, restaurant management; service provision; gastronomy; events as 'functions'	Receiving hospitality at events (being a guest) Corporate hospitality as a unique event experience		Service quality Atmospherics Technical considerations (lighting, sound, safety, health)	Business impacts Client and guest satisfaction	The competitive environment for events is dynamic Rising expectations for quality
Hospitality studies					
Studies host–guest interactions and interdependencies The nature of hospitality and service	Service quality as a determinant of future demand Growth in demand for corporate and private events as professional services				

As its core phenomenon, hospitality studies deals with formal, usually commercialized, host–guest interaction and interdependence. To be a 'host' in this context entails legal and social responsibilities, and requires an understanding of service provision both as a business, a technical skill and a fundamental aspect of human nature. Service quality is a major theme in hospitality studies, and the related theory and methods are directly applicable to event management. Customer-to-customer interaction is important in shaping the experience and perceptions of quality, and to a degree this interaction can be facilitated by managers.

Levy (2010) argued that in the design and programming of hedonic service settings such as events, managers can facilitate positive social interactions between guests. Levy's study outlined the effect of managerially facilitated consumer-to-consumer interactions on Asian and Western consumer evaluations and behavioural outcomes. A field experimental methodology was employed within the cultural group tour context. Asians are found to benefit from management facilitation of social interaction at higher levels than Westerners.

Education and interpretation

Education and informal learning are embodied in many types of planned events, notably meetings and conventions, but little attention has been paid to the educational roles of events in general and research in leisure offers a number of observations on how we examine such experiences (Dattilo and Howard 1994) as a dynamic phenomenon. A study by Gitelson *et al.* (1995) was a rare look at the educational objectives of an event, and related effectiveness. Sponsors and social marketers are very concerned with how to best get across their messages to event audiences. We also need to be concerned with how events themselves can be interpreted, for example to explain symbolic and culturally significant elements to visitors, and to engage visitors more through learning opportunities at events. The event designer and programmer therefore has to draw upon the education and interpretation fields, including their understanding and use of cognitive psychology and learning styles.

Learning theory

'Learning' is a process requiring the active involvement of the learner – knowledge cannot simply be transferred to people by teachers or any other means. 'Experience' is often said to be the best teacher, and certainly graduates are fond of saying they learned more in the first week of employment than they did in their entire academic career (teachers dispute this). In addition to basic knowledge, the learning process can be focused on physical or problem-solving skills, or shaping one's values and attitudes. Teachers generally emphasize that their job is to enable students to become life-long learners – to learn how to learn (Table 5.5).

'Bloom's Taxonomy' (Bloom 1956: 201–207) divides the learning process into a six-level hierarchy, where knowledge is the lowest order of cognition and evaluation the highest:

1. 'Knowledge' is the memory of previously learnt materials such as facts, terms, basic concepts and answers.
2. 'Comprehension' is the understanding of facts and ideas by organization, comparison, translation, interpretation and description.

Table 5.5 Education and interpretation

	Nature and meanings; the event experience	Antecedents to attending events	Planning and producing events	Outcomes and the impacted	Processes and patterns
Education					
What is knowledge? Didactics (teaching) Learning styles	Events as learning experiences	The influence of education levels on demand Desire for learning as a motive to attend events	Programming and design for learning (e.g. seminars, speakers, clinics)	What participants learn (i.e. measures of educational effectiveness)	Rising education levels affect motives and demand
Interpretation					
Theories and practice of interpretation in various settings (e.g. heritage sites, museums, events)	Interpretation through events Interpretation of the meanings of events	Availability of interpretation as it affects demand	Programming with interpretation (styles of interpretation)	Measuring the effectiveness of interpretation	Growing demand for profound experiences leads to greater need for interpretation

3. 'Application' is the use of new knowledge to solve problems.

4. 'Analysis' is the examination and division of information into parts by identifying motives or causes. A person can analyse by making inferences and finding evidence to support generalizations.

5. 'Synthesis' is the compilation of information in a new way by combining elements into patterns or proposing alternative solutions.

6. 'Evaluation' is the presentation and defence of opinions by making judgements about information, validity of ideas or quality of work based on a set of criteria.

How do people learn? The four main styles of learning can be adapted to meetings, conventions and other educational events as follows (they are not mutually exclusive and some people learn best by one style or several combined):

1. 'visual' (learn by seeing): use movies, graphics, performances;

2. 'verbal/auditory' (learn by hearing): use speakers, discussants, panels, tapes;

3. 'reading/writing' (learn by processing text): use readings and printed material; have attendees write things, make notes;

4. 'kinaesthetic' or 'experiential': involve people in creating or discussing; take field trips; get people to participate in events; run experiments; combine observation with reflection and discussion/writing.

Meeting Professionals International (MPI 2003: 62), in their *Planning Guide*, advised members they must know how adults learn. They discussed how learning can be influenced by a number of event-related facets including emotional stimulation, socializing, setting and conference programme. 'Tools of the trade' for meeting planners to foster learning experiences include case studies, lectures, discussions, poster sessions, demonstrations, participatory workshops and 'experiential learning' (i.e. learn through doing). Hilliard (2006: 46) noted that 'education is the most consistent function of associations' but there has been little research devoted to how adult learning principles should be applied at conventions. Hilliard therefore discussed how meeting planners can better achieve their goal of educating association members. Common challenges include an over-emphasis on content, rather than delivery, and a one-way flow of information rather than the creation of an interactive learning environment.

Packer and Ballantyne (2005) found that the social dimension is an important aspect of museum learning. Many visitors report having discussed or shared information with their companions. There is also evidence, however, that some museum visitors prefer to visit alone or to learn by themselves. This study explores qualitative and quantitative differences in the nature and outcomes of solitary and shared museum learning experiences. Forty solitary adults and 40 adults visiting in pairs were observed and interviewed during their visit to a museum exhibition area, and a proportion of participants were contacted by telephone four weeks after the visit. The findings challenge the supposition that social interaction is more beneficial to learning than a solitary experience and suggest that, for adult learners, solitary and shared learning experiences can be equally beneficial, but in different ways.

Interpretation

This can mean language interpretation, or the interpretation of signs and symbols (i.e. semiotics), but we are interested here in the forms of education or other communications designed to reveal meanings and relationships. Interpreters work for parks, heritage sites, zoos, museums, galleries, aquariums, theme parks and tour companies with the purpose of making certain their visitors truly understand what is being displayed, observed or otherwise experienced. The National Association for Interpretation (www.interpnet.com) is international in its membership and proclaims that 'interpretation is a communication process that forges emotional and intellectual connections between the interests of the audience and the meanings inherent in the resource'.

With regard to parks and heritage interpretation, Tilden (1957) is considered to have had the greatest influence. His six Principles of Interpretation are widely used:

1. Any interpretation that does not somehow relate what is being displayed or described to something within the personality or experience of the visitor will be sterile.
2. Information, as such, is not interpretation. Interpretation is revelation based upon information. But they are entirely different things. However, all interpretation includes information.
3. Interpretation is an art, which combines many arts, whether the materials presented are scientific, historical or architectural. Any art is in some degree teachable.
4. The chief aim of interpretation is not instruction, but provocation.
5. Interpretation should aim to present a whole rather than a part, and must address itself to the whole man rather than any phase.
6. Interpretation addressed to children (say, up to the age of 12) should not be a dilution of the presentation to adults, but should follow a fundamentally different approach. To be at its best, it will require a separate programme.

Bramwell and Lane (1993) have argued that interpretation is a cornerstone of sustainable tourism, but they identified a number of related issues or pitfalls. One concern is that interpretation can alter the meaning of cultural assets, such as by emphasizing economic roles. Deciding on what to interpret for visitors is an issue, as only a few themes or stories can be told, and this can be a political or even divisive process. Should only the unusual or spectacular be interpreted? There is also a danger of aiming interpretation only at the educated elite, while ignoring the needs of mass tourism.

Thematic interpretation

Based on cognitive psychology, 'thematic interpretation' is based on a key premise: that people remember themes far more easily than they remember facts. If event designers tap into universal belief systems, they can more easily communicate with audiences, and audiences both need and want meaningful experiences as opposed to simple entertainment. Thematic interpretation aims to create visitor experiences that have lasting impact, translating into higher levels of satisfaction, positive word of mouth, sales and repeat visits. It is best described as strategic communication.

Professor Sam Ham of the University of Idaho is most closely associated with developing and applying thematic interpretation within parks, heritage and tourism. Dr Ham, Anna Housego and Betty Weiler together authored the *Tasmanian Thematic Interpretation Planning Manual* (May 2005: available online at www.tourismtasmania.com), as part of that Australian state's innovative Experience Strategy. We can adapt their planning process to events. A convenient starting point is their definition and explanation of theme:

> *A theme is a take-home message; it's the moral of the story or main conclusion a visitor takes away.*
>
> *(Ham et al. 2005: 3)*

> *A theme is a whole idea . . . is the way you express the essence of the message you and others in your organisation want to impart to visitors; it is not necessarily the set of words you would use in direct communication to visitors . . . when a moral to the story really matters to the visitor then it touches them in lots of ways, and that's when it really sticks.*
>
> *(Ham et al. 2005: 13)*

If an event theme is thought of merely in terms of decoration or entertainment, which is appropriate at many events, then interpretation is not really required. But at cultural celebrations, religious ceremonies, arts festivals and many other planned events, we want the visitor to be emotionally and cognitively affected; we want a memorable, even transforming experience. While event guests and customers might not remember all the activities or information provided, they should be provoked into reflection and involvement by the main theme so they can make their own meanings from, and about, the event, the place and the time they spent there. Using both tangibles and intangible elements (such as symbols and emotional engagement) in interpretation makes for more powerful theming.

Ideally, the theme and various interpretive media (or tools) are targeted to various audiences depending on their levels of interest, the extent and nature of their participation, and how managers want to influence them, thereby requiring a fairly sophisticated research and evaluation process. Higher levels of effectiveness can probably be achieved through greater investment in planning and research. Evaluation of results will have to include measures of actual behaviour at the event and afterwards, questions about more intangible emotional and cognitive outcomes and effects on other people through word of mouth.

Interpretation tools

Interpretation of, and at, events can include the following tools; they can be thought of as different 'media', each with their own application depending on audiences and situations as shown in Figure 5.4.

As Arellano (2011) observed within a commemorative festival with 'street culture', producers get people to join in, and not just watch the spectacle. 'The festival goers are more than just a passive audience; they are confronted with several layers of dramatization and interpretation. Reconstruction proper, where the actor plays a historical character in the first person . . . uses spectacle to convey a passive vision.' But interpretation is also interactive, with some performers explaining to the audience what they are doing, both meanings and roles of historical characters, generating a dialogue. 'In addition to dressing in period costume and interacting with the players and actors, visitors are incorporated into the historical performance, through improvising and directing the performance, which encourages active learning, learning by doing . . .' This links with the discussion of dramaturgy which we will return to in the next chapter on the event experience.

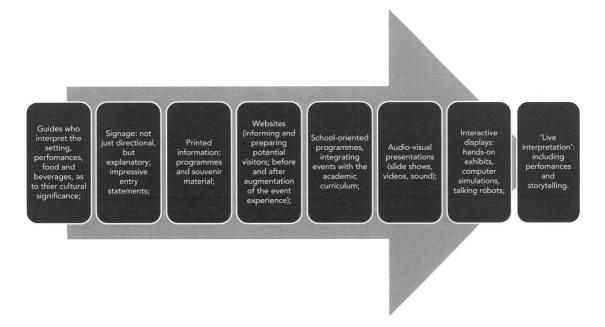

Figure 5.4 Forms of interpretation

Communications, media and performance studies

Communications can be defined as the exchange of meanings between people through a common system of symbols, such as – and especially – language. Jaworski and Pritchard (2005: 2) noted that communication 'refers to the practices, processes and mediums by which meanings are provided and understood in a cultural context'. This field covers a wide range of topics and issues, particularly speech and rhetoric, intercultural communication, information theory, public relations, propaganda and mass communications technology. It is often considered to include broadcasting, media and performance studies. Events can be considered as communication tools or artefacts, both from the point of view of event marketing (i.e. sponsors' messages at events) and as a means to interpret culture (Table 5.6). Elsewhere we have examined interpretation as a form of communication and education.

Information theory, at its most basic, is concerned with the communication process between a 'sender' (e.g. the event or some element of it) and a 'receiver' (a person or a broader audience). Masterman and Wood (2006: 4) described how the event organizer tries to convey 'messages' through specific 'media', and these messages are 'encoded' through selection of certain images, words or symbols. The target audience might fail to get the messages, owing to environmental 'noise' (i.e. all the competing stimuli and messages), or might incorrectly 'decode' (i.e. misinterpret) the messages because of ambiguity, social or cultural biases. Unless this process is monitored and evaluated, the senders could be wasting their efforts.

There are many communications and information issues: is the message clear, accurate and compelling? Does the receiver get the intended message, and act upon it in accordance with the sender's intent? Are there cultural differences that affect the communication process? Are certain channels or media more effective? These issues have obvious event-marketing implications. Communications can also be ritualistic, as with events that hold meanings such as pilgrimage and *rites de passage*. Information has to be communicated in certain ways, and perhaps only the initiated understand the true meaning. Events, in this context, can hold both superficial appeal as entertainment, and deeper cultural meanings for participants.

Media studies

Media studies covers the nature and effects of mass media upon individuals and society, as well as analysing actual media content and representations. The pioneer scholar in media studies, Marshall McLuhan, wrote in his book *Understanding Media* (1964) 'the medium is the message', which is probably one of the most misunderstood popular phrases of all times.

Our interpretation of McLuhan's dictum is that planned events are not merely communications tools, but are media for change. And we will understand events only by examining those changes, intended or otherwise. So we should not be distracted by the Internet or social media, but look always to the content and what it is changing.

The study of the effects and techniques of advertising forms a cornerstone of media studies. 'Critical media theory' looks at how the corporate ownership of media production and distribution affects society, and this can be applied to the events world by examining how sponsorship and media coverage can convert a local production into a global event, or how mega events have been converted into advertising platforms and instruments of cultural influence. As Dean (1999) noted, three advertising cues – third-party product endorsement, brand popularity and event sponsorship – have a powerful impact on how consumers perceive an event, including its esteem value. McPhail's (2006) theory of 'electronic colonialism' has gained international recognition. He argued that mass media over time will impact upon more and more individuals, primarily using the English language, resulting in greater similarities. Indigenous films and artefacts become marginalized by high-quality and mass-produced media. Perhaps this can be called the Hollywood effect.

Table 5.6 Communications, media and performance studies

	Nature and meanings; the event experience	Antecedents to attending events	Planning and producing events	Outcomes and the impacted	Processes and patterns
Communication studies					
Theories of information; symbols and semiotics; discourse Problems and methods in communications	Events as symbols and communications tools	Symbolic representations of events can encourage 'consumption'	Communication effectiveness Branding Interpretation Edutainment	Evaluation of marketing effectiveness resulting in changes in attitude or behaviour	Technological and media trends (TV coverage, virtual reality, Internet)
Media studies					
Studies the nature and influences of mass media on individuals and society Media content and representations The audience New media	Homogenization of events through mass media effects Virtual experiences	Effects of advertising on decision-making	Events designed for media audiences, both mass and segmented	Global audiences Displacement of indigenous forms of communication/events	Trends in mass media affecting the event sector
Performance studies					
The study and uses of performances, including planned events	Events as expressions of sub- and counter-cultures Create your own event experience	Desire for alternative experiences	Actors and audience merge	Personal and group identities	Values and attitudes toward performance styles

Performance studies

Schechner (2002) combined the study of anthropology with performance of all kinds, including ritual, drama, environmental theatre, political rallies, dance and music, thereby creating an intellectual-artistic field of studies. Performances, including planned events and their various performative elements, are studied from multiple perspectives in terms of their contribution to society. Wikipedia defined performance studies thus:

> *This field of study engages performance as both an object of study and as something to be experienced, practiced, enacted. Events are more than their face value. A sporting event, a ceremony, a protest are all performances in their own right. Events have specific actors, costumes, settings and audiences. Within these performances are more minute performances of self: of gender, of societal role(s), of age, of disposition(s). Examining events as performance provides insight into how we perform ourselves and our lives.*

According to Deighton (1992), consumers and events/performances interact in the following ways:

- People attend performances (passive spectators);
- People participate in performance (active roles);
- Consumers 'perform' with products (they buy goods that have symbolic meaning and use them with others, to impress them, for example, which becomes a performance (see Goffman's 1959 book *The Representation of Self in Everyday Life*));
- Products 'perform' for consumers: this is a metaphorical use of the term, as performance here means meeting technical specifications; but the marketer uses the analogy of theatrical or event performance to help sell the product (e.g. car ads that feature speed, glamour, etc. in a way that clearly suggests that buying the car will positively impact on your lifestyle).

Deighton also assessed how people assign meaning to their experiences. Photography is often a record of the good aspects of the trip or event, not the bad. When the photos are viewed at a later date, especially when shared, they are a record of the good times experienced. Given the imperfections of human memory, it is possible that we remember our remembrances (through photos and stories) more than the real experience. Telling stories – a 'narrative' – is the other common way that people assign meaning to experiences. This leads to several research methods, including asking people to construct a narrative, or analysing what people are saying on blogs. These narratives are 'social constructions' and can be heavily influenced by cultural/social conventions and interactions with fellow event-goers. They can also be quite unique, with different meanings assigned to exactly the same tangible experience.

When it comes to evaluating the quality of performances, Deighton argued that they must be considered in a different light from other goods and services. The event-goer might very well ascribe satisfaction to his or her participation or mood, or to others in the audience, rather than to the event organizers or performers. As well, surprise must be considered – people's expectations can be met and exceeded through good marketing and event design, but surprising people introduces a whole new set of factors. Is the audience delighted with the surprise, or angered?

As a consequence of temporality, people asked to evaluate satisfaction levels or quality during an event are likely to consider benefits that have not yet accrued to them, such as how they anticipate they will feel when it is over. Even when it is officially over, there is the possibility that event-goers need a lot of time to really come to a conclusion about how the event affected them, and what it means – if anything – in their lives. A good event designer also has the opportunity to educate the audience during the event, so that their evaluations at the beginning, mid-way and end might be quite different. For example, if the audience is not familiar with a particular form of interpretation, art or contest, they will need time and instruction before they can pass any judgement about the event's quality and their own satisfaction with it.

Deighton analysed performance failures related to the intention behind the performance. Expectations are a big issue. If the audience feels deceived in any way, such as if the performance was quite different from what was advertised, the quality of the performance becomes rather irrelevant to them. The skill level of performers might be judged incompetent (lip-syncing rather than live singing; rigged outcomes rather than unpredictable). A lack of originality can lead to the failure of a performance; if it is highly predictable there will be no surprise. In thrill events (races) the audience might conclude that risks were minimal, or were manipulated. Finally, if the audience is not brought into a festive event, if it lacks involvement, the organizers are likely to be blamed.

Deighton concluded that a 'show frame' rather than a 'skill frame' should be created for certain performances so that audience expectations are not disappointed as, for example, when athletes at all-star games or exhibition matches do not put everything into the contest. In the 'festive frame' organizers have to involve the audience and a certain amount of spontaneity should result. In a 'thrill frame' the risks have to be perceived to be real. Many implications for marketing and communications follow from this conclusion. As in the SERVQUAL model, consumer expectations directly impact on their evaluation of satisfaction and quality.

Performance (or 'live') art

Performance art consists of the impermanent actions of an individual or a group at a particular place and in a particular time, which of course also defines an 'event'. Presumably there has to be an audience, for can there be art without appreciation? Busking can be viewed as performance art. Martin *et al.* (2012) examined the engagement of young people with such art performances. In an extreme case, if you take away the audience, you have a flash mob, with the immediate and short-lived experience for participants overriding any concern for art.

Installation art

Sometimes artists are commissioned by governments or companies to enliven a space, get media attention or realize tourism and place-marketing aims. The installation artist can use a variety of media, and the installation is always temporary. The idea is to modify a space in terms of our tangible experience or concept of it. Most art installations are indoors, often in galleries. When they are outdoors they can attract a lot of attention, like a planned event but without a programme. Hu *et al.* (2013) examined the use of technology in creating interactive installations. Social connectedness among visitors can be facilitated and attractiveness of the experience thereby heightened.

Arts and cultural management

Superficially, arts and cultural management (or administration) is the application of management, including business practices and theory, to the operation of arts and cultural organizations and their work. It gets more complex, however, when we hear that many people in the arts or cultural sectors do not think that what they do is a business, or that normal management functions like marketing should apply. Why? The arguments are largely framed around notions of 'artistic integrity' that should not be diluted or commercialized by business methods – that audience development and accessibility are more important than pricing for profit, or that cultural tourism erodes authenticity (see Table 5.7 on this field of study).

Degree programmes in arts administration present one means of getting professionally involved with events, especially arts festivals and events held in art and cultural venues such as theatres, concert halls, museums and galleries. This is also a pathway into community outreach to foster art and cultural appreciation. In these programmes business management is applied to governmental and not-for-profit

Table 5.7 Arts and cultural management

Arts and cultural management	Nature and meanings; the event experience	Antecedents to attending events	Planning and producing events	Outcomes and the impacted	Processes and patterns
Management of arts and cultural organizations Community building through the arts and culture	Events as artistic and cultural expression Fostering appreciation and interpretation of arts and culture	Audience-building efforts generate demand for events	Management of arts and culture organizations that programme venues and produce events Volunteerism at events Partnerships for the arts/culture	Evaluating satisfaction with venues and performances Cultural impacts on society	Changing cultural norms Elitist perspectives on what is important The distribution of venues, events and organizations

Table 5.8 Cultural studies

Cultural studies	Nature and meanings; the event experience	Antecedents to attending events	Planning and producing events	Outcomes and the impacted	Processes and patterns
Critical study of popular culture and ordinary life	The appeal of art and entertainment events Importance and nature of cultural performances High and popular culture Cultural policy	Cultural capital Extrinsic motives to attend events	Linking the event sector to power and politics, gender and inequality	The distribution of costs and benefits	Culture is dynamic Cross-cultural comparisons and interactions

organizations that produce or commission events. Community building is covered, including outreach programmes, fundraising, volunteerism and partnership-building, all of which is useful to the event manager. Perhaps more importantly, the student will get an appreciation of the importance and roles of arts and culture in community life.

Cultural studies

The meanings and practice of everyday life are the subjects of cultural studies, a field that draws from anthropology, sociology and theory about all the forms of art and communications. Cultural practices comprise the ways people do particular things (such as watching television or eating out) in a given culture. Researchers examine how art, or popular activities like watching television, relate to matters of power, ideology, race, social class or gender. There can be a heavy Marxist bent to cultural studies, or a more neutral attempt to understand mass culture and how consumers attach meanings to forms of cultural expression. Hermeneutics is therefore employed to study the various 'texts' of cultural productions or artefacts (see Table 5.8 for an overview of the field).

Sport management and sport studies

Sport management focuses on sport organizations, such as professional clubs and public facilities, with specific interests in sport marketing, human resources, finance, organizational structure, organizational behaviour, ethics, information technology, policy development and communications (North American Society for Sport Management; www.nassm.com). NASSM's *Journal of Sport Management* carries articles on sport events and sport tourism, which are of particular interest to event studies. The importance of events in sport management is reflected in two handbooks, one on sport management in general (Robinson *et al.* 2013) and the most recent on sport event management (Parent and Chappelet 2015).

Sports by nature involve competitions, both regularly scheduled and one-time, so the coordination, production or marketing of events is usually an essential part of the job. This generally applies in athletics departments of educational institutions, international sport federations, professional sport clubs and leagues, sport facility and fitness club management, recreational sports (for parks and recreation departments or associations), sports commissions (city-based agencies active in event tourism development) and sport marketing firms. Graham *et al.* (1995), in their book *The Ultimate Guide to Sport Event Management and Marketing*, described this sector in detail, including types of careers and specific sport-event issues. In the book *Profiles of Sport Industry Professionals* by Robinson *et al.* (2001), numerous contributors describe their career paths and jobs, many of which involve events. The wider contribution of the subject to events is outlined in Table 5.9, with a number of these themes covered in Masterman's (2004, 2014) strategic analysis of sports event management.

Table 5.9 Sport management and sport studies

	Nature and meanings; the event experience	Antecedents to attending events	Planning and producing events	Outcomes and the impacted	Processes and patterns
Sport management					
Management of sport organizations, venues and events	Sport is both big business and public good Sport for health, fitness, mastery Sport as a social phenomenon	Unique motives for competing in or spectating at sport events Demand for sport tourism	Sport venue managers produce and host events Competitions produced by leagues and clubs Sport events bid on as part of sport tourism	Sport tourism impacts Personal well-being and social benefits of participation in sport events	Sport trends, fads (e.g. the diffusion of new sports) Sport development policy
Sport studies					
Sport psychology sociology history geography	Sport as entertainment		Social structures, patterns and organizations engaged in sport		Sport history Sport geography (patterns of sport and sport events)

Sport studies

'Sport psychology' is primarily concerned with the athlete, but the sport fan is also studied. Why does 'hooliganism' plague football, and why do fans celebrate to excess? Are there differences in motives between male and female fans and sport tourists? 'Sport sociology' relates more to event studies in that it focuses on groups and organizations engaged in sport, including those that produce and consume events. Studies of particular interest include sport subcultures, sport politics and national identity, sport and the media, violence, and sport influenced by gender, class, race or ethnicity. 'Sport anthropologists' are interested in the cultural importance of sport, and cultural differences reflected in sport.

Sport economics covers the economics of sport organizations, teams and events. Although sport-for-all and amateur athletics are often publicly supported to encourage healthy pursuits and socialization, subsidies for professional sport venues and teams have been quite controversial. Similarly, the bidding on and construction of facilities for sport events (i.e. sport tourism) almost always generates debates on costs and benefits.

Sport history includes the history of events and venues, with a great deal of attention having been paid to the Olympics; many interesting contributions can be found in the *International Journal of Sport History*. 'Sport geographers' examine the spatial distribution of sport events, and where athletes come from. The diffusion of new sports and of sport events combines the spatial and temporal dimensions and a number of interesting perspectives emerge from the work of key sport geographers (e.g. Bale and Dejonghe 2008) and the analysis of sporting events as cultural phenomena (e.g. Ferbrache 2013).

Sport tourism has emerged as a sub-field as illustrated by the *Journal of Sport and Tourism*, particularly because it has become a major element in destination competitiveness.

For example, Funk *et al.* (2007) outlined the attraction process within the Psychological Continuum Model (PCM) (Funk and James, 2001, 2006) to develop and examine five hypotheses related to motives of international participants who registered for a hallmark Australian running event. Structural equation modelling revealed that registration for the event is motivated by prior running involvement; the desire to participate in organized running events; favourable beliefs and feelings toward the host destination; and perceived travel benefits of escape, social interaction, prestige, relaxation, culture experience, cultural learning and knowledge exploration.

Venue, club and assembly management

Events are often held in single- or general-purpose arenas, convention centres, stadia or theatres, all of which can belong to the International Association of Venue Managers (www.IAVM.org). When you own or manage a venue, events are at the forefront of your mind: there are sometimes clients who pay to use the facility, and sometimes events are bid on or created to fill gaps. Hotels, clubs, restaurants and many other facilities with function spaces are also in this business. Clubs are usually private, owned by members or based on paid membership, and often closely tied to sports (e.g. golf or yacht clubs), fitness and health. Not-for-profit associations, including ethnic groups, often run clubs with facilities. The magazine *Club Management* is aimed at professional club managers, and their association is Club Managers Association of America (www.CMAA.org). Entertainment and catered events are common at clubs. Their 'events directors' might have responsibility for booking entertainment, arranging caterers or hiring decorators (see Table 5.10).

Some of the pertinent research includes the study of Preda and Watts (2003) on capacity constraints in moving people at sport-event venues. Yeoman *et al.* (2004) discussed event visitor management, including demand, flow, capacity, queuing and service.

Table 5.10 Venue, club and assembly management

Venue, club and assembly management	Nature and meanings; the event experience	Antecedents to attending events	Planning and producing events	Outcomes and the impacted	Processes and patterns
Design and management of event settings	Club membership generates expectations and participation Experience is shaped by the venue and its management	Some venues are attractions in their own right Big events usually require big arenas	Venues produce and host events Policy and regulations affecting venues and clubs	Private versus public access to venues and events Small, private events versus large, public events	Venue technologies and design Popularity of types of clubs Locational patterns (supply and demand factors)

Theatre studies

Theatre studies are liberal arts programmes that typically encompass acting, production, technical aspects of theatre and the history of theatre. At New York University's Tisch School of the Arts, the theatre studies programme aims 'to give students the artistic and intellectual foundations necessary for a successful professional life in the theatre and allied disciplines. The intensive and rigorous training received in studio is contextualized within and enriched by a knowledge of the theatre as an art and an institution, with a history, a literature, and a vital role in culture'. (http://drama.tisch.nyu.edu/object/dr_theatreStudies.html)

Theatrical productions are events. While they are typically produced as the regular business of theatrical companies, in regular seasons or programmes, they are also produced in festivals. And plays or other theatrical productions can certainly be viewed as special events from the perspective of the audience. More importantly, the very concepts of theatre and performance, steeped in tradition and culturally distinctive, lie at the foundation of event design. And theatre is relevant to all forms of event, from sports (especially 'professional' wrestling, which hopefully everyone recognizes as being staged), to meetings (the 'drama' of debate and the 'staging' of presentations), to festivals ('rites and rituals performed' for the audience and including the audience) to trade shows (replete with entertainment and 'showmanship').

Scripting events

The metaphor of events as theatre is good only to a point. First, theatres are production houses (business or not-for-profit) that create programmes of scheduled events. Second, while many event producers have a theatrical background, only certain types of planned events can be fully staged and scripted. Pine and Gilmore (1999) used the framework of Richard Schechner from the book *Performance Theory* (1988). The base is 'drama', which can be any form of story or tragedy. Drama depicts the theme of the performance, and can be expressed through different media. For a conference, the drama is the collective mission and discourse of those in attendance; for a gala banquet it can be a historical theme. The 'script' tells performers what to do, and it can include precise instructions or general directions. A script can incorporate elements of surprise or improvisation (see Table 5.11).

Table 5.11 Theatre studies

Theatre studies	Nature and meanings; the event experience	Antecedents to attending events	Planning and producing events	Outcomes and the impacted	Processes and patterns
Professional preparation for theatrical productions Drama Acting History and types of theatre	Professional theatre applied to events Events as entertainment or social commentary Cultural meanings	Cultural traditions shape demand for theatre Demand shaped by opportunity (supply) Unique theatrical productions motivate travel	Creativity Scripted performances Setting design (staging)	Personal versus societal benefits Theatre as a business	Arts and cultural policy Changing societal values

Theatre, in this framework, is the event itself – the performers implementing their script. Staff members, even volunteers at events, are performers in this theatre because they have such an important role to play in creating the desired experience. Accordingly, everyone has to have a script. What Pine and Gilmore (1999) wanted to stress is that work, in the workplace, should also be thought of as theatre. And of course if the theatre is interactive, involving the audience by way of activity and mental/emotional immersion, the experience will be that much more unique and memorable. Finally, Schechner (1988) defined 'performance' as being dependent on having an audience. Performances are perceived, or simply enjoyed. An interaction has to occur, but the 'audience' does not necessarily have to appreciate that they are part of a performance or being influenced by a script.

Forms of theatre

Schechner (1988) also differentiated between four basic forms of theatre (see Table 5.12), each embodying varying degrees of being scripted in combination with stable or dynamic performance. The first is 'improvisation' (or 'improv'), a form of theatre in which the script is very flexible and the outcomes unpredictable. It is most used for comedy, but also seems to describe many flash-mob events. Improvisation actually requires preparation and many skills to be effective as theatre or to be used in a special event. Audiences should quickly appreciate that they are part of an experiment and the journey they are taking with the performers is going nowhere in particular, or inevitably will result in surprises. At a minimum, 'improv' events need a premise or a scenario, a starting point or concept. They offer great scope for audience involvement. In stark contrast to the 'improv' is the 'platform' theatre, which we associate with plays and musicals. The performance is generally fully scripted (memorized and rehearsed) and the performers clearly separated from the audience. In these types of event the guest is seldom motivated to attend twice, unless the excellence and subtleties of the show encourage a desire for deeper understanding; unless it is so enjoyable that experiencing it again is more enjoyable!

'Matching theatre' is edited, like a film or television show. Someone has to put it together to create a coherent whole. The audience can be asked to move about a venue, as in some murder mystery

Table 5.12 Schechner's (1988) four forms of theatre

Street theatre	Improv theatre
Dynamic performance	Dynamic script
Stable script	Stable performance
Platform theatre	Matching theatre
Stable performance	Dynamic script
Stable script	Dynamic performance

performances, trying to form a mental picture of everything that is happening, despite discontinuities in both space and time.

'Street theatre', otherwise known as 'performances by buskers or travelling minstrels', can be informal and highly individualistic or packaged within festivals. The entertainers have to put on a show, first drawing the audience then engaging them sufficiently to secure a voluntary financial reward. Ordinary space has to serve as a stage, and in some cases can be incorporated into the act, becoming really unique, temporary event settings. Their script has to be relatively stable, after all they are jugglers or fire-eaters, or singers or clowns. But each performance is also going to be a unique blend of audience–performer interactions, setting (imagine the street noise) and programme (they have to possess an adaptable repertoire in terms of specific acts, and be able to alter their sequence and timing).

A. Rogers (2012), a geographer, examined in a review article how the performing arts of dance, theatre, music and live art have become established means through which cultural geographers can examine how people experience and make sense of their everyday worlds. This is a very similar theme to that of connecting festivals and events to place identity, as articulated by De Bres and Davis (2001) regarding festivals and Ramshaw and Hinch (2006) in the context of sports events.

Health studies

Mass assemblies, from a health perspective, present a huge risk and there are many historical examples such as the flu pandemic of 1918–1919 that saw such gatherings avoided (Johnson 2006). Increasingly we are seeing attention given to events from health and related fields, often combining elements of risk management, security, customer service and regulations. Event tourism is obviously impacted by disease, real or threatened (see Table 5.13), and this highlights the major role of travel medicine in informing event management and hosting (Page 2009; Al-Tawfiq and Memish 2012; Memish *et al.* 2014).

A great deal of attention must be given to mass gatherings such as the Hajj, and the visitors' well-being. One such examination of events and health was undertaken around the Athens Summer Olympics of 2004 (Tsouros and Efstathiou 2007). The main risks were identified as disease (transmitted through food, water, travellers); accidents and injuries; terrorism and crime; and weather and other environmental threats. These are broadly similar to the continuum of traveller problems identified in the scientific literature on travel medicine. Where travellers come from is a concern, as well as how many, density in and around venues, visitor flow and turnover.

Three main areas of concern are illustrated in Figure 5.5, which can form the starting point for planning.

Table 5.13 Health studies

Health studies	Nature and meanings; the event experience	Antecedents to attending events	Planning and producing events	Outcomes and the impacted	Processes and patterns
The study of injury and illness: causes, prevention, treatment	Events as factors contributing to health and well-being Safe and healthy experiences Experiences and behaviour modified by drugs and alcohol	Fear of injury and illness is a constraint Health concerns can motivate attendance at certain events (e.g. healthy living expos) Some events have a drug/alcohol culture	Health and safety regulations affect design and management Restrictions on travel or activities Need for security	Health effects of events and related activities on persons and populations Events that gain bad reputations in the community	Events and the spread of illness Statistics of injury and illnesses at events, over time

Psycho-social domain
(Who are the visitors, their motivations, behaviour, drug/alcohol use, emotions, length of stay);

Biomedical domain
(Crowd and individual health status, potential for injury and illness, age and gender, activity level of spectators and participants, temperature/weather-related physiology, alcohol and drug-related physiology);

Environmental domain
(Attendance and density, indoor or outdoor venues, terrain, type and nature of event, seated or moblie, temperature and humidity, availability of drugs/alcohol).

Figure 5.5 Planning model for events and health concerns

Health-care specialists want to assess the risks, the need for response services and the ways in which prevention or minimization can be implemented. The potential for a major incident is particularly important, including violence and the outbreak of serious disease. One important consideration when contemplating the hosting of a large-scale event is the host region's capability of dealing with a resulting disaster.

5.2 RESEARCH NOTES ON HEALTH AND EVENTS

Lee, J.-E., Almanza, B. and Nelson, D. (2010). Food safety at fairs and festivals: Vendor knowledge and violations at regional festivals. *Event Management*, 14(3), 215–223.

The concern is for food-borne illnesses at events. Researchers studied violations, and food vendors at Indiana festivals were tested. They were found to be mostly knowledgeable of regulations. Training implications were discussed.

Memish, Z. A., Zumla, A., Alhakeem, R. F., Assiri, A., Turkestani, A., Al Harby, K. D. and Al-Tawfiq, J. A. (2014). Hajj: Infectious disease surveillance and control. *The Lancet*, 383(9934), 2073–2082.

'Religious festivals attract a large number of pilgrims from all over the world and are a potential risk for the transmission of infectious diseases between pilgrims, and to the indigenous population. The gathering of a large number of pilgrims could compromise the health system of the host country. The threat to global health security posed by infectious diseases with epidemic potential shows the importance of advanced planning of public health surveillance and response at these religious events. Saudi Arabia has extensive experience of providing health care at mass gatherings acquired through decades of managing millions of pilgrims at the Hajj. In this report, we describe the extensive public health planning, surveillance systems used to monitor public health risks, and health services provided and accessed during Hajj 2012 and Hajj 2013 that together attracted more than 5 million pilgrims from 184 countries. We also describe the recent establishment of the Global Center for Mass Gathering Medicine, a Saudi government partnership with the WHO Collaborating Centre for Mass Gatherings Medicine, Gulf Co-operation Council states, UK universities and public health institutions globally.'

Urban and community studies

Urban and community studies, and its closely related professional field urban (or town) planning, deals with a variety of issues concerning the development and planning of cities and communities as well as related policy issues. It is interdisciplinary and draws heavily from geography, history, economics, sociology, architecture, design, cultural anthropology and political science and is a very productive area of research on events; its scope is illustrated in Table 5.14.

Event studies fits into any number of urban and community topics, particularly since most large-scale events and event venues are located in cities. Figure 5.6 provides examples from the recent research literature on urban studies to illustrate the important interface between urban and event studies; the journal *Urban Studies* is an important source.

One of the most influential studies on mega events and urban policy was by Roche (1994), who reviewed the influence of planning, political and urban contextual processes and factors on mega-event production. Roche illustrated these themes through a discussion of comparative event research and a case study of Sheffield's Universiade 1991. This study indicates the important influence of contextual societal change, urban leadership and non-rational planning in event production processes. Subsequently Quinn (2003) reviewed the existing literature on urban festivals and argued that city authorities tend to disregard the social value of festivals and to construe them simply as vehicles of economic generation or as 'quick fix' solutions to city image problems. Quinn argued that if arts festivals are to achieve their undoubted potential in animating communities, celebrating diversity and improving quality of life, then they must be conceived of in a more holistic way by urban managers.

Table 5.14 Urban and community studies

Urban and community studies	Nature and meanings; the event experience	Antecedents to attending events	Planning and producing events	Outcomes and the impacted	Processes and patterns
Urban development and dynamics Communities Place identity Planning, development and design	Events as urban cultural experiences Relationship to the urban setting (e.g. heritage) Larger crowds affect urban events Venues are mostly urban	Desire to escape city environments Proximity to many event venues Increased opportunity for urban-dwellers Subcultural and community influences (desire for identity and sharing)	Urban planners and designers create spaces for events, and spaces that need the animation of events Event offices within city administrations Urban-based tourism and cultural agencies	Effects of events on urban form, housing, design, liveability	The festivalization of urban policy (within the context of development and place marketing) The geography of events within cities The history and evolution of events within cities

Cornelissen, S. (2011). Mega event securitisation in a third world setting: Glocal processes and ramifications during the 2010 FIFA World Cup. *Urban Studies*, 48(15), 3221–3240.

Dawson, M. (2011). Putting cities on the map: Vancouver's 1954 British Empire and Commonwealth Games in comparative and historical perspective 1. *Urban Geography*, 32(6), 788–803.

Kontokosta, C. (2012). The price of victory: The impact of the Olympic Games on residential real estate markets. *Urban Studies*, 49(5), 961–978.

Macbeth, J., Selwood, J. and Veitch, S. (2012). Paradigm shift or a drop in the ocean? The America's Cup impact on Fremantle. *Tourism Geographies*, 14(1), 162–182.

Rota, F. S. and Salone, C. (2014). Place-making processes in unconventional cultural practices. The case of Turin's contemporary art festival Paratissima. *Cities*, 40, 90–98.

Smith, A. (2014). 'Borrowing' public space to stage major events: The Greenwich Park controversy. *Urban Studies*, 51(2), 247–263.

Taylor, T. and Toohey, K. (2011). Ensuring safety at Australian sport event precincts: Creating securitised, sanitised and stifling spaces? *Urban Studies*, 48(15), 3259–3275.

Vanwynsberghe, R., Surborg, B. and Wyly, E. (2013). When the games come to town: Neoliberalism, mega-events and social inclusion in the Vancouver 2010 Winter Olympic Games. *International Journal of Urban and Regional Research*, 37(6), 2074–2093.

Weller, S. (2013). Consuming the city: Public fashion festivals and the participatory economies of urban spaces in Melbourne. *Urban Studies*, 50(14), 2853–2868.

Figure 5.6 Recent examples of progress in urban studies and events research

Gelder and Robinson (2011: 140) emphasized the importance of arts and festivals in particular in urban policy as:

> *Arts and cultural projects have played an increasingly important role in British urban regeneration since the mid-1980s; however, the focus has shifted over the years to the capability of arts activity in supporting community-led renewal, rather than on capital projects.*

These can also be harnessed more fully in year-long cultural events, such as the European Cities of Culture, as outlined by Richards and Palmer (2010).

Rural studies

Hall and Page (2014) argue that the term 'rural', based on G. M. Robinson's (1990) synthesis, has remained an elusive one to define in academic research, although a number of popular conceptions of rural areas are based on images of rusticity and the idyllic village life.

However, Robinson argued that:

> *defining rural . . . in the past has tended to ignore common economic, social and political structures in both urban and rural areas . . . In simple terms . . . 'rural' areas define themselves with respect to the presence of particular types of problems. A selective list of examples could include depopulation and deprivation in areas remote from major metropolitan centres; a reliance upon primary activity; conflicts between presentation of certain landscapes and development of a variety of economic activities; and conflicts between local needs and legislation emanating from urban-based legislators. Key characteristics of 'rural' are taken to be extensive land uses, including large open spaces of underdeveloped land, and small settlements at the base of the settlement hierarchy, but including settlements thought of as rural.*
>
> *(Robinson 1990: xxi–xxii)*

Therefore, within events research, the term 'rural' will have a wide range of meanings and uses, ranging from very remote rural areas through to those located on the urban fringe of towns and cities. Rural areas are diverse and vary in their degree of ruralness and their attributes, but they do have an important role to play in event studies, especially given the rural lifestyle, economy and landscape (see Table 5.15).

Agricultural festivals and events as manifestations of rurality are an obvious theme (see the various studies by Janiskee), but so too is the contribution of events to rural identity and economic development. The book *Festival Places: Revitalizing Rural Australia* (edited by Chris Gibson and John Connell 2011) covers the many connections between festivals and other events and rural communities.

5.3 RESEARCH NOTE ON EVENTS AND COMMUNITIES

Gibson, C., Waitt, G., Walmsley, J. and Connell, J. (2009). Cultural festivals and economic development in nonmetropolitan Australia. *Journal of Planning Education and Research*, 29(3), 280–293.

'Examining a database of 2,856 festivals in Australia and survey results from 480 festival organizers, the authors consider how non-metropolitan cultural festivals provide constraints as well as opportunities for economic planners. Cultural festivals are ubiquitous, impressively diverse, and strongly connected to local communities through employment, volunteerism and participation. Despite cultural festivals being mostly small-scale, economically modest affairs, geared around community goals, the regional proliferation of cultural festivals produces enormous direct and indirect economic benefits. Amid debates over cultural and political issues (such as identity, exclusion and elitism), links between cultural festivals and economic development planning are explored.'

Table 5.15 Rural studies

Rural studies	Nature and meanings; the event experience	Antecedents to attending events	Planning and producing events	Outcomes and the impacted	Processes and patterns
Rural development and dynamics The nature of ruralness and rural communities Place identity Planning	Events as rural cultural experiences Relationship to heritage, colonialism, settlement patterns, migration, agriculture Venues are more likely to be outdoors	Need for entertainment and socializing Often must travel to towns and event venues Tradition and an annual events calendar (especially connected to agriculture)	Heightened need for leadership Resources for events might be scarce (financial, human) Limited choice of venues Traditional use of show/ fair grounds Use of events for positioning and tourism	Effects of events on community viability and the environment are paramount concerns	The festivalization of rural and regional policy (within the context of development and place marketing) The geography of events within large regions The history and evolution of events within rural areas

Reid (2007) identified a range of social consequences that occur as a result of hosting events, especially within rural communities. She resisted a classification into positives and negatives and looked at how impacts were socially constructed. By taking an event stakeholder perspective within three rural communities of Southwest Queensland, Australia, Reid found a number of consequences that were often ignored in the event impact literature, including trust- and respect-building, breaking down social barriers, forgetting hard times and being affiliated with a success.

Recent progress in rural studies and events is outlined in Figure 5.7, where subject-specific journals such as the *Journal of Rural Studies* have a key role to play in the theoretical development of the field.

Aboriginal, ethnic and multicultural studies

This grouping could be subsumed under cultural anthropology and cultural studies, but there are specific and important implications of aboriginal, ethnic and multicultural studies for planned events. The study of anthropology and events has a long tradition, exemplified in India with the research dating back to the nineteenth century. Indian anthropologists of the twentieth century (e.g. Naik 1948) examined the event phenomenon at a time of dramatic change within the structure of Indian society.

Numerous festivals and events are produced by, and have themes tied to, specific cultural groups, while in many countries the multicultural (or international) festival is a well-established format. Topics of concern to those who study native peoples and ethnic groups include identity (self-perception and that of others), preservation of their heritage and special challenges facing them (such as discrimination, and

Blichfeldt, B. S. and Halkier, H. (2014). Mussels, tourism and community development: A case study of place branding through food festivals in rural North Jutland, Denmark. *European Planning Studies*, 22(8), 1587–1603.

Bob, U. and Majola, M. (2011). Rural community perceptions of the 2010 FIFA World Cup: The Makhowe community in Kwazulu-Natal. *Development Southern Africa*, 28(3), 386–399.

Capriello, A. and Rotherham, I. D. (2011). Building a preliminary model of event management for rural communities. *Journal of Hospitality Marketing and Management*, 20(3–4), 246–264.

Gibson, C. and Davidson, D. (2004). Tamworth, Australia's 'country music capital': Place marketing, rurality, and resident reactions. *Journal of Rural Studies*, 20(4), 387–404.

Holloway, L. (2004). Showing and telling farming: Agricultural shows and re-imaging British agriculture. *Journal of Rural Studies*, 20(3), 319–330.

Li, M., Huang, Z. and Cai, L. (2009). Benefit segmentation of visitors to a rural community-based festival. *Journal of Travel and Tourism Marketing*, 26(5–6), 585–598.

McHenry, J. A. (2011). Rural empowerment through the arts: The role of the arts in civic and social participation in the Mid West region of Western Australia. *Journal of Rural Studies*, 27(3), 245–253.

Rich, K., Bean, C. and Apramian, Z. (2014). Boozing, brawling, and community building: Sport-facilitated community development in a rural Ontario community. *Leisure/Loisir*, 38(1), 73–91.

Figure 5.7 Recent progress in rural studies and events research

Table 5.16 Aboriginal, ethnic and multicultural studies

Aboriginal, ethnic and multicultural studies	Nature and meanings; the event experience	Antecedents to attending events	Planning and producing events	Outcomes and the impacted	Processes and patterns
The identity of racial and cultural groups Preserving cultural heritage Special challenges facing groups Aboriginal rights	Expressions of identity The desire for sharing and understanding between groups Celebration of diversity	Groups with a need to preserve or rediscover their roots and identity Learning about other cultures (search for authenticity)	Reserving sacred rituals from public view Who is in control? The need for interpretation	Threat of commodifying traditions Tourism impacts Intercultural understanding	Geographical spread of festivity and ritual Creation of new traditions and forms of events Influence on cultural and multicultural policy

native land ownership and other rights). Multiculturalism is but one approach, sometimes formalized, to bringing people together as outlined in Table 5.16. There are many connections between festivals, events and the specific cultural manifestations of ethnicity, particularly in an era of global migration and diaspora. Ethnicity can be expressed through performances (including music, costumes, song and dance), consumption (food and beverages, arts and crafts), literature, language and religion (rites and rituals).

Often the intent is to share, foster mutual understanding and encourage social integration, rather than to have a party just for one group. Carnegie and Smith (2006) provided a showcase of ethnic cultures, or an expression of 'Indianness'; the Mela in Edinburgh, and elsewhere in Europe, increasingly involves festivity with others. According to the authors it has become a mainstay of the city's summer festival season. It helps both Scots and Indians in the community to reflect on identity and togetherness. However, Carnegie and Smith suggest that the more successful it becomes as a tourist attraction, the less likely it is to remain tied to a local community. Burdseya (2008) provided a case study of the Amsterdam World Cup, an annual amateur football competition and multicultural festival. Placing the event within the context of Dutch integration policy, it examines the differing and contested conceptions of identity, community and multiculturalism articulated by participants and organizers and, more broadly, the role that 'alternative' events play in resisting or reinforcing dominant political ideologies. Other papers specific to ethnicity include those by Cheska (1981); Sofield (1991); Spiropoulos *et al.* (2006); and Brewster *et al.* (2009).

'Aboriginal' events (encompassing all native peoples) have special significance in cultural terms, raising issues of authenticity (e.g. are performances commodified for tourists?), the need for preserving the sacred by keeping certain rituals hidden and using public events to make political statements. Many native groups want to attract tourists for reasons of both cultural understanding and economic development.

Figure 5.8 provides a sample of aboriginal studies related to events. For example, Phipps (2011) provided a case study of Australia's 'most prominent Aboriginal festival', called the Garma Festival, which highlights the desires of its aboriginal producers for both equality of opportunity (necessary to redress many disadvantages) and to preserve and pursue their distinctive culture. Phipps describes such celebrations as cultural politics.

Chang, J. (2006). Segmenting tourists to aboriginal cultural festivals: An example in the Rukai tribal area, Taiwan. *Tourism Management*, 27(6), 1224–1234.

Hinch, T. and Delamere, T. (1993). Native festivals as tourism attractions: A community challenge. *Journal of Applied Recreation Research*, 18(2), 131–142.

Jackson, I. (2008). Celebrating communities: Community festivals, participation and belonging. *The Australian Centre, School of Historical Studies*, 161–172.

Lee, T. H. and Hsu, F. Y. (2013). Examining how attending motivation and satisfaction affects the loyalty for attendees at aboriginal festivals. *International Journal of Tourism Research*, 15(1), 18–34.

Phipps, P. (2011). Performing culture as political strategy: The Garma Festival, northeast Arnhem Land. In C. Gibson and J. Connell (eds), *Festival Places: Revitalising Rural Australia*, pp. 109–122. Bristol: Channel View.

Slater, L. (2010). 'Calling our spirits home': Indigenous cultural festivals and the making of a good life. *Cultural Studies Review*, 16(1), 143–154.

White, L. (2011). The Sydney 2000 Olympic Games bid: Marketing indigenous Australia for the Millennium Games. *International Journal of the History of Sport*, 28(10), 1447–1462.

White, L. (2013). Cathy Freeman and Australia's indigenous heritage: A new beginning for an old nation at the Sydney 2000 Olympic Games. *International Journal of Heritage Studies*, 19(2), 153–170.

Whitford, M. and Ruhanen, L. (2013). Indigenous festivals and community development: A sociocultural analysis of an Australian indigenous festival. *Event Management*, 17(1), 49–61.

Zeppel, H. (1999). *Aboriginal Tourism in Australia: A Research Bibliography*. Gold Coast, Queensland, Australia: CRC for Sustainable Tourism.

Figure 5.8 Sample research studies on aboriginal events

Table 5.17 Visitor studies

Visitor studies	Nature and meanings; the event experience	Antecedents to attending events	Planning and producing events	Outcomes and the impacted	Processes and patterns
Understanding and enhancing visitor experiences Interpretation and exhibition design and methods (including signage) Learning and behavioural outcomes of experiences and interpretation	Events as learning experiences Enhanced events through interpretation	Demand for learning experiences Special needs and preferences of tourists	Venues produce exhibitions and other events The effects of various settings on experiences	Measuring the effects of interpretation on visitors	Efficiency policies dictate the use of events as interpretive devices and means to attract visitors

Visitor studies

Visitor studies is an interdisciplinary theme and a set of methods, with its own professional association and research journal. The Visitor Studies Association (www.visitorstudies.org) focuses on all facets of the visitor experience in settings like museums, zoos, nature centres, visitor centres, historic sites, parks and other informal learning settings. The purpose of related research and evaluation is to understand and enhance visitor experiences in informal learning settings. Obviously tourism, hospitality, leisure, arts and event studies are all concerned with visitors and their experiences. The potential for synergies is great (see Table 5.17). Delbosc (2008) suggested a number of lines of research that bring event studies and visitor studies together, as summarized in Research Note 5.4 that follows.

5.4 RESEARCH NOTE ON FESTIVALS AT MUSEUMS

Delbosc, A. (2008). Social identity as a motivator in cultural festivals. *Visitor Studies*, 11(1), 3–15.

Delbosc argued that 'as museums continue to broaden their offers and attract increasingly diverse audiences, it becomes ever more important to understand how motivations for visitation can vary between different cultural groups. This article explores some of the reasons people visit cultural festivals at the Immigration Museum in Melbourne, Australia, combining data from 5 different festivals with a total sample of 414. The audience of these festivals contains a mix of 74 per cent cultural community members and 26 per cent non-community members, and their reasons for visiting the festivals differ in distinct ways. Among these distinctions, it was found that social identity played a role in why people chose to visit, especially for community members and at the festivals of communities that were relatively new to Melbourne.'

STUDY GUIDE

Closely related professional fields were discussed as to their links with, and contributions to, event studies. These fields all involve events to some extent, so the discipline of event studies, as it develops, can feed back important concepts to them. Note how each field has to draw upon foundation disciplines for theory and methodology, and how the ways in which they apply theory suggests possibilities and direct applications for event studies. Leisure studies offers the most in terms of theory and philosophy, because that field is specifically concerned with events and experiences. Several leisure theories and methods are vital in helping to explain motivations to attend events and event tourism. They have also developed a philosophy of leisure service that might be applicable to events.

STUDY QUESTIONS

- Are all planned events opportunities for leisure experiences?
- Distinguish between intrinsic and extrinsic motivations as they apply to events.
- Discuss the relevance of serious leisure, recreation specialization, involvement and commitment to event studies – and specifically to event tourist careers.
- In what ways can all planned events be considered part of cultural tourism?
- Is sport tourism mostly concerned with events? What else is pertinent?
- How can events contribute to destination image enhancement?
- Why exactly are venue managers and hospitality professionals involved with planned events? What can their field contribute to event studies?
- How can learning theories be applied to events?
- Discuss the meaning and applications of thematic interpretation.
- Show how to apply information theory to the study of events, and for event marketing.
- What are the fundamental principles of performance? Link performance to social interaction theory.
- Distinguish between cultural management and cultural studies.
- Apply Schechner's four forms of theatre to other forms of planned events.
- In terms of experiences, are all planned events similar to theatre?
- What are the health concerns most applicable to mass gatherings?
- How are events important to both urban and rural place identity?

FURTHER READING

Gibson, C. and Connell, J. (eds) (2011). *Festival Places: Revitalising Rural Australia*. Bristol: Channel View.

Gibson, H. (2006). *Sport Tourism: Concepts and Theories*. London: Routledge.

Page, S. J. and Connell, J. (2006). *Leisure: Critical Concepts in the Social Sciences*, 4 Volumes. London: Routledge.

Page, S. J. and Connell, J. (2010). *Leisure: An Introduction*. Harlow: Pearson Education.

Schechner, R. (2002). *Performance Studies: An Introduction*. New York: Routledge.

Stebbins, R. (2006). *Serious Leisure: A Perspective for Our Time*. Somerset, NJ: Aldine Transaction Publications.

Plate 1 Accelerating techno-culture and its VR dreamscapes promise much for the future of events. (Read more in Expert opinion: Future events and technology culture: dreamscapes or dark fantasy?, Chapter 2. p. 47)

Source: iStock (© Michal Krakowiak).

Plate 2 Glastonbury Festival, UK. Music tourism contributed £2.2 bn to the UK economy in 2012. (Read more in Events in focus: UK music festivals – scale and impact, Chapter 2, p. 70)

Source: iStock (© Anthony Brown).

Plate 3 Exhibition district in Guangzhou city in Guangdong province, China. (Read more in Research note on exhibitions in China, Chapter 2, p. 79)

Source: iStock (© Jacus).

Plate 4 Up Helly Aa in Lerwick, Scotland. More than a thousand volunteers work on the festival each year, and it is a focal point for community cohesion. (Read more in Research notes on social capital, Chapter 3, p. 99)

Source: iStock (© Andrew J Shearer).

Plate 5 Copacabana Beach, Rio de Janeiro. *Reveillon*, the New Year's Eve celebration on Copacabana beach in honour of the sea goddess, *Iemanjá*, has become a major tourist draw. (Read more in Research notes on religion, Chapter 3, p. 113)

Source: iStock (© wenht).

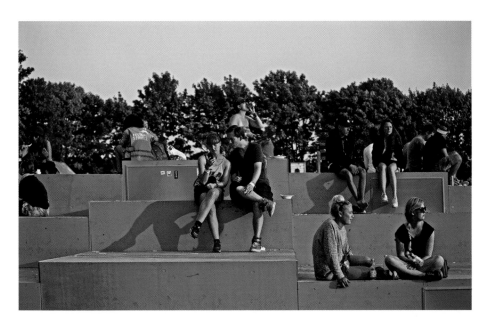

Plate 6 Roskilde Festival, Denmark. To keep ahead in the festival market, innovators in the field of managerial systems, technologies and services are deliberately invited to use the grounds as test benches for new ideas. (Read more in Research notes on innovation and festivals, Chapter 3, p. 103)

Source: iStock (© lubilub).

Plate 7 China Pavilion at World Expo 2010. Major events can have the effect of shaping an image of the host community or country, leading to its favourable perception as a potential travel destination. (Read more in Research note on hosting events, Chapter 5, p. 194)

Source: iStock (© piccaya).

Plate 8 Saudi Arabia has extensive experience of providing healthcare at mass gatherings acquired through decades of managing millions of pilgrims at the Hajj. (Read more in Research notes on health and events, Chapter 5, p. 213)

Source: iStock (© afby71).

Plate 9 Globalization and localization of Mardi Gras are occurring simultaneously with the result being a mix of homogenizing and particularizing influences in New Orleans. (Read more in Research note on Mardi Gras, Chapter 2, p. 72)

Source: iStock (© Joel Carillet).

Plate 10 While food lovers attend many festivals and other food-related events, the highly involved foodies are most likely to prefer hands-on experiences such as cooking lessons from chefs. (Read more in Events in focus: Designing food events for foodies, Chapter 7, p. 283)

Source: iStock (© PhotoTalk).

Plate 11 TransRockies Challenge mountain-bike event. Results of a survey of attendees suggest that many serious sport tourists develop travel careers centred on competitive events. (Read more in Research notes on the event travel career trajectory, Chapter 8, p. 295)

Source: iStock (© PhotoTalk).

Plate 12 Chelsea Flower Show. An analysis of the market for horticulture shows in England showed that while age is a key demographic variable, a more valuable means of segmenting the population is by their level of enthusiasm for gardening. (Read more in Research Note on consumer-show motivation, Chapter 8, p. 301)

Source: Herry Lawford.

Plate 13 Qualitative and longitudinal research conducted at the Galway Arts Festival found that festivals tend to 'emerge as bottom-up enterprises, small in size, local in scale and, initially, heavily dependent on dedicated volunteers'. (Read more in Research note on festival leadership, Chapter 9, p. 319)

Source: iStock (© rihardzz).

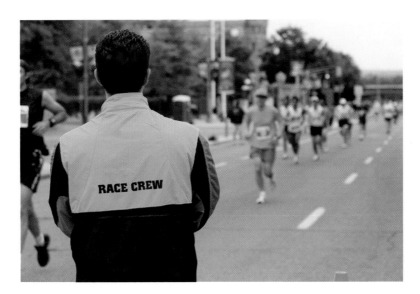

Plate 14 Recent research into volunteer motivation offers the possibility of improved recruitment and retention techniques for volunteer organizations. (Read more in Research note on volunteer motivation, Chapter 9, p. 346)

Source: iStock (© Photawa).

Plate 15 Athens Olympic Stadium. There is no 'best' right way of capturing all the impacts of a mega event like the Olympics. (Read more in Research notes on public discourse about events, Chapter 11, p. 400)

Source: iStock (© Rex_Wholster).

Plate 16 Washington, DC Cherry Blossom Festival. Researchers combined passive participant observation with the use of a checklist and photographs to document issues and visitor behaviour at this large-scale public event. (Read more in Research notes on participant observation, Chapter 12, p. 417)

Source: iStock (© OceanFishing).

Chapter **6**

The event experience and meanings

LEARNING OBJECTIVES

Upon completion of this chapter students should know the following:

- the cognitive, affective and conative dimensions of event experiences;
- leisure experiences versus work (and intrinsic versus extrinsic motivation);
- the concepts of liminality and the liminoid in the context of cultural anthropology and as applied to event experiences, with specific reference to rites and rituals;
- 'communitas' and its importance in event experiences;
- how event experiences can be different for customers/guests, spectators or participants, volunteers, organizers/staff, and other stakeholders;
- meanings attached to event experiences;
- experiences associated with planned event types, and the meanings attached to those experiences by individuals and societies;
- why some experiences are memorable or transforming;
- the scope for, and limitations related to, designing event experiences;
- the meaning of co-creation of event experiences;
- differences between constraining and liberating experiences;
- service dominant logic.

Defining 'experience'

This chapter concerns the core phenomenon of event studies – planned event experiences – and meanings attached to them. If we cannot clearly articulate what the event experience is, then how can it be planned or designed? If we do not understand what it means to people, then how can it be important? Our starting point is a discussion of definitions, noting different meanings of 'experience' and how it can be used as both a noun and a verb. We recall the interpretation of 'leisure experiences' and then return to the 'experience economy' we introduced in Chapter 1 and how the corporate world has been developing 'experiential marketing' to commercialize the experience economy, whereby two-way relationships are built with consumers and businesses beyond the conventional model of consumer marketing. The basic premise is to engage the consumer much more deeply with a focus on their emotions and in a far more personal manner than is achievable by mass-marketing methods. The significance of experiential marketing as a dimension of consumer behaviour led Miller and Washington (2011) to argue that in the USA around $37 billion is spent annually on such forms of marketing, illustrating its significance in engaging consumers.

Following a discussion of these issues around the experience economy, the chapter presents a model of the planned event experience, derived from anthropology, leisure and tourism studies. The notion of 'liminal' and 'liminoid' experiences, and the creation of special places and times, are central to the model. Specific types or forms of events are revisited, looking at the experiential dimensions associated with each, and how people might describe them. Each stakeholder group is also examined, from customers to volunteers, in order to demonstrate substantial differences in event experiences and how they are obtained. Meanings attached to event experiences are examined from the perspectives of individuals, society, culture and the corporate world.

'Experience' defined generically

In normal conversation people might use the term 'experience' in several ways, either as a noun or a verb. In each of the immediately following examples 'experience' is used as a noun. These statements illustrate key points, so a little commentary is attached to each.

'I had an intellectually stimulating experience at the meeting.'

This statement describes the experience both in terms of cognition (i.e. learning) and affect (attitude, or emotion).

'The marathon was a challenging and exhausting experience, but I was exhilarated by my success!'

The runner describes her/his experience in terms of:

- physicality (exhausting), which is the conative or behavioural dimension of experience;
- feelings about it (exhilaration is an emotional state);
- 'challenging', in this context, can relate either to the physical experience (they had to push themselves extra hard to complete the race) or to a post-event assessment of meaning, in which case the runner might be saying they felt a sense of accomplishment or mastery in the achievement of personal goals.

'I am a person with lots of event experience.'

(i.e. I have been to many events and learned a lot about them; there has been an accumulation of knowledge or skill).

'The experience of attending my first World's Fair was a highlight of my life; I will never forget it!'

The person is talking about being at the event, involving direct observation and a stream of consciousness; there is also profound, transforming meaning attached.

We also use 'to experience' (the verb) in different ways. Here are event-related examples:

'As an event manager I have experienced (i.e. lived through) many near disasters.'

This a simple statement about something that happened, not a value judgement, emotional reaction or inference of meaning.

'I want to experience the excitement of a Rolling Stones concert!'

This use of the verb is loaded with emotion or feelings, and it refers to the knowing and feeling that comes only through direct participation, or 'being there'.

'You have to get experienced in many tasks at real events before you can become a competent manager.'

Here it means to undergo a change, an accumulation of transformative experiences, becoming more knowledgeable and skilled.

Referring back to these examples, note that the 'conative' dimension of experience describes actual behaviour, the things people do including physical activity. The 'cognitive' dimension of experience refers to awareness, perception, memory, learning, judgement and understanding or making sense of the experience. This is likely to be dominant in meetings, conferences, scientific forums and some business and trade events, where education or sharing ideas and knowledge are the main goals.

The 'affective' dimension of experience concerns feelings and emotions, preferences and values. Describing experiences as fun or giving pleasure reflects emotions, while many social aspects of experience reflect values – including being with friends and family, and a sense of sharing and belonging to a wider community.

How people describe event experiences as they occur, and talk about them afterwards, remains in large part a mystery and therefore must be of considerable interest to event researchers and producers. It is certainly possible that events satisfy those in attendance at one level, but at the same time fail to achieve the organizers' intended experiences (such as learning, cultural appreciation, social integration, increased brand identity). It is also quite possible that events are determined to be successful in terms of desired outcomes (e.g. money earned, attendance, brand recognition), but the experiences of guests are unsatisfactory, even negative.

'Leisure experience' (intrinsic motivation and freedom of choice)

As Chapter 5 illustrated, Mannell and Kleiber (1997) discussed leisure experiences using the concept of 'immediate conscious experience' (or stream of consciousness) which, to understand it, requires the monitoring of real-time behaviour. To be 'leisure', the experience should be accompanied by a sense of freedom, and of competence and control. For this reason we need to understand the immediate conscious experience at events based on:

- anatomy of the experience (what happened to you? intensity; duration);
- moods, emotions, feelings (self-evaluation of the experience); intensity, relaxation, arousal, activation (bored/excited; energetic/tired; active/passive; alert/drowsy);
- involvement: perceived duration; narrow focus of attention; ego-loss;
- cognitive components (ideas, beliefs, thoughts, images/imagination, meanings attached);
- sense of competence/control;
- sense of freedom.

We will return to this approach when talking about experiential sampling, the phenomenological method used to study experiences.

The 'experience economy'

One of the most profound trends in the world of events has been the corporate sector's embracing of the desirability of using the concept of 'experiences' for purposes of marketing and branding. This has occurred because of the readily observed rise of demand for experiences rather than products, and the power of events and other 'experiences' to emotionally connect with consumers, while traditional methods of marketing have declined in impact. All of this has given rise to what some are calling the 'experience economy' and a host of 'creative industries' as we introduced in earlier chapters. Mossberg (2006: 51) suggested that 'The growth of these industries can be explained by new consumption patterns, new technology, and the need for meetings, caring, entertainment and delight.' In fact Jens (2009) identified a number of megatrends that were driving the growth of the experience economy, notably:

- globalization
- world trade
- technology
- individualization
- the search for authenticity.

There has been an explosion of literature on the 'experience economy' and 'experiential marketing'. This was, as Chapter 1 illustrated, stimulated by Pine and Gilmore who, in their influential book *The Experience Economy* (1999: 3), claimed that 'companies stage an experience whenever they engage customers, connecting with them in a personal, memorable way'. As Smidt-Jensen *et al.* (2009: 849) argue, the experience economy as conceived by Pine and Gilmore suggests 'that economic actors gain an advantage in the market by staging and selling memorable experiences that are enjoyable and personally engaging for the customer' which has redefined many elements of capitalist economies in the developed world. Smidt-Jensen *et al.* (2009: 849–850) argue that, 'This new economic evolution is argued to be based on the fact that customers are generally becoming more open to experiences and more willing to take greater risks and spend larger sums of money to experience something new, because basic goods and services no longer satisfy customers sufficiently.' This growth in industries to meet this need focused around the cultural industries, and those offering experiences we can consume are directly aligned with planned events. Conceptually, Sundbo and Bærenholdt (2007: 11) divided the experience economy into two distinct sectors:

- a primary experience sector that is composed of companies and institutions that have the production of experiences as the primary objective and
- a secondary experience sector where experiences are add-ons to artefacts or service.

For events the co-presence of the event producer and consumer need to be co-located for the experience to be realized. In their economic geography of the experience economy in Denmark, Smidt-Jensen *et al.* (2009) identified the growth of employment in these sectors that clustered around the main towns and cities.

When the customer becomes part of the interplay (i.e. a co-performer) the experience becomes individualized. Four 'realms' of experience were suggested by Pine and Gilmore (1999), derived from two intersecting dimensions as noted in Chapter 1. From an event perspective, the horizontal dimension in the Pine and Gilmore model is a simple active–passive dichotomy, reflecting the activity level of the customer or event-goer. The vertical dimension is much more interesting, reflecting the connection between customer and event. People are 'absorbed' in the experience when the performance occupies their attention and is brought into their minds. 'Immersion' is when the person is physically or virtually 'into' the experience.

Pine and Gilmore (1999: 31) referred to the *Oxford English Dictionary* to define 'entertainment' as 'the action of occupying a person's attention agreeably; amusement'. They suggested that it is one of the oldest forms of experience. In 'aesthetic' experiences (Pine and Gilmore 1999: 35) 'individuals immerse themselves in an event or environment but themselves have little or no effect on it, leaving the environment (but not themselves) essentially untouched'. Thus, 'passive participation' in the Pine and Gilmore model equates with entertainment or aesthetic experiences, while 'active participation' equates with education and escapism.

Education, to Pine and Gilmore (and many educators), should be interactive, with the onus on the learner to become involved and on the educator to facilitate it. Mental engagement is probably more difficult to realize than physical engagement, as in outdoor pursuits and recreation. Hence, physical engagement is often used to promote the mental side. As well, making education fun, as in 'edutainment', is an effective approach.

'Escapist' experiences require much greater immersion than either educational or entertainment experiences, according to Pine and Gilmore (1999: 33). 'Rather than playing the passive role of couch potato, watching others act, the individual becomes an actor, able to affect the actual performance.' This approach is counter to most theatre or concert events as entertainment, and most closely resembles the festival, party or flash mob, which all depend upon interactivity.

Theorists will see in the four-realm model of Pine and Gilmore the basic 'seeking–escaping' motivators identified by Iso-Ahola (1980, 1983) that apply to all leisure and travel, as confirmed in many studies of the motivations of event-goers. It is a very useful model in stimulating thought about the nature of designed experiences, but it is short on making explicit the theoretical underpinnings.

Pine and Gilmore on designing experiences

The Experience Economy (1999) provides details on how to create experiences, and those authors' guidelines resonate well with event professionals – although they were originally aiming their process mostly at retailers. The first task is to establish the 'theme' of the experience, including the scripting of a 'participative story' to unify all the elements (Pine and Gilmore 1999: 48).

Themes should alter the guests' sense of time, place and reality. Themes are made tangible and memorable through 'positive cues' that leave lasting impressions, notably high-quality customer service, design elements, the entertainment, food and beverages, and various other sensory stimulations. Remember how smell triggers memories! Negative cues must be eliminated. Guests should be given, or be able to purchase, memorabilia of their experience.

Surprise is a big element in the Pine and Gilmore approach, by which they mean 'staging the unexpected' (1999: 96). Surprise has to be built on customer satisfaction (basically, delivering what was promised) and eliminating customer 'sacrifice' (i.e. the difference between what they expect and what they perceive they received, often a deficit). Surprise can mean departing from the script, or including seemingly bizarre elements into it. Surprise can come from the juxtaposition of contrasting elements of style, out-of-context performance or display, humour and even fright. It will often require a preformulation of guest expectations. And it can be risky!

Taking the theatrical analogy further, Pine and Gilmore discussed the various roles and actors required for a theatrical production, all of which are directly pertinent in the events business. There are producers who financially back the event, and directors who are in charge of the actual production. 'Dramaturgs' act as interpreters of the theme or story, and in the events business they might be consultants from various backgrounds as diverse as theatre, education/interpretation, sport or commerce. Scriptwriters have to prepare the written script or other forms of directions for performers. In dance they are choreographers. In sport they are coaches and in athletics they are trainers. Singers require songwriters and voice trainers.

A host of technicians make essential services happen, while set designers make the setting work visually. In the events world, set designers and technicians can be the same, as in making a spectacle from fireworks and lasers, creating intriguing sound and light effects, or decorating tables. Chefs have to both cook and create interesting, tasteful delights. Flower and balloon arrangers stress aesthetics, but must know what will work in various circumstances. Good set designers know about environmental psychology, whether or not they have studied it formally. Prop managers, costume designers, stage crews and casting companies are also needed.

The final topic covered in *The Experience Economy* is 'transformation'. Pine and Gilmore argued that events are 'produced experiences', but transformations occur within the guest or customer. Many event designers seek to facilitate or guide such transformations, specifying outcomes in terms of health and well-being, learning, self-actualization and happiness. These arise from meaningful experiences and may be cumulative. 'When you customize an experience you change the individual' (Pine and Gilmore 1999: 165).

If an event is merely intended to inform or sell, entertain or amuse, achieving transformations will not be a goal of the designer. Increasingly, however, events are planned explicitly for this purpose. Companies want employees to become committed and achieve their full potential, so their corporate functions are intended to transform attitudes and behaviour. Governments and cause-related organizations want the public not only to give money, but to become healthier, wiser, more involved citizens.

Co-creating experiences

'Passive participation' in the Pine and Gilmore model equates with entertainment or aesthetic experiences, while 'active participation' equates with education and escapism. As an extension of this line of reasoning, we need to consider the ideas of co-creation, and liberating experiences. An experience continuum is suggested, and it clearly links to concepts of involvement, engagement, serious leisure and travel careers.

Level 1

Pure entertainment is passive, as in spectating at sports or watching a performance, with no engagement or activity ('couch potato' comes to mind!). Along these lines, spectacle is intended to overwhelm the senses, especially the visual, leaving little room for engagement or learning. Aesthetic appreciation of art is a little different, as it requires an emotional response. It is worth recalling that anything can be perceived as entertainment, especially if no interpretation of meaning is provided.

Level 2

Engagement: participation as an athlete, performer, volunteer or organizer requires engagement with the event and co-creation of its meanings. Meanings of the experience can be mediated and facilitated, but not created by the producers. Interactive audiences provide at least partial engagement, if only at the emotional and cognitive levels (e.g. conference participants, aesthetic appreciation of performances and exhibits).

Level 3

Co-creation: user innovation is part of the event production process. Experience meanings are fluid, as the concept and event progresses. While the event might be mostly entertainment in concept, co-creators feel engaged. A degree of unpredictability must be accepted.

Level 4

Liberating experiences: people reject formal planned event organization as being overly restrictive and engage in their own, possibly spontaneous 'happenings'. In this context, entertainment is a state of mind (self-entertainment), not a production. van Limburg (2008) examined co-creation as innovation in pop festivals, indicating that it adds a new dimension into the marketing policy of a company, and the research identified a seven-step model that festival managers can use to implement co-creation in their festival. This is explored further in Research Note 6.1.

6.1 RESEARCH NOTE ON CO-CREATION

van Limburg, B. (2008). Innovation in pop festivals by co-creation. *Event Management*, 12(2), 105–117.

'Co-creation adds a new dimension into the marketing policy of a company, thus developing the ultimate product or service . . . First the trends within this branch were identified. The next steps were to locate the lead users and then to analyse their experiences. Useful tools within this explorative research are communities, which are used to gain information on lead users. The experiences of lead users in the multiday pop festival branch showed the problems and needs in this branch. These findings are both scientific and practical. The scientific contribution is the question for more research of co-creation stimulating environments. The other scientific finding is the quest for research in order to make the lead user a better lead user and so more of value to a firm. The practical contribution is the delivery of a seven-step model festival managers can use to implement co-creation in their festival.'

Approaches to event experiences

Tourism experiences

Ooi (2005: 53) identified six approaches to identifying and studying tourism experiences. The first derives from cognitive psychology and relates to leisure theory. Preconceived ideas, expectations and perceptions affect how tourists consume, evaluate and experience tourism 'products'. The second approach reflects a great deal of tourism literature, all based on the assumption that travel generates positive experiences; tourism is a means to an end, resulting in learning, happiness and nice memories. In the third approach (again from leisure studies) researchers concentrate on state of mind and the depth of engagement, or 'flow' and 'optimal experiences'.

The 'phenomenological' approach is fourth, for example as proposed by Li (2000) to describe the immediacy of personal touristic experiences through rich, reflexive and intimate data. In the fifth approach, Urry's (1990, 1995, 2002) concept of the 'tourist gaze' is employed, focusing on how travellers notice differences from their own environment and daily life. But because the visitor lacks local knowledge, their experience is a reflection of their own background. In the sixth approach, the theatrical analogy is used, as by Pine and Gilmore in *The Experience Economy* (1999), arguing that 'engaging experiences' depend on the degree to which tourists interact with the 'product'.

Ooi (2005: 54) also suggested that tourist experiences are enriched or shaped by 'mediators', including guides, DMOs and the information available. These help to catch the attention of travellers and even to manage their experiences. Ooi argued that (2005: 55): 'Tourism mediators craft tourism experiences by controlling and directing tourists' attention.' People can only pay attention to one thing at a time, and we are easily overwhelmed by too much information or too many stimuli. When attention shifts, our experience is altered; individuals are both drawn to different stimuli, and react differently to the same stimuli. A further development of the experience notion is the contribution made by marketing, particularly experiential marketing.

Event experiences and marketing

Within the growth in marketing research, the experience economy has been embraced as a major area for research. This has emerged from a tradition of services marketing outlined by Baron *et al.* (2014) in their review of the field. As research on services developed, this review highlighted key phases of growth – with different strands of work – one of which was the shift from a measurement and analysis of customer service and quality issues (SERQUAL) to that known as 'service dominant logic' that has contributed to the work on the experience economy as illustrated in Figure 6.1 (see Vargo and Lusch 2004, 2006, 2008 for the basic principles, and Crowther and Donlan 2011 for a discussion of service dominant logic and events).

O'Sullivan and Spangler's (1998: 5) *Experience Marketing: Strategies for the New Millennium* stated that in the 'experience economy', there are three types of actor. 'Infusers' are manufacturers who infuse their products with experiences for marketability. 'Enhancers' are service providers who use experiences to heighten satisfaction levels, to differentiate from competitors. And 'experience makers' are service providers who create experiences as the core of their business. To O'Sullivan and Spangler (1998: 3) event experiences involve the following:

- participation and involvement in the consumption;
- the state of being physically, mentally, socially, spiritually, or emotionally engaged;
- a change in knowledge, skill, memory or emotion;

Figure 6.1 The paradigm shift from SERVQUAL to service dominant logic.

Source: Page (2015: 321). Reprinted from *Tourism Management, 5th Edition*, S. J. Page, Routledge (2015).

- the conscious perception of having intentionally encountered, gone to or lived through an activity or event;
- an effort directed at addressing a psychological or internal need.

They also identified five 'parameters' of experience (O'Sullivan and Spangler 1998: 23):

1. stages: events or feelings that occur prior to, during and after;
2. the actual experience: factors or variables that influence participation and shape outcomes;
3. needs being addressed;
4. roles of the participant and other people involved (personality, expectations, behaviour) in shaping outcomes;
5. roles of and relationships with the provider of the experience (ability and willingness to customize the experience, control it).

O'Sullivan and Spangler ask a lot of pertinent questions about the event experience. To what extent is the experience real versus virtual, customized or mass produced, unique or commonplace? Is it focused on people, an attraction, a facility, equipment or performance? Does the event experience consist of concrete or disconnected episodes? Is the guest or customer participant or spectator, facilitated or self-directed? Does the event create a temporary or transforming change, or result in pleasure or preservation? What is the level of authenticity?

The 'guaranteed' and safe experience

How do we explain the popularity of theme parks and entertainment events – including cultural productions? One answer is that they provide 'guaranteed' and safe experiences. Their predictability, combined with perceived personal security, assures the customer that they will get what they expect, even though their expectations are limited. In contrast, travel and many event experiences are somewhat unpredictable, with plenty of risks. If people are willing to sacrifice spontaneity, cultural authenticity and surprise for the safe and mundane, that is their business. The more highly 'involved' traveller, plus the many novelty seekers of the world, will certainly continue to seek out special experiences.

The WOW! factor

Event designers strive hard to impress the visitor. Citrine (n.d.) held that the 'WOW! factor' is a guiding principle for event designers. Visitors, Citrine argued, should be 'dazzled' when they arrive and leave. Is this the same as saying event designers seek to create really special, emotionally engaging and memorable experiences?

Much of what goes into 'WOW!' is art and spectacle – a visual impression which Page and Connell (2010) observed in relation to visitor attractions. Sound and smell can also be combined with decor, lighting and other programmic elements of style, so 'WOW!' can be a complete sensory reaction. Clearly this can be designed. But can you have a 'WOW!' experience in terms of learning, cultural authenticity or perhaps physical mastery? That's a little more difficult to conceptualize, let alone to design or programme.

Considerably exceeding expectations, and building in elements of surprise, could achieve the 'WOW!' reaction. So too could disappointment and failure, giving rise to the wrong kind of 'WOW!' (as in, that really stunk!). An interesting study by Morgan (2008) entitled 'What makes a good festival? Understanding the event experience' explored the nature of extraordinary experiences through a netnographic analysis of the views of committed attendees at the 2005 Sidmouth Folk Festival. The findings are illustrated in

---

6.2 RESEARCH NOTE ON EVENT EXPERIENCES

Morgan, M. (2008). What makes a good festival? Understanding the event experience. *Event Management*, 12(2), 81–93.

'This article explores the nature of extraordinary experiences through a netnographic analysis of the views of committed attendees at the 2005 Sidmouth Folk Festival. . . . To provide a framework for analysing these responses, a holistic prism model was developed from the literature to bring together the main external and internal elements of the festival experience: "Design and Programming", "Physical Organization", "Social Interaction", "Personal Benefits", "Symbolic Meanings" and "Cultural Communication". This was used to analyse the messages and explore the way in which festival-goers evaluate their experience. The findings support the view that festivals provide a space and time away from everyday life in which intense extraordinary experiences can be created and shared.'

Research Note 6.2, and they support the view that festivals provide a space and time away from everyday life in which intense extraordinary experiences can be created and shared, a theme we will return to below. Allen *et al.* (2008) point to the concept of extraordinary experiences in marketing research building on psychological constructs around achieving an extremely happy state through events where the social interaction is one of the main stimuli.

A model of the planned event experience

This conceptual model (Figure 6.2) is based largely on the social and anthropological literature discussed earlier, especially pertaining to rituals and communitas. It is not intended as a design model, but you can see general design implications. At the core of our model is a distinct experiential zone called 'liminal/liminoid'. It is a zone that must be delineated in both spatial and temporal terms. This is a 'special place' because of programming and how it is designed, all in preparation for the guests, viewers or participants. Designers can make it special through decor, entertainment, activity and sensory stimulations of all kinds, and they should use Falassi's (1987) 'valorization' concept to make event-goers aware that they are entering a space/time that has been set aside for their special purposes.

Figure 6.2 A model of the planned event experience

Meaning is conveyed through opening ceremonies, symbolism such as banners or logos, and the theme. Some event experiences can be called 'sacred' (religious, spiritual) and others 'profane' (fun, escapist). However, it should always be a 'time out of time', to use Falassi's terminology – that is, it should be perceived to be outside the normal, beyond routine, unique. To the extent possible, all those involved with the event should experience the belonging and sharing that defines 'communitas'. An interesting explanation of meaning and its role in events can be found in Events in Focus 6.1.

EVENTS IN FOCUS

6.1 Understanding event experiences in the experience economy, event meaning and event duration: new research directions

According to Kociatkiewicz and Kostera (2012) the key features of the experience economy that we need to understand in relation to events include the immediacy, subjectivity, playfulness and performativity of the experience economy. Within the context of events, their research also highlighted a number of other key concepts shaping the meaning of the event experience, notably the speed of the event and scale which begin to shape two key elements of the resulting experience – the immediate and memorable (see Figure 6.3). This provides a basis on which to begin to focus on the meaning in the experience and what key concepts will help to identify what shapes these experiences.

According to Ryan (2014: 250)

> First, the event is perceived as having meaning for the individual. There is something about an event with which the attendee identifies – it reflects degrees of interest that at the time of the event is deemed significant. Attributed significance to the nature of the event however may be either temporary or enduring, and is to be distinguished from the significance of the experience as being temporary or enduring, although the two are linked.

Ryan (2014: 251) highlighted identifiable concepts in the analysis of meaning in event experiences:

* *Enduring meaning*, something which emerges when the person attending the event has an ongoing interest with the event.

Figure 6.3 The experience economy, scale and speed in event experiences

- Attachment and identification arguing that

  The more closely is one's association with an event through interests or personal connections, the more one identifies with the desired success of the event. Identification is a two way process, and as evidenced by the literature relating to serious leisure . . . so one's own sense of being is reinforced by association with being present at, or playing an organising role in the event.

  (Ryan 2014: 251)

- *Anticipation* as determinant of the experience and the key role of media in informing and in the build up to the anticipation.
- Events as a *liminal experiences*, since they are outside of the everyday and ordinary life experiences.
- The role of the event in stimulating *emotional responses* especially communitas when being with others and other signifiers such as tee shirts, football shirts and insignia.

This led Ryan (2014) to develop Figure 6.4, based on the level of meaning in an event and the duration of interest in the event with four types of event participant identified in each of the four

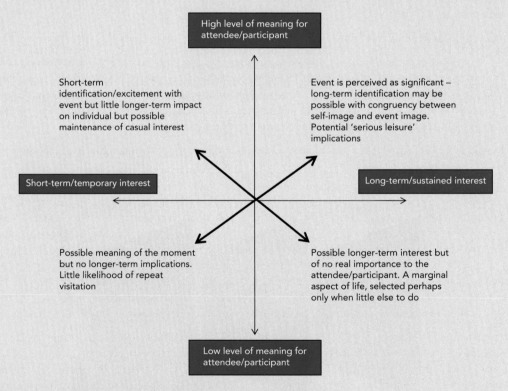

Figure 6.4 Matrix of event meaning and duration of interest.

Source: Ryan (2014: 257). Reprinted from *The Routledge Handbook of Events*, S. J. Page and J. Connell, Routledge (2014).

quadrants. In fact studies such as Scott (1995) emphasize how important many of the concepts highlighted are for event attendance in terms of meaning, with sociability and family togetherness (including communitas) and escape from routine, event excitement and curiosity noted as frequent facets underpinning the experience and meaning derived from events. Recent research by Ziakas and Boukas (2014) has suggested that we may need to adopt phenomenological research approaches to begin to understand experiences and meaning in events, understanding what is memorable, why and over what duration that memorability is retained. Additional approaches from cultural and environmental economics using valuation methods to understand the value of events to people have used the Triple-Ex approach looking at experience, extent of visit (duration) and visit expenditure (Andersson and Ambrecht 2014). More traditional research methods around notions of service quality that emanate from marketing have also been applied (e.g. Song *et al.* 2014) in relation to the experience economy, observing that aesthetics and entertainment were among the most important experiential elements of Expo visitors. Manthiou *et al.* (2014) found similar results when examining loyalty and vivid memories of attending events, with the entertainment and aesthetics elements shaping loyalty to visit. Sit and Birch's (2014) review of events in shopping malls also identified some of these components in the family-oriented events staged that were rated as relaxing and entertaining.

It is easy to think of a special place as an event venue, like an arena, theatre or convention centre. But it can also be a temporary event space, or a whole community. The question of scale is important (as illustrated in Events in Focus 6.1) along with speed, because as we move from venue to large public space to entire community, we have a much more complex and difficult job of design and programming and a different type of experience evolving from the slow to fast type. Nevertheless, many communities manage to make themselves festive throughout, or at least operate as important entrances and meeting places, during the time of special events.

Before we get to the event there is preparation and anticipation. Most people go to an event having some expectations of the experience to be obtained (or partially self-created), or at least some foreknowledge that an event is about to be experienced. Much research has been conducted on motivation to attend events, especially festivals, and it mostly confirms the 'seeking–escaping' theory, suggesting that people clearly anticipate that an event is going to be out of the ordinary. You could stumble upon an event and be surprised, but even so there will be a sense of having left somewhere and arrived at some special place. Even where expectations are completely absent, that is, the event-goer never gave it any thought at all, there still has to be the 'entering into' event that marks a transition from ordinary to extraordinary. Seeking to capture these elements and measure them remains a challenging process around the concepts in Events in Focus 6.1 (such as emotion, mood (Hull, 1990), surprise (Vanhamme and Snelders, 2001)), using in situ research methods or techniques around reminiscing or focusing on triggers such as nostalgia.

Csikszentmihalyi's theory of 'flow' (1975, 1990) fits into this model. It suggests that people seek 'optimal arousal', leading to 'flow' experiences which can be characterized by deep involvement, intense concentration, lack of self-consciousness and transcendence of self. These are intrinsically rewarding experiences. To the extent that designers can facilitate 'flow', event-goers can be expected to report exhilaration (from fantasizing or total immersion in music or activity), a sense of accomplishment (athletic achievement, mastery of a skill, intellectual stimulation) or transformation (through an intense emotional or spiritual process). How to foster a high level of involvement is the real challenge, and events that provide mere entertainment will find this illusive.

'Liminality' is not strictly dependent upon the type of event or venue. This space/time exists in the minds of the attendees and participants, not within the programme or venue itself. It can therefore be entered through the pathways of 'fantasy' (the heart of many theme parties), a willing suspension of the ordinary to play a role (as in carnival), engagement in new ideas and processes (such as discourse, clinical learning, team projects), participation with others (like celebration) or any kind of higher-than-usual level of involvement.

In the case of 'flash mobs' and other events at the fringe, it is the participants who, according to some unwritten script or external prodding, largely make their own experiences. They are temporarily using (or 'liberating') a space for their purposes, perhaps making a social or political statement in doing so, but quickly returning it to the ordinary. 'Reversion' to normal life should be accompanied by a sense of change, going from the special to the ordinary. There might be a feeling of accomplishment, renewal, transformation, relief or loss. It is important to feel something at the end, otherwise what was special or memorable about the experience? It may be possible to feel a sense of loss at the end of conferences, not necessarily because the stimulating programme is over, but because of separation from friends and colleagues. It is the loss of 'communitas', and it leads to the drive to attend future events. Anyone who is highly 'involved' or emotionally moved by events will experience this loss. It gives meaning to the event and to our ordinary lives.

To the extent that people enjoy events, or at least derive some benefits from attending, they might very well develop an event career. Similar to Pearce's 'travel career', we learn from events and perhaps desire more of the same (the loyal festival-goer), or we crave the uniqueness, even surprises that come from many different types of event (the cultural event tourist), or we want ever-increasing challenge (the amateur, competitive athlete). In fact nostalgia has a clear role to play, as demonstrated by Fairley and Gammon (see Research Note 6.3).

6.3 RESEARCH NOTE ON LIMINAL EXPERIENCES AND NOSTALGIA

Fairley, S. and Gammon, S. (2006). Something lived, something learned: Nostalgia's expanding role in sport tourism. In H. Gibson (ed.), *Sport Tourism: Concepts and Theories*, pp. 50–65. London: Routledge.

Fairley and Gammon suggested that for many sport fans there is a nostalgic desire to re-enter the liminoid space they associate with events and with the group experience of travelling to events. This space involves a strong sense of community or shared subcultural identity, and resembles the carnival in its acceptance of abandoning social norms. There is also the appeal of escape from everyday life. Nostalgia, in this context, fuels a career of event-related travel, and it relates to volunteers at events as well.

O'Dell (2005: 133) argued that we must not over-emphasize the disjuncture from ordinary life when we consider 'liminal' or 'liminoid' experiences. His point is that touristic and event experiences can only be special or exceptional when considered in light of one's ordinary life and experiences. He said: 'To a large extent people learn the ropes of "experiencing" through their daily consumption patterns. We also need to develop competencies for experiencing, and this is embodied in the concepts of serious leisure, specialization, and self efficacy.'

What makes an event experience rewarding and memorable?

Moscardo (2010) summarized the literature on effective and rewarding customer and tourist experiences, and this body of knowledge is easily adaptable to event design (see Table 6.1). Her discussion is in the context of the importance of storytelling and themes for tourist experiences. Stories are one form of thematic interpretation. Compare Moscardo's factors to the list of features that help make events 'special', to the 'elements of style', and discussions of ego involvement and serious leisure; consider which of these reflect generic versus targeted benefits. In Table 6.1, a number of event-specific references have been added. In fact a useful study that has a bearing on the memorable nature of the event experience is mindfulness. Van Winkle and Backman (2009) examined visitor mindfulness at a cultural event that revolves around the concept of mindfulness, which is a state of being that requires individuals to engage in active information processing, enabling them to be adaptive and responsive to information in their surroundings. This is explored further in Research Note 6.4.

6.4 RESEARCH NOTE ON MINDFULNESS AND EVENT EXPERIENCE

Van Winkle, C. and Backman, K. (2009). Examining visitor mindfulness at a cultural event. *Event Management*, 12(3/4), 163–169.

'Mindfulness is considered a state of being that requires individuals to engage in active information processing, enabling them to be adaptive and responsive to information in their surroundings. Mindfulness is believed to result in more learning, high satisfaction, greater understanding, and greater feeling of control over behaviour. Event managers must find ways to enhance visitor satisfaction as well as minimize negative impacts that result from events, and encouraging visitor mindfulness could contribute to these outcomes. This study took place over a two-week period in July 2005 at the Winnipeg Fringe Theatre Festival in Winnipeg, Manitoba, Canada. Results presented demonstrate that the more interested visitors were in the festival the higher they scored on the mindfulness scale. Visitor level of mindfulness was positively related to their satisfaction with the event and their feelings of control over their own contribution to impacts. Implications for event managers are discussed.'

Generic and specific types of planned event experiences

If we return to the earlier discussion of how our planned event typology is based on event forms, which are social constructs, it suggests they are not based on unique experiential components. Not only is it difficult to describe experiences, but any event can conceivably engender many different experiences. The following discussion is an attempt to show that there are both generic and specific experiences associated with types of event, but this is not the same as formulating an experiential typology of events.

Generic event experiences

'Generic experiences' are those which can occur at any event, and therefore have more to do with the individual's state of mind and particular circumstances than with the event theme, programme or setting. We are convinced that many people attend events for generic personal benefits such as entertainment and simple diversion (we can call this 'escapism') and 'having fun' is probably how most people would

Table 6.1 Factors associated with effective and rewarding customer and tourist experiences

Factors (Source: Moscardo, 2010)	References specific to events (or highly applicable)
Theme: strong, clear and consistent, supported by design and 'servicescape'	Themed events: Goldblatt 2011: 108; Targeting through theming: Getz 2005: 321. Developing the theme: Van der Wagen 2008; Getz et al. 2001, on service mapping/servicescapes; Bruwer and Kelley 2015.
Story or narrative: allows customers to play a desirable role or create their own stories to tell others	John Deighton 1992, on narratives in performance; Cruikshank 1997, on a storytelling festival; Mossberg 2008, on storytelling in hospitality; Moscardo 2010.
Perceived authenticity: access to real objects, places and people (i.e. objective authenticity); genuine interactions with others in the setting; and opportunities for activities that reflect one's true self (i.e. existential authenticity)	Boorstin 1961; Greenwood 1972, 1989; Buck 1977; Papson, 1981; Cohen 1988b; Getz 1998b; Sofield and Li 1998; Wang 1999; Robinson et al. 2004; Xie 2003, 2004; Picard and Robinson 2006a; McCartney and Osti 2007; Knox 2008; Brida et al. 2013; Robinson and Clifford 2012.
Interactive, participatory and engaging: customers as co-creators of the experience	Hilliard 2006, on meeting planning; Harvey et al. 1998, on exhibits; Ralston et al. 2007; Pine and Gilmore 1999; Bjorner and Berg 2012, on co-creation.
Uniqueness: rarity, novelty and surprise	On surprise: Schechner 1988 (theatre); Pine and Gilmore 1999; Pettersson and Getz 2009. On uniqueness: Nicholson and Pearce 2001; Ralston et al. 2007; Getz 2005; Foster and Robinson 2010.
Easy to access: easy to get to, move around and understand (i.e. legibility)	On accessibility: Severt et al. 2007; for disabled: Darcy and Harris 2003; on legibility and site design: Getz 2005.
Multisensory	Harvey et al. 1998, discovered they could more than double the time visitors spent at exhibits by making them interactive and multisensory.
Emotive	Botterill and Crompton 1996: emotional states are integral to 'optimal experiences'; Russell and Lanius 1984: the same stimulus can generate widely different affective appraisals of settings; Matheson 2008; Nelson 2009; Huang et al. 2012 on mood.
Opportunities to be social	Fairley and Gammon 2006, on nostalgia and shared experiences of sport fans; Coghlan and Filo 2013 on connectedness.
Personal relevance: making connections to personal history; can be personalized	Van Winkle and Backman (2009): mindfulness at events.
Total immersion in the setting	Harvey et al. 1998: The influence of museum exhibit design on immersion and psychological flow; Berridge 2012a.
Learning opportunities	Lee and Back 2009: the importance of learning at conferences; evaluation of an event's educational goals: Gitelson et al. 1995; visitor desire for interpretation: Xie 2004.

describe the experience (see Table 6.1). Meanings attached to these experiences would not normally be profound. We cannot expect them to be memorable or transforming, but that is possible. More important are the generic social motivations and benefits associated with leisure and travel in general, which apply to intrinsically motivated event experiences – especially to have quality time with friends and family, and to enjoy that sense of belonging and sharing we call 'communitas'.

Social experiences can occur whenever and wherever people get together, but planned events definitely facilitate them. Indeed, social and cultural groups create events specifically for this purpose, or find that certain events are good at facilitating it.

Uysal and Li (2008) presented a critical literature review of empirical studies of festival and event motivation. They identified that the most frequently mentioned dimension was socialization (24.0 per cent), followed by family togetherness (18.8 per cent), novelty (19.0 per cent) and escape (15.7 per cent). The other major dimensions were cultural exploration (5.0 per cent), entertainment (5.8 per cent) and attractions (4.1 per cent). The key role of social factors was also identified by Foster and Robinson (2010) focusing on the motivational factors that influence event attendance in family groups. The study of families with children confirmed the overriding importance of family togetherness, followed by socializing and then excitement in motivating family attendance at special events. The study concluded that families are willing to compromise on individual motivation and attend events that children will find satisfying. Families were not interested in novelty or uniqueness, they just wanted to spend time together. Similarly, Ko *et al.* (2010) examined consumer satisfaction and event quality perception at a US Open Taekwondo Championship. Their study found that 'social interaction' was a motivator for spectators at the martial arts event. We will return to this important discussion in Chapter 8, specifically dealing with festival motivations where a model is presented showing essential services, generic and event-specific benefits.

Specific event experiences

In this section we examine the kinds of experiences that can and should be associated with certain types of planned events.

Cultural celebrations

Cultural experiences in general are all about seeking knowledge, learning and understanding something new, and appreciating some aspects of culture – both the traveller's and that of the destination. The cultural tourist or cultural event-goer wants to engage emotionally and cognitively with places, people and dimensions of lifestyle, including tangible things like historic sites, cultural performances, food and beverages, or meeting local people, and with intangible aspects including the symbolism of art and architecture. Simply sightseeing, or enjoying entertainment or spectacle, does not constitute a cultural experience. Celebrations and commemorations in general reflect and foster belonging and sharing among a family, social group, community or nation. Values come to the fore, and a clear sense of place is usually present. The event's theme suggests what is to be celebrated, although in many cases it is the community itself that is the object of celebrations. In all cultural events we should be concerned with the notion of 'authenticity' and what that means in experiential terms. A detailed discussion of authenticity follows, in the section on meanings.

Festivals and carnivals

Festivals and carnivals, as discussed previously, are meant to be joyous experiences. But they can range from solemn and sacred festivals to profane carnivals marked by wild revelry. Role playing and inversion (including masquerading) are found in many carnivals. They usually embody rituals and symbolism that act as cues in suggesting the appropriate mood and emotions (see case studies of these issues in Laing and Frost 2014). These experience domains have been studied in depth by sociologists and anthropologists, such as Turner and Falassi. Many so-called 'festivals', however, seem to provide little more than packaged entertainment and a party atmosphere, leaving it up to the audience and others involved to create their own, deeper experiences – if possible. Thematic interpretation can help communicate what is culturally significant about events, including their setting (the place), symbolic elements and historic context. One area of interest among researchers is the area of music festivals. For example, Pegg and Patterson (2010) examined visitor motivations and experiences sought; they found that visitors' love of country music was the primary reason for attending the festival. However, the overall results indicated that it was the variety of activities and festival atmosphere that were considered by visitors as being the most important aspects of their participation. The atmosphere was repeatedly mentioned as a reoccurring theme, and, in particular, they stressed the casual, relaxed, family-friendly atmosphere. Visitors also commented on the welcoming feelings that they received from people who were living locally. This reflects a sense that the event attracted people with desires similar to the visitors, that is, to have a safe and enjoyable time together. Further insights are provided by Ballantyne *et al.* (2014) in their analysis of the music festival experience.

In contrast to the Tamworth (Australia) festival mentioned above by Pegg and Patterson (2010), consider this radically different experience described by an anonymous blogger who attended a drugs-infested concert:

> *Take how many times you have been offered drugs and multiply that times 1,000 and thats how many times you will be offered drugs a day at. . . . People walking around with backpacks shouting 'coke, x, molly, nugs, doses!' and every other drug you can think of. I walked by a table where people were selling nitrus in balloons. What I learned throughout this was that the people who are carrying around all of these drugs were there to screw you over and take your money. There is a system with the . . . drug world its either bring your own or make friends with hippies because they have the best stuff. We were exchanging food and beer for getting smoked up and acid.*

Religious and spiritual experiences

Sacred and spiritual experiences are not necessarily the same. 'Sacred' generally refers to established religious dogma (e.g. the Holy Scriptures are sacred; communion is a sacred rite). Spiritual experiences could be non-religious in nature, consisting of feelings of transcendence (e.g. 'I felt completely removed from, even raised above, the worries of daily life') or self-discovery ('I was on a different plain of existence where I felt connected to every thing and every one'). Timothy and Olsen (2006: 271) argued that there are significant differences between being religious and being spiritual. Spiritual refers to personal belief, a search for meaning in one's life, and so any tourist could have a spiritual experience in a sacred place or alongside religious pilgrims. Rapture, ecstasy, transcendence, revelation are terms used in conjunction with intense religious or spiritual experiences. Is this what is supposed to happen at a church service or during a papal tour? Can these experiences be designed or facilitated at religious events? Certainly there is often the intent to do so, as when a preacher calls upon people in the congregation to come forward to repent. There is also a special dimension of 'communitas' in religious events, as highlighted by the rite of 'communion'.

Reisinger (2006) saw possibilities for spiritual experiences being incorporated into, or modifying, many common forms of tourism, from nature tours to attending farm shows and harvest festivals, food and wine tastings to spa visits. While often associated with visits to sacred places, spiritual experiences are also realized through meditation, exploring and performing rituals. In this sense the search for meaning in life can propel, almost invisibly, many leisure and travel activities.

Pilgrimage

Pilgrimage is a quest, a journey and the experience of a sacred place. For many it is a duty. The entire pilgrimage can be conceptualized as a special event in a person's life, a rite of passage and a transforming experience, but there are often well-defined events associated with religious pilgrimages. Pilgrimage occurs in stages. To prepare for the Hajj in Mecca, Muslims are to put their earthly affairs in order and become spiritually prepared. The event itself involves a number of rituals, including those of purification, praise, repentance and sacrifice. Upon completion of the Hajj, one becomes 'hajji' and gains special status, making it a transforming process, at least in symbolic terms. Raj and Morpeth (2007) described the activities and experience of the Hajj, emphasizing that it was not a touristic experience, but a religious obligation, and a beautiful, once-in-a-lifetime experience.

Singh (2006: 232) argued that Hindu pilgrims 'enjoy sacred journeys as an earthly adventure from one place to another that entails the combined effects of a spiritual quest and physical hardship'. But could that not also describe the experience of a long-distance runner? Certainly the key elements that make religious quests and experiences different from other spiritual or emotionally uplifting experiences are participation in specified rituals or ceremonies that have deep meaning to the devoted and faithful. The place itself is crucial, but unlike a secular event venue, the meaning of sacred places is permanent, traditional and sanctioned by official religious bodies.

Here are remarks from 'A Pious Pilgrim's Experience', posted online:

> *The enthusiasm and devotion to the saint were evident as soon as I stepped within the grounds of the basilica. Police barricades and market stalls gave the hint that many people were expected. Little did I realise that on the second day of the three day festival a crowd estimated at about 75,000 would attend an open air mass in celebration of the relics' arrival in Bari 913 years ago. Italian fervour and Catholic piety instilled in this Anglican a true sense of emotion and joy as I tried to be faithful to the vigorous festival schedule.*

Virtual and secular pilgrimage

Only Muslims can experience the Hajj in person, but others may visit websites that provide a simulacrum of what it is like to be a pilgrim. Many tourism scholars now speak of secular pilgrimages, such as a golfer's pilgrimage to St Andrews in Scotland (the generally recognized birthplace of the game) or a wine lover's pilgrimage to the regions in which favourite wines are produced. Gammon (2004: 40) argued that pilgrimage 'will include a journey of some kind to a place (or places) which holds personal and/or collective meaning to the "pilgrim"'. The experience might provoke 'awe and wonderment', whether at a sport, shrine or holy event.

Within special interest groups, or subcultures, certain events have prestige and become must-see, must-do 'icons'. For example, marathon runners strive to qualify for the Boston Marathon, making participation in that event almost like a pilgrimage. Does this apply to music concerts or other types of events? Could consumer researchers identify a set of events that people just have to attend because of their symbolic value?

Regarding secular pilgrimages, here is an experience posted by a blogger:

> *My second pilgrimage was the Running of the Bulls in Pamplona, as made famous in Hemingway's novel, 'The Sun Also Rises.' We watched from our specially reserved balcony like 'Juliets' as 4 of our group joined the hundreds of other runners in a pilgrim's test of fearlessness and danger. One could nearly taste the adrenalin in the air. One could definitely taste the churros (donuts) and sangria!*

Political and state events

Many political and state events will have a high degree of formality, pomp and ceremony attached to them. Terms like stately, regal or dignified might be used to describe the mood. What you will experience at such events can vary greatly, depending on why you attended (to protest, participate, or report on?), what access you have to the VIPs and how you interact with security. For the politicians in attendance there should be dialogue, negotiation and public displays of diplomacy. A study by Digance (2005) examined the impact of the Commonwealth Heads of Government (CHOGM) meeting.

Arts and entertainment experiences (including the aesthetic)

By labelling entertainment an 'industry', society has created a social construct that depicts many forms of planned events (especially concerts, award shows and sports, but even festivals and art exhibitions) as entertainment. Events, for many, have become legitimate outlets for consumerism, where we spend our time and money oblivious to, or unwanting of, any deeper experience or meaning than short-lived amusement. This, of course, is a dangerous thing for anyone concerned about the arts, cultural authenticity or social values. 'Aesthetic judgement' concerns art and beauty, but is value laden and relative. What one person finds attractive, another might describe as boring or disgusting. An aesthetic experience, however, is one in which we find something to be pleasing to our senses. It can be the aesthetic appreciation of paintings, food, fashion or music. Hence it is intensely personal, which leads to the expression 'you can't please everyone'. Designers take note: aesthetic experiences are valued, and they motivate a great deal of travel and consumption, but you cannot guarantee satisfaction. For most appreciators of fine art, food, music or whatever, it is the exploration and sense of discovery that matter most.

Limited research has been reported on art exhibitions (see du Cros and Jolliffe 2014 for a review), but Axelsen and Arcodia (2004) argued that they should be viewed in the context of special-event motivation and experience. A review of the literature suggested that people attend art galleries for reasons of learning, social interaction, status and novelty. Smith (2006) discussed the rise of 'new leisure tourism', linking it to the increasing blurring of work and leisure, and to 'de-differentiation' or the breakdown of boundaries between previously distinct activities. New leisure tourists are engaging in escapism, looking for fresh experiences, wanting fun and high-quality entertainment. Novelty-seeking is a key aspect of this trend, leading Urry (2002) to suggest that people are becoming insatiable in their quest for novelty because reality never matches their expectations.

Youthful, hard-working consumers, brought up on music videos and computer entertainment, seem to have a very limited attention span and are constantly seeking stimulation. Smith (2006: 224) concluded that new leisure tourists are not interested in culture, but want playful, event-fantastical experiences. Contrived, simulated, even obviously fake settings can provide this. Interactivity is desired, but in a technological sense. Fascination with celebrities is part of this new experiential realm. Industry has responded (in the spirit of the 'experience economy') with theming, overtly catering to hedonism, celebrity endorsements, and what is being called 'shoppertainment'.

Competitive sport/recreation event experiences (for athletes)

It has to be more than just winning! Although competitive sports superficially involve games played by persons or teams with the intent of winning, that in itself does not constitute the entire experience or meaning. Many people compete for very personal reasons, such as to gain fitness and mastery, while others compete for social reasons – to be part of a group and to enjoy a social event. Bouchet *et al.* (2004) reviewed the literature on sport-tourist experiences and concluded there are four theoretical streams evident. From a 'behavioural theory' perspective, group activities and interactions are the focus. For example, Green and Chalip (1998) found that strong subcultural meanings were attached by participants to a women's sport event. From cognitive psychology comes attention to needs, motives, values and risk taking. A third approach combined the psychological and behavioural roles of travellers, and the fourth is the experiential model.

Bouchet *et al.* (2004) advanced their own approach to analysing the sport-tourist experience, encompassing considerations of self-worth (perceived risk, optimal stimulation, variety and novelty-seeking), spatial variables, or the place (including functional components and a post-modernist view of how visitors create their own experiences and living space), and interpersonal variables (new relationships and 'communitas').

What particularly distinguishes competitive sport experiences from any other event experiences is the structure (venues, rules and team versus single play), all of which are specific to each sport. Either this structure appeals to a person or it does not, and the diversity of sport gives rise to an almost infinite variety of experiential possibilities. Some are less combative than others; some require brute strength, others demand finesse and artistry. Sport is both highly personal (what the athlete accomplishes on their own) and social (the team, the community of athletes, the whole event organization).

A half-marathoner's experience was described this way, online:

> There were quite a few people running. I think about 20,000+ were on hand to run. It was pretty cool to be surrounded by a bunch of people who had the same aim, the same goal. For months, I trained alone. But on this day, I was running with 20,000 others. It was quite a rush.

The sport spectator and sport-fan experience

In the report *Travelers Who Attend Sport Events* (Travel Industry Association of America 1999), sport-event tourism was depicted as a major social and economic phenomenon, where 84 per cent of the American adults who had travelled for sport reasons had been spectators. Many of these were parents or grandparents going to watch children play in competitions. In other words there is a huge family market within sport-event tourism. Only 16 per cent travelled to participate, and some of them also spectated. Gibson (1998, 2006) found in her research that the 'active sport tourist' was mostly a male with college education and higher income. This segment, she concluded, will likely continue to travel for participation in their favourite sports well into retirement.

Attending a sport event can be motivated by a desire for entertainment and spectacle (i.e. simple diversion), the desire for emotional stimulation or having a social outing. Being a sport spectator is a role we can all play, and most spectators know that it is generally more interesting (certainly more emotionally exciting) to be at a live event as opposed to watching on TV. Being a sport 'fan', however, is something quite a bit more engaging. Wann (1995) and Wann *et al.* (1999) developed a 'sport-fan motivation scale' that covers both intrinsic and extrinsic motivation. It consists of eight common reasons for watching sport, and these can also be conceptualized as desired experiences: escape, 'eustress' (i.e. stress evoked by emotions or events, here considered to be positive stimulation), aesthetics (appreciation of the beauty of sports), self-esteem, group affiliation, family, entertainment and economic (e.g. betting). Chen (2006) provided a review of the literature on sport fans, in a paper devoted to a phenomenological study of event sport-fans' behaviour, experiences and values.

Studies of sport fans have taken psychological and social-psychological approaches (see, for example, Wann 1997; Smith and Mackie 2000). Specific attention has been given to 'affect and emotion' (Dietz-Uhler and Murrell 1999; Wann *et al.* 2002; Madrigal 2003), motives (Trail and James 2001; James and Ridinger 2002), 'identification' (Laverie and Arnett 2000), gender differences (Dietz-Uhler *et al.* 2000; James and Ridinger 2002), factors influencing fan behaviour (End *et al.* 2003) and loyalty (Mahony *et al.* 1999, 2000; Tapp 2004). Some fans can be considered to be engaging in 'serious leisure' (Gibson *et al.* 2003). It has even been determined that highly 'committed' sport fans spend more in destinations than casual fans. A summary of the motives of sport spectators can be found in Table 6.2.

Table 6.2 Motives of sport spectators

Authors	Framework	Motives
Wann (1995)	Sports Fan Motivation Scale (SFMS)	eustress, self-esteem, escape, entertainment, economic (gambling), aesthetic, group affiliation, family
Milne and McDonald (1999)	Motivation of Sport Consumers (MSC)	risk-taking, stress reduction, aggression, affiliation, social facilitation, self-esteem, competition, achievement, skill mastery, aesthetics, value development and self-actualization
Trail and James (2001)	Motivation Scale for Sport Consumption (MSSC)	achievement, acquisition of knowledge, aesthetics, drama, escape, family, physical attraction, physical skills of players, social interaction.
Funk et al. (2001, 2002, 2003)	Sport Interest Inventory (SII)	family bonding, friends bonding, drama, entertainment value, escape, excitement, player interest, role model, socialization, team interest, vicarious achievement
James and Ross (2004)	-	entertainment, skill, drama, team effort, achievement, social interaction, family, team affiliation, empathy
Mehus (2005)	Entertainment Sport Motivation Scale	social, excitement
Koo and Hardin (2008)	-	vicarious achievement, team performance, escape, family, eustress, aesthetics, entertainment value, social opportunities.

Source: Benckendorff and Pearce (2012: 170). Reprinted from *The Routledge Handbook of Events*, S. J. Page and J. Connell, Routledge (2012).

Chen concluded that most studies suggest that personally relevant values (from needs and the benefits sought), and 'identifications' (such as social identity) most explain why fans become highly involved and committed to teams (see also Wann and Branscombe 1993; Madrigal 1995; Bristow and Sebastion 2001). Chen's (2006) study determined that 'personal balance' and 'socialization' were the essential parts of the experiences being sought, and these were obtained through volunteering, being at events, travel with other fans and the team, 'pilgrimages' to places with special meanings, and non-related social and touristic activities in destinations.

Mark Cuban, owner of the Dallas Mavericks basketball team, has a unique perspective on the fan experience as reflected in these comments (from The Mark Cuban Weblog (blogmaverick.com), posted 24 December 2011):

> *Think back to the first professional sporting event you ever went to. It was probably a parent taking you to the game. What do you remember? Do you remember the score? A home run? A jump shot? A pass play? Or do you remember who you were with? I remember being with my dad at a Pirates game. My dad and my uncle at a Steelers game. Think about your fondest memories at a sporting event. Again, what do you remember? Hanging with your buddies? A first date? A last date? How you felt after the team won or lost? A business partner or customer? Or the score? I'm guessing its not the score.*
>
> *We in the sports business don't sell the game, we sell unique, emotional experiences. We are not in the business of selling basketball. We are in the business of selling fun. We are in the business of letting you escape. We are in the business of giving you a chance to create shared experiences. I say it to our people at the Mavs at all time, I want a Mavs game to be more like a great wedding than anything else.*

Exhibition experiences

According to Mair (2013) conferences and exhibitions continue to play a major role in the world of business and trade, despite the rise of social media and technology-enabled communication (e.g. Skype) for facilitating face-to-face meetings of customers and clients. A study by Jung (2005) on exhibition attendee perceptions of service quality gave some insight on desired experiences, namely the importance assigned to the number of exhibitors, quality of goods and services exhibited, and the seminars, conferences and other events that were part of it. These are all product quality items that reflect the learning and marketing content of the event.

From a trade-show blogger:

> *I left the show feeling good about the experience. I received much positive feedback and excitement about all of our current and upcoming books. Ultimately, I'm glad I was there. I do hope to eventually find out if it was worth the costs involved. Only time will tell. And, being patient will help.*

Convention and meeting experiences

It is probably assumed that people attend conferences and meetings for extrinsic reasons, because it is part of their business or job description, so very little pertinent research has been done. Certainly event marketers need to know more about how to attract and satisfy their clientele, while in event studies we want to know if these experiences are categorically different from those at other events. An interesting perspective to engage the audience at conferences is the use of drama – described by Nelson (2009) as dramaturgy. The purpose here is to enhance the experience through using creative and emotional cues that introduce a dramatic element to the experience as illustrated in Figure 6.5.

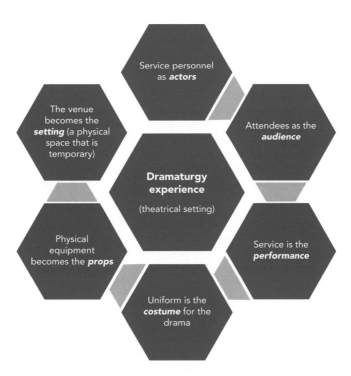

Figure 6.5 The elements of dramaturgy in conferences

Source: Developed from Nelson (2009).

Oppermann and Chon (1997) discussed the decision process, constraints, and both extrinsic and intrinsic motivations for convention attendance by members of associations. They observed both push and pull factors, and noted that many people were annual attendees. van Riper *et al.* (2013) focused on one of the key motives for conference attendance – social networking (see Research Note 6.5).

A lot of choice exists, so intervening opportunities, locational factors and destination image play a role. Davidson (2003) discussed the benefits to destinations and convention-goers in adding pleasure to their business trips. A convention might represent a rare or once-in-a-lifetime opportunity to visit an attractive area. Spouses and other family members often want to come along.

6.5 RESEARCH NOTE ON SOCIAL NETWORKING

van Riper, C. J., van Riper III, C., Kyle, G. T. and Lee, M. E. (2013). Understanding how social networking influences perceived satisfaction with conference experiences. *Annals of Leisure Research*, 16(1), 103–114.

'Social networking is a key benefit derived from participation in conferences that bind the ties of a professional community. Building social networks can lead to satisfactory experiences while furthering participants' long- and short-term career goals. Although investigations of social networking can lend insight into how to effectively engage individuals and groups within a professional cohort, this area has been largely overlooked in past research. The present study investigates the relationship between social networking and satisfaction with the 10th Biennial Conference of Research on the Colorado Plateau using structural equation modelling. Results partially support the hypothesis that three dimensions of social networking – interpersonal connections, social cohesion and secondary associations – positively contribute to the performance of various conference attributes identified in two focus group sessions. The theoretical and applied contributions of this paper shed light on the social systems formed within professional communities and resource allocation among service providers.'

Rittichainuwat *et al.* (2001) determined that attendees at a hospitality educator/researcher conference were motivated primarily by self-enhancement, business and association activities, and sightseeing. The work of Severt *et al.* (2007) reveals that different types of conference and meeting will be associated with different motivators and experiential dimensions. They studied the motivations, satisfaction and behavioural intentions of a group of small business owners and managers attending a regional-level conference with exhibition produced by a national trade association. Their most important motivations for attending, in order, were: education; educational information at exhibits; reasonable travel time to the event; networking opportunities; and business activities. Four of these five are clearly experiential in nature, while accessibility is a facilitating/constraining factor. Attendees were very satisfied with the educational component, ranking it highest. Those most satisfied with education were the most satisfied overall, and the most likely to both return and tell others to attend the conference.

The Centre for Exhibition Research (CEIR 2003) research confirms that face-to-face interaction is vital in marketing, and this will ensure the continuance of live events despite the impact of social media on networking people virtually. Indeed, it appears that although business events are the first to be cancelled in times of troubles (terrorism, pandemics and natural disasters), they bounce back very quickly and continue to grow in number.

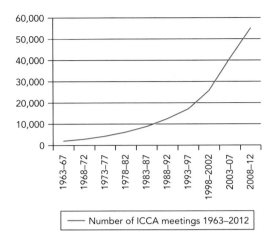

Figure 6.6 Number of ICCA meetings (based on five-year aggregated data)

Source: ICCA data cited in Page (2015).

Mair (2013) reported that many countries in Asia were facing possible over-capacity issues in venue construction as destinations have raced to develop localities to host major conferences. Even so, Page (2015) highlighted the scale of growth in the conference and convention market using the International Congress and Convention Association data as illustrated in Figure 6.6.

What this illustrates is that the demand for conferences and conventions continues apace, and the ICCA data also illustrate that the USA and Europe dominate the market for events. Clearly the rise of social media has not dampened enthusiasm for meeting face-to-face: it may have even expanded the appetite for such meetings. There really is no 'virtual event' that can simulate symbolic interaction, socializing or having fun while doing business. People love to travel and meet, and always will.

Here is a completely different kind of meeting experience, from a blogger and *Twilight* fan:

> *So I went to the Twilight Convention in San Francisco last weekend with a friend (on February 13th,) and we had a blast! We got general tickets for Saturday ($30 each) and sat in pretty good seats. The reserved seats ($50) were right beside and ahead of us, and there were plenty of spots to sit in our general seating area, so I would definitely recommend buying general tickets if you don't care about sitting right at the front of the theater. Of course, I got very tiny photos of the celebrities, but I'm okay with that. I didn't buy celebrity photos or autographs either, but I got my own candid photos at the Volturi Vampire Ball so I'm okay with that, too. I prefer to take my own photos. One of the guest celebrities (Charlie Bewley, who plays the Volturi tracker Demetri) actually ran into the audience to answer questions, so I got a close-up look at him.*

The experiences of different stakeholders

Table 6.3 lists many of the principal event stakeholders, from guest and customer to the media and general public, each of which can have quite different experiences from the same event. The event experience is always at least partially dependent upon the expectations and attitudes of those involved (as inferred above with reference to dramaturgy), and on one's willingness to enter into the spirit of the occasion. As well, different stakeholders will be directly or indirectly affected (on-site versus off) and dependent on their roles (organizers and volunteers). Accordingly, we need more understanding of the expectations people bring to events, and how they describe their experiences. Most of the experiences shown in this

Table 6.3 The experiences of different stakeholders

Groups having event experiences	Subcategories	Unique or especially important experiential dimensions
Paying customers	Sport spectators	Escaping, being entertained
	Concert audience	Belonging and sharing
	Exhibition and conference attendees	Authentic cultural experience
	Festival tourists	Emotionally involved and loyal fans (also nostalgia)
		Socializing and communitas
		Learning, and seeking self-actualization
Guests	Persons invited to a private event	Socializing, networking
	The public at free events	Being part of a community or family
	Guests of sponsors	Subcultural identity
		Being treated as honoured guests, VIPs
Participants	Athletes at competitions	Challenge and mastery
	Performers in arts competitions	Communitas and subcultural expression
Media audience	Remote TV viewers, radio listeners, webcast participants	A virtual entertainment experience shaped by the media
Performers	The entertainers at events	Professional competence, mastery
	Buskers, street performers	self-esteem
	Professional athletes	Ancillary enjoyment of the event
Producers and organizers	Owners	Might be similar to staff and volunteers
	Directors	Need to be responsive and reflective
	Managers	
Very Important People (invited VIPs)	Politicians	Doing their duty
	Celebrities	Protocol shapes their experience as 'performers'
	The Olympic 'family'	
	Investors	Being treated with honour and respect
		Gaining self-esteem
		Ancillary enjoyment of the event
Officials	Referees, timekeepers and stewards.	Professional conduct and responsibility defines their involvement
Regulators	Police, fire, health inspectors, etc.	Professional conduct and responsibility defines their involvement
Sponsors and grant givers	With their own hospitality component	Business success, networking
	Or as VIPs	Providers of hospitality to their own guests (the event is still the attraction)
		Or same as VIPs
Suppliers and vendors	External suppliers	Contractual relationships define their involvement
	Or on-site vendors	Ancillary enjoyment of the event

Table 6.3 (continued)

Groups having event experiences	Subcategories	Unique or especially important experiential dimensions
Volunteers	Board members (may be workers or VIPs at the event)	The 'cast', part of the experience for others
	Unpaid workers at the event	Enjoyment of the event
		Communitas among volunteers
		Self-fulfilment
Paid staff	Paid workers at the event	Paid employment defines their experience
	Security staff, after hours	Ancillary enjoyment of the event
The media	Official (as sponsors)	Might want a VIP experience
	Unofficial media	Professional competence
The public	Indirectly experiences the event (overspill effects or vicarious experiences)	The public's experience can range from 'psychic benefits' to being inconvenienced or harmed

table are, of course, attainable by many of the stakeholders in many event settings. What Table 6.3 sets out to list are those attributes that could be different or special, for each stakeholder – not their full range of potential experiences.

Paying customers

Many events charge admission and attract paying customers who will expect delivery of the promised product, or experience, to a high standard. They are entitled to complain if they do not get their perceived consumer benefit, to use the consumer behaviour concept. Marketers might be content with determining satisfaction levels, as that is the simplest measure of experiential effectiveness in a commercial context. 'Fans' might have other experiences on their mind, including loyalty, communitas and nostalgia (see Fairley 2003 on nostalgia). Cultural tourists might stress belonging and sharing, an authentic cultural experience and a learning experience. Satisfaction levels do not provide much insight to the event experience. Deeper inquiry can reveal how memorable the event was, its meaning to the customer (especially in terms of personal and social constructs), and whether or not the customer had a transforming experience in any way. These phenomenological measures could be potentially valuable for improving the event.

Guests

This term, 'guests', implies that the event-goer is there because they are wanted. The guest will expect to be treated like a personal guest, with hospitality being a key service quality. Guests expect to be greeted and honoured by their hosts. While guests at private parties know they were invited, which shapes their expectations about hospitality and possibly about service levels, making paying customers feel like guests is a real challenge. The guest 'experience' will inevitably include a strong social component, because they are part of an invited group. 'Communitas' is often presupposed in this context, with all guests having an existing affiliation, but it also might have to be facilitated when strangers are in the mix. The use of esoteric rituals and symbols known only to 'insiders' is one form of bonding that designers can use.

Participants

This group consists of the athletes in sports or recreational events, dancers in dance festivals, musicians in music competitions, and to a degree the delegates attending conventions. The event is all about them; it does not exist without their participation. They are likely to feel that the event is for their benefit and its organizers should respect their needs and wishes. Participants also might feel a personal responsibility for the success of the event, but that is contingent on factors such as who owns or sponsors it. To understand participants' experiences requires knowledge of their motives, expectations, activities, emotions and cognitive processes in the specific context of the event. The full range of planned event experiences can apply, but participants are typically looking for mastery through meeting challenges, learning opportunities, and subcultural identity or communitas.

Media audience

Presumably most 'virtual' experiences of planned events, especially TV coverage of sports and concerts, award ceremonies and spectacles, would be described as entertainment. A key question for event studies researchers is whether or not media experiences can be the same as live experiences in terms of emotional engagement and cognition. Can they be as memorable or transforming? We will have to rely on media studies for answers. With the ascendancy of webcasts, there is a need for researchers to examine interactive media experiences, as observed in Chapter 3.

Performers

This group consists of paid entertainers or athletes, all part of the show that customers want to experience. They have quite different motives for being at the event, and gaining a sense of professional accomplishment has to be important. If their experience is bad, it can negatively impact on the overall event quality and customer satisfaction. Producers generally know how to treat professionals with dignity and respect, and to look after their tangible and emotional needs. If the opportunity arises, some performers can also get to enjoy parts of the event themselves.

Producers/organizers

Sometimes the producers/organizers are also involved, working alongside other volunteers; in other events they are completely detached from the experiences they are seeking to create and therefore need to be responsive, and reflective on what they are doing and the feedback they are getting.

VIPs

Whether they are politicians, royalty or celebrities, being a Very Important Person by definition means that event organizers will be giving them special treatment, honour, respect and a lot of security, with protocol often determining what can and cannot be done. Their experience cannot possibly be the same as other guests or customers, and indeed they might become part of the spectacle, temporarily becoming performers. Despite these considerations it might be possible to segregate VIPs enough that they can enjoy part of the event.

Officials and security

Professional conduct and specific responsibilities govern the event experiences of referees, stewards, time-keepers and other officials. They might be almost invisible, or play an important and highly visible role in the event. Their experiences will perhaps include off-duty enjoyment of part of the event, otherwise their main concerns are purely technical. The experience of security personnel is restricted by their need for vigilance.

Regulators

This category of stakeholder (e.g. building and health inspectors) attends events to supervise and ensure compliance, but also have to be made comfortable, kept safe, and have their basic technical and human needs looked after. Professional conduct defines their roles, but might they not take a little time to actually enjoy the event? Perhaps some of them deserve to have VIP status.

Sponsors and donors

Unless they see themselves as regulators, these 'facilitating' stakeholders should be given VIP treatment at events. Corporate sponsors often want specific hospitality services for themselves and their guests, even to the point of having private and exclusive areas and mini-events. Business has to be done, and that is an experience realm that does not have to be divorced from having fun. In addition to enjoying the event, which might be of secondary importance, facilitators also have a vested interest in its success and might therefore play the role of supervisors or evaluators. Some might want status as producers or owners. Needless to say, their overall, multidimensional experience has to be made satisfactory.

Suppliers and vendors

Often these contracted service and goods providers are brought into the event as sponsors as well, giving them a vested interest in its success. They might also find time to enjoy the event. Yet they have specific, professional functions to complete which have to be supervised and evaluated by event management. That means there is a risk of 'split personality' when it comes to the event experiences of contracted suppliers. Health and safety will always be top priorities for suppliers and vendors.

Volunteers

To the extent that they interact with other people at the event, they are both helping to create, and share in, the experiences. Volunteers should have a unique perspective on the overall experience and how others are enjoying the event and have become a specific field of research within events (see Stebbins and Graham 2004 for an overview) especially in the public/not-for-profit sector. Volunteers have to be satisfied or they will not continue to volunteer. Johnston *et al.* (2000) found that sport involvement led directly to volunteering at sport events, which suggests that participants want an experience related to that sport, such as contact with its stars. Saleh and Wood (1998) found some unique motives held by volunteers at a multicultural festival (namely sharing their culture and maintaining cultural links). Elstad (1997) studied student volunteers at the Winter Olympic Games in Lillehammer, Norway, and determined that satisfaction with their experience related most strongly to expanding personal networks, being part of the event atmosphere and achieving job-related competence. In another study, Elstad (2003) found that the top reasons for event volunteers to quit were workload, lack of appreciation and poor organization, all of which suggest experiential implications.

Ralston, Lumsdon and Downward (2005) reviewed the literature on event volunteers, covering motivation, profiles, satisfaction studies and theory. The reasons why people volunteered clearly pertained to the experiences they sought, including excitement, uniqueness (the chance of a lifetime), meeting interesting people and being part of a team. Meanings attached to the experience included supporting sport, doing something useful for the community, helping the city, region and country, and using their skills. A recent review of the event-volunteer phenomenon by Schlenker, Edwards and Wearing (2014) noted the episodic nature of event volunteering related to their timing and frequency, and this also has major implications for the use of paid staff.

Paid staff

Hanlon and Jago (2014) reviewed the nature of human resource needs in event management, observing the pulsating nature of events and the unusual demands this places on human resourcing, which needs to pay particular attention to the staffing demands illustrated in Figure 6.7.

As Figure 6.7 shows, there might be quite different experiences for staff (and this applies to many volunteers as well) depending on their level of involvement through the entire planning and de-commissioning cycle. Most paid staff will be able to have some direct experience of the event, if only when off-duty, but some, like overnight security, will not. All paid staff have specific duties, so they have to be supervised and evaluated, with event enjoyment being an ancillary goal, and (ideally) secondary to the experience of professional accomplishment. There can be overlap, of course, between the roles and experiences of volunteers, paid staff and performers. This will depend on the extent to which these groups are part of the show (as 'cast members') and how dependent guests/customers are on each group for their experiences.

The media

Hopefully most media people attending the event are official sponsors, in which case they require technical support and VIP status. But there are also likely to be unofficial media whose access to the event might be restricted. Conflicts could occur between the two groups of media, between media and VIPs or performers, and between media and organizers/staff. Media relations has become a major task at events and cannot be left to chance. If people have a bad personal or professional experience, the event's image could consequently take a negative hit.

In addition to the media and event experience, Dayan (1994) examined the televising and live broadcasting of historic events such as the Olympic Games. These were described as festive television or media events; such events are therefore viewed not as routine but as cultural performances, and are exceptional planned events with the power to reach global audiences.

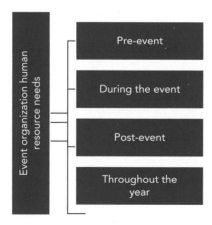

Figure 6.7 The human resource needs of event organizations

The public at large

There might be spillover effects from events, such as noise, light, traffic, smells, crowds and bad behaviour, all of which can cause bad feelings among neighbours and the wider community. The media like to focus on all these issues. The public at large, even those not attending and not interested, can nevertheless gain 'psychic benefits' from their vicarious experience of events, such as increased community pride and perceptions of economic and other impacts. Our discussion of resident perceptions and attitudes in Chapter 10 elaborates on these points.

Meanings attached to planned event experiences

Event experiences can mean as little to us as fleeting entertainment (not important and not memorable), or as much as profoundly transforming. To a community or society, events can have simple commercial meaning (as part of the 'entertainment industry') or they can be significant economic and place-marketing forces. From a cultural perspective events can be reinforcing or threatening. From an economic and tourism point of view events are products to sell, and they must generate tangible as well as image benefits. And to corporations that sponsor or produce events, they have importance in terms of marketing, branding and corporate responsibility.

Meanings attached to planned events are at once anticipatory (as in, 'we are going to the festival to celebrate our heritage'), evolving (e.g. 'the event itself was responsible for changing everyone's attitudes toward the arts') and reflective (such as, 'looking back, it was clearly an event with great economic and political impact'). Historians, and critical researchers, help to attach meanings to events. So do political ideologies and the interactions of all the stakeholders involved. Meanings that are political and societal might not impress the individual, who is, after all, able to formulate personal interpretations and meanings for any event. But, if events have little or no meaning of importance to people, they will not attend. If events lack social, cultural and economic meaning, who will support them?

Personal meanings

The meanings that individuals attach to event experiences are 'personal constructs', which can be defined as a level of cognitive significance that represents how we understand the world around us. In effect, we construct reality in our minds to explain experiences. 'Personal construct theory' posits that people attribute meanings to their experiences, and each person therefore has different experiences. Kelly (1955) theorized that a person's experiences consist of 'a set of personally construed events' that are not necessarily valid. That is, we might not get it right – they are subjective and subject to change. Based on our experiences we can anticipate and predict future experiences, which of course influences what we expect from a planned event.

Epting and Neimeyer (1984: 2) argued that these personal constructs 'serve not only as interpretation of past events but as hypotheses about events yet to be encountered'. Botterill and Crompton (1996) used personal construct theory to examine leisure/tourist experiences and concluded that emotional states are integral to 'optimal experiences' as defined by interviewees.

At one level, we can say that personal meanings relate directly to personal needs, the motives expressed for attending events, and the anticipated benefits to be obtained through the planned event experience. Ask yourself how you give meaning to your life through work, leisure and family. Where do events fit into that meaning system? The rites of passage that mark our lives are bound to be memorable, and full of personal meaning, helping to define who we are. But most of them, like birthdays, anniversaries, weddings and graduations, are also social occasions, with substantial meaning to families and wider social networks.

Experience marketers have also realized that they must engage consumers in events that hold meaning for them. Diller *et al.*, in their book *Making Meaning* (2006: 3), concluded:

> *Our own work in the field has led us to the conviction that for companies to achieve enduring competitive advantage through experience design, their innovations cannot be based simply on novelty. Increasingly, they must address their customers' essential human need for meaning. To do this, companies must first understand the role that meaning plays in people's lives, how products and services can evoke meaning, and then how to identify the core meanings they should target with their own offerings. For companies facing both globalization and the end of the mass market, 'making meaning' is one of very few strategies that will work.*

The personal benefits and meanings can include any of the following, derived from earlier discussions as well as the contribution of Diller *et al.* (2006: 320):

- communitas (as a result of belonging and sharing, from reaffirmation of roots or of connections and values);
- esteem: validation of oneself in the opinions of others; self-worth; prestige and reputation (such as may be realized through competitive or intellectual accomplishments);
- learning, enlightenment (for example, from new cultural experiences or a connoisseur's appreciation of food, art or music);
- self-discovery, self-actualization, understanding, wonder;
- transformation (religious, spiritual, personality or character, renewed, motivated);
- redemption and atonement (from failure or sins);
- mastery (from skills, physical triumph);
- accomplishment or success (from business, trade, commerce, networking, creativity, artistic expression);
- creativity or innovation (making a lasting contribution);
- fulfilment of responsibility (professionalism, or as a dedicated sport fan, or from getting involved as a volunteer);
- health and well-being (through physical activity, learning);
- security (living without fear);
- duty (military or civic) fulfilled; patriotism and loyalty to a cause;
- truth, honesty, integrity (a meaning given to relationships and to one's own behaviour);
- beauty or aesthetic appreciation;
- freedom (acting without constraint; intrinsically rewarding pursuits);
- harmony (with nature or others) and oneness (belonging, unity);
- justice (fairness and equality; democratic expression).

People might not be able to articulate the meanings they assign to event experiences; they might not think of meanings at all. You could ask them what benefits they expected and derived from the experience, and that comes close. They can be asked to respond to a list of statements or adjectives about the event to see if they found it memorable, transforming or meaningful in terms of the above-mentioned dimensions. People want to give meaning to their experiences and to their lives in general, but expressing those meanings requires deep thought and a good vocabulary! This is a real challenge for researchers and theorists. Events in Focus 6.2 highlights how positive psychology may make a significant contribution to this area.

EVENTS IN FOCUS

6.2 Using positive psychology in designing events

Coghlan, A. (2015). Tourism and health: Using positive psychology principles to maximise partici-pants' wellbeing outcomes – a design concept for charity challenge tourism. *Journal of Sustainable Tourism*, 23(3), 382–400.

A recent study of event design by Coghlan examines how to harness the key tenets of positive psychology into the design principles for events to achieve eudomonic states (i.e. the state of mind where an individual can flourish and be happy) so that their sense of well-being is enhanced. Coghlan points to five predictors of well-being that have been identified as enhancing eudomonic states as shown in Figure 6.8.

What this study emphasizes is the importance of participation in an event, and using the example of a charity event, Coghlan illustrates the underpinning principles that need to be designed in to achieve these well-being principles combined with the theory of positive psychology. Within the literature on positive psychology, Coghlan illustrates that five principles have to be incorporated into the event to leverage the well-being benefits as illustrated in Figure 6.9.

What Figure 6.9 shows is that the following principles are significant:

- *Intentional activity*, which is derived from the literature in leisure where physical activity makes a contribution to happiness (especially where combined with something like a charity event which Coghlan studied) and so this feature has to be able to derive meaning for the participant.

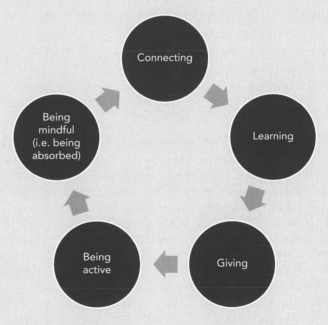

Figure 6.8 Predictors of well-being

Figure 6.9 Integrating the science of positive psychology into the design of tourism experiences: a conceptual model

Source: Coghlan (2015: 338). Reprinted from *The Journal of Sustainable Tourism*, 23, A. Coghlan, Tourism and health: using positive psychology principles to maximise participants' wellbeing outcomes, Copyright (2015), with the permission of Taylor and Francis.

- *Motivation and goal attainment*, where the event has the ability to motivate an individual's intrinsic motivation so as to achieve self-set goals which can be attained (as well as setting mini goals within the event, such as reaching half-way).

- *Signature strengths*, which Coghlan describes as the thoughts, feelings and behaviours of individuals that can contribute to the reward of participation such as endurance, a sense of community, leadership and so forth. The event needs to leverage these signature strengths to engage the participants to enhance their positive benefit from involvement.

- *Positive emotions and gratification*, where positive emotions help to achieve a state of authentic happiness which may be displayed through enjoyment, engagement and satisfaction with the event.

- *Sharing positive events*, where individuals recount and reminisce about events in the past, has the potential to achieve what Coghlan describes as capitalization, where the retelling of the event provides an opportunity to relive it.

Summarizing the findings of the study, Coghlan highlights the value of appropriate forms of event design to incorporate these principles, whereby the intentional element can be achieved from the point of sign up to the end of the charity event; connecting with others, setting goals and achieving a meaningful involvement and activating the signature strengths as well as reminiscing all have very good positive psychological benefits and a contribution to well-being. The study lays the groundwork for the further development of well-being and event research which may expand our understanding of this important area in the future.

Social meanings

These are meanings given to events by social groups, communities and society as a whole. Individuals are affected by these meanings, but are also able to make their own interpretations of events. Event types or forms, as previously discussed, are to a large extent 'social constructs', with collectively assigned and generally recognized meanings. Abrahams (1987) noted that the way we frame or attach meaning to experiences is embedded in social and cultural order. Our most popular religious holidays and civic celebrations have generally accepted meanings. For many people the sacred might have given way to the profane for holidays like Christmas; nevertheless society as a whole recognizes and needs the social and personal benefits of these holidays, despite some differences in meanings attached to them.

Forms of event, like festivals and sport competitions, are expected to conform to widely held expectations regarding where and when they are held, who attends, accepted and expected behaviours, and even their programmic elements. Going beyond the norms, as innovative event designers are wont to do, risks alienating or at least mystifying elements of the potential audience. If the changes are accepted, perhaps over a long period of time, then they are added to the social constructs we hold. We can call this process the making of tradition, or the establishment of social norms and conformity.

Social and political constructs

Roche (2000: 7; see also Roche 2006) saw events, like the global Millennium celebrations, acting as 'important elements in the orientation of national societies to international or global society'. Indeed, many countries have used mega events to gain legitimacy and prestige, draw attention to their accomplishments, foster trade and tourism, or to help open their countries to global influences. This is much more than place marketing – it is more like national identity-building. And Whitson and Macintosh (1996: 279) argued that countries and cities compete for mega-sport events to demonstrate their 'modernity and economic dynamism'.

Julie Russell (2004) examined the political meanings attached to the National Eisteddfod of Wales, which has a tradition dating back to 1176. She found that this annual competition of music and poetry is simultaneously an arena for performing arts, a forum for preserving the Welsh language, a tourist attraction, a trade fair and a platform for political acts of Welsh significance. 'As an arts and cultural festival . . . the Eisteddfod also delivers the wider range of economic and socio-linguistic benefits which embrace the interests of the Wales Tourist Board, the Arts Council of Wales, the Welsh Language Board, local authorities and others.'

Sense of community and sense of place

Derrett (2004: 48) discussed how communities share their culture through festivals and events, and how the interdependencies of residents, place and visitors help establish a valued sense of community and place:

> They celebrate a sense of place through organizing inclusive activities in specific safe environments. They provide a vehicle for communities to host visitors and share such activities as representations of communally agreed values, interests and aspirations. Thirdly, they are the outward manifestation of the identity of the community and provide a distinctive identifier of place and people.

On the other hand, 'commodification' or 'festivalization' of culture is a threat. Duffy (2000) examined the sense of place achieved through popular music festivals, and a body of work within environmental psychology has focused on the theme of place attachment (the bonding of an individual with an environment they value) and the meanings ascribed to places, which can be adapted to the notion of planned events. Scannell and Gifford (2010) reviewed the various definitions of the concept and synthesized them into a three-dimensional organizing framework. According to those authors, the 'person dimension' of place attachment refers to its individually or collectively determined meanings, the 'psychological dimension' includes the affective, cognitive and behavioural components, and the 'place dimension' emphasizes the spatial level.

Cultural meanings

Quinn (2000: 264) concluded that:

> *If at the heart of every festival are a place and a place-based community actively reproducing its shared values and belief systems, there is an important sense in which these cultural meanings are intentionally produced to be read by the outside world.*

A related challenge stems from the fact that meanings are easily and often contested, based on different values and belief systems within the same community. So while the festival is a 'text' on culture, to be interpreted, it is often an ambiguous one. In fact studies from anthropology (e.g. Rotenberg and McDonogh 1993) illustrate the significance of a body of knowledge around spatial meanings in urban studies.However, the principal challenge for event research is that these environments are essentially temporary; they pose different research problems for understanding spatial meaning.

Sport as cultural expression

'Games and sports, like religious rituals and festivals, can be interpreted as reflections of broader social relationships and cultural ideals' (Mitler *et al.* 2004: 348). To Geertz (1993) they are models of culture depicting key values and ideals, such as fair play or friendly competition. Sport can also have more sinister or controversial significance, reflecting or encouraging aggression and dominance of one group over another, or territoriality and cultural imperialism. Many people see elements of a national culture in their sports, and in the emphasis they place on sports. We should be asking, does policy regarding sport reflect or shape culture?

Cultural authenticity

There has been a great deal of debate about what an 'authentic' experience or event really is, and if it is even desired or understood by tourists or event-goers. We are speaking here of cultural authenticity, which is really the cultural meaning attached to an event. Boorstin's famous (1961) description of 'pseudo events' was really a commentary on mass tourism, as he believed that culture was being commoditized and that many events were created to cater to tourists' expectations. This belief contrasts with those of MacCannell (1973) and others, who believed that people sought out authentic cultural experiences because they lived shallow or uninteresting lives. Cohen (1979) argued that different types of tourists required different experiences, which hold different meanings, all of which are mediated by culture. He distinguished two major streams – those searching for authenticity (or on a spiritual quest) called 'modern pilgrimage', and those seeking pleasure.

Wang (1999) identified three types of authenticity. 'Object-related authenticity' pertains to the true nature of the event as a cultural expression. In this context, event producers have to ensure that their performances, design features and other programmic elements are genuine reflections of the culture being displayed. But who is to judge this?

'Constructive authenticity' is projected on to the event in terms of images, expectations, preferences and beliefs. Visitors might be fooled, and they might not care if the event is not a true cultural expression. Event producers have considerable scope for entertaining people, but should they be concerned about meanings attached by visitors? Does the event producer have an obligation (moral, or in terms of marketing) to ensure that the event is not misperceived?

To Wang 'existential authenticity' occurs because whatever the nature of the event (authentic in cultural terms, or not), event consumers might have their own, meaningful experiences which they interpret as being authentic. The theory is that authentic experiences enable discovery of one's true self. This presents a real challenge for the event producers, as they must acknowledge that their programme is (merely?) a setting or background for desired, highly individualized experiences. In a variation, Timothy and Boyd (2006) discussed 'relative authenticity', saying that authenticity is a subjective notion varying from person to person, depending on our social conditioning. Meaning is not derived from the event, in this interpretation, but from the interaction of event and visitor-created meanings.

The conclusion we are left with is that 'cultural authenticity' is a theoretically difficult concept. Our position is that when it comes to determining what is authentic or not, only the cultural groups being represented, or doing the performance, are qualified to judge. Within cultures there often rages a debate about whether modern performances are authentic and justifiable, but surely outsiders cannot be expected to decide.

There is a completely different approach to 'authentic' experiences, one that has wider application. Consider this: are sport events authentic? Not in cultural terms, but as events deserving of trust and belief in them? Despite the occasional scandal arising from gambling or bad refereeing, sports are generally considered to be authentic because the outcome is unpredictable, the players give their best, and talent plus hard work is rewarded. Many other forms of entertainment are widely thought to be contrived and unbelievable. Even so-called television 'reality shows' appear to be nothing more than stylized, scripted theatre. More research on event-consumer beliefs and on mass-media experiences related to 'authenticity' is warranted.

Contested culture, stakeholders and legitimacy

Will all stakeholders in a community agree on core values and what is to be celebrated? In fact, culture and its representations are often contested. To examine this issue, Crespi-Vallbona and Richards (2007) interviewed many stakeholders in Catalonia, finding that there were common issues surrounding festivals in that region. Cultural identity was the strongest and most common theme, reflecting this region's long struggle to establish a national identity. This was a binding factor, even though differences in meanings were evident. Nevertheless, the researchers observed tension between the local and global perspectives on events, and there was concern for preserving cultural integrity when events were also expected to serve political, economic and social goals. They observed that:

> stakeholders tend to differ more in the meanings attached to concepts such as identity, with policy makers exhibiting a greater emphasis on economic and political issues, whereas cultural producers are more concerned with social aspects of identity. However, the general consensus on the social role of cultural events between the different stakeholders may be one explanation for the relatively vibrant festival culture in Catalunya.
>
> (Crespi-Vallbona and Richards 2007: 103)

Differences in meanings attached to festivals are related to claims to power, legitimacy and urgency by the various stakeholders involved in the policy process.

Economic meanings

To a large extent we have already defined the economic meanings attached to events by looking at event tourism and the roles of attraction, catalyst, animator, image-maker and place marketer. These meanings are shaped by politicians and industry, rather than the general public or travellers themselves. Many events are also considered to be part of the 'entertainment or culture industries', or perhaps the 'creative industries', and these represent economic meanings. Within the context of 'popular culture', using the term 'industry' is likely to imply commercialization and mass consumption.

Although many events are within the realm of arts and culture, they do have to be managed as businesses. This introduces a tension between the values of arts/culture on the one hand, and the potential for hard-nosed management or commercialization on the other. Ideally the economic and arts/cultural meanings can be brought into balance. Sports as 'big business' is a recurring theme. For example, Rozin (2000) described Indianapolis as a 'classic case' of how sports can generate a civic turnaround. Sports Business Market Research Inc. (2000: 167) observed that in the 1980s and 1990s American cities 'put heavy emphasis on sports, entertainment and tourism as a source of revenue for the cities'. Gratton and Kokolakakis (1997) believed that in the UK sports events had become the main platform for economic regeneration in many cities.

Berridge (2007) observed that:

> *The discipline of events is expanding significantly from its cultural and celebratory origins and the role of events in business is changing as its effectiveness in 'brand marketing' is more clearly understood and the levels of investment increase as a result.*

Within the corporate world it is now fashionable to think of a brand in terms of relationships, with 'live communications' or 'event experiences' building and sustaining these relationships between company and customer. In this context, planned events are brand-building tools, and the experiences have to be evaluated in terms of how they meet corporate marketing aims. There is growing competition to attract and 'engage' customers this way, so events will tend to have a short life cycle. Something new will always be needed.

When companies practise corporate responsibility, their participation in events takes on new meanings. To the extent that corporations show commitment to the community and the environment out of altruism or necessity, events can be expressions of that commitment. Contemporary consumers and lobby groups expect companies to behave responsibly and that should lead to something of a reversal in the trend towards viewing participation in events as just marketing. In this context it seems reasonable to suggest that 'authenticity' and commercialism are incompatible. What do you think?

STUDY GUIDE

It is essential to be able to explain the planned event experience, and meanings attached to it – this is the core phenomenon of event studies. This chapter first explored the meaning of 'experience', including how it is conceptualized in leisure theory and within the context of the 'experience economy'. To develop a model of the planned event experience also required drawing upon anthropological theory, particularly to employ the notions of 'liminal', 'liminoid' and 'communitas'. Different event stakeholders will have different motives, experiences and meanings, so producers have to understand how, for example, paying customers are different from invited guests or VIPs. Consider how the material in this chapter aids in event design, making events 'special', and in marketing events to specific target audiences.

STUDY QUESTIONS

- What are the behavioural (conative), emotional (affective) and mental (cognitive) dimensions of 'experience'?
- What do intrinsic and extrinsic motivations have to do with event experiences?
- Why are corporations so interested in event experiences, within the context of the 'experience economy'?
- Explain why service dominant logic is a compelling new approach to experience design and event planning.
- Describe the model of planned event experiences, and specifically define 'liminal' and 'liminoid' in this context, drawing on anthropological theory.

- Discuss the concept of 'communitas' as it applies to event experiences, including why it can be a 'generic' event experience.
- How do the concepts of 'optimal arousal' and 'flow' relate to the planned event experience?
- In what ways can event experiences be 'memorable' and 'transforming'?
- What is the 'theory of spectacle' and how does it apply to event experiences?
- Give examples of how different types of planned events can facilitate both 'generic' and 'event-specific' experiences.
- Show how different stakeholders experience events in different ways, related to their motives and functions.
- Use the concepts of 'personal construct' and 'social construct' to explain various meanings attached to events.
- What is meant by 'cultural authenticity' and why is it important in event studies?

FURTHER READING

Baron, S., Warnaby, G. and Hunter-Jones, P. (2014). Service(s) marketing research: Developments and directions. *International Journal of Management Reviews*, 16(2), 150–171.

Diller, S., Shedroff, N. and Rhea, D. (2006). *Making Meaning*. Upper Saddle River, NJ: Pearson.

Gilmore, J. and Pine, J. (2007). *Authenticity: What Consumers Really Want*. Boston: Harvard Business School Press.

Morgan, M., Lugosi, P. and Ritchie, J. R. B. (2010). *The Tourism and Leisure Experience: Consumer and Managerial Perspectives*. Bristol: Channel View.

Pine, B. and Gilmore, J. (1999). *The Experience Economy: Work is Theatre and Every Business a Stage*. Boston: Harvard Business School Press.

Timothy, D. and Olsen, D. (eds) (2006). *Tourism, Religion and Spiritual Journeys*. London and New York: Routledge.

Chapter **7**

Event design

LEARNING OBJECTIVES

Upon completion of this chapter students should know the following:

- the meaning and practice of design and how it is applied to events;
- principles of psychology, sociology and other disciplines as applied to event design;
- aspects of events that are subject to design, with specific design issues:
  - ○ setting (site and venue) and atmosphere;
  - ○ theme and programme (including performers, participants and programmic elements of style);
  - ○ services (service quality; staff and volunteers as 'the cast');
  - ○ consumables (gastronomy; gifts);
- use of market intelligence to design events for special-interest groups.

What is event design?

'Design' is neither pure science nor art; it is both a technical and creative act. The chapter starts with definitions of design and the meaning of event design, addressing the basic question of whether or not planned event experiences can be designed, and if so, how. When it comes to the tools of event design, we can draw on a number of principles from psychology, environmental psychology and social psychology in particular. The opinions of a number of event designers are also presented, in order to ground the discussion in real-world professional practice. Creativity is an integral part of design, which means looking at its meaning and tools that have been used to foster creativity or innovation. This takes us into the arts, but also draws from science and engineering. Detailed discussions are presented on the event setting (the site, venue and atmosphere), the programme, including elements of style, and services that have to be managed for quality and experiential impact.

Definitions

Nathan Shedroff wrote *Experience Design* (2001) and co-authored *Making Meaning: How Successful Businesses Deliver Meaningful Customer Experiences* (Diller *et al.* 2006). This definition of design is derived from his website (www.nathan.com):

> *Design is a set of fields for problem-solving that uses user-centric approaches to understand user needs (as well as business, economic, environmental, social, and other requirements) to create successful solutions that solve real problems. Design is often used as a process to create real change within a system or market. Too often, Design is defined only as visual problem solving or communication because of the predominance of graphic designers.*

Shedroff distinguishes several fields of design applications including 'environmental design' for structures or settings, and 'experience design'. Experience, to Shedroff, consists of:

> *The sensation of interaction with a product, service, or event, through all of our senses, over time, and on both physical and cognitive levels. The boundaries of an experience can be expansive and include the sensorial, the symbolic, the temporal, and the meaningful.*

And these features are explored further in Expert Opinion 7.1 by Steve Brown.

7.1 EXPERT OPINION

Event design

Associate Professor Steve Brown is a practitioner academic who combines professional practice as an event designer with academic research, primarily in the field of audience behaviour. He was responsible for the development of the event design and management programmes at Flinders University in Adelaide, Australia and is Deputy Academic Director at the Australian Institute of Business. To him event design must have an audience orientation.

A definition

Event design is the creation, conceptual development and staging of an event using event design principles and techniques to capture and engage the audience with a positive and meaningful experience. The event designed experience that is the result of the ongoing event design process maximizes the effectiveness of communication with the audience and can both influence and modify audience behaviour which, as a consequence, increases the potential for the event to meet and exceed its stated aims and objectives while providing the foundation for the delivery of an optimal or peak experience for the audience.

My professional experience designing, managing and marketing events over the past thirty plus years – combined with over fifteen years of academic research – has convinced me that though the foundation of any successful event is strong event *management*, it is well researched and effectively applied event *design* that is the critical factor in the success and sustainability of an event.

If we are to have truly sensational experiences then events must be designed first and managed next. We need to put our audiences first and be audience-centric in our thinking, our planning and in the development of the original concept. This is where the potential for the event experience is fully realized. Event design is not an 'add-on' to an otherwise well detailed and defined and pre-scribed management process but should be the guiding direction for, and an over-arching influence on, the decision-making and action taken over the entire course of the event's life.

While event design is, of course, related to the creation of the event's aesthetic and theme, it is also inextricably linked with the event designer's deep understanding of the event's audience – their predispositions (motivations, behaviours, demographic, social identity), their behaviours and the range of known factors that affect them. It is an opportunity to engage and communicate with our audiences in new and more effective ways.

An event design approach, therefore, presupposes intent to influence both the audience and their experience.

How the audience is captured by – and, importantly, engages with – the created and staged experience is two parts of one process: the development of an event concept and then the practical application of event design principles and techniques. Doing so ensures that not only will the event achieve its aims and objectives (commercial or otherwise), but also will provide experiences where audiences are moved, engaged, connected, fascinated, thrilled, captured, convinced, saddened, delighted, elated, enthralled and even – if they are given the opportunity by us – joined as one.

Brown and James (2004: 59) argued that: 'Design is essential to an event's success because it leads to improvement of the event on every level.' The 'core values' of the event provide the starting point: why is an event held, and for whom? What are its substance and intended outcomes? Brown and James discussed five design principles for events that are incorporated into the ensuing discussion:

- scale
- shape
- focus
- timing
- build

They also emphasized the need for creativity and uniqueness in event design, as generic events offering the same benefits are unlikely to endure. This can be accomplished, in part, by incorporating the rituals and symbols of the host community.

Julia Silvers (2004: 5), in her book *Professional Event Coordination*, expressed event design thus: 'Remember that you are packaging and managing an experience. This means that you must envision that experience, from start to finish, from the guest's point of view.'

Graham Berridge, a UK event professional and lecturer, has written a book devoted to the subject. In *Event Design and Experience*, Berridge (2007) discusses the field of 'experience design' at length, stating that the subject is in its infancy. Unfortunately, the term is being used to describe the design of everything from websites (digital media) to storytelling, theme parks and corporate 'brand events'. Berridge argued that the purpose of event design is to create desired perceptions, cognition and behaviour. Building and maintaining relationships is at the core, and stimulating emotional connections through engagement is the vehicle.

Berridge (2012b: 278) also argued that it might be useful to distinguish between 'event architecture', which largely encompasses the technical, problem-solving functions of design, and the 'artistic or aesthetic design and creation' processes, both of which must be combined to create successful event experiences. Many creative challenges exist for the event experience designer, including concept and theme, entertainment, staging, ambience, decoration, and food and beverage. We often associate 'design' with fashion, aesthetics or visual graphics. Events do require aesthetic design, particularly to create the right atmosphere, but there is much more to it. Perhaps we need to think more about industrial design, with its emphasis on problem-solving. A chair has to be designed for efficiency and comfort, plus it has to be pleasing to the eye. An event, both its *tangible setting* (the site and venue), *the atmosphere* (with sensory stimulations of all kinds) and its *programme* combine to create the 'experiential components', and also have to be designed, both with the producer's goals in mind and the needs, preferences and desires of the audience or customers. If design is separated from goals and real-world needs, we are left with art for its own sake.

Can experiences be designed?

There already exists a Wikipedia definition of experience design that suggests:

> *Experience design (XD) is the practice of designing products, processes, services, events, and environments with a focus placed on the quality of the user experience and culturally relevant solutions, with less emphasis placed on increasing and improving functionality of the design. An emerging discipline, experience design draws from many other disciplines including cognitive psychology and perceptual psychology, linguistics, cognitive science, architecture and environmental design, haptics, hazard analysis, product design, theatre, information design, information architecture, ethnography, brand strategy, interaction design, service design, storytelling, heuristics, and design thinking.*

In this context, 'haptics' refers to the sense of touch and is concerned with applying the sense of touch to user interfaces (such as computer keyboards).

At this point, you may find it helpful to go back to the previous chapter and re-read the definitions of 'experience', look again at how meanings are attached to experiences and think about that long list of stakeholders (much more than guests or the audience) who are experientially influenced by planned events. It is possible to get people involved, have them do specific things and receive desired stimuli, but it is not possible to guarantee or predict what individuals actually 'experience' cognitively and emotionally as an outcome. Nor can the event designer know for a certainty what meanings will be attached to those event experiences, or whether they will have any transforming impact.

'Experienced' event producers build up an understanding of what seems to work well to make people happy, or at least to say that they are satisfied. And 'practice does make perfect' when it comes to both getting the design elements right (i.e. technically perfect, and in keeping with the designer's vision), and also in avoiding mistakes. In these ways the designer's experience and intuition go a long way to improving event experiences. But whatever the design process, there has to be research and feedback from the stakeholders leading to improvement, otherwise the designer is guilty of either taking a 'product orientation' (here is what I offer, it's good for you), or creating art for its own sake (with no problem being solved).

An experience is so highly personal that it cannot be planned, designed or even promised to event-goers. The purpose of any event is to suggest what experiences might be had (through theming and interpretation), facilitate positive experiences (through design of setting, programme, services and consumables) and to enable everyone concerned, as much as possible, to realize their goals (co-creation). On the other hand, design and management also seeks to constrain undesired experiences, including aggression, violence and over-stimulation.

Creativity and innovation

A simple definition of 'creativity' is that it is the mental process of generating new ideas or concepts. It can be equated with invention and innovation, as in the engineering and entrepreneurial contexts. Creativity is not found only in the arts – it is a fundamental part of all human endeavour. Where does it come from, and can it be taught? It does appear that some people are more naturally creative than others, perhaps benefiting from unique mental processes or their upbringing. We sometimes say that creative people show 'genius' because their ideas or their art just seem to be so novel or fresh.

With whole 'industries' now devoted to creativity and knowledge formation, it is becoming more and more unlikely that individuals will spontaneously generate truly original ideas or non-derivative art. So another approach to creativity becomes more important, and that is to actively search for, discuss and refine new associations between facts and concepts. That is one of the aims of this book – to encourage students, researchers and policy-makers to put things together in new ways – to be creative, to think in different ways, often referred to by the euphemism of 'thinking outside the box'. You not only need a lot of information as the starting point, you need some advice on how to proceed.

Richard Florida's (2002) concept of 'the creative class' is relevant here. According to Florida, creativity is a driving force in economic life, and a key source of competitive advantage. Some cities flourish because of their creative class, and Florida argued that creative-class workers choose cities for their tolerant environments and diverse populations, as well as good jobs. The event sector has to be part of this creativity, and is therefore deserving of attention by both cultural and economic policy-makers. 'Creative capital' has value, and it has to be attracted, even though the people displaying the most creative capital might otherwise be viewed as eccentric, at best, or just plain weird. Tolerance, technology and talent go together.

Creativity can certainly be taught, at least to a degree. If the social environment is supportive, more people will become artists and inventors. If the learning environment is oriented in such a way, students at all levels can learn to be more creative. Hopefully this book accomplishes something of that nature by encouraging readers to make new associations between ideas, see new problems and opportunities that emerge from a discussion of existing ones, and think up research that can lead to new knowledge.

Innovation

A simple definition of innovation is to renew (or change), with something new (an idea, a programme or an event) arising from this process. As Franchetti and Page (2009) observed, innovation is derived from the Latin term 'innovatio' which means 'to create something new'. In events, this relates to the type of experience being provided. Sundbo and Bærenholdt (2007) observed that innovation normally occurred at the level of the firm, at the level of a network and at a systems level (i.e. within government, institutions and organizations that influence the management and operation of activities). Hjalager (2009) expands upon the typical areas of innovation, basing her observations on the initial work of Schumpeter (1975), which outlined the main areas for industrial innovation. These include product innovations, process innovations (e.g. new ways of delivering services), market innovations (i.e. new ways of communicating with the customer such as the Internet) and logistical innovations (i.e. innovations in supply chain delivery of services such as vertical integration to deliver a seamless tourism experience). Therefore within an events context, achieving innovation is about organizational culture that fosters innovative (as opposed to more laggard behaviour that resists change), leadership and planning as well as harnessing the raw creativity or design around the staging of events and the experience outcome. To be innovative, event organizers must strive to constantly learn, reform and renew their approach to management and design.

Several authors have examined innovation in the events sector (van Limburg 2008; Carlsen *et al.* 2010; Jóhannesson 2010), and Research Notes 7.1 also address this theme.

7.1 RESEARCH NOTES ON INNOVATION

Larson, M. (2009). Festival innovation: Complex and dynamic network interaction. *Scandinavian Journal of Hospitality and Tourism*, 9(2–3), 288–307.

Material from case studies of three Swedish festivals showed that innovation takes place in complex networks involving many actors having various interests. Innovation networks are often highly dynamic and changing: innovation often takes place in new partnerships. The innovation work is hard to plan: it is to a large degree an emergent process and sometimes innovation originates from improvisation. Some innovation can, however, become institutionalized and embedded in the routines of the partnership interaction. Festival organizers need to reflect on their network and relate strategically to how their partners can contribute to successful festival innovation.

Hjalager, A. (2009). Cultural tourism innovation systems – the Roskilde Festival. *Scandinavian Journal of Hospitality and Tourism*, 9(2–3), 266–287.

Hjalager wrote that '[S]ince 1971, Roskilde Festival (Denmark) has developed its role as a leading element in an emerging cultural innovation system. Festival organizers maintain long-term, dense and multi-faceted relations. Funds from the (non-profit) festival are efficiently channelled into cultural and sports facilities, enhancing the attractiveness of the region. To keep ahead in the festival market, innovators in the field of managerial systems, technologies and services are deliberately invited to use the grounds as test benches for new ideas. . . . Roskilde is a not static event. Since 2001 especially, wider ranging organizational structures have been constructed and politically enforced with the aim of nurturing spin-offs, and including strong representation within the educational and research sectors.'

Foundations of event design

The foundations of event design, as depicted in Figure 7.1, consist of setting, management and people, all with the aim of facilitating unique, satisfying and memorable experiences that will attract guests, customers and participants – hopefully creating loyal audiences. It is the combination of these basic elements, within the almost limitless parameters of the elements of style, that is in the realm of design. And remember that every time an event is offered, the experiences of those involved will be different – if only because their expectations, moods and behaviour will differ.

Nelson (2009) was concerned about creating enhanced experiences for event attendees through the application of Goffman's (1959) dramaturgical perspective and the components of atmospherics (Kotler 1973) and servicescape (Bitner 1992). Goffman, according to Nelson, stressed the setting components of furniture, decor, physical layout, and other background items that supply the scenery and stage props. Attendees enter a specially designed setting for the performance of the event. Physical and ambient factors are part of the designer's repertoire: lighting, colour, quality of materials, layout, music, entertainment, fragrance and room temperature. Signs, symbols and artefacts are also employed to create the right atmosphere and a functional servicescape.

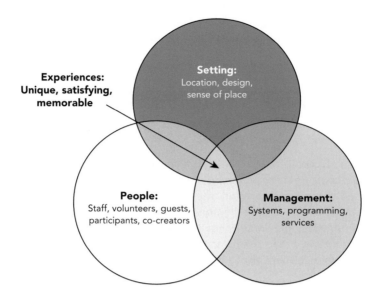

Figure 7.1 Foundations of event design

Designing the setting

Event settings, first of all, are places that have to be defined as 'special' for the duration of the 'time out of time' that constitutes a planned event. The main initial considerations are location (e.g. centrality and accessibility), site characteristics (is it suitable for the event?) and the social–cultural context (has it historic and cultural meaning?). Infrastructure and management systems then have to be developed or modified, including basic services, theme and programme, amenities and guest services, security and controls. Both site planning and aesthetic design are important.

Settings and management systems will interact with the people dimension (staff, volunteers, participants, performers, other guests and customers) in shaping the event experiences. There are unlimited ways to combine setting, management and people, yielding great opportunities for creative event design. However, each setting poses its own challenges and opportunities, some of which are identified in the ensuing discussion of generic event settings. By 'generic', we mean all events will fit into one or more of them because they are defined by function.

Assembly

Conventions, concerts, festivals and spectator sports – any event bringing together large numbers of people – require settings that provide for sitting, viewing and listening. The event manager can often rent 'assembly' venues that have their own management systems, including convention centres, hotel ballrooms, exposition halls, concert halls, auditoria and arenas.

Major design challenges include the fact that many venues are either halls or arenas with no inherent aesthetics, or require substantial modification on technical or creative grounds to suit the event. This negative factor might be compensated adequately by the presence of staff and systems to facilitate events. Opportunities for using unique and even strange venues abound. Meeting planners seek out venues in special places with inspiring or provocative features.

Advice on meeting and convention venue design can be found in Meeting Professionals International (2003), *Meetings and Conventions: A Planning Guide*. Party design is covered by Bailey (2002) and Lena Malouf's (2002) *Parties and Special Events: Planning and Design*.

Procession

Parades, flotillas, cavalcades, marches and other similar events are linear, mobile forms of entertainment, spectacle or ritual with special design and management requirements. The audience might be standing, seated or moving along with the procession. The most common linear setting, however, is a street with a static audience along the route. Some processions pass through seating areas and even stadia, where they take on the form of theatre.

Logistics for such events are challenging, such as getting everyone in a parade or race mobilized for proper sequencing, the likelihood of causing traffic disruption and congestion, and the fact that most streets are unsuited for spectating. Gregson (1992) gave advice on using pavements, streets and buildings to stage events, noting that architects generally fail to take account of seasonal changes and the needs of public gatherings. Also refer to IFEA's publication *Parades* (2000).

Linear-nodal

Many sport events involve races or other linear forms of activity, including long-distance running and auto racing, which combine elements of procession with nodes of activity. Usually the audience congregates at the nodes, such as start, finish and transition points. The event designer will often have to provide live video feeds from the linear portions to the places where fans congregate. Service points for athletes and vehicles are also needed.

Open space

Frequently, events make use of parks, plazas and closed-off streets, especially in publicly sponsored events designed to appeal to mass audiences. Free movement is a feature of these settings, but they usually also contain sub-areas for assembly, procession and exhibition/sales. European cities seem to have the advantage in terms of beautiful, culturally significant squares for events, while North American cities tend to have more space, such as waterfronts and natural parks to use for large public gatherings (Getz 2001). Environmental concerns are important in parks, while potential damage to buildings is a concern in urban plazas.

Exhibition/sales

Purpose-built exhibition and convention centres are the best suited for trade and consumer shows, although any event can incorporate areas for food and beverage or other merchandise sales and demonstrations. These settings are designed to entice entry and circulation, browsing and sales. Sometimes the audience merely views the exhibits; at other venues, sales are made. Since the purpose of these events is usually commerce, a number of principles from environmental psychology have to be applied to the design in order to ensure that interpersonal contacts are facilitated. Good circulation is necessary, but it is also desirable to have people linger and talk. See *The Art of the Show* (Morrow 1997) for details on exhibition design.

Events as theatre

Theatre is one form of planned event, but as already discussed it is also a metaphor for performances and events of all kinds. Certainly there is ample scope for the event designer to draw upon theatrical productions to enhance event settings and experiences. 'Experience design' according to Haahti and Komppula (2006) draws heavily on 'dramaturgy', which is part of theatre and performance studies. They provide examples in which high-contact, high-involvement tourists co-create experiences with professional 'stagers' or facilitators. Ideas for 'manuscripts' and 'staged experiences' have to be generated with the needs and expectations of guests in mind, embodying myths, stories and history from the place or event. 'This enables the creation of a place and a space for being together and the development of a group identity in experiencing' (Haahti and Komppula 2006: 103). In this approach, the 'stage' is whatever venue the experience takes place in, but it has to be appropriate to the design.

Staging

This is the most fundamental theatrical concept, based on the fact that plays and many other performances are usually produced in a specific (assembly) venue with a stage and an audience. 'Staging' or 'stagecraft' applies to both the layout of this type of setting and to what is done on the stage (or within the entire performance space, whatever it is) to facilitate the performance and enhance the audience's experience. The basic components are illustrated in Figure 7.2.

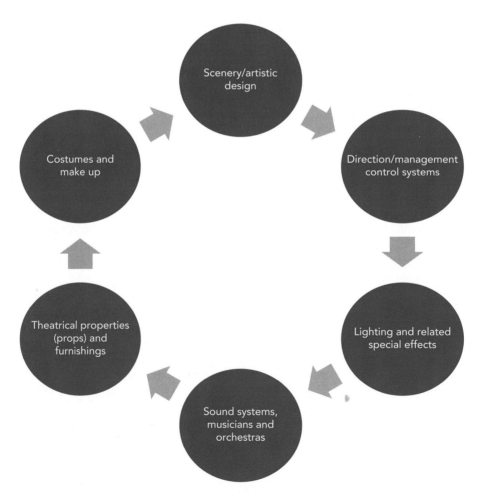

Figure 7.2 The elements associated with enhancing the audience experience

Brown and James (2004) discussed five specific theatrical applications to events. Scale, shape and focus apply to the setting, whereas timing and build come under the heading of scripting or programming.

SCALE

It is important to match the scale of the event or activity to the venue, in part to ensure the audience can see and understand what is happening. This principle will affect decisions on whether to stress the visual over the aural, and three-dimensional over two-dimensional. The audience needs enclosure, but does not want to feel restricted.

SHAPE

Drawing from environmental psychology, knowledge of how an audience relates to and moves within an environment is essential. Removing visual and tangible clutter or distractions, and keeping things simple and legible, are important design principles for event settings.

FOCUS

The use of blocking techniques from theatre and film direction ensures that the audience concentrates on what the designer/programmer wants it to focus on. Consider how lighting, colour, movement and shape affect people (this draws on both cognitive and environmental psychology).

Sensory stimulation at events

There is both art and science in the following specific design elements. Environmental psychology provides the theoretical foundation for researchers who want to know to what extent these variables can affect the event experience. These are summarized in Figure 7.3 and each is examined in turn.

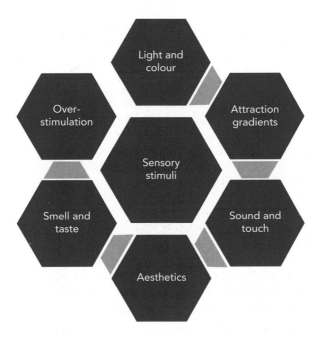

Figure 7.3 Types of sensory stimulation at events

Light

Experiments have shown that lower levels of light result in greater interpersonal intimacy and quieter or reduced conversation. So event designers reduce lighting just before the curtain rises or the speakers take the stage in order to quiet the audience. On the other hand, soft lighting during a banquet will likely encourage conversation. Lighting also impacts on functionality. If the event purpose is to discuss important topics, dim lighting will be counter-productive. If it requires audience attention on a stage or person, then dim ambient lights plus a spotlight are effective. Light shows, often including lasers, provide a lot of mental stimulation and generate emotional arousal.

Too much light stimulation can be counter-productive if the audience is expected to calm down immediately afterwards. Light stimulation generates a lot of brain activity that is difficult to turn off, hence you are wise to avoid watching television before sleep time, and do not want to have a strobe-light effect just before listening to a speaker.

Colour

People have colour preferences, and colours affect mood. Colour can be manipulated through lighting or other design features. Perceived spaciousness can be influenced by colours and lighting, helping to reduce feelings of crowding. 'Colour theory' relates to how specific media affect colour appearance (i.e. the effects of context on colour appearance) whereas 'colour psychology' considers the effects of colours on feelings and behaviour (e.g. will a pink room really calm prisoners and a red room increase tension? Does blue make people feel calm and cool?). 'Colour symbolism' is culturally defined, as in whether red suggests heat, anger or danger.

Sound

Loud noise is universally shunned, as it both physically hurts and gets in the way of desired conversations or other interactions. Quiet, ambient music has been found to be relaxing, although many people are rather sick of the elevator music we are too often subjected to.

Aesthetics

Art, colour, light and decoration all have aesthetic effects. We either like some art and designs or we do not. Aesthetic stimulation might lead to conversation, intellectual appreciation, quiet contemplation – or it might be ignored. Aesthetic design elements might also hold symbolic meaning, and this can be manipulated by event designers. For example, certain colours, design features (like expensive art) and shapes or patterns are associated with political ideologies, royalty, lifestyles, social class, or other potentially unifying or controversial themes. Being in a pleasant setting can also impact on people's willingness to help each other, but it might prove to be a distraction if serious business discussion is required.

Smell

Food-service professionals know that their best advertisement is often the smell of cooking. In a newly renovated shopping centre on either side of the entrance were a coffee shop and a cinnamon-bun dealer. The smells were strategically intended to get consumers in the mood for shopping. If we are hungry, the right smells can invoke salivation. The wrong smells can make people physically ill. Indeed, the military has experimented with smell as a weapon!

Over-stimulation or complexity

The well-known phenomenon of 'museum fatigue' has to be understood by event designers. Whatever is on display, or used in learning situations, people only devote so much attention before becoming mentally fatigued. In a museum, visitors eventually start passing by many exhibits without stopping or even looking, because they have already absorbed enough. The same kind of mental fatigue can result in conventioneers skipping sessions, students falling asleep in class (boredom might also be a factor there) or visitors to art exhibits merely glancing at outstanding works of art. Event designers can plan their setting to focus attention quickly on the primary exhibits or other features, to reach visitors prior to fatigue setting in. Lecturers can hit the highlights first, then go on to the mundane details.

Attraction gradients

When designing for pedestrian flow, ask what is in the event or its design that will most attract people. Exhibition planners know that the best sites are right at the entrance, facing those entering the hall. After that, there is a gradient of desirable locations based on visitor movements (often towards the centre, or to the exits, or the food, or the washrooms), although the movement can be influenced by both overall design and individual exhibit design.

Taste

While this is obviously the critical factor in dining experiences, and at food festivals, taste can be manipulated in other event environments to stimulate emotional and behavioural responses.

Touch

Exhibit designers understand that involvement with displays is better than mere visual stimulation. Getting people to touch and try is one key step towards learning, or buying. Harvey *et al.* (1998) discovered that they could more than double the time visitors spent at exhibits by making them interactive and multisensory, and providing better lighting and easier-to-read lettering. Visitors felt more immersed in the overall museum experience.

Preferences

The Kaplan (1987) model helps to predict people's preferences for various types of environment:

- 'coherence': the scene is organized, everything hangs together;
- 'legibility': we can categorize or understand the setting, everything is clear to us;
- 'complexity': a measure of the number and variety of elements in the setting;
- 'mystery': hidden information is present and we are drawn into the setting to learn more.

Too much complexity or mystery, however, can be a bad thing. Too much mystery can be incompatible with legibility, and can become frightening. If the event designer provides light and dark contrasts, the viewer might be drawn in, whereas too dark a room can be scary and might discourage entry. Also, consider an empty room versus one in which people are present. Are we normally inclined to enter a space in which no other people are present? What appeals to people for meetings, trade shows and learning seminars might be quite different from settings for sports, public celebrations and private parties.

Cognitive mapping and wayfinding

We know that coherence and legibility are important when it comes to environmental preferences, so how do we translate that into event design, and how does it impact on event experiences? Bateson (1989) said that 'legibility' is crucial in all 'servicescapes', because customers arrive with expectations of how the site will function. These are, of course, social constructs, such as the notion that festival sites should always have a main stage and a food/beverage area.

Kevin Lynch (1960) provided the classic approach to cognitive mapping in cities, with implications for event settings. His key principles should be applied to event site planning so that people can easily understand the layout and efficiently navigate within it. The larger and more complex the site, the more important it is to strive for coherence and legibility. Lynch stressed the following features for wayfaring:

- 'nodes': activity places (provide a central stage and entertainment area within a park; arrange the venue to have multiple, easily located focal points);
- 'paths': routes people follow (direction and flow within an event venue has to be controlled; use signs and edges);
- 'landmarks': shapes, signs or symbols that everyone can see and refer to (e.g. every world's fair builds a monument, usually in the centre);
- 'districts': neighbourhoods, shopping centres and other themed areas (group compatible activities together);
- 'edges': perceptual or real barriers between districts (people should recognize where they are in relation to other districts).

Lynch also found age and gender differences in how people wayfare, and there are probably many cultural differences as well. This suggests a research project for application to a variety of event sites.

Barker's (1968) behaviour settings can be adapted to fit different circumstances and goals. The three generic means of control pertain to:

- 'access' (who gets in, or under what schedule);
- 'design capacity' (i.e. the numbers allowed; consider peak and average attendance);
- 'flow' (time spent on site; turnover rates).

It is also necessary to consider accessibility for persons with physical and other disabilities or special needs (see Fleck 1996). Darcy and Harris (2003) showed how to do an accessibility plan for events that provides for all needs.

Traffic management in and around events presents serious challenges, and practical advice is available from a number of sources. The UK National Outdoor Events Association has a manual on traffic (see: www.noea.org.uk), and from New South Wales, Australia, there is *Traffic Management for Special Events* (www.rta.nsw.gov.au).

Architecture and settings

Architect David Rockwell in the book *Spectacle* (Rockwell and Mau 2006: 20) said that: 'The experience of making connections in real time and real space has always fascinated me. Spectacle celebrates events that offer a time and a space for live, shared experience.' Rockwell believes that events provide opportunities for creative risk taking. While architecture has not traditionally been associated with event design, and is not in our opinion a closely related field, there is obviously plenty of scope for applications. *Spectacle* provides mostly visual examples of mass gatherings, most contemporary but some historical, in which architectural design shapes the setting and the experience.

The affective quality of places

A model by Russell and Lanius (1984), called 'adaptation level and the affective appraisal of environments', seems very applicable to events. The basic premise is that emotional reactions to environments can be described in words along two continua: from pleasant to unpleasant, from arousing to sleepy. Forty descriptors were developed through research, falling into the four quadrants:

1. highly arousing and highly pleasant (e.g. exciting, exhilarating, interesting);
2. highly arousing and unpleasant (e.g. distressing, frenzied, tense, hectic);
3. unarousing and unpleasant (e.g. dull, dreary, unstimulating);
4. unarousing but pleasant (e.g. serene, tranquil, peaceful, restful).

Is quadrant 1 close to the 'WOW!' factor desired by many event designers? Note that the descriptors are not specifically experiences, only reactions to stimuli.

Russell and Lanius determined through experimentation that the same stimulus (they used photographs) can generate widely different affective appraisals. In other words, setting designers cannot be certain that their work will elicit the intended emotional response. One major reason is that people adapt to the environment and particular stimuli, so they react differently the next time.

AROUSAL

Interpersonal and environmental stimuli cause responses, both physiological and psychological, triggering behavioural responses. Sometimes event designers want to increase arousal, as in fostering celebration or revelry, and at other times they decrease stimulation in order to foster reverence or attentiveness. People have a limited capacity for dealing with a lot of stimulation and can become over-stimulated. When this happens it can trigger a response such as withdrawal or anxiety, and it will usually result in a filtering of stimuli to focus on the necessary or desirable inputs. Another strategy frequently employed by people is to attempt to eliminate or adjust the stimulus, such as by screening information, turning down noise and light levels, or engaging in conversation in order to mask an annoying or boring speaker.

OPTIMAL STIMULATION

People have their own ways of finding optimal arousal levels, and this can be accomplished through escaping or seeking stimulation. This is at the core of leisure and travel theory, based on the notion that motivation or need for leisure and travel is a result of simultaneously seeking and escaping. Continuous exposure to simulation can result in 'adaptation', such as people in cities adapting to higher levels of noise or crowding.

BEHAVIOUR CONSTRAINTS

Loss of perceived control is the first step in the behavioural constraints model. It leads to discomfort and 'reactance' – that is, we try to regain control. Even the anticipation of loss of control, or another threat, can trigger reactance. If people are constantly told they cannot do something, a possible consequence is 'learned helplessness'. People are likely to give up trying to make changes after a while, and that can apply to any consumer of any product or service.

ENVIRONMENTAL STRESS

What causes us stress? Certainly when things feel out of control, beyond our ability to cope, we feel stress. But environmental factors can also cause stress, such as event settings or programmes that generate sensory overload, overcrowding, nasty surprises, bad behaviour on the part of other guests, or poorly managed environmental systems leading to bad air. Fear causes stress, and a lack of knowledge about what is happening can generate fear.

Personal space

What is the difference between intimacy, personal distance, social distance and public distance? We want intimacy with lovers and family, but not strangers. We tolerate crowds, even seek them out, when a certain atmosphere is desired. At meetings, we might feel uncomfortable if the seats are too close.

Hall (1966) identified the four spatial zones, with 'intimate distance' being 0 to 1.5 feet (touching and feeling distance, with lots of contact and various sensory exchanges). 'Personal distance' is 1.5 to 4 feet (mostly verbal and visual contacts; contacts with friends and regular acquaintances). 'Social distance' is 4 to 12 feet (impersonal and business-like eye and voice contacts, no touching, normal voice levels). Fourth, 'public distance' is over 12 feet (formality, as in students' relationship to a lecturer in a classroom; when the need exists for technical assistance or raising one's voice).

Environmental psychologists have studied personal space in various settings, using laboratory experiments and simulations or field methods. For event researchers, field observations and tests will yield the best results. Remember that cultural factors are likely to be important, and that age and gender have to be considered.

'Personal space' can be used by event designers to help achieve goals. For example, it is well known and easily observed that communication effectiveness diminishes with distance from the speaker. That is why classrooms are designed as amphitheatres and not long halls. There have been studies of optimal spacing in learning environments, for professional interaction and for facilitating group processes. 'Sociopetal' distance brings people together, such as the circular or opposite layout of chairs in one's living room, while 'sociofugal' spacing diminishes interaction (e.g. rows of chairs).

A related concept is 'territoriality', which refers to a tendency for similar groups to stick together and apart from other groups. Within- and between-group interactions are easy to observe in most social settings, such as the little cliques that form at parties. If you want people to join in, leave an obvious opening, as in a crescent, but if you feel exclusionary, form a tight little knot with everyone facing inwards. Another form of territoriality occurs when people protect space for themselves or their group, like reserving seats or claiming tables at a banquet. Is this a good or bad thing?

Crowding

'Density' is an objective measure of how many people there are in a given area, but 'crowding' is how people feel about the situation. Studies have shown that in wilderness settings, even the sight of a few other canoeists is crowding. Although a potential problem at events, people often expect crowds and they can even add to our enjoyment (Lee *et al*. 1997; Wickham and Kerstetter 2000; Mowen *et al*. 2003).

Some of our reaction to the presence of others is related to the size of the group and our personal space – this is 'social density' (Bell *et al*. 2001: 296), whereas some of it depends on how much space there is – that is, 'spatial density'. It is the difference between too many people to interact with, versus not enough space. Freedom to move, perceived control and risks can also be factors. For example, what would happen in a panic – can we escape? Certainly the context also influences our judgement of what is crowding. Researchers have found that males and females are equally affected by high social density, but males suffer more from high spatial density. Friends and social support mitigate stress or anxiety caused by crowding. Evidence linking crowding with aggression or other anti-social behaviour is not clear, especially within event settings.

Bell *et al.* (2001: 315) compared various theoretical models pertaining to crowding. Critical causes of crowding (not of density, but the resultant feeling) have been attributed to excessive social contact and social stimulation, reduced freedom (e.g. to move about), scarcity of resources (bathrooms?), violations of personal space, unwanted contacts (groping?), interference with desired behaviour and lack of privacy. Possible coping mechanisms for crowding include withdrawal, attempts to reduce stimulation/arousal, escape, aggressive behaviour, territoriality and other attempts to maintain freedom, control or privacy. Some of these coping mechanisms might be desirable even if the crowding is considered to be, overall, unavoidable or fun. Cutting across most of these models is the notion of perceived control. If we believe we can take control of the situation, the negative impacts will be diminished.

Freedman's (1975) 'density-intensity model' appears to have great relevance to events, although it has been controversial. His model suggests that density intensifies reactions that would otherwise occur given the particular situation, so that high density heightens the importance of other people and magnifies our reactions to them. High density therefore intensifies the pleasantness of positive situations (e.g. a party or celebration) and intensifies the negativity of situations we would rather avoid. Accordingly, your expectations, desires and mood upon entering an event setting will directly impact on your reaction to density – whether or not you feel crowded. Mowen *et al.* (2003) found that crowding at events is more likely to be a positive factor at the entertainment stage, and negative at food and beverage outlets; it varies by zone and activity.

Stressors

'Stressors' at events can lead to problems. These include: excessive waiting; overcrowding; excessive sensory stimulation; overwhelming security, regulation or threats; fencing that prevents escape (people feel trapped) and other restrictions on movement.

Berlonghi (1990: 73) concluded that panic at events is likely to stem from real or perceived threats, and he discussed eight crowd characteristics to help managers or security identify crowd problems and security threats.

Freedman (1975) also experimented with 'contagion', which is the rapid spread of emotions or behaviour through a group or crowd. This phenomenon obviously has a direct bearing on events, as in some cases we want to foster positive contagion (especially celebration and humour) and in others it is very bad (fear and fighting).

Crowd management and crowd control

'Crowd management' has to be integrated throughout the design process and management systems. The purpose is to both prevent problems and facilitate good experiences. 'Crowd control', on the other hand, involves security and other measures that only become necessary when there is a problem and should be handled by experts (Rutley n.d.).

Setting a firm site capacity (or 'design capacity'), in terms of the number of people invited or permitted, is one way to prevent overcrowding and related problems. Similarly, managers can try to regulate the flow and turnover of patrons. Other capacity and crowd management techniques include advance and group ticketing (to avoid bottlenecks), physical barriers and activity spacing, information provision and the management of queues (Mowen *et al.* 2003). See also Ammon and Fried (1998) for advice on event crowd management.

7.2 RESEARCH NOTE ON CROWD PSYCHOLOGY AND POLICING

Reicher, S., Stott, C., Cronin, P. and Adang, O. (2004). An integrated approach to crowd psychology and public order policing. *Policing: An International Journal of Police Strategies and Management*, 27(4), 558–572.

'This paper uses recent developments in crowd psychology as the basis for developing new guidelines for public order policing. [It] argues that the classical view of all crowd members as being inherently irrational and suggestible, and therefore potentially violent, is both wrong and potentially dangerous. It can lead to policing strategies that respond to the violence of some in the crowd by clamping down on all members, and therefore lead all members to perceive the police as hostile and illegitimate. In such conditions, even those who were initially opposed to violence may come to side with more conflictual crowd members and hence contribute to an escalation in the level and scope of collective conflict. This paper argues that police officers need to concentrate on understanding the collective identities, priorities and intentions of different groups in the crowd and give the same priority to facilitating the lawful intentions of some groups as to controlling the unlawful intentions of others.'

Theme and programme design

A 'theme' is a unifying idea or concept which gives meaning to the event, or is the object of celebration or commemoration. It can be a visual or sensory theme, in the realms of decorators and chefs, an activity theme (styles of sport, play, recreation), a fantasy theme (usually combining decor and entertainment), an emotional theme (such as a celebration of something of value), or it can be intellectual in nature (such as the conference topic or workshop problem).

Recalling our earlier discussion of 'thematic interpretation', the theme should be stimulating and provocative, embodying tangible and intangible elements. Memorable themes tap into universal belief systems and should provide the take-home message – the moral of the story. Many entertainment or decoration themes do not do that, nor is it necessarily appropriate at concerts, parties and other social gatherings. Whatever goes into the event programme, from sensory stimulation to entertainment and spectacle, should ideally reflect and reinforce the theme.

Programme planning

A programme is the scheduled or 'scripted' activities for the audience and other participants. A concert programme can be quite simple, consisting of the order of artists or musical pieces. A festival programme might be complex, involving multiple days and venues with numerous activities and performances. Sport events have scheduled times for competitions and award ceremonies. Meetings and conventions typically operate with tight agendas to make sure the programme of speakers, plenary and breakout sessions, meals, coffee breaks and social events keeps to the schedule.

Programme 'portfolios' consist of all the different activities and services provided at events. They have to meet multiple objectives, appeal to diverse audiences and ideally be sustainable. To evaluate feasibility, desirability and continuance requires measures that reflect underlying goals and values. For example, commercial events have to monitor economic demand and profits, while public festivals might be focused on fulfilling social aims, like awareness-building or providing cultural opportunities to specific groups in the community. Other possible values and measures include image, tradition, stakeholder desires, market potential and share, and growth potential.

The 'programme planning process' usually starts with an evaluation of existing programming and/or new idea generation. It is generally wise to test ideas, although for planned events this can be difficult. At a basic level, focus groups can be held to test programme ideas with potential patrons or with stakeholder groups, and at a more costly level mini-events can be held to see if the concept is feasible and satisfies target segments.

'Life-cycle' considerations are important. Some programmes and services can be slated for a short life expectancy, including planned termination, while others can be allowed to run a full course through growth, maturity and decline. If sales and profits are the primary measure of success, a programme or service will have to be terminated or 'rejuvenated' through reinvestment and repositioning when profit margins shrink. Community-service and goodwill programmes do not have to be terminated because of cost and revenue considerations, but their ongoing effectiveness has to be demonstrated.

Sustaining traditional programmic elements, while innovating regularly to test new ones, is a model followed by many events including the Calgary Stampede (see Getz 1993b, 1997). At some point, changes to programming can be so substantial as to constitute repositioning of the entire event.

Scripting and choreography

In most forms of theatrical performance the 'script' is followed to the letter. How appropriate this is at other events is a matter of style and intent. In some respects a schedule of activities, or the event programme, is a script. Specific elements of an event can be scripted while the overall 'performance' is improvised or merely themed.

'Choreography', borrowed from dance, is an alternative approach for events. Here, characters and interactions are suggested through notations, but the actual behaviour of 'performers' is somewhat creative and unpredictable.

Timing and build

'Timing', or scheduling, has to consider the audience's attention span and responses to stimuli, keeping in mind that 'event time is different from real time and audiences respond differently to it'. In general, Brown and James (2004: 61) recommended programming 'tightly' and accurately to maintain 'flow' and contact with the audience. In contrast, 'build' is the use of time and programming, including ebbs and peaks of intensity, to maximize impact on the audience. There is a skill in using limited resources to achieve great emotional or intellectual stimulation.

Programmic elements of style

'Style' means a characteristic way of doing things (to create a unique event), excellence of artistic expression (a measure of product or programme quality) or fashion (which always changes). We can say that designers have their own style, and that all events are stylistically different. Recall our earlier discussions of aesthetics and beauty, because style is largely subjective and therefore subject to widely different interpretations. Each 'programmic element of style' has a creative and a technical component. Elements can be combined in unlimited combinations to design a unique event programme. Generally the elements have to be designed in concert with the setting and implemented through physical development and all the management systems.

Some programmic elements of style are 'hallmarks' of particular types of event. That is, the event form requires it by definition, or, as a social construct, this element is closely associated with it. For example, business and trade events like fairs and trade shows involve commerce by nature. Festivals are celebrations, so they have to incorporate belonging and sharing, emotional stimulation, rituals and symbolism. Sports and recreation must involve games or competition. But standing alone, one element of style looks bare and will generate a rather narrow range of experiences. Sports are packaged as festivals for a good reason, to expand their appeal and generate additional benefits. Business events are serious, but they almost always base part of their appeal on social and touristic opportunities.

One way to specify programmic elements of style is to list the actions a programmer or designer can include, or the activities that participants and guests are to engage in. These are the main activity elements subject to design, but keep in mind that each one can have varying cognitive and affective outcomes:

- teach, interpret, inform; engage people in discourse or problem-solving;
- play and compete (games; mental and physical activity);
- amuse (use of humour and surprise);
- entertain (including spectacle, performances);
- engage in rites and rituals (including symbolism and protocol; cultural authenticity must be considered);
- exhibit (art; goods and services for marketing purposes);
- buy, sell, trade (commerce);
- mix and mingle (socializing, partying, group discussion);
- sensory stimulation (sight, sound, touch, taste, hearing);
- hospitality (welcoming, guiding, services, satisfying basic needs such as eating, drinking, resting, toilets).

We have already examined the main programmic elements that constitute sensory stimulation, so here we need to add a list of ways to stimulate emotions. Just about any combination of activities and sensory stimulation can provoke emotional and cognitive responses, but these elements are tried and true in the context of politics, patriotism, religion and affinity groups:

- ritual and symbolism that reflects or suggests cultural and social identity; the display of sacred or respected artefacts;
- direct verbal appeals to loyalty, pride, community or faith (i.e. preaching and propaganda);
- celebrity endorsements and the charisma of speakers, especially from recognized leaders;
- selected information and interpretation (as social marketing and propaganda).

For event designers and programmers there can be a fine line between emotional or cognitive stimulation and exploitation, between facilitating a powerful, transforming experience and provoking a negative, even violent response. 'Playing with emotions' should always be undertaken with the benefit of research and evaluation, and this has often, sadly, been ignored.

Programme (or 'product') quality

Getz and Carlsen (2006: 146) discussed the main dimensions of event quality. Quality begins with the organization: its mandate and vision, philosophy and customer orientation; the competence of its staff and volunteers; its governance; and effectiveness of its management. Programme (or product) quality is experiential and subject to qualitative evaluation by all the stakeholders. Customers evaluate quality by expressing their level of satisfaction with the event overall, or with the quality of what is being presented to them in the form of sport competition, the musical performance, the speakers at a convention, art at an exhibit, food at a banquet, etc. Product quality can also be assessed through benchmarking against other events, the opinions of expert judges, or through experiential research.

Love and Crompton (1996) tested the hypothesis, based on the works of Herzberg (1966), that some event elements are 'dissatisfiers' which can undermine the visitor experience, while others are 'satisfiers' which provide benefits. 'Dissatisfiers' are like Herzberg's 'maintenance' factors – they must be provided to expected levels of quality, but in themselves do not satisfy visitors. The researchers argued that most of the physical factors at events, such as parking, rest rooms and information, are dissatisfiers, while ambiance, fantasy, excitement, relaxation, escape and social involvement are satisfiers. High-quality events must meet expectations in both categories, but they are non-compensatory in that a single or small number of attributes can determine perception of overall quality. Tentative support for this model was confirmed, and the researchers believed that certain attributes were perceived to be of so poor or high quality that visitors disregarded or discounted other attributes in giving their overall appraisal.

Baker and Crompton (2000) determined that generic and entertainment features of an event are more likely to generate increased satisfaction and motivate return visits or positive word-of-mouth recommendations. Saleh and Ryan (1993) found that quality of the music programme is the most important service factor in attracting people to jazz festivals. Overall satisfaction levels affected the intention for repeat visits. Similarly, Thrane (2002) explored the link between satisfaction and future intentions of festival-goers. The most important conclusion from his study in Norway was that event managers must try to improve programme quality (in this case music) *and* be concerned with other factors that shape overall satisfaction.

Ryan and Lockyer (2002) studied satisfaction levels of participants in the South Pacific Masters games in New Zealand – a friendly, multi-sport event for older athletes. The results showed that sport-event managers need to pay particular attention to improving items of high importance but low satisfaction. In this sample the prime motivators – seeking challenge and fun – were found to be satisfied by the event. A factor analysis was also used to identify five components of importance to participants, namely: social (social events plus meeting people); registration (good communications); challenge; after-event communication; and that the competition is both fun and serious.

Service design and quality

Researchers have demonstrated that event satisfaction is primarily dependent upon the core elements of the programme, whether this is music or sport competition, and that is exactly what theme and programme design seeks to accomplish. In this context, the setting, service delivery and consumables are supporting factors. An exception is for food and beverage events, where consumables are the core, or commerce events where people purchase tangible products. Nevertheless, service delivery is important, as bad service easily displeases people. It is a design process because good service is both technical (e.g. no errors made, everything is done on time) and creative/qualitative (staff are friendly and helpful; staff as part of the experience).

There is a huge body of literature on service marketing, quality and delivery, especially for the tourism and hospitality sectors (see, for example, Prideaux *et al.* 2006). Applied to event design, the basic principle is that all management systems as well as staff and volunteer actions directly affect the customers' perceptions of quality and therefore their level of satisfaction with the event experience.

Drummond and Anderson (2004) discussed the meaning of quality and how service management impacts on events. They explained what has to be done to create a satisfying 'service experience' before, during and after the event. They argued that service enables the guest or customer to more fully enjoy the product or experience. Wicks and Fesenmaier (1993) studied differences between visitors and vendors in their perceptions of service quality at an event. A comparison of alternative approaches to evaluating event quality was undertaken by Crompton and Love (1995).

Service blueprinting and service mapping

'Blueprinting' is a tool with value in all the services, but its application to planned events has been minimal. The idea is to create a chart or 'blueprint' based on the flow of intended visitor activities and experiences, and to show how the experiences are facilitated by the setting (or 'servicescape'), all the management systems and human contacts. The service 'map' is a diagnostic or evaluation tool which can precede blueprinting, or test its effectiveness.

In a research article by Getz *et al.* (2001), which received the best paper award for that year from the *Journal of Travel Research*, two service maps show the results of a team of nine researchers (the three authors and six trained students) who conducted an on-site evaluation of the event. Triangulation was employed, including (1) direct observation of the site and audience, using standard checklists, (2) a visitor survey, mostly about satisfaction, and (3) logbooks reflecting participant observation (i.e. documenting their event experiences).

Stage One provides an overview of the entire event experience, from approach to departure, whereas Stage Two looks at details of the range of possible on-site experiences: consumption, viewing, interacting, essential services. The more complex the event, the more researchers will be needed, and many maps might result. Once the evaluation has been completed, 'blueprints' for the next event can be prepared. Alternatively, the evaluators start with a blueprint to see how well it has been implemented.

Customer actions

The blueprint anticipates the flow of customer actions, starting with approach to the site and ending with departure. If there are many activity options or venues it will be necessary to have multiple blueprints, some in great detail and one for the overall process. Although the blueprint specifies actions in settings, it should consider the intended customer or guest experience. For example, 'viewing art in gallery' can be expanded into 'the guest will enjoy a quiet, aesthetic experience, aided by interactive information about the artists and their displays'. This experiential elaboration will greatly assist in planning the 'physical evidence' and staff–guest interactions.

When doing a service mapping exercise, as evaluation, multiple observers (engaged in direct and participant observation) will be needed to plot the actual flow and activities of guests and to summarize the experiential dimensions.

Tangible evidence of product and service quality

The blueprint specifies all the physical evidence of quality, such as entertainment, the competition, exhibits, facilities, signs, equipment and audio-visual effects, and these are depicted on the diagram in the area above the customer-actions flow chart. Include the hygiene factors like toilets and soap, water and comfort stations. Anticipate everything the guest will need or desire and specify the quality standards. In the case of evaluations, describe gaps and flaws in tangible evidence, such as crowding, unanticipated behaviour, safety and health hazards, obvious customer confusion and inadequate signage or direction. Describe programme or product quality as experienced by observers.

'Hygiene factors' have been found to be extremely important at events, not in motivating people to attend or affecting their assessment of overall programme quality, but in terms of causing dissatisfaction (these include security, cleanliness, comfort). Event quality can also be assessed by reference to its impacts, through measuring the attainment of positive goals and avoidance or amelioration of negative outcomes.

Visible staff contacts

For each customer action, or experience setting, the blueprint has to specify staff or volunteer support that will, or could, involve staff–guest interaction. These also define potential 'critical incidents' where service failure could occur. This line, under the flow chart, also quantifies human resource needs, in terms of staffing levels, duties and necessary training.

Viewed as 'cast members', staff and volunteers have both technical roles to play in delivering essential services, and an experiential role to play in facilitating desired experiences. Their appearance and demeanour are important to theming as well as service. In terms of service marketing theory (i.e. SERVQUAL, developed by Parasuraman *et al.* 1988), staff and volunteers have to exhibit 'responsiveness' (willingness to help; promptness), 'assurance' (knowledge and courtesy; convey trust and inspire confidence), 'empathy' (caring; providing individual service) and 'reliability' (ability and dependability).

Invisible management processes

The usual practice is to draw a line under the 'visible staff contacts' and in this bottom space on the blueprint to indicate the management systems that have to be in place to support the entire service process (which, at events, inevitably means the programme as well). In evaluations, the observers can work backwards from obvious failures or problems to determine what was missing or flawed in these hidden systems (for example: police should have regulated the approach road).

Importance-performance (IP) measurement

It is one thing to know how satisfied a guest is, another to understand if the items being rated were important to their decision to attend or their overall satisfaction with the event. Satisfaction usually links to future behaviour such as word-of mouth recommendations and repeat visits. The IP technique is quite versatile and generates numeric scores and graphics that are fairly easy to interpret and communicate.

For example, those attending music concerts can usually be expected to give a high score to the quality and reputation of performers as motivators for attending, and as the main sources of satisfaction or dissatisfaction. Ideally, the manager wants to find out that they performed very well in providing the entertainment that consumers valued the highest. You do not want to find out that toilets were ranked 'very poor' and provided a great source of dissatisfaction.

As illustrated in the Research Note 7.3, IP grid analysis can be usefully combined with other quantitative techniques.

7.3 RESEARCH NOTE ON IMPORTANCE-PERFORMANCE MEASUREMENT

Smith, S. and Costello, C. (2009). Culinary tourism: Satisfaction with a culinary event utilizing importance-performance grid analysis. *Journal of Vacation Marketing*, 15(2), 99–110.

'The aim of this research was to provide a practical method for assessing satisfaction at a culinary event. Twenty-seven culinary event attribute items were analysed from an international culinary event. MANOVA was employed to identify differences between importance and performance measures. Importance-performance analysis (IPA) was subsequently used to assist culinary event organizers while identifying critical performance attributes in order to improve customer satisfaction. Findings revealed food and beverage prices, come/go, convenient parking and food tasting had high importance scores, yet low performance measures. The use of multiple regression analysis confirmed three out of the four attribute items had a predictive effect on overall satisfaction.'

Experience factor model

Ralston *et al.* (2007) developed an 'experience factor model' for event design, which combines experiential and service quality elements. The 'experience factors' consist of themed experiences, targeted impressions, reducing negative cues, engaging multiple senses, providing a mix in memorabilia, customizing to the individual, getting into and staying in character, and performing to appropriate form. The service factors are those of SERVQUAL: tangibles, reliability, responsiveness, empathy, assurance, recovery, competence, courtesy, security, access/welcome and communications.

Their model can be used as a diagnostic tool, using a type of SWOT analysis, which includes independent assessment of critical incidents, to assess an event's or attraction's 'experience quotient' and 'service quotient'. Service quality has to be high in order to achieve a high 'experience quotient' (i.e. to achieve memorable and transforming experiences), so the model encompasses an 'experience threshold'. This zone separates displeasure from enjoyment.

Design of gastronomy and other consumables

At many events the food and beverage service is incidental to the main theme and programme, but at others it is experientially paramount. This is true at food and wine festivals, gala dinners and other events that stress cultural authenticity. Tellstrom *et al.* (2006: 130) stressed that: 'Food and meals are a central field in the communication of culture.'

In terms of quality and design, this is the realm of the chef and banquet manager, who are in turn dependent on suppliers for quality. Eating at many events is nothing more than a basic service, but it should be an experience. Lashley *et al.* (2004) defined the dimensions of this eating experience: the occasion; the company one dines with; atmosphere; food; service; and setting.

Gustafsson *et al.* (2006) noted that the meal product consists of visual effect, taste/expectation compliance, reflection of style and standard of service. They argued (2006: 89) that 'the whole product process requires both craftsmanship, science and aesthetical/ethical knowledge in order to produce good meals and result in the optimum experience for the guest/diner'. All the senses have to be stimulated, 'and in harmony to create agreement that it was a good meal experience' (Gustafsson *et al.* 2006: 90).

Gift-giving is also important at some events, including those in which sponsors provide samples to take home, or when employers reward their staff. In these cases the tangibles are a key part of the event experience, so their inherent (or perceived) quality, and how they are presented, are critical. To marketers, each gift is a branding exercise – sponsors want guests to go away with favourable and enduring perceptions of their brand. To employers rewarding staff, the symbolic value of the gift is usually more important.

In Events in Focus 7.1, a design model for food events targeted at highly involved foodies is presented, based on published research papers and the book *Foodies and Food Tourists* (Getz *et al.* 2014). A similar concept for designing ecotourism events has also been developed (see Getz 2013b).

7.1 Designing food events for foodies

Most food and beverage events are focused on consumption – eating and drinking! Throw in some entertainment and family fun and the typical food festival emerges. But this is not what highly involved food lovers (foodies) want from their event experiences. Based on large-scale, multi-country research, an event design model was generated. Researchers used ego-involvement theory to identify the core characteristics of being a foodie, then pinpointed the crucial role of attending events in differentiating dynamic foodies who travel a lot for food experiences. While food lovers attend many festivals and other food-related events, the highly involved foodies are most likely to prefer tactile or hands-on experiences (such as cooking lessons from chefs) and events focused on learning, cultural authenticity and creativity.

Conceptually, Figure 7.4 shows the necessity for positioning food events in such a way that they can attract dedicated food tourists, and not merely provide generic benefits for residents. The targeted event can be separate from, or part of, a larger event, such as a festival. The programmer/designer starting with this concept can manifest the various core benefits with actual programming. For example, the learning benefit includes mastery of techniques, leading to cooking classes with chefs. The creativity benefit includes aesthetic appreciation, such as a focus on serving food and wine/food pairings. Making the event culturally authentic can be accomplished through rituals and celebrations with like-minded foodies (i.e. communitas) and through heritage interpretation – telling stories, for example, of why and how various foods have become traditions in local cuisine.

This is an example of how event design for special-interest segments should be based on research, with the emphasis placed on identifying the main benefits desired by target markets.

It reflects demand-side thinking in which design follows from market intelligence. Of course many existing food-related events are based on tradition and will not necessarily want to

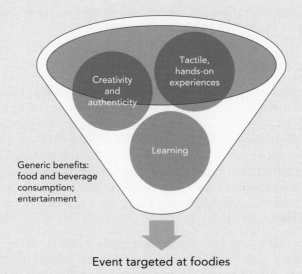

Figure 7.4 Developing food events for tourists

follow this approach; it is most appropriate for event-tourism purposes and the private sector seeking profit.

Sources: Getz et al. (2014, 2015); Getz and Robinson (2014a, b); Robinson and Clifford (2012); Robinson and Getz (2013, 2014).

Designing 'slow events'

There are slow food, slow villages and now slow events! The slow movement has evolved and as Page (2015: 129) summarized

> *the notion was also popularised at a city-destination level by the Cittaslow (Slow City) movement based on three underpinning concepts:*
> * *Do things at the right speed*
> * *Adapt one's attitude towards time and one's use of it*
> * *The pursuit of quality over quantity.*

Simons (2015) has applied principles from the slow movement to the design of events, stressing that such events should:

- be organized in a bottom-up manner with all stakeholders involved in decision-making;
- ensure that benefits flow to the community;
- be rooted in locality, reflecting a sense of place and providing identity; visitors should be able to connect to locality through stories;
- stress community development, not growth or profit.

Regarding the critical element of time, both frequency and duration of slow events, Simons (2015: 75) argued that, 'A slow event takes the time that is necessary for the event to be experienced to the fullest by the people involved in the event as well as by the visitors.'

Liberating versus constraining

Event planning and management can often be described as constraining, that is, we use combinations of setting, programme design and management systems to prevent certain actions (often in the name of safety) or to remove the possibility of distractions and confounding environmental forces like noise. Barriers and gates are erected, flows of people are tightly regulated, security has to be visible and police should be ready to react, schedules must be met, and so on. Do people find this stifling? Does it limit experience to only the manageable and predictable? At some point, event designers and planners must ask themselves if their events have become standardized, contrived, boring or sanitized to the point where innovation and new artistic expression has moved elsewhere. How long can a particular form of event remain popular before it becomes mundane?

We should ask ourselves what we can do to enable liberating experiences, rather than constrain them. This will represent a fundamental shift in event planning and design. Perhaps the starting points are already clear, whether in the form of installation art (temporary and challenging), forms of interactive theatre where unpredictable outcomes are encouraged, the growing necessity to surprise people in order to exceed their ever-more demanding expectations, in those (seemingly unplanned) events at the margin described earlier, or in the co-production of events through producer–audience collaboration.

Of the three dimensions of experience, the conative (behavioural) is most constrained by event management. The setting constrains movement, the schedule constrains temporal experiences – forcing the guest into the designers' timeframe. Of course, people enter into the event space (a time out of time in a special place) willingly, and suspend their normal behaviours in favour of the anticipated experience, but there is no reason why the event time/space cannot also be liberating in particularly pleasant and memorable ways. Let's look at how this can be accomplished.

We can break the spatial constraints by:

- online interconnectivity (have an interactive virtual experience ready for everyone);
- involve the wider community, not just guests/customers (e.g. take aspects of your event to them; outreach programmes to schools);
- site planning that facilitates fluid entrance and exit (also a key safety consideration) and suggests permeability with the wider community and/or natural environment; open the site for wide vistas; make barriers and edges almost invisible; design for extra space and easy movement.

We can break the temporal constraints by:

- co-creation of the event through ongoing consultations and feedback;
- encouraging participants/customers to take the event experience home with them (e.g. souvenirs, DVDs, follow-up events and real-time communications);
- media coverage, live and delayed.

The cognitive dimensions (i.e. thinking) can also be liberated by being prepared to:

- maximize mental engagement and learning opportunities;
- mentally challenge guests/customers/virtual audiences;
- build in novelty and surprise.

The affective dimensions perhaps require more thought, but are equally amenable to liberating practices whereby we can:

- foster emotional responses that are normally inhibited (e.g. laughter and other verbalizations, tears and other forms of sympathy, surprise and shock, fear and repulsion);
- use sensory stimulation to encourage the formation of permanent and pleasant memories (remember the value of smell in memory formation and recall).

The challenge of enabling or liberating practices is critical. If people fail to get the desired experience in planned events, they are very likely to try others, to give up on the sector altogether or to start inventing their own. Clues to what the future might hold are often apparent online, in blogs and other social media devoted to event experiences, where members of myriad communities of interest or social worlds interact. A disquieting possibility is that recreational rioting and other forms of anti-social behaviours might become more common as people seek to be liberated from stifling social environments and legal constraints.

Future directions

According to Richards *et al.*'s (2014) *Event Design: Social Perspectives and Practices* events should be designed as value-creation platforms, and evaluators should judge them according to how well the aims have been met. The study reflected on a number of important design-related themes that require more research and attention, including the somewhat slippery concept of co-creation. While it is true that all events provide some degree of shared experience creation, being social in nature, there are elements of design that can advance this concept and engage visitors even more. Crowther and Orefice (2015) argued strongly for co-creation by design, rather than by default. Technology can enable more before, during and after-event interaction and social media is a vehicle for creating experiences without the direct influence of producers and managers. Taken even further, the concept leads to self-organizing events and liberation, as previously discussed.

According to Richards *et al.* (2014) another design theme to explore is 'curation'. Content curators filter or screen information to reduce volume/flow and make it more targeted to the users' interests and needs; this could apply to messaging, raw data, programming content and other design elements. The time element is always of interest, witness the example of 'slow events' mentioned earlier. Event-related experiences are being extended to the before and after phases, and presumably leading to the next experience! Those enthusiasts pursuing event-tourist careers know this very well. And finally, it is worth mentioning that events are designed at various policy levels, such as being instruments of city design/positioning, and increasingly as assets in broad portfolios. As yet, the design of event portfolios and populations has not been a topic of research.

STUDY GUIDE

Although experiences can neither be designed nor guaranteed, event producers and designers must do their best to specify intended experiences, and to anticipate the motives, needs and desired experiences of all the stakeholders. Design is both a technical and creative process to meet goals and solve problems. While some authors and event professionals take a holistic view of design, applying it to the entire planning and production process, this chapter has stressed four elements of the planned event that are clearly the realm of designers. The interactions of setting design with theme and programme, service quality and provision of consumables have direct bearing on experiences. The discussion of service mapping and blueprinting has many applications to design and evaluation, but also contains a number of theoretical foundations from the mainstream literature on service management and marketing.

STUDY QUESTIONS

- Define 'design' and discuss its importance in event studies.
- Do you believe experiences can be designed? How?
- Explain the necessity to base event setting design on theory from cognitive and environmental psychology. Give specific applications.
- In what ways can the event designer adapt principles from theatre?
- Give examples of how coherence and legibility can be achieved in event site planning.
- Do people have preferences for event settings? Are these 'social constructs'?
- Discuss how 'crowding' is more than just the number of people at an event.
- What are the main tools in crowd management and crowd control?
- Illustrate how various 'programmic elements of style' can be used for learning, sensory and emotional stimulation.
- What is programme and service quality, and how can they be measured or evaluated?
- Describe 'service blueprinting' as an event design tool, including reference to 'the cast'.
- Describe market research that can inform the design of an event for a special-interest segment such as foodies or ecotourists.
- Why and how can planned-event experiences be made more liberating?

FURTHER READING

Berridge, G. (2007). *Event Design and Experience*. Oxford: Butterworth Heinemann.

Getz, D., Robinson, R., Andersson, T. and Vujicic, S. (2014). *Foodies and Food Tourism*. Oxford: Goodfellow.

Halsey, T. (2010). *Freelancer's Guide to Corporate Event Design*. Oxford: Elsevier.

Matthews, D. (2008). *Special Event Production: The Resources*. Wallingford: CABI.

Prideaux, B., Moscardo, G. and Laws, E. (eds) (2006). *Managing Tourism and Hospitality Services: Theory and International Applications*. Wallingford: CABI.

Richards, G., Marques, L. and Mein, K. (2014). *Event Design: Social Perspectives and Practices*. Oxford: Routledge.

Chapter **8**

Antecedents and decision-making

LEARNING OBJECTIVES

Upon completion of this chapter students should know the following:

- relationships between personal antecedents to event attendance (or participation), the barriers and constraints, decision-making, post-experience evaluation and future decisions;
- differences between intrinsic and extrinsic motives and how they lead to participation in, and travel to attend, events;
- specific constraints influencing the decision to attend events, and how people negotiate through barriers to achieve their goals;
- reasons why some people do not attend events;
- how different stakeholders make decisions about attending events, including guest/consumers/participants, organizers and volunteers, sponsors and suppliers.

What are antecedents?

Why do you attend an event? Surely there are myriad reasons, depending on your own needs and motives, the circumstances and the types of events that you can choose from. Event-related behaviour is complex and probably ever changing, but there are theoretical fundamentals that will help us understand the process and apply this knowledge to all planned events.

'Antecedents' are all those influences that shape interest in, and demand for, choices, and actual event attendance or participation. We start with needs, which are closely linked to intrinsic (self-directed) and extrinsic (from outside) motives. A discussion of demand takes us from social psychology to economics, then we draw upon consumer research to explore decision-making. Leisure theory provides a solid base for examining barriers and constraints, and how people overcome or negotiate through them to achieve their goals.

To start the discussion, a conceptual model of the main factors shaping participation in, or attendance at, planned events is presented (Figure 8.1). Numerous models and frameworks are available from consumer research in general and, more specifically, tourism (see overviews in Ryan 2002; Crouch *et al.* 2004; Decrop 2006) and leisure (see Walker and Virden 2005; Hinch *et al.* 2006). Benckendorff and Pearce (2012) developed a very useful framework for applying psychological theory to event participation. They considered pre-event, on-site and post-event experiences, for spectators, attendees, performers and elite participants. They stressed that psychological theory on personality, motivation and involvement is important when looking at antecedents, while role theory, identity, liminality, flow, mindfulness, emotional and performative labour, and experience analysis can be applied to the event experience itself. Satisfaction, loyalty, self-actualization and personal development apply after an event experience, according to Benckendorff and Pearce.

Although this framework is designed as a process, it is not predictive. It shows all the main factors we need to understand, and suggests how they interconnect, but it is not possible to forecast that any particular set of antecedents will result in certain decisions, or that certain experiences lead to predictable future behaviour. The rest of the chapter reflects the main elements of the model, with sections on barriers and constraints, decision-making, evaluation and feedback.

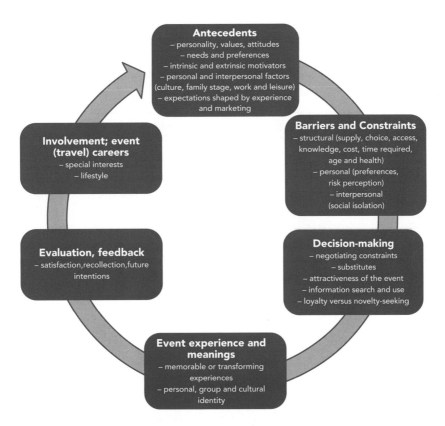

Figure 8.1 Antecedents and decision-making process

Personality

Personality, values, attitudes and lifestyle preferences are the psychological factors that lie at the foundation of human behaviour. Individuals will show a propensity for certain behaviour as a result of these factors, but that does not necessarily mean they will act, or act consistently on them.

'Personality types' were previously explored, noting that some people have a higher propensity to seek novelty or take risks. Some people, in the terminology of Stanley Plog (1987), are more 'adventuresome' than others, leading them to seek out unique leisure and travel experiences. Others have a greater need for consistency and therefore a higher tolerance of boredom.

According to the theory of 'personality–environment congruence', 'extroverted' risk takers will be happy at raucous concerts, but probably shy 'introverts' will not. Events often cater to certain personality types without the organizers being aware of it. Another theory of potential relevance is that of 'optimal challenge', which suggests that in event programming the matching of challenges with participants' skills will likely produce the desired 'flow' experience. This is more critical for sport events that attract competitors at different levels, for educational events where people want to learn different things and for recreational events where there are certain risks involved. Csikszentmihalyi (1975, 1990) concluded that boredom results when challenges are too low, and anxiety stems from challenges that are too great.

Values

Values are subjective reactions to, and assessments about, the world. They are deeply held, and in behavioural terms they imply a conscious assessment of the desirability of alternative behaviours, including what is right and wrong. Values are shaped by experience, religious or political affiliations, general social and cultural influences, and perhaps by personality. Do you value freedom of choice? Having decisions made for you by government? Environmental responsibility? How are your personal values different from the important people in your life? And do your values shape your interest in events or tourism?

8.1 RESEARCH NOTE ON SUBCULTURES

Green, C. and Chalip, L. (1998). Sport tourism as the celebration of subculture. *Annals of Tourism Research*, 25(2), 275–291.

Green and Chalip determined that participants in the Key West Women's Flag Football Tournament sought (beyond the usual mastery and competency motives in sport participation) the opportunity to get together to celebrate their subculture (i.e. to meet affiliation needs). The place of the event could be much less important than the nature of the event, especially the opportunities provided for both formal and informal socializing and celebration. The overall event package, they recommended, should be designed to appeal to particular subculture values.

Attitudes

Allport (1937) provided the classic definition of attitude as a 'learned predisposition to respond to an object or class of objects in a consistently favorable or unfavourable way'.

Attitudes are theorized to contain 'conative' (action and behavioural intention), 'affective' (evaluation and affect, or emotion) and 'cognitive' (perception and belief) components. Note that this trilogy is also used, in a slightly different way, to describe the dimensions of 'experience'.

Within the context of the 'theory of planned behaviour' (Ajzen 1991), researchers have examined attitudes towards leisure participation. Many other factors influence actual behaviour, but measuring attitudes can be a good predictor if the attitude is linked to specific behaviour, such as 'how do you feel about attending a rock concert/cultural festival/art exhibition in the next 12 months?', as opposed to general behaviour (such as 'how do you feel about attending special events?'). What are the influences shaping attitudes towards planned events? Some combination of personal, social and cultural factors lies at the base of beliefs and predispositions.

Lifestyle

'Lifestyles', as unique patterns of thinking and behaving, arise from personality, values and attitudes. Some researchers refer to these, together, as 'psychographics'. According to Decrop (2006: 11), lifestyles reflect the 'self-concept' of people. Although seldom explored in the context of planned events, as opposed to leisure and travel in general, there must be lifestyles that predispose or facilitate participation in events. Examples could be dedicated marathon runners whose 'lifestyles' are built around training and travelling to events, or the 'lifestyles' of food and wine connoisseurs, which predispose them to attend certain festivals and exhibitions.

If it is accepted that many people value experiences more than objects and consumables, so that (for example) foodies and food tourists are willing and often eager to pay for rewarding and novel experiences, then consumption of experiences must hold symbolic value. Consistent patterns of symbolic consumption generate and help define discernible lifestyles. In the 'foodie' lifestyle examined by Getz *et al.* (2014), events figure prominently in shaping and reinforcing identity, with some specialized events holding high symbolic value and therefore becoming 'iconic' to those with a special interest in food.

The term 'lifestyle' has a number of possible connotations, including the view that a healthy or moral lifestyle is highly desirable (such as being environmentally and socially responsible), or that some people have enviable or lamentable lifestyles (e.g. lifestyles of the rich and famous). In this context, being a foodie, or demonstrating any other form of lifestyle through leisure and travel, might attract criticism. That is why lifestyle cannot be separated from values and social norms.

Needs

According to Maslow (1954, 1968) 'needs' are both physiological (what we need to live and be safe) and socially learned (what we need to belong and be happy). The following four were said to be 'deficit' needs, and people instinctively seek to meet them. In times of stress regression can occur, but people are said to move from the lower- to the higher-order needs in a developmental process:

- physiological: survival needs, including water, food and shelter;
- safety and security needs: stability, order, protection, structure;
- love and belonging needs: social needs, a wish for affection and to show affection, a sense of community;
- esteem needs: hierarchical, with the lower order consisting of respect of others, status and recognition; higher order – self-respect, competence, independence, achievement and mastery.

Others have argued that there are additional needs, and that the hierarchical nature of Maslow's theory is unsupportable. However controversial, Maslow's hierarchy of needs has been tremendously influential, and is referenced again in our discussion of volunteer motivation.

Self-actualization and peak experiences

Maslow's hierarchy is often shown as a pyramid with self-actualization at the top. Maslow believed that certain people, only 2 per cent of the population, could be called 'self-actualized', and they have many more 'peak experiences' than others. A 'peak experience' is available to all, and self-actualization is 'growth motivation', or a process of seeking.

'Peak experiences' were described as sudden feelings of intense happiness and well-being. They are non-religious, quasi-mystical or mystical in nature, and possibly accompanied by awareness of 'ultimate truth' and the unity of all things. Also accompanying peak experiences is a heightened sense of control over the body and emotions, and a wider sense of awareness. The experience fills the individual with wonder and awe.

Maslow described 'peak experiences' as self-validating, self-justifying moments with their own intrinsic value; never negative, unpleasant or evil; disoriented in time and space (which sounds like the liminal/liminoid zone of Turner (1974), as well as Csikszentimihalyi's (1975) 'flow'); and accompanied by a loss of fear, anxiety, doubts and inhibitions. Critics argue that anybody, whether good or evil, could have one of these peak experiences, so it has no moral basis. Others find it unscientific and untestable.

'Benefits' are what people believe they will obtain from consumption or participation, and these are generally expressed in terms related to need fulfilment. For example, of all the benefits provided by leisure services and sport, improved health has to be near the top of the list. People 'want' many things or experiences, but that is not necessarily the same as needing them. Only the individual can decide when a want becomes a need, although society often makes judgements as to what is a basic need. Often potential substitution comes into play, because many needs and wants can be met through different means.

Do people need events?

The answer is yes, sort of! People might not respond to questions by saying they need to attend a party or cultural celebration, but they do need the socializing, relaxation or escapism that events offer. People need to discover, learn and fulfil their aesthetic ambitions, and attending events provides these benefits. Companies have to market and do business, so they need exhibitions and consumer shows. Associations have to meet. Humans need to recreate, leading to sport events. Events of all kinds have been successful because they meet so many fundamental personal, social, cultural and economic needs.

One question that gets at the heart of the issue is this: if all festivals were removed, would people create new ones? If sports events were cancelled, would there be high demand to bring them back? If conferences ceased because of terrorism, how long would it be before companies and associations found alternative ways to get their people together? Clearly, there is demand for events, and history has demonstrated that this growing level of demand reflects underlying, fundamental needs. Individual events may be substitutable, and people have lots of choices, but events do meet basic human needs.

Motivation and motives

'Personality traits' have a rather permanent influence on behaviour, whereas 'motivation' is dynamic, it can and does change. 'Motivation' refers to the process by which people are driven to act in a certain way (Decrop 2006: 9). Iso-Ahola (1980, 1983) took a more comprehensive approach in saying that motivations are internal factors that arouse, direct and integrate behaviour. Another way to look at 'motivation' is to think of a need or 'disequilibrium', which is accompanied by an expectation that action will reduce it. If the expectation is met, satisfaction results. The experience of, or failure to attain, satisfaction influences future behaviour (i.e. there is a feedback mechanism).

'Motives', by contrast, are specific reasons for doing something, and they have to follow from underlying needs and motivation. For example, people who are 'highly involved' in a sport or lifestyle pursuit (like running) have a strong 'motivation' to attend events where their specific needs can be satisfied. But their 'motives' for deciding to attend a specific event might include consideration of who else is attending, the entertainment opportunities and the attractiveness of the location.

It is common in the tourism literature to use the terms 'push factors' or 'drivers', and 'pull factors' or 'attraction/attractiveness' to cover travel motivation (Dann 1977, 1981; Crompton 1979). When we speak of the interaction of push and pull factors, Iso-Ahola's (1980, 1983; Mannell and Iso-Ahola 1987) 'seeking and escaping' model comes to the fore. Seeking and escaping motivation simultaneously influences our decisions because we are both seeking to find personal and interpersonal rewards and hoping to escape aspects of personal and interpersonal environments that bother us. Both seeking and escaping are forms of intrinsic motivation, or what we want to do for its own sake.

In escaping our everyday environment we seek change and novelty, especially new experiences. 'Under-' or 'over-arousal' gives rise to this need for escape, but of course we also have to seek out something to alter our arousal levels – hence the need for 'optimal arousal' at events. Have a look at travel and entertainment marketing to see the importance of 'escapism' in motivating consumer choices. When it comes to 'seeking' motives, personal satisfaction or rewards can be obtained through relaxation, exploration, learning, aesthetic experiences, meeting challenges or mastery (a sense of competence). Interpersonal rewards can include social contacts and connectedness (belonging and sharing).

Motivational studies have been frequent in the events literature (for example: Mohr *et al.* 1993; Uysal *et al.* 1993; Leibold and van Zyl 1994; Backman *et al.* 1995; Scott 1995; Nogawa *et al.* 1996; Crompton and McKay 1997; Oppermann and Chon 1997; Formica and Murrmann 1998; Formica and Uysal 1998; Green and Chalip 1998; Raybould 1998; Pitts 1999; Ngamson and Beck 2000; Nicholson and Pearce 2001; McGehee *et al.* 2003; Xiao and Smith 2004; Ryan and Trauer 2005; Funk *et al.* 2007) including review articles by Lee *et al.* (2004), Gibson's (2004) review of sport tourism motivation, and a review by Li and Petrick (2006). Benckendorff and Pearce (2012) reviewed motivational studies, with an emphasis on sport spectators and attendees – a subject that is further developed in the *Routledge Handbook of Sports Event Management* (Parent and Chappelet 2015). Mair (2013) has reviewed the motivational studies conducted on convention attendees.

Li and Petrick (2006) found that most such studies were theoretically grounded in, and gave support to, the 'seeking-escaping' motivation theory, and the similar push/pull model. Some more recent motivation studies are presented later, as research notes, focusing on festivals, business events and sports.

The event travel career trajectory

The notion of a motivational trajectory in which motivation changes over time, through travel experiences, came from Pearce and Caltabiano (1983) and was later largely refuted by Pearce and Lee (2005), who concluded that multiple, generic motives apply to all leisure travel. However, the trajectory appears to apply much more to special interests than it does to general travel motivation, so it has been hypothesized that motivations should change over time as amateur athletes become more involved (Getz 2008; Getz and McConnell 2011; Getz and Andersson 2010). If this is true, then the motivations of highly involved event tourists should differ significantly from the lesser involved. In particular, the highly involved should stress personal development motives, rather than those relating to the lower-order needs (from Maslow 1954) such as relaxation and socializing.

General pleasure-travel motivation will often be different from special-interest travel. Indeed, a considerable amount of research and theory-building has occurred within the field of sport tourism, with particular relevance to sport-event motivation. Gibson (1998) described 'active sport tourists' as those most likely to travel for participation in favourite pursuits, and they often do this well into retirement. Gibson also referred to involvement and specialization theories to help explain motivation and travel behaviour.

The term 'career' implies 'serious leisure' as theorized by Stebbins (discussed on pp. 187–188). What we want to look for – and researchers have so far only scratched the surface in this context – are people who for reasons of their 'involvement' or 'commitment' not only attend many events, but demonstrate a progression or pattern of event participation and attendance that stems from their increasing experience and shifting motivation.

Jones and Green (2006) explained the relevance of serious leisure and social worlds to sport tourism studies. They said that: 'Serious sport tourism (that is, travel to participate in serious leisure) is able to provide individuals with a positive social identity' and 'Travel to participate in a sport or leisure activity puts one in an extended contact with other participants . . . outside of everyday experience, and often includes more experienced members of the subculture' (Jones and Green 2006: 43, 44). In this context, sport events provide spaces for social identity formation and reinforcement.

McGehee *et al.* (2003) found that highly involved recreational runners travelled more on overnight trips to participate in events, compared with medium-involved runners. This confirmed the well-established proposition that greater involvement results in higher levels of participation, and for runners this means participation in competitive events. Although they found that runners did not attend all the races they would have liked to, owing to a number of constraints such as family obligations, they did not examine race characteristics or destination choices. Interestingly, highly involved runners also participated in more races in their own communities. Once attracted, the authors suggested that highly involved recreational runners could become repeat visitors, assuming they had a good overall race and destination experience.

Shipway and Jones (2008) applied the serious leisure framework to runners' experiences at a major marathon. They classified runners as 'serious sport tourists' on the basis of the level of ability needed to compete in a marathon, length of trip and stay necessitated by participation, and relatively high cost of training for the event (2008: 65). 'Discussion between participants emphasized the importance of travel, in that races that were held in distant or unusual locations held greater perceived capital than those within the UK' (2008: 68). Discussion of past event experiences was very pronounced. Running careers were discussed. The marathon for some was a 'career marker', 'representing a confirmation of their progression to confirmed serious runner' (2008: 72). The collection of subculture capital leads to 'the desire to travel and collect places' (2008: 72), leading to a lot of storytelling. The durable benefits of running were identified as 'developing and overcoming personal challenges, experiencing a heightened sense of achievement and self-esteem, fun and happiness, healthy living, weight loss and physical well-being, injury rehabilitation' (2008: 73).

A related trajectory construct is the 'sports tourism demand continuum' developed by Jackson and Weed (2003), in which athletes can progress from incidental participation through sporadic, occasional, regular and committed levels all the way to 'driven'. However, this model is more relevant to professional and elite athletes. In a modification, Weed and Bull (2004) take into account the importance of travel to participants, with those at the 'driven' level taking part in more sport tourism.

Main hypotheses for the event travel career trajectory

A considerable amount of research will be required to test and develop this theoretical construct. So far the basic hypotheses[1] have been stated this way, for runners:

- H1 (Motivation): highly involved runners will be motivated significantly more by higher-order needs related to self-actualization. In the context of competitive sport, this translates into personal motivations like meeting challenges and self-improvement, as opposed to social and relaxation motivation; by implication, motivations should be revealed to change over time.

- H2 (Travel Style): highly involved runners will be significantly different from others participating in the event. They should travel to more events, possibly more with partners and family, and combining events with general holidays.

- H3 (Temporal): the highly involved runners will exhibit less seasonality in their travel, as they seek out specific events; destinations employ events to counter normal demand peaks and troughs.

- H4 (Spatial): highly involved runners will travel farther, longer and more by air. An advancing career in running should result in higher-level competition at the national and international levels.

- H5 (Event Types): highly involved runners will participate in different types of events, related to their prestige, novelty or perceived challenge. Certain events are iconic within social worlds; experienced runners should also be novelty-seekers.

- H6 (Destination and Event Choice Criteria): the importance of various criteria when selecting events and destinations will differ significantly between higher- and lesser-involved runners. The ideal holiday destination for the highly involved will provide the opportunity to participate in an event, and to satisfy partners or family members.

The Research Notes 8.2 provide evidence in support of these hypotheses.

8.2 RESEARCH NOTES ON THE EVENT TRAVEL CAREER TRAJECTORY

Getz, D. and McConnell, A. (2011). Event tourist careers and mountain biking. *Journal of Sport Management*, 25(4), 326–338.

'This paper seeks to advance theory pertaining to serious sport tourism, through the application of serious leisure and ego-involvement theory and the analysis of a survey of participants in the TransRockies Challenge mountain-bike event. Participants were questioned post-event about their motives, involvement in their sport, event-related travel, and destination and event preferences. Analysis revealed that most respondents were highly involved in competitive mountain biking, and were primarily motivated by self-development through meeting a challenge . . . . Results suggest that many serious sport tourists develop travel careers centred on competitive events. A hypothetical framework for assessing six dimensions of event travel career trajectories is developed, leading to consideration of practical management implications and research needs.'

Getz, D. and Andersson, T. (2010). The event-tourist career trajectory: A study of high-involvement amateur distance runners. *Scandinavian Journal of Hospitality and Tourism*, 10(4), 468–491.

'As a partial test of the event-tourist career trajectory, a large sample of registrants for a half-marathon in Sweden was questioned in a pre-event survey about their motives, involvement in their sport and event-related travel. Employing an involvement scale specific to amateur distance runners, analysis revealed that most runners were not highly involved in this sport. However, a comparison of the most highly involved (constituting the top decile of the sample) and the remainder revealed many significant differences that do support the hypotheses in all six dimensions.'

Lamont, M., Kennelly, M. and Wilson, E. (2012). Competing priorities as constraints in event travel careers. *Tourism Management*, 33(5), 1068–1079.

This paper applies the concept of an event travel career to non-elite triathletes. For these active sport tourists, ongoing pursuit of an event travel career is arguably constrained by competing priorities that intervene between everyday life and their pursuit of an event travel career. In-depth interviews were conducted with 21 triathletes identified as pursuing an event travel career. Interpretive analysis revealed seven domains of competing priorities that could work to constrain their event travel career aspirations. These domains included familial relationships, domestic responsibilities, sociability, finances, leisure, well-being and work/education.

Getz, D. and McConnell, A. (2014). Comparing trail runners and mountain bikers: Motivation, involvement, portfolios, and event-tourist careers. *Journal of Convention and Event Tourism*, 15(1), 69–100.

'Amateur trail runners and endurance mountain bikers are compared with regard to motivation, involvement in their sport, competitive-event portfolios and event travel careers. . . . The two "destination events" differ considerably in terms of the gender of participants, with a much higher proportion of females in the running event. Both samples were revealed to have a fairly high level of involvement in their sport, but a large proportion of participants in both events also participated in a wider portfolio of challenging sports. . . . This involvement has led a majority to develop an event travel career.'

Figure 8.2 is supported by research, but remains hypothetical – especially as it might apply to other sports, arts, hobbies and lifestyle pursuits. There is no inevitability to progression, as many people remain at a beginner's level, or they progress then fall back in terms of their commitment and involvement.

Much more research is needed along these lines. What are the short-term and ultimate goals of highly involved event participants? Do some 'iconic' events compel them forwards, training harder, searching for better performance? How do they combine their interest in running, or art, or any other pursuit with more general leisure and travel preferences? How can event designers maximize the desired experiences of the

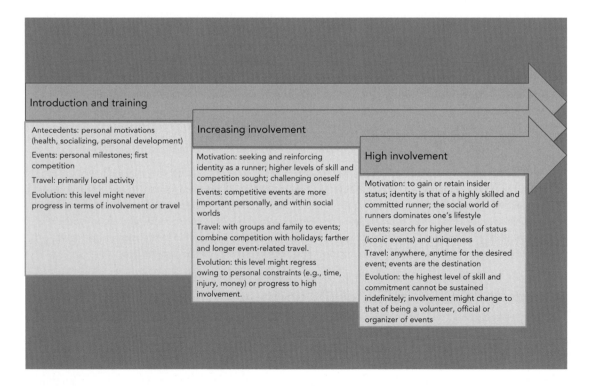

Figure 8.2 Hypothetical event travel career trajectory for amateur distance runners

'highly involved' as well as those for whom the event is only of general interest? Comparative research among leisure interest and social worlds is required. There is reason to believe that travel careers develop within arts, sports, hobbies and various lifestyle pursuits such as an interest in food and wine. Business people and professionals, including academics, also develop event careers related to advancement and changing needs on the one hand and increasing ability to travel on the other.

Personal and interpersonal factors

Sport, entertainment and business events are an integral part of many cultures. A person's cultural background can have a profound influence on their perceptions of their need for, or their interest in, certain types of planned events. In some societies individuals are encouraged to think in terms of hedonistic consumption, leading to event 'consumption', but in others the collective will or religious/political doctrine generates a quite different pattern of socially acceptable behaviour.

There are many common reasons for attending cultural celebrations, including entertainment, spectacle and social, but we also need to focus on the cultural antecedents. For traditional events, people are expected to participate and even organize them because of the cultural norms existing in their communities.

How much does social obligation impact on attendance and participation in cultural celebrations? Some take on the status of institutions, thereby attracting volunteers who gain prestige or social standing. Buying tickets to some arts festivals might be considered the thing to do if one is in the higher social classes, while travelling to the annual Wagnerian opera festival in Bayreuth, Germany, might be considered both a pilgrimage and a chance to meet the European elite.

Lifestyle is in part a social construct, dependent on other factors such as reference points and participants. Peers are an especially important element in events that have subcultural dimensions, including cultural celebrations and sports.

Expectations

Needs and motives give rise to expectations that certain behaviours will yield desired benefits, and this is the essence of the 'theory of planned behaviour'. Expectations are also shaped by communications (advertising and image-making) on the part of events, and particularly by word-of-mouth recommendations or expressed opinions from valued reference groups.

The 'travel career trajectory' is also applicable, as the more experience one has with events (either particular events or events in general), the more it will affect expectations. For example, marathoners will build up specific expectations of what the event should offer by way of challenge, services to runners and the nature of their own experience. The greater the involvement in, or commitment to, a particular pursuit, the more it will shape expectations and future participation.

Festival motives

Many of the event motivation studies mentioned earlier were directed at festivals. Probably the most important conclusion, reinforced by the ensuing Research Note 8.3, is that generic motives predominate (i.e. family togetherness, socializing, group identity), while event-specific motives (the programme, the art form, uniqueness features) are likely to be important to niche segments and relatively more important for tourists. Certainly festival motivators are primarily intrinsic, that is, for leisure and other personally/socially rewarding reasons, whereas for other types of event extrinsic motivators might also apply (e.g. for work and business).

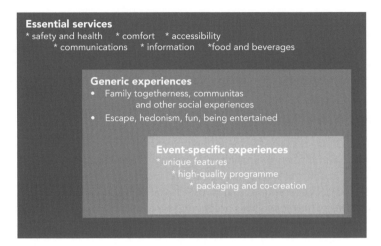

Figure 8.3 Generic and event-specific motivators

Festival motivation: generic and targeted benefits

There is enough evidence to support the proposition that festival attendance is largely driven by generic benefits. In Figure 8.3 the generic and event-specific motivators, that is, the experiences desired, are combined with essential services to provide a model of value to event designers and marketers. The essential services can be called 'hygiene factors' or 'dissatisfiers' (after Herzberg 1966) because they do not motivate, yet they can dissatisfy customers.

Generic benefits attract the widest possible audiences, but are also highly substitutable. Event-specific experiences, or benefits offered, will attract those seeking something special such as unique, one-time-only and high-quality programming. The highly involved are motivated by experiences they can share with others in their social worlds. A mix of generic and targeted benefits, built on a foundation of high-quality service, is essential for events to compete with other events and other forms of entertainment and especially to attract tourists.

The importance of socializing has been highlighted by Nordvall *et al.* (2014), with implications for design of all festivals and events – see the accompanying Research Note 8.3.

8.3 RESEARCH NOTES ON FESTIVAL MOTIVATION

Gelder, G. and Robinson, P. (2009). A critical comparative study of visitor motivations for attending music festivals: A case study of Glastonbury and V Festival. *Event Management*, 13(3), 181–196.

'Most importantly, the article supported the notion that multiple motivations come into play and it suggests that it is risky for festival managers to rely solely on the theme of the event itself. It is equally important to create a fun and festive atmosphere that offers ample opportunity to socialize and have new and non-musical experiences.'

McClinchey, K. and Carmichael, A (2014). The future of local community festivals and meanings of place in an increasingly mobile world. In I. Yeoman, M. Robertson, U. McMahon-Beattie, E. Backer and K. Smith (eds), *The Future of Events and Festivals*, pp. 140–156. Abingdon: Routledge.

The authors of this chapter studied a multicultural festival in Canada as a cultural space that conveys meanings of hope, pride and celebration and allows ethnic groups to organize, practise and perform authentic cultural traditions. This provides a sense of belonging to the wider community while fostering cultural identity. To others, attending a multicultural festival reflects a search for authenticity and simplicity in a mobile world, where finding one's identity has become difficult. The festival provides a meaningful space to connect visitors and participants.

Andersson, T. and Mossberg, L. (2014). Interest in food events: Some insights from Swedish consumers. In A. Cavicchi and C. Santini (eds), *Food and Wine Events in Europe*, pp. 201–212. Oxford: Routledge.

The authors concluded that 'When food festivals are congruent with symbolic values this will hypothetically enhance the enjoyment value of food festivals and thus the interest in food festivals' (2014: 208). Foodies, or highly involved food lovers, are more likely to attend festivals and other food-related events that build and reinforce identity.

Nordvall, A., Pettersson, R., Svensson, B. and Brown, S. (2014). Designing events for social interaction. *Event Management*, 18(2), 127–140.

'Socialization motivates people to visit events and social interactions between event visitors influence their experience of the event. The conclusions are based on a literature review and empirical data collected at a Swedish music festival. The research found that social interactions between event visitors are an important part of the event experience and the level of satisfaction for the individual attending an event. Social interactions consist of three main types: known-group socialization; external socialization; audience socialization. Every part of the event (theme and programme, setting, consumables, service) can be designed to facilitate positive experiences and to constrain negative experiences related to such interactions.'

Festival types

There are many types of festival, so event-specific motivators always have to be considered. A number of research notes have been provided to illustrate some key differences. Perhaps the most challenging type is that of the so-called 'community festival', which often means a multi-purpose event intended to appeal to the widest possible audience. While such festivals tend to celebrate the community itself, or have the aim of social integration, they might also contain programmic elements that are designed to attract tourists (especially entertainment and participatory sports). Usually they are organized and/or supported by local government, but might be managed by a not-for-profit society or a consortium of local organizations.

Jepson and Clarke (2014) and Jepson et al. (2013) explore the community festival from the perspective of social inclusion and power relations. They utilized the motivation–opportunity–ability (MOA) model as an analytical framework to explore decision-making, and argued that both inclusivity and public engagement are necessary for the creation of successful community events. What this implies for motivation theory is that unless residents feel empowered and take a sense of ownership in community festivals, they are unlikely to feel comfortable in attending them.

Festivals and cultural tourism

Many event tourists are 'cultural tourists' – that is, they are seeking cultural experiences – while other events certainly can be designed to deliver cultural experiences. The Travel Industry Association of America, together with the *Smithsonian Magazine* (2003), reported on *The Historic/Cultural Traveler*. They found an ever-increasing demand, with 81 per cent of Americans who had travelled in the past year considered to be 'historic/cultural', based on their interests and activities. For 30 per cent of travellers, their choice of destination was influenced by a specific cultural event or activity.

Although there are many definitions of cultural tourism in the literature, McKercher and du Cros (2002: 3) said that it can be approached from four perspectives: 'tourism derived' (a form of special interest travel; a product); 'motivational' (what travellers are looking for, including visits to the arts, monuments, festivals); 'experiential' (an emphasis on cultural learning; the quest for understanding and self-fulfilment) and 'operational' (related to the purpose of the study, as in this case to examine festivals as a form of cultural tourism). They also postulated (2002: 16) seven possible relationships between tourism and cultural heritage assets, ranging from 'full cooperation' to 'full conflict', and this provides a framework for investigating the marketing and tourism orientation of cultural festivals. The in-between categories include 'working relationships', 'peaceful co-existence', 'parallel existence/blissful ignorance', 'mild annoyance' and 'nascent conflict'.

In terms of planning and developing cultural tourism, McKercher and du Cros (2002: 186) employed a 'market appeal-robusticity' matrix which bases tourism potential on an evaluation of the asset's (in our context, planned events) market appeal and its ability to cope with visitors 'or to be modified in a way that does not compromise its values'. Different strategies are therefore required for festivals that have strong touristic appeal but are not robust, compared with those with little appeal but substantial robusticity. Although criteria were suggested for tangible heritage assets (2002: 191), little has been said about events – especially regarding their robustness/adaptability versus cultural significance and authenticity. In other words, is it possible and legitimate to turn any or all cultural festivals into tourist attractions?

Ideally, many events should attract a segment that McKercher and du Cros (2002: 148) called the 'purposeful cultural tourist', who wants a deep cultural experience and has been motivated to travel to a destination by its cultural attractions. However, the event organizer must also prepare for visitors with a lesser need for cultural experiences, including those who are not really attracted by culture at all (in other words, they are seeking other benefits such as fun and social opportunities, or are motivated by escapism).

Motivational research on business events

We should expect that motivations to attend meetings and business-related events will be quite different from leisure motivations, specifically that extrinsic motives will often dominate: being required to attend (lack of choice), seeking a reward for attending (learning something useful, developing a personal or business network) and a mix of extrinsic and intrinsic rewards (i.e. combining business with pleasure). Business-event organizers often stress the social programme as well as pre- and post-event tours.

Mair (2013) reviewed the literature on convention motivation, observing that the main topics explored by researchers were the desire for networking and professional development/education. Constraining factors included cost, timing, accessibility, location attractiveness and health or safety concerns. See Research Notes 8.4 for elaboration.

8.4 RESEARCH NOTES ON BUSINESS-EVENT MOTIVATIONS

Mair, J. and Thompson, K. (2009). The UK association conference attendance decision-making process. *Tourism Management*, 30(3), 400–409.

This paper reports on research carried out into the consumer behaviour displayed by UK association conference delegates when deciding to attend a conference. Examination of the available literature suggested that there has been little investigation of the delegate's perspective on attending a conference, as most research into business events has traditionally been centred on the supply side, particularly convention destination image and association site selection. The paper found six underlying dimensions of the UK association conference delegate decision-making process – personal/professional development, networking opportunities, cost, location, time and convenience, and health and well-being. Additionally, regression analysis showed that two of the dimensions (networking opportunities and cost) were significant predictors of intention to attend the conference again in the future.

Fjelstul, J., Severt, K. and Breiter, D. (2010). Building association attendance: Differences between chapter, regional, and annual meetings from the perception of the association members. *Event Management*, 14(3), 183–192.

'The objective of this study was to identify meeting patterns and trends related to chapter, regional and/or annual conference attendance. Factors likely to increase attendance, attendance trends over a five-year period, recommendations by association members and the preferred mode of delivery were identified. Results will assist meeting planners in providing maximum benefits to association members and to potentially increase attendance at each conference level.

The most important factors that will increase attendance were found to be relevance of the programme, better speakers and receiving employer financial support.'

Consumer-show motivations

Although this kind of show or exhibition is often lumped together with other business events, since they generally seek to make a profit, the motivations of consumers are going to be different from those attending for professional or business reasons.

8.5 RESEARCH NOTE ON CONSUMER-SHOW MOTIVATION

Fox, D. and Edwards, J. (2009). A preliminary analysis of the market for small, medium, and large horticultural shows in England. *Event Management*, 12(3–4), 199–208.

'This study analysed the socio-demographic and other characteristics of actual and potential visitors to three styles of English horticultural shows. The shows selected varied in terms of their status (national, regional, local), the number of visitors they attract and the length of time they are open to the public. The analysis of the findings of a survey of residents in southern England suggests that while age is a key demographic variable, a more valuable means of segmenting the population is by their level of enthusiasm for gardening. Furthermore, it is proposed that demand for the largest shows, held nationally, can be established not only through these factors but also by the potential visitors' history of attending smaller horticultural shows.'

Rittichainuwat, B. and Mair, J. (2011). Visitor attendance motivations at consumer travel exhibitions. *Tourism Management*, 33(5), 1236–1244.

'The findings suggest that visitors to consumer travel exhibitions have multiple motivations: acquiring purchase information, being attracted by the theme or being encouraged to visit by media coverage. Half of the visitors perceived travel fairs to be an important distribution channel through which they could get special deals on travel to desirable destinations (or at least source information on travel). It seems likely that consumer travel show attendance may be closely linked with the individual leisure desires of the visitor. The study suggests two clusters: (1) shopper cluster, whose major motivation is purchasing, and (2) total visitors, whose motivation is to undertake an ongoing information search and attend seminars to maintain their awareness of new trends in the tourism industry.'

Motivational research on sport fans and spectators

In applying psychological ideas to sport event participation, Benckendorff and Pearce (2012: 166) distinguished between spectators and attendees, performers and participants, and elite participants. Fans were considered to be a special segment. Personality, role theory, involvement, motivation and the actual experience plus post-experience are important considerations. Identity theory suggests that people attend sport and other types of event that carry symbolic significance, thereby helping to define themselves.

Li and Petrick's (2006) literature review related to sports resulted in several important conclusions. First, a general motivation scale for sport event attendance by fans or spectators has been developed and widely applied (see Wann 1995; Wann *et al.* 1999). Second, studying potential attendees adds to our understanding (as opposed to surveys of actual attendees), and third, travel and event motivation might be different – a finding of significance for sport tourism.

Perspectives of all the stakeholders involved with sports events are covered in the *Routledge Handbook of Sports Event Management* (Parent and Chappelet 2015). Bodet (2015) reviewed the spectator's perspective and the literature on fans and spectators, concluding that while most literature has focused on devoted and fanatical fans, sports crowds are in fact very heterogeneous; segmentation is always necessary to identify important differences in characteristics, needs and expectations. More research is needed on the attitudes and experiences of both casual and interactive spectators.

8.6 RESEARCH NOTE ON SPORT FAN MOTIVATIONS

Wann, D., Grieve, F., Zapalac, R. and Pease, D. (2008). Motivational profiles of sport fans of different sports. *Sport Marketing Quarterly*, 17(1), 6–19.

'This investigation examined sport type differences in eight fan motives: escape, economic (i.e. gambling), eustress (i.e. positive arousal), self-esteem, group affiliation, entertainment, family and aesthetics. Participants (final sample $N = 886$) completed a questionnaire packet assessing their level of fandom and motivation for consuming one of 13 target sports classified into three different dichotomies: individual (e.g. figure skating, golf) versus team (e.g. professional baseball, college basketball); aggressive (e.g. professional wrestling, professional football) versus non-aggressive (e.g. professional baseball, figure skating); and stylistic (e.g. figure skating, gymnastics) versus non-stylistic (e.g. professional hockey, tennis).'

The sample was of young college students, but it revealed there were substantial motivational differences among the types of sports studied – with the exception of the 'escape' motive which did not differ significantly.

Motivational research on sport participation

The previous discussion of serious sport tourism and the event travel career trajectory identified key motives for amateur participation and sport tourism, and in particular the importance of challenging oneself through physical activity. Additional insights can be found in the *Handbook of Sports Event Management* chapter by Young *et al.* (2015) on Masters Sport Perspectives. They discuss the research done on involvement and commitment to sport in general, then summarize what is known about Masters competitors. The reasons frequently given for competing in Masters Games include improving health and fitness and dealing with or combating older age, enjoyment, seeing new places and having cultural experiences, social affiliation and, of course, meeting personal challenges.

8.7 RESEARCH NOTE ON SPORT EVENT MOTIVATION

Funk, D., Toohey, K. and Bruun, T. (2007). The role of socio-psychological and culture-education motives in marketing international sport tourism: A cross-cultural perspective. *Tourism Management*, 28(3), 806–819.

The authors conducted a survey among international runners at the 2005 Gold Coast (Australia) Marathon. Several well-tested scales were used: Personal Involvement Inventory, Strength of Motivation Scale, Attitude Towards Australia, Knowledge-Learning Scale, Cultural Experience Scale and Cultural Learning Inventory. 'The study found that participants, regardless of cultural background, had a positive attitude toward Australia, a high level of running involvement, and a strong desire to participate in organized running events.' Running was the primary travel motive, but Japanese runners in particular also wanted to learn about Australia and Australian culture (leisure activities, music and art and lifestyle).

Barriers and constraints

All the antecedents we have considered act together to shape a person's desire and propensity for certain event experiences, but there are often constraints on our actions, especially time and money, and specific barriers to overcome. The next section deals with 'leisure constraint theory' applied to events. There is no comparable theory for extrinsically motivated event participation, but it is probable that a mix of intrinsic and extrinsic motivation applies to many business-event decisions (see Figure 8.4).

Leisure constraints theory

Why do some people not participate in events? This question is vital in marketing, but there are also important theoretical considerations that get to the nature of motivation, benefits and the nature of the event experience. In event studies the challenge is not to only identify constraints on attendance but to examine how people overcome constraints to attend, and how that knowledge might affect both event planning and marketing. In the context of 'serious leisure' or frequent event participation by 'high-involvement' types, we should be studying how constraints are 'negotiated' over a lifetime.

The leisure researchers Crawford *et al.* (1991) identified three general categories of constraints to participation: 'structural', 'personal' and 'interpersonal'. They are not necessarily hierarchical, and might be interactive. These are set out in Figure 8.4 and each is now examined in turn.

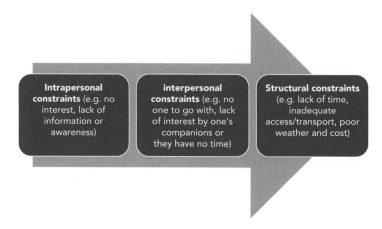

Figure 8.4 Barriers to event attendance

Source: Developed from Lee and Palakurthi (2013).

Structural constraints

The first and foremost of these is accessibility, which stems from the location and timing of events of all kinds – they are simply not always available, convenient or known by all potential participants. All aspects of supply analysis come into play here, as do marketing and communication. For example, it has long been observed that there is a huge gap between tourists' interest in attending cultural events in other countries and actual participation. Why? Because they have imperfect knowledge of what's available, and are most likely to be in an area when the events are not held. This is also why we are so interested in the 'dedicated event tourist' who travels specifically because of events.

Time and cost are always structural constraints. On the one hand, we need to identify who is left out of the arts, or sports, or any other type of event because they are unable to afford it or cannot make the necessary time. On the other hand, 'not enough time or money' are convenient excuses, and might often mean the person does not assign any priority to a given opportunity. The first is a constraint issue, the second pertains more to preferences.

Age and health are obvious factors to consider. In youth we cannot get about on our own, and until we have income we cannot do what we want. With advancing age and declining health (or at least specific health problems) interest and participation in many leisure and work-related events will likely decline. For events, there is a need to combine both life-cycle and work/career evolutionary approaches.

Personal constraints

These are individual psychological conditions, including personality and moods, that hold us back from participating. Some people are predisposed to social activities, others to introversion. Sometimes we want to mix, at other times we need to be left alone. This category is similar to our earlier discussion of personality, values, attitudes and lifestyle.

Risk perception, and tolerance for risk, enters into many leisure and travel decisions. Do we want to have a thrill if it means assuming personal risks, or can we afford to spend time and money on an event that might not satisfy us? How preferences are first formed for events or event experiences has not been researched, but for ongoing participation there are explanations within the concepts of 'serious leisure', 'recreation specialization', 'commitment' and 'involvement'.

Interpersonal constraints

These constraints arise within social contexts, taking into account the influence of others. This might take the form of letting significant others make decisions for us, being influenced by peer pressure (e.g. fear of ridicule) or being subjected to discrimination. Social isolation is often a limitation, especially for certain types of events – after all, who wants to go to a party or celebration alone? On the other hand, events are often great places to meet people.

A lot of research has documented gender differences in travel, leisure and sport, but little of this has been applied to events. More research on why people do not attend events is necessary, such as in Research Note 8.8.

8.8 RESEARCH NOTE ON EVENT NON-ATTENDEES

Miller, L., Jago, L. and Deery, M. (2004). Profiling the special event nonattendee: An initial investigation. *Event Management*, 8(3), 141–150.

A representative telephone interview sample of residents of Melbourne, Australia, was undertaken to examine why some people did not attend festivals or other special events in the city. Theoretical underpinning of the research came from leisure constraint research. Results highlighted that older age explained a lot of non-interest in events, and older widows, especially, were not going to events. Being single or having younger children at home was positively associated with attending events. Full-time employment resulted in greater participation than part-time work. The fact that demographic variables explained attendance seems to be in contradiction to findings of festival-motivation research, but there are theoretical differences between motivation and attendance/non-attendance. Specific identified barriers included health, lack of time, perceptions of crowding and accessibility concerns, while a general lack of interest was the biggest reason given. The authors suggested that future research should try to determine if a lack of interest in events is absolute, related to life-stage or a result of situational constraints. Finally, it is worth noting that only 13 per cent of respondents had *not* attended an event in the past five years.

8.9 RESEARCH NOTE ON EVENTS AND LEISURE CONSTRAINTS

Lee, D. and Palakurthi, R. (2013). Marketing strategy to increase exhibition attendance through controlling and eliminating leisure constraints. *Event Management*, 17, 323–336.

This is one of the first articles to explicitly address the leisure constraints theory and literature within the context of event studies focusing on the exhibition sector in South Korea. These exhibition centres encourage business interaction, including consumer shows. The study identified 19 leisure constraints from the existing research and theoretical models on this theme. The main findings were that:

- Four intrapersonal constraints dominated, namely 'no concern to visit, no interest, not being comfortable in the venue' (perhaps due to crowding). Three interpersonal constraints dominated (i.e. a companion's lack of time to participate, a companion's lack of economic resources/support to visit and a lack of companions).

- Structural constraints consisted of a lack of opportunity to participate, a lack of entertainment facilities at the venues and a lack of exciting programmes to attract the visitor, although the importance of these different constraints varied geographically between four locations studied (Seoul, Incheon, Gyeonggi and Chungcheung).

Among the implications which the authors drew from the study were:

- Married attendees had to make a bigger financial commitment to visit than unmarried attendees due to higher levels of interpersonal constraint, indicating that family promotions might help attract more price-sensitive attendees.
- Those aged 35–44 displayed the greatest intrapersonal and interpersonal constraints due to a lack of time and resources, reflecting their stage in the family life cycle.
- Those attendees with the highest levels of educational attainment had the lowest levels of intrapersonal constraints.
- Distance had a distinct spatial impact on attendance.
- Distinct cultural and idiosyncratic differences exist between South Korean attendees and those from other Western countries. For example, South Koreans may be more inclined to attend exhibitions which are relatively new events and they also expect entertainment when they visit.

Constraint negotiation

As constraints almost always exist, how do people who do participate in, or attend, events overcome them? 'Negotiation' of constraints is the individual process of finding ways to do what we want to do. If we really want to attend a concert, how do we get the money, make the time, find someone to go with and book the tickets? The issue of constraints and how you negotiate them to overcome them has been a significant area of research within leisure for over 20 years. The seminal study in the field was by Jackson *et al.* (1993), who discussed generic strategies for negotiating constraints as illustrated in Figure 8.5. What Jackson *et al.* found was that people have to strike a balance between constraints and their motivations to participate. Negotiating these barriers or constraints and balancing with motivation results in different

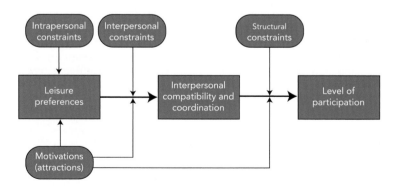

Figure 8.5 Jackson, Crawford and Godbey's balance proposition: leisure participation as a product of a balance between constraints and motivations

Source: Jackson *et al.* (1993). Reprinted from *Leisure sciences*, 15(1), Jackson, E. L., Crawford, D. W., & Godbey, G. Negotiation of leisure constraints, Copyright (1993) with the permission of Taylor and Francis.

strategies being employed. 'Cognitive' strategies are the internal, psychological ways we deal with constraints. For example, the theory of 'cognitive dissonance' can be applied by suggesting that if we cannot attend a concert because of high costs, we will devalue the artist or type of music and do something else that we perceive to provide equal benefits. In this sense, when people say they do not like certain types of event, they might mean they cannot afford them. We all want to feel good about the choices we make, even if they are influenced by constraints.

'Behavioural' strategies include better time management, learning new skills, earning more money or modifying our routines in order to do what we want to do. Some people turn leisure into work, or vice versa. For 'serious leisure', one generally has to acquire knowledge to get the most out of the experience, and this applies to many volunteers at events. In order to think of oneself as an expert or connoisseur, say for the purpose of getting the most from a wine festival, advanced wine knowledge is essential. Similarly, to really be satisfied with your performance at the next Masters Games or X Games, you need to advance your skills through training and competition. To even compete in many sport events you have to qualify through lower-level competitions.

'Time management' is something we all try to improve, particularly in an age when a majority of people complain about time pressures, or lack of time to get active. 'Multi-tasking' (or 'pluriactivity') is the norm for most students, working people and homemakers. Mannell and Zuzanek (1991) reported that even retired seniors felt that a lack of time was a serious leisure constraint.

Setting priorities is the key. Generally, when respondents to a survey say they did not do something because of time or money constraints, they are probably truthful in a general sense. But this common response might very well be hiding a conscious or subconscious prioritization, so they really mean 'attending the event is not high enough on my current list of priorities to justify making the effort or paying the price'. So the researcher will have to dig deeper. It seems paradoxical, but the most constrained people are sometimes the most active! How do they manage to engage in preferred leisure pursuits when others give up? The fact is that many people find innovative ways to overcome or negotiate through constraints (see Hinch et al. 2006, for a discussion and references).

Setting affordances

Pertinent to the analysis of antecedents and event studies is 'setting affordances', which are those objective characteristics of the venue or setting that make certain actions and behaviours possible. For example, an attractive, spacious function room presents many social possibilities to dinner guests, but without wheelchair accessibility some people cannot enter. 'Affordance' is also a concept rooted in cognition and environmental psychology, placing the emphasis on 'perceived affordances'. Regardless of the venue manager's or event producer's intentions, people's perception of what is possible, and what is a barrier, can differ greatly.

Decision-making

Negotiation of constraints is both a background antecedent and a key part of specific decision-making processes. Then it is necessary to study how people search for and use information, especially because events are very time-sensitive opportunities. As well, in the context of economic 'demand' for events, we have to consider their 'attractiveness', the possibility of substitute experiences (including competition) and whether or not people are loyal to certain events.

Information search and use

An important consideration is whether the decision is 'routine' or 'unique'. For some sport events and concert series a consumer can buy season tickets, or multi-day passes, thereby necessitating one big purchase decision – but there will still be a decision required for attending each and every game or concert. Loyal festival fans can also return year after year, in which case most of the same variables enter into the decision. When decision-making becomes 'routine', the person does not need a lot of information (or perceives this to be true), takes less time and already has a predisposition.

Most event opportunities are likely to be 'unique' decision-making episodes, especially when a purchase decision is required. In these cases the consumer needs lots of information and might take a lot of time obtaining it. Part of the appeal of modern Internet marketing is that the time component can be reduced substantially, and research has found that Internet shoppers tend to use only a few sites, thereby limiting their time expenditure. The risk factor also has to be considered, because every new decision to attend or participate in an event poses risks such as wasted time and money, bad experiences, and health and safety concerns.

8.10 RESEARCH NOTES ON INFORMATION SEARCH

Chen, A. and Wu, R. (2009). Understanding visitors' involvement profile and information search: The case of Neimen Song Jiang Battle Array Festival. *Event Management*, 13(4), 205–222.

'The construct of involvement has become a promising variable to help understand and explain individuals' leisure behaviours. Researchers have examined involvement in various areas. However, few studies have focused on its relationship to information search in the context of the eastern world. This study identified the relationship of involvement dimensions to information search among Chinese participants. Results indicated that higher levels of involvement were associated with higher levels of information search. Specifically, self-expression and greater culture-related activity participation were effective determinants of information search.'

Filo, K., Funk, D. and Hornby, G. (2009). The role of web site content on motive and attitude change for sport events. *Journal of Sport Management*, 23(1), 21–40.

'Using the Psychological Continuum Model (PCM) as its theoretical framework, this article presents two studies examining information requirements for sport event web sites and evaluating the impact of web site communications on consumer motivation and attitudes towards the event. This research provides evidence that web site marketing communication does activate attitude change within consumers, as well as empirical support for attitude change within the PCM framework. Findings highlight the potential strategic use of web site communication for sport event organizers to enhance consumer attitudes towards the event and increase attendance.'

Demand

'Demand' is often equated with how many people will come to an event, or pay for it. More correctly, in economic terms, it is a function of the relationship between price and the quantity 'demanded' for an event in particular circumstances. For each price, the demand relationship tells the quantity the buyers want to buy at that corresponding price.

Consider other related factors. Usually price is a monetary cost, as in how much an admission ticket costs, but you might also want to put a value on the consumer's time and energy expended, especially if travel is involved. What about 'free' events? For these it is common to measure demand in terms of attendance, but organizers have to be cautious about interpreting this. Many people might not pay anything for an event that is currently free. Research on 'willingness to pay' is then required.

Attractiveness of the event

A related concept is 'attractiveness'. This means the 'drawing power' or 'pull' of an event, both its general appeal (generic benefits) and its targeted benefits for specific needs and interests. In the context of economic 'demand', attractiveness could be equated with 'market potential' and measured by 'penetration rates'. That is, within a given market area, how many purchases can be expected, expressed as a percentage of the population? (If half the people come twice, that is considered to be 100 per cent.) Different market areas also have to be considered, such as local, regional, national and international zones.

As an example of 'attractiveness' or 'drawing power', note how *Runners' World* magazine ranked the top ten marathons (see www.runnersworld.co.uk), all of which are in world-class cities: London, Chicago, Berlin, New York, Boston, Stockholm, Paris, Honolulu, Amsterdam and Rotterdam. What were the criteria? They favoured the point of view of ordinary, not elite runners, and scored them according to beauty, atmosphere and speed. In describing the top ten, they mentioned the following attractiveness factors:

- a festive or party atmosphere; entertainment along the route; fireworks;
- the route (historic sites; flat and fast or highly challenging; interesting things like views, crossing bridges);
- well organized;
- size (number of participants – either many and crowded or few and intimate; number of spectators);
- age and prestige (especially Boston);
- exclusivity (qualifying times required);
- climate (mild, sunny).

Substitution

Just about every leisure and travel pursuit can be substituted. We do not absolutely need to go to a specific destination or participate in a specific event and (this is assuming free choice); there are always alternative ways to meet our leisure needs. Thinking again of the theory of 'cognitive dissonance', we can easily convince ourselves that one form of music appreciation or sport or hobby is as good as another, even if we were influenced by constraints.

If extrinsic motivations to attend an event apply, substitution takes on a different meaning. We might be able to learn what we need to know from different trade shows, or meet the necessary contacts at different conventions, but these choices are less common than in the leisure realm. Many event attendees go to a specific event because it is the only one, or the best one to satisfy their purposes.

The theory of 'leisure substitution' suggests that if a person cannot do one thing, he or she will choose another that provides similar psychological experiences, satisfactions and benefits (Brunson and Shelby 1993). This appears to be very true for primarily social experiences, where the activity, setting or event is of secondary concern. Events offering 'targeted benefits' for highly involved persons are less substitutable than those offering only 'generic benefits'.

Decision to attend or participate

Wanting to attend, even planning to, is quite different from going to an event. At some point commitment is made, perhaps money spent on travel or tickets, but something might still intervene to prevent attendance. Researchers therefore seek to discover the links between levels of awareness, interest in attending, forming a specific intention to go and actual attendance.

How are decisions made to attend or travel to events, and what factors are considered? Consider all the context and choices we have to understand:

1. 'Consumers' decide to spend money on a concert ticket or sport event (Go alone or with others? Which day and hour, if there are choices? Is overnight travel necessary or desirable? What seat, depending on availability? How much can I afford to/want to pay?);

2. 'Guests' decide whether or not to accept an invitation to a party, wedding or company function (What's in it for me? Who else is going? Who will be offended if I do not go? What will I wear? Was it fun last time?);

3. 'Volunteers' decide if they will be part of the community festival (Can anyone take my place? Will I be rewarded? How much time is required? Am I skilled enough?).

Decision-making occurs in stages, with feedback called 'post-purchase evaluation'. There is an awareness and opinion-forming stage, which might be combined with information gathering (even if it's no more than asking for someone's advice), during which the consumer forms an intent, rejects the opportunity or waffles indecisively.

Loyalty versus novelty-seeking

Loyalty in the events sector is a tricky concept – it is not at all similar to being loyal to a car brand or a favourite restaurant. For one thing, except for professional sports and regular theatrical productions, most events are unique opportunities. Numerous event-related decisions are never exactly repeated. As well, it is known that many people engage in novelty-seeking in travel and leisure, generally preferring something new each time a decision is made.

But event loyalty does exist in some forms, as indicated by ample research on sport-fan loyalty to teams. Loyalty to periodic conferences and exhibitions exists, both because of the business or professional advantages and the enjoyment of socializing with friends who always meet there. Many people do go to the same festivals year after year, especially those that have become traditions in their home communities. Hypothetically, event loyalty is likely to result from obtaining specific benefits, especially those related to special interests. Loyalty might also be a lifestyle factor stemming from events that fit one's work-life and social calendar.

8.11 RESEARCH NOTE ON LOYALTY

Okayasu, I., Nogawa, H. and Morais, D. (2010). Resource investments and loyalty to recreational sport tourism event. *Journal of Travel and Tourism Marketing*, 27(6), 565–578.

'Generally, as many researchers indicated, participants' loyalty will lead to repeat attendance or purchase. However, there is no consensus as to how loyalty develops. In the files of recreational sport tourism event research, the process leading to participants' loyalty with a specific event is not evident.

The purpose of this article is to test a conceptual framework of the development of loyalty that is grounded in resource theory. According to the proposed model, when participants and organizers invest specific profiles of resources in each other, the participants tend to develop a bond with the customer and become dedicated to maintaining a stable relationship.'

Post-experience evaluation and feedback

Satisfaction, meanings and transformation

Was the event experience as expected? Was it merely satisfactory or in some way exceptional, even surprisingly pleasant? Presumably people who have disappointing event experiences are less likely to become loyal or to develop an event career. However, novelty-seekers might very well seek out new events regardless of the quality of a given event, simply because they get easily bored or constantly need new experiences. By contrast, do loyal event-goers necessarily have a low level of need for novelty?

If events are memorable, assigned profound personal and social meanings, or somehow transform the individual, then surely this will encourage loyalty or development of an event career? That is a hypothesis to be tested. The 'event careerist' might be constantly engaged in evaluation and planning for new events. One leads to another, until some point of diminishing returns is reached (i.e. 'satiation') or certain constraints (perhaps health) become insurmountable.

Creating memorable, transforming event experiences is the goal of many event producers, and if people really do enjoy and recollect events they are more likely to return or seek out comparable experiences. As noted by Gibson (2005), in Research Note 8.12, nostalgia can be an important motivator.

8.12 RESEARCH NOTE ON NOSTALGIA

Gibson, H. (2005). Understanding sport tourism experiences. In J. Higham (ed.), *Sport Tourism Destinations: Issues, Opportunities and Analysis*. Oxford: Elsevier.

According to Gibson, in this review, some research evidence suggests that sport tourism fans and participants value ritual and nostalgia. As sport tourists enter the 'liminoid' space/time (based on Turner's theory of ritual process) formed by an event or trip, they are able to put aside normal behaviour and enjoy a new, often social experience, free from norms and values that govern everyday work and home life. Competition-related rituals, shared with a like-minded group of peers, define these experiences and give rise to considerable nostalgia about them. The event itself can be merely a facilitator of these shared, valued memories. Repeat sport tourism behaviour might often be motivated by attempts to re-create past, shared experiences. Gibson also referred to involvement and specialization theories to help explain motivation and travel behaviour.

Future intentions

Intentions can be measured, and in the context of the 'theory of planned behaviour' a specific intent to attend an event is a very good measure of demand. In fact, it is commonly used in attendance forecasting for major events, following the logic that within specific markets (geographically or otherwise segmented) awareness has to build, then interest, and finally clear intent to travel or make the purchase.

This brings us full circle in the model, stressing that antecedents include the influence of previous experience. What is not shown are the effects of other kinds of experience on event-related behaviour. Also, broader forces are at work, including a person's experiences with entertainment, sport or business in general. At what point do events become part of the opportunities people are willing to consider? How is a festival substitutable with all other forms of entertainment? There is so much to study!

STUDY GUIDE

In this chapter a model was illustrated to shape the discussion of all the main factors considered in order to understand decisions and choices leading to event attendance. This is partly the realm of psychology and consumer research, but also the economics of supply and demand, and of cultural and social forces. The discussion started with personal factors, specifically personality, values, attitudes and lifestyle. Then needs, motivations and motives were examined, including the travel career trajectory and how it can help explain event-related behaviour. The event travel career trajectory is new theory, under development, linking back to earlier discussions of serious leisure, involvement, commitment and intrinsic motivation. Try to apply it to other leisure pursuits, including different sports, art forms, hobbies, and lifestyle interests such as food and wine. Also try to apply the model of basic services, generic and targeted (or specific) benefits to different forms of planned events, from festivals to trade shows.

STUDY QUESTIONS

- Explain how 'personality', 'values', 'attitudes' and 'lifestyle' relate to interest in, and demand for, event experiences.
- What are basic human 'needs', and how do they link to 'motivation'?
- Explain the 'travel career trajectory' and show how it can be adapted to understanding the antecedents to attending planned events.
- How important are 'seeking' versus 'escaping' motivations in explaining event attendance? What have researchers found that confirms or rejects this theory when applied to events?
- Do most people attend festivals for generic or specific benefits? Where do essential services enter the decision-making process?
- How are 'expectations' formed? Consider post-event evaluation.
- Explain 'leisure constraint theory' and how it applies to events. Differentiate between the main types of 'constraints', and give event-specific examples.
- Use the concepts of 'serious leisure', 'commitment', 'ego involvement' and 'recreation specialization' to help explain how people develop event careers and negotiate constraints.
- What is 'demand' for events? How are 'attractiveness' and 'substitution' related to demand?
- What factors help explain the differences between 'loyalty' and 'novelty-seeking' with regard to event behaviour? Where does 'nostalgia' fit in?

NOTE

1 A hypothesis is an idea or proposition which you construct and test through the research process to assess its validity. The construction of the hypothesis may have been constructed to test the existing theories or wisdom on the subject and it follows a scientific process of testing and verification.

FURTHER READING

Decrop, A. (2006). *Vacation Decision Making*. Wallingford: CABI.

Funk, D. (2008). *Consumer Behaviour in Sport and Events: Marketing Action*. Oxford: Butterworth-Heinemann.

Gibson, H. (ed.) (2006). *Sport Tourism: Concepts and Theories*. London: Routledge.

Parent, M. and Chappelet, J.-L. (eds) (2015). *Routledge Handbook of Sports Event Management*. Oxford: Routledge.

Chapter **9**

Planning and management of events

LEARNING OBJECTIVES

Upon completion of this chapter students should know the foundation concepts and main research approaches to increasing knowledge about the following dimensions of event planning and management:

- leadership (including organizational culture);
- organizational and inter-organizational behaviour (including organizational structure, coordination and stakeholder management);
- planning (strategic, project, business) and decision-making;
- sustainability as a concept and a process;
- operations and logistics (including service quality management);
- human resources (including volunteer management);
- financial management and control (including sponsorship);
- marketing and communications;
- risk, health and safety;
- research, evaluation and information systems.

Introduction

This is not a chapter on *how to* plan and manage events, but on what we need to know to study the management of events. By increasing knowledge, we make the job of event planning, design and management easier and more effective. Management is a broad field, encompassing business, not-for-profit and public administration, and planned events fall into all three categories. Most of the management functions associated with events are discussed in this chapter; however, programming and design have already been covered. There is no correct place to start, as all the management functions are crucial, but we have elected to start with leadership, including a discussion of event founders and organizational culture. For each management function a figure is provided to summarize major themes or topics covered, an indication of the disciplinary foundations for theory and methods, and unique issues or applications for events.

Leadership, founders and organizational culture

A 'leader' is someone who provides direction, or examples that others follow. Leadership is the pivotal role of managers (Mintzberg 1994) and of boards of directors. Of course, in many small organizations and informal events everyone chips in as needed, in which case leadership is somewhat of a collective process. Leadership in events requires the setting of a vision, developing strategies and goals, and inspiring everyone to work together towards those goals. Oakley and Krug (1991) believed that creative leaders empower their workers, but also take responsibility for all the decisions made by workers; they focus on goals and results, are both current and future oriented.

Group leadership, where no one dominates and all decisions are taken democratically, is an alternative approach, but difficult to implement – especially in projects where rapid decision-making is necessary. Events typically require both artistic and management leadership. An over-emphasis on business might stifle artistic innovation, whereas an over-emphasis on creativity might compromise the event's financial viability.

Leadership ability is essential for owners and founders of events, but leadership skills come to the fore, and have to be learned, as workers become supervisors and progress to become managers. Technical skills and hands-on operations have to give way to people skills such as motivating and problem-solving. At the highest management levels, conceptual knowledge (theory) is needed, as well as the ability to formulate visions, goals and strategies, alongside research and evaluation skills.

Derrett (2015: xiii) observed that: 'Some practitioners suggest that two vital characteristics of enduring festivals are vision and leadership.' Assuming that many events want to endure, their leadership and culture need to be focused on what it takes to succeed in meeting their most important goals. Other terms that help describe 'enduring' include 'sustainable', 'flourishing', 'resilient' and 'thriving'. Many would insist that 'profitable' or 'competitive' be added to this list. 'Resilience' is a key concept, as many events face crises that threaten their very existence; they must be able to recover or reinvent themselves. Elsewhere in this book we examine the concept of institutionalization, and it is highly relevant to leadership and culture (see Table 9.1).

Table 9.1 Leadership, founders and organizational culture

Leadership, founders, organizational culture	Foundations	Unique issues or applications for events
Leadership roles and styles	Psychology (personality)	Are event founders and leaders unique?
Power	Sociology and anthropology (culture; social groups)	
Organizational culture		Balancing creativity with managerial competence
Entrepreneurship	Economics (theories of the firm)	
Intrapreneurship		Business and social entrepreneurship

Power

Power and leadership go together. Owners of companies and events typically have the legal power to compel obedience, just as in the military. Boards of directors can use legal power to enforce their policies. Managers often have 'legitimate' power (Mintzberg 1983) by virtue of their position to direct or coerce the actions of subordinates. Other sources of power identified by Mintzberg include 'reward power' (the ability to bestow or withhold tangible and intangible rewards), 'expert power' (people follow because of superior knowledge or ability), 'information power' (obtained through control of vital information) and 'referent power' (stemming from loyalty and admiration).

Power and knowledge are inseparable, according to Stadler (2013). Drawing from the theories of Foucault (e.g. 1969, 1982), Stadler examined power–knowledge relations within the Queensland Music Festival community cultural development project and drew conclusions about how new knowledge was created within the community as well as the organization. With regard to community festivals, Clarke and Jepson (2011) looked at how a steering committee exercised power in restricting knowledge within the community; this exercise of power resulted in the communities not being able to feel ownership of the festival.

Leadership styles and roles

Boella (1992) discussed generic leadership styles, many of which are found but have not been studied within the events context. They include charismatic, autocratic, democratic, bureaucratic, inspirational, artistic, technocratic, entrepreneurial and visionary. While some managers seek to lead through a vision and setting a good example, others merely give orders. What is most effective in any given event setting is difficult to say, and deserves serious research. Van der Wagen (2006: 152) argued that leadership for events must be more flexible than in a typical business setting, sometimes being autocratic, as in a crisis, and at other times collaborative and appreciative.

Leadership roles

For the Sydney Summer Olympic Games of 2000 a graphical leadership model was developed, which placed the various leadership roles in a circle to emphasize the need for a non-linear approach (see Van der Wagen 2006). The three most important roles were thought to be 'energizing', 'appreciating' and 'managing time and stress' (this latter one is not usually considered in management texts). The more usual roles of planning, coordinating, controlling, directing, decision-making and informing were also included. 'Energizing' (2006: 151) was thought to be essential in celebrations, to create and sustain the right atmosphere for guests, staff and volunteers. The longer the timeframe, the more difficult it is to keep everyone's energy levels high.

9.1 RESEARCH NOTES ON LEADERSHIP

Davies, A. (2011). Local leadership and rural renewal through festival fun: The case of Snowfest. In C. Gibson and J. Connell (eds), *Festival Places: Revitalising Rural Australia*, pp. 61–73. Bristol: Channel View.

'Festivals catalyse social networking, capacity building and entrepreneurial capacities.' This chapter focuses on how festivals catalyse local leadership of the transformational kind, that is, not just getting the festival job done, but fostering a sense of moving beyond immediate problems and self-interest to benefit the wider community. The leader and followers engage in an exchange process whereby leaders inspire (they are charismatic), stimulate (intellectually) and give individualized attention to their followers. Results, unfortunately, cannot easily be measured. But Davies asserts there were noticeable attitude changes towards the value of local participation in socio-economic adaptation processes and in particular towards the benefits of tourism.

Reversté, F. and Izard, O. (2011). The role of social and intangible factors in cultural event planning in Catalonia. *International Journal of Event and Festival Management*, 2(1), 37–53.

'This study considers three elements of social capital which play a role in event planning (motivation, internal network creation and leadership) and analyses their impact on the local tourism industry. This study's primary conclusion is that events with SC elements which strengthen their social cohesion, view and justify the event as a socializing fact, regardless of the scope of tourism at these functions. Additionally, research showed that the creation of relationship networks strengthened the community's internal cohesion, representativeness and sense of identity. Finally, leadership elements which increase visibility and connect the event to external networks explain the current differences between events' tourism appeal and impact.'

Can leaders be trained?

Goldblatt (2004) suggested that event leaders need to have the qualities of integrity, confidence, persistence, collaboration, problem-solving, communication skills and vision. Locke (1991) identified personality traits found in successful leaders, but many people reject the notion that leaders (or entrepreneurs) are born, or that certain traits lead to success. Van der Wagen (2006: 222) describes an approach to event leadership training that includes imparting knowledge about the event, the organization, the workforce/volunteers and their tasks. Potential leaders also engage in self-analysis of their own attributes and potential strengths or deficiencies. Specific advice from experienced event leaders can help to develop decision-making ability and lead to desirable behaviour.

The event founder as leader

How do events get started? Somebody, or a group, has to take the initiative, and this leadership can continue well into the lifespan of the event and its organization. One of the leadership styles is entrepreneurial, and we need to explore this in more detail because of its importance in both business and the other management environments.

Entrepreneurs (social and private)

The term 'entrepreneur' is not easy to define, and there are two major schools of thought about entrepreneurship: that it is a personality trait held by rather unique persons; or that it is one or more actions that can be observed and measured. Furthermore, entrepreneurship can apply to personal business ventures or to social situations. The 'personality trait theory' suggests that entrepreneurs are born, not made. Some people are compelled (or have an inborn propensity) to create businesses or events, seek out opportunities that others ignore (especially in terms of finding a niche in the marketplace), pull together resources (often through personal networking), take personal risks and (but not necessarily) create personal wealth. Innovation or creativity is often thought to be inherent in entrepreneurs, and this is certainly evident among those who establish festivals and other events.

Being one's own boss, or wanting to take a hands-on approach to work, is also a personality trait clearly associated with people who start up new businesses or events. Entrepreneurs are not discouraged by failures, and often bounce back from a failure to try again. 'Serial entrepreneurs' keep starting new ventures in a rather restless fashion, which leads some observers to think of them as socially dysfunctional or psychologically disturbed.

If the motivations driving entrepreneurs are mostly personal, or connected to family values and goals, they are clearly within the realm of business and microeconomics. But there is little doubt that 'social entrepreneurs' are very active in the arts, leading to establishment of many not-for-profit festivals and events. A 'social entrepreneur' might also work within governmental or not-for-profit organizations to create profits (or profitable events) to be used for social projects. Cause-related events can be created this way.

'New venture' creation is the starting point for discussing entrepreneurship as observable activity. Starting up an event could be motivated by the desire for profit or social good. Risks are inherent in this process, especially when it comes to acquiring and spending one's own and other people's money. Reputations are also at stake. The entrepreneur's personal network can be vital at this start-up stage and in the subsequent years when vital support and resources have to be sustained through effective stakeholder management.

Intrapreneurship

Within organizations 'intrapreneurship' can be a valuable process, but it usually has to be fostered. Can a whole organization, or a group within, really behave as if they were private entrepreneurs? The object would be to encourage innovation in particular, hopefully leading to higher profits or other forms of corporate effectiveness. In this context it is possible to establish new events, or bid on them, within a government or tourist agency. Another application would be within an event production company that wants to stay ahead of the competition, or within a large corporation that sponsors or produces its own events.

Often it is necessary to set up specific intrapreneurial units to achieve these corporate goals, and such units need leadership. By nature, persons attracted to government and corporate employment might be lacking in those entrepreneurial traits necessary for innovation. Or at least they might lack experience in new venture creation. In such cases there is a serious risk of creating a culture clash!

Organizational culture

Culture in general is based on shared beliefs, values, practices or attitudes, and it is a concept of importance to companies and other organizations. Schein (1985) defined organizational culture as:

> *A pattern of shared basic assumptions that the group learned as it solved its problems of external adaptation and internal integration, that has worked well enough to be considered valid and, therefore, to be taught to new members as the correct way you perceive, think, and feel in relation to those problems.*

In a strong cultural context everyone works together towards common goals because they share the vision and underlying values of the organization. This is where event founders have the greatest influence, in establishing the 'core values', but this unity of purpose can fade with time. In other organizations, recruitment, indoctrination and compulsory conformity to norms ensures that values are preserved, but at the cost of individual choice and expression. In both situations, if everyone thinks the same way – called 'groupthink' – there is a serious risk that innovation will be stifled.

According to Schein an observer can assess organizational culture by first identifying superficial but 'tangible attributes' such as facilities, rewards, dress and interactions. The 'professed culture' of an organization is reflected in its mission statements, codes of conduct, public statements, and the expressed values and attitudes of members. At the third and deepest level are an organization's 'tacit or unseen assumptions'. They can be unspoken rules, guiding behaviour and decisions in a taken-for-granted manner. The researcher or member might have to spend a lot of time within an organization to come to any conclusion about its deepest cultural values.

Hofstede (1980) demonstrated that there are national and regional cultural groupings that affect the behaviour of organizations. These five characteristics of culture can be influential in all organizations:

1. 'power distance' – refers to the degree to which a society expects that some individuals wield larger amounts of power than others;

2. 'uncertainty avoidance' – reflects the extent to which a society accepts uncertainty and risk; this is associated with entrepreneurship;

3. 'individualism versus collectivism' – refers to the extent to which people are expected to act on their own versus being a loyal group member;

4. 'masculinity versus femininity' – male values supposedly include competitiveness, assertiveness, ambition, and the accumulation of wealth and material possessions;

5. 'long- versus short-term orientation' – describes the importance attached to the future (fostering stewardship and sustainable development) versus immediate profit or gratification.

There is no doubt that organizations evolve in terms of their culture, and this affects other management functions in profound ways. Getz (1993a) observed that festival organizations exhibited life-cycle dynamics, and that festival founders did shape their culture. Several festivals in Calgary were seen to have experienced cultural crises, such as changes in strategic direction, which occurred when founders were replaced by newcomers.

O'Toole and Mikolaitis (2002) emphasized the importance of understanding culture when producing corporate events. Such events have to 'fit' in terms of company values, goals, politics and style. But despite the importance of culture within mainstream management theory and practice, there have been few event-related studies published that even mention the concept.

Strategic event creation and public policy

Perhaps the most significant aspect of modern planned events is their elevation from the private, community and institutional domains to a formal incorporation into numerous public policy domains. Events of all kinds are being supported, created and bid on, to meet diverse, strategic goals of society. This has several important implications related to leadership, culture and management. For example, those who plan and produce events are often dealing with a single client but are held accountable to a very wide group of stakeholders. This fact also applies to many events produced for corporations and non-profit societies.

Researchers have examined various policy domains that lead to strategic creation, subsidy or facilitation of planned events and their venues. Strategic tourism roles have been well explored (e.g. Stokes 2008). Swart (2005) argued for strategic planning of sport-event tourism in South Africa. Presenza and Sheehan (2013) commented on the strategic value of a portfolio of sport events in destination development, and it is inevitable that portfolios and populations of events are strategically planned in the future.

Mules (1993) pointed out the roles of events in urban renewal strategies, a theme which has since been expanded to include urban economic and social revitalization and repositioning from a branding perspective (e.g. Duignan 2013). Pugh and Wood (2004) examined multiple reasons for event support in London, including place marketing, pride and economic development. Cultural development is also a well-explored theme, particularly in the context of cities of culture (Richards 2007a; Richards and Palmer 2010).

While in many countries local and regional/state governments and their agencies have been at the forefront, national-level policies and strategies related to events cannot be ignored. Khodr (2012) scrutinized political reasons for Qatar's event strategy, concluding that explanatory factors include economic sustainability and diversification, tourism, and social development strategies; these factors can be viewed in the light of globalization and modernization trends. Houlihan *et al.* (2015) identify reasons why countries host major sport events, including: a desire for increased legitimacy and positive image; boosting sport participation and competitiveness; being a catalyst for urban economic regeneration; economic modernization; allowing for diplomatic initiatives connected to international relations; nation and city identity-building and branding, and fostering social integration.

Resources utilized by events are often heavily competed for, by groups with many legitimate and appealing claims about their cultural, social, economic or environmental benefits. Therefore, the allocation of public resources (including subsidies) to events generally requires their organizers and producers to explicitly justify their public benefits.

Those who produce events that are at least partially in the public domain have a far greater planning, control and evaluation challenge than those who produce small, private events. Professionalism and the credentialling of event managers are increasingly demanded by funding agencies because of the need for open, public accountability and for liability reasons. Finally, the sustainability of periodic events is of public interest and is directly linked to specific policies on funding, regulations, subsidies, facility development, etc.

9.2 RESEARCH NOTE ON FESTIVAL LEADERSHIP

Quinn, B. (2006). Problematising 'festival tourism': Arts festivals and sustainable development in Ireland. *Journal of Sustainable Tourism*, 14(3), 288–306.

Qualitative and longitudinal research was conducted on the Wexford Festival Opera and Galway Arts Festival through archival research, interviews, resident and visitor questionnaires. In terms of their management, Quinn found that festivals tend to 'emerge as bottom-up enterprises, small in size, local in scale and, initially, heavily dependent on dedicated volunteers'. Wexford's emerged from the city's social and economic elite, but they were careful to involve a broad section of the community. 'Politicians lobbied for resources, business people sought financial support from local businesses and the church leaders praised the festival in their Sunday sermons.' Festival relationships with the Arts Council of Ireland, state tourism agency, national media and commercial sponsors 'have all placed increasing pressure on the festival organisations to view the arts through economic lenses'. Tourism has been especially important for Wexford in terms of paying audiences and protection from arts critics. Being a successful tourist attraction makes both the Wexford and Galway festivals worthy of state support and corporate sponsorship (i.e. committed stakeholders).

Organizational and inter-organizational behaviour

Organizations are social groups, and therefore sociology and social psychology have made substantial theoretical contributions to our understanding of how they function and change (see Table 9.2). Microeconomics is also relevant, pertaining especially to how firms acquire and utilize resources. In the research literature little attention has been paid to event organizations, although some progress has been made in examining events in the context of collaboration and stakeholder management, and regarding human resources and especially volunteers.

Table 9.2 Organizational and inter-organizational behaviour

Organizational and inter-organizational behaviour	Foundations	Unique event issues or applications
Ownership	Sociology and social psychology (social groups and networks)	How are public, for-profit and not-for-profit events different?
Governance		
Organizational structures	Economics (theories of the firm)	Governance and management challenges facing the volunteer event organization
Open-system diagnostics		
Organizational quality		Special challenges facing one-time and pulsating events
Evolutionary stages		
Bureaucratization		
Institutionalization		
The learning organization		
Inter-organizational relationships (stakeholders)		

Ziakas and Costa (2010) employed network analysis to examine the inter-organizational patterns that shape a host community's capacity to capitalize on its event portfolio. This method allows for the identification of linkages, both strong and weak, central organizations and the nature of interactions. These researchers believe that analysis of inter-institutional networks can suggest a community's capacity for building and managing an event portfolio, and can be used as a strategic tool.

Ownership, governance and organizational structure

There are three generic ownership, or legal, models found in the events world: (1) private, for-profit companies that produce events; (2) government agencies (such as parks and recreation, sport or arts and culture) that produce or facilitate events; and (3) the large not-for-profit sector that includes clubs, charities and event-specific organizations like festival societies. Andersson and Getz (2009) systematically compared festivals in four countries in terms of their ownership, governance, structure and content. They concluded that although the festivals offered a similar product and had similar mandates, they differed considerably in terms of revenue sources, cost structure, use of volunteers, corporate sponsorship and decision-making. These differences are potentially important to destinations that view festivals as attractions and use them in place marketing.

There has been little research published on the relative advantages or problems associated with these ownership types, or the business models they follow to provide their 'products' and 'services'. One important question to be addressed is whether or not they are substitutable. For example, in China and other countries local authorities are the dominant producers of festivals and other events. Can they create private or not-for-profit organizations to take over from the public sector? Clearly legal and cultural constraints exist, especially in societies without a strong volunteering or entrepreneurial tradition. And how is a festival or event different, better or more sustainable if it is produced by one of these forms of organization? From a tourism or economic development perspective, is it better to work with public-sector events or the other types?

'Governance' is a big issue. In for-profit companies there are owners and employees, so the question of who runs the business is generally clear. In government agencies there can be a confusing and stifling bureaucracy to deal with. Within not-for-profit societies, the relationships between boards of directors and professional staff have to be sorted out. Who sits on the board is a major issue, especially with regard to the pros and cons of involving key stakeholders. In all-volunteer events, governance and coordination present special challenges, and the organizations can be faced with dissenting opinions within or takeover attempts by organized, external interest groups.

Dredge and Whitford (2011) viewed governance as a form of public/private policy-making that requires stakeholders to get together for discussion and to take action to achieve common goals. This approach embodies the notion of collaboration and the process of consensus-building.

This entire area of organizational structure and coordination (both internal and external) has largely been untouched by event researchers, although plenty of advice is available through professional associations and books written by experts. It ties closely to other topics covered in this chapter, including decision-making and planning. The second level of concern is organizational structure, which has a direct bearing on stakeholder relationships, internal coordination and control. A number of typical structures are illustrated and discussed in Getz (2005), including single and multi-organizational structures. Festivals are often produced by clubs, internally, and by stand-alone not-for-profit societies, but it is also common to find different organizations cooperating to produce events. As well, sport events are frequently produced through formal links between governing bodies and local organizing committees.

Open-system theory and the learning organization

No organization can exist independently of its environment; indeed it has to be 'open' to obtain resources. Its impacts (especially for events) are also felt by the community and environment, giving rise to many stakeholder claims. There is a 'general environment' in which global forces have to be considered through environmental and future scanning, and a 'community context' which includes most event stakeholders and the origin of most 'inputs' (information, support and resources). The 'internal environment' is the organization that produces the event, and all its management systems.

In this conceptualization (see Figure 9.1), the event (its theme, programme, facilitated experiences) is a 'transforming process' intended to achieve specific desired outcomes. There can also be unintended 'outcomes', and 'externalities' – like pollution – that are not normally accounted for by the event organizers. However, multiple stakeholders will evaluate the event and its organization, and this process is labelled 'external evaluation'. The 'internal evaluation' process is the task of managers or owners who have to determine if they are meeting their goals (i.e. their effectiveness) and how efficiently they are utilizing their resources. Evaluation and feedback should influence future decision-making through strategic planning.

'Open-system diagnostics' involves using this model to identify problems and to improve both efficiency and effectiveness. 'Effectiveness' means the degree to which goals are obtained or the organization fulfils its mandate. Use of the model helps in identifying how the mandate and goals are externally driven by various stakeholders and environmental forces, and how transforming processes are directed towards achieving those goals. Evaluation systems have to be directed towards identifying goal attainment, although the 'goal-free evaluation' approach sometimes has benefits. 'Efficiency' refers to how well resources are used to generate the desired outcomes. The model suggests ways to improve the flow and use of resources, to cut costs (such as heavy administration costs) and to evaluate outcomes achieved in terms of resources required (i.e. measures of costs and benefits).

Note that 'outcome', 'output', 'impacts' and 'consequences' are often used synonymously. However, the term 'output' is usually reserved for a mechanical or manufacturing process. Elsewhere, we use the term 'impact' in a different sense, stressing that impacts are often perceived or felt in a subjective way.

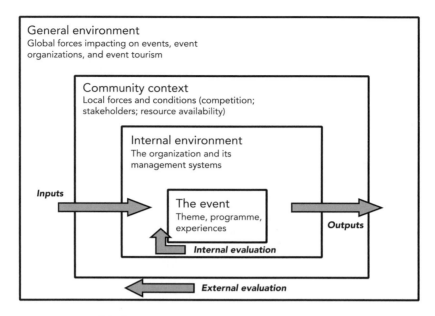

Figure 9.1 Open-system model of event management

Source: Adapted from Getz and Frisby (1988).

How do organizations 'learn' and retain memory? Senge (1990: 3) said that the 'learning organization' is one in which 'people continuously expand their capacity to create the results they truly desire, where new and expansive patterns of thinking are nurtured, where collective aspiration is set free, and where people are continually learning to learn together' (also see Senge *et al.* 1994). In part, this is a reflection of organizational culture, and in part it can be facilitated through constant research, evaluation and reflection. The open-system model is a good starting point for structuring the learning process.

'Benchmarking' against other events is another way by which managers learn. To a degree, studying other events is both inevitable and good, but it can and does result in copying and standardization. Proper benchmarking looks at the ways successful organizations do things, in other words their processes or 'best practices'. Getz (1998a) studied the searching and sharing practices of festival organizers and classified them as being 'inward or outward-looking organizations'. Searching was either formal or informal in nature, and varied a lot in terms of space (local through international), substance (comparisons with similar festivals versus all events) and theoretical (education) versus experiential (learning though visits and conversations).

Organizational quality and standards

Any discussion of event programme or service quality has to include the 'quality' of the organization producing the event. The people producing events have to demonstrate professionalism and competency, trustworthiness and reliability. Policy on organizational quality is a direct reflection of culture and vision. It will have to cover organizational philosophy, ensure proper documentation in all the management systems, effectively engage all staff and volunteers, and take into account all outcomes. Bowdin and Church (2000) argued that quality programmes cost money, but the investment is quickly recovered by reducing waste and eliminating failures. Over time the costs of auditing and evaluation decline.

Standards prepared for the meetings industry have been developed. These are called MBECS and they have been reviewed by Cecil *et al.* (2013). Professional standards of this kind provide the basis for curriculum design and for continuous learning. They do not (like EMBOK and other body-of-knowledge systems) actually provide the knowledge or skills, as that role falls to educators and occurs through real-life experience.

The ISO 21021 standards for 'Sustainable Events Management' (download at www.iso.org) fall into this category as they lay out procedures for event organizations to follow in pursuit of a 'triple-bottom-line' approach to sustainability. These types of standards are intended to lead to improved organization and planning, with the aim of preventing or ameliorating negative impacts and maximizing desired outcomes. They typically include the following:

- designing a sustainability policy;
- issue identification and evaluation;
- stakeholder identification and engagement;
- objectives, targets and plans;
- performance against principles of sustainable development;
- operational controls;
- competence and training;
- supply chain management;
- communication;
- monitoring and measurement;
- corrective and preventive action;
- management system audits;
- management review.

Evolution, bureaucratization and institutionalization

Organizations have to be created, as in the establishment of a legal corporation or not-for-profit society, or they evolve from informal organizations. For example, many professionally managed festivals and events have evolved from club-produced events. Once established, there can be an evolution towards greater 'formality', emergence of leadership and increasing 'professionalization' (in terms of hiring professional staff and professional conduct) and 'bureaucratization' including formal committee systems and strategic planning (Katz, 1981).

Frisby and Getz (1989) modelled this hypothetical evolution for festivals, noting that at each evolutionary stage there was a risk of having to return to the previous stage owing to failure or loss of resources. They also suggested that in cities, with larger populations and presumably more resources to draw on, festivals were more likely to professionalize.

Richards and Ryan (2004) adapted the Frisby and Getz (1989) model by suggesting three axes: (1) 'informal/ grassroots resource base'; (2) 'organizational age'; and (3) 'organized public and private sector involvement'. They argued (1989: 96) that 'being a grassroots event does not preclude the adoption of a formal or professional approach to event organization'. Professionalism, they said, can be externally imposed on an event organization.

In Schein's (1985) conceptualization of the evolution of organizational culture, various crises are likely to occur as the organization evolves, linked to leadership changes and value conflicts, particularly as sub-cultures emerge. Richards and Ryan (2004), through their historical assessment of the evolution of the Aotearoa Traditional Maori Performing Arts Festival in New Zealand, agreed that various crises will accompany event maturation. In their case study the issues or crises stemmed from the need to achieve financial stability, addressing the festival's cultural orientation and significance, gender issues, the increasing roles of media and sponsors, the representations of groups and regions, and tensions between competitive and performative orientations.

Why do some events, like the Calgary Stampede (profiled in Getz 1993b, 1997, 2005), become permanent institutions in their communities? Can all events aspire to this status, and should they? One meaning of the word 'institution' is that of 'constraints or rules that induce stability in human interaction' (Voss 2001). These arise because societies face recurrent problems, so that when we call an organization an 'institution', we are saying that it exists to deal with a fundamental – or at least important – social need (including cultural and economic needs). Since not all people can be directly involved in creating institutions, a set of actors, or stakeholders, has to decide on – or establish through repeated interactions or interdependencies – the rules or the organizations to deal with major social problems. Stability in these institutions has direct benefit to the stakeholders, or society as a whole, and should ideally generate increased efficiency in resource use.

The study of institutions is very well established. Selznick (1957) distinguished between institutions as tools to accomplish specific tasks, and institutions to which people formed commitments. Emile Durkheim (as reported in Traugott 1978) argued that sociological analysis should discover the causes, mechanisms and effects of institutions on societal life. Essentially, institutions regularize social life, and may foster cooperation and increase efficiency. Applicable to many festivals, it can also be said that institutions are like 'public goods' in that all members of society may benefit from them, whether or not they contribute to their establishment and upkeep. Coleman (1988, 1990) believed that institutions are part of what is often called 'social capital'. An anthropological perspective (Sahlins 1976) suggests that cultural institutions mainly serve symbolic purposes.

Another way of looking at institutions is through the lens of evolutionary game theory. Young (1998) showed that certain institutions arise as equilibria in games played by members of a population of agents who recurrently interact. This ties institutional theory directly to stakeholder and network theory. As well, since powerful agents or special interest groups might create and support institutions, there is a need to take a political science and welfarist approach to their study.

A central focus of the 'old' study of institutions is the evolving relationship between an organization and its environment, which of course includes all its stakeholder interactions. 'New institutionalism', according to Heimer (2001), is an outcome of organizational sociology. It focuses on the process (symbolic reasons are emphasized) by which a practice or structure is diffused, becomes a prerequisite for legitimacy (among key stakeholders), is taken for granted and is expected.

By definition, therefore, an event that becomes an 'institution' exists with a specific mandate or purpose, is permanent, and fulfils an important social role or solves social problems. A community cannot do without its institutions, and when threatened they will receive strong support; if they disappear, others will have to be created to carry on their functions. Very few events fit these criteria, yet recent research involving a survey of festivals in Sweden suggests that many festival managers actually believe their event to be an 'institution' (Getz and Andersson 2008).

Figure 9.2 (adapted from Getz and Andersson 2008) suggests the process by which an event (as a permanent organization) might evolve or strategically become a permanent institution in its community. The key process is transitioning from an internal to an external orientation, as many events – especially in their early years – are very focused on their internal processes and stakeholders. Relationships with external stakeholders will probably increase in number and complexity over time, and the most important of them can be brought into legal or moral 'ownership' (through share offerings or board directorships) or other forms of long-term partnership, including sponsorship.

It appears that increasing dependency on committed stakeholders is a large part of becoming an institution. In other words, independence might have to be sacrificed for sustainability. The Stampede reflects this evolution, with the City of Calgary owning the land, having a permanent representative on the Stampede board, and assisting the Stampede in its ongoing development plans. Richards and Ryan (2004: 115) also concluded that the history of the Aotearoa Traditional Maori Performing Arts Festival

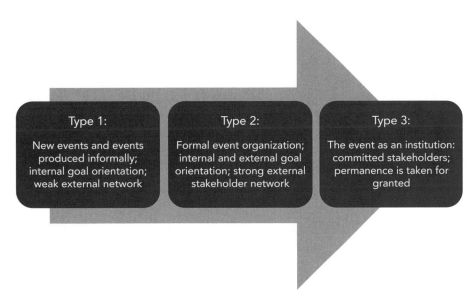

Figure 9.2 Hypothetical institutionalization process for events

Source: adapted from Getz and Andersson (2008).

> *illustrates that cultural festivals mirror many different dynamics and are places of discourse between different paradigms of traditional and evolving culture, between minority and majority groupings, between a need for independence and a dependency, usually on public authorities that might in other circumstances be seen as part of the majority-dominated structures.*

Another way to look at this institutionalization process is to think of what it means to become a 'hallmark event'. If the destination and event are co-branding, their images mutually reinforcing, this suggests institutional status.

One-time versus permanent event organizations

There are big differences between permanent event organizations, such as festival societies that produce annual events, and one-time organizations that have to be decommissioned when the event is over. Little attention has been paid to the one-time event organization from a theoretical or even a comparative perspective. Typically established for major sport events or world's fairs, the one-time event organization has to engage in project planning and apply a project management organizational model.

One of the unique aspects of permanent event organizations is their 'pulsating' nature (Hanlon and Cuskelly 2002). They need a permanent, small core of volunteers and professionals, but must be able to substantially expand their staff and volunteer force to produce the event. This is examined later in the Human Resources section.

Inter-organizational behaviour

The need for resources requires that organizations engage with individuals (like customers) and with other organizations. Theories of resource dependency, population ecology, collaboration, network and stakeholder theory are powerful when trying to explain external relationships. Another look at stakeholder theory is warranted here, as some pertinent research has been completed regarding events.

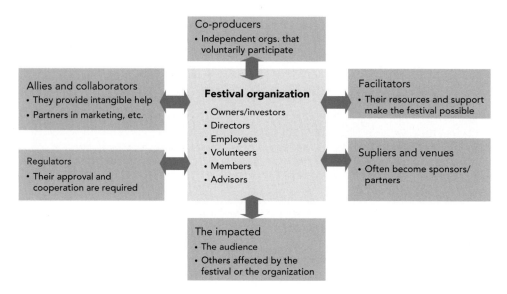

Figure 9.3 Major stakeholder types and roles in festival networks

Source: Getz *et al.* (2007). Reprinted from *Event Management*, 10 (2/3), Getz, D., Andersson, T., and Larson, M. Festival stakeholder roles: Concepts and case studies 103–122. Copyright (2007) with the permission of Cognizant Communication Corporation.

Stakeholder management

The paper by Getz *et al.* (2007) described and classified external festival stakeholders based on case studies from Sweden and Calgary. Figure 9.3 shows the resulting conceptualization. The various categories are not mutually exclusive, and indeed the research showed clearly that some stakeholders have multiple roles. For example, city government is often simultaneously a 'facilitator' (giving grants and other resources), 'co-producer' (sharing staff and venues), 'owner/controller' (being on the board of directors) and 'regulator', which can make its event-related policies confusing or contradictory.

'Suppliers and venues' are often brought into the festival organization as sponsors; this is generally recognized as being a good strategy for reducing dependency and costs. 'Allies and collaborators' might include marketing partnerships with tourism or the collaborative work of professional and affinity groups. How these stakeholders wield power and negotiate the goals and strategies of the event can be referred to as a 'political market square' (Larson and Wikstrom 2001; Larson 2002).

9.3 RESEARCH NOTES ON STAKEHOLDER MANAGEMENT

Parent, M. and Slack, T. (2008). Conformity and resistance: Preparing a francophone sporting event in North America. *Event Management*, 11(3), 129–143.

'This article seeks to examine the competing conforming and resistance pressures for an organizing committee. Findings from a case study relating to the *Jeux de la Francophonie*, or Games of La Francophonie, highlighted the presence of conflicting pressures between the North American context of the organizing committee and the European, Francophone context of the event's international body, which impacted goal setting, funding/commercialization, athlete/artist calibre, sanctioning, and international government relationship and VIP treatment. The nature of the event, the stakeholders involved and the event's setting or context were found to be interrelated sources of pressures on the organizing committee.'

Izzo, F., Bonetti, E. and Masiello, B. (2012). Strong ties within cultural organization event networks and local development in a tale of three festivals. *Event Management*, 16, 223–244.

'The purpose of this article is to provide a deeper understanding of successful event networks and offer a conceptual framework which can be used to analyse their impact on local development. In particular, this study addresses two research questions. First, how does network structure affect the success of the event and its outcomes on local development, other than in economic terms? Second, which main capabilities does the "network orchestrator" need to promote the effectiveness of the event network? By analysing three different Italian cultural festivals – "Festivaletteratura" ("Festival of Literature" – Mantua), "Festival della Scienza" ('Festival of Science" – Genoa) and "Festivalfilosofia" ("Festival of Philosophy" – Modena, Carpi, Sassuolo) – this article sheds light on: (a) the features of successful event networks, (b) the dynamics linking network structure and the social outcomes generated, and (c) the typical bundle of relational capabilities that network orchestrators need. Then it draws some implications for management and offers some remarks to stimulate further research in the field of special events.'

Corporate social responsibility and a social licence to operate

Powerful event owners and their backers can usually achieve what they want through the complicity of political and industry collaborators, often resulting in a complete absence of meaningful community input, and, in the worst cases, the actual suppression of dissent. This runs counter to the principles of CSR, in which corporations (including events) should seek a licence to operate from the affected community. For permanent events, this is a matter of stakeholder inclusion and becoming an institution, whereas for one-time events it is a risky proposition. What if the community objects and politicians are faced with angry mobs? Should those planning a mega event subject themselves to such a process? On the other hand, building community trust well in advance should result in increased ticket sales and volunteering.

9.4 RESEARCH NOTE ON CORPORATE SOCIAL RESPONSIBILITY

Dowling, M., Robinson, L. and Washington, M. (2013). Taking advantage of the London 2012 Olympic Games: Corporate social responsibility through sport partnerships. *European Sport Management Quarterly*, 13(3), 269–292.

'This research explores the ways in which corporate organizations leveraged corporate social responsibility (CSR) through a sport initiative that was conceived, implemented and mediated by the British Olympic Association (BOA) preceding the London 2012 Olympic Games. This research aimed to evaluate the initiative in order to understand the benefits, barriers and partnership working and sought to answer the question: how is CSR being leveraged through sport by corporate organizations in the lead up to mega-sporting events?'

Planning and decision-making

Planning is a future-oriented process in which organizations set goals and put in place actions to attain them. It is always political, with groups in society or within organizations competing for influence or resources. Although planning by nature should be a rational process, it is clear that decisions in the events sector are often made in an irrational manner (for examples, see Armstrong 1985; Butler and Grigg 1987; Bramwell 1997).

Planning is often focused on conflicts and problems, and researchers Phi and Dredge (2014) have examined events in this light using Q method. They explored problem structuring through a case study of the Australian World Rally Championship.

Decision-making

Are leaders and managers 'rational' when it comes to making decisions? Surely the whole emphasis on planning and research is intended to produce rational decisions that achieve goals, yet Bramwell (1997) concluded that for mega events, there was little evidence of a rigorous application of the full planning cycle as advocated in planning texts. Laybourn (2004) explored theory on decision-making and applied it to the events sector. She found that the generic literature supports the contention that decision-makers are not naturally rational! They tend to use simplifying short-cuts called 'heuristics'. In particular, potential negative impacts are commonly underestimated, which has serious implications for risk assessment and management at events. When people stand to gain from a decision they tend to be more cautious than when they stand to take a loss. And of course everyone notices when something goes wrong, whereas competency and success might be ignored.

Current decisions are strongly influenced by previous decisions, especially when a lot of money has been invested, leading to 'entrapment'. There is a natural tendency to want to recover 'sunk costs' (i.e. money already spent) and maximize return on investments made. This can help explain why risky decisions are made, and the frequent pursuit of losing courses of action, despite obvious and compelling arguments to the contrary. There are always costs of withdrawal to consider, but perhaps more important is 'losing face'.

Laybourn also emphasized that decision-making is affected by personality, perceptions, emotions and moods, social factors, experience, the cost of information, time constraints and gender. There are many constraints on perfect knowledge and perfect judgement, so people should be trained in effective decision-making. A variety of techniques can be used to aid decision-making, including the 'decision tree', or mathematical modelling as found in operations research and management science (see Table 9.3). But do event planners and managers use them?

Table 9.3 Planning and decision-making

Planning and decision-making	Foundations	Unique event issues or applications
Rationality vs. irrationality	Psychology (cognition and environmental)	Events are projects
Heuristics		The need for event producers to think strategically, and to manage the organization like a business
Incrementalism	Sociology (social groups and networks)	
Advocacy		
Feasibility	Mathematics and engineering (systems modelling)	High likelihood of organizational crises
Project planning		
Strategic planning		
Business planning		

Planning theory

'Rational planning' is always future oriented, involving a vision, the setting of goals, consideration of alternative courses of action and their potential consequences, the formulation and implementation of strategies and actions to realize goals, and continuous evaluation and feedback in order to improve the system. It is a process – it is continuously evolving and hopefully learning from past mistakes. Planning is always political, especially when public agencies or public money are involved, but even within organizations 'politics' (that is, the resolution of competing claims and goals) is always a factor.

Not everyone believes in or practises rational planning (for general reviews of planning theory and practice see Mandelbaum *et al.* 1996; Sandercock 1998; and Campbell and Fanstein 2003). 'Muddling through' and 'incrementalism' are alternative approaches to managing organizations and events, although few professionals would admit to being 'muddlers'. 'Incrementalism', that is, developing or progressing slowly, in measured steps, is a defensible approach when uncertainty or complexity is high. It does not attempt to be comprehensive, but attacks problems and policy issues with precision instruments rather than broad strategies. It is also closely connected to the notion of a 'political market square', in which decisions are made through bargaining and the exercise of power among all the stakeholders, rather than by professional planners or technocrats. 'Collaborative' or 'consensus-building processes' are similarly intended to involve all parties and points of view, but with the emphasis on formal issue identification and conflict resolution. It is arguable, however, whether rational planning or incrementalism is more democratic or effective.

'Advocacy' is another approach to planning, policy and decision-making that might have relevance to the events sector. Advocacy is based on the premise that disadvantaged and marginalized groups in society are normally left out of planning and policy-making and therefore their interests must be represented by others. To the degree that citizen involvement or 'community-based planning' works, advocacy should not be needed, but that is a seldom-achieved ideal.

Various approaches to planning for leisure, sport and tourism, most of which have some application in the field of events planning, were explained by Veal (2010: 160). The first is 'fixed standards of provision', and this one is more suitable for parks and sport/recreation facilities than for services and events. It is difficult to imagine any government setting standards such as 'a festival for every 100,000 persons', or 'a consumer show every six months in every city'. It makes little sense to take this approach, yet if a whole-population approach is taken (discussed elsewhere) there might be some justification for public authorities to set targets for celebrations and sports. Veal argued that standards are often based on conditions that no longer apply, or on a specific value set from interest groups, so the process of setting standards is political.

Providing opportunities (i.e. events) for a diverse range of business and leisure interests is another approach. In a commercial context it means that companies and organizations respond to expressed demand or felt needs and the government does not intervene. For public agencies it means ensuring that there are sufficient numbers and types of events to please most segments of the population. There is no published evidence that this is part of any government policy, although it is a logical implication of taking a whole-population approach. More likely is the provision of festivals and events for 'deprived' segments of the population (especially those with low incomes) and in areas where better social integration is desired. Those are both needs-based approaches.

In a stakeholder-based or community-development approach, facilities and services – and possibly events – would be planned according to democratic means, from the ground up. A bottom-up approach has the clear advantage of gaining political legitimacy and reflecting the perceived needs and priorities of the residents who are served. In many places this is done indirectly, and incompletely, through the actions of not-for-profit organizations which often claim to meet public needs and fill gaps in government services. Two major issues will arise in the bottom-up approach: where do the resources come from to meet stakeholder demands? And are all residents and groups equally consulted and served?

From a free-market approach, it could also be suggested that public demand, manifested in ticket sales, should determine what events are held. This could be modified for event tourism as specific target segments are of high value, within the context of a strategic, portfolio approach to bidding on and creating events. That approach is unique to event tourism, as it follows from specific economic and place-marketing goals.

If the desired outcomes can be expressed for specific events and whole populations, employing a triple-bottom-line approach, then events planning can devise strategies to achieve these goals. This leads to our later discussions of impact assessments and the difficulty of proving that events achieve certain benefits, or that benefits outweigh costs. The easiest case to prove is that of tourism attractiveness, as event tourists can generally be identified and their economic impacts estimated fairly accurately. Unfortunately, not all costs are considered in many impact studies. One goal, borrowed from leisure, sports and the arts that does make perfect sense for events planning, is that of achieving increases in public participation through the vehicle of providing and hosting events. If there are more participatory events that create leisure, sport and artistic opportunities, then we should see increased participation leading to other benefits. Less certain is the often-made claim that hosting spectator and mega events will generate increased participation.

Events as a sector are not generally the subject of direct government planning, as they become subsumed under the headings of sport, arts/culture, leisure or business/trade. Tourism planning for events is at an immature stage in most countries and cities, remaining largely ad hoc and opportunistic.

Project planning and feasibility studies

Rooted in engineering, where project planning is a vital skill, and in logistics (which has to be mastered in the military), project planning is applicable to all events – even those produced by permanent organizations which also do strategic planning. The basic nature of events is that they are defined by time (a limited duration) and their schedule is announced and usually fixed well in advance. This necessitates getting all the planning and preparations done according to a fixed and often tight schedule. According to O'Toole (2000), many event projects fail, or overrun their budget and schedule, and perhaps this is due to poor planning or control systems.

'Feasibility studies' should ideally precede, or at least accompany, project planning. In a rational planning process we do not commit to an event until we know it is affordable, desirable, environmentally sound, marketable and manageable. All too often, however, events are bid on and planned without full feasibility studies or cost and benefit forecasts, generally arising from corporate and political influences rather than public input.

Two key books which focus on this topic are *Events Feasibility and Development: From Strategy to Operations* (O'Toole 2011) and *Corporate Event Project Management* by O'Toole and Mikolaitis (2002). Specific tools are employed in project planning, including project scoping, work breakdown and task analysis, costing, risk analysis, and scheduling and controlling with critical paths. Management of time is critical, and often time pressures lead to modifications or political actions to get the job done. A full life-cycle approach is recommended, including how to wind up the event and deal with the legacy.

Far too little attention is given to feasibility within the context of portfolios and populations of events. While a single event can be rationally assessed as to costs and impacts, its effects on other events are harder to evaluate. Long-term feasibility and sustainability of all events presents quite different issues from single-event feasibility.

Business planning

Ample advice is available on how to prepare and use a business plan for events, as well as reasons for doing it (see Getz 2005). In the book *New Tourism Ventures* (Tassiopoulos 2011) detailed business planning for new ventures is covered. Unfortunately, the business plan is often overlooked or done only for show. It is a convenient and useful way to summarize the event concept, its feasibility in financial and marketing terms, and its management. At the core of every business plan is a believable budget, with costs fully estimated and revenues realistically forecast.

It is the budget, or financial feasibility, that sinks many events. 'Costs' are viewed as commitments and the money is spent in preparation for the event. However, 'revenue' forecasts contain a lot of wishful thinking or just plain guesswork. So money gets spent but projected income does not materialize, resulting in shortfalls, debt and ultimately failure. Cash-flow projections and management are also vital components in business plans. Many events have to spend up-front, but earn most of their revenue only at the time of the event through sales – or even afterwards when grants come in.

Strategic planning

Although there is no real evidence to support the claim that strategic planning results in better events or more sustainable organizations, it seems inconceivable that event producers would not want to have a vision, set goals and make strategies for the long term. One-time events also need goals and a plan, and if the planning period is measured in years, it will have strategic elements built in.

What separates strategic planning from project planning, in theory, is first of all the principle of 'adaptability'. A project usually has a fixed goal, an event with known form, timing and programme – like a sport competition or exhibition. But permanent events and their organizations have to adapt to changes in their environment – their goals are changeable, and the events evolve. Being a 'learning organization' improves adaptability. Strong external stakeholder relationships help to ensure permanence and diverse inputs. The mandate or mission of the organization needs to be periodically reviewed, leading to a re-assessment of goals and strategies.

'Strategy' is the second main difference, in the sense that a project has a single outcome (the event) whereas strategy to implement goals or fulfil a mandate can evolve and be multidimensional. Perhaps goals can be achieved by changing, terminating or replacing the event. A 'strategy' is defined as an integrated set of policies, programmes and actions intended to fulfil the organization's mandate, realize its vision and achieve its goals.

In contrast to rationally planned strategies, 'emergent strategy' just happens as a consequence of the many decisions taken or untaken, and is often only realized in hindsight. For example, a manager might say 'it was not until years later that I could identify our strategy as one of accommodating and integrating key stakeholders, bringing them in as partners; it just seemed the right way to develop'.

A lot of research has to accompany the process of strategic planning, including 'environmental and future scanning' (forces and trends), 'situation analysis' (where we are, our current situation), stakeholder input and issues identification, and market and consumer research (including strengths, weaknesses opportunities and threats relative to competitors). Specific outputs in the process typically include a vision statement, goals, strategies, action or implementation plan (actions, costs, schedule and responsibilities defined) and a marketing/communications plan.

Operations and logistics

'Operations' refers to all those systems that must be in place and the actions that have to be taken to produce the event. Clearly these have to be planned well in advance, unless you are doing a 'flash mob'. Operations can also be thought of as the day-to-day decisions and actions within the event organization or company, as opposed to strategic and business-level actions (see Table 9.4).

Table 9.4 Operations and logistics

Operations and logistics	Foundations	Unique issues and challenges for events
Transforming processes	Engineering and mathematics (systems modelling)	Complex and risky event settings and programmes
Customer, supplier-oriented and communication systems		Crowd emotions and behaviour
Procurement	Social psychology (crowd behaviour; perceptions of risk; behavioural controls)	Lack of experience for one-time events
Supply chain management		
Critical path analysis	Environmental sciences (reduce, reuse, recycle)	Peak demand periods and simultaneous entry or exit from venues
Queuing theory		
Risk assessment and management	Environmental psychology (design for crowds and security)	The perishability of event capacity
Security		The need to be 'green'
Environmental management systems		

Operations and logistics generally apply to three subsystems, namely:

1. customer oriented (traffic, queuing, ticketing, information, essential services, comfort and safety, crowd management);
2. supplier oriented (utilities, infrastructure, technical services, security systems);
3. communications (equipment, procedures, accreditation, hosting the media, scheduling).

The book *Management of Event Operations* by Tum *et al.* (2006) provides a more comprehensive event operations model. Its main components are the analysis stage (environmental scanning and situational analysis), the operations planning process – both strategic and detailed – implementation and delivery, and performance evaluation. The basic theory and methods come from 'operations management' and from project planning and management.

Tum *et al.* (2006) use the concept of 'transforming processes' (as in our open-systems management model) to describe operations. Resources and other inputs are converted into the desired outputs, namely the event or other services and products. Operations in this context are influenced by four major event characteristics:

1. size and volume of output (how many guests, how many transactions?);
2. complexity and variety of services/products offered to the consumer (size of the site, complexity of the programme);
3. uncertainty (of attendance, costs, time, technical requirements);
4. interactions (extent and nature of contacts between guests and staff).

Logistics

The basic idea of 'logistics' is to move people, goods and equipment (even money and tickets) to the right place at the right time. The event producer could take the approach of trying to schedule it all to perfection, as in 'just-in-time delivery', or simply get everything and everyone together at one place at one time and then try to sort it out. Obviously, this latter approach could prove chaotic.

People movement

There has to be a plan for traffic and parking, including policing and security. Site planning takes into account accessibility, flow and emergency evacuation. Queuing and service provision efficiency are related issues. Some event production companies also engage in 'destination management', which in terms of logistics involves greeting and transporting arriving guests/participants, getting them from place to place, and even providing tours and entertainment. Registration and ticketing are key elements; as these often cause bottlenecks, it's best to do them in advance, electronically. Security can be a nightmare if everybody has to be searched, and preventing a crowd-rush to the stage is always necessary.

Queuing theory

For many events, especially meetings and sport competitions, everyone arrives and leaves at roughly the same time, often resulting in traffic congestion and long line-ups. To the extent that arrivals and departures can be staggered, congestion can be reduced. 'Batch' arrivals and departures can be utilized to ease the problem, such as by assembling guests at various external points and then bringing them to the venue in groups. Reservation systems, specifying times and places for guests, are an alternative solution.

How to manage people in queues or line-ups is another management challenge. Theme parks have become skilled at both the psychological and physical management of queues, including offering people the option of paying extra to avoid them! Tum *et al.* (2006: 210) provided a queuing formula that can help event managers. It considers the rate of arrivals and average service time (e.g. how fast are people arriving and how long does it take to get them through the gates?). The resultant measure of 'customer intensity' shows the probability of queuing and queue lengthening.

Critical path analysis

Critical path analysis (CPA) is the best way to schedule complex projects and event programmes. It starts with the work breakdown and task analysis, involves staffing and costing estimates, and works backwards from the event date or programme start time to demonstrate the fastest possible path to getting the necessary tasks accomplished. Detailed examples are provided in Getz (2005) and Tum *et al.* (2006).

Procurement and supply chain management

Many goods and services (including information) have to be purchased or subcontracted, which is 'procurement'. The 'supply chain' refers to how needed information, goods and services flow through the event system, corresponding to the inputs, transforming processes and outputs in the open-systems model. For events, a failure in the supply chain could mean cancellation, programme reduction or quality problems.

Supply chains should be managed to achieve a number of objectives:

- maximize efficiency (no waste or time delays; getting only what was ordered);
- ensure quality (through setting standards and inspections);
- minimize costs (e.g. through competitive bidding);
- bring suppliers into the event as sponsors or partners;
- ensure security (theft protection) and safety;
- benefit the host community (source locally);
- ensure a green event, by requiring all suppliers to conform to environmental management standards.

A key decision for any organization is that of outsourcing versus internal supply. It might look attractive to avoid external supply costs by doing it yourself, but that strategy entails many potential costs and risks. Tum *et al.* (2006: 123) provided an illustration of the 'chain of decisions and decision points' associated with supply chain management. Clearly the process requires a technical knowledge of the event's needs as well as how to work with suppliers.

Capacity management

How much is needed: of food, water, tents, car parking, staff? Being able to forecast attendance and other needs is critical to supply management. It is a very high-risk strategy to allow unlimited access to an event and then try to match supplies to the actual demand. The safer alternative is to establish a 'design capacity', then restrict attendance to numbers that can be accommodated (with reference to both physical capacity and desired level of service quality). Modularization of an event can be used to combine these strategies: set design capacities for critical elements (such as concerts) and allow open attendance at others (e.g. parades).

How long does it take to sell tickets, get people through security, for customers to buy food or to use the toilets? Efficiency studies are often needed to identify bottlenecks and management solutions. Capacity can often be increased, and wait times reduced, by either physical redesign, changes in staffing, or the addition or deletion of certain services within the site or venue.

One of the severe challenges facing many event producers is the fact that if tickets are not sold (for concerts, dinners, etc.), the lost revenue cannot be made up later. In technical terms, this kind of capacity cannot be stored, it is 'perishable'. That is why the practice of revenue or yield management is required.

9.5 RESEARCH NOTES ON OPERATIONS AND COMMUNICATIONS

Papagiannopoulos, P., Xenikos, D. and Vouddas, P. (2009). Event management and group communications: The case of the 2004 Olympic Games in Athens. *Event Management*, 13(2), 103–116.

'The latest developments in information and communication technologies (ICT) revolutionize the way security, reliability and efficiency of administration action is assured in large-scale events. This report draws from the experience of the 2004 Olympic Games and models the use of ICT for wireless group communications in operations management. It examines (1) the structure and the information content of the communication routes for management, (2) the criteria for selection of a wireless telecommunications technology appropriate for the event, and (3) the reproducibility of important work parameters related to communications during typical operations or emergency conditions.'

Ogbeide, G., Fenich, G., Scott-Halsell, S. and Kesterson, K. (2013). Communication preferences for attracting the millennial generation to attend meetings and events. *Journal of Convention and Event Tourism*, 14(4), 331–344.

'The purpose of this study was to explore the communication channels considered the most useful for attracting and meeting the needs of Millennials with regard to meetings, events and/or conventions. The results of this study indicated that the preferred channels of communication among Millennials were face-to-face communication, directly followed by e-mail, and then text messaging. The results also indicated that the Millennial generation appreciated the use of technology for communication (e.g. Wi-Fi and audience polling for immediate feedback) and expected it to be accessible during meetings and events.'

Marketing and communications

Although the practice of marketing is often reduced to, or confused with, advertising and sales, it is best described as the management of the interface (or 'exchange relationships') between an organization and its stakeholders, in pursuit of achieving the organization's goals. Communications are a key element in this ongoing process. Marketing requires research to gain understanding of customers' and other stakeholders' needs, motives and choices, the effectiveness of communications, and the influences of price and supply. Its theoretical foundations lie mainly in psychology and economics.

Customers are not the only group that requires relationship management – that task starts internally with staff and volunteers and extends externally through 'facilitators' and 'regulators'. The essence of 'exchange relationships' is that the organization offers something of value that others are willing to buy or support; it has to be a voluntary and mutually beneficial process. In our case, events are offered as an experience for consumers to buy or guests to enjoy, a product to be delivered to clients, or a marketing tool for corporations.

The marketing concept: customer versus product orientation

The classic 'marketing' concept embodies the principle of 'customer orientation', which means the organization develops events that are in demand by clearly defined customers or clients (see Table 9.5). In contrast, a product orientation is often found in the events sector, particularly in the arts, where the event is presented as a work of art that has value on its own, regardless of economic demand or support. Art event producers do not necessarily have to sell their concepts to paying customers, but they do have to 'sell' to public grant-giving agencies and corporate sponsors.

We should modify the classic marketing concept in at least two important ways. The first is to argue that the customer is not always right, and event producers should not merely provide the entertainment and spectacle that will generate the highest profit. Customers do need to be educated, and many will be happy to have their tastes modified, their minds stimulated, their emotions uplifted. And even if customers are happy to pay for unsafe or environmentally destructive events, that is not an adequate reason to provide

Table 9.5 Marketing and communications

Marketing and communications	Foundations	Unique issues and challenges for events
Marketing concept	Psychology (perceptions, attitude formation, involvement, communications, motivations, decision-making)	Many event producers are product oriented
Customer orientation		
Marketing mix		Marketing the one-time event (e.g. demand forecasting is problematic)
Relationship marketing	Economics (demand and pricing; competition)	The need for multiple target markets for many events
Demand forecasting		
Segmentation	Social psychology (group influences on consumer decisions)	Events are experiences, not consumable products
Marketing strategies		
Target marketing	Anthropology (the planned event experience)	One-time events have to be pre-sold (little time for recovery)
Positioning and branding		
Communications mix		Co-branding and marketing augmentation through sponsorship
Product life cycle		Create a tourism orientation

them. A second modification is to note that many events exist in the realm of public policy or social services, and do not need to respond only to market forces. But they do need to practise marketing in the form of relationship management.

Mayfield and Crompton (1995) studied the marketing orientation of festivals in Texas, revealing substantial differences. Interestingly, older events tended to have less of a marketing orientation, perhaps reflecting complacency or lack of professionalism compared with younger organizations. A related study was completed by Mehmetoglu and Ellingsen (2005), with the conclusion that there were multiple reasons why none of the small Norwegian festivals in their sample demonstrated a full marketing orientation.

The marketing mix

The 'marketing mix' consists of the elements that can be managed to build and sustain those essential stakeholder relationships. We prefer the '8 Ps' approach of Alastair Morrison (1995), but have grouped them into 'experiential' and 'facilitating elements'. The 'product' is in fact the event experience, and We believe marketers have to learn a lot more about experiential marketing through research and theory-building. There have been a lot of naïve opinions expressed about how retail, brand and entertainment 'experiences' can change people and make companies successful.

The other marketing mix elements that directly affect the experience are 'place' (site, venue or setting), 'programming' (including the theme) and 'people' (interactions among staff, volunteers, guests, participants). Facilitating components consist of 'partnerships', 'promotions' (i.e. communications), 'packaging', including distribution, and 'price'. Partnerships refer to all the external stakeholder relationships that have to be managed. Packaging, especially in the context of event tourism, can sometimes be thought of as a 'product'. That is because the tourist often prefers to buy travel, accommodation and events all at once. Distribution is the process of communicating with customers and selling the products, including by means of the Internet, in-person sales and packages sold through agents. Finally, 'price' is a facilitating component because it determines who can, or wants to, make the purchase. Price can also affect the experience in the sense that perceived value for money impacts on a consumer's overall satisfaction.

The communications mix (integrated marketing communications)

In the book *Innovative Marketing Communications: Strategies for the Events Industry*, Masterman and Wood (2006) not only deal with the traditional 'communications mix' by which the event reaches its targets, but also examine how events are used as communications tools. They emphasize 'integrated marketing communications' (IMC), which has been advanced in response to perceived failures of mass media, new media options and demands from clients for demonstrating the return on investment from marketing efforts. IMC is highly targeted (both customer and multi-stakeholder oriented), combines all the communications tools for consistency and synergy, and stresses relationship and branding goals.

It is difficult to keep up with ICT advances. Severt *et al.* (2013) have examined information communication technology preferences of Generation Y, while Hudson and Hudson (2013) and Hudson *et al.* (2015) have focused on social media use in the marketing of events. Social media have an increasing role to play not only in the communications mix but in co-creation of the experience before, during and after events.

Research, evaluation and information management for event marketing

Wood (2004) outlined the main marketing information needs for events, starting with setting event objectives. Research and information are also needed in the context of environmental scanning, customer analysis (including segmentation and targeting, satisfaction and expectations), competitor analysis and positioning, tactical marketing decisions, impacts and strategic planning. The main research and data collection tools of event marketers include surveys, interviews, focus groups and observation. Attendance counts (or estimates) and evaluation of marketing effectiveness are important tasks.

Wood (2004: 152) graphically illustrated and discussed a comprehensive marketing information management system for events organizations. It covers both internal and external data sources, stakeholder information files (customers and others) and the various applications of research and analysis.

Segmentation and target marketing

This is one topic in event management that has received a lot of research attention, and segmentation is often tied to motivation studies. For example, see Taylor and Shanka (2002), who profiled wine festival attendees, and Oakes (2003), who segmented visitors to music festivals. Basic variables used in market segmentation for events start with simple geography (market areas), demographics (age and gender) and socio-economics (income and class), and can proceed to more challenging variables including benefits sought (generic versus specific), consumption patterns (what people buy, how and where) and visitation patterns (repeat visits, loyalty, seasonality). Many studies have segmented event visitors on the basis of motivation, including Lee *et al.* (2004) and Barbieri *et al.* (2008). Psychographics is the most complex approach, dealing with lifestyles and values – as illustrated in Research Note 9.6.

9.6 RESEARCH NOTE ON LIFESTYLE AND VALUES SEGMENTATION

Hede, A., Jago L. and Deery, M. (2004). Segmentation of special event attendees using personal values: Relationships with satisfaction and behavioural intentions. *Journal of Quality Assurance in Hospitality and Tourism*, 5(2/3/4), 33–55.

Lifestyle segmentation identifies similar groups based on attitudes, opinions and interests and is therefore an application of psychographics. Personal values are at the root of attitudes and much behaviour. In this study, patrons of a musical theatre show were surveyed over a ten-month period. The sample was mostly married, working females. Factor analysis of results from the value scale revealed three personal value domains: 'extrinsic' (to have a sense of belonging; to be well respected; to be in warm relationships and to have security); 'hedonistic' (to have fun and enjoyment; to have excitement); and 'achievement-based' (to be self-fulfilled, and to have a sense of accomplishment). Then exploratory hierarchical cluster analysis was used for segmentation purposes.

Prentice and Anderson (2003) segmented visitors to the Edinburgh Festival on the basis of 'tourism styles', which is similar to a benefits-sought approach. Seven clusters of 'consumption style' were identified, reflecting different interest levels in international or Scottish performing arts, and in the historic city.

Interesting variations on segmentation variables include: serious leisure (Mackellar 2009, 2013a); ego involvement (Robinson and Getz 2013); expenditure (Dixon *et al.* 2012); planned behaviour theory (Horng *et al.* 2013); how stakeholders segment event audiences (Tkaczynski 2013); music genre preferences (Kruger *et al.* 2011); skill and expertise in the context of recreation specialization (Lamont and Jenkins 2013); and leisure benefits (Lyu and Lee 2013). It should be kept in mind that segmentation is designed to aid marketing, but can also provide new insights on fundamental questions of need, motivation and benefits obtained.

Positioning, branding and co-branding

Although branding is a huge marketing topic, and has been studied in the context of event tourism and destinations (e.g. Chalip and Costa 2006; Chen 2012; Bodet and Lacassagne 2012), little work has been published on branding specific events. Examples include art exhibitions (Camarero *et al.* 2010) and the perspective of exhibitors (Jin and Weber 2013). Research Note 9.7 features branding of a unique marathon.

9.7 RESEARCH NOTE ON BRANDING

Oldberding, D. and Jisha, J. (2005). 'The Flying Pig': Building brand equity in a major urban marathon. *Sport Marketing Quarterly*, 14, 191–196.

Oldberding and Jisha reported on how this marathon, established in 1999, became a 'must-run' event, first attracting 6,000 participants and growing to 12,000 by 2004 (counting marathon runners and walkers, relay racers and walkers, 5-mile, 5K, 10K and 'piglet' categories). The organizers specifically wanted to create distinct positioning, with a brand that would appeal to the target segment. The organizers (the Cincinnati Marathon Inc.) recognized the potential for a niche-market event that focused on the new marathoners – first-timers, and older runners who were less interested in their times.

Mossberg and Getz (2006) used case studies to examine a number of concepts and issues involving festival branding. One of the standard approaches is to use a city's name, often in conjunction with specification of the festival genre, as in Calgary Children's Festival. Another common approach, at least in North America, is co-branding with a corporate sponsor including the selling of title rights (e.g. 'TD Canada Trust Calgary International Jazz Festival'). One conclusion of the Mossberg and Getz (2006) study was that festival managers were not fully applying branding theory to their events.

Resources and financial management

Very little research has been conducted on events as businesses, or from a business and management perspective, so their comparative financial operations are little understood. Perhaps this is because so many events are in the public domain and not subject to normal business management principles, or because not-for-profit event organizations somehow believe they do not have to operate like a business. The basic facts, however, are that all events have to secure, manage and account for their resources, and that financial problems are the main source of business and event failure (see Table 9.6).

Sponsorship and other sources of revenue

Purely as a business venture, events would have to sell products (i.e. merchandise) and services (i.e. admission fees for entertainment) that are in demand in order to generate sufficient revenue to survive, or sufficient profit to justify investment. But many other resources are actually relied upon, including grants and subsidies from public authorities, sponsorship revenue and in-kind support from private sponsors, and fundraising through many activities. For-profit event firms might have a more difficult time getting grants, but might actually have an advantage in obtaining commercial partners.

Sponsorship has received the greatest amount of attention from practitioners and researchers, undoubtedly as a reflection of its global importance in the events sector. It can best be defined in economic and

Table 9.6 Financing, financial management and control systems

Resources and financial management	Foundation theories and concepts	Event-specific issues and applications
Resources and dependency	Economics (theories of the firm; supply and demand; pricing; valuation)	Huge capital costs for mega events
Business models		Making money from 'free' events
Pricing theory and strategies		Events as public services (subsidies; break-even; underwriting financial losses)
Revenue or yield management	Political science (policy to support events)	
Return on investment		Cash-flow problems arise because revenue is earned only at or after the event
Financial risk	Sociology (social networks)	
Controls and accountability		Multiple sources of financing are needed
Valuation (what's an event worth?)		Multi-stakeholder perspectives on success and ROI
Sponsorship		Sponsorship as co-branding

marketing terms as an exchange relationship involving payments made to events by external organizations (these can and do include public agencies) or persons, for specific benefits provided by the events. Discussion and advice on event sponsorship can be found in Skinner and Rukavina's book (2003) *Event Sponsorship*, and in Getz (2005). The International Events Group (IEG) specializes in seminars and publications on event sponsorship, including a legal guide to sponsorship. Most event associations have publications and hold seminars on sponsorship.

Catherwood and van Kirk (1992) commented on the growth of corporate sponsorship after the commercial success of the Los Angeles Olympic Games. Crompton (1993, 1995) reviewed reasons for sponsorship growth, and examined criteria used by corporations when deciding on what events to sponsor. Weppler and McCarville (1995) conducted research on how corporate decisions on event sponsorship were actually made. Two studies, by Wicks (1995) and by Mount and Niro (1995), examined event sponsorship in small communities. In this environment decisions are often made on the basis of community goodwill and civic duty. Perhaps the same thing occurs at the community level or among distinct social and cultural groups.

There are numerous issues and risks associated with corporate sponsorship. Events have to worry about 'goal displacement', with the interests of commercial sponsors possibly taking over. Dependency on one or a few sponsors is potentially a problem. Sponsors face risks from 'ambush marketers' and a loss of goodwill if the event goes wrong for them. Indeed, it is a form of co-branding that impacts on both parties.

Some research on the effectiveness of event sponsorship has been done. Kerstetter and Gitelson (1995) and Coughlan and Mules (2002) tested sponsorship recall among event patrons, revealing that it is not easy to obtain positive results. The mainstream marketing literature has many more studies on effectiveness, benefits and risks – mostly from the sponsors' points of view. Increasing attention is being given to how sponsors evaluate the effectiveness of their investments in events.

Sponsorship has to be researched and understood from many perspectives. It relates to stakeholder management, strategic planning, organizational culture and its evolution, risk management, financial controls, marketing and communications, legal issues and branding. For example, Drengner *et al.* (2011) researched event–brand congruence, and Andersson *et al.* (2013b) assessed strategies for events to acquire sponsorship revenue.

There remains a need for research aimed at improving our understanding of the multidimensional effects of sponsorship in the events world. Maestas (2009) considered return on investment (ROI), return on objectives, media exposure analysis and market value analysis as methods in use. Since ROI looks at impacts on a company' profits, it is difficult and expensive to assess.

Return on investment (ROI)

The professionals who plan and organize business events are increasingly being required to justify the event, and account for its return on investment. In Phillips *et al.* (2008) *Return on Investment in Meetings and Events*, the authors deal explicitly with the needs of meeting professionals, as represented by MPI (Meeting Professionals International). A paradigm shift is evident, with meeting planners (and therefore those seeking to attract and host events) being required to justify the events up-front and account for their efficiency and effectiveness afterwards. Previously, it was adequate to merely document what the event programmed, and the activities undertaken by attendees. Philips *et al.* (2008) provide many measures of impact, not all of which are tangible or measurable in monetary terms. To get the necessary feedback requires detailed research and evaluation. The categories of research and data in their recommended process include the following:

● inputs: what the event actually consists of (number of attendees, what they did, etc.);
● reaction and perceived value (were the attendees satisfied and how do they rate their experiences and the programme);
● learning (what did attendees learn);
● application and implementation (what was made of the gained/shared knowledge after the event);
● impact and consequences (effects of the learning on business performance);
● ROI (compares the monetary benefits to the costs of the meeting).

Convention centres, hotels/resorts and destinations that are competing for, and hosting, business events, must be aware of this paradigm shift. It cannot be taken for granted that the rapid growth of business events will continue, especially during times of economic downturn, and it must be recognized that increasingly the businesses and associations that hold meetings and conventions want to know exactly what they are worth.

There is a potential problem when destinations and convention centres want more meetings and higher-spending business-event tourists, and measure only economic impacts from the destination's perspective. They cannot ignore what the meeting organizers want, and should become partners in providing the data and analysis necessary to justify meetings.

ROI has different meanings to other event stakeholders. Tourism officials generally measure their return on investment from events as total economic impact for the destination (which generally leads to exaggerations). In social or cultural policy fields, ROI is not usually used, but it could be measured by reference to specific outcomes like changes in awareness and attitude or behaviour.

9.8 RESEARCH NOTE ON SPONSORSHIP

Nadav, S., Smith, W. and Canberg, A. (2010). Examining corporate sponsorship of charitable events in the greater Charleston area. *Event Management*, 14(3), 239–250.

'The purpose of this study is to develop an event sponsorship decision-making model based on how companies in the greater Charleston, South Carolina area choose and evaluate sponsorship of local charitable events. The findings in this study suggest that six primary factors influence event sponsorship decision-making: business policy, type of organization, event type, marketing strategy, projected outputs and perceived value. The emphasis on each of these factors in the decision-making process was also influenced by the business's orientation towards pure marketing or pure philanthropy.'

Resources and dependency

Theories of the firm were examined in Chapter 4, demonstrating the importance of having a competitive advantage in securing resources and other forms of capital. While it might appear to be desirable in all circumstance to avoid becoming dependent, some degree of dependency on committed stakeholders might actually be a wise strategy to pursue. Indeed, it seems to be a precondition to becoming a permanent institution. Researchers are just beginning to look at resource acquisition and management strategies for events.

The event as a business venture

Very little research has been undertaken on events as business ventures, so our knowledge of microeconomics in the events sector is limited. The key question has to be: how effective are events at generating revenues and profits? Wanhill (2006) is one of only a few researchers to have examined event finances. Pricing theory and related marketing strategies are relevant here.

9.9 RESEARCH NOTE ON EVENT ECONOMICS

Wanhill, S. (2006). Some economics of staging festivals: The case of opera festivals. *Tourism, Culture and Communication*, 6(2), 137–149.

Wanhill examined how a Finnish opera festival secured resources and sustained itself financially. Its pricing reflects its charitable status and public-service aims, and its capacity is fixed, so that rising costs cannot be matched by revenue from ticket sales. However, the government of Finland subsidizes the organization as a way to support opera and cultural tourism. The researcher recommended a revenue management model to improve decision-making, specifically to assess pricing strategies.

The study by Andersson and Getz (2007) on a single festival's costs and revenue management, and related issues, showed that strong stakeholders (particularly entertainment booking agents) could inflict higher costs on an event, while the event organizers had the potential to keep costs under control from weak stakeholders (i.e. where choices were available). A related issue is the fact that so many events are produced in the public (governmental) sector and by not-for-profit societies. To some extent they are isolated from market forces, or the normal laws of supply and demand. Government subsidies can support events, for the 'public good', that could not survive on their own. Not-for-profit organizations can sometimes continue to produce events even when in chronic debt because stakeholders, including sponsors, value what they do or trust them.

Revenue or yield management

McMahon-Beattie and Yeoman (2004) discussed revenue management for events. Similar to 'yield management', as practised by hotels and airlines, this financial management approach is suitable for events with a fixed and 'perishable' capacity (i.e. only so many tickets to sell, but if unsold the capacity is wasted) and predictable demand fluctuations (by day, week, hour). Using historical data on demand fluctuations, or forecasts, revenue managers adjust prices or make special offers to entice customers in what would otherwise be low-demand periods. This can affect programming and staffing as well. Season tickets, multi-entry passes, discounts for seniors or other groups, and various other pricing and promotion tactics have to be integrated with revenue management. So far no one has reported research on the application or effectiveness of such techniques at events.

Controls and accountability

This is definitely a neglected area of research (and probably within event management as well). Raj (2004) examined the human, or behavioural, aspects of financial management for events. This approach covers not only professionalism but also internal relationships and morale. It was stressed that 'budgeting' is not just financial planning, it is also designed to influence human behaviour and goal-setting. Barbato and Mio (2007) examined accounting practices and the development of management control at the Venice Biennale.

Human resources and volunteer management

Human resources management for planned events includes the normal considerations of staffing common to all forms of organization, plus several unique challenges. There is the special importance of volunteers and external suppliers or contractors, and unique characteristics of events in terms of how they are governed; the need for project planning and management, and their fluctuating need for workers, are special considerations. Lynn Van der Wagen (2006: preface) in the book *Human Resource Management for Events: Managing the Event Workforce*, emphasizes that: 'There is no more challenging environment for human resource management than the event business.' She shows how the challenges stem from a combination of the importance people assign to events, the nature of project planning and management, numerous stakeholders to consider, and the risks associated with every aspect of event production.

Events have unique human resource needs and challenges, especially because of their usual reliance on volunteers. 'Pulsating' event organizations have to manage resources quite differently from permanently staffed organizations. Planned event experiences are also often dependent on staff and volunteers for providing service quality as well as being part of the performance. Sometimes a lack of professionalism is an issue, especially where leadership and organization are informal.

Research on careers

Surprisingly little is known about careers in the events sector, despite a surge in popularity of event management and closely related educational programmes around the world. Researchers are just beginning to study the nature and challenges of professional event careers. The book edited by Baum *et al.* (2009), entitled *People and Work in Events and Conventions*, was the first to cover research on HR issues in the events sector. In that book, Jago and Mair (2009) discuss career theory applied to major events, pointing out a number of important trends and issues. They referred to McCabe's (2008) identification of a career pattern called 'butterflying', at least applicable to convention and exhibition professionals (see Research Note 9.10), and they noted the difficulties associated with 'pulsating' event organizations and one-time events. Many event professionals, out of preference and necessity, do not stay long in one job and full-time traditional careers are in short supply (this might not hold true for festivals, however) (see Table 9.7). One consequence is the rotating of key staff between major events, and a career pattern that is described

9.10 RESEARCH NOTES ON CAREERS

McCabe, V. (2008). Strategies for career planning and development in the convention and exhibition industry in Australia. *International Journal of Hospitality Management*, 27(2), 222–231.

'This paper examines the career planning and development strategies of individuals in the convention and exhibition industry in Australia. Through a structured questionnaire, career information was received from a sample of individuals (*N* = 126) employed within the industry and then analysed using a range of descriptive and evaluative techniques. Results indicate that the convention and exhibition sector is dominated by well-educated, career-mobile females who follow a strategy of "butterflying" between jobs and subsectors of the industry. They also use a range of personal career planning and development strategies that may be affected by their age, but not their gender. Findings from the research have implications for the individual and the employing organization.'

Ladkin, A. and Weber, K. (2010). Career aspects of convention and exhibition professionals in Asia. *International Journal of Contemporary Hospitality Management*, 22(6), 871–886.

'The paper reviews the key literature relating to life and work history research, career profiles and human capital, which is followed by a discussion of findings of an online survey of C&E industry professionals in Asia. . . . Findings indicate that there is no specific career route/path into the industry, with experience being generated in a wide variety of sectors, and primarily gained in management, sales and marketing roles. Professionals show a high level of career commitment and face a variety of challenges relating to environmental, customer and job demands.'

Table 9.7 Human resources and volunteer management

Human resources and volunteer management	Foundations	Unique event issues and applications
Motivation (discipline and rewards; burn-out and rust-out)	Psychology (needs, motivation, cognition, learning)	Pulsating events need periodic, large-scale infusions of workers
Locus of control (supervision; team work)	Sociology (social groups)	Heavy reliance on volunteers, both in governance and operations
Induction or indoctrination		
Training and professional development	Anthropology (culture)	Staff and volunteers as 'cast' members (part of the experience)
Careers	Education (training)	
Risk management (health and safety)		

as 'episodic' – moving from one major event to another, in sequence. In this way, expertise from the Olympics, for example, gets transferred to the next one. Another trend is for private firms to provide staff to multiple events, or to produce many events professionally, for profit.

Careers related to meetings, conventions and exhibitions have been studied the most, presumably because they are usually associated with major venues. Similar research on festivals and sport-event careers is needed.

HR planning

Getz (2005) and Van der Wagen (2006) both provided detailed HR planning models. Van der Wagen's approach starts with the event's purpose and strategic plan, and integrates HR within project planning and across all the functional areas – from accreditation to workforce planning. Key steps include: an HR strategic plan; work breakdown structure; assessment of labour needs forecast versus supply assessment (considering paid staff, volunteers and contractors); risk assessment; HR operational plan and budget; recruitment and selection; training; staffing logistics; performance management; recognition and reward system; and post-event evaluation.

Hanlon and Stewart (2006) conducted a study of staffing for a major sport-event organization, raising the question of what strategies are best. A mix of full-time, outsourced, seasonal and volunteer personnel might be involved. A complex structural arrangement can exist, numbers fluctuate and everyone is on a defined-term contract. Temporary work teams are one solution. Hanlon and Stewart made a number of recommendations for strategy, documentation and practice.

Legal and ethical issues will inevitably arise for events, including laws applying to who can be hired, on what basis applicants can be rejected (certain questions or security checks might not be permitted) or employees terminated. Another common issue is the reality and appearance of discrimination, especially on boards of directors, and the desirability of having staff and volunteers reflect the social and cultural mix of the community.

Motivation

Several theoretical approaches can be applied to the task of recruiting and motivating event workers. A quick overview is provided before getting into more detail on the volunteer.

Herzberg's two-factor theory

It is sometimes called the 'motivator-hygiene theory', and is closely related to Maslow's hierarchy of needs. Herzberg's workplace studies (1966) caused him to conclude that 'hygiene factors', like salary, security and other benefits, do not motivate people but can cause dissatisfaction. What motivates people to work (or work better) are challenges, recognition and responsibility.

An interesting adaptation of this theory in event studies is its use to explain customer or guest satisfaction. In this context 'hygiene factors' like inadequate toilets, parking problems or long waits cause dissatisfaction but do not motivate people to attend events or lead to perceptions of overall quality.

McGregor's Theory X and Theory Y

Managers who believe (consciously or instinctively) in 'Theory X' think that workers are inherently lazy, so structure and discipline (or the threat of punishment) are needed to motivate them. This is in accord with Skinner's (1938) 'behavioural modification' approach, requiring reward and discipline. However, McGregor (1960) determined that at higher levels of Maslow's hierarchy, praise, respect, recognition, empowerment and a sense of belonging are far more powerful motivators than money. Accordingly, the 'Theory Y' manager tries to remove barriers to creativity and self-fulfilment, provide a comfortable work environment, and treat employees or volunteers with a great deal of respect.

Vroom's expectancy theory

'Expectancy theory' (Vroom 1964) states that workers have a variety of goals (particularly to avoid pain and experience pleasure) and that they can be motivated if they believe that there is a positive correlation between efforts and performance, that favourable performance will result in an outcome, that the outcome's value to the employee can be determined, and the desire to satisfy the need is strong enough to make the effort worthwhile. It is sometimes called 'expectancy-valence theory', where 'valence' refers to the emotional orientations people hold with respect to outcomes.

Professionalism

Event management is slowly becoming accepted as a quasi-profession, and this acceptance is linked to the increasing number of graduates from various educational programmes as well as holders of designations from certifying professional associations. Getz and Wicks (1994) argued that event management can aspire to quasi-professional status on a par with recreation and leisure managers, but the typical absence of government licensing prevented full professional status. Professionalism remains an important topic. Bladen and Kennell (2014) have considered the necessary pedagogy, while Brown (2014) and Jiang and Schmader (2014) have examined the case for professionalism from the perspective of practitioners.

In part, the EMBOK project is intended to provide the body of knowledge necessary to permit licensing. However, Harris (2004) argued that a lack of common purpose and unity currently precludes professional status. Harris's conclusion clearly reflects the split between professional associations dedicated to specific event forms, and their rivalry for members and credibility. It is in their self-interest to perpetuate differences, but eventually they will all have to deal with the fact that 'event management' has become the academic standard, not meeting management or exhibition management and the like. They can all certainly maintain their event-specific focus to some degree, but will have to reconcile their specialization with the emerging generic professional designation of 'event manager'.

Event managers are already expected to conduct themselves as professionals, regardless of their backgrounds, affiliations, or status as volunteer, owner or employee. This expectation rests on the need for minimum standards of education, training and experience, adherence to professional codes of conduct (ethics) and legal responsibility for actions.

Harris (2004: 107) provided a model for professionalization that encompasses three approaches to defining professionals. These are the 'trait approach' (including skills based on professional, full-time occupation, provision of training, proof of competency, organization, code of conduct and altruistic service), a 'functionalist approach' (systematic knowledge, common interest, recognition by society, control of behaviour, work socialization, system of rewards and community of spirit) and a 'business approach' (commercial vision, effective response to market and client demands, managerial skills, entrepreneurial skills and success through profit).

The ethics standards, or codes of conduct, prepared by major international event organizations are documented in Getz (2005), along with advice on how event professionals should create and govern their conduct by their own values and standards. Ethical issues, and how values and ethics are being used in practice throughout the event sector, require research and debate.

As professionalism increases there will be a need for more focused research on what constitutes professionalism, and on the related career issues for practitioners. Research has been done on leadership training for events (Tzelepi and Quick 2002, regarding the Sydney Olympics) and Hanlon and Cuskelly (2002) studied generic induction (or orientation) methods for events, including the need for detailed manuals. Induction and training are particularly crucial for one-time events. Sheehan *et al.* (2000) profiled meeting planners based on hotels and conference centres, while O'Brien and Shaw (2002) profiled independent meeting planners in Canada.

Research on event volunteer recruitment and motivation

Key questions for volunteer management are 'What motivates event volunteers, and how can their commitment and productivity be maximized and sustained?' Volunteering is not uniformly valued and practised, being in part a reflection of cultural norms, political systems, economic conditions and living standards. Generic information is available from many countries on who volunteers, why, and for what (see, for example, US Department of Labor 2005; Australian Bureau of Statistics; Imagine Canada; UK Institute for Volunteering), which is always a good starting point for any discussion of volunteers.

Volunteer management for events requires specialized knowledge within HR, as well as event-specific strategies and practices, reflecting both the size and nature of the event. A lot of research has been conducted on the Olympics, but those findings are not necessarily applicable to small events or other types. Specific to events, a growing body of research evidence exists on volunteer motivation, satisfaction, commitment and experience. Studies include those by: Williams and Harrison (1988); Ryan and Bates (1995); Williams *et al.* (1995); Elstad (1997, 2003, 2009); Farrell *et al.* (1998); Green and Chalip (1998, 2004); Saleh and Wood (1998); Johnston *et al.* (2000); Coyne and Coyne (2001); Strigas and Newton-Jackson (2003); Leigh *et al.* (2013); Ralston *et al.* (2005); Monga (2006); Bendle and Patterson (2008); Lockstone and Baum (2009); Bang *et al.* (2009); Fairley *et al.* (2013); Neufeind *et al.* (2013); Gallarza *et al.* (2013); Allen and Bartle (2014); and Treuren (2014).

Underlying motivation to volunteer for events can include generic motivations like doing good ('altruism'), looking for social and career benefits (networking), and challenge. Volunteers particularly enjoy the belonging and sharing, or 'communitas' that can occur through their event experiences. Volunteering can also be one manifestation of 'serious leisure', and it is clear that some people volunteer at many events. Those who have a great experience at an event are likely to become motivated to volunteer at others.

We know from research that involvement in a sport leads to volunteering at sport events of the same type, and that the prestige of an event makes a big difference. Also, research has shown that community pride is an important factor. Monga (2006) concluded that multiple motivations apply to event volunteers, but that affiliatory reasons, or attachment to the event's theme or activity, are strongest.

There are many other issues to be considered. What are the reasons for gender and age differences, and what is the influence of location and ethnicity or race on event volunteering? How can we explain discrepancies in where and how people volunteer – are some causes more popular than others? Where volunteering is considered to be only a source of cheap labour, or is viewed as taking away paid jobs, how can it be developed?

Indoctrination, training and supervision all have to be directed towards service quality and the participation of all staff, volunteers and suppliers to the facilitation of designed experiences. A serious question to be asked is the degree to which satisfactory staff/volunteer/supplier experiences contribute to guest and other stakeholder experiences. This is much more than a service quality issue, as it gets to the heart of how experiences are shaped.

9.11 RESEARCH NOTE ON VOLUNTEER MOTIVATION

Treuren, G. J. M. (2014). Enthusiasts, conscripts or instrumentalists? The motivational profiles of event volunteers. *Managing Leisure*, 19(1), 51–70.

'Recent research into volunteer motivation offers the possibility of improved recruitment and retention techniques for volunteer organizations by designing organizational recruitment messages to match volunteer motivations. Using a sample of event volunteers ($N = 488$) drawn from five event organizations, this paper tests for the existence of distinct groups of volunteers with similar bundles of motivations (motivational profiles), using cluster analysis. This paper finds six

distinct motivation profiles: three types of enthusiasts who love different aspects of the volunteering experience; two types of conscripts, who serve with varying degrees of reluctance;
and instrumentalists, who choose to volunteer to obtain some form of material benefit. This
finding has potentially great significance for volunteer managers, enabling them to recruit the
type of volunteer they want, to be able to identify the volunteer type they do not want, and
to design volunteer management practices that better meet the needs of the volunteers they
want to retain.'

Risk, health, safety and security

'Health and safety management' aims to ensure that all event participants and attendees, as well as
those affected by an event, are protected from threats to their health and safety. It is people-focused, and
includes the very important crowd management and security tasks. 'Risk management' can be defined as
the process of anticipating, preventing or minimizing potential costs, losses or problems for the event,
organization, partners and guests. Ask the question: 'What is at risk? Is it the loss of money, reputation
and survival of the event and its organizers, or personal safety and health? Risk, health and safety management has to cut across all the other systems in event management. In this section, just the basic principles
are covered, together with some of the related issues (see Table 9.8).

Unique risk elements and challenges for events

Numerous threats or hazards face the event producer, all of which pose risks. Researchers have examined
many of these, including: protests (Henderson 2008; Horne and Whannel 2010); terrorism (Toohey 2008);
riots (Cunneen and Lynch 1988); health issues (Earl *et al.* 2005; Ahmed *et al.* 2006; Choi and Almanza
2012); crowd problems (Earl 2008); crime (Barker *et al.* 2002; George and Swart 2012; Campaniello 2013;
Matheson and Finkel 2013); and alcohol (Pegg *et al.* 2011). Many problems and threats are correlated with
the size of events and their ability to attract media coverage. Terrorism and crime in particular necessitate
high-level security and control measures. Bad weather and unpredictable environmental forces, including
the state of the economy, can drastically affect turnout and sales. Attracting the wrong people or incompatible segments could lead to trouble.

Table 9.8 Risk, health and safety

Risk, health and safety	Foundations	Unique event issues and applications
Risk planning and management integrated in all management functions	Psychology and sociology (crowding, aggression, territoriality, perception of risks)	Some events are inherently risky, and this is part of their appeal
Legal liability		Crowds generate risks
Insurance	Environmental psychology (human–setting interactions)	Some events are associated with alcohol, partying and revelry, which can lead to problems
Health standards	Operations management	
Safety standards	Planning theory and rational decision-making	Volunteers might not be able to cope
Security systems		

Many events, like motor sports, are inherently risky; this is part of their appeal, and imposes a dilemma for policy-makers and producers. How far can one err on the side of caution before shutting down the risks or thrills that make an event attractive? Risky activities include sports, running with the bulls and similar rites, eating and drinking, or just plain assembling in a large crowd. Celebration and revelry are hallmarks of festivals and carnivals, parties and many concerts. Any use of animals can be risky.

Risks also arise from organizational and managerial actions, such as the employment of untrained staff or volunteers, the absence of proper management systems and controls, or a general lack of professionalism. Choosing the wrong setting, such as a sensitive environment or an area known for its natural hazards, can be a serious mistake. The wrong date can lead to competition and conflict, and the wrong price or programme affects image and sales. Quality control is particularly difficult at events, owing to the use of many volunteers, reliance on numerous suppliers, and the difficulty of retaining staff or volunteers. Systems often have to be reinvented annually.

Whatever the hazard or threat, the risks accrue to guests and participants, organizers, other stakeholders and the environment. Risks generate problems in terms of personal health and injuries, money (financial losses), marketing (tarnished image, loss of demand), the law (lawsuits for negligence), community relations and political support (owing to negative impacts).

Risk planning and management

Guidance is available from IFA and Argonne Productions (1992), Berlonghi (1996) and textbooks by Tarlow (2002) and Silvers (2008). A very useful manual (*The Event Safety Guide*, revised 1999) on health and safety planning for music events has been prepared in the United Kingdom by the Health and Safety Executive of the central government. In the UK and other jurisdictions, it is a requirement of law for events and facilities to produce a policy and plan for health and safety, and there are government inspectors to ensure compliance with all pertinent laws and regulations. Johnson (n.d.: 71) also called for all events to have a written 'emergency action plan' to ensure that staff and volunteers will respond promptly and adequately to both predictable and unusual problems.

The planning process begins with the identification of possible threats and hazards in various risk 'fields', such as finance, health or the environment. This can accompany 'task analysis' in project planning, as recommended by O'Toole and Mikolaitis (2002). Next, an assessment of 'risk probabilities' (how likely they are to occur) and 'severity' (how serious are the consequences) leads to a matrix analysis of probability times severity. Priorities can then be determined, leading to action. Silvers (2008) integrates the risk management process with the various elements of EMBOK (Event Management Body of Knowledge).

According to Berlonghi (1990) there are several generic strategies for events to follow: 'avoidance' (the hazard, such as a programme activity or venue, should be eliminated); 'reduction' (some hazards can be minimized or kept to an acceptable level through better management, training or operations, or actions focused on reducing the potential severity of damage or losses); 'diffusion' (spreading risks among stakeholders or over time and space); 'reallocation' (risks can be reallocated completely, as where a parent body or municipality absorbs risks for specific events; users have to sign waivers).

Insurance providers can help in the whole process, as they learn the risks and consequences through experience, and some have developed specific guidelines that event organizers must follow in order to even qualify for insurance. Activities and whole events have been cancelled because of the cost or lack of insurance. Professional associations and cities have resorted to self-insurance schemes just to be able to continue producing events.

9.12 RESEARCH NOTE ON RISK STRATEGIES

Leopkey, B. and Parent, M. (2009). Risk management strategies by stakeholders in Canadian major sporting events. *Event Management*, 13(3), 153–170.

'Two Canadian sporting events – the ISU (International Skating Union) 2006 World Figure Skating Championships and the U-20 FIFA (*Fédération Internationale de Football Association*) World Cup Canada 2007 – provided the platform for a comparative case study that was built using archival material and interviews. Key findings included a breakdown of risk management strategy types and an analysis of common strategies used across the various stakeholder groups. Seven risk strategy categories were identified by the various stakeholder groups: reduction, avoidance, reallocation, diffusion, prevention, legal and relationship management. As a result, a strategic framework for dealing with risk management issues experienced at sporting events is provided.'

Security

Security is a big part of risk planning and a key element in event operations and logistics. Understanding crowd emotions and behaviour is essential for most events, with the threat of terrorism at major events being an added worry. In the book *Event Risk Management and Safety*, Tarlow (2002: 135) drew attention to the links between events and terrorism, specifically why they make such inviting targets:

- proximity of events and event venues to major transportation routes and centres;
- potentially large-scale business and tourism disruption from cancellation or postponement;
- media attention is immediate, on-site;
- customers at many events are unknown, and anonymous in crowds.

In a special issue of *Sport in Society* on security and sport mega events, editors Mastrogiannakis and Dorville (2013) reviewed the contributions, including papers on football-related hooliganism and violence and the roles of technology, such as surveillance, in combating threats.

9.13 RESEARCH NOTE ON SAFETY AND SECURITY

Markwell, K. and Tomsen, S. (2010). Safety and hostility at special events: Lessons from Australian gay and lesbian festivals. *Event Management*, 14(3), 225–238.

'The article reports on the results of an Internet-based questionnaire survey that sought information concerning gay, lesbian and queer participants' perceptions and experiences of hostility, threats and violence on the basis of their sexual identity before, during and after these events. Event organizers and public officials involved in planning and management emphasize the order and goodwill of these occasions. Nevertheless, participants from these sexual minorities feel notably unsafe or threatened in relation to significant aspects of attendance at large-scale night-time events with a wide heterosexual participation, and this may prove to be an important factor in the long-term viability of these events.'

Table 9.9 Research, evaluation and information systems

Research, evaluation and information systems	Foundations	Unique event issues and applications
Applied research	The field of information management	The challenge of organizational learning and memory in pulsating organizations
Internal evaluation	Computer science	Need for information from many, diverse sources
External evaluation and accountability	Evaluation as a field of study	
Information systems	Research methods from many disciplines and fields	The gap between academics and practitioners
		Many external stakeholders requiring information and demanding accountability

Research, evaluation and information systems

All the management functions have to be supported by research, evaluation and information systems. The open-system model of events illustrates that information is an essential input, and that both internal and external evaluations are crucial for accountability, improvement and learning. Although fundamental research can be useful to managers, they mostly want applied research to solve immediate problems. Increasingly, accountability to external stakeholders is placing heavy information demands on event organizers.

'Pulsating' events have a special challenge to become learning organizations with solid 'memories', as they have only a few permanent staff. Can they develop partnerships for this purpose? All-volunteer event organizations are especially challenged, and probably have to rely on external sources. Owing to the chronic gap between academics and practitioners, it would make sense for institutions and professional event associations or local event groups to combine efforts.

The event manager first has to establish an overall process for collecting information and doing research and evaluation (i.e. be a learning organization), then determine how best to analyse, disseminate and utilize it. Storage is an issue, although more from the perspectives of security, access and convenience. Having staff responsible for information management and technology, or outsourcing the work, are options.

Numerous software programs are available for aspects of event information management, especially regarding conference registration, project management and budgeting. The various specialized textbooks for event managers provide suitable starting points for developing specific research, evaluation and information systems. An article by Wood (2004) documented marketing information needs, and this is probably the most-discussed management function from a research perspective. Attention is required for all the other functions, and for an integrated event information management system (see Table 9.9).

As technological advances are frequent, managers and theorists are concerned about how event design, marketing, operations and experiences are being affected. The notion of a technology acceptance model has been examined by Kim *et al.* (2011) and it raises the question of what technology will be used and how it will impact on event studies.

STUDY GUIDE

Each of the main event management functions has been considered (programming and design excepted) with the emphasis placed on what we need to know about them, and how to do related research. Researchers have not comprehensively attacked the management functions related to events, leaving some of them very under-developed in terms of theory and method. Link the discussion of careers back to the introductory chapter, and consider how various motivational theories apply to volunteers and professionals – what are the differences? The institutionalization model is new theory under development for events, and, so far, is only considered in the context of periodic festivals. Do you think it applies to other types of event?

STUDY QUESTIONS

- Define 'leadership', 'power', 'leadership styles' and 'leadership roles' in the context of planned events.
- Distinguish between 'entrepreneurship' and 'intrapreneurship' as applied to events; how is social entrepreneurship relevant?
- How do founders shape 'organizational culture', and why is it important?
- What are the main differences between governmental, profit and non-profit structures in the events sector? Link ownership to stakeholder theory and resource dependency.
- Explain the interrelationships between the concepts of sustainability, enduring events and 'institutionalization' for events
- How can events become 'learning organizations'?
- What is 'rational' planning and decision-making, and why is it not always applied to events?
- Distinguish between 'strategic', 'project' and 'business' planning for events.
- Explain the three key operation subsystems for events and discuss key 'logistics' issues.
- What is 'capacity management' for events? Give examples.
- Should the 'marketing concept' always be fully applied to events? Explain in the context of special-interest event tourism and event-related careers.
- How do 'segmentation' and 'target marketing' relate to needs, motives and benefits sought?
- Should all events be run as a 'business'? What exactly would that mean?
- Discuss theories of motivation as they apply to event volunteers.
- Show how to recruit, motivate and keep committed volunteers for specific types of event.
- Why are events unique in terms of risk management? Explain the research and evaluation necessary to support risk planning and management.
- What research, evaluation and information systems should be in place to support event management? Tie your answer to the open-system model.

FURTHER READING

Baum, T., Deery, M., Hanlon, C., Lockstone, L. and Smith, K. (2009). *People and Work in Events and Conventions*. Wallingford: CABI.

Derrett, R. (2015). *Creating Enduring Events*. Hoboken, NJ: Wiley.

O'Toole, W. (2011). *Events Feasibility and Development: From Strategy to Operations*. Oxford: Butterworth-Heinemann.

Phillips, J., Breining, M. and Phillips, P. (2008). *Return on Investment in Meetings and Events*. Oxford: Elsevier.

Silvers, J. (2008). *Risk Management for Meetings and Events*. Oxford: Butterworth-Heinemann.

Tum, J., Norton, P. and Wright. J. (2006). *Management of Event Operations*. Oxford: Butterworth-Heinemann/Elsevier.

Van der Wagen, L. (2006). *Human Resource Management for Events: Managing the Event Workforce*. Oxford: Butterworth-Heinemann/Elsevier.

Chapter

10

Outcomes and the impacted

LEARNING OBJECTIVES

Upon completion of this chapter students should know the following:

- forces and stressors which generate event-related outcomes, both intended and unintended;
- the potential positive and negative social, cultural, environmental and economic impacts of events and event tourism;
- why and how to evaluate tangible and intangible costs and benefits from multiple stakeholder perspectives;
- policy implications of event outcomes;
- the importance and methods of assessing the worth of an event.

What are outcomes and impacts?

Planned events always have a purpose and goals. This means that certain 'outcomes' are both desired and predicted, but it is also possible that unanticipated and negative outcomes are also generated. Indeed, an event, or events collectively and cumulatively, might initiate or be part of a change process acting at a large scale on society and the environment.

The term 'outcomes' in this chapter is derived from the open-system model wherein 'transforming processes' (management systems and the event itself) convert 'inputs' to 'outputs' or 'outcomes'. 'Impacts' have a more specific meaning within this approach. People who experience the outcomes of events feel 'impacted'. The economy is 'impacted' by changes related to the event.

Evaluators typically set out to demonstrate that the event was 'effective', or successful in achieving its goals, and sometimes they also assess 'efficiency' (how well resources were used). Tzelepi and Quick (2002) identified various approaches to evaluating 'effectiveness' that are relevant to events, namely: 'goal attainment' (assuming goals were predetermined), 'systems resource approach' and 'internal process approach' (using the open-system model as a diagnostic tool); 'competing values' (within the organization); and 'strategic constituencies' (considering the views of all stakeholders).

Clients and other key stakeholders in events typically want a report on how their resources were used and the degree to which their specific objectives were met. All too often no one is willing to examine 'externalities' – such as impacts on those not directly involved in the event's production, or environmental pollution. A full event evaluation takes into account costs and benefits and their distribution.

In 'goal-free evaluation' no assumptions are made about purposes or goals, so evaluators seek to demonstrate what happened, whether intended or unintended. Sometimes this approach is taken when long-term, expensive programmes are evaluated, as in health care and education. Government agencies will want to ensure that major policies are being implemented 'effectively' and 'efficiently', plus they want to avoid negative impacts in other policy fields.

In policy terms, the primary need is for a comprehensive events and event tourism policy, fully integrated with closely related policy domains including leisure, sport, culture, the arts, health, economic development and tourism, the environment, community and social development. In the ensuing sections, specific policy implications related to social, cultural, economic and environmental impacts are discussed.

In each of the main sections of this chapter a table is presented both to summarize the contents and to suggest the process at work. It starts with 'stressors', which are really 'change actors' or 'causal forces'. There is no positive or negative connotation to the term 'stressor'; the potential outcomes in the frameworks can often be interpreted as positive or negative. The third column examines possible responses, which for personal outcomes refers to individual responses, but, for the others, is the realm of policies and strategies.

There is nothing predictive about these tables, and they are not intended to be all-inclusive. They do provide a good starting point for considering the sources and nature of event-related outcomes, and what can be done about them. The chapter ends with a detailed discussion of 'impact assessment' and 'cost–benefit evaluation', mainly because these should be comprehensive in terms of individual, social, economic and environmental outcomes – should be, but usually are not.

Personal outcomes

The personal dimension, from antecedents to experiences to outcomes, is the least researched and most poorly understood theme in event studies. Leisure theorists have a lot to offer here, but their concerns do not apply to all types of event setting and experience. We will have to go back to the disciplinary foundations for inspiration and guidance in pursuing knowledge of how individuals are affected by events (see Table 10.1).

Stressors, or causal forces

How do planned event experiences change people? Revisit the framework for studying antecedents and choices for planned events to see the main considerations. For the individual, the event experience can be memorable and transforming, but only in the context of anticipation/expectations, travel (if relevant) and post-event evaluation, which includes assigning or modifying meanings attached to the experience.

Table 10.1 Personal outcomes

Stressors or causal forces	Potential personal outcomes	Possible responses
The individual's actions in attending events are the stressors or causal factors. These actions relate to: • anticipation • travel to the event • the event experience • post-event evaluation	**Negative experience:** • the event was boring or over-stimulating; did not meet expectations (in terms of quality and/or experience) • perceived lack of value for money or a 'waste of time' **Positive experience:** • met or exceeded expectations • pleasantly surprised • achieved peak or flow experience • satisfaction; happiness • attitude change (towards the event, sponsors, causes, or events in general) • transformation (fundamentally changed by the experience in terms of personality, values, lifestyle)	**Negative experience:** • loss of interest in event or event type; no intent to repeat • negative word-of-mouth communications **Positive experience:** • increased interest in the event or event type • positive word-of-mouth communications • loyalty to specific events • higher level of involvement or specialization (in specific pursuits) resulting in increased event participation • development of an 'event career'
• general social, economic and environmental circumstances surrounding the event (or events) as they impact on individuals • a dominant view of the event (or events) might arise through media coverage and other opinion-shaping forces • the influence of organizers, designers and managers on personal experiences at events	**Negative perceptions:** • direct and indirect effects • the event (or events) considered to be harmful, a threat or undesirable **Positive perceptions:** • direct and indirect effects • the event (or events) considered to be useful, beneficial or desirable	• perceptions affect attitudes toward the event or events in general • political action might result

How one 'experiences' an event is crucial. In all three experiential domains, 'conative', 'affective' and 'cognitive', the individual can direct the process, or simply go along with the flow of events. People who are interested, perceptive and engaged are going to have different kinds of experiences and outcomes.

Many environmental forces act on individual event experiences, and these too are 'stressors'. 'Social representations' are formed of events, through the media and the influence of reference groups, and these shape expectations and event-related behaviour. The experiences people have at events are also in part predetermined by the organizers, designers and managers.

Potential personal outcomes

We have to be able to determine if expectations are met, and – with greater theoretical and practical difficulty – try to understand if specific needs and motivations have been fulfilled. These can include learning, aesthetic appreciation, mastery, self-actualization or (most difficult of all) transformation. It becomes even more challenging if we want to link concepts like involvement, serious leisure or event careers to personal outcomes, or to measure socialization and acculturation through event experiences. We also want to consider how personal meanings attached to event experiences can be measured and evaluated.

Other perspectives have to be considered as well, including those of sponsors who typically want to see changes among event consumers' awareness, image and intention towards corporations, brands and products, as well as grant-givers who might want to see attitudinal changes arising from communications at events.

Both positive and negative outcomes are possible. The experience might be judged negatively if 'optimal arousal' was not achieved, quality was disappointing or it was not as advertised. Positive experiences should follow from having expectations met or exceeded. Many contributors to positive, memorable and transforming experiences are actually beyond the control of the organizers and designers, who can only hope to suggest and facilitate great experiences.

Within a more general context, a person not attending the event might still form a perception of how he or she has been impacted, either positively or negatively. 'Social exchange theory' can explain some of this, as people who believe they benefit from the event are likely to think more highly of it. Others may form a negative opinion, believing they have been harmed or impeded in some way.

Possible responses

Satisfaction generally predicts whether people will want to repeat the experience, become loyal fans/consumers, or spread positive word-of-mouth about a service or product. Positive experiences can be expected to influence future behaviour, particularly where individuals develop event careers (or become more serious, involved, committed or specialized) as a consequence of event experiences. Dissatisfied event-goers, on the other hand, might lose interest, stay away in the future, or try something else to achieve the same benefits.

Persons indirectly forming a negative perception of an event's impact on themselves are likely to hold negative attitudes towards it, and perhaps to events in general. This could result in political action. Support for events should increase when residents feel they benefit in some way.

Considerable scope exists for research on personal outcomes, with the challenge of ultimately attempting to prove cause and effect. Many assertions have been made about transformation effects (see Research Notes 10.1 below) linked to the influence of participation, but which comes first – involvement or participation? Where do event travel careers begin? Other possible social and personal outcomes of sport have been considered in a special issue of *Sport in Society* (see Spaaij 2009), including the empowerment of women or social groups, social inclusion, health and identity.

10.1 RESEARCH NOTES ON PERSONAL AND SOCIAL OUTCOMES

Watson, R., Tucker, L. and Drury, S. (2013). Can we make a difference? Examining the transformative potential of sport and active recreation. *Sport in Society*, 16(10), 1233–1247.

This paper focuses around the transformative potential of sport and active recreation and is premised on an assertion that sport in its broadest sense is a political project. It draws on three different empirical studies to critically assess ways in which involvement for participants can be (potentially) transformative, transformational and transforming. The first study focuses on gay sport and gay football, the second looks at a recreational football team where the manager is seeking to actualize participation as transformational for players to challenge practices of discrimination including sexism and racism. The third study focuses on dance and masculinity and considers how transforming practices are embodied and expressed in complex ways. The paper argues that attention needs to be paid to the nature and type of activities being assessed and emphasizes the importance of context-specific empirical research to engage more fully with claims pertaining to transformative potential.

Hixson, E. (2014). The impact of young people's participation in events: Developing a model of social event impact. *International Journal of Event and Festival Management*, 5(3), 198–218.

'This paper aims to explore the social impact that two events, the Adelaide Fringe Festival and the Clipsal 500, have on young residents (16–19 years old) of Adelaide. The purpose of this paper is to examine how young people participate in these events and how this affects their sense of involvement in the event and contributes to their identity development. A mixed methods approach was adopted in which focus groups and questionnaires were conducted with secondary school students. This study found that young people demonstrated more involvement in the Adelaide Fringe Festival and their identities were more influenced by this event. Further investigation of the Adelaide Fringe Festival also indicated that level of participation affects the social outcomes gained, with those participating to a greater degree achieving higher involvement and increased identity awareness.'

An enduring issue stems from the oft-made claim that sport events generate interest in activity leading to increased participation, with presumed health improvement. This imputed outcome is linked to the effects of media exposure and the influence of celebrities and heroes in the sport domain. But it is difficult to prove, and many scholars have concluded that such positive impacts do not occur or are only temporary. For example, Sousa-Mast *et al.* (2013) believed that claims about sport participation legacies of mega events continue to be made despite a lack of evidence.

Social, cultural and political outcomes

Social, cultural and political outcomes of events stem from the five categories of stressors or forces shown in Table 10.2. First, there is the monetary 'investment' or other use of resources to create events, giving rise to economic change and a flow-through to social, cultural and environmental consequences. To the extent that tourists are attracted, or 'consume' events, their travel and presence in the host community leads to impacts. The event itself, its physical development, surrounding traffic and on-site activities also generate outcomes. The extent and nature of community involvement in the event (such as policy involvement or volunteering) has an influence on its effects and how they are perceived. Finally, the media can have a powerful influence on how events are perceived, and even influence the impacts of events on remote audiences.

Deery and Jago (2010) reviewed the research literature on the social impacts of events and concluded that social exchange theory predominated as a theoretical perspective. In this construct, people who feel they gain from events and or event tourism should be supportive, and perceive fewer or lesser negative

Table 10.2 Social, cultural and political outcomes

Stressors or causal forces	Potential social, cultural and political outcomes	Possible responses
Expenditure/ investment in events	Opportunity costs (money diverted from or not available for other social and cultural needs) Stimulation of the economy; job creation Inflation in cost of living	Exchange theory suggests that those who benefit will support events; others might feel marginalized or disadvantaged Support for, or opposition to, event tourism or visitors
Event tourism; host–guest interactions	Tourism influx results in many host–guest interactions Demonstration effects and acculturation Spread of disease Possible conflict over venue and resource use	Boundary maintenance (to keep tourism out of the community)
Event-related development, activities and traffic	Congestion, amenity loss, crime and other disruption Unruly behaviour at or surrounding events	Health and safety standards imposed on events Calls for control and change Higher or lower levels of event participation
Community involvement in events	Events as entertainment Feeling of ownership and control, or of exclusion and 'them versus us' Development of skills and networks Community pride and integration, or divisiveness Preservation of traditions, or threat to authenticity of traditions Consumer surplus or psychic benefits derived from events in the community	Political action based on degree of perceived ownership and control Social responses based on integration or divisiveness (participation, withdrawal) Cultural transformation Promote social integration and civic pride Events become permanent institutions
Media coverage	Changes in perceptions and attitudes resulting from media coverage (social representations formed)	Public pressure for political action in response to dominant views of events

effects. They determined that communities are never homogeneous in their perceptions of event impacts. Social representation theory has also been suggested (Pearce *et al.* 1996), and in this construct it cannot be assumed that people rationally assess the costs and benefits of events or tourism, and they hold representations of these objects based on personal experience and media coverage. Most studies focused on assessing resident perceptions of social impacts, employing various scales, but little attention has been given to the consequences of negative impact perceptions among a resident population. Their work on anti-social behaviour at events suggested that it could destroy community pride and lead to opposition to events.

Major themes on social impact research and theory development have been covered in the book *Exploring the Social Impacts of Events*, edited by Richards *et al.* (2013). Social capital certainly has become a major area of interest for researchers, including questions of its definition, origins and uses. This connects to all discussions of event goals and legacies, as social concerns have come to the fore. Individual, group, place and national identity have been attracting a lot of attention from event scholars and others. As mentioned above, and covered in the research notes, engagement, involvement and transformational outcomes are a challenging topic. Other important topics, many in need of development, include: events as places for socialization (linked to co-creation of experiences and social integration); social inclusion (also see power and equity); host–guest bridging and the fostering of understanding; elitism versus democratization; emancipation of women or groups without power; attracting attention and the legitimation of groups, nations and ideals; the capacity of communities to host events (also see discussions on portfolios and populations); the growing use of social media; inputs from and impacts on diverse stakeholders.

Cultural themes should be given more prominence. These range from the engagement of audiences in arts and traditions, which is often seen as arts development, to the roles of events in preserving authenticity in performances or other art forms. Our earlier discussions of cultural anthropology and authenticity are relevant here.

Stressors: expenditure and investment in events

The first stressor or causal force is economic, relating to investments and event-related expenditures. Invested money could be spent elsewhere (i.e. events have 'opportunity costs'), resulting in a potential diminishment of social and cultural expenditure. On the other hand, new wealth created through investments and tourism could be used to enhance social and cultural programmes. If the economy prospers, everyone potentially gains in social and cultural terms. Economic benefits can be maximized when money flows directly from tourists into a community-controlled event and locally owned businesses. This is usually a convincing argument made in favour of mega events in particular, and event tourism in general.

'Social exchange theory' suggests that some groups in society will not perceive benefits, and might actually have costs or other negative impacts imposed upon them, resulting in disadvantage, dissatisfaction and, potentially, political action. Researchers studying the Gold Coast (Australia) Indy races determined that where one lived in relation to the races, and respondents' occupations, helped explain positive and negative attitudes towards the event (Fredline and Faulkner 1998, 2002a, 2000b).

Politicians and other influential stakeholders should be explicitly accountable for the potential costs and benefits. If they have formulated sound policies, and commit to ongoing evaluation of costs and benefits, then we can say their actions are rational.

Event tourism and host–guest interactions

To the degree that events generate tourism, then direct and indirect interactions between hosts (residents) and guests (tourists) will result. Many social scientists have argued that tourism in general is a destructive force in cultural terms, and that cultural events in particular are easily 'commodified' as tourist attractions.

Some authors have worried about the negative influence of tourism on traditional cultures (e.g. Greenwood 1972; Jordan 1980; Wilson and Udall 1982). Often these effects are most visible in the area of cultural productions such as rituals, music, dance and festivals, and particularly those which incorporate traditional costumes. Residents of destination areas quickly learn that culture can become a 'commodity' for which tourists will pay a great amount, resulting in either the transformation of occasional, sometimes sacred events into regular performances, or the modification of rituals into forms of entertainment which are easier to perform or please the audiences more. In both cases, the rewards become monetary and divorced from their cultural meanings.

However, there is little agreement on tourism being bad for cultural events, or on how and why negative impacts occur (see, for example, Noronha 1977; Macnaught 1982; Getz 1998b). Some authors have argued that tourism actually helps to preserve or revive traditions and strengthen indigenous cultures (e.g. Boissevain 1979; Cheska 1981), and events are one of the most common mechanisms. Sofield (1991) examined a successful, traditional event in the South Pacific and drew conclusions regarding the analysis and attainment of sustainability for indigenous cultural tourism developments.

Events and event tourism can be transforming forces/processes, changing entire communities or social groups. Outcomes can be variously interpreted as positive or negative, depending on one's point of view and the information available. The entire community or society might adapt a particular stance towards them, such as events are good for the community/economy, or event tourism is bad for the environment/ culture. Inevitably, a political response is necessary to perceived negatives and hostile attitudes, although it is wise to have policy and strategy in place before the problems arise.

Shaw and Williams (2004: 175) modelled 'stages in cultural commodification' for festivals and events affected by tourism, arguing that 'commodification' was part of consumer culture, that commodification and consumerism lead to dependency in tourist destination areas, and that the commodification of social and ritual events leads to 'an erosion of meaning, accompanied by community fragmentation'. Their stages are:

1. independent travellers take an interest in local events; they observe, but do not necessarily understand meanings;
2. growth in organized tourism occurs;
3. tour operators market local culture as an attraction;
4. events become staged for tourists, leading to a loss of meaning for local people (the event is a commodity) and tourists are observing 'pseudo events'.

Shaw and Williams (2004: 177) also discussed how events negotiate or mediate commodification, drawing on a number of specific cases reported in the literature. Laxson (1991) described how Native Americans limited access by tourists to their own pueblo culture, keeping some aspects of their rituals secret. Other native communities have denied access to sacred rituals but have made other performances a regular part of pow-wows that seek to attract tourists. Picard (1996) reported that some Balinese dances performed for tourists are 'staged authenticity' because they do not contain elements that are reserved for authentic rituals.

Cultural celebrations have cultural and social impacts, perhaps reinforcing traditions or a dominant value set. The authenticity question requires careful consideration of what it means and how it can be evaluated from multiple perspectives. 'Festivalization' is both a powerful economic and tourism force in terms of its impacts, but to some observers it is a negative cultural force. Differences of opinion are the norm when-ever cultural values are being discussed.

Health concerns are ever increasing, especially because of the widespread fear that global pandemics are looming. The first things to be shut down when a serious threat is perceived will be travel and events. Ironically to bounce back, destinations will employ events and media coverage to broadcast that they are safe and open for tourism.

Conflicts over resource or venue use are a very specific form of host–guest interaction. Do residents feel deprived when tourism-oriented events are held in their parks and theatres? Or does the additional reve-nue generated help support local parks, recreation and cultural programming?

Community involvement in events

The extent to which residents are involved with events, from volunteering to ownership, and including citizen power to influence the decision-making process, can determine or moderate many social, cultural and political outcomes. To what extent can events contribute to social integration, combating social conflict, or build community pride? Largely unproven claims have been made about the socially transforming power of events, so more research is definitely justified here. Similarly, do cultural events promote and enhance appreciation of, and support for, the arts and other cultural pursuits?

Waitt's (2004) critical examination of the 2000 Sydney Olympic Games provides an example of how 'civic boosterism' was employed to create a dominant, positive representation of the Games, and to exclude or silence its critics. While the Games were used to reposition Sydney in the world context, they also had to be sold to the population through the exploitation of Olympic symbolism and rhetoric, and through promises of major, lasting benefits. Another study, abstracted in Research Note 10.2 below, looked at residents of Salt Lake City.

10.2 RESEARCH NOTE ON RESIDENT PERCEPTIONS

Gursoy, D. and Kendall, K. (2006). Hosting mega events: Modelling locals' support. *Annals of Tourism Research*, 33(3), 603–623.

Research concerned the 2002 Winter Olympic Games in Salt Lake City. Resident support for the event was found to rely heavily on perceived benefits, which supports social exchange theory. The authors concluded that a collaborative decision-making model for events is desirable, and as an important input the residents should be consulted or canvassed on their concern for, and attachment to, the community, because high levels lead to support for mega events. Strong ecocentric values (i.e. positive towards the environment) do not necessarily translate into opposition, but such people will pay more attention to the costs.

Other researchers have found that support for mega events varies over time, and a sampling of public opinion after an event will likely reveal a lowered impression of benefits. Euphoria and heavy political support beforehand will persuade many people that the event is worthwhile, but afterwards they look for benefits that might not have accrued (Mihalik 2001).

Delamere (2001) and Delamere *et al.* (2001) developed a scale to measure attitudes towards the social impacts of community festivals. Fredline and Faulkner (1998, 2002a, 2000b) and Fredline (2006) noted that there are two traditions of research on event and event-tourism impacts on host communities. Some studies look at broad, general impacts, while others look at how specific groups are impacted or feel about tourism and events. Recent attention has concentrated on measuring resident perceptions and attitudes towards events, as in the research by Fredline *et al.* (2003). Those authors argued that more effort is needed to develop consistent measures of social impacts. The concept of 'social capital' is relevant – i.e. what citizens, organizations, corporations and government agencies 'invest' in making more liveable, safe and healthy communities. Anything that impacts on 'quality of life' is part of the social impact concept developed by these authors.

The ultimate in community acceptance is that events become recognized as permanent 'institutions' in their community. Elsewhere we discussed this in the context of stakeholder theory and noted that key supporters have to become committed to the event, generally taking some level of ownership or at least responsibility for it. It can also be suggested that 'institutions' can only emerge through strong community support as measured by loyal attendance, committed volunteers and political support – especially in a time of crisis. Certainly a congruence of values is required between the event and its community.

10.3 RESEARCH NOTES ON RESIDENT PERCEPTIONS OF IMPACTS

Yang, J., Zeng, X. and Gu, Y. (2010). Local residents' perceptions of the impact of 2010 Expo. *Journal of Convention and Event Tourism*, 11(3), 161–175.

'A survey using a 42-item impact scale was conducted in Shanghai. The results showed that there were five factors of positive impacts and three of negative impacts. The majority of respondents perceived the impacts of 2010 EXPO positively, particularly those who were employed in the industries closely related to city image enhancement and consolidation. Based on their different perceptions, residents were classified into three groups: Favourers, Realists and Haters. This study contributes to the existing body of knowledge in an attempt to understand local residents' perceptions of a mega event in different economic and cultural settings.'

Lorde, T., Greenidge, D. and Devonish, D. (2011). Local residents' perceptions of the impacts of the ICC Cricket World Cup 2007 on Barbados: Comparisons of pre- and post-games. *Tourism Management*, 32(2), 349–356.

'Statistically significant differences between pre- and post-games perceptions were found for all seven factors: benefits of cultural exchange, social problems, economic benefits, natural resource and cultural development, traffic congestion and pollution, price increases, and construction costs. While pre-games expectations were that the costs of hosting CWC 2007 would outweigh the benefits, after the games Barbadians perceived that the benefits had outweighed the costs. Within this context, it is recommended that there be a greater level of engagement with local residents prior to hosting a mega event, to maximize benefits, minimize costs and ensure successful outcomes.'

Event researchers have begun to examine personal and societal benefits, including identity formation and the creation of social and cultural capital. Misener and Mason (2006) concluded that hosting sporting events offers opportunities for generating social capital and community development through building community networks related to events. Arai and Pedlar (2003: 185) believed that public celebrations and other community gatherings engender social capital through enhanced social cohesion, trust, mutuality, cooperation and openness:

> *Participation in communities of celebration entails people coming together in sports, festivals, hobbies, volunteering, and the arts, and finding in these leisure activities common and public goods. This communitarian conceptualization of leisure stands in stark contrast to the privatization of leisure that has become commonplace in recent decades.*

Sharpe (2008), in the context of a community music festival, focused on how the leisure context of the event shaped the approach, style and efficacy of the attempt to foster social change – in other words, leisure and events as political tools. Doherty (2009) employed social exchange theory to examine event volunteers and concluded that their intentions for future volunteering were influenced by experienced benefits of the event, including social enrichment, community contribution and a positive life experience. This and other studies of event volunteers link specifically to volunteering as serious leisure.

Di Giovine (2009) used ethnographic fieldwork to explore the emergence of Hoi An from a sleepy Vietnamese town into the country's most popular destination. Residents implemented a monthly Lantern

Festival that 'ritually refreshes their sense of communitas and reinforces the unique temporality in which they live'. Roemer (2007: 185) studied a Japanese *matsuri* (festival) demonstrating how

> *ritual participation yields a strong sense of community, and this is connected with several forms of social support . . . the main participants in this month of rites and festivities gain a sense of belonging and emotional support based on their roles in this historically and culturally significant shrine-related festival.*

Chalip (2006) argued that the celebratory nature of events

> *engenders a liminoid space that can foster social value, particularly through a sense of communitas. In order to enable and amplify liminality and communitas, event organisers and host community planners should foster social interaction and prompt a feeling of celebration by enabling sociability among event visitors, creating event-related social events, facilitating informal social opportunities, producing ancillary events, and theming widely.*

Event-related development, activities and traffic

This category could be broken down into a number of forces or stressors, but they all relate to the operation of the event itself. Events generally produce positive impacts for some, and negative effects for others, often with spatial implications. Impacts of noise, congestion, crime or other disruption to community life occur in spatial and temporal patterns. For an example of research on events and crime see Barker *et al.* (2003).

The first comprehensive, and landmark, study of event impacts (Adelaide's Grand Prix, by Burns *et al.* 1986) examined how residents were affected in their homes and while conducting their normal business, such as by increased commuting times. Accident rates were also analysed, revealing a so-called 'hoon effect' attributed to the atmosphere of the races and the nature of those attracted to them. Ritchie (1984) suggested that the socio-cultural impacts of events could include the benefits of an increase in activities associated with the event (e.g. arts or sports) and strengthening of regional values or traditions.

A fascinating account of a special event gone wrong was provided by Cunneen and Lynch (1988). They described how the annual Australian Grand Prix Motorcycle Races had become the scene for institutionalized rioting, despite, or perhaps because of, the efforts of organizers and police to control crowd behaviour. After some time, people came for the riots rather than the races. Obviously a major repositioning of the event was necessitated.

Media coverage

Media coverage of events can have global reach, influencing people around the world, and must be managed if destination promotion is to be positively enhanced (Getz and Fairley 2004). Conversely, media attention focused on events can impact on the host community. Using events for image enhancement, branding or repositioning can also have unexpected social and cultural consequences. Do residents support the images in question, or in general favour exploitation of their culture in tourism marketing?

'Social representation theory' (Pearce *et al.* 1996) suggests that communities or societies build up representations of events based on experiences, social interaction, available information and the media. These representations are resistant to change and may influence attitudes towards new events. In some communities, therefore, we can expect to find dominant attitudes that events are good, or a threat. Such attitudes might not be strictly rational.

Hall (1992) also noted that major events, particularly those with global media coverage, tend to attract potentially violent protests and political demonstrations. This has obvious security implications and might discourage some communities from promoting their events.

Economic outcomes

The economic impacts of events (see Table 10.3) have received enormous research attention, and have generated considerable controversy over methods and applications. While this has been an inevitable occurrence, given the politics of events and tourism, it also has distracted from the advancement of research tools and convincing measures of social, cultural and environmental outcomes (Carlsen *et al.* 2000).

Comprehensive overviews of the literature have been provided by Dwyer *et al.* (2010) in the book *Tourism Economics and Policy*, and by Dwyer and Jago (2012) in a chapter entitled 'The economic contribution of special events'. Research Note 10.4 provides details on a novel approach to triple-bottom-line evaluation of events in which monetary values are assigned to economic, social and environmental impacts.

A secondary line of economic research has examined other benefits such as urban renewal, increased trade and industrial productivity. These are usually related to large events that require substantial public and private investments. Much less well researched and understood is the economics of organizing and

Table 10.3 Economic outcomes

Stressors or causal forces	Potential economic impacts	Possible responses
Investment and new money	New money flows into area and generates income and wealth	Perceived economic benefits drive event tourism policy and marketing; subsidies for event bidding and organizations are justified
Construction of event venues	Opportunity costs mean that other development actions are not taken	
Sponsorship and grants	Event organizers might lose money	Cost–benefit evaluation called for
Organizational expenditure	New event venues and infrastructure builds tourism and event capacity	Strategic planning for event tourism; partnerships with sponsors and between agencies of government
	Inflation of prices for residents	Develop and use local suppliers
Event tourism	Mass tourism or niche markets	Competitive strategy (bidding, producing, facilitating events)
		Packaging for extended stays and spreading the benefits more widely
		Leverage events for trade and development
		Market to high-yield event tourists
Activities at and surrounding events	Isolation or spread of economic benefits through tourist spending	Planned leveraging of event benefits involves many partners
Land use changes	Creation of event zones	Integrated urban development and renewal involves events and venues
	Restructuring of areas has both positive and negative impacts on businesses and residents	
Individual and community involvement	Capacity building for economic development	Distribution of costs and benefits should be a major policy issue
Media coverage	Fair coverage of costs and benefits?	Media impact on policy

---

10.4 RESEARCH NOTE ON ECONOMIC IMPACTS

Andersson, T. and Lundberg, E. (2013). Commensurability and sustainability: Triple impact assessments of a tourism event. *Tourism Management*, 37, 99–109.

In this study, a model for measuring impacts of a tourist event from sustainability perspectives and in a common monetary metric is developed. The aim is to achieve commensurability. The proposed model is tested on a three-day music festival and the results demonstrate a possibility to produce a sustainability impact analysis in a uniform metric. Measured in monetary terms, socio-cultural impacts carry weight just as economic impacts do whereas environmental impacts have little importance for the total assessment. This illustrates how the low market value of emission rights makes environmental concerns negligible from an economic perspective. Finally, issues related to scope of the assessment, commensurability and opportunity cost are discussed and possibilities for future studies are suggested.

---

producing events as a business venture (this is an application of microeconomics), or in the not-for-profit sector (where a combination of business and institutional/philanthropic values is at work).

Investment and new money

Economic benefits are generated when events can be shown to attract new (or 'incremental') money into an area from investment, grants, sponsorship and tourists. Where the money comes from, and who is liable for ongoing operating costs or losses, is a big issue. When it comes to employment effects, typically only one-time mega events generate a lot of construction and thereby stimulate employment growth.

It is still sometimes argued by event 'boosters' that mega events generate huge benefits from the legacy of infrastructure and venues, but this assertion can easily be wrong. The investments in infrastructure and venues are true costs of holding events, and area residents are liable to pay for these 'investments' over many years. Perhaps the event is a catalyst for accelerating investments in infrastructure or venues that would otherwise be needed. Also, the 'investment' might have a long-term benefit in generating new tourism business through the hosting of events that could not otherwise have occurred. Remember that the term 'investment' implies a future return, and this has to be carefully scrutinized for events.

To argue that a city will gain facilities from an event that it otherwise would not have makes economic sense only if these facilities are completely paid for (capital and future operating costs) by external agents, such as central government or sponsors. Otherwise, residents should decide if they really need, or want, to pay for them. As well, if a higher level of government is paying, then one city gains at the expense of all others. The central government would have to show that the 'investment' is good for the whole country.

It is also pointless to say that needed facilities will be developed sooner, as a legacy of the event, if those facilities are not really affordable. For example, can a city really afford a new train system that is needed primarily because it will host a mega event? This is tantamount to mortgaging the future, because it imposes higher taxation on future generations of residents. On the other hand, action now might prevent or solve future congestion problems, so it becomes a difficult decision.

A related issue is that of surplus capacity. Many communities have publicly financed parks, recreation and cultural facilities that are under-utilized. To the extent that events make better use of these public assets, specifically by generating increased revenues through tourism and additional consumer spending, then some degree of public subsidy is also warranted.

Governments usually realize a substantial tax return from events, whether they 'invest' in them or not. Studies of event impacts have clearly demonstrated the tax benefits for all layers of government (see, for example, Taylor and Gratton 1988; Coopers and Lybrand 1989; Turco 1995; Andersson and Samuelson 2000). A major reason is that travel and events result in more consumption of heavily taxed goods and services, as well as bringing in new tourism revenue. Dimanche (1996) studied the infrastructural developments associated with the New Orleans World's Fair, saying it created a legacy in terms of new hotels, transportation and other facilities that benefited tourism – and thereby led to future tax gains.

Event tourism

The most-studied event impact stems from the role events play in attracting visitors to an area who would not otherwise travel there. There can be no doubt that events in general are tourist motivators, or increase a destination's appeal, but it cannot be assumed that events have tourism-related economic impacts. They have to be shown to motivate travel that would not otherwise occur. Numerous reports on tourism impacts exist, and the section on impact assessment ending this chapter provides references on how it should be done validly. Despite the state-of-the-art being well documented, some event tourism impact studies still make fundamental mistakes like failing to prove the event motivated new travel and spending, or by not discounting for time switching, casual attendees or displacement effects.

Throughout this book, attention is paid to reasons for attending events, including travel motivations and event careers. Events also attract many people for generic benefits, usually entertainment and socializing in nature, but it is likely the most beneficial events from a tourism perspective are those that attract people seeking specific benefits (i.e. the niche markets). These include participation events and events organized by and for special interest groups. Mackellar (2006) examined this issue specifically by comparing nine events in one Australian region, and found that they variously attracted 'community social seekers' to 'leisure fanatics'. A 'special interest event spectrum' was suggested as a way to classify events, and develop a portfolio, using the ratio of visitors to locals.

The economic benefits of event tourist segments have been studied, but not in any systematic, comparative way. Grado *et al.* (1998) and Dwyer (2002) looked at the convention tourist's impacts. Andersson and Solberg (1999) examined sport event tourists, and Solberg *et al.* (2002) studied business travellers to sport events (the media, etc.). The economic benefits derived from festival tourists have been researched by Crompton *et al.* (2001) and the British Arts Festivals Association (2000, 2002, 2007). Impacts of visitors to a travelling art exhibition were examined by Mihalik and Wing-Vogelbacher (1992). Major studies of festival tourism impacts have been carried out in Canada's National Capital Region (Coopers and Lybrand 1989) and in Edinburgh (Scotinform 1991).

Increasing attention has been given to 'leveraging' events in order to improve tourism impacts, stimulate local businesses (e.g. Chalip and Leyns 2002) or increase trade in general (Brown 2002). The aim of 'leveraging' strategies is to generate greater economic benefits from events, over a longer period of time, and to spread them more widely. This can be accomplished through encouraging tourism pre- and post-event, packaging event visits with wider travel itineraries, and joint marketing among attractions and destinations. Fostering trade and industrial spin-offs is another approach, and it requires sophistication in managing diverse stakeholders such as sponsors who bring their business partners to events for hospitality.

Globally, the competition for event tourism has become fierce. Destinations establish event development corporations or units, and employ professionals who bid on events that can be moved about, including world's fairs and the Olympics. In developing event 'portfolios' for the destination, thought has to be given to the individual and cumulative impacts of events, using a variety of potential measures of outcomes and value.

Activities at and surrounding the event

Sometimes the concentration of economic activity at an event actually hurts other businesses. People might stay away from business areas because they fear the event-related crowds, while others are motivated to leave town or stay at home. These are all 'displacement' effects. To combat this potential problem requires 'leveraging' the event with a variety of businesses in the community to ensure they all benefit.

Chalip and Leyns (2002) showed how local businesses could increase their benefits from events through partnerships. Pennington-Gray and Holdnak (2002) researched a tourism event that was unfortunately 'disconnected' from its region, thereby minimizing the spread of benefits. They recommended ways to promote the event and destination together, for mutual benefits.

10.5 RESEARCH NOTE ON DIRECT SPENDING

Case, R., Dey, T., Hobbs, S., Hoolachan, J. and Wilcox, A. (2010). An examination of sporting event direct-spending patterns at three competitive levels. *Journal of Convention and Event Tourism*, 11(2), 119–137.

Results of this study showed that participant-oriented sporting events generate significant amounts of direct spending for host communities at various competitive levels. It was found that the amount of spending per person increases as one moves to higher levels of competition. Demographic factors, such as age, gender, race, education and income levels, appear to be consistent across competitive levels, but spending patterns of participants change at the higher levels. Travel patterns and lodging accommodation choices seem to be different as one moves from lower to higher competitive levels.

Land use changes

Large-scale events are typically planned with urban renewal and development in mind, thereby potentially creating permanent alterations to the landscape and civic economy. Some cities, like Gothenburg in Sweden, have developed permanent event and entertainment zones that perform important social and economic roles.

Carlsen and Taylor (2003) looked at the ways in which Manchester used the Commonwealth Games to heighten the city's profile, give impetus to urban renewal through sport and commercial developments, and create a social legacy through cultural and educational programming.

Individual and community involvement

Economic change in the long run, related to events, will require a strategic approach, and high levels of involvement from local businesses and the community at large. This can be called 'capacity-building', or making certain that a single event or multiple ones lead to improved ability and willingness to attract and host higher-yielding visitors in the future.

Ways to maximize local economic benefits from events were discussed in Getz (2005). To the extent possible, 'leakages' from the local economy should be minimized by the use of resident staff and local suppliers, thereby increasing 'backward linkages'. Reinvesting profits or surplus earnings in the host community is a good way to boost support for events.

Media coverage

We have already discussed the imputed benefits of media coverage, and how destination images and branding are potentially enhanced through events. It should not be forgotten that negative images can also be communicated widely, with potentially damaging consequences to the destination.

A common concern is the fairness and completeness of media reporting on event costs and benefits, and the related issue of how authorities and event boosters might exploit the media to achieve public support for their plans.

Environmental outcomes

Ecological footprint analysis and carbon calculators

Conducting EIAs (environmental impact assessments) before and after events should be the norm, but it is not (see Figure 10.1). The Olympics has an environmental policy that goes some way to ensuring that host cities implement green operations and sustainable design measures. But the sheer size of mega events, especially those requiring new venue construction, ensures that claims to being green and sustainable are often met with scepticism.

All events leave a 'footprint', although there is a big difference between small street festivals, major tourist events and the large-scale construction projects associated with mega events. Ecological footprint analysis has been applied to events in Sweden by Andersson and Lundberg (2013); however, regions and countries need to develop their own data as land values and other inputs vary a great deal (see Table 10.4). For other applications, see Collins and Flynn (2008) and Research Note 10.6.

Investment and development

The construction of new venues can have huge impacts on the physical environment and ecological systems, both immediately and in the long run. Consequently it is generally wiser to utilize existing facilities to the fullest. A full life-cycle accounting process should ensure that event facilities are planned to be waste-reducing, energy efficient and recyclable.

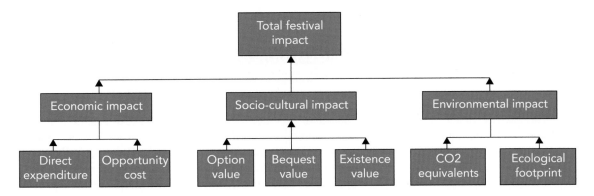

Figure 10.1 A measurement model describing the total impact from a sustainability perspective

Source: Andersson and Lundberg (2013). Reprinted from *Tourism Management*, 37, Tommy D. Andersson, Erik Lundberg, Commensurability and sustainability: Triple impact assessments of a tourism event, 99–109. Copyright (2013) with the permission of Elsevier.

Table 10.4 Environmental outcomes

Stressors or causal forces	Potential environmental impacts	Possible responses
Investment and development	Direct impacts on land, wildlife and resources Subsequent generation of waste and ongoing resource use Urbanization process Aesthetics	Avoid sensitive areas Regulate development for environmental sustainability Impose full life-cycle accounting Use development to clean up damaged areas Impose design standards
Event tourism	Generates traffic, congestion Consumes energy and releases carbon into the atmosphere	Favour/require mass transit Concentrate events spatially Stress small-scale events
Activities	Visitor activities and crowding can be harmful to the environment directly (e.g. trampling and erosion) or indirectly (through resource consumption and waste generated)	Require green event practices (reduce, reuse, recycle) Clean up after events Educate visitors (social marketing for attitude and behaviour change)
Land use changes	Environmental legacy of positive change, or damaged ecosystems	Community-based planning to accommodate and regulate events
Individual and community involvement	Personal and community-felt impacts on daily life	Enhanced pressure or support for environmental management Lobbying by special interest groups Multi-stakeholder inputs needed
Media coverage	Balanced coverage of environmental issues?	Role in shaping public opinion and policy

10.6 RESEARCH NOTE ON FOOTPRINT ANALYSIS

Collins, A., Jones, C. and Munday, M. (2009). Assessing the environmental impacts of mega sporting events: Two options? *Tourism Management*, 30(6), 828–837.

'This paper examines two such approaches for quantitative impact assessment of selected environmental externalities connected with visitation at sporting events. The paper considers the use of Ecological Footprint analysis and Environmental Input–Output modelling. It provides examples of the applications of these techniques to discrete sporting events in a UK region, and discusses whether these techniques are appropriate for exploring the environmental impacts of mega events.'

Collins *et al.* concluded that the greatest impact was generated by travel to the event, especially by car, followed by food and beverage consumption. Both methods have difficulties in terms of data required and assumptions made.

Although building greener and more sustainable infrastructure for events is obviously wise, the very need for large-scale, new venues is hard to justify in environmental terms. Cities wanting the new development have to come up with integrative strategies and justifications that are convincing to many interest groups.

Event tourism

Although highly valued for their tourism impacts, the resultant travel has an environmental cost. 'Green events' (e.g. Laing and Frost 2010) have to encompass more than on-site considerations; they have to look at the entire travel and hosting process. How can total travel be reduced by locating the event optimally, relative to the market? Can public transport be used more efficiently, especially to reduce congestion? What size of event is tolerable or sustainable in any given environment?

Tourism itself consumes vast quantities of fuel and generates untold amounts of greenhouse gasses. There are many who argue for less tourism, and therefore would approve of events that are local in orientation. Until the travel industries convert to alternative, cleaner and renewable fuels, this criticism will continue to intensify.

Activities

What do visitors do when they attend events, both on-site and in the area? Can they be educated on environmental and social responsibility, to avoid negative impacts? Specific concerns include resultant traffic and congestion, the possibility of damage to sensitive areas, and the addition to waste and pollution. The 'greening' of events will remain a major issue, with the Olympics leading the way by implementing its own environmental programme. A good example of how an event can become more environmentally friendly is that of the Cherry Creek Arts Festival in Denver, Colorado (profiled in Getz 1997, 2005). Events can also be positive tools in conservation, such as festivals and shows held to raise awareness or funds.

Events will increasingly be evaluated by reference to principles of sustainable development. Currently many events are not sustainable when it comes to some or all of the following criteria:

- minimization of waste, energy consumption and pollution;
- keeping private travel to a minimum;
- protecting resources for the future;
- fostering a positive environmental attitude;
- reusing facilities; not building needless infrastructure;
- avoiding damage to wildlife habitat and ecological systems.

Land use changes

Community-based planning is needed to accommodate and regulate events, the construction of venues and the establishment of event zones in cities. Mega events resulting in large-scale venue and infrastructure development will permanently alter the landscape, and in many circumstances this is a valued and planned-for outcome. When it is not part of the initial event concept, or bid, it can be expected that long-term benefits will be harder to achieve.

Individual and community involvement

Economic and social impacts of events might be more obvious, but a loss of amenity, destruction of habitat and disruption of wildlife, will be noticed by residents. Their reaction will typically be negative, stimulating a policy debate and response. In Calgary, for example, the frequent use of a city park (Princes Island) for events led to neighbourhood protests and the imposition of time and noise restrictions.

More proactive community involvement, especially in policy-making for events, should aim to prevent negative impacts and install a more comprehensive evaluation and management system for the whole event sector. A feeling of 'community ownership' in specific events should translate into better environmental management.

Media coverage

The media might have to be educated on environmental impacts, especially regarding subtle, cumulative changes in land use, ecological processes and amenity loss. Environmental issues tend to receive less attention than economic impacts, yet strong coverage by the media can have real influence on public environmental attitudes, as demonstrated by the building of awareness and interest in global warming issues.

Impact assessment and cost–benefit evaluation

Economic impact studies for events have often been flawed, and in some cases deliberately (Crompton and McKay 1994). For political reasons, it can be advantageous to exaggerate benefits and minimize costs. Forecasting big benefits before an event is common practice, followed by secrecy when it comes to releasing post-event evaluations. With time, these shoddy and unethical practices will become impossible to continue in the face of public outrage and media scepticism.

The state-of-the art in economic impact assessments for events has progressed to the point where we can say there is no excuse for invalid and unreliable studies. The first comprehensive economic assessment of a major Australian event, by Burns *et al.* (1986), laid most of the foundations, including economic cost–benefit evaluation. Burgan and Mules (1992) reported on the economic impacts of sport events, while Crompton's (1999) report for the National Parks and Recreation Association provided specific guidelines for municipalities to conduct valid event impact studies.

Two landmark journal articles by Dwyer *et al.* (2000a, 2000b), published in *Event Management,* laid out the requirements for assessing and forecasting event impacts; they were based on a kind of meta-analysis of Australian event impact studies, as well as economic theory. Dwyer *et al.* (2006a) have recommended use of 'computable general equilibrium models' for assessing the economic impacts of events beyond the local area, rather than input–output models. The input–output approach, they argued, contains an upward bias if used for broad regions or nations.

The Cooperative Research Centre in Sustainable Tourism in Australia has published a series on event impacts including the book *Economic Evaluation of Special Events: A Practitioner's Guide,* by Jago and Dwyer (2006), and the ENCORE toolkit for conducting studies (see www.sustainabletourismonline.com).

The main potential error in traditional economic impact studies is a failure to clearly identify 'new' or 'incremental' income for the region, that is, money that would not have entered the economy if it was not for the event. All benefits have to be 'attributed' to the event this way, and not to tourism in general. For example, only the money spent by tourists who travelled because of the event should be included.

Related measurement issues that have to be considered include the identification of 'time switching' (the visitors would have come to the destination anyway, they merely changed their time to correspond with the event) and 'casual tourists' who travelled for other reasons but also attended the event. 'Displacement' is another issue, as events might attract tourists who take rooms from regular visitors (this happens during peak travel seasons), or residents might refrain from shopping because of congestion associated with the event. Amongst the biggest weaknesses of traditional economic impact assessments is that they are too narrow in scope. Essentially, such studies look for tourism-generated benefits and tend to ignore costs and negative outcomes. Hence we need comprehensive cost and benefit evaluations, as recommended by Mules and Dwyer (2006), and especially to assist public policy on financial support for events.

Comprehensive cost and benefit evaluation

The main costs and benefits to be evaluated are:

- Tangible benefits: expenditure of sponsors and other investors (e.g. external grants); new facilities and venues (if funded externally); new employment; event tourist expenditures (and the 'multiplier' effect); positive media coverage resulting in tourism gains; general economic growth and trade; increased capacity (marketing and accommodation) resulting in future tourism growth; retained resident expenditure (this is controversial).
- Tangible costs: capital and construction costs; wages and other employment costs; essential services (police, infrastructure, etc.); long-term maintenance of venues.
- Intangible benefits: community pride; cultural renewal; increased interest and investment in the host community or destination; enhanced real estate values.
- Intangible costs: crowding and inconvenience; noise and visual pollution; personal crime and property damage; resident exodus and tourist avoidance of the area.

Costs or problems not taken into the accounts of events are termed 'externalities', and they include indirect and intangible problems like pollution and amenity loss, social and cultural disruption. 'Opportunity costs' should also be considered. These are all the alternative uses that could be made of capital, human effort and other resources. If events constitute good investments, it has to be asked if the same resources would generate more benefits when applied to other projects.

It should always be asked 'who gains and who pays?' for events. The distribution of costs and benefits might very well be the most important issue, especially because it often seems that industry and the community's powerful elite realize huge profits at the taxpayer's expense, even while poor people are displaced or the middle class has its taxes increased to pay for the mega event or new event venue. Is this just perception or a myth? If so, why are so few cost–benefit or post-event impact assessments conducted, and why do government agencies or event development corporations behave so secretly when it comes to accounting for expenditure on events?

The legacy

Evaluation of events often has to consider long-term, indirect, often subtle impacts. The term 'legacy' applies to all that is left over from the event (or events) as a positive inheritance for future generations, or as problems to deal with (for discussions of event 'legacies' see: Hall 1994b; Andersson et al. 1999; Getz 1999; Ritchie 2000; Sadd and Jackson 2006; Preuss, 2007; Quinn 2010b; Sadd 2010).

Sometimes the true value of an element of the legacy will not be clear for a very long time, or a consensus on the value might never be achieved. The Calgary experience is informative, as this host city of the 1988 Winter Olympic Games reputedly realized a surplus of C$ 300 million, which has grown substantially and provides ongoing support for facility maintenance, amateur sport initiatives, a winter festival, and event bidding and hosting.

Mega events especially are often 'sold' to the public (and they need selling, given the high public costs) on the basis of many benefits plus the creation of a permanent legacy. To the extent that the legacy is intangible, consisting of national pride or increased legitimacy in the international community, an economic and business case does not really have to be made. But all claims made about increased tourism and the benefits of new infrastructure require careful economic assessment.

What usually happens is that mega events are justified in advance in economic and business terms, but a full cost–benefit accounting is never forthcoming, for purely political reasons. Many costs are typically hidden, or treated as externalities, the big items being transportation improvements and security. The so-called induced tourism, supposedly generating a 'quantum leap' in tourist demand (Getz 1999), seldom materializes, and if tourism does flourish in the aftermath it is impossible to prove that it happened because of the event.

The concepts of 'net present value' and 'future earnings' can be useful in evaluating the legacy. As pointed out by many economists, the development of new infrastructure for events is a cost of hosting the event, and not a benefit. Any derived, future benefits first have to be justified in terms of future earnings, and then discounted because of depreciation, increasing maintenance costs, and of course normal investment opportunity costs. Many so-called legacies have turned into expensive, useless 'white elephants'.

What is an event worth?

What is an event worth? Although most evaluation in the events realm is of a technical nature and concerned with management problems, the most difficult challenge is to place a value on single events, portfolios and populations. There is no absolute answer, so let's examine the different ways of addressing this question.

Economic impact

The calculation of economic impact is generally restricted to 'new money' coming into an area because of the event, and its 'multiplier' effect. This estimate is mostly expressed in terms of 'income' or 'value added' to the area. Many authors have used multipliers, which are problematic in both theory and practical application (see, for example, Vaughan 1979; Archer 1982; Burns *et al.* 1986; Fleming and Toepper 1990; Crompton and McKay 1994; Crompton 1999; Dwyer *et al.* 2000a, 2000b; Yu and Turco 2000; Tyrrell and Johnston 2001; Jago and Dwyer 2006; Lee *et al.* 2010). As noted above, this approach is narrow and often ignores costs.

Total revenue

A simple calculation of how much revenue or 'new money' an event brings into the area is useful. Consider not just consumer spending, but also ticket and retail sales, rents and commissions, donations, grants and sponsorship revenue. This is usually going to be equal to the revenue or income side of the budget.

Return on investment

To private investors, the 'ROI' is their measure of value. In other words, for every dollar invested, what are their profits or earnings? Tourism agencies investing in events often equate 'economic impact' with ROI. For social or cultural investments more intangible measures of ROI are required, such as changes in awareness, attitudes and behaviour.

Consumer surplus and existence values

The event is worth the value that consumers assign to it in terms of 'willingness to pay'. Their 'utility value' (i.e. benefits gained from the event) might be higher than the cost they have to pay or the value of the resources consumed to produce the event. This approach to valuation is difficult, given that people are possibly unable or unwilling to talk about hypotheticals like 'what would you pay if . . .?' Andersson and Samuelson (2000) advised on the use of the 'contingent valuation method' for events.

Similarly, the 'existence value' of an event could be measured by asking residents what they would pay to create or keep an event, say from their own wallets or in increased taxes. The theory is that people value things even if they do not see or use them. Researchers could also ask who will support or rescue a threatened event; is it worth enough to the community to bail out more than once, and what might the rescue package legitimately cost?

Papers published by Armbrecht (2014), Andersson and Lundberg (2013) and Andersson and Armbrecht (2014) detail the theory behind and use of contingent valuation and its application to determining various use and non-use values attributable to events. Research clearly reveals that people value events even if they do not attend them, as events provide real choices, preserve traditions and enrich communities in different ways. 'Bequest value' pertains to the roles events can play in preserving traditions (to be passed on to future generations) but might also relate to the value of certain events for youth (the next generation). 'Option value' clearly stems from the choices events provide, and most people would agree that communities without events would be very boring! 'Existence value' covers the range of possible social, economic cultural and environmental benefits that events can bring to communities. However, just because people recognize these values does not necessarily mean they are happy to see governments lavish money on them, or to have their taxes raised to support them – that is a subject for public discourse and political decision-making.

An additional category can be suggested, that of 'acceptance value'; in the modern world people do not agree with everything governments spend money on, or with social trends, but they accept them as part of life in pluralistic and democratic societies. Acceptance value, in this sense, is part of social capital.

Sponsorship potential

One approach is to determine the value of events to sponsors, as properties for investment and co-branding. In other words, how much will the 'title' and all other sponsors pay (or commit 'in-kind'/'contra') to the event? This is useful because a not-for-profit or public organization can put a commercial value on the event. International Events Group (IEG 1995: 19) advised event owners to consider that qualitative benefits offered to sponsors are more important than the value of tangible things like tickets and gifts. Prestige has a value, but only a surrogate measure of it can be made.

Media value

Many events assign a dollar value to the media coverage they get by valuing the coverage at the same price you would have to pay if it was advertising. For example, news reports about the event could be given a dollar value based on the cost of an equivalent paid advertisement. But this practice ignores the fact that advertising is targeted and usually repetitive, with its timing and reach under control. It also tends to ignore the content by looking mainly at quantity. Finally, it says nothing about the potential effects of the coverage on audiences.

Shibli and the Sport Industry Research Centre (2002) took a sample of television viewers in the UK to measure the average and peak size of the live broadcast audience for a snooker championship in Sheffield, England. As well, they determined its television 'rating' (i.e. the percentage of all viewers watching a single programme). The volume of clearly visible or audible exposure for sponsors' logos or messages was calculated using specially trained observers and software, then a cash equivalent value was calculated based on how much it would cost to purchase television advertising in the form of 30-second messages.

The same was done for messages about Sheffield. The report emphasized that there is no guarantee that such media exposure is effective.

Psychic benefits

Burns *et al.* (1986) determined that the Adelaide Grand Prix imposed costs and problems on the resident population, but a large majority still thought the event was desirable and should be held again. In other words, it had 'psychic value' for them, which was at least equal to the monetary value of all those personal and community-felt costs.

Multiple perspectives on value

As argued throughout this book, a multi-stakeholder approach is important. What does the community think about the event? Its sponsors and grant-givers? Its suppliers, volunteers, staff? The tourism and hospitality sectors, and the arts community? There really is no one measure of value that sums up all these perspectives, so all their views should be solicited. Together, they constitute the community that can help an event be accepted or validated, even becoming a permanent institution.

Also, principles of 'sustainable development' can be applied to evaluating the worth of an event. Ask these questions: did the event (or events) make it more costly or difficult for future generations to enjoy an equal or better quality of life? Were irreplaceable resources used up? Do events add to global environmental problems, or help solve them? Could the long-term impacts be predicted and, where necessary, were preventative and ameliorative actions implemented?

Triple-bottom-line and values-based evaluation

In a 2009 article in the *Journal of Policy Research for Tourism, Leisure and Events*, Getz argued for a comprehensive, triple-bottom-line approach to event evaluation, essentially adopting principles of sustainable development and corporate social responsibility. This is a values-based approach, rather than a technical exercise in proving cause and effect. It relates to the major issue of what events are worth. Arguments made in that article drew upon the ideas of Pumar (2005), who had outlined a process for achieving the institutionalization of a new paradigm, such as acceptance of the idea of global warming. In this approach, we collectively need to accomplish the following:

- establish a global research agenda for sustainable and responsible events (and compare results);
- lobby for events-domain policy development in every country (that is, explicit policy devoted to the events sector), with all stakeholders involved;
- find champions to popularly communicate the new paradigm (people willing to speak out, for example, about the worth of events from multiple perspectives and the weaknesses of focusing on economic and tourism benefits);
- establish new, more comprehensive information-sharing networks;
- seek to transform, or replace traditional marketing organizations (DMOs) with bodies that have research, policy and evaluation mandates pertinent to events; event development agencies should have a broader mandate, with all stakeholders involved;
- institutionalize event-studies research and policy.

In a response to that article, Dredge and Whitford (2010) called for a more nuanced approach to events policy in which the complexity of stakeholder interests is recognized. They prefer a context-specific approach, although a framework was not provided. Discourse of this type is clearly necessary, and no one perspective on events is likely to hold sway over the entire research or policy-making community.

In addition, those authors differentiated between policy research *of* versus policy research *for* events. Research is needed both on the how, why, when, where and for whom policy is made, together with research investigating the policy-making processes to increase understanding of the characteristics of policy-making.

STUDY GUIDE

Outcomes should be considered in the context of the open-system model of event organizations. There are intended outcomes, with the event being a transforming process, and evaluation is required to determine the 'effectiveness' of the system in attaining these goals. 'Efficiency' also has to be evaluated, because resources are generally scarce. Some outcomes are unintended, and even 'external' to the event and the organization. External stakeholders are likely to focus on these impacts. Those who are 'impacted' by events are legitimate stakeholders, including those who represent environmental, social and cultural concerns.

When conducting impact assessments, or evaluations of outcomes, 'stressors' or 'causal factors' should first be identified. It is not just the event itself that can cause changes, so we have to consider related investments, tourism, physical developments and media effects. The degree to which the community is involved in the event, or in policy formulation related to events, will also have an important bearing on outcomes and on how people feel they have been impacted. Stressors then have to be linked to the full range of potential outcomes, both desired and unintended, internal and external. Whether impacts are positive or negative will depend on one's perspective and on the research and evaluation methods used. This analysis leads to policy, strategy and other possible responses.

STUDY QUESTIONS

- Discuss 'outcomes' and their evaluation in the context of the open-system model of event management.
- What are 'stressors' or 'causal forces'?
- Identify the key forces that shape personal event outcomes; discuss how and why people might find their event experiences satisfactory or not (or positive/negative).
- How do individuals respond to their direct and indirect event experiences?
- Explain how events can cause social, cultural and political outcomes (i.e. stressors plus potential impacts). Refer specifically to 'exchange theory'.
- What is 'commodification' of culture and how is it related to authenticity in planned events?
- Why and how should we study resident perceptions and attitudes towards events?
- What generates the economic benefits attributed to events? Include 'new money'.
- How might events cause environmental impacts?
- How can events be made sustainable? Take a triple-bottom-line approach.
- What research is required in order to perform an economic impact assessment for an event? In what ways is this type of assessment limited in its usefulness for policy?
- Provide a detailed explanation of cost–benefit evaluation for events, including discussion of 'opportunity costs' and the 'distribution' of impacts.
- How can you answer the question 'what is an event worth?'

FURTHER READING

Goldblatt, S. and Goldblatt, J. (2011). *The Complete Guide to Greener Meetings and Events*. New York: Wiley.

Jones, M. (2010). *Sustainable Event Management: A Practical Guide*. London: Earthscan.

Chapter **11**

Events and public policy

LEARNING OBJECTIVES

Upon completion of this chapter students should know the following:

- ways in which planned events fit into various public policy fields;
- justifications for public-sector intervention in, and support for, planned events;
- how policy involving events is formed in a political environment;
- how policy affects event production and management.

Public policy and events

The staging of planned events cannot ignore the many public policies and resulting regulations or laws that impact on the event sector. Conversely, policy-makers in many public policy domains have to gain a better understanding of planned events of all types in order to ensure that events can be a sustainable force for cultural, social and economic progress. Ideally, governments at all levels will create a vision and take an integrated approach to events, or at least ensure that policies affecting events are proactive and coordinated.

In this chapter, we commence with a discussion of the significance of event policy and how it has developed as a key area along with some of the wider theoretical issues which impact upon the analysis of policy issues in events. This is followed by a discussion of the nature of public policy and the meaning of 'policy domains'. The second section examines justifications for public intervention in the event sector through discussion of the concepts of 'public goods', 'ideology', 'market failure' and 'efficiency'.

Then each major policy domain related to planned events receives a more detailed examination, covering economic policy (development, tourism), social (leisure, sport, health and well-being), cultural (arts) and the environment. Finally, the chapter concludes with a look at the policy-making process as applicable to the event sector.

The evolution of policy analysis in events

According to Foley *et al.* (2012), the evolution of policy analysis in events research has been a phase of development that has contributed to the development of event studies (see Figure 11.1) as it has developed from a focus entirely dominated by event management to the position marked by this book – the emergence of event studies. Within that transition, policy analysis has focused on a range of issues, but a dearth of studies identified by Foley *et al.* (2012) was a defining feature of this area of study within events.

However, Hall (2014: 188) adopts a more explicit theoretical analysis, noting that 'political analysis is closely related to public policy analysis' and making a case that the political analysis of events does in fact have a much longer pedigree and contribution to the policy debate as noted in Chapter 4. In theoretical terms, Hall (2014) argues that the political analysis of events reflects the wider concern of politics, which is about power and who gets what, where and how, a fundamental concern which was also central in the welfare geography work of D. M. Smith (1977), with an implicit focus on the territorial inequalities that arose from the distribution of goods and benefits in society. In this respect, politics and and the analysis of power should be a central concern in event studies as power shapes the public policies and influences the ways in which events are developed and staged, and beneficiaries and losers emerge. This is not deemed to be a popular pastime for researchers, as it often involves critiquing the very bodies funding and hosting events even though there are many good reasons for greater transparency and accountability in event research if events are to benefit the wider public good.

What is public policy?

'Public policy' consists of a goal-directed process by governments and their agencies, manifested in laws, regulations, decisions (both actions and inaction) and intentions of governments regarding specific problems or general areas of public concern. Policy can be viewed in terms of 'power', because political parties, special interest groups and their professional lobbyists constantly seek to influence policy.

Figure 11.1 Evolution of research on events policy in relation to the transition from event management to event studies

Source: Developed from Foley *et al.* (2012).

Political scientists and other researchers can study inequities in who has power, and what interests are actually taken into account when event policy is established.

Policies of government are often based on 'ideology', arising from party-political manifestos. However, determining what is a government's policy in many cases has to be deduced from what they do, or avoid doing, and this might simply reflect the dominant values of society at the time. It might also be difficult to discern the rationality behind government actions, and indeed it often appears that there is no coherent policy on events.

A 'policy domain' is a broad area of government responsibility or interest, such as culture, the economy, the environment or health, which usually encompasses a variety of departments, agencies, laws, regulations and programmes. Planned events cross a number of policy fields, often involving two or three levels of government, so it will be necessary to develop liaison between agencies on event-related issues, and to develop integrating policies.

If a sector or subsector (like tourism or sport tourism, planned events in general, or cultural festivals) achieves a high enough profile, perhaps due to concerted lobbying or changes in ideology, it can become a policy domain with its own ministry, agency and explicit policy. This should result in a higher profile and more effective governmental action. In many countries, tourism successfully lobbied governments to be considered as an 'industry', and in many cases this has resulted in increased planning, better marketing, direct government involvement through funding or the establishment of industry-led tourism commissions. Nothing like this has happened for events, yet, but arts and cultural organizations have in general been fairly successful in being recognized either as an 'industry' or as a policy domain.

The institutional framework

Hall and Rusher (2004) noted that the policy dimensions related to events include the political nature of the policy-making process, public participation, sources of power, exercise of choice by policy-makers in a complex environment and perceptions of the effectiveness of policy. To study event policy therefore requires knowledge of the various institutions involved, and how they interact and make policy. These include the legislators (elected or otherwise), government agencies (such as culture, tourism, sport and economic development), the courts, law enforcement, public–private partnerships, quasi-governmental organization, regulators, and other organizations with power, such as trade unions and political parties.

Increasingly cities, regions and countries are creating event-specific agencies or companies to bid on, facilitate or produce events. Unfortunately, public policy gets confusing, and perhaps becomes counterproductive, when governments delegate authority to 'independent' agencies. This can result in secrecy, lack of accountability, and decisions made without regard to public needs or preferences.

Each policy field will involve a different network of stakeholders, yet tourism, culture, sports, events and other networks of agencies and interests overlap considerably. Finding one's way through these networks can be a challenge. Within them, who has power and how is it used? Intra- and intergovernmental conflicts, or lack of integration, also influence event-related policy. National governments typically promote tourism, but often it is local governments who have to provide the infrastructure; it is their voters who feel the immediate impacts. Sport and events might appear to be perfect partners, but each interest group probably wants something different and might fight over resources.

The concept of 'policy regimes' is of direct relevance, especially when it comes to the very big issues like hosting mega events. Richards and de Brito (2013: 227) noted that 'More recent studies of events have also underlined the importance of policy regimes to provide the "political will" necessary to derive lasting benefits from events.' A 'regime' could be defined by alliances, networks and power brokers. Often there are elite groups in society that have the ability to make things happen because of their collective power.

Justifying public-sector involvement

At least at election time, most governments try to justify their policies. They also put forward clearly different policy platforms, based on ideology or the need for positioning. Many voters are swayed by specific proposals or measures, while others are impressed more by values and policies that suggest the general direction a government will take.

Veal (2006) observed that the critical approach to sociological research and theory has raised many public policy questions. For example, who is being served by public expenditure on festivals? Probably the most obvious public policy that relates to planned events is funding, so what is the case for public funding of events? Practice varies widely, with money coming from a variety of public agencies, all aimed at different outcomes. Increasing scrutiny of policy, or of government inaction, leads to many questions being raised in the media and at the community level.

The main lines of justification for public funding or other forms of intervention (like regulations, direct production of events or marketing) start with ideology – namely, what is a 'public good'? After that, 'market failure' or market inadequacies are often cited, and achieving greater efficiency is also used as justification. When we addressed possible responses to outcomes and the question of 'what is an event worth' in the previous chapter, we were setting up this discussion of policy justification. Some of it goes back to the disciplinary overview of economics, and there are other threads of justification running throughout the book, including 'leisure benefits'.

The public good argument, and ideology

The key to this powerful argument is to demonstrate important benefits from events that accrue to society as a whole – or to the economy (which should clearly benefit us all) and to the environment (everyone supports a healthier, safer, more sustainable environment). It should also be made clear by policy-makers that the benefits from events can only be achieved through support and investment in events, or at least that the benefits of events are equal to those from other expenditure/investment opportunities. When backed by research, expert testimony and public opinion surveys showing support for events, the 'public good' argument cannot easily be refuted.

Therefore, in order to make the 'public good' argument valid and convincing, the following criteria have to be met:

- events fit into accepted policy domains (culture, health, economics, etc.);
- public benefits are substantial (it's worth our while to get involved), inclusive (everyone gains) and they can be demonstrated or proved;
- there are rules and accountability for money spent and other actions taken.

11.1 RESEARCH NOTE ON EVENTS AS PUBLIC GOODS

Solberg, H. and Preuss, H. (2007). Major sport events and long-term tourism impacts. *Journal of Sport Management*, 21(2), 213–234.

'Hosting major sport events can cause positive shifts in tourism demand on a long-term basis, but the additional revenues might not counterbalance the investment costs that are required of the host destination. Many of the benefits from sport events fall into the category of public goods. This represents a rationale for governmental funding if those who benefit are driven by free-rider incentives. The prospect of governmental funding, however, provides motives to exaggerate the socio-economic value of the events. This complicates the job of deciding which events to support and by how much. In conclusion, the challenge for policy-makers is to evaluate the true costs, benefits, risks and leveraging strategies that each event offers.'

Ideology

Political parties take different approaches to event funding or regulation, and in general to culture, economic development or leisure and sport, based on ideologies. 'Ideology' is rooted in philosophies, value sets and even religious beliefs. Seldom do political parties engage in ideologically based debate over policies towards planned events, but it does happen around specific issues and events – especially for spending on mega events or event venues, and sometimes regarding the funding of festivals and sports.

In terms of ideological differences, observers can look for the following indicators of substantial differences between party positions, and then assess how they will affect the events sector:

- a general belief in government intervention, which leads to many programmes of funding as well as to many regulations – versus a general belief in free enterprise, the marketplace and individual rather than collective responsibility;
- policies that result in governments taking a proactive lead, versus a problem-solving approach (e.g. formulating pro-event policy or merely reacting to issues);
- a belief that culture, sport and leisure are matters of health and public welfare, versus the view that they are best left to individual consumption decisions;
- a belief that tourism is business and best left to the industry, rather than being a social, environmental or cultural issue;
- responsiveness to special interest groups (which reveals power bases).

Veal (2010) has reviewed the effects of ideology and political parties on sport, leisure and tourism. He also considered movements or philosophies, including feminism and environmentalism. By way of summary, Veal (2010: 42) said that none of the ideologies focus on leisure, sport or tourism, but each provides a 'distinctive perspective for viewing the role of these phenomena in contemporary society, and the role of the state in relation to their provision and regulation'.

Social equity

The 'social equity' principle is really a part of the 'public good' justification. In the context of planned events it can be stated this way:

> *Where events provide a 'public good' (i.e. benefits accrue to society as a whole), it is justifiable for governments to intervene by way of subsidies (to events or participants) or direct provision of events, in order to ensure that everyone has the means to attend or otherwise benefit from events.*

'Social equity' literally means that access to a public good or service, and to the benefits of public investment, is based on principles of fairness, justice and need. This is not the same as 'equality', wherein everyone gets exactly the same thing. For example, 'equal access' to events or the benefits of events would mean that everyone gets the same, but that principle is not widely held to be feasible or desirable.

Equity is a serious issue for the event sector, particularly because many governments value events in the context of culture, social integration, leisure and health. If left to the free market, it is probable that many people will not be able to participate in some events because of high cost, inaccessibility or lack of knowledge about opportunities. While the equity principle justifies subsidies and direct provision, the value of events to society can and should be measured. Over-development of economic impact assessment has left us weak on demonstrating social and cultural values.

Sometimes government action related to events directly violates the equity principle. We see this occur in the arts sector when heavily subsidized institutions and events (such as symphony, ballet, opera, theatre) still charge high ticket prices, making it impossible for the poor to attend. This contravenes the equity principle and has to be corrected. One solution is to maintain high nominal prices (the rich hardly notice it) but to ensure that low-cost tickets are available to those in need. Another is to proactively take art and events to the people.

Failure (or inadequacies) of the marketplace

This economic justification for public involvement rests on the premise (or ideological belief) that economic development in general is best left in the hands of the private sector, but in some cases the 'free market' does not provide sufficient incentive or reward to stimulate entrepreneurial activity or to generate public goods and services. Accordingly, giving money to tourism marketing organizations, participating in joint ventures with the private sector or providing tax incentives or subsidies to investors (including events) can all be justified as a necessary means to achieve public policy aims.

This argument is sometimes extended to providing assistance for the non-profit sector. For example, non-profit organizations produce many festivals and other events in an inherently risky environment, and so they deserve assistance as long as the public good can be demonstrated.

Why economic 'laws' fail in the event sector

Burgan and Mules (2001) and Mules and Dwyer (2006) argued that fewer sporting venues would be built and fewer events would occur without public support, because 'market forces' will not support them. Yet many of the direct benefits accrue to the hospitality and travel industry, so why should the public sector intervene?

The supply of events would eventually reach equilibrium with demand (i.e. what consumers are willing to pay) only if a completely free market existed. At that equilibrium point there would theoretically exist the number and types of events that were 'demanded' by paying customers. But a relatively 'free market' really only exists for certain types of events: those produced by for-profit corporations for companies or consumers that are looking for specific entertainment, learning or marketing opportunities that can only be met by these types of events (perhaps weddings or private parties). But most event entrepreneurs have to compete with subsidized events and event venues in the public or non-profit domains, which distorts the marketplace.

Imagine trying to produce a private music festival for profit in a city that also hosts a dozen or more annual non-profit events, each with some degree of government subsidy. This was the case of one festival in Calgary, which only lasted two years and saw the private investors lose a lot of their own money. Try to imagine a free market for the Olympics, a world's fair or all the sporting events that are put out to bidders every year. And can there be a free market for conventions and fairs if most are produced in publicly financed convention centres?

Return on investment and economic efficiency

Governments can make money! Numerous studies have shown that governments at all levels realize substantial tax gains from tourism in general, and event tourism in particular. Events stimulate consumption of goods and services that are heavily taxed. Purely on a profit basis, public-sector investment is thereby justified. However, there has to be proven feasibility, accountability and professional management in place.

Increasingly the public sector in many countries has engaged in 'downsizing' and 'outsourcing' to save the taxpayer money. Really this is a way of saying that the services need to be provided, but the private sector can do it more efficiently. Some cities have developed festivals and events, then put them out to tender. Publicly funded facilities are managed, for profit, by private companies that use events to generate both tourism and private profits.

Efficiency is also gained when events with surplus capacity are marketed to tourists, and when events are held in public facilities and spaces that both have surplus capacity and need additional revenue. In these cases, spending a little on events can realize important benefits for residents.

Justifications based on intangible benefits (psychic and existence values)

'Psychic benefits' accrue to people when they value something more than its related costs, as was calculated in the landmark event impact study by Burns *et al*. (1986). This is similar to 'consumer surplus', meaning that people are willing to pay more than the actual cost to them.

Researchers might also be able to show that people value an event, even when they do not attend, because it leads to pride in their community or they anticipate indirect benefits. This 'existence' value can be given weight through the use of 'contingent valuation methods'. Andersson (2006) concluded that researchers have generally found citizens to approve of public expenditure on culture, whether or not they are users. Indeed, one of the frontiers in justifying events is that of establishing use and non-use values. Researchers in the Sunshine Coast, Australia, employed the use/non-use methodology pioneered in Sweden by Andersson and Lundberg (2013) and Andersson and Armbrecht (2014), with the aim of valuing the entire population of events within a municipality. The authors of the report (Getz *et al*. 2013) drew a number of conclusions that can help advance this line of research to aid policy-making and strategy for events development (see Events in Focus 11.1).

EVENTS IN FOCUS

11.1 Policy-making and strategy for events development

Selected conclusions from: Getz, D., Gration, D., Raciti, M., Sie, L. and Frost, D. (2013b). *Final Report: Sunshine Coast Event Portfolios Valuation Research*.

The overall purpose of this research was to pilot an innovative approach to determine the value of portfolios of planned events in a community or destination, with implications for policy and strategy making. Both resident and tourist input was obtained. Use and non-use values were examined, attempting to create both an economic valuation in monetary amounts and a social perception of the worth of events.

Researchers at both the University of Queensland and the University of the Sunshine Coast collaborated in conducting a pilot survey followed by a large-scale online survey of residents and tourists during 2013. Usable responses to the major online survey were obtained from 1,085 residents and 384 non-residents.

Major conclusions are as follows:

1. Residents of the Sunshine Coast greatly value their planned events, with substantial direct use value accruing from attendance, active participation (e.g. as athletes and artists) and volunteering.

2. Residents gave strong recognition to the economic, personal and social values of planned events, regardless of whether they used them or not.

3. Non-use values recognized by residents include 'option value' (i.e. having more to chose from), 'bequest value' (i.e. valued traditions; creating a legacy for future generations; more for youth to do), and 'existence value' (i.e. events are good for the community in multiple ways).

4. Residents largely believe that planned events are not causing significant social or environmental problems.

5. From a policy perspective, planned events represent a major field in which both economic gain and general public good are being created, with even greater potential to grow.

6. Residents especially support festivals and cultural celebrations, and a range of events and event venues are also supported.

7. There is only limited support among residents to accept tax increases to pay for new events or venues; this could be controversial, and a full justification for new capital expenditures and ongoing support should always be provided to residents.

Implications for policy and strategy

1. Development of a portfolio of planned events and venues should:
   a. maximize the joint value of events and venues for both residents and tourists;
   b. incorporate an events awareness and community benefits communication strategy;
   c. provide a range of celebrations, entertainment, participation and spectator sports that meet contemporary needs and anticipate emerging needs;
   d. facilitate direct involvement of residents as organizers, volunteers, athletes and artists;
   e. develop at least one event into international, hallmark-event status;
   f. provide ongoing evidence of the benefits events and venues bring to residents;

2. a managed portfolio of events for the Sunshine Coast should stress balance by types and sizes, and all-year opportunities for celebration and participation.

It is highly desirable to combine regular event visitor surveys with specific questions concerning willingness to pay, perceptions of the overall attractiveness of events in the destination and ideas for improvements; questions on relationships with residents and the environment would also be useful, in order to identify potential problems. Periodic surveys of residents are important in order to ask questions similar to those included in the current research: willingness to pay; different kinds of engagement with events; events attended; preferences for venues and events; percep-tions of positive and negative impacts.

Because public authorities and publicly subsidized events need to demonstrate the creation of 'public goods' (that is, benefits that are realized and appreciated by everyone, or at least by all taxpayers), it is important to be able to show levels of public support and to identify and deal with issues raised; care should be taken to obtain the input of specific segments of the population that might be excluded through typical survey methods, including seniors, youth and economically disadvantaged groups.

The 'health' (or sustainability) of an event population can be measured, in part, by residents' impact perceptions and their changing levels of support for policies and strategies; for tourists, direct measures of demand and expenditure are useful for evaluating overall portfolio health.

The law of the commons

Culture, public lands and facilities, scenery and other natural resources exploited for tourism and events can be considered 'common' assets. Their benefits should accrue to everyone, and they need to be protected (this is the 'stewardship' principle in sustainability theory). Only government policy and action can protect common assets.

If 'common' assets are used for tourism or events without regulation, by whoever takes initiative, benefits will accrue only to a few and the resources will potentially be depleted. Accordingly, public policy and action is justified on sustainability grounds, not necessarily in the form of investment, but at least in the form of regulation and, when needed, rationing. This is certainly a good reason for initiating public policy discussions.

Counter-arguments

Counter-arguments are also available. Money given to special interest groups often attracts opposition, especially from groups that do not get similar treatment. Sometimes there are strong cultural or political forces opposing government spending on projects that are claimed to be 'elitist' (e.g. performing arts), 'harmful' (risky sports), 'perverse' (gay or lesbian pride) or 'narrow' (i.e. the benefits accrue only to tourism or to private companies).

A lack of involvement with tourism or events might occur because attention is turned elsewhere (so do policy-makers have the facts? Are they effectively lobbied?). And because governments are faced with virtually unlimited spending opportunities, and limits on resources, they have to constantly prioritize. It is certainly reasonable for policy-makers and political parties to say they have more important priorities than planned events, but that is not very convincing when policy already exists for directly related domains like sport, the arts, tourism and economic development.

11.2 RESEARCH NOTE ON POLITICS

Reid, G. (2006). The politics of city imaging. A case study of the MTV Europe Music Awards Edinburgh '03. *Event Management*, 10(1), 35–46.

This event became politicized because of a large public subsidy that was intended to generate local economic benefits and help portray Edinburgh in a new light. The event was part of the city's ongoing repositioning strategy. Although Reid says the event did generate some benefits, local media were very critical. Issues of power, media management, how events are justified and what exactly is culture are all addressed in this article.

Why national governments are involved with events

Many governments at all levels are developing policies and strategies regarding the events sector – often with tourism as the main priority, but increasingly adding social, cultural and environmental goals as well. Examples from Scotland and New Zealand can be found in Events in Focus 11.2.

EVENTS IN FOCUS

11.2 Events sector policies and strategies: examples from Scotland and New Zealand

Scotland (www.eventscotland.org)

'The Perfect Stage' is Scotland's national events strategy which outlines our mission and vision for attracting and hosting events up to 2020. The strategy defines Scotland's key assets, which have made it a world leading events destination.

Scotland's cultural identity and heritage are strong differentiating factors and the friendliness of our people is renowned throughout the world. Scotland boasts a rich natural landscape as well as impressive architecture and cityscapes and a range of sports facilities and arenas. Scotland has a range of iconic sporting and cultural events, which form the backbone of our events portfolio and reinforce our reputation as a world leading events destination.

The strategy also defines the seven key impacts by which EventScotland will measure the successes of Scotland's events industry: tourism; business; image and identity as a nation; media; participation and development; environment and social and cultural benefits.

Scotland has earned its place and reputation in hosting major world class events and, through this visionary and aspirational events strategy, will continue to do so.

Scotland: The Perfect Stage outlines a clear mission and vision for building and strengthening Scotland's events industry and leading that industry into the future.

Major Events New Zealand (www.med.govt.nz/majorevents/new-zealand-major-events/strategy)

The New Zealand Government, through New Zealand Major Events, works in partnership with the event sector to support New Zealand's growing reputation as an attractive destination for major events of global significance. The government invests in major events that generate significant immediate and long-term benefits and align with wider government objectives through leverage and legacy opportunities.

Our vision is that New Zealand becomes a world class event destination where major events generate economic, social and cultural benefits to New Zealand.

New Zealand Major Events' priorities are to attract, retain, grow and enhance tourism.

Major events have the potential to:

- increase tourism revenue
- increase opportunities for New Zealand brand promotion
- create new business and trade opportunities, reinforcing high achievement and increasing participation in sports and arts

- strengthen national pride and identity
- enhance the capability of the events sector.

Over the long term major event outcomes include:

- a high value economy
- vibrant communities and culture
- a flourishing events sector.

New Zealand Major Events' priority actions include:

- smart investment of the Major Events Development Fund in events with the most potential for economic return
- continue to ensure that events activate leverage and legacy plans that deliver on wider government objectives
- implement the revised decision-making structure for the Major Events Development Fund – including establishing the Major Events Ministers Group and Major Event Investment Panel
- develop a prospecting plan to enhance New Zealand's ability to attract major events
- develop a stronger model for evaluating the economic, social and cultural benefits of major events
- continue to implement the Business Events Strategic Approach alongside Tourism New Zealand
- more effectively communicate the government's Major Events Strategy to the New Zealand events sector and reinforce New Zealand's reputation as a world-class events destination
- continue to support sector capability building through the Major Events Resource Bank.

11.1 EXPERT OPINION

Socio-cultural trends and issues relating to tourism, festivals and cultural events

Dr Philip Long, Bournemouth University, UK

The development and promotion of festivals and cultural events that are aimed, at least in part, at attracting tourists, continues to be of interest to researchers, policy-makers and practitioners in the arts, community development, regeneration and tourism worldwide. Connections are also being made between festivals and showcasing the work of sectors within the so-called 'creative industries' (e.g. film, literature, visual and performing arts, fashion and emerging media technologies). This political and professional recognition is testimony to the importance of festivals in people's lives and their intrinsic and extrinsic socio-cultural and economic values, even though these can be contentious and are not necessarily well understood, with a tendency for 'benefits' to be hyped in justifying public and private funding.

However, reductions in public-sector funding and private-sector sponsorship following the global economic crisis continue to be threats to the festival sector. In the United Kingdom, and elsewhere, a decline in disposable income among the 'squeezed middle classes' is also of concern to those arts festivals that seek to attract such audiences.

More positively, however, many festivals continue to have an enduring appeal and 'place in the calendar' and some may benefit from people substituting spending on long-haul, expensive holidays for more local leisure pursuits, including attendance at festivals that involve shorter travel distances (the so-called 'staycation' phenomenon in the UK, for example).

This last observation extends beyond economic considerations to focus on socio-cultural trends and issues that may have implications for the festivals sector. Such 'trends' are difficult to identify categorically and of course vary across societies, cultures, national and even local and regional boundaries. This very brief review outlines some dimensions of socio-cultural change that are prominent in media discourse at least in the UK and that are also the subject of academic research and policy papers that go beyond the festival and tourism literature.

In no particular order, the following issues may be discerned. First, in the UK and elsewhere there has been a policy emphasis on the scaling-back of the state and promotion of a 'localist' agenda. Festivals that celebrate the distinctive nature of local places are pertinent here. Second and related to localism is the promotion of volunteering. The encouragement of volunteering at festivals and events both large and small scale is a prominent feature of voluntarism. Third, there are ongoing concerns in many societies surrounding migration and the integration of ethnic minority communities with some emphasis now on an 'inter-cultural' discourse and the 'failure' of a multicultural approach. Again, festivals that celebrate communities and that bring together people across ethnic 'divides' have a large role to play. Fourth, new and emerging media have implications for festival practitioners in relation, for example to the application of such technologies to festival programmes (digital arts festivals, for example) and in audience engagement through mobile devices and apps. Fifth, demographic changes reflected in the ageing population in many societies have important implications for festivals in terms of programming, audiences, access, etc. A final socio-cultural consideration in this brief and far from exhaustive review is a fashionable topic derived from economic and social theorists on the political economy of happiness and well-being. Again, at least in theory, festivals and cultural events have much to contribute to social and individual well-being and contentment.

In the sections below, we look more closely at the economic, cultural, social and environmental policy domains as they relate to planned events. For each, goals are suggested, then related policy initiatives and appropriate performance measures are discussed.

Economic policy and events

Much of the importance attached to planned events is related to their economic benefits, leading many governments to view event development as a legitimate, strategic policy field. While this has resulted in considerable growth in the events sector, it is a limited view of planned events and does result in some negative consequences (see Table 11.1).

Foster event tourism

Tourism 'boosterism' has led many policy-makers to believe that events are good, and that investment in them is justified, because they attract tourists and media attention. Event tourism clearly can generate foreign currency and enhance a destination's image development, but these benefits cannot be taken for granted. There are too many variables at play to ensure success: witness the downturn in tourist arrivals

Table 11.1 Economic policy and events

Possible goals	Related policy initiatives	Performance measures
Foster event tourism	Establish event tourism as a policy domain	Measure event tourism yield relative to other tourists
Leverage events for general economic development	Develop an event portfolio strategy for the community or destination	
Use events to maximize venue efficiency	Integrate event policy with venue investment and operations	Tourism growth
		Demonstrable 'legacy' benefits
Use events in place marketing (e.g. image enhancement)	Integrate event policy with place marketing and other economic development	Evaluation of image enhancement

to Australia following the 2000 Sydney Olympic Games. The Olympics were oversold on the basis of long-term tourism benefits, but who could predict the tragedy of 9/11 the following year?

Event tourism is a truly global phenomenon, and is highly competitive, but many destinations and cities do not have a specific policy or strategy for it. Event tourism policy should be fully integrated with policy for venues (e.g. convention centres, sport and cultural facilities) and for place marketing and economic development.

Developing a 'portfolio' of events (see Getz 2005) is a good strategy. At the base of the portfolio 'pyramid' are small, local events which meet resident needs, animate the destination and perhaps have some tourism growth potential. The top of the pyramid should be an occasional mega event, but for most destinations it is probable that enduring benefits are more attainable through the development of one or more periodic 'hallmark events' that fit the brand and boost the destination's image. As well, many regional-scale events will provide tourism benefits. One essential component of the portfolio approach is to recognize that events have different value (e.g. sustainability, high-yield, growth potential, market share, cost) and that portfolios can be developed for different types of events and for all seasons.

Strategic consideration should also be given to the desirability and means for growing events in size and tourism significance, such as by increased marketing and lengthening of their duration. Some events can be transformed from resident to visitor dominated, although with caution to avoid displacement or disgruntlement of residents.

The selection of performance measures is important. Too many tourism organizations rely on volume measures, as if having more tourists is inherently good and without costs. Every destination should instead concentrate on yield and sustainability. Event tourists tend to be high in yield relative to mass, packaged tourists, and this has clearly been documented for convention tourists and types of participant-sport tourist. The sustainability of tourists in this context refers both to their long-term demand (will they come back?) and their appropriateness in terms of achieving sustainable development goals.

11.2 EXPERT OPINION

Asset management, portfolio management, process mapping and the gulf

Below is a personal view by event producer and consultant William (Bill) O'Toole on event development in the Middle East (also see his website: www.epms.net).

The countries surrounding the Arab Gulf are focusing on events and festivals as a tool to enable business and social development. The culture of these countries is well attuned to some events, such as meetings and conferences. Almost all private houses have a meeting area for discussion and hospitality called the *majlis*. Exhibitions have been around for thousands of years with the caravan routes and the souks. Public festivals, product launches and marketing events are relatively new to the region.

Saudi Arabia recently announced the creation of the Saudi Exhibitions and Conventions Bureau. It has built upon the work over ten years to develop local tourism festivals and events that created the foundation for an events industry. The SECB aims to develop the necessary infrastructure and attract events into the region.

The governments are embarking on developing event strategies. As part of their strategy, Dubai gained the World Expo for 2020 and is developing it into a significant event for the whole region. They have created the Dubai Event Calendar to consolidate and support events and festivals. The local online industry website, SourceME, lists over 600 event companies and organizers in the Gulf region, most of which have their office in Dubai.

In response to this rapid development over the past 15 years and the resulting complexity, the governments are turning towards an events portfolio or asset management approach to their events so they can direct the development, invest in successful events and devolve the events that are simply not working. As described in the textbook *Events Feasibility and Development* (O'Toole 2011: 8), 'the tools of physical asset management can be taken across to the event industry. They provide a ready made language to describe the event portfolio and enable the comparison of the event assets to other tangible and intangible assets.'

At the same time the policies and procedures involved in the event management and the events portfolio management need to be understood and described. The tool employed for this is process mapping. Process mapping describes the workflow and therefore includes the time and tasks. 'Process mapping involves extracting the [event management] processes, describing them and their interactions. By doing this, the processes may be improved, delegated and, in some cases, automated though software. Attendee registration is an example of a process used in certain events, repeated many times and is ultimately automated' (O'Toole 2011: 8).

The result is a rational system for events development. Asset management creates a long-term view of value so as to apportion resources to events with a positive impact over years. The process mapping allows the rationalizing of the internal management of each event. Governments in Dubai, Saudi Arabia, Abu Dhabi and Doha as well as the major companies such as the investment banks have all begun this transformation. The next step is the creation and implementation of event management standards and, possibly, the licensing of event companies.

Leverage events for general economic development

Event tourism policy and strategy have been expanding to focus on 'leveraging' events more comprehensively, including using events to foster trade and economic diversification. Plans also have to be in place to realize the potential urban renewal benefits of mega events and to ensure that facilities built for events will remain viable and efficiently utilized in the long term.

The employment-creation potential of most events is small, although mega events can generate substantial short-term growth in construction jobs. To maximize employment benefits, event policy has to be tied closely to tourism, sport and culture/arts development in general, and to venue construction and operations.

Suitable performance measures can include jobs created and sustained, the spread of event benefits in time and space, stakeholder satisfaction, new trade and business links formed, and start-up businesses related to events.

Use events to maximize venue efficiency

Funding and building convention and exhibition centres, arts and sports facilities has a major impact on events and event tourism. What is surprising is that massive infrastructure investments are frequently made without a supporting events policy. It seems to be assumed that cities need impressive facilities, and that most publicly funded event venues will be permanently subsidized by government.

How many events are held, and their economic benefits, is one measure of venue efficiency. Building them is expensive, but easy, whereas making good use of facilities in the long term is the real challenge. A balance between tourist and resident use is also desired.

Use events in place marketing

Exploiting events for image-building, branding, repositioning or place marketing in general requires policy and a strategy. Competitive advantages are being gained by destinations that have the knowledge and vision to integrate events with other place-marketing efforts, including film development, familiarization tours, trade missions, and city or regional branding.

Because economic impact and growth measures are most in use, there needs to be more effort expended on developing and testing social, cultural and environmental performance measures in event tourism. Some intangible measures, including image enhancement, are difficult to formulate and research. Even more difficult, both in theoretical and methodological terms, is to prove that image enhancement increases tourism demand.

Cultural policy and events

Next to economics, events are most often seen as being in the domain of cultural policy. This relates mostly to festivals and the arts, but there is no reason why all planned events cannot facilitate cultural experiences and meet other cultural development goals (see Table 11.2).

Foster arts and cultural development

A number of studies have examined the aims or mandates of festivals and events. A survey of Irish festivals (Goh 2003) asked organizers to indicate and prioritize their aims, revealing that the top goal was

Table 11.2 Cultural policy and events

Possible goals	Related policy initiatives	Performance measures
Foster arts and cultural development through investment in events	Integrate events in cultural policy and arts development strategies	Assess the overall effectiveness of arts and cultural development in the community
Leverage events for general and traditional/indigenous cultural development	Develop specific event funding programmes	
Use events to maximize venue efficiency	Develop cultural themes and programming for all events	Develop and employ specific measures of cultural event success and its benefits
Foster sustainable cultural event tourism		

to promote artistic excellence. This was followed very closely by increasing tourism and area promotion (both place-marketing goals). Other aims (in descending order) were to showcase local heritage or arts, boost the local economy, celebration, encourage social inclusion, and education.

'Development' in the arts and cultural domains has to encompass increased awareness of what is available and its benefits to the community, audience-building through direct involvement of people in the arts, generating revenue (such as by facilitating corporate sponsorship and targeting grants), fostering traditional or indigenous talent and expression, and even providing free entertainment for the public.

Radbourne (2002) said that the most common argument for government involvement is that 'arts and cultural activity enrich a society and that all people have the right of access and participation'. Because public benefits are generated (although these are frequently in dispute), and because the private sector will not provide the necessary supply (a 'failure of the marketplace'), direct government action is needed. Basically this is the 'social equity argument' – that many people cannot afford the arts without government intervention. More recently, claims have been growing that the arts and cultural activity in general make for an attractive living and working environment, stimulating innovation and competitive advantage (e.g. Florida, 2002 and the 'creative economy').

All events can provide cultural experiences through appropriate theming and programming. There is no reason why business and political events cannot provide cultural experiences for visitors, such as through authentic entertainment, meaningful host–guest interactions, interpretation, and additional pre- or post-cultural opportunities.

11.3 RESEARCH NOTE ON ARTS, FESTIVALS AND POLICY

Quinn, B. (2010a). Arts festivals, urban tourism and cultural policy. *Journal of Policy Research in Tourism, Leisure and Events*, 2(3), 264–279.

'Arts festivals are in the ascendant. Framed within an array of neoliberal, culture-led urban regeneration strategies, they are now a mainstay of urban tourism and urban policy-making. As such, they face growing competitive pressures and competing agendas, and the need for a set of coherent goals and policy frameworks is vital. While a review of the literature clearly shows that arts festivals can deliver a series of benefits that separately meet the cultural policy and urban tourism policy objectives, there is little to suggest that cities normatively engage in comprehensive, integrated policy-making for urban arts festivals.'

Foster sustainable cultural event tourism

Ali-Knight and Robertson (2004: 8) outlined the Edinburgh Cultural Policy, and the subsequent Festivals Strategy launched in 2001 in tandem with an Events Strategy. These policy initiatives reflected the city's commitment to its positioning as the 'festival city', in recognition of the contribution of events to both the economic and cultural viability of the city. The Festivals Strategy emerged from stakeholder consultations, in both the tourism and festival sectors, discussions with core groups like the Joint Festivals Working Group, and extensive desk research including benchmarking against other cities.

Some of the key goals of the Festivals Strategy were to develop a year-round programme of events, and to ensure their independence and a balance of creativity, social objectives and commercial viability. Other aims covered social inclusion (getting a broad range of residents involved) and securing adequate funding.

There will remain, inevitably, many tensions between culture and the growing 'instrumentalist' or 'strategic' approaches to festivals and events. Waterman (1998) highlighted latent tensions between festival as art and economics, between culture and cultural politics. He concluded that support for the arts is part of a process used by elites to establish social distance between themselves and others, and that festival development is related to place promotion, which encourages 'safe' art forms.

Traditional culture

As illustrated in Research Note 3.1 by Xie (2003), official Chinese policy both helped convert the bamboo-beating dance on Hainan Island to a tourist-oriented spectacle and, ironically, helped turn it into an authentic tradition for the Li people. This aspect of cultural policy is often overlooked in developed countries because traditional events and indigenous peoples are either non-existent or have been marginalized. It is more likely that native celebrations, like the North American pow-wow, will be viewed as tourist attractions and marketed accordingly, rather than viewed as being on a par with opera or theatre.

11.4 RESEARCH NOTE ON CONTESTED MEANINGS AND PLACES

Adams, K. (2011). Public interest anthropology, political market squares, and re-scripting dominance: From swallows to 'race' in San Juan Capistrano, CA. *Journal of Policy Research in Tourism, Leisure and Events*, 3(2), 147–169.

'This article explores a disturbing irony of certain touristic festivals and heritage sites: although these festivals and sites tend to draw heavily on the language of shared heritage and community, the dominant narratives and cultural symbols embodied in these venues sometimes celebrate more traditional and problematic "racial", ethnic and gender hierarchies. Via a case study of the annual swallows festival – held in the California mission town of San Juan Capistrano, this article offers an illustration of the value of embracing a public interest anthropology (PIA) framework for identifying and addressing the hidden racisms underlying some heritage tourism sites. Moreover, the article suggests that the political market square metaphor for conceptualizing tourism festival management could be productively reframed and paired with a PIA approach to facilitate more inclusive, colour-blind approaches to developing tourism policy.'

Social policy and events

Foster social integration

In many communities, including small towns and city neighbourhoods, events can be catalysts for community development. Their organization and revenue-making potential can foster self-sufficiency and pride in accomplishment. Community identity and pride can be heightened through sharing with outsiders. Integration of diverse or conflicted social groups should be a specific aim, to be realized through planning and decision-making, all the way through social interaction and interpretation at events.

Public services and resources provided to events (e.g. police, fire, traffic control, transport, physical infrastructure) are often viewed as expenses to be recovered, but should be provided within the context of social and cultural policy. In many cases direct provision of events, and subsidies for using public services, are warranted.

Who should have access to public spaces and venues? Many governments license all events and ban or shut down informal gatherings, but does this policy always serve social and other goals? It can certainly be argued that in a free society people have the right to assemble and hold spontaneous events, although this has to be balanced by responsible behaviour. How should potentially conflicting aims be resolved?

Combat social problems

What constitutes anti-social behaviour versus permissible civil disobedience? Preventing and reacting to social problems at or surrounding events is a matter of social policy. It is not just a security issue, but should integrate public awareness and education, event management including crowd controls, venue design and travel restrictions.

Leverage events for urban renewal

Mega events in particular are viewed as opportunities for large-scale redevelopment or urban renewal projects. Cities create tangible legacies in terms of monuments and landmarks, culture and entertainment precincts, fresh design and aesthetics, and hopefully renewed residential value. History has demonstrated that these benefits must be planned in advance, not left to chance, and that events can be a powerful planning and renewal tool (see Table 11.3).

Use events to enhance health and wellness

Events can be used as social marketing tools (requiring education and thematic interpretation) and to provide activities for encouraging healthy lifestyles. There will be direct tie-ins to sport, parks and recreation. Examples include food and beverage festivals with nutritional themes, sport competitions stressing safe play, and 'edutainment' events in parks. Health concerns and regulations have to be applied across the spectrum of events and event venues, so why not make them proactive to encourage health and wellness?

'Social tourism' is a related policy field, entailing the subsidization of holidays or other leisure activities, especially for the economically disadvantaged or persons with special needs. 'Sport For All' and sport youth festivals can yield psychological as well as health benefits. Because so many sports glorify violence, policy should be directed towards the counter-message that sport can be safe, friendly and fun. Hooliganism and other social problems associated with certain sport events have to be combated through a multidimensional approach including legal prohibitions against travel, public education, venue design, crowd management/controls and security regimes.

Table 11.3 Social policy and events

Possible goals	Related policy initiatives	Performance measures
Foster social integration and community development through a programme of public events	Integrate events with urban renewal, social and community development policy	Assess the overall effectiveness of social policy; develop and employ specific measures of event success and its benefits
Combat social problems at and surrounding events (hooliganism, crime, etc.)	Integrate events with health and wellness policy	
	Integrate events with policy for sport, parks and recreation	
Leverage events for urban renewal	Provide resources for combating social problems associated with events	
Use events to enhance health and wellness	Formulate policy regarding the use of public spaces for events, both formal and informal	

Public subsidy for professional sports and private sport venues is controversial. A lot of evidence suggests it is not economically beneficial to cities, and typically it is done for reasons of prestige and political expediency. Are there any social benefits that can justify this form of subsidy?

Recreation events can be viewed as a public good, particularly when they encompass a variety of social and cultural aims. Events in parks should provide for safe social interaction and should foster environmental responsibility.

11.5 RESEARCH NOTE ON LOCAL AUTHORITY POLICY IN WALES

O'Sullivan, D., Pickernell, D. and Senyard, J. (2009). Public sector evaluation of festivals and special events. *Journal of Policy Research in Tourism, Leisure and Events*, 1(1), 19–36.

Research in Wales on local authority involvement with events demonstrated that goals for local or community events were primarily related to (in descending order) community well-being, economic development, image enhancement, extension of the tourism season, local culture and arts and civic pride. But when it came to evaluation, it was primarily oriented towards management improvement and economic impacts, with social-cultural impacts not being sufficiently considered. The authors called for a more balanced, triple-bottom-line approach to event evaluation.

Community resilience

Derrett (2008: 107) has developed a model to show how festivals can develop community resilience, defined as the 'future capacity of that community to meet challenges that might beset them'. The key elements in the process are participation (collaboration, engagement from multiple stakeholders), governance (leadership, learning) and the nature and context of the event. The aims are to foster social-cultural well-being, environmental sustainability and economic prosperity. In effect, events are a catalyst in this complex process of community and economic development, in a triple-bottom-line approach. All this should be viewed in the context of development of a sense of place and community.

Social marketing

Many uses of events as policy instruments can be considered as 'social marketing', designed to change attitudes and behaviour of the public – for the better. The focus is on populations, not individuals, and positive results can be very difficult to prove. Probably the best-known examples are from the health policy domain, particularly stop-smoking campaigns. When events are intended to change attitudes and behaviour, new research methods and measures will be required.

Lefebvre (2011) outlined a social marketing approach focused on audiences. The four rings of the model have audiences in the middle, and it is essential to specify what are the benefits to the target audience. Benefits should tap into deep motivations. The social context must be understood, both with regard to current attitudes and desired behaviours, and both determinants and consequences of attitudes and behaviour. Methods of branding and positioning should be used to communicate the ideal, in terms that the target audience find appealing. It has to mean something positive to them, such as health, pride, happiness and well-being. The full marketing mix can then be employed, including economic and non-economic aspects of price (such as the cost of social problems in a community).

Applied to events there are many challenges, not the least of which is being able to demonstrate that holding events, and getting people to participate, will achieve desired goals. Sometimes these things just have to be accepted on faith, and that is part of what a philosophy of planned events should encompass – just as it does for leisure in general.

Environmental policy and events

Robert Case (2013) authored the book *Events and the Environment*, emphasizing the various relationships that have to be considered: the entire supply chain for events; venues, permanent and temporary; micro and macro impacts (from waste and noise to climate change); legacies such as regeneration; and the various environmental constraints and determinants such as weather and landscape. The book covers legislation and standards applicable to the events sector, at various levels of government. One interesting observation made by Case is that small events are not scrutinized in the same way as large events, and perhaps do not even have to account for environmental impacts.

Require green and sustainable events and event venues

The basic policy imperative is to ensure that all events are 'green', meeting the minimum RRR standards (i.e. reduce, reuse and recycle), and integrate with conservation and environmental management policies, land-use planning and controls, noise and traffic by-laws, and other environmental influencers (see Table 11.4). Beyond that, a policy to foster sustainable events (a 'triple-bottom-line' approach: economic, social, environmental) will go much further to conserve the environment and ensure long-term support for events, although it cannot be expected that all stakeholders will share this comprehensive perspective (Hede 2007).

In the UK, a Sustainable Events Management System has been developed (British Standards Institute 2006) and this suggests a likely global trend. The document provides several reasons for developing standards, including social and client expectations, legislative compliance and the delivery of better outcomes at lower cost. Issues to be considered under the heading of sustainable events are diverse: global climate change; air and water use and quality; land use; biodiversity; heritage; emissions and waste; product stewardship (ethics and values); health, safety and comfort. A lot of emphasis is placed on organization and management systems, including risk assessment, working with stakeholders and supply chain controls.

Tribe (2005: 380) discussed sustainable development from an economics perspective, and we can apply these principles to events. Renewable resources are at the base of many sustainable development strategies, so what in the events sector is truly renewable? Culture is renewable, but it changes and can be

Table 11.4 Environmental policy and events

Possible goals	Related policy initiatives	Performance measures
Require green and sustainable events and event venues	Integrate event policy with planning, land use and all environmental management systems	Develop comprehensive environmental standards and evaluation measures for events and event venues
Leverage events for environmental education and development	Supply chain controls	Evaluate the social marketing effectiveness of environmental messages at events
Foster events with environmental themes	Full life-cycle accounting	

impacted negatively. Cultural differences that we value, such as traditions, costumes, foods and symbols, should be protected. Events that have a negative effect on the environment, generate excessive waste or foster consumptive attitudes cannot be justified in this context.

A related concept is that of 'capacity to absorb' events, or to tolerate change without detrimental impacts on culture or the environment. Each event has potential impacts, but what can we say about cumulative event impacts? Little attention has been paid to this issue. Design capacity for venues is a related concept, and event managers are forced to examine maximum attendance and the activity load of events for safety, health and experiential reasons.

The 'precautionary principle' comes up whenever sustainability is discussed, but it is controversial. Some people believe that if we can anticipate that an event might cause negative impacts, we should not produce it. This is extreme in my view, as it can be misused to preclude just about any activity or development. In the same way, the principle of 'no irreversible change' is open to considerable misuse as a way to prevent desired and necessary action. The fact is that almost any development results in irreversible changes.

Finally, we have already mentioned economic 'externalities'. A logical response to the externality problem is to require that polluters pay for their actions, and that anyone causing public costs should be held accountable. If this principle gets applied uniformly it will mean that no event organizer will be able to ignore costs and impacts that extend beyond the event. However, this principle can also be abused. Consider that events often result in traffic congestion, albeit temporarily, and some people not attending the event might lose time and money as a consequence. Should they be compensated by the event organizers? What about people impacted by event-caused noise?

Certainly it is important to consider all these costs and benefits in the feasibility study and in post-event evaluations, but it is also important to realize that society is almost always paying some price for economic activity; we tolerate congestion and noise as a normal consequence of living in cities and fostering economic growth. The same argument applies to any event that provides a 'public good' – we should be willing to collectively tolerate some degree of inconvenience or amenity loss in pursuit of social and cultural growth. To what extent we tolerate them, and how we deal with externalities, is a matter of debate and public decision-making.

Economic tools exist for influencing the marketplace and fostering sustainable development. Price mechanisms generally work well, either using high prices to discourage consumption or subsidized prices to encourage it. If society believes that attending cultural festivals is a form of sustainable development, but participation in off-road motorcycle races is not, price manipulation can be made through differential taxation, subsidies or other means. Still more effective, of course, is direct prevention of undesirable events through licensing or other regulatory devices.

Leverage events for environmental education and development

The goal here is to infuse environmental education into events, as a form of 'social marketing'. Visitors should be made aware of green operations and sustainability principles applied to the event they are attending, and they could also be informed of how to extend these actions to their home and work settings. Obviously events with environmental themes are best able to educate visitors about conservation, sustainability and other issues, but they might not attract as broad an audience.

Foster events with environmental themes

Events with explicit environmental themes have been growing in number, including global movements like Earth Day and interest-specific themes like bird watching. The tools of 'thematic interpretation' should be employed to make sure the message provokes a positive reaction from guests. Many such events will be exercises in 'social marketing' by environmental agencies, but special interest groups like 'birders' are also active in this sphere.

Public policy-making

If events are considered a 'public good', on par with – or an element in – social, leisure, health, sport and culture policy, then there should be a planning process in place to ensure adequate provision. The following system could be put in place:

- needs assessment; issues identification; multi-stakeholder input;
- developing a portfolio of events to meet specific needs in specific places;
- setting standards of provision and accessibility;
- funding and facilitation programmes tied to public agencies and venues;
- organizational development to ensure implementation; community capacity-building;
- research, monitoring and impact evaluation;
- review and policy refinement.

It seems likely that most authorities will not develop such an integrated events policy, but within the closely related policy domains, the same planning approach can be applied:

- issues (why are we interested in events? justification for intervention);
- purpose and goals (what we want to accomplish with events – the desired outcomes);
- research, consultations and the planning process;
- evaluation and accountability (e.g. performance measures, monitoring and feedback);
- implementation: laws and regulations; event development or bidding agencies; event-funding programmes.

Policy considerations

Hall and Page (2006: 335) identified a number of policy-related considerations that should be applied to the events sector.

What is the policy environment?

This includes the basic form of government (is it democratic?), the distribution of power and how society is structured. The dominant and varied values of political parties (i.e. ideology) are key forces, especially the emphasis on a free market versus interventionism.

'Institutional arrangements' must be considered. Where exactly is event-related policy formed, and how is it implemented at all levels of government and within quasi-public agencies? Unless there exists an event development agency (these are common in Australia), or an events office within city hall (for example, in the Chicago Mayor's Office), who even speaks for events? There are many voices to be heard, and not all of them are effective in lobbying.

This introduces the notion of a 'policy arena' in which special interest groups engage in lobbying, institutions interact, individuals and groups achieve influence, and leadership might or might not be effective. The notion of a 'political market square' is pertinent, as the various stakeholders have varying degrees of power and influence, form alliances or collaborate, negotiate and seek to influence policy. The openness of this process should be a matter of concern to everyone. In most places the policy arena for events is fractured, consisting of the often-competing voices of sport, arts, heritage, culture and tourism, and further subdivided by professional associations representing specific types of event.

Specific policy issues have to be considered within the general policy domains discussed above. Policies and programmes are formulated for specific purposes, then must be evaluated in terms of their impact, effectiveness and efficiency. Policy should be continuously reviewed and improved, and with full stakeholder input. A great deal of technical support is required for this process, including research and information dissemination. Finally, there is the important matter of accountability – how are officials and others held accountable for their policies and actions?

Options for events policy and strategy

Getz and Frisby (1991) developed a framework for local government policy-making in the events sector, and their framework can be applied to event-related policy in general. The basic logic also applies to other agencies, such as tourism, which get involved with events. The basic premise is that some level of policy or direct intervention in the events sector is desired and practical. First, several optional roles have to be considered:

- 'direct provision': government or agencies produce and own events;
- 'equity approach': do not produce, but invest in events (in this case 'equity' means the capital invested);
- 'sponsorship': act like corporations and make sponsorship deals for specific benefits (such as image-making, social marketing);
- 'facilitate': through various policy initiatives, facilitate event creation or operations.

The 'facilitation' role leads to various assistance options:

- financial: grants, loans, lines of credit, debt relief, subsidies (e.g. for use of police, traffic services, venues), tax relief, awards and prizes;
- technical: professional advice; training; research and information; office space;
- marketing: overall or event-specific promotions; inclusion in government materials, websites, etc.;
- regulatory: fast-tracking; release from onerous obligations;
- infrastructure: provision and improvement of necessary services (roads, water, etc.) and public venues (e.g. theatres, arenas, parks, plazas).

In this interventionist approach a number of other policy issues arise. To whom should assistance be given? Should all organizations and events be treated the same, or should they have to meet specific criteria like proof of managerial competence? Under what conditions should assistance be given? There could be annual applications mandated, and grants could be in the form of one-time-only seed money versus continuous support. And all systems need procedures and accountability, including formal applications, monitoring and periodic audits.

Regulating the events sector

Event producers have to satisfy and manage relationships with numerous regulatory agencies and their officials. A majority of these are at the local level, but sometimes multi-level approvals are needed:.

- police: security requirements; police presence;
- traffic: accessibility, parking, public transport, control;
- fire: maximum capacity; accessibility and evacuation procedures; materials;
- health and safety: hazardous materials; fireworks and lasers; food and beverage preparation and storage standards; electricity; waste disposal;
- building inspection: new construction or allowable temporary structures;

- land use: where events can be held; where venues can be built; size limits; site planning requirements;
- noise control: noise levels and dispersion; hours of operation;
- labour: minimum wages; age restrictions; work hours; certification of professionals and trades people;
- environmental: emission standards (smoke, pollutants); recycling; wastes;
- consumer protection: price controls, guarantees, refunds.

Policy formulation at the community level: collaboration and consensus-building

Policy-making for events can range from a top-down approach, dictated by government or specific agencies, to bottom-up, arising from community needs assessments and the input of many stakeholders. Event tourism policy tends to be top-down (at least in Australia, as demonstrated by Whitford 2004a, 2004b), mainly because it is seen as legitimate economic development, but also because so much bidding on events is opportunistic.

When developing policy open to stakeholder input, a number of collaborative, consensus-building approaches can be used. Hall and Rusher (2004: 225) gave an example of effective community involvement in events policy. In New Zealand the Alexandra Blossom Festival illustrates 'how the complex social structures of the community have shaped the political environment and how this in turn has evolved into a relationship with local government that ensures a high degree of community input into policy development'. The festival has sought to be inclusive of various interests and values in the community.

Research, evaluation and public policy

What do we need to formulate and effectively administer events-related policy? Both practitioners and academics have a role to play, not just the policy-makers themselves.

To analyse policy, or strategy, one should examine the following:

- intention, expressed purpose (is it economic/development-oriented, or community/culture-oriented; goals and performance criteria);
- contents (responsibilities of the agencies involved, types of events covered, applicability in different settings);
- implementation (programmes and schedules, funds allocated, regulations, evaluation and accountability);
- results (multiple, independent evaluations of intended and unintended outcomes; feedback and revisions).

Robertson *et al.* (2009) believe there is general agreement that events have the potential to offer sustainable benefits, but there is rarely clear guidance as to how this will be determined or measured. Often social and cultural goals are paralleled by tourism and place-marketing goals, raising fears of goal displacement. There are contested meanings to many festivals, depending on stakeholder interests. Policy and institutional networks can be important when assessing impacts, as festivals can be catalysts for future action. This creation of social or cultural capital is difficult to measure. The authors surveyed festival directors in the UK and concluded that the age and type of event was important when it came to how festival evaluations were conducted and the impacts judged to be important.

Public discourse and policy

We cannot expect rational and sustainable decision-making until and unless there is a full, open and honest public discourse on events and their cost and impacts. Such a discourse is also essential for the institutionalization of a new paradigm, such as a sustainable events or triple-bottom-line approach.

What gets covered in the press, and the issues talked about by residents, constitute important elements in the public discourse. Researchers and practitioners have a moral responsibility to engage politicians and the public, in large part by offering evidence and informed opinions about the impacts of events.

The following Research Notes 11.6 make it clear that public discourse on events is often difficult, and even deliberately manipulated.

11.6 RESEARCH NOTES ON PUBLIC DISCOURSE ABOUT EVENTS

Theodoraki, E. (2009). Organisational communication on the intended and achieved impacts of the Athens 2004 Olympic Games. *Journal of Policy Research in Tourism, Hospitality and Events*, 1(2), 141–155.

The researcher examined how and what the Athens Olympic Committee (2004) communicated with different audiences, over the life cycle of the event. It is stressed that there is no 'best' right way of capturing all the impacts of a mega event like the Olympics, and that they are subject to the influence of multiple stakeholders. Theodoraki concluded that consideration of impacts at the bid stage was very weak, with no quantifiable targets or commitments. Anticipated positive economic impacts were stressed by proponents. Social benefits were also raised, but there was no evidence cited to support forecasts of benefits. Post-event statements by organizers ignored sport and political impacts, and made unsupported claims about tourism and other economic gains. Environmental and social benefits were also claimed, using only opinion surveys that appeared to be public-relations exercises. No real impact study was conducted after the Games. It was concluded that most of the communications from organizers were intended to create a positive image of the IOC and the Games. Pressures on staff to report only positive effects were observed. Greek officials wanted public support for infrastructure and redevelopment projects.

Weed, M. and Dowse, S. (2009). A missed opportunity waiting to happen? The social legacy potential of the London 2012 Paralympic Games. *Journal of Policy Research in Tourism, Hospitality and Events*, 1(2), 170–174.

The authors observed considerable interest in the media and public in discussing the potential impacts of the Olympics on the UK. There were a lot of official Olympic and oppositional narratives being circulated, each serving the interests of different groups. Weed and Dowse concluded that (2009: 170) 'the dominant public discourse has been about the potential to develop economic legacies'. The Paralympic Games were seldom discussed, presumably because they were felt to offer fewer economic benefits, or were simply lumped into the overall Olympic legacy. Too much emphasis was placed on developing elite Paralympic athletes, as a legacy, and the authors worried about opportunity costs if money was taken from other programmes for the disabled to pay for the mega event. These researchers favour using the Games to help change public and official attitudes. Most evidence supporting claims about social impacts were really opinion pieces, and the proof does not exist.

STUDY GUIDE

The nature of public policy was discussed at the beginning of this chapter, leading to an exploration of how public involvement in the events sector can be justified. Specifically this included the 'public good' argument and 'equity principle', which are linked to ideology, and, borrowing from economics, the 'failure of the marketplace' justification. Additional justification is related to 'efficiency', as in getting the most out of public infrastructure and venues, and the intangible or psychic benefits that accrue to people even if they do not attend events.

Public discourse surrounds many events, especially the ones that require huge public investments. The best way to see policy and planning at work is to follow the whole process from beginning to end. In the case of the Olympics or a world's fair, this process takes many years. You can also go back through various media reports to see how public debate (if any) evolves.

STUDY QUESTIONS

- What is 'public policy' and what are 'policy domains'?
- Explain how governmental intervention in the event sector can be justified, including the 'public good' and 'equity' arguments, 'market failure' and 'efficiency'.
- Discuss economic, social, cultural and environmental policy domains as they pertain to planned events. Give examples of major possible goals, related policy initiatives and performance measures.
- What factors are important in shaping the policy-making process for events? Include 'ideology' and 'institutional arrangements'.
- What process should governments follow to develop policies for events?

FURTHER READING

Case, R. (2013). *Events and the Environment*. Oxford: Routledge.

Veal, A. (2010). *Leisure, Sport and Tourism: Politics, Policy and Planning* (3rd edn). Wallingford: CABI.

Chapter **12**

Science, knowledge and theory for event studies

LEARNING OBJECTIVES

Upon completion of this chapter students should know the following:

- how knowledge is created in event studies;
- the main paradigms of knowledge and knowledge formation;
- the main research methodologies and methods from disciplines and closely related fields;
- how research is justified in applied, theoretical and policy contexts;
- how theory is developed specifically for event studies;
- the meaning and importance of convergence of forms and functions in events;
- major knowledge gaps and research priorities in event studies.

A framework for knowledge creation

This chapter is about creating knowledge in event studies, most of which will come from doing research. But where do good research ideas come from? How do we know if a research project is worth doing? Most event-related research has stemmed from sheer curiosity, or from a management or policy need. Because event studies is a new field, a lot of pertinent research has been within well-established disciplinary lines of inquiry. To progress towards interdisciplinarity, wherein event studies will have its own theories and methodologies, we will have to focus more on the core phenomenon and related themes.

This is not a chapter on research methods, although many are mentioned. It is intended to provide an overview of the entire knowledge-creation and research process, starting with a conceptual model, then

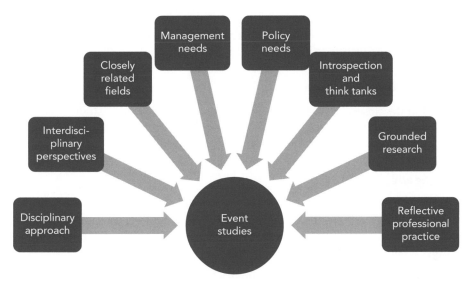

Figure 12.1 Creating knowledge and doing research in event studies

proceeding to discussion of basic research paradigms, methodologies and methods. Pertinent research-method books have been written for the events sector (Fox *et al.* 2014), leisure and tourism (Veal 2011), arts and events management (Veal and Burton 2014), and sport studies and sports management (Veal and Darcy 2014)

Figure 12.1 depicts the various ways in which knowledge can be created and a research project can begin, applied to event studies. At the centre is our new field of studies, and we will naturally have to rely on established disciplines and closely related professional fields for ideas, theories and methods.

Disciplinary perspectives

Anyone doing research on events should view the established disciplinary perspectives as a legitimate starting point. Even if the research problem is rooted in a policy or management need, it is highly possible that sociology, economics or another discipline already provides an answer or a solid foundation for doing the research. However, within these disciplines the study of events is often incidental to a broader issue or theoretical problem, or the focus is not on the core phenomenon of the planned event experience.

When two or more disciplinary foundations are applied to the problem we enter the realm of interdisciplinary research, with the long-term goal being to establish unique, event-specific interdisciplinary theory and knowledge.

Interdisciplinary approach

Event studies fits best into the social sciences, mainly because of its heavy reliance on the human and behavioural disciplines, but it also is eclectic in drawing from arts, sciences, engineering and design – really any other area of study can offer something of value. An interdisciplinary approach to event studies means integrating the concepts and methods of two or more disciplines. This can be done by diverse research teams, or by a single researcher who brings together, for example, economic theory on supply and demand with sociological theory on social networking, for some new insights. The ultimate goal is to create theory specifically applicable to events.

Closely related professional fields

Work being done in the closely related professional fields, especially leisure studies and tourism, offers a foundation for event studies research. These fields not only have a head start in applying various disciplines to their problems and issues, but events already figure prominently in their contents.

Management needs

Much of the event-related research done to date has been applied, related to the practice of event management or event tourism. Researchers and practitioners have to continue to work together, and to close the natural gap between them, in order to ensure that research is timely and useful. But not all event studies research needs to be, or should be, applied.

Ensuring that knowledge grows over time is the aim of a learning organization, and it depends on a formal evaluation system being in place. For one-time events, knowledge transfer is more difficult, as the next organizers might be in a different country, and get started years later. The Olympics Transfer of Knowledge (TOK) programme is designed to build on previous experiences and make it easier to get the mega event produced as promised. Beginning with the Sydney 2000 Olympic Summer Games, the process includes observers who complete reports, visual evidence (videos, photos) and debriefings. Pre-bid research is also conducted according to IOC protocols in potential host cities.

Evaluation is also needed on the numerous one-time events that do not have formal requirements for TOK. This should be the role of tourism organizations that bid, and venues that host events. Standard methods and measures are needed to make results comparable.

Reflective professional practice

It has always proved difficult to get practitioners to contribute research papers or case studies to the refereed, academic literature. The starting point is for practitioners to be reflective, not just focused on the tasks at hand, and to use this reflection in part to initiate research projects. Often the applied needs of practitioners can dovetail nicely with the more theoretical and long-term goals of academics.

Introspection and think tanks

Knowledge also comes from individual reading and introspection, group brainstorming (the 'think-tank' approach) or pure serendipity (i.e. good luck). When research institutions are established, or groups of academics and research students interact at universities, a lot of new thinking and theorizing occurs almost naturally. To date, only a few such clusters of event scholars have been established. One of their aims has to be a closer link with professional practitioners.

Grounded research

In grounded research we do not start with a problem, theory or hypothesis in mind, but with our interest in the core phenomenon (planned event experiences). The grounded approach rests on the premise that researchers should not carry preconceived notions into their projects, but construct research in such a way that knowledge and theories emerge from data and structured analysis. We always hope that completely fresh insights arise from grounded research. More discussion on grounded research follows in this chapter.

Policy needs

While general research is needed to support policy, in turn policy-makers will require a variety of studies – often evaluations – to initiate the process or support and improve their efforts. This generates some tension between researchers, politicians and bureaucrats, as witnessed in the ensuing Research Note 12.1.

12.1 RESEARCH NOTE ON POLICY AND RESEARCH

Best, J. (2009). What policy-makers want from research; what researchers want to tell them. *Journal of Policy Research in Tourism, Hospitality and Events*, 1(2), 175–178.

Jon Best notes that claims about the non-sporting benefits of sports (and sport events) are largely unsubstantiated by empirical research. Health benefits are known to accrue from activity, but this is not the same as claims that sport leads to improved health. Because of the known difficulties in establishing cause and effect, more theoretical approaches are being developed: theory-based evaluation, theories of change, logic models and scientific realism. But policy-makers wanting simplistic answers might not be happy with complex theoretical explanations of impacts.

Philosophy and knowledge

What is knowledge? How do we 'know' anything? These questions are at the heart of epistemology, methodology and ontology. Disciplines have their own perspectives on the best and proper ways to do research, and scholars subscribe to one or more research paradigms.

Science and the pursuit of knowledge are not the same. 'Scientific method' is all about a prescribed process and theory-building, whereas 'knowledge' can be developed from original thinking (creativity), synthesis (reflective thought by informed, wise people) and serendipity (unplanned discovery). In this section a number of important terms and concepts are examined so that event-studies researchers will understand where their work fits into the bigger picture of science and knowledge creation. It will become clear that there is a lot of disagreement about the very meaning or usefulness of science and scientific method.

Philosophy of science, epistemology and ontology

'Philosophy of science' consists of the philosophical foundations, assumptions and implications of natural and social sciences. It seeks to explain such things as the nature of scientific statements and concepts, and the formulation and use of the scientific method.

'Epistemology' specifically deals with knowledge, the relationships between the 'knower' and 'that which is to be known', and the justification of 'knowledge claims'. Modern science is dominated by 'empiricists' who believe that all knowledge is ultimately derived from some experience that requires research and analysis.

Adapting Tribe's (1997: 639) approach from tourism studies, the 'epistemology of event studies' should be concerned with the character of knowledge about planned events, the sources of such knowledge, the validity and reliability of claims of knowledge about planned events, the use of concepts, the boundaries of event studies, and the categorization of event studies as a discipline or field.

Tribe's arguments about tourism ring true for event studies as well. If we limit event studies to the use of 'scientific method', we will miss out on large parts of the phenomenal world of planned events that are not scientifically quantifiable and are not, in fact, scientific puzzles. More appropriately, event studies needs greater epistemological breadth, encompassing philosophical, moral, aesthetic, historical and sociological inquiry and discourse.

'Ontology' is a branch of philosophy concerning the origins, essence and meaning of 'being', or what it means to exist. It can also be defined as dealing with conceptualizations of reality. In research, ontology usually refers to how knowledge is represented and the vocabulary being used to describe it.

In the social sciences there are four main ontological approaches. 'Realism' is based on the idea that 'the truth is out there', or that researchers can indeed discover facts and establish a true picture of reality. For example, marketing researchers might believe they can determine exactly who prefers certain types of events, and why. This leads to 'empirical research', and it can be said that 'empiricism' entails making observations about the real world, which can be evaluated in relation to facts.

'Empiricism' is what separates 'science' from philosophy or theology. 'Positivism' is the scientific approach most associated with experimentation, quantitative techniques and the assumption that researchers are discovering the truth. The fourth ontological approach, 'post-modernism', rejects the notion that we discover the truth through empiricism, and proclaims that every observation or measurement is open to interpretation.

Positivism has guided most of the natural sciences and strongly influenced the social sciences, so we will discuss it in greater detail below. Later, more attention is given to post-modernism and contemporary discourse on research and knowledge.

Ontological mapping

The literature pertinent to event studies falls into three major subdivisions, as discussed in Chapter 1, and each of these can be considered to be an academic discourse (discussed below). In this context, ontology refers to the knowledge being created and discussed within event management, event tourism and various disciplines. Ontological mapping identifies the main concepts and terminology employed in these discourses so that we can see how they are evolving, how they interconnect, and gaps that need filling.

Complete ontological mapping of each discourse, and of event studies in total, is an enormous job and has just begun. This book covers the main concepts and terms being used, but ontological mapping should ideally be based on systematic analysis of all the pertinent literature, and it should be hierarchical in nature. Major concepts are most important, and each can usually be subdivided. The only application found within event studies has been by Singh *et al.* (2008), who employed this method in developing an ontology specific to a knowledge-based system for safe festivals and events.

As a tool in discourse analysis, ontological mapping should reveal the dominant terms and concepts being employed in the literature (in this case the published research literature), which in itself helps differentiate established lines of inquiry and simultaneously enables interconnections to be made. Beyond that, different critical perspectives can be applied, such as determination of bias reflecting power or dominant values.

If you refer back to the earlier discussion of event management, event tourism and the 'classical' discourse from sociology and anthropology, in each of these discussions are key concepts and terms being used by scholars which cover the main areas of knowledge creation. For example, in the 'classical' discourse ritual, symbolism and festivity cover major bodies of knowledge and continuous lines of research and theory development. Event tourism, being instrumentalist, is preoccupied with research and theory pertaining to the roles of events in tourism development and place marketing, with the seasonality problem and the nature of attractions being central. EMBOK is an ontological system, as it defines the main skills and areas of knowledge required by event professionals, but it is not an academic discourse.

Discourse

'Discourse' can be narrowly defined as a conversation, or in a more formalized way as a rule-based dialogue among parties. An event can be interpreted as a discourse. Crespi-Vallbona and Richards (2007) viewed festivals as 'arenas of discourse enabling people to express their views on wider cultural, social and political issues'. But we are here more concerned with academic discourses pertaining to festivals and other events.

Foucault (1969) saw discourse as a system of ideas or knowledge, with its own vocabulary; this can result in the power to monopolize communications and debate, and to enforce particular points of view. My preference is to follow along the lines of Foucault, viewing a discourse as a system, or structured line of reasoning, ideas and approaches to knowledge creation, including theory development and practical applications. Meaning is assigned within a discourse, based on researchers' values, so that the language and concepts define and delimit what is legitimate or expected of those contributing to it; as well, some understandings are marginalized or ignored completely.

For example, Tribe (2004: 57) argued that 'the business discourse' in tourism has 'some coherence and structure, and a framework of theories and concepts (borrowed from the field of business studies)', and that tourism studies tends to crystallize around this interdisciplinary approach. Translated into the subject of this chapter, the business discourse becomes 'event tourism' and is also applicable to the profession of 'event management'. Tribe also argued that the other main area of knowledge creation in tourism studies, undertaken by researchers not interested in the business approach, draws from specific disciplines and leads to interdisciplinarity.

If it is simply asked, 'what is being researched pertaining to planned events?', then the answer is found in an extensive and systematic literature review identifying the terminology and concepts employed by researchers. From reviews conducted by the authors, three discourses were identified, encompassing both the concepts and research themes within event studies and related debate and argument – including contested meanings and the appropriateness of applying particular theories and methodologies. The matter of research and theory-building paradigms comes into question, although individual scholars might never question where they stand on such philosophical issues.

To illustrate, consider that the knowledge domain of event tourism includes considerable attention to economic impact assessment and related issues such as the 'attribution problem' (i.e. what criteria and evidence are necessary to attribute impacts to a particular event?). This is part of the study of event tourism but is neither theoretical nor debated, it simply has to be understood and applied. However, the concept of 'authenticity' is often hotly debated, such as through claims that tourism commodifies festivals and renders them culturally inauthentic. The 'classical' discourse is rooted in social sciences and seems to naturally foster debate and philosophizing, whereas festival tourism and management is much more applied, and less critical. Scholars seeking greater interdisciplinarity are generally responsible for bringing challenging concepts and theoretical/philosophical debate into the tourism and management discourses.

'Discourse' on any subject, such as a political process for determining support for cultural festivals, involves two-way or multi-stakeholder communications, with the aim of ensuring mutual understanding. It is a rule-based process in which arguments are evaluated for their validity, and it facilitates shared decision-making or consensus-building. Stating one's opinion is not discourse, nor are propaganda and advertising. Argument without rules is not discourse. Allowing statements to be made that cannot be verified as to fact or source violates the principles of discourse.

Conflicting views exist on discourse, including those of Foucault (1969) and Habermas (1973). Foucault, the French philosopher, saw discourse as a system of ideas or knowledge, with its own vocabulary (such as the way academics speak to each other). This can result in the power to monopolize communications and debate, and to enforce particular points of view. For example, if only certain people can speak the language of event studies, their 'discourse' will dominate. It is far better that everyone is able to participate.

To Jaworski and Pritchard (2005: 1), discourse is 'a semiotic system': textual-linguistic, visual or any other 'system of signification'. Discourse can mean conversation and language use, whereas 'critical discourse' examines cultural/social practice and processes including politics, values, norms, ideologies (Jaworski and Pritchard 2005: 4). 'Social lives are constructed in and through language/discourse' (Jaworski and Pritchard (2005: 5).

Positivism

Similar to natural scientists, positivists adopt an external (i.e. the researcher's) perspective on discovering the truth and formulating theories that are both explanatory and predictive. Social scientists and management researchers wanting to be more like the 'hard sciences' have adopted a positivistic approach which stresses the 'scientific method' to prove cause and effect, or otherwise employs reliable and valid methods to discover the 'truth' about the world and how people and societies function in it. Positivists separate values from research. Most research done on events has been in this tradition, if only because most event-related research has been concerned with marketing and economics.

When visitor surveys are done at events, for example, researchers try to obtain a random or systematic sample so that estimates can be made about the whole population of event attendees. Conclusions are drawn regarding average spending, motivations to attend, etc. When a household survey is conducted to assess resident perceptions of, and attitudes towards, events, a similar sampling process occurs and the resulting data are subjected to statistical tests to reveal patterns and explain differences. All of this can be used in theory-building. Researchers assume that they are discovering, measuring or explaining the ways in which real people think and act. Are they wrong to think this?

'Experimentation' is also at the heart of positivism. Experiments are used to test hypotheses, requiring that controls be put in place to compare cause and effect among groups. While experiments are rare in applied management fields like tourism or events, the method has been widely used in some of the disciplines that contribute to our knowledge of events, especially in psychology and its subdisciplines.

One of the oft-proclaimed advantages of scientific method is the removal of subjectivity and the imposition of strict protocols for data collection and analysis – including ethical research behaviour. For example, no student doing research for a thesis or dissertation would be allowed to draw conclusions about how events cause economic impacts without convincing supervisors and examiners that data collection and analytical techniques are sound. There is a firm understanding that researchers do not make up results, that studies can be replicated and that conclusions can be tested.

But this scientific 'advantage' also attracts dissatisfaction and criticism when researchers study humans and societies. There is, first of all, real doubt about how well experiments and survey methods reveal the truth, or get at the complexity of individuals and groups.

Second, there is a concern that 'objective' research treats people as 'objects', and that the subjects of research should be part of the process and benefit from it. In fact, some research might actually do harm to people either by way of the dynamics of the research (such as observing people and thereby interfering with their lives or work) or its results (such as by exposing divisions and biases).

Schultz and Lavenda (2005) discussed how anthropologists have questioned positivism as the dominant research paradigm. Assumptions about how the world really worked, and about the ethics and politics of their research (particularly about participant observation), started to be challenged in the 1960s and

1970s. As researchers began to de-emphasize scientific detachment and entered into dialogues with informants and respondents, a greater emphasis was placed on interpretation and differences in opinion.

Schultz and Lavenda (2005: 43) argued that collaborative dialogues achieve 'intersubjective meanings' in which researchers and informants gain a new, shared understanding of the world. According to these anthropologists, researchers are to be 'reflexive', or always critically thinking about the experience of research and how it is done. Do researchers and informants share enough, in cultural terms, to really understand each other?

The nature of 'proof', and cause–effect relationships

One of the main tenets of positivism and the scientific method is that we can 'prove' that certain actions cause certain effects. This is not nearly as simple as it sounds, and within event studies there are only a few problems amenable to this application of scientific method.

Cause and effect relationships are demonstrable for economic impacts. A rigorous methodology that incorporates random or systematic sampling of visitors and a theoretically correct attribution of visitor expenditure (based on determination of reasons for travel) is a proven way to show that event tourism generates economic benefits. Of course, if a full cost and benefit evaluation is not undertaken, the results of economic impact assessments will be interpreted out of context.

Similarly, research can prove that events and event tourism cause environmental change, although sometimes interpretation of positive and negative changes will be open to dispute. Clear examples of cause and effect are to be found when crowds at events trample vegetation, or when construction for events pollutes the water or air. But at a macro level, say in a large city, the relative contribution (compared with industry and transport) of events and tourism to air and water pollution might be insignificant.

While considerable progress has been made in evaluating the various positive and negative impacts attributable to events and event tourism, little if anything has been 'proven' of cause and effect in social or cultural terms. There are many confounding variables that could explain why residents perceive good or bad impacts (see social exchange theory and social representation theory). It is too simplistic to argue that a community or city gains specific social benefits like integration or pride from events, as there are clearly many policy and action paths towards the same outcomes. For many purposes, therefore, resident perceptions and attitudes will remain the best indicators of event impacts.

Post-modernism

To post-modernists, there is no single truth, and all 'meta-narratives' and 'paradigms' like religion and political doctrine are rejected. Jennings (2006: 3) said:

> *The postmodern paradigm disputes grand theory and views the world (its ontological perspective) as being constructed of multiple realities and that no one reality has favour over another. A central tenet is the deconstruction of the surface features of phenomena in order to expose the underlying core realities.*

'Axiology' is the study of values, value judgements and ethics. Most writers of journal articles present their data, analysis and conclusions in a way that implies complete objectivity and scientific rigour. But some academics are now trying to explain how their own values might affect their research, analysis and conclusions. And it has become fashionable to require students writing theses and dissertations to discuss their entire ontological and methodological approach, and to disclose their values or biases. That is a good idea for theses and dissertations, if only to make everyone aware of the thought and assumptions that went into the student's research and analysis.

Theories and models

Klemke *et al.* (1998) asserted that 'theories' have the following properties:

- may be stated as laws or assertions about existence;
- exhibit generality or comprehensiveness;
- explain not one law or phenomenon, but many;
- have explanatory and predictive ability;
- unify diverse phenomena and laws;
- aim at deep understanding of phenomena;
- contain terms referring to unobservable entities or properties.

Klemke *et al.*'s assertions about theory might not be fully applicable to event studies. 'Theory' is a much overused and misused term. Much of the so-called 'theory' seen in the academic literature consists not of explanatory and predictive modelling that withstands the test of time (i.e. permanence), as a good physics or chemistry theory would, but of conceptualizations and propositions. Within the social sciences, humanities and management studies, we probably cannot generate explanatory/predictive theory, nor is it necessarily a worthwhile pursuit.

A more appropriate approach to theory development comes from John Kelly (1987: 2) in his book *Freedom to Be: A New Sociology of Leisure*. Kelly argued that all theoretical models share the following:

- they are acts of explanation, communicated to others;
- they are systematic and disclose their presuppositions and evidence;
- they are always subject to question and criticism.

Theory development, to Kelly, is something we do 'whenever we attempt to explain to others the antecedents and conditions of occurrences'. In the context of event studies, each of the chapters on the five themes of event studies contains a lot of theory development. The application of all the theories and models from other disciplines to the study of planned events is also theory development.

Neuman (2003) said that a 'conceptual model' is a collection of concepts that together form a web of meaning and represent a simplified description of complex phenomena. Models usually serve to depict the believed or proposed structure of interrelationships of factors which help explain a higher-order concept. Accordingly, theories in our field are never truly complete nor are they completely generalizable, but they do contribute to knowledge-building and stimulate debate. Basically, we have no distinct theory of planned events. At this stage we have to rely on borrowing and adapting theories from pertinent disciplines.

Propositions and hypotheses

'Propositions' can form the basis of a conceptual model and can be important in building theory. If we have deep understanding of some aspects of events we can legitimately propose that certain things are true, or will be discovered. Propositions need to be debated or tested, and in that sense they can be turned into 'hypotheses' for other researchers.

Propositions are generally stated in the following way:

> *P1: (It is proposed that) what people think of as types or forms of event, such as 'festival', 'convention' or 'sport competition', are social constructs in terms of expected setting and programme, and in terms of their meaning; these constructs will vary from culture to culture and will evolve over time.*

Throughout this book there are other observations or conclusions that can easily be stated as propositions, useful either for generating research hypotheses or policy action.

Research methodologies

Disciplines have their own methods, rules or postulates that together constitute 'methodologies', or accepted ways of conducting research and generating knowledge. Methodology is rooted in philosophical assumptions (i.e. epistemology, ontology) and provides the rationale for conducting research in accepted ways.

In 'positivism', reality is assumed to be objective, independent of the researcher/observer, and the truth can be discovered by the methodologies of the 'scientific method' such as experimentation. As discussed earlier, 'science' has been the dominant methodology and it remains the most accepted way of doing things in event studies. Note that many 'qualitative' methods are also part of this tradition, and indeed have considerable credibility within the social 'sciences'.

Deductive research

In the positivistic tradition, the starting point is a proposition or hypothesis, generally derived from previous research and existing theory. Data are collected with the specific intent of testing the hypothesis through statistical techniques, such as comparing means on scores from Likert scales to 'prove' that members of one racial or cultural group hold different attitudes towards an event when compared with another group. This can, indeed, add considerable understanding to our problem of why some events do not engage all members of the community. Whether or not the resultant theory-building is the same, or better/worse than that arising from inductive or grounded research, is difficult to say. In the social sciences there is no real test other than the test of time and criticism.

Inductive and grounded research

The starting point for 'inductive' and 'grounded research' is some kind of observation or data collection, leading to analysis. The researcher is to have no preconceived notion of findings. This leads to explanation or theory-building. In inductive or grounded research there might emerge many possible explanations for an observed phenomenon, and they all have to be considered.

Grounded research draws mostly from the work of Glaser and Strauss (1967). In their approach, various types of coding are employed to reach a 'saturation point' where no additional understanding of relationships or abstractions is gained from the data. Theories are built upon categorized data that help to describe and explain the research focus. It should be said that many researchers find a rigorous application of the Glaser and Strauss methodology to be impractical, but the general principle of working inductively from data in steps that lead to theory is sound. Research by Xiao and Smith (2004) in Research Note 12.2 shows an application of this methodology to event studies.

12.2 RESEARCH NOTE ON INDUCTIVE REASONING AND GROUNDED RESEARCH

Xiao, H. and Smith, S. (2004). Residents' perceptions of Kitchener-Waterloo Oktoberfest: An inductive analysis. *Event Management*, 8(3), 161–175.

This paper employs inductive analysis of answers to an open-ended question from a questionnaire survey of residents, namely: 'If you were trying to describe Kitchener-Waterloo Oktoberfest in a few words to a friend who has never attended before, what would you tell him or her?' All 232 responses to the question were initially subjected to 'unrestricted coding' which meant that bits of data were sorted and assigned conceptual codes. These codes included phrases like fun, good time, enjoyment, excellent music, relaxation, ethnic culture, meeting strangers. Looking at the relationships between codes, four main categories of Oktoberfest supporters emerged: seeking entertainment/fun; seeking cultural experience; seeking socialization; and vitalizing the local economy.

Interpretivism

'Interpretivism' arises from the belief that the study of humans is different from the natural sciences, so positivism is not necessarily the best methodology. Sociology, for example, is split between 'structuralists', who favour positivism, and 'interactionists', who favour interpretivism.

While positivism views reality as single, objective and tangible, interpretivism believes in multiple, socially constructed realities (Decrop 2006: 47). In other words, your world-view is quite different from mine. Interpretivists seek understanding, but do not make firm predictions (no explanatory/predictive models). Interpretivist research tends to focus on that which is unique, even deviant, rather than seeking global generalizability. The knowledge generated is contextual, being value and culture-bound. Researchers are likely to interact and cooperate with their subjects and to use holistic-inductive methodology (or naturalistic inquiry). 'Naturalistic inquiry' is the non-manipulative study of real-world situations, as opposed to experimentation. A lack of predetermined constraints on findings makes it similar to grounded research.

Social constructivism

Social scientists often engage in debates about the extent to which theories are shaped by their social and political context. In this way 'social constructivism' postulates that social factors play a large role in the acceptance of new scientific theories. Jennings (2006: 3) described it this way: 'Social constructivism has an ontological position that acknowledges the multiple realities of the people (sometimes called actors) participating in the research.' It is contrary to 'postpositivists', who still perceive a reality. 'The epistemological position of social constructivism is a subjective and value-laden one. Moreover, researchers utilize primarily qualitative methodology and engage in an intrinsic, instrumental, and transactional axiology' (Jennings 2006: 3).

Semiotics

'Semiotics', or 'semiology', is the study of signs, sign systems and their meanings. 'Signs' are also symbols, standing for something else. For example, semiotics can be applied to words and texts, body movements or the clothes people wear. In contrast, 'communication' is the process of transferring data and is concerned with the media of communication. In both communications and semiotics there is a concern for how receivers interpret and give meaning to signs and communications.

According to Echtner (1999), in ontological terms the 'semiotics paradigm' views reality as being socially constructed, and consisting of systems of signs such as language. Semioticians seek to uncover recurring patterns and layers of meanings. Applied to events, we need to understand interactions among 'signs' (advertisements, branding, theming, explicit and implicit communications about the event and within the event) and the 'interpretants' – those people in attendance, or our target markets.

Ryan (2000) believed that tourist space is a locus of selected meanings where the visitor brings their own interpretations. Signs and symbols are interpreted to create meanings, with one implication being that meanings are only in part shaped by the event planner, and another implication being that multiple meanings are often the norm.

Critical theory

According to Habermas (1973) the role of the critical researcher is to reveal conflicts and contradictions and help eliminate the causes of alienation or domination. Jennings (2006: 3) described the 'critical theory paradigm' as adopting

> *an ontological position that the social world is constrained by rules, although these rules can be changed. Its epistemological position is halfway between subjectivism and objectivism. Axiologically, this paradigm should lead to transformational change, as the aim of research in this paradigm is to alter the social circumstances of those being studied.*

Within event studies this approach has not frequently been evident, although some authors do appear to take a critical theory perspective on issues like race (Adams 2011), aboriginal events (Phipps 2011), gender and sexuality (Hughes 2006; Finkel 2011). Coughlin (2010) employed methodology from 'feminist cultural criticism' in her study of ritual spectacle, festivals, art and cultural tourism in nineteenth-century Brittany.

Tribe (2008) concluded that a number of tourism-related issues in particular require the application of critical theory, including sustainability, terrorism and peace, globalization and community tourism, ethical tourism and social exclusion, equity and poverty elimination. To these could be added identity (personal, group and place), commodification and authenticity, spectacle, contested meanings of celebration, freedom to travel and assemble, ethnic and aboriginal events, the tensions between liberating and constraining forces, recreational rioting and protests.

In applying critical theory, the researcher must not unwittingly accept dominant ideologies or worldviews. Respondents might not be telling the truth and they might be ignorant of the way things really work. Neither is the researcher generally free of bias.

Research purposes and methods

Veal (2006: 3) provided a typology of research from the perspective of its purpose or utility. 'Exploratory' or 'descriptive' research seeks to uncover facts or describe a situation. This simplest type of research is commonplace in emerging fields like event studies and might consist of inventories, mapping and classifications of events, case histories, profiles of event organizations, or compilations of facts about policies and regulations affecting the event sector. A trend analysis of demand for events is descriptive, whereas an analysis of factors causing the trend is explanatory.

'Explanatory' research seeks understanding. In a positivist tradition there is often an assumption of cause and effect, such as: the growth in demand for entertainment events is explained by the rise of disposable incomes enabling more people to engage in hedonistic pursuits. If we can explain why something happens, then a predictive model should be possible.

'Evaluative research' is essential in event management and in policy development. 'Internal evaluation' of an organization's effectiveness (in attaining goals) and efficiency (the best use of its resources) is a responsibility of management. 'External evaluation' is conducted by stakeholders who want to know if their 'investment' or support for the event has been worthwhile, or to otherwise examine the impacts of the event.

'Formative' evaluation includes needs assessments, feasibility studies and demand forecasting, anything to do with shaping future decisions and actions. 'Process evaluation' occurs during an event or programme, with a view to correcting mistakes or improving it while it is running. 'Outcome evaluation' includes impact assessments and other after-the-event surveys and analysis, all intended to determine accurately what happened, and why.

Quantitative methods

Quantitative methods are associated with positivism, and qualitative with interpretivism, but there is absolutely no reason why both cannot be combined in any given piece of event-related research or evaluation. The difference is not one of good technique, but of what you need to know and how best to find it out. Often an exploratory, qualitative stage, using focus groups, interviews and observation, precedes a more quantitative stage.

Secondary data analysis

Especially when used as a starting point in research projects, existing sources such as large data sets on leisure, travel or consumer behaviour can provide new insights. Have all analytical tools been used on the existing data? Can new hypotheses be tested? It can also be a useful exercise for students to examine general tourism data, for example, to search for event-specific behaviour and motivations.

Systematic observation

As employed in the Getz *et al.* (2001) study of a surfing event, nine trained observers used temporal and areal stratification of an event to observe and record information about the setting and the audience. This is a quantitative method insofar as the data collected can be analysed in the same way as survey data. Remember that observation can also yield qualitative insights.

Questionnaire surveys

These are probably the most popular research method, because you can get lots of data cheaply, and sometimes quickly. In the positivistic tradition a random sample or complete census is necessary to make generalizations about a population. Surveys can follow a number of procedures.

'Self-completion, intercept surveys' are a very common way to get immediate feedback from festival-goers, on site. 'Intercepts' can also be done of cars on roads, or of persons at airports. Usually the researcher wants a random sample (e.g. every n'th person through the gate) but might settle for a 'systematic sample' (such as you can obtain through spatial and temporal stratification).

'Post-event, mail-back' surveys: often a two-stage approach is best (Pol and Pak 1994), such as getting people at the event to provide a little information and having them agree to a postal follow-up. The post-event portion is best for getting more accurate data on total expenditures and an assessment of the overall experience.

The 'telephone survey' is a good way to cover a market area, such as doing a survey of awareness of an event in a city two hours away by car. Sampling problems are common with this method, so often a 'quota' sample is taken (i.e. get so many males, females and families). 'Quota sampling' is useful in market research where you want a balanced response from males and females, or perhaps you only need the opinions of older tourists. Instruct canvassers to obtain a specific number from each target category.

'Convenience sampling' is generally not recommended, but is easy and cheap – just take anybody that you can get to answer your questions. It can be combined with quota sampling, and a useful variation is to sample willing people in a particular location or at an event, which has the advantage of a common frame of reference (the place or the event).

The 'captive sample': this method works well at meetings and other events where participants feel obligated to respond or cannot avoid doing the survey. Students are often a 'captive sample'!

A number of scholars have compared different survey methods applied to events, such as comparing log books with self-completion questionnaires (Faulkner and Raybould 1995; Breen *et al.* 2001). Quite a few studies have been aimed at perfecting attendance counts and improving attendance estimates at events (e.g. Brothers and Brantley 1993; Raybould *et al.* 2000).

Qualitative methods

Qualitative methods generally do not attempt a numerical analysis, and are more focused on discovering people's attitudes, feelings, motives or perhaps meanings attached to an event experience. Often the numbers of respondents involved are small, as the appropriate methods (e.g. participant observation, interviews, focus groups) are time consuming. Of special interest might be the interactions between people in a focus group setting, which need to be recorded and later interpreted, or perhaps the language used by people in a self-reporting situation (e.g. do event-goers use words like 'self-fulfilling' or 'mastery' when describing their event experiences?).

Phenomenology and hermeneutics

'Phenomenology' as a method attempts to obtain a direct description of a person's experience, ignoring for the moment any causation or motivation. 'Hermeneutics' is a Greek word for interpretation. All writing and symbolic communication (including performances and sports) can be viewed as 'text', and that text can be interpreted.

Hayllar and Griffin (2004) employed 'hermeneutic phenomenology' to explore tourists' experience of a tourist space, the 'Rocks' in Sydney. They engaged visitors in lengthy, structured interviews about the area and their experiences in it. In effect, visitors interpreted their own experiences, then researchers interpreted the 'text' of those interviews by examining themes in the recounted experiences. The results of such research are insights about experiences, but this is not 'objective' in the positivistic tradition and therefore is regarded as qualitative research. Chen's (2006) use of phenomenology (see Research Note 3.5 in Chapter 3) is one of the few examples specific to events.

Netnography

A possible substitute for field research is to assess the meanings of what people say on web logs, or in other written texts. Netnography is the branch of ethnography that analyses the free behaviour of individuals on the Internet and uses online marketing research techniques to provide useful insights. It provides information on the symbolism, meanings and consumption patterns of consumer or leisure groups (Kozinets 2010). It can be passive and hidden, or researchers can declare their aims and interact openly with online respondents.

By way of example of passive netnography, read this first-hand account, taken anonymously from a web posting, from someone who attended a festival.

> *About fifteen years ago I went to my first [festival name and location deleted], and I fell in love with the sacred fire circle and the festival space around it. The strength and magic of this sacred container rocked my world. I can honestly say I have never experienced anything like it in my life. Those 5 days were the most memorable ones I have ever had and cannot wait to return this*

summer. The festival's an incredible experience. Unbelievable! I just can't explain it! I wouldn't miss it for anything in the World! It keeps me happy! It's a really intense experience if you enjoy the music because there's so much of it! Memories are made here. The kind that really make a difference in your life.

It appears to have been a truly memorable, even transforming festival experience, and there are clues as to the nature of the experience. But what is really meant by 'magic' and 'intense'? We cannot get clarification from the written text. And how can we interpret the phrase 'rocked my world'? More questions are raised than can possibly be answered.

The following two blog quotations are from marathon runners.

I run because it makes me feel alive. It challenges me like nothing else. I have run each decade of my life. The pain brings me a reminder that life is not easy. The feeling when you cross the finish line reminds me that nothing worthwhile in life comes easy.

I ran the first marathon to see if I could do it. I continue to run more marathons to see if I can improve my time, and maybe one day qualify for Boston . . . I run to stay in shape, get away for a while, and to compete. Compete against myself to see if I can become a better runner. It's important because it helps keep me in shape and gives me a goal to shoot for. Plus the interaction with other runners is awesome.

One cannot understand the competitive athlete who participates in many events without paying attention to their fundamental motivations. The quotations suggest that these runners are creating meanings for the events in terms of mastery and self-development, with social or affiliation experiences being important.

This quote is from a student who attended a multicultural youth science forum.

Although this trip was academically very enriching, it is the social and cultural exchange along with the bonds we formed that will be cherished forever. This was my first trip to another country as a student and I have certainly gained a lot of confidence from it.

Clearly 'communitas' was at the core of this event experience, the sense of belonging and sharing reflected in the word 'bonds'. But it was also a learning experience and one of self-growth.

When reading first-person accounts of experiences, a basic interpretive problem is that the researcher had no control over the writer. They might be posturing, lying, exaggerating; who knows? If you take the accounts at face value they will probably mislead you. If you assume there is some grain of truth in them, collectively, it will probably result in improved understanding and maybe play a part in developing theory. It seems like a good, qualitative starting point for more in-depth phenomenological research.

There might be ethical questions to consider when analysing texts. Is it possible to identify the sources of the above blog quotes? Can they be slightly disguised while still retaining their authenticity?

Experiential sampling

This method (see Csikszentmihalyi and Csikszentmihalyi 1988) provides a means to collect information about the context and content of daily life, or some element of leisure such as event experiences. It can be thought of as 'systematic phenomenology', allowing people to report on the cognitive and affective elements of their lived experiences. It is particularly relevant to event experiences (although we have not found this application reported in the literature) because questions can cover the physical setting, social context, activities, thoughts, feeling, moods and other self-appraisals.

Diaries can be used, although there is the problem of recollection bias and memory failure. Getting people to write down or record their thoughts and feelings while engaged in the experience is preferable, but intrusive. Not everyone will agree to participate, and some will either do a poor job or quit.

In most experiential sampling projects the respondents have been given a signalling device such as a pager or beeper. Random beeps then trigger self-completion of a brief set of questions, the idea being to intrude as little as possible yet cover the full extent of the experience. Current technology allows for wireless Internet contact and instant communication back to the researchers.

In terms of an event, it would probably be best to start experiential sampling during the anticipation and approach stage, while afterwards it might be better to address experiences through direct debriefing. Here are some ideas on what to ask:

- where are you right now? (perhaps requiring a map of the setting);
- who are you with? (prompt with categories);
- what are you doing? (prompt with categories but allow for the unexpected);
- describe your mood (a seven-point scale with paired opposites describing moods can be used);
- what are you thinking about?
- your level of concentration (e.g. paying attention to the show, or daydreaming);
- perceived control (e.g. are you free to do what you want, or under some obligation).

Larson and Csikszentmihalyi (1983) and Hektner and Csikszentmihalyi (2002) also provided advice on how to conduct experiential sampling, including a draft instrument, and they advised that it is probably best to use this technique in combination with other methods.

Content analysis

What are the newspapers saying about the impacts of an event, or the wisdom of bidding on a world's fair? How have event-goers described their experiences on blogs? Content analysis can employ specific techniques such as hermeneutics to compile and interpret what has been said.

Observation and participant observation

Carlsen (2004) outlined a number of event evaluation methods including observation and participant observation techniques. These were used in a study by Getz *et al.* (2001) of a surfing event. Their direct observation employed checklists and spatially/temporally stratified sampling. Participant observation consisted of each of nine researchers 'enjoying' as much of the event as they could. Each observer then recorded their general observations and impressions, and when these qualitative (and subjective) insights were combined with systematic observation and interviews a service quality map was prepared. With three convergent methods being used, this research illustrates the principle of 'triangulation'.

12.3 RESEARCH NOTES ON PARTICIPANT OBSERVATION

Park, M., Daniels, M., Brayley, R. and Harmon, L. (2010). Analysis of service provision and visitor impacts using participant observation and photographic documentation: The National Cherry Blossom Festival. *Event Management*, 14(2), 167–182.

The researchers combined passive participant observation with the use of a checklist and photographs to document issues and visitor behaviour at this large-scale public event. Six days were covered, in different locations, by the team. This allowed for more in-depth understanding of the visitor experience over the entire event. Researchers concluded that the nature of this event in Washington, DC, led to 'intense, concentrated consumption and usage of facilities, services, and natural resources, making it difficult for management to keep up with visitor demand and risking long-term degradation of the natural resources'. They feared that the area's carrying capacity would be exceeded.

Mackellar, J. (2013b). Participant observation at events: Theory, practice and potential. *International Journal of Event and Festival Management*, 4(1), 56–65.

'A review of the literature examines applications of the research method and discusses the steps of the research cycle. Using the example of the Swell Sculpture Festival, participant observation is demonstrated to be a highly appropriate method to gather data on interactions and relationships through the recording of behaviour, conversation and experience in situ. The paper suggests that methods of participant observation can be used to gain a deeper understanding of social dynamics of audiences and the affective dimensions of their behaviour. It is suggested that the method is highly appropriate to the context of event environments, where the use of surveys can interrupt the flow of the event experience for audiences, or be made impossible by the structure of the event. The case study demonstrates the application of the methodology by event managers to gaining a better understanding of audience behaviour and expectations.'

Interviews

One can often learn more from a few interviews than from a large-scale questionnaire, but perhaps both are desirable. 'Formal interviews' are structured, and sometimes it is best for interviewees to know the topics in advance so they can be prepared – especially if they are being consulted because of their professional position. 'Informal interviews' do not have a firm structure, although the topics have to be clear in the mind of the researcher. Interviews can be analysed systematically, using content analysis, or interpreted as to the key points.

'In-depth interviews' are a time-consuming method intended to cover a lot of ground and obtain considerable detail, usually from a few respondents. They are very useful with key informants who know a lot, such as interviewing event managers about their stakeholder relationships and strategies (see Getz *et al.* 2007). This method can be a part of researching the case histories of events or in conducting cross-case analysis.

'Group interviews' and 'focus groups' encourage interaction among respondents within a controlled setting. A synergistic affect is usually desired, such as getting a group of event managers together and asking them to identify all the funding issues faced by the festival sector. However, a strong personality can potentially influence everyone's opinion. Focus groups are a staple in consumer research, but of course you cannot draw generalized conclusions from the input. They are usually the starting point.

'Ethnography' traditionally involved living in a place, being submersed in a society or cultural group. Favoured by early anthropologists, this obviously time-consuming and challenging research method yields a lot of insights. But there will always be the issues of observer bias, interaction effects (changing what you are observing) and information being withheld and deliberate misrepresentation by the 'observed'. 'Participant observation' can be ethnography at a small scale.

Case studies

Case study method has seen a massive growth from the initial edition of Yin's (2014) seminal book in the field over 30 years ago. It has been described by Yin (2014) as a key research method to use when seeking to ask questions such as 'How' or 'Why' in social research as well as a technique to gather in-depth knowledge about a specific phenomena. Yet it should not be construed, as Yin (2014) argues, to be a soft approach to research, as one simply associated with the description of events and experiences. The ability to derive generalizations and broader findings from single cases is both challenging and difficult.

Getz *et al.* (2007) used the case study method to compare festivals in Canada and Sweden on the topics of stakeholder types, relationships, management and issues. 'Cross-case analysis' is a powerful tool in exploratory research, as it can generate numerous insights. Findings from case studies are not generalizable, but do play an important role in creating new knowledge, generating hypotheses or propositions, and testing existing theory.

Time-budget studies

How much time do people spend attending events of different kinds, or how much time do marathoners use in preparing for and travelling to races? Time is the fundamental determinant of whether people attend planned events and its analysis has largely been undertaken within leisure studies, as Roberts (2006) has demonstrated. The fundamental determinants of whether people actually have time to undertake or attend planned events can be demonstrated in Figure 12.2, which illustrates the three broad categories of time that exist within a given day comprising 1,440 minutes. Current debates around such time-related studies by Gershuny (2011) indicate that trends towards greater time spent on leisure since the nineteenth century have begun to change with greater time pressures on families, households and individuals in many modern societies. Among current research concerns are those related to personal well-being and issues such as work-life balance and greater pressures in balancing the different daily and weekly household obligations as demonstrated in Figure 12.2. This area of research is certainly a fruitful area of inquiry for event studies as the discussion in Events in Focus 12.1 shows.

EVENTS IN FOCUS

12.1 The use of time-budget studies in event research: a novel area for research

The importance of events within the everyday lives of people poses a unique research challenge in seeking to utilize a research method or methods that can encapsulate the entirety of an individual's daily/aggregated use of time and how planned events feature in these lives. Within leisure studies research, largely informed by research in sociology, three distinct types of research approach have been used.

Techniques developed in leisure and recreation studies to assess time use

- A continuous record of recreation activities of a sample population for a given time period which involves respondents keeping a diary of activities (the time-budget approach). This has a long history of use in social science and leisure research, as outlined by Gershuny (2011), which can be dated to nineteenth-century Russia. Its use in the UK is documented by Pember-Reeves (1913) and in the USSR by Sorokin and Berger (1939). Mass observation in the UK was conducted between 1937 and 1955, together with more recent studies of leisure such as Zuzanek *et al.*'s (1998) cross-national survey of Dutch and Canadian use of time.

- Questionnaire surveys, which require respondents to recall activities in the form of an individual case study. Such case studies are detailed and sometimes contain both qualitative and quantitative questions, and they are inevitably small-scale due to the time involved in in-depth qualitative interviews.
- Questionnaire surveys which are large scale, enabling statistically significant subsamples to be drawn. Such surveys may be derived using simple and unambiguous questions that focus on a specific recreation activity or one that covers the entire spectrum of leisure activities.

Source: Based on Hall and Page (2014).

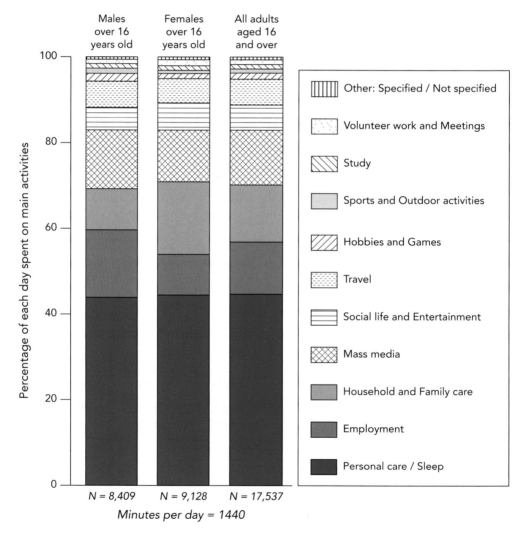

Figure 12.2 Time budgets for males, females and the total population of adults aged 16 and over in 2000

Source: Based on Office for National Statistics, UK 2002 data reproduced with permission from C. M. Hall and S. J. Page, *The Geography of Tourism and Recreation*, 4th edition, Routledge (2014).

What these studies illustrate is that time budgets record a person's use of time, describing:

● the duration
● sequence and
● timing of a person's activities for a given period, usually of between a *day* and a *week*.

In the analysis of time budgets, Thrift (1977) provided an assessment of three principal constraints on our daily activity patterns, which are:

● comparability constraints (e.g. the biologically based need for food and sleep)
● coupling constraints (e.g. the need to interact and undertake activities with other people)
● authority constraints (e.g. where activities are controlled, not allowed or permitted at a certain point in time).

These need to be superimposed on the three techniques.

Gershuny (2011) has reviewed the scope and scale of time-budget studies undertaken by different countries across the world as well as the differing methods of data collection and analysis used. Two examples that are often referred to are the UK and USA respective studies, which are highlighted. In both cases, planned events as a category are not collated as specific pieces of data and this highlights the importance of further studies which will reveal more specific event-related perspectives around an individual's use of time. Typically data are scattered across different categories of time use, where planned events may be associated with cultural activities, sporting events, socializing and, more broadly, leisure pursuits.

As Hall and Page (2014) illustrated, the UK 2000 Time Use Survey (ONS 2002), which set out to measure how people spent their time, comprised a representative sample of households and individuals within households, based on a household questionnaire survey and diaries, and a one-week work and education time sheet. It was undertaken in 2000–2001 and no further studies have occurred. Therefore, the results can only be indicative of what time use looks like from an aggregated perspective and they pre-date the rise of social media and personal technology (e.g. mobile phone and tablet use). As Figure 12.2 shows, time use was calculated over a typical day and it illustrates the following headline statistics based on Hall and Page (2014):

● Almost 44 per cent of male and just over 44 per cent of female time is spent on personal care and sleeping each day, followed by employment.
● Leisure activities (e.g. sport, hobbies, games, social life, entertainment and mass media): the data found that 20 per cent of male and 20.33 per cent of female time is devoted to such pursuits.

Longitudinal data calculated by Gershuny (2011) indicated that ONS studies found that home leisure (in which planned events will feature) grew in the UK from 87 minutes a day in 1961 to 121 minutes in 1983–1984, to 136 minutes in 2000–2001.

A survey that has been consistently undertaken since 2003 is the American Time Use Survey by the Bureau of Labor, which surveys 9,000 people and identifies different categories to the ONS. The 2013 data depict a broadly consistent pattern for weekday activities, where around 4.5 hours a day is spent on work-related activities, 4.74 hours a day on leisure and sports during the week and 6.4 hours a day at weekends. The survey breaks the categories for leisure and sport into five broad categories (socializing, relaxing and leisure; relaxing and leisure; arts and entertainment; sports, exercise and recreation; and travel related to leisure and sport). The growth of social media and networking is reflected in the 0.16 hours per week spent on these activities and 0.13 hours per day spent on telephoning, emailing and mail. There are clear male–female differences, with males spending more time on leisure (5.61 hours a week compared with 4.94 hours for women, though this is most marked at weekends where the difference is 7.07 hours for men and 5.89 for women). Age differences also exist, with those aged over 65 years of age enjoying at least seven hours of leisure per week compared with those working individuals, aged from 25 to 54 years old, who typically have just over four hours of leisure a week. This also varied by ethnicity, with those of Hispanic origin enjoying the least leisure time, at 4.61 hours a week, compared with those of Black or African-American origin, who enjoyed six hours a week. These figures also varied in the weekday and weekend and activities undertaken. Those who were employed in the survey had diminishing leisure hours depending upon salary level, as the higher salary earners had less leisure time. Likewise, the presence of young children also reduced available leisure time.

What time-budget studies do is help us to understand how the prioritization of planned events fits within individual and household time budgets, which is a key starting point for further behavioural studies on individuals to assess the motivations underlying participation in, spectating at and engagement with such events.

Action research

'Action researchers' are usually involved in a programme or project that is intended to have specific outcomes, and the entire process continuously needs to be evaluated and revised. There is plenty of scope for learning about what works and what does not, but also the risk of involvement bias.

We have not seen any application of 'action research' in the events sector, but it can work this way: the researcher joins the team planning and implementing an event, all the while both contributing as an equal and observing/analysing how decisions are made and which stakeholders have the greatest impact. Usually action research is devoted to social causes, so a more typical application would be for the participant/ researcher to work with a community group to develop and evaluate a festival intended to solve some local problems.

Historical research

The history of a specific event or class of event is a subject for historians, yet it has to be put into a social, cultural, environmental and economic context. The historical researcher has to have a point of view, or methodology. For example, how have both politics and technological innovation affected the origin and evolution of international expositions, particularly world's fairs? Why are the Olympics such a sought-after, iconic event? Keep in mind that historiographers will assess the relevance and validity of information used and its analysis within historical research.

Longitudinal research and concatenation

A great deal can be learned by time-sampling, or otherwise studying a phenomenon like an event over a long period of time. This can be an important part of historical research, but just as much an element in policy and programme evaluation. For example, looking at the impacts of event tourism on a community at one point in time is quite limiting, so why not conduct surveys every year for a decade?

A linked series of research projects constitutes concatenation, and this will be increasingly important as research centres and consortia focus on particular aspects of event studies. The aim is to build cumulative knowledge and to develop theory. While this can occur by carefully positioning a research project in the context of similar studies by others, it probably works best when the same team undertakes the work. Two examples are found in the events literature. The first example is by Shipway and Jones (2007, 2008) on amateur running. Another ambitious concatenation, concerning festival management, has been summarized in the article by Getz *et al.* (2010), in which data from identical surveys in four countries were compared. Some of those results are presented elsewhere in this book.

Futures research

Can we really conduct research on the future? There are trend extrapolation, Delphi panels and future scenarios to help envisage and plan for the future, whereas longitudinal research will tell us if we got it right. Remember that speculation and prophecy are completely different exercises.

More and more we will be required to deal with the reality of climate change. If predictions come true, the world will change in profound ways. The various scenarios prepared by experts have to be translated into implications for events, leisure and tourism. Most of the implications will be pessimistic, but the future can also be shaped by policy made today, and we should aim to get certain events considered alongside other important issues. The worse things get, the more we need them!

Meta-analysis

This research method has had limited application in the events field, mainly because so few research studies yield comparable data. The work of Dwyer *et al.* (2000a, 2000b) in developing an approach to event-impact forecasting and evaluation was a kind of meta-analysis in that various impact studies were compared and general conclusions drawn, both about the methods employed (and how they needed to be improved and standardized) and the nature of event impacts.

Cross-cultural research

Event studies must also develop through cross-cultural research, and this is rarely attempted. Schneider and Backman (1996) tested a 'Western' motivation scale in Jordan and found that it generally worked well. Kay (2004) conducted a review of research 'of relevance' to cultural event tourism, but that review found that few studies systematically compared or contrasted between cultures. Kay addressed the questions of what should be the focus of cross-cultural research, and how it should be conducted, but the sphere of concern was restricted to gaining improved understanding of who attends events, and why.

The greater need is for seeking understanding of all the elements and processes in our event-studies framework within and between different cultures (including countries) and cultural groups in society (including ethnic and affinity groups and subcultures). The vast majority of the available literature is Western, thereby limiting its generalizability, and in this book (and in most pertinent sources) only English-language literature has been considered.

When comparing cultures, it is almost certain that the personal and social constructs attached to planned events will be different, giving rise to varying levels of significance assigned to events in a policy context. However, the power of globalization has to be taken into account, particularly through the influence of mass media and the Internet, so we also have to look for diffusion and adaptation within the world of planned events.

Theory development for event studies

It is difficult to imagine one grand, unifying theory of planned events, but the field of event studies does need its own theoretical constructs, and they will certainly be derived from interdisciplinary theory-building, as Events in Focus 12.2 illustrates.

EVENTS IN FOCUS

12.2 Progress in events research

The past decade has seen a monumental increase in research activity in events research, reflected in the growing quantum of research publications and number of books and publications both within the academic and public sector charting the important role of events. As this book illustrates, this continued growth in research poses several challenges for the student of events, to understand how all this research is progressing, how it fits together and what the hot topics are for further study at Masters and Ph.D. levels. While texts such as this book have an important role in synthesizing the nature of event studies and how it contributes to the further development of the subject area, there is also a role for more substantive studies of two to three times the size of this book to take stock of how the subject is developing. This was the objective of the recently published *Routledge Handbook of Events* (Page and Connell 2011) in which key researchers in the field outlined how their respective subject area or contemporary theme had developed and the key debates associated with its development.

This *Handbook* represents the first major research work to outline the state of events research since its rapid growth in the 1980s. It is pertinent to briefly outline some of the key features of the *Handbook*, which has a relevance for readers of this book as a reference source to further extend their study of events by looking at cutting-edge reviews of the subject area. Contents of the book cover a wide range of social science subject areas that have contributed to the evolution of event studies through to key management-related topics and a number of contemporary themes.

It is impossible, in a short snapshot such as this, to identify all of the major contributions in detail, but a number of key threads run throughout many of the chapters in the *Handbook*. First, much of the progress in the development of a distinct subject knowledge, which we are now labelling 'event studies', is emerging from social science and a number of other areas of management science such as human resource management, risk management and finance as well as marketing. Notable areas of development that have shaped the intellectual development of the subject have come from the areas of geography, planning, economics, sociology, anthropology and psychology and the intersection of these areas in new foci points such as the event experience and event design.

These subject areas are working on the cutting edge of social and management science, developing a holistic view of what makes events special and successful for different stakeholders and destinations, particularly the growing volume of event impact research. It is also evident that the political environment associated with events has also grown in significance, as funding decisions to support event development are usually political decisions. There is also growing evidence that new research agendas associated with the wider development of research on the cultural industries has also influenced the debates now permeating event research, such as the rise of specific themes like the spread of night-time cities, multicultural event destinations and global concerns associated with safety, security and the surveillance society.

In terms of research methodology, many of the chapters also review the long-term evolution of research methods now being employed to study events (quantitative and non-quantitative), reflecting the wider developments in social science research. There is also growing evidence of new themes such as sustainability playing a greater role in shaping the operation and management of events. What the *Handbook* shows is that the state of research in events is continuing to develop along two interrelated directions: pure academic research using the concepts and tools from social science and management science, and more applied research that is operational in focus and often undertaken by industry, public-sector bodies and consultants in a problem-solving context. Event studies remains in a state of constant evolution and its continued development offers many fascinating opportunities for all types of researchers.

A number of overarching questions require attention:

- Why are planned events found in all societies, as they have been throughout history? (Their *raison d'être*; values to various societies and cultures.)
- Do all societies institutionalize generic types of events, and are their functions identical? Are the functions enduring or constantly evolving?
- What are the basic functions they perform, or the goals they meet (from multiple stakeholder perspectives)?
- Why do people want to, or need to, attend events, and how do they select them? (This is not merely a marketing issue, as we need to explain how various events are perceived and attitudes shaped towards them, in different cultures and settings.)
- How do individuals and groups experience different events, and how are these experiences affected by management and other variables?
- How are people changed (if at all) by event experiences?
- In what ways are planned events evolving (through policy, strategy, social and individual action)?
- What is the future of planned events (and related professions)? Can virtual events replace in-person experiences?

Exchange and convergence theory on the forms and functions of planned events

There is an existing, multidimensional construct, called exchange theory, which answers many fundamental questions about planned events. A common theme in all planned events is exchange, because they are all social experiences with a purpose – whether economic, social, cultural or familial in scope. From an economics perspective we can see planned events as cooperation mechanisms to facilitate necessary exchanges, primarily economic in nature. This especially applies to markets, fairs and exhibitions, but also covers many meetings, conventions, corporate and political events. Social order arises from the necessity and the social conventions associated with these events. Festivals and other cultural celebrations appear to conform more to the anthropological approach to exchange theory, as they clearly embody ritual and symbolism, but these elements are found in many events.

In Figure 12.3, four dimensions are shown, based on the premise that any event can potentially embody both economic and social/cultural exchanges, and possess symbolic and ritualistic value. As well, many event experiences are highly personal in nature, pertaining to entertainment at one end and self-development at the other. Planned events both arise from social order and help define and maintain it. Increasingly, we look to planned events as institutionalized forms of business, a means of personal or group expression, social order and celebration.

At the innermost zone of convergence, major festivals and events of all forms can possess high value on social, economic, personal and symbolic dimensions. This reflects, in part, their scale and related attractiveness to residents, tourists and the media – they generate substantial economic exchanges even if that is not their goal. Individuals will find ample scope for meeting their self-development needs through volunteering and direct participation. These events – often called mega, iconic, hallmark or

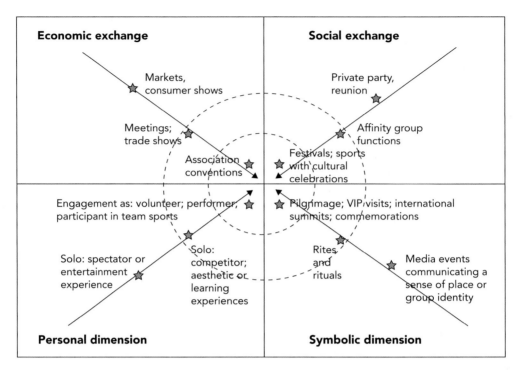

Figure 12.3 Types and functions of planned events: four dimensions and zones of convergence

Note: Events in the inner ring maximally possess a mix of economic, social, personal and symbolic value.

signature – are symbols for their host communities/nations and foster pride, identity and cohesion. By their nature, permanent events in this zone tend to become institutions, supported by powerful stakeholders because they perform all these necessary functions. As well, they tend to converge in terms of form, with a high degree of blending of all the elements of style.

At the outermost range of the economic exchange dimension are events – like attending a market to shop, or a consumer show to look around and learn – that are low in social exchange (individuals or small groups attend and group experiences are not facilitated), symbolic value and personal development. But a trade show, while ostensibly all about business for particular industry groups, does also embody social and symbolic dimensions. Although meetings and conventions are often conducted for business reasons, they can also be positioned (alternatively or equally) in the social exchange dimension for purposes of group identity-building and cohesion. Those attending events targeted at specific groups generally experience a sense of communitas.

The social exchange dimension emphasizes the importance of events as both reflections and facilitators of essential social exchanges, the kinds that form and reinforce group identity – from the level of friends and family, through all kinds of affinity groups and subcultures, all the way to city and national identity. Private parties are at the outer range, while public festivals/celebrations are within the inner zone. The largest and most public events also generate economic activity by attracting sponsors, grants and tourists; they are typically high in symbolic value, with the event being iconic within some groups and important to places, as in hallmark events. These planned events typically combine elements such as sports with festivals and exhibitions, or conventions with gala banquets and tours. And they offer many opportunities for personal engagement and growth.

These elements are shown in Figure 12.3. Along the continuum representing the personal dimension, the individual displays a range of levels of involvement or engagement, beginning with being a solo spectator at a sport competition or concert in which entertainment/spectacle prevails. Solo experiences in social events are frequent, such as running in a race or going to an event as a learning or aesthetic opportunity (e.g. art exhibitions). Within the inner zone, the individual experiences a high level of engagement (or involvement), such as in team sports, as a volunteer or performer, and these experiences are associated with both personal development (or self-actualization) and socializing.

All events can hold symbolic value to persons and groups, but many fall primarily within this dimension. Events broadcast to the community or world are often intended to foster a positive image, community pride and group identity; they may be any type of event, or expressly produced as media events with small numbers of direct participants or guests. A panoply of rites and rituals exist that are more social in nature, clearly engaging individuals and groups in symbolic activities: from birthdays and anniversaries to bar mitzvahs and religious processions. Parades, read as social texts, can easily fit into this category. Within the inner zone of convergence are large-scale, social events that also have economic significance such as pilgrimages, VIP visits, international summits and heritage commemorations. Individuals can experience these events as being spiritually, culturally or intellectually rewarding, and even transforming.

Maximizing the 'power' of planned events

Public policy-makers, corporations and the tourism industry all pursue strategies for augmenting the communicative and instrumentalist power of events; that is, to make them more effective in achieving their varied (and often converging) goals. Larger public and media events are doing this already, combining multiple forms of event, adding symbolic content, and making them meaningful and valuable to many stakeholders. Remember McLuhan's (1964) dictum: the medium – an event – is the message. The powerful event speaks clearly and loudly, it contributes to creativity and innovation in society, and it stands for all things good and wonderful. We hope.

But what of small and single-form events? To augment their power, first consider their purpose and strengths. If they are primarily organized for private groups or companies, in what ways can they generate benefits for others? If the event is high on social exchange, organized for example to celebrate belonging and sharing within a social world, to what extent can it become important in an economic sense, such as through event tourism? Wherever possible, maximize the potential for involving individuals in ways that facilitate personal development and socializing.

Perhaps the most neglected power concept is that of deliberately augmenting the symbolic value of events. Many organizers appear to be reluctant to do this, perhaps fearing the alienation of one group when dominant-group symbols are utilized. This can be dealt with in several ways, starting with the planned inclusion of obvious stakeholders and many communities. But symbolism can also be neutral, accepted by most groups through constant media exposure, and universal in meaning. Consider the following examples:

- brands that stand for quality;
- symbols of the nation and the local community (we all live somewhere!);
- symbols associated with charities, good works and fine people;
- rituals that convey gravity, prestige, triumph;
- music and art as a universal language.

Yes, it is likely that somebody will object to every symbol, some group will be offended. It is truly impossible to please everyone all the time. That should not prevent us from trying to enhance the integrative power of events – to bring us all together in communitas.

A research agenda for event studies

Shaw and Williams (2004: 275) put forward a general research agenda for tourism studies that can readily be adapted to event studies. In their view, researchers have to be critical (not just have a management or business-driven agenda), employ diverse disciplinary and methodological perspectives, and be holistic. This means positioning event studies within broad social, economic and environmental discourses.

Being 'critical', as used by Shaw and Williams, means to not simply adhere to a research agenda driven by event management, event tourism or event policy. Researchers (including students) have to be free to challenge established practices and paradigms and to generate new ideas and approaches. Second, being 'critical' suggests the adoption of a particular approach to research. Just remember that critical theory and critical thought are only useful if they help create new understanding and build better methods and skills. My point is that researchers do not have to buy into any school of thought to be critical and constructive.

Within our discussion of each of the main themes of event studies, a large number of research ideas and needs were generated, and these are summarized below. It is not useful to assign priorities to them, because depending on one's perspective any of them could be important. A starting point for doing event-related research can be disciplinary, so that only those questions framed within sociology, for example, would be important. Other starting points are management needs, policy evaluation or personal interest in a topic.

For each of the themes a few key questions are asked, and possible research methods suggested. This is not in any way to limit the range of research possibilities, but is a starting point.

A research agenda for planned event experiences and meanings

This is the core of event studies and therefore demands constant attention from researchers and theorists and Table 12.1 outlines an agenda. According to Borrie and Birzell (2001) there have been four common approaches to studying visitor experiences:

1. The 'satisfaction approach' is really a surrogate measure, as it asks if people were satisfied with their experiences – not what those experiences were or what they meant. This line of research has generated both practical and theoretical understanding, but does not go far enough in exploring experiences.
2. The 'benefits approach' asks respondents to indicate their level of agreement with statements regarding the benefits they might have received, such as to escape, to relax, to learn, etc. It is similar to asking about motivations to attend an event. A priority here is examining and comparing motives/benefits at all types of events, in different cultures and settings.
3. 'Experience-based' methods involve reporting on thoughts, feelings or moods during daily life, a trip or event. Phenomenological approaches should be a top priority in event studies, particularly for gaining better theoretical understanding of immediate conscious experience; experiential sampling should be utilized in a variety of event circumstances.
4. A 'meanings-based' approach requires deep insights obtained through participant observation or interviews, or the application of hermeneutic phenomenology; life-enriching stories are elicited. We need considerably more research on social and personal constructs of event meanings.

A research agenda for antecedents and choices

Generic consumer research and evaluation methods have to be adapted better to event-related problems, especially because we are dealing with experiences that embody many personal, social and cultural meanings. A considerable volume of research has been undertaken on motivation, which gives clues as to needs, experiences and outcomes, but these are all conceptually different and their interactions are complex.

Table 12.1 Research agenda: planned event experience and meanings

Event studies themes	Key research questions	Possible research methods
The planned event experience and meanings	How do people describe, explain and assign meaning to various event experiences within each of these dimensions: conative (behaviour), affective (emotional) and cognitive?	Hermeneutics (analysis of texts; self-reporting)
	Describe and explain the formation of personal and social constructs regarding event experiences.	Phenomenology (e.g. in-depth interviews at events)
	How does level of involvement or engagement affect the event experience?	Direct and participant observation
	Examine 'arousal' and 'flow' within different event settings.	Experiential sampling (diary or time-sampling with standard questions)
	What makes event experiences memorable and transforming?	
	How does 'communitas' form at events? Can it be facilitated?	
	Is there a measurable 'WOW!' factor?	
	Systematically compare different event experiences (for all stakeholders, from paying customers and guests to the general public, and between types of event, from sport to carnival).	

For example, do people believe they 'need' events, and where do such needs come from? Table 12.2 outlines a research agenda for this theme.

Leisure constraints theory offers considerable scope for examining why some people attend events and others do not. Constraint negotiation applied to intrinsically and extrinsically motivated event attendance should be examined. Economic theories and methods should be applied to gain a better understanding of supply and demand issues that influence event attendance, and particularly willingness to pay and pricing.

Research agenda: management, planning, design and operations of events

In an article in the first issue of the *International Journal of Event and Festival Management*, Getz et al. (2010) put forward a very detailed research agenda for festival management studies and Table 12.3 extends this thinking. A real need was identified for comparative and cross-cultural research, and much of the analysis was based on a four-country comparison employing the same questionnaire for festival managers – research that is summarized in the article. Table 12.3 provides only a starting point, and readers should see the 2010 article for detailed recommendations.

Research agenda for patterns and processes

So little historical and historiographic research has been undertaken on planned events that it is practically an untouched theme. How has the profession of event management evolved, from the earliest times? The Olympics have been over-analysed, but what about other forms of event that have a long lineage? Multi- and cross-cultural studies are essential.

Table 12.2 Research agenda: antecedents and choices

Event studies themes	Key research questions	Possible research methods
Personal antecedents Barriers and constraints Decision-making Post-event evaluation and feedback	What are the main cultural variables affecting the perceived value and attractiveness of events? Examine the relative importance and nature of generic versus specific (targeted) needs, motives and benefits that are sought through different planned event experiences. Develop marketing implications. Do people believe they 'need' events? How is economic demand for events shaped by price, competition, substitution, policy and other factors? How are event careers developed? Use ego-involvement, social worlds, recreation specialization and commitment theories. In what ways does 'serious leisure' affect events? What constraints are most important in shaping demand and attendance at different types of event? How are constraints negotiated for intrinsically and extrinsically motivated event attendance? How do different segments use the Internet and other media for searching and decision-making in the events sector? Can planned events be substituted by other forms of entertainment and business practices?	General consumer and market area surveys Focus groups Social needs evaluation Supply–demand assessment In-depth interviews Time-budget studies Longitudinal studies of event travel careers and constraint negotiation Comparisons among leisure pursuits, hobbies, sports, the arts and lifestyle

Histories of individual events are interesting, but only theoretically important if they can be systematically compared and analysed within a theoretical framework such as resource dependency or institutionalism and Table 12.4 outlines a range of productive lines of inquiry. Historians can also make a major contribution by reassessing history through the lens of major planned events and numerous personal events, as that is how many people remember and give meaning to the flow of time.

Geographic research on planned events has been given a solid foundation by Robert Janiskee and a few others, but there has been no consistent spatial-temporal approach. In cities, what has been the distribution and evolution of events, and how are they to be explained? Have resources, culture or strategy been most responsible for the observable portfolios of events in any given area? When or how does an area or community reach saturation level in terms of the numbers and types of events? How do events interact? What are their cumulative impacts? Some of the answers will assist in event-strategy formulation, policy-making and marketing.

In terms of future studies of planned events, the slate is blank. There has been lots of speculation on how virtual events might evolve, possibly threatening 'live events', but we cannot believe this for a moment.

Table 12.3 Research agenda: management, planning, design and operations

Event studies themes	Key research questions	Possible research methods
Leadership Organizational culture Planning and decision-making Design Marketing and communications Finances, financial management and controls Operations and logistics Human resources Risk, health and safety Research, evaluation, and information systems	What leadership styles are most effective for different types of events and event settings? How can creativity and management competency be balanced in the event sector? What strategies are most effective in achieving event sustainability and institutional status? Which stakeholder management strategies work best? Does rational planning and decision-making work better for events than incrementalism or advocacy? Compare one-time and periodic events. How do various stakeholders perceive and manage the risks associated with events? What are the potential effects of sensory and emotional stimulation at events? How can theory from environmental psychology improve event logistics and crowd management? What are the main determinants of customer satisfaction at events? What volunteer careers exist in the event sector, and how do they foster commitment and professionalism?	Case studies and cross-case analysis Historical research Open-system audits Stakeholder mapping Organizational ethnography Surveys of owners and managers Consumer experiments Financial audits and ROI studies Whole population studies (over time)

There is simply no substitute for 'being there' and for 'live experiences'. However, advances in technology and communications in particular are shaping the events field, and we have to pay attention to these forces and trends. For example, convention centres are now designed as both live and virtual event venues, to reach a global audience.

We need some 'futurists' in this field. We will play the role, for now, by offering the following propositions, each of which should suggest more than one research project:

> *FP 1 (Future proposition 1): Planned, live events, both personal and societal in scale and meaning, will always be a prominent feature of civilization, in all societies and cultures.*

> *FP 2: Virtual events will gain in frequency and importance in response to advances in global technology, and because of globalization forces and the costs or risks of travel, but they will be in addition to, and not a substitute for, live event experiences.*

> *FP 3: Corporate influence on the field of planned events will continue to increase, especially in terms of events produced as manifestations of marketing and branding.*

> *FP 4: The strategic justifications for public-sector involvement with events, especially mega events bearing heavy costs, will be increasingly scrutinized and more difficult to defend, while social, cultural and environmental justifications will become more acceptable.*

Table 12.4 Research agenda: patterns and processes

Event studies themes	Key research questions	Possible research methods
History Geography Future studies Policy	In what fundamental ways have various types of events evolved, in different cultures? Do events progress naturally through life cycles? What factors most shape their evolution? Do communities or destinations reach event saturation? What explains different patterns of events in time and space? What are the forces shaping the future of events? Can they be controlled? How do events adapt? What are the ways in which stakeholders exercise power, and negotiate, to develop events and event-related policy? Who gets excluded or marginalized? How do we know when event policies are effective and efficiently administered? Which justifications for public involvement in events are supported, and why? What are the ideological foundations of event policy? How are events shaping urban form and urban society? What measures will demonstrate the social and cultural benefits of planned events?	Document review Interviews with people who shaped history Mapping Delphi panels Trends analysis Scenario-making Policy reviews

FP 5: Generic 'event management' professionals will become the norm, forcing the various professional associations to adapt their recruitment appeal and to demonstrate their added value.

FP 6: The event professional of the future will be competent in event management theory and applications, knowledgeable about the importance of events in society, an effective advocate for event-related policy, and a constant learner within the field of event studies.

FP 7: Even if travel and tourism collapse, possibly because of the cascading effects of global warming, another energy crisis, war, terrorism or global pandemics, events will still remain important globally because they meet fundamental human needs.

Some really big future issues

There are many major forces propelling the events sector in terms of growth in numbers and diversity, the attention we pay to them, their perceived value and cumulative impacts. Both supply and demand-side forces are at work. Leisure and tourism are driven by population and economic growth, especially personal disposable incomes. The all-pervasive and global mass media, more and more the Internet, shape consumer demand for events. Economic growth and the forces of globalization (such as free trade and integrated economies) stimulate more business travel, meetings, conventions and exhibitions. Nations and cities compete heavily to attract and develop events for strategic reasons. But will all these forces continue unabated?

Global warming threatens the world's coastlines and ski resorts, and might very soon alter the ways in which we do business, travel and consume. The very mention of 'global pandemic' sends chills down the collective spines of everyone in the tourism and events industries. Why? Travel and events are the first things to be cancelled when disease breaks out, and dire predictions about the ravages of bird flu, SARS or something else abound. Add the constant threat of wars and terrorism, and the increasing inconveniences caused by security, and the potential for disruption will remain high. If the world is perceived to be unhealthy or unsafe, people will stay at home. And if energy costs continue to accelerate, or shortages are experienced, many will have no choice but to stay close to home. Will that be the end of planned events?

We can foresee a future (this is scenario-making) in which event tourism diminishes greatly because of the counter-forces mentioned above. Whole regions of the planet might lie devastated and mass migrations occur. The economy might suffer and consumerism disappear as a social and economic force. But, perhaps ironically, planned events will then become more important, not less. Instead of event tourism we will have to rely more on media events to stay connected globally. Instead of mega events that move from country to country, each nation, region and community will require its own celebrations, meetings and games to bring people together for live experiences. Because events have met essential needs throughout history, in all civilizations, it is safe to conclude that they will endure and adapt.

Policy questions

A major research priority is to examine how event policy is formulated within the context of power, negotiation, stakeholder and public input. It is equally important to determine why event policy is either not formulated, or is not integrated with other policy fields. Performance evaluation is necessary, including the developing of effectiveness and efficiency measures for policies affecting planned events. Little attention has been given to the justifications used for public-sector involvement with events, including the ideological bases, and how the public perceives the justifications (or values events in general).

Research agenda: outcomes and the impacted

Most event-impact-related research to date has been focused on tourism and economics, leaving a huge gap in terms of social, cultural and environmental impact knowledge. Event policy and management cannot advance without addressing this issue.

There have been some specific and substantial contributions to our understanding of the social and cultural impacts of planned events, but it cannot be said that there is a comprehensive or systematic approach and Table 12.5 outlines a range of productive lines of further inquiry. Anthropologists and sociologists have paid a lot of attention to festivals in particular, and to certain event-related issues, but they have had their own theoretical agendas. Their collective contributions do not constitute sufficient knowledge about the real or potential outcomes of all planned events.

The valuation of planned events has to be completely re-evaluated and redirected away from predominantly economic measures. Most planned events, from personal rites of passage to cultural celebrations, from trade shows to world's fairs, meet fundamental social and cultural needs. Who gives value to these meanings and roles?

Final comments

In this third edition of *Event Studies* most of the original material remains intact. Some material has indeed been deleted, in order to make room for new topics and research notes, for expert opinions and new figures. As the core and peripheral literature on planned events continues to grow, it has become impossible to

Table 12.5 Research agenda: outcomes and the impacted

Event studies themes	Key research questions	Possible research methods
Personal Social, cultural and political Economic Environmental	How do people describe and explain why events are satisfying, memorable or transforming? What are the personal and social consequences of negative event experiences? What performance measures exist and are needed for the social, cultural and environmental policy domains? How does exchange theory influence various stakeholder perceptions of event impacts? How are social representations of events formed? How does the nature and extent of community involvement influence event success and outcomes? Under what circumstances are events commodified and authenticity lost, versus traditions renewed and culture revitalized? How are the benefits and costs of events distributed through the population? What strategies work best for maximizing local economic benefits? Who are the high-yield event tourists, and how should they be attracted? How can events be made more environmentally sustainable? What are the cumulative impacts of an event and events in general, within a community or ecosystem? What is the value of any given event?	Focus groups In-depth interviews Consumer and social surveys Media content analysis Stakeholder consultations Ethnography Comprehensive cost–benefit evaluations Business surveys Market research Environmental audits and formal impact assessments Valuations

incorporate all of the good material into one book, or even to reference it, so we have become more selective. More important than including all the useful references and great research examples is the goal of keeping up with the new ideas, issues and methods.

Event studies remains open to definition and development, drawing as it must from all the traditional disciplines and many closely related professional fields. It can never have fixed boundaries, and both knowledge creation for, and the nature of, event studies has to remain a process of adding, refining, testing and debating.

STUDY GUIDE

Before beginning research it is important to consider a number of philosophical issues regarding the meaning and creation of knowledge, hence a discussion of epistemology, ontology, positivism and post-modernism. Research in event studies should not be confined to any particular research paradigm, rather it should be inclusive and integrative.

Positivism, associated with quantitative, scientific methods (including experimentation), has led to substantial theory development in the foundation disciplines, much of which is necessary for event studies. Yet the experiential nature of events, and the diverse meanings attached to them, necessitate alternative approaches such as phenomenology, ethnography and inductive, grounded research in general. An interpretivist perspective, recognizing socially constructed realities, will definitely help progress the field.

Research and evaluation purposes and methods were then discussed, revealing the broad range of approaches that can be useful. Throughout the book examples of many methods have been provided, hopefully making it clear that no particular approach or technique should have pre-eminence. Finally, a research agenda for event studies was presented, including key research questions and appropriate methods. This agenda is really just a starting point and is not, indeed, to limit research. Priorities will be different depending on one's perspective on events, as outlined in our framework for creating knowledge.

STUDY QUESTIONS

- Is event studies a 'discipline', 'multidisciplinary' or 'interdisciplinary'? Why?
- Explain the ways in which knowledge can be created for event studies.
- Define these terms and explain how they affect the creation of knowledge: 'epistemology'; 'ontology'; 'positivism'; 'post-modernism'.
- Why are 'theories' needed in event studies? How are they developed?
- Show how 'deductive' and 'inductive' methodologies are both appropriate in event studies.
- What are the main purposes and uses of research and evaluation?
- Give examples of established research methods from foundation disciplines that can be applied in event studies.
- Illustrate 'quantitative' and 'qualitative' research that has been applied to the study of planned events.
- Explain 'phenomenology' and why it is important in event studies.
- Suggest and justify research priorities for each of the main themes in event studies.

FURTHER READING

Fox, D., Gouthro, M., Morakabati, Y. and Brackstone, J. (2014). *Doing Events Research. From Theory to Practice*. Oxford: Routledge.

Goodson, L. and Phillimore, J. (eds) (2004). *Qualitative Research in Tourism: Ontologies, Epistemologies and Methodologies*. London: Routledge.

Tribe, J. (ed.) (2009). *Philosophical Issues in Tourism*. Bristol: Channel View.

Veal, A. (2011). *Research Methods for Leisure and Tourism: A Practical Guide* (4th edn). Harlow: Prentice Hall.

Veal, A. and Burton, C. (2014). *Research Methods for Arts and Event Management*. Harlow: Pearson.

Veal, A. and Darcy, S. (2014). *Research Methods in Sport Studies and Sport Management: A Practical Guide*. Oxford: Routledge.

References

Abbott, J. and Geddie, M. (2000). Event and venue management: Minimizing liability through effective crowd management techniques. *Event Management*, 6 (4), 259–270.

About Italy News Blog (http://newsblog.aboutitaly.net, accessed 25 August 2015).

Abrahams, R. (1982). The language of festivals: Celebrating the economy. In V. Turner (ed.), *Celebration: Studies in Festivity and Ritual*, pp. 160–177. Washington DC: Smithsonian Institution Press.

Abrahams, R. (1987). An American vocabulary of celebrations. In A. Falassi (ed.), *Time Out of Time, Essays On the Festival*, pp. 173–183. Albuquerque, NM: University of New Mexico Press.

Action.Ran.Org (http://action.ran.org, accessed 25 August 2015).

Adams, K. (2011). Public interest anthropology, political market squares, and re-scripting dominance: From swallows to 'race' in San Juan Capistrano, CA. *Journal of Policy Research in Tourism, Leisure and Events*, 3 (2), 147–169.

Addo, P. A. (2009). Anthropology, festival, and spectacle. *Reviews in Anthropology*, 38 (3), 217–236.

Agrusa, J., Maples, G., Kitterlin, M. and Tanner, J. (2008). Sensation seeking, culture, and the valuation of experiential services. *Event Management*, 11 (3), 121–128.

Ahmed, Q. A., Arabi, Y. M. and Memish, Z. A. (2006). Health risks at the Hajj. *The Lancet*, 367 (9515), 1008–1015.

Ahmed, Z. (1991). Marketing your community: Correcting a negative image. *Cornell Quarterly*, 31 (4), 24–27.

AIEST (1987). *Editions AIEST, Vol. 28, The Role and Impact of Mega-Events and Attractions on Regional and National Tourism*. St Gallen, Switzerland.

Ajzen, I. (1985). From intentions to actions: A theory of planned behaviour. In J. Kuhl and J. Beckmann (eds), *Springer Series in Social Psychology*, pp. 11–39. Berlin: Springer.

Ajzen, I. (1991). The theory of planned behavior. *Organizational Behavior and Human Decision Processes*, 50 (2), 179–211.

Ajzen, I. and Fishbein, M. (1973). Attitudinal and normative variables as predictors of behaviour. *Journal of Personality and Social Psychology*, 27 (1), 41–57.

Ali-Knight, J. and Robertson, M. (2004). Introduction to arts, culture and leisure. In I. Yeoman, M. Robertson, J. Ali-Knight, S. Drummond and U. McMahon-Beattie (eds), *Festivals and Events Management*, pp. 3–13. Oxford: Elsevier.

Ali-Knight, J., Robertson, M., Fyall, A. and Ladkin, A. (2008). *International Perspectives of Festivals and Events: Paradigms of Analysis*. Oxford: Butterworth-Heinemann.

Al-Kodmany, K. (2013). Crowd management and urban design: New scientific approaches. *Urban Design International*, 18 (4), 282–295.

Allen, J. (2008, 2nd edn 2014). *Event Planning: The Ultimate Guide to Successful Meetings, Corporate Events, Fundraising Galas, Conferences and Conventions, Incentives and Other Special Events*. Mississauga, ON: Wiley Canada.

Allen, J. and Bartle, M. (2014). Sport event volunteers' engagement: Management matters. *Managing Leisure*, 19 (1), 36–50.

Allen, J. and Cochrane, A. (2014). The urban unbound: London's politics and the 2012 Olympic Games. *International Journal of Urban and Regional Research*, 38 (5), 1609–1624.

Allen, J., Massiah, C., Cascio, R. and Johnson, Z. (2008). Triggers of extraordinary experiences within a sub-cultural consumption event. *Advances in Consumer Research*, 35, 711–713.

Allen, J., O'Toole, W., Harris, R. and McDonnell, I. (2011). *Festival and Special Event Management* (5th edn). Milton, QLD: John Wiley & Sons Australia.

Allix, A. (1922). The geography of fairs: Illustrated by old-world examples. *Geographical Review*, 12 (4), 532–569.

Allport, G. (1937). *Personality: A Psychological Interpretation*. New York: Holt, Rinehart & Winston.

Al-Tawfiq, J. A. and Memish, Z. A. (2012). Mass gathering medicine: A leisure or necessity? *International Journal of Clinical Practice*, 66 (6), 530–532.

American Anthropological Association (www.aaa.net.org, accessed 25 August 2015).

American Council for the United Nations University (2007). *State of the Future, the Millennium Project* (www.unmillenniumproject.org; www.acunu.org, accessed 25 August 2015).

American Historical Association (www.historians.org, accessed 25 August 2015).

America's Cup Office (1987). *America's Cup Defence Series, 1986/87: Impact on the Community*. Prepared for Government of Western Australia and Commonwealth America's Cup Support Group, Centre for Applied and Business Research, Nedlands, W.A.

Ammon, R. and Fried, G. (1998). Crowd management practices. *Journal of Convention and Exhibition Management*, 1 (2/3), 119–150.

Anand, N. and Watson, M. R. (2004). Tournament rituals in the evolution of fields: The case of the Grammy Awards. *Academy of Management Journal*, 47 (1), 59–80.

Ancient History Sourcebook (www.fordham.edu/HALSALL/ancient/asbook.html, accessed 25 August 2015).

Andersson, I. and Niedomysl, T. (2010). Clamour for glamour? City competition for hosting the Swedish tryouts to the Eurovision Song Contest. *Tijdschrift voor Economische en Sociale Geografie*, 101 (2), 111–125.

Andersson, T. (2006). The economic impact of cultural tourism. In T. Andersson, B. Holmgren and L. Mossberg (eds), *Cultural Tourism: Visitor Flows, Economic Impact and Product Development*, pp. 33–46. Published for the European Cultural Tourism Network at the School of Business, Economics and Law, University of Gothenburg, Sweden.

Andersson, T. and Armbrecht, J. (2014). Use-value of music event experiences: A 'triple ex' model explaining direct and indirect use-value of events. *Scandinavian Journal of Hospitality and Tourism*, 14 (3), 255–274.

Andersson, T. and Getz, D. (2007). Resource dependency, costs and revenues of a street festival. *Tourism Economics*, 13 (1), 143–162.

Andersson, T. and Getz, D. (2008). Stakeholder management strategies of festivals. *Journal of Convention and Event Tourism*, 9 (3), 199–220.

Andersson, T. and Getz, D. (2009). Tourism as a mixed industry: Differences between private, public and not-for-profit festivals. *Tourism Management*, 30 (6), 847–856.

Andersson, T. and Lundberg, E. (2013). Commensurability and sustainability: Triple impact assessments of a tourism event. *Tourism Management*, 37, 99–109.

Andersson, T. and Mossberg, L. (2014). Interest in food events: Some insights from Swedish consumers. In A. Cavicchi and C. Santini (eds), *Food and Wine Events in Europe*, pp. 201–212. New York: Routledge.

Andersson, T. and Samuelson, L. (2000). Financial effects of events on the public sector. In L. Mossberg (ed.), *Evaluation of Events: Scandinavian Experiences*, pp. 86–103. New York: Cognizant.

Andersson, T. and Solberg, H. (1999). Leisure events and regional economic impact. *World Leisure and Recreation*, 41 (1), 20–28.

Andersson, T., Getz, D. and Mykletun, R. (2013a). Sustainable festival populations: An application of organizational ecology. *Tourism Analysis*, 18, 621–634.

Andersson, T., Getz, D., Mykletun, R., Jaeger, K. and Dolles, H. (2013b). Factors influencing grant and sponsorship revenue for festivals. *Event Management*, 17 (3), 195–212.

Andersson, T., Persson, C., Sahlberg, B. and Strom, L. (eds) (1999). *The Impact of Mega Events*. Ostersund, Sweden: European Tourism Research Institute.

Andrews, H. and Leopold, T. (2013). *Events and the Social Sciences*. Abingdon: Routledge.

Arai, S. and Pedlar, A. (2003). Moving beyond individualism in leisure theory: A critical analysis of concepts of community and social engagement. *Leisure Studies*, 22 (3), 185–202.

Archer, B. (1982). The value of multipliers and their policy implications. *Tourism Management*, 3 (4), 236–241.

Archibald, M. (2007). An organizational ecology of national self-help/mutual-aid organizations. *Nonprofit and Voluntary Sector Quarterly*, 36 (4), 598–621.

Arellano, A. (2011). A history of Quebec – branded: The staging of the New France Festival. *Event Management*, 15 (1), 1–12.

Armbrecht, J. (2014). Use value of cultural experiences: A comparison of contingent valuation and travel cost. *Tourism Management*, 42, 141–148.

Armstrong, J. (1985). International events: The real tourism impact. In *Conference Proceedings of the Canada Chapter, Travel and Tourism Research Association*, pp. 9–37. Edmonton.

Atkinson, M. (2008). Triathlon, suffering and exciting significance. *Leisure Studies*, 27 (2), 165–180.

Australian Bureau of Statistics, Voluntary Work (www.abs.gov.au, accessed 25 August 2015).

Australian Centre for Event Management (www.acem.uts.edu.au, accessed 25 August 2015).

Axelsen, M. and Arcodia, C. (2004). Conceptualising art exhibitions as special events: A review of the literature. *Journal of Convention and Event Tourism*, 6 (3), 63–80.

Babiak, K. and Wolfe, R. (2006). More than just a game? Corporate social responsibility and Super Bowl XL. *Sport Marketing Quarterly*, 15 (4), 214.

Babiak, K. and Wolfe, R. (2009). Determinants of corporate social responsibility in professional sport: Internal and external factors. *Journal of Sport Management*, 23 (6), 717–742.

Backman, K., Backman, S., Uysal, M. and Sunshine, K. (1995). Event tourism: An examination of motivations and activities. *Festival Management and Event Tourism*, 3 (1), 15–24.

Bailey, P. (2002). *Design for Entertaining: Inspiration for Creating the Party of Your Dreams*. Weimar, TX: Culinary and Hospitality Industry Publications Services.

Baker, D. and Crompton, J. (2000). Quality, satisfaction and behavioral intentions. *Annals of Tourism Research*, 27 (2), 785–804.

Baker, S. A. and Rowe, D. (2014). Mediating mega events and manufacturing multiculturalism: The cultural politics of the world game in Australia. *Journal of Sociology*, 50 (3), 299–314.

Bakhtin, M. (1993). *Rabelais and His World*. Translated by H. Iswolsky. Bloomington: Indiana University Press (written in 1941, first published in 1965).

Bale, J. and Dejonghe, T. (2008). Editorial. Sports geography: An overview. *Belgeo. Revue belge de géographie*, (2), 157–166.

Ballantyne, J., Ballantyne, R. and Packer, J. (2014). Designing and managing music festival experiences to enhance attendees' psychological and social benefits. *Musicae Scientiae*, 18 (1), 65–83.

Bandura, A. (1977). Self-efficacy: Toward a unifying theory of behavioral change. *Psychology Review*, 84 (2), 191–215.

Bandura, A. (1986). *Social Foundations of Thought and Action: A Social Cognitive Theory*. Englewood Cliffs, NJ: Prentice-Hall.

Bang, H., Alexandris, K. and Ross, S. D. (2009). Validation of the revised volunteer motivations scale for international sporting events (VMS-ISE) at the Athens 2004 Olympic Games. *Event Management*, 12(3/4), 119–131.

Bang, H., Won, D. and Kim, Y. (2009). Motivations, commitment, and intentions to continue volunteering for sporting events. *Event Management*, 13 (2), 69–81.

Barbato, M. and Mio, C. (2007). Accounting and the development of management control in the cultural sphere: The case of the Venice Biennale. *Accounting, Business and Financial History*, 17(1), 187–208.

Barbieri, C., Mahoney, E. and Palmer, R. (2008). RV and camping shows: A motivation-based market segmentation. *Event Management*, 12 (2), 53–66.

Barker, M. (2000). *An Empirical Investigation of Tourist Crime in New Zealand: Perceptions, Victimisation and Future Implications*. Unpublished Ph.D. thesis, Centre for Tourism, University of Otago, Dunedin, New Zealand.

Barker, M. and Page, S. J. (2002). Visitor safety in urban tourism environments: The case of Auckland, New Zealand. *Cities*, 19(4), 273–282.

Barker, M., Page, S. and Meyer, D. (2001). Evaluating the impact of the 2000 America's Cup on Auckland, New Zealand. *Event Management*, 7 (2), 79–92.

Barker, M., Page, S. J. and Meyer, D. (2002). Modeling tourism crime: The 2000 America's cup. *Annals of Tourism Research*, 29 (3), 762–782.

Barker, M., Page, S. and Meyer, D. (2003). Urban visitor perceptions of safety during a special event. *Journal of Travel Research*, 41 (4), 355–361.

Barker, R. (1968). *Ecological Psychology: Concepts and Methods for Studying the Environment of Human Behavior*. Stanford, CA: Stanford University Press.

Barnett, R. (1990). *The Idea of Higher Education*. Buckingham: Open University Press.

Barney, J. (1991). Firm resources and sustained competitive advantage. *Journal of Management*, 17 (1), 99–120.

Baron, R. and Byrne, D. (2000). *Social Psychology* (9th edn). Boston, MA: Allyn and Bacon.

Baron, S., Warnaby, G. and Hunter-Jones, P. (2014). Service(s) marketing research: Developments and directions. *International Journal of Management Reviews*, 16 (2), 150–171.

Barron, P. and Leask, A. (2012). Events management education. In S. J. Page and J. Connell (eds), *Routledge Handbook of Events*, pp. 473–488. Abingdon: Routledge.

Barros, C. P. (2006). Evaluating sport events at European level: The Euro 2004. *International Journal of Sport Management and Marketing*, 1 (4), 400–410.

Bateson, J. (1989). *Managing Services Marketing: Text and Readings*. Chicago, IL: The Dryden Press.

Batty, M., DeSyllas, J. and Duxbury, E. (2003). The discrete dynamics of small-scale spatial events: Agent-based models of mobility in carnivals and street parades. *International Journal of Geographical Information Science*, 17 (7), 673–697.

Baudrillard, J. (1998). *The consumer society: Myths and Structures*. London: Sage.

Baum, J. (1996). Organizational ecology. In S. Clegg, C. Hardy and W. Nord (eds), *Handbook of Organization Studies*, pp. 77–115. London: Sage.

Baum, J. and Oliver, C. (1992). Institutional embededdness and the dynamics of organizational populations. *American Sociological Review*, 57 (4), 540–559.

Baum, J. and Oliver, C. (1996). Toward an institutional ecology of organizational founding. *Academy of Management Journal*, 39 (5), 1378–1427.

Baum, T. and Lundtorp, S. (eds) (2001). *Seasonality in Tourism*. Oxford: Pergamon.

Baum, T., Deery, M., Hanlon, C., Lockstone, L. and Smith, K. (2009). *People and Work in Events and Conventions*. Wallingford: CABI.

Baumann, R., Ciavarra, T., Englehardt, B. and Matheson, V. A. (2012). Sports franchises, events, and city livability: An examination of spectator sports and crime rates. *The Economic and Labour Relations Review*, 23 (2), 83–97.

BBC News Northern Ireland, online service, 14 July 2010 (http://www.bbc.co.uk/news/northern_ireland, accessed 25 August 2015).

Becken, S. (2015). *Tourism and Oil: Preparing for the Challenge*. Bristol: Channel View.

Becker, D. (2006). *The Essential Legal Guide to Events: A Practical Handbook for Event Professionals and Their Advisers*. Self-published.

Becker, H. (1960). Notes on the concept of commitment. *American Journal of Sociology*, 66 (1), 32–40.

Belghazi, T. (2006). Festivalization of urban space in Morocco. *Critique: Critical Middle Eastern Studies*, 15 (1), 97–107.

Bell, P., Greene, T., Fisher, J. and Baum, A. (2001). *Environmental Psychology* (5th edn). Belmont, CA: Thomson Wadsworth.

Benckendorff, P. and Pearce, P. (2012). The psychology of events. In S. J. Page and J. Connell (eds), *Routledge Handbook of Events*, pp. 165–185. Abingdon: Routledge.

Bendle, L. and Patterson, I. (2008). Serious leisure, career volunteers and the organization of arts events in a regional Australian city. *International Journal of Event Management Research*, 4 (1), 1–11.

Benedict, B. (1983). *The Anthropology of World's Fairs*. Berkeley, CA: Scolar Press.

Berlonghi, A. (1990). *The Special Event Risk Management Manual*. Self-published (A. Berlonghi, PO Box 3454 Dana Point, California 92629).

Berlonghi, A. (1996). *Special Event Security Management, Loss Prevention, and Emergency Services*. Self-published (A. Berlonghi, PO Box 3454 Dana Point, California 92629).

Berridge, G. (2007). *Event Design and Experience*. Oxford: Butterworth Heinemann.

Berridge, G. (2010). Event pitching: The role of design and creativity. *International Journal of Hospitality Management*, 29 (2), 208–215.

Berridge, G. (2012a). Event experience: A case study of differences between the way in which organizers plan an event experience and the way in which guests receive the experience. *Journal of Park & Recreation Administration*, 30 (3), 7–23.

Berridge, G. (2012b). Designing event experiences. In S. J. Page and J. Connell (eds), *Routledge Handbook of Events*, pp. 273–288. Abingdon: Routledge.

Berryman, J. (2013). Art and national interest: The diplomatic origins of the 'blockbuster exhibition' in Australia. *Journal of Australian Studies*, 37 (2), 159–173.

Best, J. (2009). What policy-makers want from research: What researchers want to tell them. *Journal of Policy Research in Tourism, Hospitality and Events*, 1 (2), 175–178.

Beverland, M., Hoffman, D. and Rasmussen, M. (2001). The evolution of events in the Australasian wine sector. *Tourism Recreation Research*, 26 (2), 35–44.

Billinge, M. (1996). A time and place for everything: An essay on recreation, re-creation and the Victorians. *Journal of Historical Geography*, 22 (4), 443–459.

Bitner, M. J. (1992). Servicescapes: The impact of physical surroundings on customers and employees. *Journal of Marketing*, 56 (2), 57–71.

Bjorner, E. and Berg, P. O. (2012). Strategic creation of experiences at Shanghai World Expo: A practice of communification. *International Journal of Event and Festival Management*, 3 (1), 30–45.

Bladen, C. and Kennell, J. (2014). Educating the 21st century event management graduate: Pedagogy, practice, professionalism, and professionalization. *Event Management*, 18 (1), 5–14.

Blake, A. (2005). *The Economic Impact of the London 2012 Olympics, Research Report 2005/5*. Christel DeHaan Tourism and Travel Research Institute, Nottingham University.

Blichfeldt, B. S. and Halkier, H. (2014). Mussels, tourism and community development: A case study of place branding through food festivals in rural North Jutland, Denmark. *European Planning Studies*, 22 (8), 1587–1603.

Bloom, B. (ed.) (1956). *Taxonomy of Educational Objectives: The Classification of Educational Goals*. Chicago: Susan Fauer Company, Inc.

Bob, U. and Majola, M. (2011). Rural community perceptions of the 2010 FIFA World Cup: The Makhowe community in Kwazulu-Natal. *Development Southern Africa*, 28 (3), 386–399.

Bodet, G. (2015). The spectators' perspective. In M. Parent and J.-L. Chappelet (eds), *Routledge Handbook of Sports Event Management*, pp. 163–180. Abingdon: Routledge.

Bodet, G. and Lacassagne, M.-F. (2012). International place branding through sporting events: A British perspective of the 2008 Beijing Olympics. *European Sport Management Quarterly*, 12 (4), 357–374.

Boella, M. (1992). *Human Resource Management in the Hospitality Industry* (5th edn). Cheltenham: Stanley Thornes.

Bohlin, M. (2000). Traveling to events. In L. Mossberg (ed.), *Evaluation of Events: Scandinavian Experiences*, pp. 13–29. New York: Cognizant.

Boissevain, J. (1979). Impact of tourism on a dependent island: Gozo, Malta. *Annals of Tourism Research*, 6 (1), 76–90.

Boissevain, J. (ed.) (1996). *Coping with Tourists: European Reactions to Mass Tourism*. Oxford: Bergahn Books.

Bonthuys, E. (2012). The 2010 Football World Cup and the regulation of sex work in South Africa. *Journal of Southern African Studies*, 38 (1), 11–29.

Boo, S. and Busser, J. (2006). Impact analysis of a tourism festival on tourists' destination images. *Event Management*, 9 (4), 223–237.

Booch, G. (2014). The human and ethical aspects of big data. *IEEE Software*, 31 (1), 20–22.

Boorstin, D. (1961). *The Image: A Guide to Pseudo-Events in America*. New York: Harper and Row.

Borrie, B. and Birzell, R. (2001). Approaches to measuring quality of the wilderness experience. In W. Freimund and D. Cole (eds), *Visitor Use Density and Wilderness Experience: Proceedings*, pp. 29–38. Ogden, UT: US Department of Agriculture, Forest Service, Rocky Mountain Research Station.

Bos, H. (1994). The importance of mega-events in the development of tourism demand. *Festival Management and Event Tourism*, 2 (1), 55–58.

Botterill, D. and Crompton, J. (1996). Two case studies: Exploring the nature of the tourist's experience. *Journal of Leisure Research*, 28 (1), 57–82.

Bouchet, P., LeBrun, A. and Auvergne, S. (2004). Sport tourism consumer experiences: A comprehensive model. *Journal of Sport Tourism*, 9 (2), 127–140.

Bourdieu, P. (1972). *Esquisse d'une théorie de la pratique, précédé de trois études d'ethnologie kabyle* (Outline of a Theory of Practice). Cambridge: Cambridge University Press.

Bourdieu, P. (1986). The forms of capital. In J. Richardson (ed.), *Handbook of Theory and Research in the Sociology of Education*. New York: Greenwald Press.

Bowdin, G. and Church, I. (2000). Customer satisfaction and quality costs: Towards a pragmatic approach for event management. In J. Allen, R. Harris and L. Jago (eds), *Events Beyond 2000 – Setting the Agenda*. Sydney: Australian Centre for Event Management, University of Technology, Sydney.

Bowdin, G., Allen, J., O'Toole, W., Harris, R. and McDonnell, I. (2011). *Events Management* (3rd edn). Oxford: Butterworth-Heinemann.

Boyd, D. and Boyd, L. (1998). The home field advantage: Implications for the pricing of tickets to professional team sporting events. *Journal of Economics and Finance*, 22 (2–3), 169–179.

Bramwell, B. (1997). Strategic planning before and after a mega-event. *Tourism Management*, 18 (3), 167–176.

Bramwell, B. and Lane, B. (1993). Interpretation and sustainable tourism: The potential and the pitfalls. *Journal of Sustainable Tourism*, 1 (2), 71–80.

Breen, H., Bull, A. and Walo, M. (2001). A comparison of survey methods to estimate visitor expenditure at a local event. *Tourism Management*, 22 (5), 473–479.

Brennan-Horley, C., Connell, J. and Gibson, C. (2007). The Parkes Elvis Revival Festival: Economic development and contested place identities in rural Australia. *Geographical Research*, 45 (1), 71–84.

Brewster, M., Connell, J. and Page, S. (2009). The Scottish Highland Games: Evolution, development and role as a community event. *Current Issues in Tourism*, 12 (3), 271–293.

Brida, J. G., Disegna, M. and Osti, L. (2013). The effect of authenticity on visitors' expenditure at cultural events. *Current Issues in Tourism*, 16 (3), 266–285.

Bristow, D. and Sebastion, R. (2001). Holy cow! Wait 'til next year! A closer look at the brand loyalty of Chicago Cubs baseball fans. *Journal of Consumer Marketing*, 18 (3), 256–275.

British Arts Festivals Association (2000, 2002, 2007). *Festivals Mean Business* (www.artsfestivals.co.uk, accessed 25 August 2015).

British Columbia Sports Branch (www.tsa.gov.bc.ca/sport, accessed 25 August 2015).

British Standards Institute (2006). *Sustainable Event Management System: Specification with Guidance for Use*. London: BSI.

British Triathlon (britishtriathlonmedia.org, accessed 25 August 2015).

Britton, S. G. (1982). The political economy of tourism in the Third World. *Annals of Tourism Research*, 9 (3), 331–358.

Brothers, G. and Brantley, V. (1993). Tag and recapture: Testing an attendance estimation technique for an open access special event. *Festival Management and Event Tourism*, 1 (4), 143–146.

Brotherton, B. and Himmetoğlu, B. (1997). Beyond destinations – special interest tourism. *Anatolia*, 8 (3), 11–30.

Brown, G. (2002). Taking the pulse of Olympic sponsorship. *Event Management*, 7 (3), 187–196.

Brown, G., Chalip, L., Jago, L. and Mules, T. (2001). The Sydney Olympics and Brand Australia. In N. Morgan, A. Pritchard and R. Pride (eds), *Destination Branding: Creating the Unique Destination Proposition*, pp. 163–185. Oxford: Butterworth-Heinemann.

Brown, K. (2010). Come on home: Visiting friends and relatives – the Cape Breton experience. *Event Management*, 14 (4), 309–318.

Brown, S. (2014). Emerging professionalism in the event industry: A practitioner's perspective. *Event Management*, 18 (1), 15–24.

Brown, S. and James, J. (2004). Event design and management: Ritual sacrifice? In I. Yeoman, M. Robertson, J. Ali-Knight, S. Drummond and U. McMahon-Beattie (eds), *Festivals and Events Management*, pp. 53–64. Oxford: Elsevier.

Brunson, M. and Shelby, B. (1993). Recreation substitutability: A research agenda. *Leisure Sciences*, 15 (1), 67–74.

Bruwer, J. and Kelley, K. (2015). Service performance quality evaluation and satisfaction in a USA wine festivalscape: Buying behavioural effects. *International Journal of Event and Festival Management*, 6 (1), 18–38.

Bryan, H. (1977). Leisure value systems and recreation specialization: The case of trout fishermen. *Journal of Leisure Research*, 9 (3), 174–187.

Buck, R. (1977). Making good business better: A second look at staged tourist attractions. *Journal of Travel Research*, 15 (3), 30–31.

Burdseya, D. (2008). Contested conceptions of identity, community and multiculturalism in the staging of alternative sport events: A case study of the Amsterdam World Cup football tournament. *Leisure Studies*, 27 (3), 259–277.

Bureau International des Expositions (www.bie-paris.org, accessed 25 August 2015).

Burgan, B. and Mules, T. (1992). Economic impact of sporting events. *Annals of Tourism Research*, 19 (4), 700–710.

Burgan, B. and Mules, T. (2001). Reconciling cost–benefit and economic impact assessment for event tourism. *Tourism Economics*, 7 (4), 321–330.

Burns, J. and Mules, T. (1989). An economic evaluation of the Adelaide Grand Prix. In G. Syme, B. Shaw, D. Fenton and W. Mueller (eds), *The Planning and Evaluation of Hallmark Events*, pp. 172–185. Aldershot: Gower.

Burns, J., Hatch, J. and Mules, T. (eds) (1986). *The Adelaide Grand Prix: The Impact of a Special Event*. Adelaide: The Centre for South Australian Economic Studies.

Burr, S. and Scott, D. (2004). Application of the recreational specialization framework to understanding visitors to the Great Salt Lake Bird Festival. *Event Management*, 9 (1/2), 27–37.

Butler, R. (1980). The concept of a tourist area cycle of evolution: Implications for management of resources. *Canadian Geographer*, 24 (1), 5–12.

Butler, R. W. (2001). Seasonality in tourism: Issues and implications. In S. Lundtorp and T. Baum (eds), *Seasonality in Tourism*, pp. 5–21. Oxford: Pergamon.

Butler, R. and Grigg, J. (1987). The hallmark event that got away: The case of the 1991 Pan American Games in London, Ontario. In *PAPER 87, People and Physical Environment Research Conference*. Perth: University of Western Australia.

Butler, R. and Mao, B. (1997). Seasonality in tourism: Problems and measurement. In P. Murphy (ed.), *Quality Management in Urban Tourism*, pp. 9–24. Wiley, Chichester.

Butler, R., Hall, C. M. and Jenkins, J. (1997). *Tourism and Recreation in Rural Areas*. Chichester: John Wiley & Sons.

Camarero, C., Garrido, M. J. and Vicente, E. (2010). Components of art exhibition brand equity for internal and external visitors. *Tourism Management*, 31 (4), 495–504.

Cameron, C. (1989). Cultural tourism and urban revitalization. *Tourism Recreation Research*, 14 (1), 23–32.

Campbell, S. and Fainstein, S. (eds) (2003). *Readings in Planning Theory*. Malden, MA: Blackwell.

Campaniello, N. (2013). Mega events in sports and crime: Evidence from the 1990 Football World Cup. *Journal of Sports Economics*, 14 (2), 148–170.

Canadian Heritage (www.canadianheritage.gc.ca, accessed on 25 August 2015).

Can West News Service. 14 December 2005, p. A3. Santarchists (www.canada.com/calgaryherald, accessed on 25 August 2015).

Capriello, A. and Rotherham, I. D. (2011). Building a preliminary model of event management for rural communities. *Journal of Hospitality Marketing and Management*, 20 (3–4), 246–264.

Carlsen, J. (2004). The economics and evaluation of festivals and events. In I. Yeoman, M. Robertson, J. Ali-Knight, S. Drummond and U. McMahon-Beattie (eds), *Festivals and Events Management*, pp. 246–259. Oxford: Elsevier.

Carlsen, J. and Taylor, A. (2003). Mega-events and urban renewal: The case of the Manchester 2002 Commonwealth Games. *Event Management*, 8 (1), 15–22.

Carlsen, J., Andersson, T., Ali-Knight, J., Jaeger, K. and Taylor, R. (2010). Festival management innovation and failure. *International Journal of Event and Festival Management*, 1 (2), 120–131.

Carlsen, J., Getz, D. and Soutar, G. (2000). Event evaluation research. *Event Management*, 6 (4), 247–257.

Carnegie, E. and Smith, M. (2006). Mobility, diaspora and the hybridisation of festivity: The case of the Edinburgh Mela. In D. Picard and M. Robinson (eds), *Festivals, Tourism and Social Change: Remaking Worlds*, pp. 255–268. Clevedon: Channel View.

Carnival of Venice (www.carnivalofvenice.com, accessed on 25 August 2015).

Carroll, G. (1984). Organizational ecology. *Annual Review of Sociology*, 10, 71–93.

Carroll, G. (1985). Concentration and specialization: Dynamics of niche width in populations of organizations. *American Journal of Sociology*, 90 (6), 1262–1283.

Carroll, G. and Hannan, M. (2000). *The Demography of Corporations and Industries*. Princeton, NJ: Princeton University Press.

Case, R. (2013). *Events and the Environment*. Abingdon: Routledge.

Case, R., Dey, T., Hobbs, S., Hoolachan, J. and Wilcox, A. (2010). An examination of sporting event direct-spending patterns at three competitive levels. *Journal of Convention and Event Tourism*, 11 (2), 119–137.

Castells, M. (2010). *The Rise of the Network Society*. Malden, MA: Wiley-Blackwell.

Catherwood, D. and van Kirk, R. (1992). *The Complete Guide to Special Event Management*. New York: Wiley.

Cavalcanti, M. (2001). The Amazonian Ox Dance Festival: An anthropological account. *Cultural Analysis*, 2, 69–105.

Cavicchi, A. and Santini, C. (2014). *Food and Wine Events in Europe*. Abingdon: Routledge.

Cecil, A., Fenich, G. G., Krugman, C. and Hashimoto, K. (2013). Review and analysis of the new international meeting and business events competency standards. *Journal of Convention & Event Tourism*, 14 (1), 65–74.

Center for Exhibition Industry Research. 26 March 2003, news release. CEIR (www.ceir.org, accessed 25 August 2015).

Chalip, L. (2006). Towards social leverage of sport events. *Journal of Sport and Tourism*, 11 (2), 109–127.

Chalip, L. and Costa, C. (2006). Building sport event tourism into the destination brand: Foundations for a general theory. In H. Gibson (ed.), *Sport Tourism: Concepts and Theories*, pp. 86–105. London: Routledge.

Chalip, L. and Leyns, A. (2002). Local business leveraging of a sport event: Managing an event for economic benefit. *Journal of Sport Management*, 16 (2), 132–158.

Chalip, L., Green, C. and Hill, B. (2003). Effects of sport media on destination image and intentions to visit. *Journal of Sport Management*, 17 (3), 214–234.

Chang, J. (2006). Segmenting tourists to aboriginal cultural festivals: An example in the Rukai tribal area, Taiwan. *Tourism Management*, 27 (6), 1224–1234.

Chang, S. and Mahadevan, R. (2014). Fad, fetish or fixture: contingent valuation of performing and visual arts festivals in Singapore. *International Journal of Cultural Policy*, 20 (3), 318–340.

Chang, W. and Yuan, J. (2011). A taste of tourism: Visitors' motivations to attend a food festival. *Event Management*, 15 (1), 13–23.

Chatterjee, K. and Gordon, A. (2006). Planning for an unpredictable future: Transport in Great Britain in 2030. *Transport Policy*, 13 (3), 254–264.

Chen, A. and Wu, R. (2009). Understanding visitors' involvement profile and information search: The case of Neimen Song Jiang Battle Array Festival. *Event Management*, 13 (4), 205–222.

Chen, N. (2012). Branding national images: The 2008 Beijing Summer Olympics, 2010 Shanghai World Expo, and 2010 Guangzhou Asian Games. *Public Relations Review*, 38 (5), 731–745.

Chen, P. (2006). The attributes, consequences, and values associated with event sport tourists' behaviour: A means-end chain approach. *Event Management*, 10 (1), 1–22.

Cheng, T.-M. and Chen, M.-T. (2014). Image transformation for Mazu Pilgrimage and festival tourism. *Asia Pacific Journal of Tourism Research*, 19 (5), 538–557.

Cheska, A. (1981). Antigonish Highland Games: An ethnic case study. Paper presented at the North American Society of Sport History, ninth annual convention, Hamilton.

Chien, P. M., Ritchie, B. W., Shipway, R. and Henderson, H. (2012). I am having a dilemma: Factors affecting resident support of event development in the community. *Journal of Travel Research*, 51 (4), 451–463.

Choi, J.-K. and Almanza, B. (2012). An assessment of food safety risk at fairs and festivals: A comparison of health inspection violations between fairs and festivals and restaurants. *Event Management*, 16 (4), 295–303.

Chwe, M. (2013). *Rational Ritual: Culture, Coordination, and Common Knowledge*. Princeton, NJ: Princeton University Press.

Citrine, K. (n.d.) Site planning for events. In *Event Operations*, pp. 17–19. Port Angeles, WA: International Festivals and Events Association.

Clarke, A. and Jepson, A. (2011). Power and hegemony within a community festival. *International Journal of Event and Festival Management*, 2 (1), 7–19.

Clarke, J. (2003). How journalists judge the 'reality' of an international 'pseudo-event': A study of correspondents who covered the final withdrawal of Vietnamese troops from Cambodia in 1989. *Journalism*, 4 (1), 50–75.

Clawson, M. and Knetsch, J. (1966). *Economics of Outdoor Recreation*. Baltimore, MD: Johns Hopkins University Press.

Club Managers Association of America (www.cmaa.org, accessed 25 August 2015).

Coghlan, A. (2015). Tourism and health: using positive psychology principles to maximise participants' wellbeing outcomes – a design concept for charity challenge tourism. *Journal of Sustainable Tourism*, 23 (3), 382–400.

Coghlan, A. and Filo, K. (2013). Using constant comparison method and qualitative data to understand participants' experiences at the nexus of tourism, sport and charity events. *Tourism Management*, 35, 122–131.

Cohen, E. (1979). A phenomenology of tourist experiences. *Sociology*, 13 (2), 179–201.

Cohen, E. (1988a). Traditions in the qualitative sociology of tourism. *Annals of Tourism Research*, 15 (1), 29–46.

Cohen, E. (1988b). Authenticity and commoditization in tourism. *Annals of Tourism Research*, 15 (3), 371–386.

Coleman, J. (1988). Social capital in the creation of human capital. *American Journal of Sociology*, 94, S95–120. In the Supplement: Organizations and Institutions: Sociological and Economic Approaches to the Analysis of Social Structure.

Coleman, J. (1990). *Foundations of Social Theory*. Cambridge, MA: Belknap Press of Harvard University Press.

Collins, A. and Flynn, A. (2008). Measuring the environmental sustainability of a major sporting event: A case study of the FA Cup Final. *Tourism Economics*, 14 (4), 751–768.

Collins, A., Jones, C. and Munday, M. (2009). Assessing the environmental impacts of mega sporting events: Two options? *Tourism Management*, 30 (6), 828–837.

Collins-Kreiner, N. (2010). Researching pilgrimage: Continuity and transformations. *Annals of Tourism Research*, 37 (2), 440–456.

Columbus, G. (2011). *The Complete Guide to Careers in Special Events*. New York: Wiley.

Comas, M. and Moscardo, G. (2005). Understanding associations and their conference decision-making processes. *Journal of Convention & Event Tourism*, 7 (3–4), 117–138.

Connell, J. and Page, S. J. (2005). Evaluating the economic and spatial effects of an event: The case of the world medical and health games. *Tourism Geographies*, 7 (1), 63–85.

Connell, J. and Page, S. (eds) (2010). *Event Tourism: Critical Concepts in Tourism. Volume 1–4*. Abingdon: Routledge.

Connell, J. Page, S. J. and Meyer, D. (2015). Visitor attractions and events: Responding to seasonality. *Tourism Management*, 46, 283–298.

Convention Industry Council (www.conventionindustry.org, accessed 25 August 2015).

Coopers and Lybrand Consulting Group (1989). *NCR 1988 Festivals Study Final Report*, Vol. 1. Ottawa: Report for the Ottawa-Carleton Board of Trade.

Cornelissen, S. (2011). Mega event securitisation in a Third World setting: Glocal processes and ramifications during the 2010 FIFA World Cup. *Urban Studies*, 48 (15), 3221–3240.

Cornish, E. (2004). Futuring: The exploration of the future. In *Futuring: The Exploration of the Future*. Bethesda, MD: World Future Society.

Coughlan, D. and Mules, T. (2002). Sponsorship awareness and recognition at Canberra's Floriade festival. *Event Management*, 7 (1), 1–9.

Coughlin, M., Coughlan, D. and Mules, T. (2010). The spectacle of piety on the Brittany coast. *Event Management*, 14 (4), 287–300.

Coyne, B. and Coyne, E. (2001). Getting, keeping and caring for unpaid volunteers for professional golf tournament events. *Human Resources Development International*, 4 (2), 199–214.

Craven, J. (1990). *Introduction to Economics: An Integrated Approach to Fundamental Principles*. Oxford: Blackwell.

Crawford, D., Jackson, E. and Godbey, G. (1991). A hierarchical model of leisure constraints. *Leisure Sciences*, 13 (4), 309–320.

Crespi-Vallbona, M. and Richards, G. (2007). The meaning of cultural festivals: Stakeholder perspectives in Catalunya. *International Journal of Cultural Policy*, 13 (1), 103–122.

Crompton, J. (1979). Motivations for pleasure vacation. *Annals of Tourism Research*, 6 (4), 408–424.

Crompton, J. (1993). Understanding a business organization's approach to entering a sponsorship partnership. *Festival Management and Event Tourism*, 1 (3), 98–109.

Crompton, J. (1995). Factors that have stimulated the growth of sponsorship of major events. *Festival Management and Event Tourism*, 3 (2), 97–101.

Crompton, J. (1999). *Measuring the Economic Impact of Visitors to Sports Tournaments and Special Events*. Ashburn, VA: Division of Professional Services, National Recreation and Park Association.

Crompton, J. (2006). Economic impact studies: Instruments for political shenanigans? *Journal of Travel Research*, 45, 67–82.

Crompton, J. (2011). Using external reference price to reduce resistance to leisure service pricing increases. *Managing Leisure*, 16 (3), 207–215.

Crompton, J. and Love, L. (1994). Using inferential evidence to determine likely reaction to a price increase at a festival. *Journal of Travel Research*, 32 (4), 32–36.

Crompton, J. and Love, L. (1995). The predictive validity of alternative approaches to evaluating quality of a festival. *Journal of Travel Research*, 34 (1), 11–24.

Crompton, J. and McKay, S. (1994). Measuring the economic impact of festivals and events: Some myths, misapplications and ethical dilemmas. *Festival Management and Event Tourism*, 2 (1), 33–43.

Crompton, J. and McKay, S. (1997). Motives of visitors attending festival events. *Annals of Tourism Research*, 24 (2), 425–439.

Crompton, J., Lee, S. and Shuster, T. (2001). A guide for undertaking economic impact studies: The Springfest example. *Journal of Travel Research*, 40 (1), 79–87.

Cronin, M. and Adair, D. (2004). *The Wearing of the Green: A History of St Patrick's Day*. London: Routledge.

Cross, G. (1986). The political economy of leisure: Britain and France and the origins of the eight hour day, 1885–1920. *Leisure Studies* (January), 69–90.

Cross, G. (1993). *Time and Money: The Making of Consumer Culture*. London: Routledge.

Crouch, G., Perdue, R., Timmermans, H. and Uysal, M. (2004). Building foundations for understanding the consumer psychology of tourism, hospitality and leisure. In G. Crouch, R. Perdue, H. Timmermans and M. Uysal (eds), *Consumer Psychology of Tourism, Hospitality and Leisure*, Vol. III, pp. 1–10. Cambridge, MA: CABI.

Crowther, P. and Donlan, L. (2011). Value-creation space: The role of events in a service-dominant marketing paradigm. *Journal of Marketing Management*, 27 (13–14), 1444–1463.

Crowther, P. and Orefice, C. (2015). Co-creative events: Analysis and illustrations. In G. W. Richards, L. Marques and K. Mein (eds), *Event Design: Social Perspectives and Practices*, pp. 122–136. Abingdon: Routledge

Cruikshank, J. (1997). Negotiating with narrative: Establishing cultural identity at the Yukon International Storytelling Festival. *American Anthropologist*, 99 (1), 56–69.

Csikszentmihalyi, M. (1975). *Beyond Boredom and Anxiety: The Experience of Play in Work and Leisure*. San Francisco, CA: Jossey-Bass.

Csikszentmihalyi, M. (1990). *Flow: The Psychology of Optimal Experience*. New York: Harper Perennial.

Csikszentmihalyi, M. and Csikszentmihalyi, I. (1988). *Optimal Experience: Psychological Studies of Flow on Consciousness*. Cambridge, MA. Cambridge University Press.

Cudny, W. (2014). Festivals as a subject for geographical research. *Geografisk Tidsskrift-Danish Journal of Geography*, 114 (2), 132–142.

Cunneen, C. and Lynch, R. (1988). The social meanings of conflict in riots at the Australian Grand Prix Motorcycle Races. *Leisure Studies*, 7 (1), 1–19.

Cusack, C. M. and Digance, J. (2009). The Melbourne Cup: Australian identity and secular pilgrimage. *Sport in Society*, 12 (7), 876–889.

Daniels, M. (2007). Central place theory and sport tourism impacts. *Annals of Tourism Research*, 34 (2), 332–347.

Daniels, M. and Norman, W. (2005). Motivations of equestrian tourists: An analysis of the Colonial Cup races. *Journal of Sport Tourism*, 10 (3), 201–210.

Dann, G. (1977). Anomie, ego-involvement and tourism. *Annals of Tourism Research*, 4, 184–194.

Dann, G. (1981). Tourist motivation: An appraisal. *Annals of Tourism Research*, 8 (2), 187–219.

Darcy, S. and Harris, R. (2003). Inclusive and accessible special event planning: An Australian perspective. *Event Management*, 8 (1), 39–47.

Darian-Smith, K. (2011). Histories of agricultural shows and rural festivals in Australia. In C. Gibson and J. Connell (eds), *Festival Places: Revitalising Rural Australia*, pp. 25–43. Bristol: Channel View.

Dashper, K., Fletcher, T. and McCullough, N. (eds) (2014). *Sports Events, Society and Culture*. Abingdon: Routledge.

Dattilo, J. and Howard, D. (1994). The complex and dynamic nature of leisure experience. *Journal of Leisure Research*, 26 (3), 195–211.

Davidson, R. (2003). Adding pleasure to business: Conventions and tourism. *Journal of Convention and Exhibition Management*, 5 (1), 29–39.

Davidson, R. and Cope, B. (2003). *Business Travel: Conferences, Incentive Travel, Exhibitions, Corporate Hospitality and Corporate Travel*. Harlow: Pearson.

Davidson, R. and Rogers, T. (2006). *Marketing Destinations and Venues for Conferences, Conventions and Business Events*. Oxford: Butterworth-Heinemann.

Davies, A. (2011). Local leadership and rural renewal through festival fun: The case of SnowFest. In C. Gibson and J. Connell (eds), *Festival Places: Revitalising Rural Australia*, pp. 61–73. Bristol: Channel View.

Dawson, M. (2011). Putting cities on the map: Vancouver's 1954 British Empire and Commonwealth Games in comparative and historical perspective 1. *Urban Geography*, 32 (6), 788–803.

Dayan, D. (1994). *Media Events*. Cambridge, MA: Harvard University Press.

Dean, D. H. (1999). Brand endorsement, popularity, and event sponsorship as advertising cues affecting consumer pre-purchase attitudes. *Journal of Advertising*, 28 (3), 1–12.

Debord, G. (1983). *Society of the Spectacle*. Translated by Ken Knabb (from the French original of 1967). London: Rebel Books.

De Bres, K. and Davis, J. (2001). Celebrating group and place identity: A case study of a new regional festival. *Tourism Geographies*, 3 (3), 326–337.

Deci, E. and Ryan, R. (1985). *Intrinsic Motivation and Self-Determination in Human Behavior*. New York: Plenum.

Deci, E. and Ryan, R. (2000). The 'what' and 'why' of goal pursuits: Human needs and the self-determination of behavior. *Psychological Inquiry*, 11 (4), 227–268.

Decrop, A. (2006). *Vacation Decision Making*. Wallingford: CABI.

Deery, M. and Jago, L. (2010). Social impacts of events and anti-social behavior. *International Journal of Event and Festival Management*, 1 (1), 8–28.

De Geus, A. P. (1988). Planning as learning. *Harvard Business Review*, 66 (2), 70–74.

De Grazia, S. (1962). *Of Time, Work, and Leisure*. New York: Twentieth Century Fund.

De Groote, P. (2005). A multidisciplinary analysis of world fairs (expos) and their effects. *Tourism Review*, 60 (1), 12–19.

Deighton, J. (1992). The consumption of performance. *Journal of Consumer Research*, 19 (3), 362–372.

Delamere, T. (2001). Development of a scale to measure resident attitudes toward the social impacts of community festivals: Part 2: Verification of the scale. *Event Management*, 7 (1), 25–38.

Delamere, T., Wankel, L. and Hinch, T. (2001). Development of a scale to measure resident attitudes toward the social impacts of community festivals: Part 1: Item generation and purification of the measure. *Event Management*, 7 (1), 11–24.

Delbosc, A. (2008). Social identity as a motivator in cultural festivals. *Visitor Studies*, 11 (1), 3–15.

Deloitte (www2.deloitte.com, accessed 25 August 2015).

Della Bitta, A., Loudon, D., Booth, G. and Weeks, R. (1977). Estimating the economic impact of a short-term tourist event. *Journal of Travel Research*, 16 (2), 10–15.

Delpy, L. and Li, M. (1998). The art and science of conducting economic impact studies. *Journal of Vacation Marketing*, 4 (3), 230–254.

Deng, Q. and Li, M. (2014). A model of event–destination image transfer. *Journal of Travel Research*, 53 (1), 69–82.

Denton, S. and Furse, B. (1993). Visitation to the 1991 Barossa Valley Vintage Festival: Estimating overall visitor numbers to a festival encompassing several venues and events. *Festival Management and Event Tourism*, 1 (2), 51–56.

Derrett, R. (2004). Festivals, events and the destination. In I. Yeoman, M. Robertson, J. Ali-Knight, S. Drummond and U. McMahon-Beattie (eds), *Festivals and Events Management*, pp. 33–50. Oxford: Elsevier.

Derrett, R. (2008). How festivals nurture resilience in regional communities. In J. Ali-Knight, M. Robertson, A. Fyall and A. Ladkin (eds), *International Perspectives of Festivals and Events: Paradigms of Analysis*, pp. 107–124. Oxford: Butterworth-Heinemann.

Derrett, R. (2015). *Enduring Festivals*. New York, NY: John Wiley & Sons.

Dewar, K., Meyer, D. and Li, W. M. (2001). Harbin, lanterns of ice, sculptures of snow. *Tourism Management*, 22 (5), 523–532.

De Young, R. (1999). Environmental psychology. In D. Alexander and R. Fairbridge (eds), *Encyclopedia of Environmental Science*. Hingham, MA: Kluwer Academic Publishers.

Dickson, C. and Arcodia, C. (2010). Promoting sustainable event practice: The role of professional associations. *International Journal of Hospitality Management*, 29 (2), 236–244.

Dietz-Uhler, B. and Murrell, A. (1999). Examining fan reactions to game outcomes: A longitudinal study of social identity. *Journal of Sport Behavior*, 22 (1), 15–27.

Dietz-Uhler, B., Harrick, E., End, C. and Jacquemotte, L. (2000). Sex differences in sport fan behavior and reasons for being a sport fan. *Journal of Sport Behavior*, 23 (3), 219–231.

Digance, J. (2005). Intergovernmental conferences: The CHOGM experience. *Journal of Convention & Event Tourism*, 7 (3–4), 65–8.

Di Giovine, M. (2009). Revitalization and counter revitalization: Tourism, heritage, and the Lantern Festival as catalysts for regeneration in Hôi An, Viêt Nam. *Journal of Policy Research in Tourism, Leisure and Events*, 1 (3), 208–230.

Dijck, J. V. (2013). *The Culture of Connectivity: A Critical History of Social Media*. Oxford: Oxford University Press.

Diller, S., Shedroff, N. and Rhea, D. (2006). *Making Meaning*. Upper Saddle River, NJ: Pearson.

DiMaggio, P. and Mukhtar, T. (2004). Arts participation as cultural capital in the United States, 1982–2002: Signs of decline? *Poetics*, 32 (2), 169–194.

Dimanche, F. (1996). Special events legacy: The 1984 Louisiana World Fair in New Orleans. *Festival Management and Event Tourism*, 4 (1), 49–54.

Dixon, A., Backman, S., Backman, K. and Norman, W. (2012). Expenditure-based segmentation of sport tourists. *Journal of Sport & Tourism*, 17 (1), 5–21.

Doherty, A. (2009). The volunteer legacy of a major sport event. *Journal of Policy Research in Tourism, Leisure and Events*, 1 (3), 185–207.

Donaldson, L. (1996). The normal science of structural contingency theory. In S. Clegg, C. Hardy and W. Nord (eds), *Handbook of Organization Studies*, pp. 57–77. London: Sage.

Donaldson, T. and Preston, L. (1995). The stakeholder theory of the corporation: Concepts, evidence, and implications. *Academy of Management Review*, 20 (1), 65–91.

Dowling, M., Robinson, L. and Washington, M. (2013). Taking advantage of the London 2012 Olympic Games: Corporate social responsibility through sport partnerships, *European Sport Quarterly*, 13 (3), 269–292.

Dredge, D. and Whitford, M. (2010). Policy for sustainable and responsible festivals and events: Institutionalisation of a new paradigm – a response. *Journal of Policy Research in Tourism, Leisure and Events*, 2 (1), 1–13.

Dredge, D. and Whitford, M. (2011). Event tourism governance and the public sphere. *Journal of Sustainable Tourism*, 19 (4–5), 479–499.

Dredge, D., Airey, D. and Gross, M. (eds) (2014). *The Routledge Handbook of Tourism and Hospitality Education*. Abingdon: Routledge.

Dredge, S. (2014). Facebook closes its $2bn Oculus Rift acquisition. What next? *The Guardian* (http://www.theguardian.com/technology/2014/jul/22/facebook-oculus-rift-acquisition-virtual-reality, accessed 23 August 2014).

Drengner, J., Jahn, S. and Zanger, C. (2011). Measuring event–brand congruence. *Event Management*, 15 (1), 25–36.

Driver, B., Brown, P. and Peterson, G. (eds) (1991). *Benefits of Leisure*. State College, PA: Venture Publishing.

Drummond, S. and Anderson, H. (2004). Service quality and managing your people. In I. Yeoman, M. Robertson, J. Ali-Knight, S. Drummond and U. McMahon-Beattie (eds), *Festival and Events Management*, pp. 80–96. Oxford: Elsevier.

Du Cros, H. and Jolliffe, L. (2014). *The Arts and Events*. Abingdon: Routledge.

Duffy, M. (2000). Lines of drift: Festival participation and performing a sense of place. *Popular Music*, 19 (1), 51–64.

Duignan, M. (2013). Events and urban regeneration: The strategic use of events to revitalise cities. *Journal of Policy Research in Tourism, Leisure and Events*, 5 (3), 307–309.

Dungan, T. (1984). How cities plan special events. *The Cornell HRA Quarterly* (May), 83–89.

Durant, H. (1938). *The Problem of Leisure*. London: George Routledge and Sons.

Durkheim, E. (1965). *The Elementary Forms of the Religious Life* (written in French in 1912; translated by Joseph Swain in 1915). New York: The Free Press.

Duvignaud, J. (1976). Festivals: A sociological approach. *Cultures*, 3, 13–28.

Dwyer, L. (2002). Economic contribution of convention tourism: Conceptual and empirical issues. In K. Weber and K. Chon (eds), *Convention Tourism: International Research and Industry Perspectives*, pp. 21–35. New York: Haworth.

Dwyer, L. and Forsyth, P. (2009). Public sector support for special events. *Eastern Economic Journal*, 35 (4), 481–499.

Dwyer, L. and Jago, L. (2012). The economic contribution of special events. In S. J. Page and J. Connell (eds), *Routledge Handbook of Events*, pp. 129–147. Abingdon: Routledge.

Dwyer, L., Forsyth, P. and Dwyer, W. (2010). *Tourism Economics and Policy*. Bristol: Channel View.

Dwyer, L., Forsyth, P. and Spurr, R. (2004). Evaluating tourism's economic effects: New and old approaches. *Tourism Management*, 25, 307–317.

Dwyer, L., Forsyth, P. and Spurr, R. (2005). Estimating the impacts of special events on the economy. *Journal of Travel Research*, 43, 351–359.

Dwyer, L., Forsyth, P. and Spurr, R. (2006a). Assessing the economic impacts of events: A computable general equilibrium approach. *Journal of Travel Research*, 45 (1), 59–66.

Dwyer, L., Forsyth, P. and Spurr, R. (2006b). Assessing the economic impacts of special events. In L. Dwyer and P. Forsyth (eds), *International Handbook of Tourism Economics*. Cheltenham: Edward Elgar.

Dwyer, L., Mellor, R., Mistillis, N. and Mules, T. (2000a). A framework for assessing 'tangible' and 'intangible' impacts of events and conventions. *Event Management*, 6 (3), 175–189.

Dwyer, L., Mellor, R., Mistillis, N. and Mules, T. (2000b). Forecasting the economic impacts of events and conventions. *Event Management*, 6 (3), 191–204.

Eagleton, T. (1981). *Walter Benjamin: Towards a Revolutionary Criticism*. London: Verso.

Earl, C. (2008). Crowds at outdoor music festivals: An examination of crowd psychology and its implications for the environmental health practitioner. *Environmental Health*, 8 (1), 34–43.

Earl, C., Parker, E. and Capra, M. (2005). Planning and management for public health impacts of outdoor music festivals: An international study. *Environmental Health*, 5 (1), 50–61.

Easto, P. and Truzzi, M. (1973). Towards an ethnography of the carnival social system. *Journal of Popular Culture*, 6 (3), 550–566.

Echtner, C. (1999). The semiotic paradigm: Implications for tourism research. *Tourism Management*, 20 (1), 47–57.

Echtner, C. and Jamal, T. (1997). The disciplinary dilemmas of tourism studies. *Annals of Tourism Research*, 24 (4), 868–883.

Economic Planning Group and Lord Cultural Resources (1992). *Strategic Directions for the Planning, Development, and Marketing of Ontario's Attractions, Festivals, and Events*. Toronto: Ministry of Culture, Tourism, and Recreation.

Edinburgh Festivals Impact Study 2011, BOP Consulting. (http://www.eventimpacts.com/pdfs/Edinburgh FestivalsFinalReport.pdf, accessed 25 August 2015).

Edwards, R. (2012). Gympie's country music Muster: Creating a cultural economy from a local tradition. *Journal of Rural Studies*, 28 (4), 517–527.

Ehrenreich, B. (2006). *Dancing in the Streets: A History of Collective Joy*. New York: Metropolitan Books.

Ellis, M. (1973). *Why People Play*. Englewood Cliffs, NJ: Prentice Hall.

Elstad, B. (1997). Volunteer perceptions of learning and satisfaction in a mega-event: The case of the XVII Olympic Winter Games in Lillehammer. *Festival Management and Event Tourism*, 4 (3/4), 5–83.

Elstad, B. (2003). Continuance commitment and reasons to quit: A study of volunteers at a jazz festival. *Event Management*, 8 (2), 99–108.

Elstad, B. (2009). Kongsberg Jazz Festival, Norway: Motivating and retaining episodic and bounce-back volunteers at an annual festival. In K. Holmes and K. Smith (eds), *Managing Volunteers in Tourism Attractions, Destinations and Events*, pp. 205–214. Oxford: Butterworth-Heinemann.

Ekman, A. (1999). The revival of cultural celebrations in regional Sweden: Aspects of tradition and transition. *Sociologia Ruralis*, 39 (3), 280–293.

Emery, P. (2001). Bidding to host a major sports event. In C. Gratton and I. Henry (eds), *Sport in the City: The Role of Sport in Economic and Social Regeneration*, pp. 91–108. London: Routledge.

Encyclopaedia Britannica Online. Economics. (www.britannica.com, accessed 25 August 2015).

End, C., Dietz-Uhler, M. and Demakakos, N. (2003). Perceptions of sport fans who BIRG. *International Sports Journal*, 7 (1), 139–150.

Environmental Protection Agency Victoria (Australia) (www.epa.vic.gov.au, accessed 25 August 2015).

Epting, F. and Neimeyer, R. (1984). *Personal Meanings of Death: Applications of Personal Construct Theory to Clinical Practice*. New York: Hemisphere.

Equations (2010). Humanity-Equality-Destiny? Implicating Tourism in the Commonwealth Games 2010. Bengaluru: *Equations* (www.equitabletourism.org, accessed 5 October 2010).

Evans, W. D. (2013). *Psychology of Branding*. New York: Nova Science Publishers.

Fairley, S. (2003). In search of relived social experience: Group-based nostalgia sport tourism. *Journal of Sport Management*, 17 (3), 284–304.

Fairley, S. and Gammon, S. (2006). Something lived, something learned: Nostalgia's expanding role in sport tourism. In H. Gibson (ed.), *Sport Tourism: Concepts and Theories*, pp. 50–65. London: Routledge.

Fairley, S., Lee, Y., Green, B. C. and Kim, M. L. (2013). Considering cultural influences in volunteer satisfaction and commitment. *Event Management*, 17 (4), 337–348.

Falassi, A. (ed.) (1987). *Time Out of Time: Essays on the Festival*. Albuquerque, NM: University of New Mexico Press.

Farber, C. (1983). High, healthy and happy: Ontario mythology on parade. In F. Manning (ed.), *Celebration of Society: Perspectives on Contemporary Cultural Performance*, pp. 33–50. Bowling Green, OH: Bowling Green Popular Press.

Farrell, J., Johnston, M. and Twynam, D. (1998). Volunteer motivation, satisfaction, and management at an elite sporting competition. *Journal of Sport Management*, 12 (4), 288–300.

Faulkner, B. and Raybould, M. (1995). Monitoring visitor expenditure associated with attendance at sporting events: An experimental assessment of the diary and recall methods. *Festival Management and Event Tourism*, 3 (2), 73–81.

Faulkner, B., Chalip, L., Brown, G., Jago, L., March, R. and Woodside, A. (2000). Monitoring the tourism impacts of the Sydney 2000 Olympics. *Event Management*, 6 (4), 231–246.

Federation European Carnival Cities (www.carnivalcities.com, accessed 25 August 2015).

Federman, M. (2004). (www.mcluhan.utoronto.ca, accessed 25 August 2015).

Fenich, G. (2005). *Meetings, Expositions, Events, and Conventions: An Introduction to the Industry*. Upper Saddle River, NJ: Pearson.

Fenich, G., Scott-Halsell, S. and Hashimoto, K. (2011). An investigation of technological uses by different generations as it relates to meetings and events: A pilot study. *Journal of Convention and Event Tourism*, 12 (1), 53–63.

Ferbrache, F. (2013). Le Tour de France: A cultural geography of a mega-event. *Geography*, 98, 144.

Ferreira, S. and Donaldson, R. (2013). Global imaging and branding: Source market newspaper reporting of the 2010 Fifa World Cup. *Tourism Review International*, 4, 253–265.

Filep, S. and Pearce, P. (2013). *Tourist Experience and Fulfilment: Insights from Positive Psychology* (Vol. 31). Abingdon: Routledge.

Filo, K., Funk, D. and Hornby, G. (2009). The role of web site content on motive and attitude change for sport events. *Journal of Sport Management*, 23 (1), 21–40.

Findling, J. E. and Pelle, K. D. (eds) (2008). *Encyclopaedia of World's Fairs and Expositions*. Jefferson, NC: McFarland.

Finkel, R. (2011). Dancing around the ring of fire: Social capital, tourism resistance, and gender dichotomies at Up Helly Aa in Lerwick, Scotland. *Event Management*, 14 (4), 275–285.

Fishbein, M. (1980). A theory of reasoned action: Some applications and implications. In H. Howe and M. Page (eds), *Nebraska Symposium on Motivation*, 27, pp. 65–116. Lincoln, NE: University of Nebraska Press.

Fishbein, M. and Ajzen, I. (1975). *Belief, Attitude, Intention, and Behavior: An Introduction to Theory and Research*. Reading, MA: Addison-Wesley.

Fjelstul, J., Severt, K. and Breiter, D. (2010). Building association attendance: Differences between chapter, regional, and annual meetings from the perception of the association members. *Event Management*, 14 (3), 183–192.

Flashmobs (www.flashmob.com; see also: MashFlob.com, www.carnivalcities.com, accessed 25 August 2015).

Fleck, S. (1996). Events without barriers: Customer service is a key in complying with the Americans With Disabilities Act. *Festivals*, March, pp. 34–35. International Festivals and Events Association.

Fleischer, A. and Felsenstein, D. (2002). Cost–benefit analysis using economic surpluses: A case study of a televised event. *Journal of Cultural Economics*, 26 (2), 139–156.

Fleming, W. and Toepper, L. (1990). Economic impact studies: Relating the positive and negative impacts to tourism development. *Journal of Travel Research*, 29 (1), 35–42.

Flinn, J. and Frew, M. (2014). Glastonbury: Managing the mystification of festivity. *Leisure Studies*, 33 (4), 418–433.

Florida, R. (2002). *The Rise of the Creative Class: And How It's Transforming Work, Leisure, Community and Everyday Life*. New York: Basic Books.

Foley, M., McGillivray, D. and McPherson, G. (2011). *Event Policy: From Theory to Strategy*. Abingdon: Routledge.

Foley, M., McGillivray, D. and McPherson, G. (2012). Policy pragmatism: Qatar and the global events circuit. *International Journal of Event and Festival Management*, 3 (1), 101–115.

Foley, M., McPherson, G. and McGillivray, D. (2008). Establishing Singapore as the events and entertainment capital of Asia: Strategic brand diversification. In J. Ali-Knight, M. Robertson, A. Fyall and A. Ladkin (eds), *International Perspectives of Festivals and Events: Paradigms of Analysi*s, pp. 53–64. Oxford: Butterworth-Heinemann.

Ford, R. C. and Peeper, W. C. (2007). The past as prologue: Predicting the future of the convention and visitor bureau industry on the basis of its history. *Tourism Management*, 28 (4), 1104–1114.

Formica, S. (1998). The development of festivals and special events studies. *Festival Management and Event Tourism*, 5 (3), 131–137.

Formica, S. and Murrmann, S. (1998). The effects of group membership and motivation on attendance: An international festival case. *Tourism Analysis*, 3 (3/4), 197–207.

Formica, S. and Uysal, M. (1998). Market segmentation of an international cultural-historical event in Italy. *Journal of Travel Research*, 36 (4), 16–24.

Foster, K. and Robinson, P. (2010). A critical analysis of the motivational factors that influence event attendance in family groups. *Event Management*, 14 (2), 107–125.

Foucault, M. (1969). *The Archaeology of Knowledge*. First translated from the French (*L'Archeologie du Savoir*) and published in English in 1972 by Tavistock Publications, London.

Foucault, M. (1982). The subject and power. *Critical Inquiry*, 8 (4), 777–795.

Fourie, J. and Santana-Gallego, M. (2011). The impact of mega-sport events on tourist arrivals. *Tourism Management*, 32 (6), 1364–1370.

Fox, D. and Edwards, J. (2009). A preliminary analysis of the market for small, medium, and large horticultural shows in England. *Event Management*, 12 (3/4), 199–208.

Fox, D., Gouthro, M., Morakabati, Y. and Brackstone, J. (2014). *Doing Events Research. From Theory to Practice*. Abingdon: Routledge.

Franchetti, J. and Page, S. J. (2009). Entrepreneurship and innovation in tourism: Public sector experiences of innovation activity in tourism in Scandinavia and Scotland. In A. Ateljevic and S. J. Page (eds), *Tourism and Entrepreneurship: International Perspectives*, pp. 109–130. Oxford: Butterworth-Heinemann.

Frank, S. and Roth, S. (2000). Festivalization and the media: Weimar, culture city of Europe 1999. *International Journal of Cultural Policy*, 6 (2), 219–241.

Fredline, E. (2006). Host and guest relations and sport tourism. In H. Gibson (ed.), *Sport Tourism: Concepts and Theories*, pp. 131–147. London: Routledge.

Fredline, E. and Faulkner, B. (1998). Resident reactions to a major tourist event: The Gold Coast Indy car race. *Festival Management and Event Tourism*, 5 (4), 185–205.

Fredline, E. and Faulkner, B. (2002a). Residents' reactions to the staging of major motorsport events within their communities: A cluster analysis. *Event Management*, 7 (2), 103–114.

Fredline, E. and Faulkner, B. (2002b). Variations in residents' reactions to major motorsport events: Why residents perceive the impacts of events differently. *Event Management*, 7 (2), 115–125.

Fredline, E., Jago, L. and Deery, M. (2003). The development of a generic scale to measure the social impacts of events. *Event Management*, 8 (1), 23–37.

Freedman, J. (1975). *Crowding and Behavior*. San Francisco, CA: Freeman.

Freeman, L., White, D. and Romney, A. (1992). *Research Methods in Social Network Analysis*. New Brunswick, NJ: Transaction Publishers.

Freeman, R. (1984). *Strategic Management: A Stakeholder Approach*. Boston, MA: Pitman.

Frew, M. (2014). Events and media spectacle. In R. Finkel, M. McGillivray, G. McPherson and P. Robinson (eds), *Research Themes for Events*. London: CABI.

Fridgen, J. D. (1984). Environmental psychology and tourism. *Annals of Tourism Research*, 11 (1), 19–39.

Frisby, W. and Getz, D. (1989). Festival management: A case study perspective. *Journal of Travel Research*, 28 (1), 7–11.

Frost, W. and Laing, J. (2013). *Commemorative Events: Memory, Identities, Conflict*. Abingdon: Routledge.

Frost, W., Wheeler, F. and Harvey, M. (2008). Commemorative events: Sacrifice, identity and dissonance. In J. Ali-Knight, M. Robertson, A. Fyall and A. Ladkin (eds), *International Perspectives of Festivals and Events: Paradigms of Analysis*, pp. 161–171. Oxford: Butterworth-Heinemann.

Funk, D. (2008). *Consumer Behaviour in Sport and Events: Marketing Action*. Oxford: Butterworth-Heinemann.

Funk, D. (2012). *Consumer Behaviour in Sport and Events*. Abingdon: Routledge.

Funk, D. and Bruun, T. (2007). The role of socio-psychological and culture-education motives in marketing international sport tourism: A cross-cultural perspective. *Tourism Management*, 28 (3), 806–819.

Funk, D. and James, J. (2001). The psychological continuum model: A conceptual framework for understanding an individual's psychological connection to sport. *Sport Management Review*, 4 (2), 119–150.

Funk, D. and James, J. (2006). Consumer loyalty: The meaning of attachment in the development of sport team allegiance. *Journal of Sport Management*, 20 (2), 189–217.

Funk, D. C., Mahony, D. F. and Ridinger, L. L. (2002). Characterizing consumer motivation as individual difference factors: Augmenting the Sport Interest Inventory (SII) to explain level of spectator support. *Sport Marketing Quarterly*, 11 (1), 33–43.

Funk, D. C., Ridinger, L. L. and Moorman, A. M. (2003). Understanding consumer support: Extending the Sport Interest Inventory (SII) to examine individual differences among women's professional sport consumers. *Sport Management Review*, 6 (1), 1–31.

Funk, D., Toohey, K. and Bruun, T. (2007). International sport event participation: Prior sport involvement; destination image; and travel motives. *European Sport Management Quarterly*, 7 (3), 227–248.

Gabrenya, W. and Hwang, K. (1996). Chinese social interaction: Harmony and hierarchy on the good earth. In H. Bond (ed.), *The Handbook of Chinese Psychology*, pp. 309–322. Hong Kong: Oxford University Press.

Gallarza, M. G., Arteaga, F. and Gil-Saura, I. (2013). The value of volunteering in special events: A longitudinal study. *Annals of Tourism Research*, 40, 105–131.

Gammon, S. (2004). Secular pilgrimage and sport tourism. In B. Ritchie and D. Adair (eds), *Sport Tourism: Inter-relationships, Impacts and Issues*, pp. 30–45. Clevedon: Channel View.

Gartner, W. and Holocek, D. (1983). Economic impact of an annual tourism industry exposition. *Annals of Tourism Research*, 10 (2), 199–212.

Geertz, C. (1993). *The Interpretation of Cultures*. London: Fontana Press.

Gelder, G. and Robinson, P. (2009). A critical comparative study of visitor motivations for attending music festivals: A case study of Glastonbury and V Festival. *Event Management*, 13 (3), 181–196.

Gelder, G. and Robinson, P. (2011). Events, festivals and the arts. In P. Robinson, S. Heitmann and P. Dieke (eds), *Research Themes in Tourism*, pp. 128–145. Wallingford: CABI.

van Gennep, A. (1909). *The Rites of Passage* (1960 translation by M. Vizedom and G. Coffee). London: Routledge and Kegan Paul.

George, R. and Swart, K. (2012). International tourists' perceptions of crime-risk and their future travel intentions during the 2010 FIFA World Cup™ in South Africa. *Journal of Sport & Tourism*, 17 (3), 201–223.

Gershuny, J. (2011). Time use surveys and the measurement of national well-being, Centre for Time Use Research, University of Oxford (http://www.timeuse.org/node/4486www.carnivalcities.com, accessed 25 August 2015).

Getz, D. (1991). *Festivals, Special Events, and Tourism*: New York: Van Nostrand Reinhold.

Getz, D. (1993a). Corporate culture in not-for-profit festival organizations: Concepts and potential applications. *Festival Management and Event Tourism*, 1 (1), 11–17.

Getz, D. (1993b). Case study: Marketing the Calgary Exhibition and Stampede. *Festival Management and Event Tourism*, 1 (4), 147–156.

Getz, D. (1997). *Event Management and Event Tourism* (1st edn). New York: Cognizant.

Getz, D. (1998a). Information sharing among festival managers. *Festival Management and Event Tourism*, 5 (1/2), 33–50.

Getz, D. (1998b). Event tourism and the authenticity dilemma. In W. Theobald (ed.), *Global Tourism*, pp. 409–427 (2nd edn). Oxford: Butterworth-Heinemann.

Getz, D. (1999). The impacts of mega events on tourism: Strategies for destinations. In T. Andersson, C. Persson, B. Sahlberg and L. Strom (eds), *The Impact of Mega Events*, pp. 5–32. Ostersund, Sweden: European Tourism Research Institute.

Getz, D. (2000a). Festivals and special events: Life cycle and saturation issues. In W. Garter and D. Lime (eds), *Trends in Outdoor Recreation, Leisure and Tourism*, pp. 175–185. Wallingford: CABI.

Getz, D. (2000b). Developing a research agenda for the event management field. In J. Allen, R. Harris and L. Jago (eds), *Events Beyond 2000: Setting the Agenda, Proceedings of Conference on Event Evaluation, Research and Education*, pp. 10–21. Sydney: Australian Centre for Event Management, University of Technology, Sydney.

Getz, D. (2001). Festival places: A comparison of Europe and North America. *Tourism*, 49 (1), 3–18.

Getz, D. (2002). Why festivals fail. *Event Management*, 7 (4), 209–219.

Getz, D. (2004). Bidding on events: Critical success factors. *Journal of Convention and Exhibition Management*, 5 (2), 1–24.

Getz, D. (2005). *Event Management and Event Tourism* (2nd edn). New York: Cognizant.

Getz, D. (2008). Event tourism: Definition, evolution, and research. *Tourism Management*, 29 (3), 403–428.

Getz, D. (2009). Policy for sustainable and responsible festivals and events: Institutionalization of a new paradigm. *Journal of Policy Research in Tourism, Leisure and Events*, 1 (1), 61–78.

Getz, D. (2010). The nature and scope of festival studies. *International Journal of Event Management Research*, 5 (1) (www.ijemr.org, accessed 25 August 2015).

Getz, D. (2013a). *Event Tourism: Concepts, International Case Studies, and Research*. New York: Cognizant.

Getz, D. (2013b). Ecotourism Events. In R. Ballantyne and J. Packer (eds), *International Handbook on Ecotourism*. Cheltenham: Edward Elgar.

Getz, D. and Andersson, T. (2008). Sustainable festivals: On becoming an institution. *Event Management*, 12 (1), 1–17.

Getz, D. and Andersson, T. (2010). The event-tourist career trajectory: A study of high-involvement amateur distance runners. *Scandinavian Journal of Tourism and Hospitality*, 19 (4), 468–491.

Getz, D. and Carlsen, J. (2006). Quality management for events. In B. Prideaux, G. Moscardo and E. Laws (eds), *Managing Tourism and Hospitality Services*, pp. 145–155. Wallingford: CABI.

Getz, D. and Fairley, S. (2004). Media management at sport events for destination promotion. *Event Management*, 8 (3), 127–140.

Getz, D. and Frisby, W. (1988). Evaluating management effectiveness in community-run festivals. *Journal of Travel Research*, 27 (1), 22–27.

Getz, D. and Frisby, W. (1991). Developing a municipal policy for festivals and special events. *Recreation Canada*, 19 (4), 38–44.

Getz, D. and McConnell, A. (2011). Event tourist careers and mountain biking. *Journal of Sport Management*, 25 (4), 326–338.

Getz, D. and McConnell, A. (2014). Comparing trail runners and mountain bikers: Motivation, involvement, portfolios, and event-tourist careers. *Journal of Convention & Event Tourism*, 15 (1), 69–100.

Getz, D. and Page, S. J. (2015). Progress and prospects for event tourism research. *Tourism Management* (in press).

Getz, D. and Patterson, I. (2013). Social worlds as a framework for event and travel careers. *Tourism Analysis*, 18 (5), 485–501.

Getz, D. and Robinson, R. N. S. (2014a). Foodies and food events. *Scandinavian Journal of Hospitality and Tourism*, 14 (3), 315–330.

Getz, D. and Robinson, R. N. S. (2014b). Foodies and their travel preferences. *Tourism Analysis*, 19 (6), 659–672.

Getz, D. and Wicks, B. (1994). Professionalism and certification for festival and event practitioners: Trends and issues. *Festival Management and Event Tourism*, 2 (2), 103–109.

Getz, D., Andersson, T. and Carlsen, J. (2010). Festival management studies: Developing a framework and priorities for comparative and cross-cultural research. *International Journal of Event and Festival Management*, 1 (1), 29–59.

Getz, D., Andersson, T. and Larson, M. (2007). Festival stakeholder roles: Concepts and case studies. *Event Management*, 10 (2/3), 103–122.

Getz, D., Andersson, T., Vujicic, S. and Robinson, R. N. S. (2015). Food events in lifestyle and travel. *Event Management*, 19 (3), 407–420.

Getz, D., Gration, D., Raciti, M., Sie, L. and Frost, D. (2013). *Final Report: Sunshine Coast Event Portfolios Valuation Research*. Presented to Tourism and Events Queensland, Sunshine Coast Council, Sunshine Coast Destination Ltd, and Tourism Noosa. The University of Queensland and Sunshine Coast University.

Getz, D., Macdonald, D. and Parent, M. (2015). The sport event owners' perspective. In M. M. Parent and J.-L. Chappelet (eds), *Routledge Handbook of Sports Event Management*, pp. 91–108. Abingdon: Routledge.

Getz, D., O'Neil, M. and Carlsen, J. (2001). Service quality evaluation at events through service mapping. *Journal of Travel Research*, 39 (4), 380–390.

Getz, D., Robinson, R., Andersson, T. and Vujicic, S. (2014). *Foodies and Food Tourism*. Oxford: Goodfellow.

Getz, D., Svensson, B., Pettersson, R. and Gunnerval, A. (2012). Hallmark events: Definition and planning process. *International Journal of Event Management Research*, 7 (1/2), 47–67.

Gibson, C. and Connell, J. (eds) (2011). *Festival Places: Revitalising Rural Australia*. Bristol: Channel View.

Gibson, C. and Connell, J. (2012). *Music Festivals and Rural Development in Australia*. Farnham, England: Ashgate Publishing.

Gibson, C. and Davidson, D. (2004). Tamworth, Australia's 'country music capital': Place marketing, rurality, and resident reactions. *Journal of Rural Studies*, 20 (4), 387–404.

Gibson, C., Waitt, G., Walmsley, J. and Connell, J. (2009). Cultural festivals and economic development in nonmetropolitan Australia. *Journal of Planning Education and Research*, 29 (3), 280–293.

Gibson, H. (1998). Sport tourism: A critical analysis of research. *Sport Management Review*, 1, 45–76.

Gibson, H. (2004). Moving beyond the 'what is and who' of sport tourism to understanding 'why'. *Journal of Sport Tourism*, 9 (3), 247–265.

Gibson, H. (2005). Understanding sport tourism experiences. In J. Higham (ed.), *Sport Tourism Destinations: Issues, Opportunities and Analysis*. Oxford: Elsevier.

Gibson, H. (2006). Towards an understanding of 'why sport tourists do what they do'. In H. Gibson (ed.), *Sport Tourism: Concepts and Theories*, pp. 66–85. London: Routledge.

Gibson, H., Willming, C. and Holdnak, A. (2003). Small-scale event-sport-tourism: Fans as tourists. *Tourism Management*, 22 (3), 181–190.

Gilmore, J. and Pine, J. (2007). *Authenticity: What Consumers Really Want*. Boston, MA: Harvard Business School Press.

Gitelson, R., Kerstetter, D. and Kiernan, N. (1995). Evaluating the educational objectives of a short-term event. *Festival Management and Event Tourism*, 3 (1), 9–14.

Giulianotti, R. and Klauser, F. (2011). Introduction: Security and surveillance at sport mega events. *Urban Studies*, 48 (15), 3157–3168.

Glaser, B. and Strauss, A. (1967). *Discovery of Grounded Theory: Strategies for Qualitative Research*. Chicago, IL: Aldine.

Gleick, J. (2000). *Faster: The Acceleration of Just About Everything*. New York: Pantheon Books.

Glenn, J. and Gordon, T. (eds) (2008). *Futures Research Methodology* (www.acunu.org/millennium, accessed 25 August 2015).

Glenn, J., Gordon, T. and Florescu, E. (2014). *2013-14 State of the Future*. Published by the Millennium Project (http://millennium-project.org/millennium/201314SOF.html, accessed 25 August 2015).

Glyptis, S. A. (1981). Leisure life-styles. *Regional Studies*, 15 (5), 311–326.

Godbey, G. and Shim, J. (2008). The development of leisure studies in North America: Implications for China. *Research Journal of Zhejiang University*, July.

Goffman, E. (1959). *The Presentation of Self in Everyday Life*. Garden City, NY: Doubleday.

Goffman, E. (1974). *Frame Analysis: An Essay on the Organization of Experience*. New York: Harper and Row.

Goh, F. (2003). *Irish Festivals – Irish Life: Celebrating the Wealth of Ireland's Festivals. Executive Summary*. Dublin: Association of Irish Festival Events.

Gold, J. R. and Gold, M. M. (eds) (2010). *Olympic Cities: City Agendas, Planning, and the World's Games, 1896–2016*. Abingdon: Routledge.

Goldblatt, J. (1990). *Special Events: The Art and Science of Celebration*. New York: Van Nostrand Reinhold.

Goldblatt, J. (2004). *Special Events: Event Leadership for a New World*. New York: Wiley.

Goldblatt, J. (2011). *Special Events: A New Generation and the Next Frontier* (6th edn). New York: Wiley.

Goldblatt, J. (2014) *Special Events: Event Leadership for a New World* (7th edn.) New York: Wiley.

Goldblatt, S. and Goldblatt, J. (2011). *The Complete Guide to Greener Meetings and Events*. New York: Wiley.

Goodson, L. and Phillimore, J. (eds) (2004). *Qualitative Research in Tourism: Ontologies, Epistemologies and Methodologies*. London: Routledge.

Gotham, K. (2005a). Theorizing urban spectacles. *City: Analysis of Urban Trends, Culture, Theory, Policy, Action*, 9 (2), 225–246.

Gotham, K. (2005b). Tourism from above and below: Globalization, localization and New Orleans' Mardi Gras. *International Journal of Urban and Regional Research*, 29 (2), 309–326.

Gottlieb, U., Brown, M. and Ferrier, L. (2013). Consumer perceptions of trade show effectiveness: Scale development and validation within a B2C context. *European Journal of Marketing*, 48 (1/2), 5–5.

Grado, S., Strauss, C. and Lord, B. (1998). Economic impacts of conferences and conventions. *Journal of Convention and Exhibition Management*, 1 (1), 19–33.

Graham, S., Goldblatt, J. and Delpy, L. (1995). *The Ultimate Guide to Sport Event Management and Marketing*. Chicago, IL: Irwin.

Grant, P. S. (2014). Understanding branded flash mobs: The nature of the concept, stakeholder motivations, and avenues for future research. *Journal of Marketing Communications*, (ahead of print) 1–18.

Grant, R. (1996). Toward a knowledge-based theory of the firm. *Strategic Management Journal*, 17 (2), 109–122.

Gratton, C. and Kokolakakis, T. (1997). *Economic Impact of Sport in England 1995*. London: The Sports Council.

Gray, N. and Porter, L. (2014). By any means necessary: Urban regeneration and the 'State of Exception' in Glasgow's Commonwealth Games 2014. *Antipode*, 47 (2), 380–400.

Green, C. and Chalip, L. (1998). Sport tourism as the celebration of subculture. *Annals of Tourism Research*, 25 (2), 275–291.

Green, C. and Chalip, L. (2004). Paths to volunteer commitment: Lessons from the Sydney Olympic Games. In R. Stebbins and M. Graham (eds), *Volunteering as Leisure/Leisure as Volunteering: An International Assessment*, pp. 49–68. Wallingford: CABI.

Green and Gold Inc. (1999). *Environmental Management and Monitoring for Sport Events and Facilities, for the Department of Canadian Heritage, Sport Canada* (www.greengold.on.ca, accessed 25 August 2015).

Greenfield, G. (2010). Reveillon in Rio de Janeiro. *Event Management*, 14 (4), 301–308.

Greenwood, D. (1972). Tourism as an agent of change: A Spanish Basque case study. *Ethnology*, 11 (1), 80–91.

Greenwood, D. (1989). Culture by the pound: An anthropological perspective on tourism as cultural commodification. In V. Smith (ed.), *Hosts and Guests: The Anthropology of Tourism* (2nd edn), pp. 171–185. Philadelphia: University of Pennsylvania Press.

Gregson, B. (1992). *Reinventing Celebration: The Art of Planning Public Events*. Orange, CT: Shannon Press.

Grippo, R. (2004). *Macy's Thanksgiving Day Parade*. Charleston, SC: Arcadia.

Gripsrud, G., Nes, E. and Olsson, U. (2010). Effects of hosting a mega-sport event on country image. *Event Management*, 14 (3), 193–204.

Grix, J. (2013). Sport politics and the Olympics. *Political Studies Review*, 11 (1), 15–25.

Grunwell, S. and Inhyuck, S. (2008). Film festivals: An empirical study of factors for success. *Event Management*, 11 (4), 201–210.

Gumbel, A. (2014). Oculus Rift hands-on: Why the latest version is a watershed moment for gaming. *The Guardian* (http://www.theguardian.com/technology/2014/sep/21/oculus-virtual-reality-headsets-gear-crescent-bay-review, accessed 25 September 2014).

Gunn, C. (1979). *Tourism Planning*. New York: Crane Rusak.

Gursoy, D. and Kendall, K. (2006). Hosting mega events: Modelling locals' support. *Annals of Tourism Research*, 33 (3), 603–623.

Gustafsson, I., Ostrom, A., Johansson, J. and Mossberg, L. (2006). The five aspects of meal model: A tool for developing meal services in restaurants. *Journal of Foodservice*, 17 (2), 84–93.

Gyimóthy, S. (2009). Casual observers, connoisseurs and experimentalists: A conceptual exploration of niche festival visitors. *Scandinavian Journal of Hospitality and Tourism*, 9 (2–3), 177–205.

Haahti, A. and Komppula, R. (2006). Experience design in tourism. In D. Buhalis and C. Costa (eds), *Tourism Business Frontiers: Consumers, Products and Industry*, pp. 101–110. Oxford: Elsevier.

Habermas, J. (1973). *The Theory of Communicative Action: Reason and Rationalization of Society*. Boston, MA: Beacon.

Haid, O., Picard, D. and Robinson, M. (2006). Christmas markets in the Tyrolean Alps: Representing regional traditions in a newly created world of Christmas. In D. Pacard and M. Robinson (eds), *Festival Tourism and Social Change – Remaking Worlds*, pp. 209–211, Clevedon: Channel View.

Halal, W. and Marien, M. (2011). Global megacrisis: Four scenarios. Two perspectives. *The Futurist* (May/June).

Hall, C. M. (1989). The definition and analysis of hallmark tourist events. *GeoJournal*, 19 (3), 263–268.

Hall, C. M. (1992). *Hallmark Tourist Events: Impacts, Management and Planning*. London: Belhaven.

Hall, C. M. (1994a). *Tourism and Politics: Policy, Power and Place*. Chichester: Wiley.

Hall, C. M. (1994b). Mega-events and their legacies. In P. Murphy (ed.), *Quality Management in Urban Tourism: Balancing Business and Environment*, pp. 109–123. Victoria, British Columbia: University of Victoria.

Hall, C. M. (2005). *Tourism: Rethinking the Social Science of Mobility*. Harlow: Pearson.

Hall, C. M. (2006). Urban entrepreneurship, corporate interests and sports mega-events: The thin policies of competitiveness within the hard outcomes of neoliberalism. *The Sociological Review*, 54 (2), 59–70.

Hall, C. M. (2012). Sustainable mega-events: Beyond the myth of balanced approaches to mega-event sustainability. *Event Management*, 16 (2), 119–131.

Hall, C. M. (2014). The political analysis and political economy of events. In S. J. Page and J. Connell (eds), *Routledge Handbook of Events*, pp. 186–201. Abingdon: Routledge.

Hall, C. M. and Page, S. (2006). *The Geography of Tourism and Recreation: Environment, Place and Space* (3rd edn). London: Routledge.

Hall, C. M. and Page, S. J. (2010). The contribution of Neil Leiper to tourism studies. *Current Issues in Tourism*, 13 (4), 299–309.

Hall, C. M. and Page, S. J. (2012) Geography and the study of events. In S. J. Page and J. Connell (eds), *Handbook of Events*. Abingdon: Routledge.

Hall, C. M. and Page, S. J. (2014). *The Geography of Tourism and Recreation: Environment, Place and Space* (4th edn). Abingdon: Routledge.

Hall, C. M. and Rusher, K. (2004). Politics, public policy and the destination. In I. Yeoman, M. Robertson, J. Ali-Knight, S. Drummond and U. McMahon-Beattie (eds), *Festival and Events Management*, pp. 217–231. Oxford: Elsevier.

Hall, C. M. and Selwood, H. J. (1989). America's Cup lost, paradise retained? The dynamics of a hallmark tourist event. In G. J. Syme, B. J. Shaw, D. M. Denton and W. S. Mueller (eds), *The Planning and Evaluation of Hallmark Events*. Avebury: Aldershot.

Hall, C. M. and Sharples, L. (2008). *Food and Wine Festivals and Events around the World*. Oxford: Butterworth-Heinemann.

Hall, C. M. and Wilson, S. (2011). Neoliberal urban entrepreneurial agendas, Dunedin Stadium and the Rugby World Cup: Or 'If you don't have a stadium, you don't have a future'. In D. Dredge and J. Jenkins (eds), *Stories of Practice: Tourism Policy and Planning*, pp. 133–152. Farnham: Ashgate.

Hall, C. M., Selwood, J. and McKewon, E. (1995). Hedonists, ladies and larrikins: Crime, prostitution and the 1987 America's Cup. *Visions in Leisure and Business*, 14 (3), 28–51.

Hall, E. (1966). *The Hidden Dimension*. New York: Doubleday.

Hall, J., Basarin, V. and Lockstone-Binney, L. (2010). An empirical analysis of attendance at a commemorative event: Anzac Day at Gallipoli. *International Journal of Hospitality Management*, 29 (2), 245–253.

Halsey, T. (2010). *Freelancer's Guide to Corporate Event Design*. Oxford: Elsevier.

Ham, S., Housego, A. and Weiler, B. (2005). *Tasmanian Thematic Interpretation Planning Manual* (http://www.tourismtasmania.com.au/publications/thematic_interpretation_manual, Accessed 25 August 2015).

Handelman, D. (1990). *Models and Mirrors: Towards an Anthropology of Public Events*. Oxford: Berghahn Books.

Hanlon, C. and Cuskelly, G. (2002). Pulsating major sport event organizations: A framework for inducting managerial personnel. *Event Management*, 7 (4), 231–243.

Hanlon, C. and Jago, L. (2014). Staffing for successful events: Having the right skills in the right place at the right time. In S. J. Page and J. Connell (eds), *Routledge Handbook of Events*, pp. 304–315. Abingdon: Routledge.

Hanlon, C. and Stewart, B. (2006). Managing personnel in major sport event organizations: What strategies are required? *Event Management*, 10 (1), 77–88.

Hannan, M. and Carroll, G. (1992). *Dynamics of Organizational Populations*. New York: Oxford University Press.

Hannan, M. and Freeman, J. (1977). The population ecology of organizations. *American Journal of Sociology*, 82 (5), 929–964.

Hannan, M. and Freeman, J. (1984). Structural inertia and organizational change. *American Sociological Review*, 49 (2), 149–164.

Hannan, M., Polos, L. and Carroll, G. (2007). *Logics of Organization Theory: Audiences, Code, and Ecologies*. Princeton, NJ: Princeton University Press.

Happel, S. and Jennings, M. (2002). Creating a futures market for major event tickets: Problems and prospects. *Cato Journal*, 21 (3), 443–462.

Harris, M. (2003). *Carnival and Other Christian Festivals: Folk Theology and Folk Performance*. Austin, TX: University of Texas Press.

Harris, R., Jago, L., Allen, J. and Huyskens, M. (2001). Towards an Australian event research agenda: First steps. *Event Management*, 6 (4), 213–221.

Harris, V. (2004). Event management: A new profession. *Event Management*, 9 (1/2), 103–109.

Hartmann, R. (1986). Tourism, seasonality and social change. *Leisure Studies*, 5 (1), 25–33.

Harvey, M., Loomis, R., Bell, R. and Marino, M. (1998). The influence of museum exhibit design on immersion and psychological flow. *Environment and Behavior*, 30 (5), 601–627.

Häussermann, H. and Siebel, W. (eds) (1993). *Festivalisierung der Stadtpolitik. Stadtentwicklung durch grosse Projekte*. Leviathan: Sonderheft 13.

Havitz, M. and Dimanche, F. (1999). Leisure involvement revisited: Drive properties and paradoxes. *Journal of Leisure Research*, 31 (2), 122–149.

Hawkins, D. and Goldblatt, J. (1995). Event management implications for tourism education. *Tourism Recreation Research*, 20 (2), 42–45.

Hayllar, B. and Griffin, T. (2004). The precinct experience: A phenomenological approach. *Tourism Management*, 26 (4), 517–528.

Hede, A. (2005). Sports-events, tourism and destination marketing strategies: An Australian case study of Athens 2004 and its media telecast. *Journal of Sport Tourism*, 10 (3), 187–200.

Hede, A. (2007). Managing special events in the new era of the triple bottom line. *Event Management*, 11 (1/2), 13–22.

Hede, A. and Jago, L. (2005). Perceptions of the host destination as a result of attendance at a special event: A post-consumption analysis. *International Journal of Event Management Research*, 1 (1) (an e-journal, online at www.ijemr.org, accessed 25 August 2015).

Hede, A., Jago, L. and Deery, M. (2002). Special event research 1990–2001: Key trends and issues. In *Proceedings of International Event Research Conference*, pp. 305–338. Sydney: University of Technology Sydney, Australian Centre for Event Management.

Hede, A., Jago, L. and Deery, M. (2003). An agenda for special event research: Lessons from the past and directions for the future. *Journal of Hospitality and Tourism Management*, 10 (3), 1–14.

Hede, A., Jago, L. and Deery, M. (2004). Segmentation of special event attendees using personal values: Relationships with satisfaction and behavioural intentions. *Journal of Quality Assurance in Hospitality and Tourism*, 5 (2/3/4), 33–55.

Heimer, C. (2001). Law: New institutionalism. In *International Encyclopedia of the Social and Behavioral Sciences*, pp. 8534–8537. Oxford: Elsevier.

Hektner, J. and Csikszentmihalyi, M. (2002). The experience sampling method: Measuring the context and content of lives. In R. Bechtel and A. Churchman (eds), *Handbook of Environmental Psychology*, pp. 233–243. New York: Wiley.

Henderson, E. and McIlwraith, M. (2013). *Ethics and Corporate Social Responsibility in the Meetings and Events Industry*. Chichester: Wiley.

Henderson, J. (2008). Hosting major meetings and accompanying protestors: Singapore 2006. *Current Issues in Tourism*, 10 (6), 543–557.

Hernández-Ehrisman, L. (2008). *Inventing the Fiesta City: Heritage and Carnival in San Antonio*. Albuquerque: UNM Press.

Hesmondhalgh, D. (2007). *The Cultural Industries*. Los Angeles, CA: Sage.

Herbert, D. T. (1988). Work and leisure: Exploring a relationship. *Area*, 241–252.

Herzberg, F. (1966). *Work and the Nature of Man*. Cleveland: World Publishing Co.

Higham, J. and Hinch, T. (2009). *Sport and Tourism: Globalization, Mobility and Identity*. Oxford: Butterworth-Heinemann.

Hiller, H. H. (1990). The urban transformation of a landmark event: The 1988 Calgary Winter Olympics. *Urban Affairs Review*, 26 (1), 118–137.

Hiller, H. (2000a). Toward an urban sociology of mega-events. *Research in Urban Sociology*, 5, 181–205.

Hiller, H. (2000b). Mega-events, urban boosterism and growth strategies: An analysis of the objectives and legitimations of the Cape Town 2004 Olympic bid. *International Journal of Urban and Regional Research*, 24 (2), 439–458.

Hiller, H. (2012). *Host Cities and the Olympics: An Interactionist Approach*. Abingdon: Routledge.

Hilliard, T. (2006). Learning at conventions: Integrating communities of practice. *Journal of Convention and Event Tourism*, 8 (1), 45–68.

Hinch, T. and Delamere, T. (1993). Native festivals as tourism attractions: A community challenge. *Journal of Applied Recreation Research*, 18 (2), 131–142.

Hinch, T., Jackson, E., Hudson, S. and Walker, G. (2006). Leisure constraint theory and sport tourism. In H. Gibson (ed.), *Sport Tourism: Concepts and Theories*, pp. 10–31. London: Routledge.

Hixson, E. (2014). The impact of young people's participation in events: Developing a model of social event impact. *International Journal of Event and Festival Management*, 5 (3), 198–218.

Hjalager, A. (2009). Cultural tourism innovation systems – the Roskilde Festival. *Scandinavian Journal of Hospitality and Tourism*, 9 (2/3), 266–287.

Hofstede, G. (1980). *Culture's Consequences: International Differences in Work Related Values*. Beverly Hills, CA: Sage.

Holloway, I., Brown, L. and Shipway, R. (2010). Meaning not measurement: Using ethnography to bring a deeper understanding to the participant experience of festivals and events. *International Journal of Event and Festival Management*, 1 (1), 74–85.

Holloway, L. (2004). Showing and telling farming: Agricultural shows and re-imaging British agriculture. *Journal of Rural Studies*, 20 (3), 319–330.

Holmes, K. and Smith, K. (eds) (2009). *Managing Volunteers in Tourism Attractions, Destinations and Events*. Oxford: Butterworth-Heinemann.

Hoppen, A., Brown, L. and Fyall, A. (2014). Literary tourism: Opportunities and challenges for the marketing and branding of destinations? *Journal of Destination Marketing and Management*, 3 (1), 37–47.

Hormans, G. (1958). Social behavior as exchange. *American Journal of Sociology*, 63 (6), 597–606.

Horne, J. (2006). The unknown knowns of sports mega-events. In M. Robertson (ed.), *Sporting Events and Event Tourism: Impacts, Plans and Opportunities*. Leisure Studies Association Publication 91, pp. 1–15. Eastbourne: The University of Brighton.

Horne, J. and Manzenreiter, W. (2006). An introduction to the sociology of sports mega-events. *Sociological Review*, 54 (issue supplement s2), 1–24.

Horne, J. and Whannel, G. (2010). The 'caged torch procession': Celebrities, protesters and the 2008 Olympic torch relay in London, Paris and San Francisco. *Sport in Society*, 13 (5), 760–770.

Horng, J.-S., Su, C.-S. and So, S.-I. (2013). Segmenting food festival visitors: Applying the theory of planned behavior and lifestyle. *Journal of Convention & Event Tourism*, 14 (3), 193–216.

Houlihan, B., Tan, T.-C. and Park, J. (2015). The national government's perspective. In M. Parent and J.-L. Chappelet (eds), *Routledge Handbook of Sports Event Management*, pp. 289–305. Abingdon: Routledge.

Hoyle, L. (2002). *Event Marketing: How to Successfully Promote Events, Festivals, Conventions, and Expositions*. New York: Wiley.

Hu, J., Le, D., Funk, M., Wang, F. and Rauterberg, M. (2013). Attractiveness of an interactive public art installation. In N. Streitz and C. Stephanidis (eds), *Distributed, Ambient, and Pervasive Interactions*, pp. 430–438. Berlin: Springer.

Huang, Y., Scott, N., Ding, P. and Cheng, D. (2012). Impression of Liusanjie: Effect of mood on experience and satisfaction. *International Journal of Tourism Research*, 14 (1), 91–102.

Hudson, S. and Hudson, R. (2013). Engaging with consumers using social media: A case study of music festivals. *International Journal of Event and Festival Management*, 4 (3), 206–223.

Hudson, S., Getz, D., Miller, G. and Brown, G. (2004). The future role of sporting events: Evaluating the impacts on tourism. In K. Weiermair and C. Mathies (eds), *The Tourism and Leisure Industry – Shaping the Future*, pp. 237–251. Binghampton, NY: Haworth.

Hudson, S., Roth, M., Madden, T. and Hudson, R. (2015). The effects of social media on emotions, brand relationship quality, and word of mouth: An empirical study of music festival attendees. *Tourism Management*, 47, 68–76.

Hughes, G. (1999). Urban revitalization: The use of festival time strategies. *Leisure Studies*, 18 (2), 119–135.

Hughes, H. (1993). Olympic tourism and urban regeneration. *Festival Management and Event Tourism*, 1 (4), 157–162.

Hughes, H. (2006). Gay and lesbian festivals: Tourism in the change from politics to party. In D. Picard and M. Robinson (eds), *Festivals, Tourism and Social Change: Remaking Worlds*, pp. 238–254. Clevedon: Channel View.

Huizinga, J. (1955). *Homo Ludens: A Study of the Play Element in Culture*. Boston, MA: Beacon Press (first published in German in 1944).

Hull, R. B. (1990). Mood as a product of leisure: Causes and consequences. *Journal of Leisure Research*, 22 (2), 99–111.

Hultkrantz, L. (1998). Mega-event displacement of visitors: The World Championship in Athletics, Goteborg 1995. *Festival Management and Event Tourism*, 5 (1/2).

Imagine Canada (www.imaginecanada.ca, accessed 25 August 2015).

International Association of Assembly Managers (www.IAAM.org, accessed 25 August 2015).

International Association for Exhibition Management (www.IAEM.org, accessed 25 August 2015). Renamed as International Association of Exhibitions and Events in 2006.

International Association of Fairs and Expositions (IAFE) (www.fairsandexpos.com, accessed 25 August 2015).

International Association of Venue Managers (www.iavm.org, accessed 25 August 2015).

International Events Group (IEG) (1995). *IEG's Complete Guide to Sponsorship*. Chicago, IL: IEG Inc.

International Festivals Association (IFA) (n.d.). *IFA's Official Guide to Sponsorship*. Port Angeles, WA.

International Festivals Association (IFA) and Argonne Productions (1992). *Festival Sponsorship Legal Issues*. Port Angeles, WA.

International Festivals and Events Association (IFEA) (n.d.). *Event Operations*. Port Angeles, WA.

International Festivals and Events Association (IFEA) (2000). *Parades*. Port Angeles, WA. IFEA (www.ifea.com, accessed 25 August 2015).

International Special Events Society (www.ISES.com, accessed 25 August 2015).

Iso-Ahola, S. (1980). *The Social Psychology of Leisure and Recreation*. Dubuque, IA: Brown.

Iso-Ahola, S. (1983). Towards a social psychology of recreational travel. *Leisure Studies*, 2 (1), 45–57.

Iso-Ahola, S., Jackson, E. and Dunn, E. (1994). Starting, ceasing and replacing leisure activities over the life-span. *Journal of Leisure Research*, 26 (3), 227–249.

Izzo, F., Bonetti, E. and Masiello, B. (2012). Strong ties within cultural organization event networks and local development in a tale of three festivals. *Event Management*, 16 (3), 223–244.

Jackson, E. (ed.) (2005). *Constraints on Leisure*. State College, PA: Venture Publishing.

Jackson, E. L., Crawford, D. W. and Godbey, G. (1993). Negotiation of leisure constraints. *Leisure Sciences*, 15 (1), 1–11.

Jackson, G. and Weed, M. (2003). The sport–tourism interrelationship. In B. Houlihan (ed.), *Sport and Society*. London: Sage.

Jackson, I. (2008). *Celebrating Communities: Community Festivals, Participation and Belonging*, pp. 161–172. The Australian Centre, School of Historical Studies.

Jackson, P. (1988). Street life: The politics of carnival. *Environment and Planning D: Society and Space*, 6 (2), 213–227.

Jaeger, K. and Mykletun, R. J. (2009). The festivalscape of Finnmark. *Scandinavian Journal of Hospitality and Tourism*, 9 (2/3), 327–348.

Jafari, J. (1987). Tourism models: The sociocultural aspects. *Tourism Management*, 8 (2), 151–159.

Jafari, J. (1990). Research and scholarship: The basis of tourism education. *Journal of Tourism Studies*, 1 (1), 33–41.

Jago, L. and Dwyer, L. (2006). *Economic Evaluation of Special Events: A Practitioner's Guide*. Cooperative Research Centre for Sustainable Tourism: Gold Coast, Australia.

Jago, L. and Mair, J. (2009). Career theory and major event employment. In T. Baum, M. Deery and C. Hanlon (eds), *People and Work in Events and Conventions: A Research Perspective*, pp. 65–74. Wallingford: CABI.

Jago, L. and Shaw, R. (1999). Consumer perceptions of special events: A multi-stimulus validation. *Journal of Travel and Tourism Marketing*, 8 (4), 1–24.

Jago, L., Chalip, L., Brown, G., Mules, T. and Ali, S. (2002). The role of events in helping to brand a destination. In *Proceedings of International Event Research Conference*, pp. 111–143. Sydney: University of Technology Sydney, Australian Centre for Event Management.

Jago, L., Chalip, L., Brown, G., Mules, T. and Shameem, A. (2003). Building events into destination branding: Insights from experts. *Event Management*, 8 (1), 3–14.

Jaimangal-Jones, D., Pritchard, A. and Morgan, N. (2010). Going the distance: Locating journey, liminality and rites of passage in dance music experiences. *Leisure Studies*, 29 (3), 253–268.

Jamal, T. and Getz, D. (1995). Collaboration theory and community tourism planning. *Annals of Tourism Research*, 22 (1), 186–204.

James, J. and Ridinger, L. (2002). Female and male sport fans: A comparison of sport consumption motives. *Journal of Sport Behavior*, 25 (3), 260–278.

James, J. D. and Ross, S. D. (2004). Comparing sport consumer motivations across multiple sports. *Sport Marketing Quarterly*, 13 (1), 17–25.

Janiskee, R. (1980). South Carolina's harvest festivals: Rural delights for day tripping urbanites. *Journal of Cultural Geography* (October), 96–104.

Janiskee, R. (1985). Community-sponsored rural festivals in South Carolina: A decade of growth and change. Paper presented to the Association of American Geographers, Detroit.

Janiskee, R. (1991). Rural festivals in South Carolina. *Journal of Cultural Geography*, 11 (2), 31–43.

Janiskee, R. (1994). Some macroscale growth trends in America's community festival industry. *Festival Management and Event Tourism*, 2 (1), 10–14.

Janiskee, R. (1996). The temporal distribution of America's community festivals. *Festival Management and Event Tourism*, 3 (3), 129–137.

Janiskee, R. and Drews, P. (1998). Rural festivals and community reimaging. In R. Butler, M. Hall and J. Jenkins (eds), *Tourism and Recreation in Rural Areas*, pp. 157–175. Chichester: Wiley.

Japanese Connection (www.thejapaneseconnection.com/Glossary/festival.htm, accessed 25 August 2015).

Jarvie, G. (1991). *Highland Games: The Making of the Myth*. Edinburgh: Edinburgh University Press.

Jawahar, I. and McLaughlin, G. (2001). Toward a descriptive stakeholder theory: An organizational life cycle approach. *Academy of Management Review*, 26 (3), 397–414.

Jaworski, A. and Pritchard, A. (eds) (2005). *Discourse, Communication and Tourism*. Clevedon: Channel View.

Jennings, G. (2006). Perspectives on quality tourism experiences: An introduction. In G. Jennings and N. Nickerson (eds), *Quality Tourism Experiences*, pp. 1–21. Oxford: Elsevier.

Jennings, W. (2013). Governing the games: High politics, risk and mega-events. *Political Studies Review*, 11 (1), 2–14.

Jens, C. (2009). *The Business of the Experience Economy*. Aarhus: Aarhus University Press.

Jepson, A. and Clarke, A. (eds) (2014). *Exploring Community Festivals and Events*. Abingdon: Routledge.

Jepson, A., Clarke, A. and Ragsdell, G. (2013). Applying the motivation-opportunity-ability (MOA) model to reveal factors that influence inclusive engagement within local community festivals: The case of UtcaZene 2012. *International Journal of Event and Festival Management*, 4 (3), 186–205.

Jiang, J. and Schmader, S. (2014). Event management education and professionalism: The view from the trenches. *Event Management*, 18 (1), 25–37.

Jin, X. and Weber, K. (2013). Developing and testing a model of exhibition brand preference: The exhibitors' perspective. *Tourism Management*, 38, 94–104.

Jin, X., Weber, K. and Bauer, T. (2010). The state of the exhibition industry in China. *Journal of Convention and Event Tourism*, 11 (1), 2–17.

Jin, X., Weber, K. and Bauer, T. (2012). Impact of clusters on exhibition destination attrativeness: Evidence from mainland China. *Tourism Management*, 33 (6), 1429–1439.

Jóhannesson, G. (2010). Emergent Vikings: The social ordering of tourism innovation. *Event Management*, 14 (4), 261–274.

Johnsen, B. (2009). What a maritime history! The uses of maritime history in summer festivals in southern Norway. *Journal of Tourism History*, 1 (2), 113–130.

Johnson, D. (n.d.). Festival risk management: Success with safety. In *Event Operations*, pp. 71–73. Port Angeles, WA: International Festivals and Events Association.

Johnson, N. (2006). *Britain and the 1918–19 Influenza Pandemic: A Dark Epilogue*. London: Routledge.

Johnston, M., Twynam, G. and Farrell, J. (2000). Motivation and satisfaction of event volunteers for a major youth organization. *Leisure*, 24 (1), 161–177.

Joliffe, L., Bui, H. and Nguyenm, H. (2008). The Buon Ma Thuot coffee festival, Vietnam: Opportunity for tourism? In J. Ali-Knight, M. Robertson, A. Fyall and A. Ladkin (eds), *International Perspectives of Festivals and Events: Paradigms of Analysis*, pp. 125–137. Oxford: Butterworth-Heinemann.

Jones, H. (1993). Pop goes the festival. *Marketing Week*, 16 (23), 24–27.

Jones, I. and Green, C. (2006). Serious leisure, social identity and sport tourism. In H. Gibson (ed.), *Sport Tourism: Concepts and Theories*, pp. 32–49. London: Routledge.

Jones, M. (2010). *Sustainable Event Management: A Practical Guide*. London: Earthscan.

Jordan, J. (1980). The summer people and the natives: Some effects of tourism in a Vermont vacation village. *Annals of Tourism Research*, 7 (1), 34–55.

Jordan, L. (2006). Staging the Cricket World Cup 2007 in the Caribbean: Issues and challenges for small island developing states. In M. Robertson (ed.), *Leisure Studies Association No. 91, Sporting Events and Event Tourism: Impacts, Plans and Opportunities*, pp. 17–42. Eastbourne: The University of Brighton.

Jung, M. (2005). Determinants of exhibition service quality as perceived by attendees. *Journal of Convention and Event Tourism*, 7 (3/4), 85–98.

Jutbring, H. (2014). Encoding destination messages in media coverage of an international event: A case study of the European athletics indoor championships. *Journal of Destination Marketing & Management*, 3 (1), 29–36.

Kachun, M. (2003). *Festivals of Freedom: Memory and Meaning in African American Emancipation Celebrations, 1808–1915*. Amherst, MA: University of Massachusetts Press.

Kaku, M. (2012). *Physics of the Future: The Inventions That Will Transform Our Lives*. London: Penguin Books.

Kang, Y. and Perdue, R. (1994). Long term impact of a mega-event on international tourism to the host country: A conceptual model and the case of the 1988 Seoul Olympics. In M. Uysal (ed.), *Global Tourist Behavior*, pp. 205–225. New York: International Business Press.

Kaplan, S. (1987). Aesthetics, affect, and cognition: Environmental preference from an evolutionary perspective. *Environment and Behavior*, 19 (1), 3–32.

Kaplanidou, K. and Vogt, C. (2010). The meaning and measurement of a sport event experience among active sport tourists. *Journal of Sport Management*, 24 (5), 544–566.

Katz, A. (1981). Self help and mutual aid: An emerging social movement. *Annual Review of Sociology*, 7, 129–155.

Kay, P. (2004). Cross-cultural research issues in developing international tourist markets for cultural events. *Event Management*, 8 (4), 191–202.

Kelly, G. (1955). *The Psychology of Personal Constructs: Vol. I*. New York: Norton.

Kelly, J. (1985). *Recreation Business*. New York: Macmillan.

Kelly, J. (1987). *Freedom to Be: A New Sociology of Leisure*. New York: Macmillan.

Kendrick, V., Haslam, R. and Waterson, P. (2012). Planning crowd events to achieve high participant satisfaction. *Work: A Journal of Prevention, Assessment and Rehabilitation*, 41 (1), 3223–3226.

Kentucky Derby Festival (http://derbyfestival.org, accessed 25 August 2015).

Kerstetter, D. and Gitelson, R. (1995). Perceptions of sponsorship contributors to a regional arts festival. *Festival Management and Event Tourism*, 2 (3/4), 203–209.

Khodr, H. (2012). Exploring the driving factors behind the event strategy in Qatar: A case study of the 15th Asian Games. *International Journal of Event and Festival Management*, 3 (1), 81–100.

Kim, D.-Y., Jang, S. and Morrison, A. M. (2011). Factors affecting organizational information technology acceptance: A comparison of convention and visitor bureaus and meeting planners in the United States. *Journal of Convention & Event Tourism*, 12 (1), 1–24.

Kim, J., Kang, J. and Kim, Y.-K. (2014). Impact of mega sport events on destination image and country image. *Sport Marketing Quarterly*, 23 (3), 161–175.

Kim, S., Ao Y., Lee, H. and Pan, S. (2012). A study of motivations and the image of Shanghai as perceived by foreign tourists at the Shanghai EXPO. *Journal of Convention & Event Tourism*, 13 (1) 48–73.

Kim, S., Park, J. and Lee, J. (2010). Predicted economic impact analysis of a mega-convention using multiplier effects. *Journal of Convention and Event Tourism*, 11 (1), 42–61.

Kim, S., Scott, D. and Crompton, J. (1997). An exploration of the relationships among social psychological involvement, behavioral involvement, commitment, and future intentions in the context of birdwatching. *Journal of Leisure Research*, 29 (3), 320–341.

Kipper, G. and Rampolla, J. (2013). *Augmented Reality: An Emerging Technologies Guide to AR*. Waltham: Elsevier.

Kleiber, D. A. (1999). *Leisure Experience and Human Development: A Dialectical Interpretation*. New York: Basic Books.

Klemke, E., Hollinger, R. and Rudge, D. (eds) (1998). *Introductory Readings in the Philosophy of Science*. New York: Prometheus Books.

Knox, D. (2008). Spectacular tradition Scottish folksong and authenticity. *Annals of Tourism Research*, 35 (1), 255–273.

Ko., Y., Kim, M. K., Kim, Y. K., Lee, J.-H. and Cattani, K. (2010). Consumer satisfaction and event quality perception: A case of US Open Taekwondo Championship. *Event Management*, 14 (3), 205–214.

Kociatkiewicz, J. and Kostera, M. (2012). The speed of experience: The co-narrative method in experience economy education. *British Journal of Management*, 23 (4), 474–488.

Kontokosta, C. (2012). The price of victory: The impact of the Olympic games on residential real estate markets. *Urban Studies*, 49 (5), 961–978.

Koo, G. Y. and Hardin, R. (2008). Difference in interrelationship between spectators' motives and behavioral intentions based on emotional attachment. *Sport Marketing Quarterly*, 17 (1), 30.

Kotler, P. (1973). Atmospherics as a marketing tool. *Journal of Retailing*, 4, 48–64.

Kotler, P., Bowen, J. and Maken, J. (1999). *Marketing for Hospitality and Tourism*. New Jersey: Prentice-Hall.

Kotler, P., Haider, D. and Rein, I. (1993). *Marketing Places*. New York: The Free Press.

Kozinets, R. V. (2010). *Netnography. Doing Ethnographic Research Online*. Thousand Oaks, CA: Sage.

Kruger, M., Saayman, M. and Ellis, S. (2011). Segmentation by genres: The case of the Aardklop National Arts Festival. *International Journal of Tourism Research*, 13 (6), 511–526.

Krugman, C. and Wright, R. R. (2006). *Global Meetings and Exhibitions*. Hoboken, NJ: Wiley.

Kurzweil, R. (2008). *The Singularity is Near: When Humans Transcend Biology*. London: Duckworth Overlook.

Kyle, G. and Chick, G. (2002). The social nature of leisure involvement. *Journal of Leisure Research*, 34 (4), 426–448.

Kyle, G., Absher, J., Norman, W., Hammitt, W. and Jodice, L. (2007). A modified involvement scale. *Leisure Studies*, 26 (4), 399–427.

Ladkin, A. and Weber, K. (2010). Career aspects of convention and exhibition professionals in Asia. *International Journal of Contemporary Hospitality Management*, 22 (6), 871–886.

Laing, J. and Frost, W. (2010). How green was my festival: Exploring challenges and opportunities associated with staging green events. *International Journal of Hospitality Management*, 29 (2), 261–267.

Laing, J. and Frost, W. (eds) (2014). *Rituals and Traditional Events in the Modern World*. Abingdon: Routledge.

Lamont, M. and Jenkins, J. (2013). Segmentation of cycling event participants: A two-step cluster method utilizing recreation specialization. *Event Management*, 17 (4), 391–407.

Lamont, M., Kennelly, M. and Wilson, E. (2012). Competing priorities as constraints in event travel careers. *Tourism Management*, 33 (5), 1068–1079.

Lankford, S. V. (1996). Crime and tourism: A study of perceptions in the Pacific northwest, In A. Pizam and Y. Mansfeld (eds), *Tourism, Crime and International Security Issues*, pp. 51–58. Chichester: John Wiley & Sons.

Larson, M. (2002). A political approach to relationship marketing: Case study of the Storsjöyran Festival. *International Journal of Tourism Research*, 4 (2), 119–143.

Larson, M. (2009a). Festival innovation: Complex and dynamic network interaction. *Scandinavian Journal of Hospitality and Tourism*, 9 (2/3), 288–307.

Larson, M. (2009b). Joint event production in the jungle, the park, and the garden: Metaphors of event networks. *Tourism Management*, 30 (3), 393–399.

Larson, M. and Wikstrom, E. (2001). Organising events: Managing conflict and consensus in a political market square. *Event Management*, 7 (1), 51–65.

Larson, R. and Csikszentmihalyi, M. (1983). The experience sampling method. In H. Reis (ed.), *Naturalistic Approaches to Studying Social Interaction*, pp. 41–56. San Francisco, CA: Jossey-Bass.

Lashley, C., Morrisson, A. and Randall, S. (2004). My most memorable meal ever! Hospitality as an emotional experience. In D. Sloan (ed.), *Culinary Taste: Consumer Behaviour in the International Restaurant Sector*, pp. 165–184. Oxford: Butterworth-Heinemann.

Lashua, B., Spracklen, K. and Long, P. (2014). Introduction to the special issue: Music and tourism. *Tourist Studies*, 14 (1), 3–9.

Lavenda, R. H. (1980). The festival of progress: The globalizing world-system and the transformation of the Caracas Carnival. *Journal of Popular Culture*, 14 (3), 465–475.

Laverie, D. and Arnett, D. (2000). Factors affecting fan attendance: The influence of identity salience and satisfaction. *Journal of Leisure Research*, 32 (2), 225–246.

Laxson, J. (1991). How 'we' see 'them': Tourism and native American Indians. *Annals of Tourism Research*, 18 (3), 365–391.

Laybourn, P. (2004). Risk and decision making in events management. In I. Yeoman, M. Robertson, J. Ali-Knight, S. Drummond and U. McMahon-Beattie (eds), *Festivals and Events Management*, pp. 286–307. Oxford: Elsevier.

Lee, C., Lee, Y. and Wicks, B. (2004). Segmentation of festival motivation by nationality and satisfaction. *Tourism Management*, 25 (1), 61–70.

Lee, C. K., Mjelde, J. W., Kim, T. K. and Lee, H. M. (2014). Estimating the intention–behavior gap associated with a mega event: The case of the Expo 2012 Yeosu Korea. *Tourism Management*, 41, 168–177.

Lee, D. P. and Palakurthi, R. (2013). Marketing strategy to increase exhibition attendance through controlling and eliminating leisure constraints. *Event Management*, 17 (4), 323–336.

Lee, H., Kerstetter, D., Graefe, A. and Confer, J. (1997). Crowding at an arts festival: A replication and extension of the outdoor recreation crowding model. In W. Kuentzel (ed.), *Proceedings of the 1966 Northeastern Recreation Research Symposium* (USDA Forest Service Ge. Tech. Rep. NE–232), pp. 198–204. Radnor, PA: Northeastern Forest Experiment Station.

Lee, J. (1987). The impact of Expo '86 on British Columbia markets. In P. Williams, J. Hall and M. Hunter (eds), *Tourism: Where is the Client?* Conference Papers of the Travel and Tourism Research Association, Canada Chapter.

Lee, J. (2014). Visitors' emotional responses to the festival environment. *Journal of Travel and Tourism Marketing*, 31 (1), 114–131.

Lee, J. and Back, K. (2005). A review of convention and meeting management research. *Journal of Convention and Event Tourism*, 7 (2), 1–19.

Lee, J. and Kyle, G. (2013). Segmenting festival visitors using psychological commitment. *Journal of Travel Research*, 53 (5), 656–669.

Lee, J.-E., Almanza, B. and Nelson, D. (2010). Food safety at fairs and festivals: Vendor knowledge and violations at regional festivals. *Event Management*, 14 (3), 215–223.

Lee, J.-S. and Back, K. (2009). Examining the effect of self-image congruence, relative to education and networking, on conference evaluation through its competing models and moderating effect. *Journal of Convention and Event Tourism*, 10 (4), 256–275.

Lee, J.-S., Lee, C.-K. and Yoon, Y. (2009). Investigating differences in antecedents to value between first-time and repeat festival-goers. *Journal of Travel and Tourism Marketing*, 26 (7), 688–702.

Lee, K. H., Alexander, A. C. and Kim, D. Y. (2013). Motivational factors affecting volunteer intention in local events in the United States. *Journal of Convention and Event Tourism*, 14 (4), 271–292.

Lee, S., Boshnakova, D. and Goldblatt, J. (2015). *The 21st Century Meeting and Event Technologies*. Waretown, NJ: Apple Academic Press.

Lee, S. and Crompton, J. (2003). The attraction power and spending impact of three festivals in Ocean City, Maryland. *Event Management*, 8 (2), 109–112.

Lee, T. H. and Hsu, F. Y. (2013). Examining how attending motivation and satisfaction affects the loyalty for attendees at Aboriginal festivals. *International Journal of Tourism Research*, 15 (1), 18–34.

Lee, Y., Datillo, J. and Howard, D. (1994). The complex and dynamic nature of leisure experience. *Journal of Leisure Research*, 26 (3), 195.

Lefebvre, H. (1991). *The Production of Space*, translated by Donald Nicholson-Smith, originally published in 1974. Oxford: Basil Blackwell.

Lefebvre, R. (2011). An integrative model for social marketing. *Journal of Social Marketing*, 1 (10), 54–72.

Leibold, M. and van Zyl, C. (1994). The Summer Olympic Games and its tourism marketing: City tourism marketing experiences and challenges with specific reference to Cape Town, South Africa. In P. Murphy (ed.), *Quality Management in Urban Tourism: Balancing Business and the Environment, Proceedings*, pp. 135–151. Wellington: University of Victoria.

Leigh, J., Lamont, M. J. and Cairncross, G. (2013). Towards a process model of induction and training for young event volunteers. *International Journal of Event Management Research*, 8 (1), 1–20.

Leiper, N. (1981). Towards a cohesive curriculum in tourism. The case for a distinct discipline. *Annals of Tourism Research*, 8 (1), 69–84.

Leiper, N. (1990). Tourist attraction systems. *Annals of Tourism Research*, 17 (3), 367–384.

Leiper, N. (2008). Why 'the tourism industry' is misleading as a generic expression: The case for the plural variation, 'tourism industries'. *Tourism Management*, 29 (2), 237–251.

Lennon, J. and Foley, M. (2000). *Dark Tourism: The Attraction of Death and Disaster*. London: Continuum.

Leopkey, B. and Parent, M. (2009). Risk management strategies by stakeholders in Canadian major sporting events. *Event Management*, 13 (3), 153–170.

Leung, R. and Law, R. (2010). A review of personality research in the tourism and hospitality context. *Journal of Travel and Tourism Marketing*, 27 (5), 439–459.

Levermore, R. (2010). CSR for development through sport: Examining its potential and limitations. *Third World Quarterly*, 31 (2), 223–241.

Levy, S. (1959). Symbols for sale. *Harvard Business Review*, 37, 117–124.

Levy, S. (2010). The hospitality of the host: A cross-cultural examination of managerially facilitated consumer-to-consumer interactions. *International Journal of Hospitality Management*, 29 (1), 319–327.

Li, M., Huang, Z. and Cai, L. (2009). Benefit segmentation of visitors to a rural community-based festival. *Journal of Travel and Tourism Marketing*, 26 (5–6), 585–598.

Li, R. and Petrick, J. (2006). A review of festival and event motivation studies. *Event Management*, 9 (4), 239–245.

Li, X. and Vogelsong, H. (2005). Comparing methods of measuring image change: A case study of a small-scale community festival. *Tourism Analysis*, 10 (4), 349–360.

Li, Y. (2000). Geographical consciousness and tourism experience. *Annals of Tourism Research*, 27 (4), 863–883.

Liburd, J. (2008). Tourism and the Hans Christian Andersen bicentenary event in Denmark. In J. Ali-Knight, M. Robertson, A. Fyall, and A. Ladkin (eds), *Perspectives of Festivals and Events: Paradigms of Analysis*, pp. 41–52. Oxford: Butterworth-Heinemann.

van Limburg, B. (2008). Innovation in pop festivals by cocreation. *Event Management*, 12 (2), 105–117.

Ling, T. (1998). Exploring the environment for healthcare. *The Madingley Scenarios*. (http://www.cambridgeforesight.c, accessed 25 August 2015).

Locke, E. (1991). *The Essence of Leadership*. New York: Lexington Books.

Locke, M. (2010). A framework for conducting a situational analysis of the meetings, incentives, conventions, and exhibitions sector. *Journal of Convention and Event Tourism*, 11 (3), 209–233.

Lockstone, L. and Baum, T. (2009). 2006 Melbourne Commonwealth Games, Australia: Recruiting, training and managing a volunteer program at a sporting mega event. In K. Holmes and K. Smith (eds), *Managing Volunteers in Tourism Attractions, Destinations and Events*, pp. 215–223. Oxford: Butterworth-Heinemann.

Lockstone-Binney, L., Whitelaw, P., Robertson, M., Junek, O. and Michael, I. (2014). The motives of ambassadors in bidding for international association meetings and events. *Event Management*, 18 (1), 65–74.

London 2012 (www.london2012.com, accessed 25 August 2015).

Long, P. (2000). After the event: Perspectives on organizational partnership in the management of a themed festival year. *Event Management*, 6 (1), 45–59.

Long, P. and Robinson, M. (eds) (2004). *Festivals and Tourism: Marketing, Management and Evaluation*. Sunderland: Business Education Publishers.

Long, P., Robinson, M. and Picard, D. (2004). Festivals and tourism: Links and developments. In P. Long and M. Robinson (eds), *Festivals and Tourism: Marketing, Management and Evaluation*, pp. 1–14. Sunderland: Business Education Publishers.

Lord Cultural Resources Planning and Management (1993). *The Cultural Tourism Handbook*. Toronto: Province of Ontario.

Lorde, T., Greenidge, D. and Devonish, D. (2011). Local residents' perceptions of the impacts of the ICC Cricket World Cup 2007 on Barbados: Comparisons of pre- and post-games. *Tourism Management*, 32 (2), 349–356.

Louviere, J. J. and Hensher, D. A. (1983). Using discrete choice models with experimental design data to forecast consumer demand for a unique cultural event. *Journal of Consumer Research*, 10, 348–361.

Love, L. and Crompton, J. (1996). A conceptualization of the relative roles of festival attributes in determining perceptions of overall festival quality. Paper presented to the Research Symposium, annual conference of the International Festivals and Events Association (unpublished).

Lynch, K. (1960). *The Image of the City*. Cambridge, MA: MIT Press.

Lyu, S. and Lee, H. (2013). Market segmentation of golf event spectators using leisure benefits. *Journal of Travel and Tourism Marketing*, 30 (3), 186–200.

Mabrey, V. and Gerstein, T. (2010). Philadelphia moves to nip flash mobs in bud: Mayor calls for parents to monitor teens' texts after incidents of mob vandalism, 23 April (http://abcnews.go.com, accessed 25 August 2015).

MacAloon, J. (1984). Olympic Games and the theory of spectacle in modern societies. In J. MacAloon (ed.), *Rite, Drama, Festival, Spectacle: Rehearsals Towards a Theory of Cultural Performance*, pp. 241–280. Philadelphia, PA: Institute for the Study of Human Issues.

Macbeth, J., Selwood, J. and Veitch, S. (2012). Paradigm shift or a drop in the ocean? The America's Cup impact on Fremantle. *Tourism Geographies*, 14 (1), 162–182.

McCabe, V. (2008). Strategies for career planning and development in the convention and exhibition industry in Australia. *International Journal of Hospitality Management*, 27 (2), 222–231.

MacCannell, D. (1973). Staged authenticity: Arrangements of social space in tourist settings. *American Journal of Sociology*, 79 (3), 589–603.

MacCannell, D. (1976). *The Tourist: A New Theory of the Leisure Class*. New York: Schocken Books.

McCarthy, M. (2012). *Ireland's 1916 Rising: Explorations of History-Making, Commemorations and Heritage in Modern Times*. Aldershot: Ashgate.

McCartney, G. and Osti, L. (2007). From cultural events to sport events: A case study of cultural authenticity in the dragon boat races. *Journal of Sport and Tourism*, 12 (1), 25–40.

McClinchey, K. and Carmichael, A. (2014). The future of local community festivals and meanings of place in an increasingly mobile world. In I. Yeoman, M. Robertson, U. McMahon-Beattie, E. Backer and K. Smith (eds), *The Future of Events and Festivals*, pp. 140–156. Abingdon: Routledge.

McGehee, N., Yoon, Y. and Cardenas, D. (2003). Involvement and travel for recreational runners in North Carolina. *Journal of Sport Management*, 17 (3), 305–324.

McGregor, D. (1960). *The Human Side of Enterprise*. New York: McGraw Hill.

McGillivray, D. (2014). Digital cultures, acceleration and mega sporting event narratives, *Leisure Studies*, 33 (1), 96–109.

McHenry, J. A. (2011). Rural empowerment through the arts: The role of the arts in civic and social participation in the Mid West region of Western Australia. *Journal of Rural Studies*, 27 (3), 245–253.

Mackellar, J. (2006). Special interest events in a regional destination – exploring differences between specialist and generalist events. In C. Arcodia, M. Whitford and C. Dicksen (eds), *Global Events Congress Proceedings*, pp. 176–195. Brisbane: University of Queensland.

Mackellar, J. (2009). An examination of serious participants at the Australian Wintersun Festival. *Leisure Studies*, 28 (1), 85–104.

Mackellar, J. (2013a). *Event Audiences and Expectations*. Abingdon: Routledge.

Mackellar, J. (2013b). Participant observation at events: Theory, practice and potential. *International Journal of Event and Festival Management*, 4 (1), 56–65.

Mackellar, J. and Nisbet, S. (2014). Sport events and integrated destination development. *Current Issues in Tourism*, 14 (2) 183–189.

McKercher, B. and du Cros, H. (2002). *Cultural Tourism*. New York: Haworth.

McKercher, B., Mei, W. and Tse, T. (2006). Are short duration festivals tourist attractions? *Journal of Sustainable Tourism*, 14 (1), 55–66.

McLuhan, M. (1964). *Understanding Media: The Extensions of Man*. New York: McGraw Hill.

McMahon-Beattie, U. and Yeoman, I. (2004). The potential for revenue management in festivals and events. In I. Yeoman, M. Robertson, J. Ali-Knight, S. Drummond and U. McMahon-Beattie (eds), *Festivals and Events Management*, pp. 202–214. Oxford: Elsevier.

Macnaught, T. (1982). Mass tourism and the dilemmas of modernization in Pacific island communities. *Annals of Tourism Research*, 9 (3), 359–381.

McPhail, T. (2006). *Global Communication: Theories, Stakeholders, and Trends* (2nd edn). Oxford: Blackwell Publishers.

Madden J. (2006). Economic and fiscal impacts of mega sporting events: A general equilibrium assessment. *Public Finance and Management*, 6 (3), 346–394.

Madrigal, R. (1995). Cognitive and affective determinants of fan satisfaction with sporting event attendance. *Journal of Leisure Research*, 27 (3), 205–207.

Madrigal, R. (2003). Investigating and evolving leisure experience: Antecedents and consequences of spectator affect during a live sporting event. *Journal of Leisure Research*, 35 (1), 23–45.

Maestas, A. (2009). Guide to sponsorship return on investment. *Journal of Sponsorship*, 3 (1), 98–102.

Mahony, D., Madrigal, R. and Howard, D. (1999). The effect of self-monitoring on behavioral and attitudinal loyalty towards athletic teams. *International Journal of Sport Marketing and Sponsorship*, 1, 146–167.

Mahony, D., Madrigal, R. and Howard, D. (2000). Using the psychological commitment to team (PCT) scale to segment sport consumers based on loyalty. *Sport Marketing Quarterly*, 9 (1), 15–25.

Mair, J. (2010). Profiling conference delegates using attendance motivations. *Journal of Convention and Event Tourism*, 11 (3), 176–194.

Mair, J. (2012). A review of business events literature. *Event Management*, 16 (2), 133–141.

Mair, J. (2013). *Conferences and Conventions: A Research Perspective*. Abingdon: Routledge.

Mair, J. and Jago, L. (2010). The development of a conceptual model of greening in the business events tourism sector. *Journal of Sustainable Tourism*, 18 (1), 77–94.

Mair, J. and Thompson, K. (2009). The UK association conference attendance decision-making process. *Tourism Management*, 30 (3), 400–409.

Mair, J. and Whitford, M. (2013). An exploration of events research: Event topics, themes and emerging trends. *International Journal of Event and Festival Management*, 4 (1), 6–30.

Major Events New Zealand (www.majorevents.govt.nz, accessed 25 August 2015).

Mallen, C. and Adams, L. (2008). *Sport, Recreation and Tourism Event Management: Theoretical and Practical Dimensions*. Oxford: Butterworth-Heinemann.

Malouf, L. (2002). *Parties and Special Events: Planning and Design*. Texas: Culinary and Hospitality Industry Publications Services.

Malouf, L. (2011). *Events Exposed: Managing and Designing Special Events*. Chichester: Wiley.

Mandelbaum, S., Mazza, L. and Burchell, R.W. (eds) (1996). *Explorations in Planning Theory*. New Brunswick, NJ: Center for Urban Policy Research, Rutgers University.

Mannell, R. and Iso-Ahola, S. (1987). Psychological nature of leisure and tourist experiences. *Annals of Tourism Research*, 14 (3), 314–331.

Mannell, R. and Kleiber, D. (1997). *A Social Psychology of Leisure*. State College, PA: Venture Publishing.

Mannell, R. and Zuzanek, J. (1991). The nature and variability of leisure constraints in daily life: The case of the physically active leisure of older adults. *Leisure Sciences*, 13 (4), 337–351.

Manning, F. (ed.) (1983). *The Celebration of Society: Perspectives on Contemporary Cultural Performance*. Bowling Green, OH: Bowling Green University Popular Press.

Mansfield, V. (1998). Time and impermanence in middle way Buddhism and modern physics. Talk at the Physics and Tibetan Buddhism Conference, University of California, Santa Barbara, 30–31 January 1998 (http://www.buddhanet.net/timeimpe.htm, accessed 25 August 2015).

Manthiou, A., Lee, S. A., Tang, L. R. and Chiang, L. (2014). The experience economy approach to festival marketing: Vivid memory and attendee loyalty. *Journal of Services Marketing*, 28 (1), 22–35.

Mark Cuban (2010). Weblog. The Fan Experience at Sporting Events – Never Look Down. 10 September, 11:13 AM (http://blogmaverick.com, accessed 25 August 2015).

Markus, H. and Kitayama, S. (1991). Culture and the self: Implications for cognition, emotion, and motivation. *Psychological Review*, 98 (2), 224–253.

Markwell, K. and Tomsen, S. (2010). Safety and hostility at special events: Lessons from Australian gay and lesbian festivals. *Event Management*, 14 (3), 225–238.

Marris, T. (1987). The role and impact of mega-events and attractions on regional and national tourism development: Resolutions of the 37th Congress of the AIEST, Calgary. *Revue de Tourisme*, 42 (4): 3–12.

Marshall, G. (1998). Exchange theory. In *A Dictionary of Sociology* (www.encyclopedia.com/doc/1O88-exchangetheory.html, accessed 24 December 2009).

Martin, A. J., Anderson, M. and Adams, R. J. (2012). What determines young people's engagement with performing arts events? *Leisure Services*, 34 (4), 314–331.

Maslow, A. (1954). *Motivation and Personality* (2nd edn). New York: Harper and Row.

Maslow, A. (1968). *Toward a Psychology of Being* (2nd edn). Toronto: Van Nostrand Rheinhold.

Masterman, G. (2004, 3rd edn 2014). *Strategic Sports Event Management: An International Approach*. Abingdon: Routledge.

Masterman, G. and Wood, E. (2006). *Innovative Marketing Communications: Strategies for the Events Industry*. Oxford: Butterworth-Heinemann.

Mastrogiannakis, D. and Dorville, C. (2013). Security and sport mega-events: A complex relation. *Sport in Society*, 16 (2), 133–139.

Matheson, C. and Finkel, R. (2013). Sex trafficking and the Vancouver Winter Olympic Games: Perceptions and preventative measures. *Tourism Management*, 36, 613–628.

Matheson, C. M. (2008). Music, emotion and authenticity: A study of Celtic music festival consumers. *Journal of Tourism and Cultural Change*, 6 (1), 57–74.

Matheson, V. (2002). Upon further review: An examination of sporting event economic impact studies. *The Sport Journal*, 5 (1), 1–3.

Matheson, V. and Baade, R. (2003). Bidding for the Olympics: Fools gold? In C. Barros, M. Ibrahim and S. Szymanski (eds), *Transatlantic Sport*. London: Edward Elgar Publishing.

Matthews, D. (2008). *Special Event Production: The Resources*. Wallingford: CABI.

Mayfield, T. and Crompton, J. (1995). The status of the marketing concept among festival organizers. *Journal of Travel Research*, 33 (4), 14–22.

Meeting Professionals International (2003). *Meetings and Conventions: A Planning Guide*. Mississauga, ON: MPI. (www.mpiweb.org, accessed 25 August 2015).

Mehmetoglu, M. and Ellingsen, K. (2005). Do small-scale festivals adopt 'market orientation' as a management philosophy? *Event Management*, 9 (3), 119–132.

Mehus, I. (2005). Sociability and excitement motives of spectators attending entertainment sport events: Spectators of soccer and ski-jumping. *Journal of Sport Behavior*, 28 (4), 333.

Memish, Z. A., Zumla, A., Alhakeem, R. F., Assiri, A., Turkestani, A., Al Harby, K. D. and Al-Tawfiq, J. A. (2014). Hajj: Infectious disease surveillance and control. *The Lancet*, 383 (9934), 2073–2082.

Mendell, R., MacBeth, J. and Solomon, A. (1983). The 1982 world's fair – a synopsis. *Leisure Today, Journal of Physical Education, Recreation and Dance* (April), 48–49.

Merkel, U. (ed.) (2013). *Power, Politics and International Events: Socio-cultural Analyses of Festivals and Spectacles*. Abingdon: Routledge.

Merrilees, B., Getz, D. and O'Brien, D. (2005). Marketing stakeholder analysis: Branding the Brisbane Goodwill Games. *European Journal of Marketing*, 39 (9/10), 1060–1077.

MidSumma (www.midsumma.org.au/, accessed 25 August 2015).

Miffling, K. and Taylor, R. (2007). Investigating the importance of youth culture in successful youth events. *Journal of Contemporary Issues in Business and Government*, 13 (2), 65–80.

Mihalik, B. (1994). Mega-event legacies of the 1996 Atlanta Olympics. In P. Murphy (ed.), *Quality Management in Urban Tourism: Balancing Business and Environment*. Proceedings, pp. 151–162. University of Victoria.

Mihalik, B. (2001). Host population perceptions of the 1996 Atlanta Olympics: Support, benefits and liabilities. *Tourism Analysis*, 5 (1), 49–53.

Mihalik, B. and Wing-Vogelbacher, A. (1992). Travelling art expositions as a tourism event: A market research analysis for Ramesses the Great. *Journal of Travel and Tourism Marketing*, 1 (3), 25–41.

Mill, R. and Morrison, A. (1985). *The Tourism System: An Introductory Text*. Englewood Cliffs, NJ: Prentice Hall.

Millennium Project (http://millennium-project.org/, accessed 25 August 2015).

Miller, L., Jago, L. and Deery, M. (2004). Profiling the special event nonattendee: An initial investigation. *Event Management*, 8 (3), 141–150.

Miller, R. and Washington, K. (2011). *Consumer Behaviour*. Rockville, MD: Richard K. Miller and Associates.

Milne, G. R. and McDonald, M. A. (1999). *Sport Marketing: Managing the Exchange Process*. Sudbury, MA: Jones & Bartlett Learning.

Mintzberg, H. (1983). *Power In and Around Organizations*. Englewood Cliffs, NJ: Prentice Hall.

Mintzberg, H. (1994). *The Rise and Fall of Strategic Planning*. New York: The Free Press.

Misener, L. and Mason, D. (2006). Creating community networks: Can sporting events offer meaningful sources of social capital? *Managing Leisure*, 11 (1), 39–56.

Mishra, D. P., Bobinski Jr, G. S. and Bhabra, H. S. (1997). Assessing the economic worth of corporate event sponsorships: A stock market perspective. *Journal of Market-Focused Management*, 2 (2), 149–169.

Mitchell, R., Agle, B. and Wood, D. (1997). Towards a theory of stakeholder identification and salience: Defining the principle of who and what really counts. *Academy of Management Review*, 22 (4), 853–886.

Mitler, B., van Esterik, P. and van Esterik, J. (2004). *Cultural Anthropology* (2nd Canadian edn). Toronto: Pearson Education, Canada.

Mohr, K., Backman, K., Gahan, L. and Backman, S. (1993). An investigation of festival motivations and event satisfaction by visitor type. *Festival Management and Event Tourism*, 1 (3), 89–97.

Molnár, V. (2014). Reframing public space through digital mobilization: Flash mobs and contemporary urban youth culture. *Space and Culture*, 17 (1), 43–58.

Monga, M. (2006). Measuring motivation to volunteer for special events. *Event Management*, 10 (1): 47–61.

Monroe, J. and Kates, R. (2005). *Art of the Event: Complete Guide to Designing and Decorating Special Events*. Chichester: Wiley.

Morgan, M. (2008). What makes a good festival? Understanding the event experience. *Event Management*, 12 (2): 81–93.

Morgan, M. and Wright, R. (2008). Elite sports tours: Special events with special challenges. In J. Ali-Knight, M. Robertson, A. Fyall, and A. Ladkin (eds), *International Perspectives of Festivals and Events: Paradigms of Analysis*, pp. 187–204. Oxford: Butterworth-Heinemann.

Morgan, M., Lugosi, P. and Ritchie, J. R. B. (2010). *The Tourism and Leisure Experience: Consumer and Managerial Perspectives*. Bristol: Channel View.

Morgner, C. (2014). The evolution of the art fair. *Historical Social Research*, 39 (3), 318–336.

Morrison, A. (1995). *Hospitality and Travel Marketing* (2nd edn). Albany, NY: Delmar.

Morrow, S. (1997). *The Art of the Show: An Introduction to the Study of Exhibition Management*. Dallas, TX: International Association for Exhibition Management.

Moscardo, G. (2010). The shaping of tourist experience: The importance of stories and themes. In M. Morgan, P. Lugosi and J. R. B. Ritchie (eds), *The Tourism and Leisure Experience: Consumer and Managerial Perspectives*, pp. 43–50. Bristol: Channel View.

Moser, G. and Uzzell, D. (2003). Environmental psychology. In T. Millon and M. Lerner (eds), *Comprehensive Handbook of Psychology: Volume 5: Personality and Social Psychology*. New York: John Wiley and Sons.

Mossberg, L. (2000). Effects of events on destination image. In L. Mossberg (ed.), *Evaluation of Events: Scandinavian Experiences*, pp. 30–46. New York: Cognizant.

Mossberg, L. (2006). Product development and cultural tourism. In T. Andersson (ed.), *Cultural Tourism: Visitor Flows, Economic Impact and Product Development*, pp. 47–59. Published for the European Cultural Tourism Network at the School of Business, Economics and Law, University of Gothenburg, Sweden.

Mossberg, L. (2008). Extraordinary experiences through storytelling. *Scandinavian Journal of Hospitality and Tourism*, 8 (3), 195–210.

Mossberg, L. and Getz, D. (2006). Stakeholder influences on the ownership and management of festival brands. *Scandinavian Journal of Hospitality and Tourism*, 6 (4), 308–326.

Mount, J. and Niro, B. (1995). Sponsorship: An empirical study of its application to local business in a small town setting. *Festival Management and Event Tourism*, 2 (3/4), 167–175.

Mowen, A., Vogelsong, H. and Graefe, A. (2003). Perceived crowding and its relationship to crowd management practices at park and recreation events. *Event Management*, 8 (2), 63–72.

Moyer, K. (1968). Kinds of aggression and their physiological basis. *Communications in Behavioral Biology* (Part A), 2 (2), 65–87.

Mules, T. (1993). A special event as part of an urban renewal strategy. *Festival Management and Event Tourism*, 1 (2), 65–67.

Mules, T. and Dwyer, L. (2006). Public sector support for sport tourism events: The role of cost-benefit assessment. In H. Gibson (ed.), *Sport Tourism: Concepts and Theories*. London: Routledge.

Mules, T. and McDonald, S. (1994). The economic impact of special events: The use of forecasts. *Festival Management and Event Tourism*, 2 (1), 45–53.

Nadav, S., Smith, W. and Canberg, A. (2010). Examining corporate sponsorship of charitable events in the greater Charleston area. *Event Management*, 14 (3), 239–250.

Naik, T. (1948). Aboriginal festivals in Gujrat. *Eastern Anthropologist*, 2 (1), 16–21.

National Association for Interpretation (www.interpnet.com, accessed 25 August 2015).

National Association of Sports Commissions (www.sportscommissions.org, accessed 25 August 2015).

North American Society for Sport Management (www.nassm.com, accessed 25 August 2015).

Nelson, K. B. (2009). Enhancing the attendee's experience through creative design of the event environment: Applying Goffman's dramaturgical perspective. *Journal of Convention and Event Tourism*, 10 (2), 120–133.

Neufeind, M., Güntert, S. T. and Wehner, T. (2013). The impact of job design on event volunteers' future engagement: Insights from the European Football Championship 2008. *European Sport Management Quarterly*, 13 (5), 537–556.

Neulinger, J. (1974). *Psychology of Leisure: Research Approaches to the Study of Leisure*. Springfield, IL: Charles C. Thomas.

Neuman, W. (2003). *Social Research Methods: Qualitative and Quantitative Approaches* (4th edn). Boston, MA: Allyn and Bacon.

New South Wales. *Traffic Management for Special Events* (www.rta.nsw.gov.au, accessed 25 August 2015).

Ngamson, B. and Beck, J. (2000). A pilot study of motivations, inhibitors, and facilitators of association members in attending international conferences. *Journal of Convention and Exhibition Management*, 2 (2/3), 97–111.

Nicholson, R. and Pearce, D. (2001). Why do people attend events: A comparative analysis of visitor motivations at four South Island events. *Journal of Travel Research*, 39 (4), 449–460.

Nickerson, N. and Ellis, G. (1991). Traveler types and activation theory: A comparison of two models. *Journal of Travel Research*, 29 (3), 26–31.

Nogawa, H., Yamaguchi, Y. and Hagi, Y. (1996). An empirical research study on Japanese sport tourism in Sport-for-All events: Case studies of a single-night event and a multiple-night event. *Journal of Travel Research*, 35 (2), 46–54.

Nordvall, A., Pettersson, R., Svensson, B. and Brown, S. (2014). Designing events for social interaction. *Event Management*, 18 (2), 127–140.

Noronha, R. (1977). Paradise reviewed: Tourism in Bali. In E. de Kadt (ed.), *Tourism: Passport to Development?* pp. 177–204. Oxford: Oxford University Press.

Nurse, K. (2004). Trinidad Carnival: Festival tourism and cultural industry. *Event Management*, 8 (4), 223–230.

Oakes, S. (2003). Demographic and sponsorship considerations for jazz and classical music festivals. *Service Industries Journal*, 23 (3), 165–178.

Oakley, E. and Krug, D. (1991). *Enlightened Leadership: Getting to the Heart of Change*. New York: Simon and Schuster.

O'Brien, D. (2005). Event business leveraging: The Sydney 2000 Olympic Games. *Annals of Tourism Research*, 33 (1), 240–261.

O'Brien, E. and Shaw, M. (2002). Independent meeting planners: A Canadian perspective. *Journal of Convention and Exhibition Management*, 3 (4), 37–68.

O'Dell, T. (2005). Management strategies and the need for fun. In T. O'Dell and P. Billing (eds), *Experience-scapes: Tourism, Culture, and Economy*, pp. 127–142. Copenhagen Business School Press.

Office for National Statistics (2002). *Time Use Survey*. London: ONS.

Ogbeide, G., Fenich, G., Scott-Halsell, S. and Kesterson, K. (2013). Communication preferences for attracting the millennial generation to attend meetings and events. *Journal of Convention and Event Tourism*, 14 (4), 331–344.

Okayasu, I., Nogawa, H. and Morais, D. (2010). Resource investments and loyalty to recreational sport tourism event. *Journal of Travel and Tourism Marketing*, 27 (6), 565–578.

Oldberding, D. and Jisha, J. (2005). 'The flying pig': Building brand equity in a major urban marathon. *Sport Marketing Quarterly*, 14 (3), 191–196.

Olds, K. and Ley, D. (1988). Landscape as spectacle: World's fairs and the culture of heroic consumption. *Environment and Planning D: Society and Space*, 6, 191–212.

Oliver, R. (1977). Effect of expectation and disconfirmation on postexposure product evaluations – an alternative interpretation. *Journal of Applied Psychology*, 62 (4), 480–486.

Oliver, R. (1980). A cognitive model of the antecedents and consequences of satisfaction decisions. *Journal of Marketing Research*, 17 (3), 460–469.

Olsen, K. (2002). Authenticity as a concept in tourism research: The social organization of the experience of authenticity. *Tourist Studies*, 2 (2), 159–182.

Olson, J. and Reynolds, T. (2001). *Understanding Consumer Decision Making: A Means End Approach to Marketing and Advertising Strategy*. Mahwah, NJ: Lawrence Erlbaum Associates.

Ooi, C. (2005). A theory of tourism experiences. In T. O'Dell and P. Billing (eds), *Experience-scapes: Tourism, Culture, and Economy*, pp. 51–68. Copenhagen: Copenhagen Business School Press.

Oppermann, M. and Chon, K. (1997). Convention participation decision-making process. *Annals of Tourism Research*, 24 (1), 178–191.

O'Sullivan, D., Pickernell, D. and Senyard, J. (2009). Public sector evaluation of festivals and special events. *Journal of Policy Research in Tourism, Leisure and Events*, 1 (1), 19–36.

O'Sullivan, E. and Spangler, K. (1998). *Experience Marketing: Strategies for the New Millennium*. State College, PA: Venture Publishing.

Otnes, C. and Peck, E. (2003). *Cinderella Dreams: The Allure of the Lavish Wedding*. Berkeley, CA: University of California Press.

O'Toole, W. (2000). The integration of event management best practice by the project management process. *Australian Parks and Leisure*, 3 (1), 4–8.

O'Toole, W. (2011). *Events Feasibility and Development: From Strategy to Operations*. Oxford: Butterworth-Heinemann.

O'Toole, W. and Mikolaitis, P. (2002). *Corporate Event Project Management*. New York: Wiley.

Packer, J. and Ballantyne, R. (2005). Solitary vs. shared learning: Exploring the social dimension of museum learning. *Curator: The Museum Journal*, 48 (2), 177–192.

Page, S. J. (1994). Perspectives on tourism and peripherality: A review of tourism in the Republic of Ireland. In C. Cooper and A. Lockwood (eds), *Progress in Tourism, Recreation and Hospitality Management: Volume 5*, pp. 26–53. London: Belhaven.

Page, S. J. (2009). *Transport and Tourism*. Harlow: Pearson.

Page, S. J. (2015). *Tourism Management* (5th edn). Abingdon: Routledge.

Page, S. J. and Connell, J. (2006). *Leisure: Critical Concepts in the Social Sciences, 4 Volumes*. Abingdon: Routledge.

Page, S. J. and Connell, J. (2010). *Leisure: An Introduction*. Harlow: Pearson Education.

Page, S. J. and Connell, J. (eds) (2011). *Routledge Handbook of Events*. Abingdon: Routledge.

Page, S. J. and Connell, J. (2014). *Tourism: A Modern Synthesis* (4th edn). Andover: Cengage.

Page, S. J., Yeoman, I., Connell, J. and Greenwood, C. (2010). Scenario planning as a tool to understand uncertainty in tourism: The example of transport and tourism in Scotland in 2025. *Current Issues in Tourism*, 13 (2), 99–137.

Palma, M. L., Palma, L. and Aguado, L. F. (2013). Determinants of cultural and popular celebration abundance: The case study of Seville Spring Fiestas. *Journal of Cultural Economics*, 37 (1), 87–107.

Papagiannopoulos, P., Xenikos, D. and Vouddas, P. (2009). Event management and group communications: The case of the 2004 Olympic Games in Athens. *Event Management*, 13 (2), 103–116.

Papastergiadis, N., McQuire, S., Gu, X., Barikin, A., Gibson, R., Yue, A. and Jones, M. (2013). Mega screens for mega cities. *Theory, Culture and Society*, 30 (7–8), 325–341.

Papson, S. (1981). Spuriousness and tourism: Politics of two Canadian provincial governments. *Annals of Tourism Research*, 8 (2), 503–507.

Parasuraman, A., Berry, L. and Zeithaml, V. (1988). SERVQUAL: A multiple-item scale for measuring consumer perceptions of service quality. *Journal of Retailing*, 64 (1), 12–40.

Parent, M. and Chappelet, J.-L. (eds) (2015). *Routledge Handbook of Sports Event Management*. Abingdon: Routledge.

Parent, M. and Seguin, B. (2007). Factors that led to the drowning of a world championship organizing committee: A stakeholder approach. *European Sport Management Quarterly*, 7 (2), 187–212.

Parent, M. and Slack, T. (2008). Conformity and resistance: Preparing a francophone sporting event in North America. *Event Management*, 11 (3), 129–143.

Park, M., Daniels, M., Brayley, R. and Harmon, L. (2010). Analysis of service provision and visitor impacts using participant observation and photographic documentation: The National Cherry Blossom Festival. *Event Management*, 14 (2), 167–182.

Patterson, I. and Getz, D. (2013). At the nexus of leisure and event studies. *Event Management*, 17 (3), 227–240.

Pearce, P. (1998). Marketing and management trends in tourist attractions. *Asia Pacific Journal of Tourism Research*, 3 (1), 1–8.

Pearce, P. and Caltabiano, M. (1983). Inferring travel motivation from travelers' experiences. *Journal of Travel Research*, 22 (2), 16–20.

Pearce, P. and Lee, U. (2005). Developing the travel career approach to tourist motivation. *Journal of Travel Research*, 43 (3), 226–237.

Pearce, P., Moscardo, G. and Ross, G. (1996). *Tourism Community Relationships*. Oxford: Pergamon.

Pearlman, D. and Gates, N. (2010). Hosting business meetings and special events in virtual worlds: A fad or the future? *Journal of Convention and Event Tourism*, 11 (4), 247–265.

Pegg, S. and Patterson, I. (2010). Rethinking music festivals as a staged event: Gaining insights from understanding visitor motivations and the experiences they seek. *Journal of Convention and Event Tourism*, 11 (2), 85–99.

Pegg, S., Patterson, I. and Axelsen, M. (2011). Sporting events and the use of alcohol by university students: Managing the risks. *Event Management*, 15 (1), 63–75.

Pennington-Gray, L. and Holdnak, A. (2002). Out of the stands and into the community: Using sports events to promote a destination. *Event Management*, 7 (3), 177–186.

Penrose, E. (1959). *The Theory of the Growth of the Firm*. New York: Wiley.

People and Physical Environment Research Conference (1987). Perth: Centre for Urban Research, University of Western Australia.

Pernecky, T. (2015). *Approaches and Methods in Event Studies*. Abingdon: Routledge.

Pernecky, T. and Luck, M. (2013). *Events, Society and Sustainabilty: Critical and Contemporary Approaches*. Abingdon: Routledge.

Persson, C. (2002). The Olympic Games site decision. *Tourism Management*, 23 (1), 27–36.

Peters, M., Piazolo, F., Köster, L. and Promberger, K. (2010). The deployment of intelligent local-based information systems (ILBI): A case study of the European Football Championship 2008. *Journal of Convention and Event Tourism*, 11 (1), 18–41.

Pettersson, R. and Getz, D. (2009). Event experiences in time and space. A study of visitors to the 2007 World Alpine Ski Championships in Åre, Sweden. *Scandinavian Journal of Tourism and Hospitality Research*, 9 (2/3), 308–326.

Pettersson, R. and Zillinger, M. (2011). Time and space in event behaviour: Tracking visitors by GPS. *Tourism Geographies*, 13 (1), 1–20.

Pfeffer, J. (1981). *Power in Organizations*. London: Pitman.

Pfeffer, J. and Salancik, G. (1978). *The External Control of Organizations: A Resource Dependence Perspective*. New York: Harper and Row.

Phi, G., Dredge, D. and Whirford, M. (2014). Understanding conflicting perspectives in event planning and management using Q method. *Tourism Management*, 40, 406–415.

Phillips, J., Breining, M. and Phillips, P. (2008). *Return on Investment in Meetings and Events*. Oxford: Elsevier.

Phipps, P. (2011). Performing culture as political strategy: The Garma Festival, northeast Arnhem Land. In C. Gibson and J. Connell (eds), *Festival Places: Revitalising Rural Australia*, pp. 109–122. Bristol: Channel View.

Picard, D. and Robinson, M. (2006a). Remaking worlds: Festivals, tourism and change. In D. Picard and M. Robinson (eds), *Festivals, Tourism and Social Change: Remaking Worlds*, pp. 1–31. Clevedon: Channel View.

Picard, D. and Robinson, M. (eds) (2006b). *Festivals, Tourism and Social Change: Remaking Worlds*. Clevedon: Channel View.

Picard, M. (1996). *Bali: Cultural Tourism and Touristic Culture* (2nd edn). Singapore: Archipelago Press.

Pieper, J. (1952). *Leisure: The Basis of Culture*. Translated by Alexander Dru. London: Faber and Faber (originally published as *Muße und Kult*. Munich: Kösel-Verlag, 1948).

Pigram, J. (1983). *Outdoor Recreation and Resource Management*. London: Croom Helm.

Pike, S. and Page, S. J. (2014). Destination marketing organizations and destination marketing: A narrative analysis of the literature. *Tourism Management*, 41, 202–227.

Pillow Fight Club (www.pillowfightclub.org, accessed 25 August 2015).

Pillow Fight Day (www.pillowfightday.com, accessed 25 August 2015).

Pine, B. and Gilmore, J. (1999). *The Experience Economy: Work is Theatre and Every Business a Stage*. Boston, MA: Harvard Business School Press.

Pitts, B. (1999). Sports tourism and niche markets: Identification and analysis of the growing lesbian and gay sports tourism industry. *Journal of Vacation Marketing*, 5 (1), 31–50.

Pizam, A. (1978). Tourism's impacts: The social costs to the destination community as perceived by its residents. *Journal of Travel Research*, 16 (4), 8–12.

Plog, S. (1972). Why destination areas rise and fall in popularity. Paper presented to the Travel Research Association Southern California Chapter, Los Angeles.

Plog, S. (1987). Understanding psychographics in tourism research. In J. Ritchie and C. Goeldner (eds), *Travel, Tourism and Hospitality Research*, pp. 302–313. New York: Wiley.

Plutschow, H. (2013). *Matsuri: The Festivals of Japan: With a Selection from PG O'Neill's Photographic Archive of Matsuri*. Routledge. (First published in 1996.)

Pojani, D. (2014). Urban design, ideology, and power: Use of the central square in Tirana during one century of political transformations. *Planning Perspectives*, 30 (1), 67–94.

Pol, L. and Pak, S. (1994). The use of a two-stage survey design in collecting data from those who have attended periodic or special events. *Journal of the Market Research Society*, 36 (4), 315–326.

Ponsford, I. and Williams, P. (2010). Crafting a social license to operate: A case study of Vancouver 2010's Cypress Olympic venue. *Event Management*, 14 (1), 17–36.

Pop, C. (2013). The modern Olympic Games – a globalised cultural and sporting event. *Procedia – Social and Behavioral Sciences*, 92, 728–734.

Porter, M. (1980). *Competitive Strategy: Techniques for Analyzing Industries and Competitors*. New York: The Free Press.

Porter, P. (1999). Mega-sports events as municipal investments: A critique of impact analysis, in J. L. Fizel, E. Gustafson and L. Hadley (eds), *Sports Economics: Current Research*. New York: Praeger Press.

Poynter, G. and MacRury, I. (eds) (2009). *Olympic Cities: 2012 and the Remaking of London*. Aldershot: Ashgate Publishing.

Prahalad, C. and Ramaswamy, V. (2004). Co-creation experiences: The next practice in value creation. *Journal of Interactive Marketing*, 18 (3), 5–14.

Prebensen, N. (2010). Value creation through stakeholder participation: A case study of an event in the high north. *Event Management*, 14 (1), 37–52.

Preda, P. and Watts, T. (2003). Improving the efficiency of sporting venues through capacity management: The case of the Sydney (Australia) Cricket Ground Trust. *Event Management*, 8 (2), 83–89.

Prentice, R. and Anderson, V. (2003). Festival as creative destination. *Annals of Tourism Research*, 30 (1), 7–30.

Presenza, A. and Sheehan, L. (2013). Planning tourism through sporting events. *International Journal of Event and Festival Management*, 4 (2), 125–139.

Preston, C. (2012). *Event Marketing: How to Successfully Promote Events, Festivals, Conventions, and Expositions*. Chichester: Wiley.

Preuss, H. (2004). *The Economics of Staging the Olympics: A Comparison of the Games 1972–2008*. Cheltenham: Edward Elgar.

Preuss, H. (2007). The conceptualisation and measurement of mega sport event legacies. *Journal of Sport and Tourism*, 12 (3/4), 207–228.

Preuss, H. (2009). Opportunity costs and efficiency of investments in mega sport events. *Journal of Policy Research in Tourism, Leisure and Events*, 1 (2), 131–140.

Preuss, H. (ed.) (2013). *Impact and Evaluation of Major Sport Events*. Abingdon: Routledge.

Prideaux, B., Moscardo, G. and Laws, E. (eds) (2006). *Managing Tourism and Hospitality Services: Theory and International Applications*. Wallingford: CABI.

Professional Convention Management Association (www.pcma.org, accessed 25 August 2015).

Pugh, C. and Wood, E. (2004). The strategic use of events within local government: A study of London Borough councils. *Event Management*, 9 (1/2), 61–71.

Pumar, E. (2005). Social networks and the institutionalization of the idea of sustainable development. *International Journal of Sociology and Social Policy*, 25 (1/2), 63–86.

Putnam, R. (2004). *Democracies in Flux: The Evolution of Social Capital in Contemporary Society*. New York: Oxford University Press.

Pyo, S., Cook, R. and Howell, R. (1988). Summer Olympic tourist market – learning from the past. *Tourism Management*, 9 (2), 137–144.

Quinn, B. (2000). Whose festival? Whose place? An insight into the production of cultural meanings in arts festivals turned festival attractions. In M. Robinson, P. Long, N. Evans and R. Sharpley (eds), *Expressions of Culture, Identity and Meaning in Tourism*. Sunderland: Centre for Travel and Tourism Research/Business Education Publishers.

Quinn, B. (2003). Symbols, practices and myth-making: Cultural perspectives on the Wexford Festival Opera. *Tourism Geographies*, 5 (3), 329–349.

Quinn, B. (2005). Arts festivals and the city. *Urban Studies*, 42 (5–6), 927–943.

Quinn, B. (2006). Problematising 'festival tourism': Arts festivals and sustainable development in Ireland. *Journal of Sustainable Tourism*, 14 (3), 288–306.

Quinn, B. (2010a). Arts festivals, urban tourism and cultural policy. *Journal of Policy Research in Tourism, Leisure and Events*, 2 (3), 264–279.

Quinn, B. (2010b). The European Capital Culture initiative and cultural legacy: An analysis of the cultural sector in the aftermath of Cork 2005. *Event Management*, 13 (4), 249–264.

Quinn, B. (2013). *Key Concepts in Event Management*. London: Sage.

Radbourne, J. (2002). Social intervention or market intervention? A problem for governments in promoting the value of the arts. *International Journal of Arts Management*, 5 (1), 50–61.

Raj, R. (2004). The behavioural aspects of financial management. In I. Yeoman, M. Robertson, J. Ali-Knight, S. Drummond and U. McMahon-Beattie (eds), *Festivals and Events Management*, pp. 273–285. Oxford: Elsevier.

Raj, R. and Morpeth, N. (eds) (2007). *Religious Tourism and Pilgrimage Festivals Management: An International Approach*. Wallingford: CABI.

Raj, R. and Musgrave, J. (2009). *Event Management and Sustainability*. Wallingford: CABI.

Raj, R., Walters, P. and Rashid, T. (2008). *Event Management: An Integrated and Practical Approach*. London: Sage.

Ralston, L., Ellis, D., Compton, D. and Lee, J. (2007). Staging memorable events and festivals: An integrated model of service and experience factors. *International Journal of Event Management Research*, 3 (2) (www.ijemr.org/docs/Vol3–2, accessed 25 August 2015).

Ralston, R., Lumsdon, L. and Downward, P. (2005). The third force in events tourism: Volunteers at the XVII Commonwealth Games. *Journal of Sustainable Tourism*, 13 (5), 504–519.

Ramshaw, G. and Hinch, T. (2006). Place identity and sport tourism: The case of the Heritage Classic Ice Hockey Event. *Current Issues in Tourism*, 9 (4–5), 399–418.

Rapoport, R., Rapoport, R. N. and Strelitz, Z. (1975). *Leisure and the Family Life Cycle*. London: Routledge & Kegan Paul.

Ravenscroft, N. and Mateucci, X. (2002). The festival as carnivalesque: Social governance and control at Pamplona's San Fermin fiesta. *Tourism Culture and Communication*, 4 (1), 1–15.

Raybould, M. (1998). Participant motivation in a remote fishing event. *Festival Management and Event Tourism*, 5 (4), 231–241.

Raybould, M., Mules, T., Fredline, E. and Tomljenovic, R. (2000). Counting the herd: Using aerial photography to estimate attendance at open events. *Event Management*, 6 (1), 25–32.

Reeves, K., Bird, G., James, L., Stichelbaut, B. and Bourgeois, J. (eds) (2015). *Battlefield Events: Landscape, Commemoration and Heritage*. Abingdon: Routledge.

Reicher, S., Stott, C., Cronin, P. and Adang, O. (2004). An integrated approach to crowd psychology and public order policing. *Policing: An International Journal of Police Strategies and Management*, 27 (4), 558–572.

Reid, G. (2006). The politics of city imaging: A case study of the MTV Europe Music Awards in Edinburgh '03. *Event Management*, 10 (1), 35–46.

Reid, S. (2007). Identifying social consequences of rural events. *Event Management*, 11 (1/2), 89–98.

Reisinger, Y. (2006). Travel/tourism: Spiritual experiences. In D. Buhalis and C. Costa (eds), *Tourism Business Frontiers: Consumers, Products and Industry*, pp. 148–167. Oxford: Elsevier.

Reunion Network (www.reunionfriendly.com, accessed 25 August 2015).

Reversté, F. and Izard, O. (2011). The role of social and intangible factors in cultural event planning in Catalonia. *International Journal of Event and Festival Management*, 2 (1), 37–53.

Rice, E. (1983). *The Grand Procession of Ptolemy Philadelphus*. Oxford: Oxford University Press.

Rich, K., Bean, C. and Apramian, Z. (2014). Boozing, brawling, and community building: Sport-facilitated community development in a rural Ontario community. *Leisure/Loisir*, 38 (1), 73–91.

Richards, G. (1996). European cultural tourism: Trends and future prospects. In G. Richards (ed.), *Cultural Tourism in Europe*, pp. 311–333. Wallingford: CABI.

Richards, G. (2007a). The festivalization of society or the socialization of festivals? The case of Catalunya. In G. Richards (ed.), *Cultural Tourism: Global and Local Perspectives*, pp. 257–269. New York: Haworth.

Richards, G. (2007b). Culture and authenticity in a traditional event: The views of producers, residents, and visitors in Barcelona. *Event Management*, 11 (1–2), 33–44.

Richards, G. and Palmer, R. (2010). *Eventful Cities: Cultural Management and Urban Revitalization*. Oxford: Butterworth-Heinemann.

Richards, G., de Brito, M. and Wilks, L. (2013). *Exploring the Social Impacts of Events*. Abingdon: Routledge.

Richards, G., Marques, L. and Mein, K. (eds) (2014). *Event Design: Social Perspectives and Practices*. Abingdon: Routledge.

Richards, P. and Ryan, C. (2004). The Aotearoa traditional Maori performing arts festival 1972–2000: A case study of cultural event maturation. *Journal of Tourism and Cultural Change*, 2 (2), 94–117.

Riggio, M. (2004). *Carnival: Culture in Action: The Trinidad Experience*. New York: Routledge.

van Riper, C. J., van Riper III, C., Kyle, G. T. and Lee, M. E. (2013). Understanding how social networking influences perceived satisfaction with conference experiences. *Annals of Leisure Research*, 16 (1), 103–114.

Ritchie, B., Sanders, D. and Mules, T. (2006). Televised events: Shaping destination images and perceptions of capital cities from the couch. In C. Arcodia, M. Whitford and C. Dicksen (eds), *Global Events Congress, Proceedings*, pp. 286–299. Brisbane: University of Queensland.

Ritchie, J. R. B. (1984). Assessing the impacts of hallmark events: Conceptual and research issues. *Journal of Travel Research*, 23 (1), 2–11.

Ritchie, J. R. B. (2000). Turning 16 days into 16 years through Olympic legacies. *Event Management*, 6 (2), 155–165.

Ritchie, J. R. B. and Beliveau, D. (1974). Hallmark events: An evaluation of a strategic response to seasonality in the travel market. *Journal of Travel Research*, 13 (2), 14–20.

Ritchie, J. R. B. and Lyons, M. (1990). Olympulse VI: A post-event assessment of resident reaction to the XV Olympic Winter Games. *Journal of Travel Research*, 28 (3), 14–23.

Ritchie, J. R. B. and Smith, B. (1991). The impact of a mega-event on host region awareness: A longitudinal study. *Journal of Travel Research*, 30 (1), 3–10.

Rittichainuwat, B. and Mair, J. (2011). Visitor attendance motivations at consumer travel exhibitions. *Tourism Management*, 33 (5), 1236–1244.

Rittichainuwat, B., Beck, J. and LaLopa, J. (2001). Understanding motivations, inhibitors, and facilitators of association members in attending international conferences. *Journal of Convention and Exhibition Management*, 3 (3), 45–62.

Robbe, D. (1999). *Expositions and Trade Shows*. New York: Wiley.

Roberts, K. (2006). *Leisure in Contemporary Society* (2nd edn). Wallingford: CABI.

Robertson, M. and Frew, E. (eds) (2007). *Events and Festivals: Current Trends and Issues*. Routledge (previously published as a special issue: *Managing Leisure*, 2007, 12 (2/3)).

Robertson, M., Rogers, P. and Leask, A. (2009). Progressing socio-cultural impact evaluation of events. *Journal of Policy Research in Tourism, Hospitality and Events*, 1 (2), 156–169.

Robinson, G. (1990). *Conflict and Change in the Countryside. Rural Society, Economy and Planning in the Developed World*. London: Belhaven Press.

Robinson, L., Chelladurai, P., Bodet, G. and Downward, P. (2013). *Routledge Handbook of Sport Management*. Abingdon: Routledge.

Robinson, M., Hums, M., Crow, R. and Philips, D. (2001). *Profiles of Sport Industry Professionals: The People Who Make the Games Happen*. Gaithersburg, MD: Aspen Publishers.

Robinson, M., Picard, D. and Long, P. (2004). Festival tourism: Producing, translating, and consuming expressions of culture(s). *Event Management*, 8 (4), 187–189.

Robinson, R. N. S. and Clifford, C. (2012). Authenticity and festival foodservice experiences. *Annals of Tourism Research*, 39 (2), 571–600.

Robinson, R. N. S. and Getz, D. (2013). Food enthusiasts and tourism: Exploring involvement dimensions. *Journal of Hospitality and Tourism Research* (first published on 26 September 2013 as doi:10.1177/1096348013503994).

Robinson, R. N. S. and Getz, D. (2014). Profiling potential food tourists: An Australian study. *British Food Journal*, 116 (4), 690–706.

Roche, M. (1994). Mega-events and urban policy. *Annals of Tourism Research*, 21 (1), 1–19.

Roche, M. (2000). *Mega-Events and Modernity: Olympics and Expos in the Growth of Global Culture*. London: Routledge.

Roche, M. (2006). Mega-events and modernity revisited: Globalization and the case of the Olympics. *Sociological Review*, 54 (2), 25–40.

Rockwell, D. and Mau, B. (2006). *Spectacle*. London: Phaidon Press.

Roemer, M. (2007). Ritual participation and social support in a major Japanese festival. *Journal for the Scientific Study of Religion*, 46 (2), 185–200.

Rogers, A. (2012). Geographies of the performing arts: Landscapes, places and cities. *Geography Compass*, 6 (2), 60–75.

Rogers, E. (1995). *Diffusion of Innovations*. New York: The Free Press.

Rogers, T. (1998). *Conferences: A Twenty-First Century Industry*. Harlow: Addison Wesley Longman.

Rogers, T. (2013). *Conferences and Conventions: A Global Industry* (3rd edn). Oxford: Butterworth-Heinemann.

Rojek, C. (1995). *Decentring Leisure*. London: Sage.

Rojek, C. (2005). *Leisure Theory: Principles and Practice*. Basingstoke: Palgrave Macmillan.

Rojek, C. and Urry, J. (eds) (1997). *Touring Cultures: Transformation of Travel and Theory*. London: Routledge.

Roman Empire (www.roman-empire.net, accessed 25 August 2015).

Rota, F. S. and Salone, C. (2014). Place-making processes in unconventional cultural practices. The case of Turin's contemporary art festival Paratissima. *Cities*, 40, 90–98.

Rotenberg, R. L. and McDonogh, G. W. (1993). *The Cultural Meaning of Urban Space*. Toronto: ABC-CLIO.

Rothman, R. A. (1978) Residents and transients: Community reaction to seasonal visitors. *Journal of Travel Research*, 16 (winter), 8–13.

Rothman, R. A., Donnelly, P. G. and Tower, J. K. (1979). Police departments in resort communities: Organisational adjustments to population undulation. *Leisure Sciences*, 2, 105–118.

Rowntree, B. S. and Lavers, G. R. (1951). *English Life and Leisure: A Social Study*. London: Longmans, Green.

Rozin, S. (2000). The amateurs who saved Indianapolis. *Business Week*, 10 April.

Runners World magazine (www.runnersworld.co.uk, accessed 25 August 2015).

Running USA. *The 2014 State of the Sport (Part I: Non-Traditional Running Events)* (www.runningusa.org, accessed 25 August 2015).

Ruperto, A. and Kerr, G. (2009). A study of community events held by not-for-profit organizations in Australia. *Journal of Nonprofit and Public Sector Marketing*, 21 (3), 298–308.

Russell, J. (2004). Celebrating culture, energising language, transforming society. In M. Robinson, *Conference Proceedings, Journeys of Expression III*. Centre for Tourism and Cultural Change, Sheffield-Hallam University (Compact Disc).

Russell, J. and Lanius, U. (1984). Adaptation level and the affective appraisal of environments. *Journal of Environmental Psychology*, 4 (2), 119–135.

Rutley, J. (n.d.). Security. In *Event Operations*, pp. 75–83. Port Angeles, WA: International Festivals and Events Association.

Ryan, C. (2000). Tourist experiences, phenomenographic analysis, post positivism and neural network software. *International Journal of Tourism Research*, 2 (2), 119–131.

Ryan, C. (2002). *The Tourist Experience* (2nd edn). London: Continuum.

Ryan, C. (2014). The experience of events. In S. J. Page and J. Connell (eds), *Routledge Handbook of Events*. Abingdon: Routledge.

Ryan, C. and Bates, C. (1995). A rose by any other name: The motivations of those opening their gardens for a festival. *Festival Management and Event Tourism*, 3 (2), 59–71.

Ryan, C. and Lockyer, T. (2002). Masters' Games – the nature of competitors' involvement and requirements. *Event Management*, 7 (4), 259–270.

Ryan, C. and Trauer, B. (2005). Sport tourist behaviour: The example of the Masters Games. In J. Higham (ed.), *Sport Tourism Destinations: Issues, Opportunities and Analysis*. Oxford: Elsevier.

Ryan, C., Smee, A., Murphy, S. and Getz, D. (1998). New Zealand events: A temporal and regional analysis. *Festival Management and Event Tourism*, 5 (1/2), 71–83.

Rybczynski, W. (1991). *Waiting for the Weekend*. New York: Viking.

Sadd, D. (2010). What is event-led regeneration? Are we confusing terminology or will London 2012 be the first games to truly benefit the local existing population? *Event Management*, 13 (4), 265–275.

Sadd, D. (2014). The future is virtual. In I. Yeoman, M. Robertson, U. McMahon-Beattie, E. Backer and K. Smith (eds), *The Future of Events and Festivals*, pp. 209–218. Abingdon: Routledge.

Sadd, D. and Jackson, C. (2006). Planning for resort regeneration. In M. Robertson (ed.), *Sporting Events and Event Tourism: Impacts, Plans and Opportunities*, pp. 43–64. Leisure Studies Association Publication 91. Eastbourne: The University of Brighton.

Saget, A. (2006). *The Event Marketing Handbook: Beyond Logistics and Planning*. Chicago, IL: Dearborn Trade Publishing.

Sahlins, M. (1976). *Culture and Practical Reason*. Chicago, IL: University of Chicago Press.

Saleh, F. and Ryan, C. (1993). Jazz and knitwear: Factors that attract tourists to festivals. *Tourism Management*, 14 (4), 289–297.

Saleh, F. and Wood, C. (1998). Motives and volunteers in multi-cultural events: The case of Saskatoon Folkfest. *Festival Management and Event Tourism*, 5 (1/2), 59–70.

Sandercock, L. (ed.) (1998). *Making the Invisible Visible: A Multicultural Planning History*. Berkeley, CA: University of California Press.

Santos, J. (2014). Brazil: An emerging power establishing itself in the world of international sports mega-events. *International Journal of the History of Sport*, 31 (10), 1312–1327.

Scannell, L. and Gifford, R. (2010). Defining place attachment: A tripartite organizing framework. *Journal of Environmental Psychology*, 30 (1), 1–10.

Schechner, R. (1988). *Performance Theory*. New York: Routledge.

Schechner, R. (2002, 2013 3rd edn). *Performance Studies: An Introduction*. Abingdon: Routledge.

Schein, E. (1985). *Organizational Culture and Leadership*. San Francisco, CA: Jossey-Bass.

Scheyvens, R. (2002). *Tourism for Development*. Harlow: Prentice-Hall.

Schlenker, K., Edwards, D. and Wearing, S. (2014). Volunteering and events. In S. J. Page and J. Connell (eds), *Routledge Handbook of Events*. Abingdon: Routledge.

Schlentrich, U. (2008). The MICE industry: Meetings, incentives, conventions and exhibitions. In B. Brotherton and R. Wood (eds), *The Sage Handbook of Hospitality Management*, pp. 400–420. London: Sage.

Schmidt, E. and Cohen, J. (2013). *The New Digital Age: Reshaping the Future of People, Nations and Business*. London: John Murray.

Schneider, I. and Backman, S. (1996). Cross-cultural equivalence of festival motivations: A study in Jordan. *Festival Management and Event Tourism*, 4 (3/4), 139–144.

Schnell, T. and Pali, S. (2013). Pilgrimage today: The meaning-making potential of ritual. *Mental Health, Religion & Culture*, 16 (9), 887–902.

Schultz, E. and Lavenda, R. (2005). *Cultural Anthropology: A Perspective on the Human Condition*. Oxford: Oxford University Press.

Schumpeter, J. (1975 [1942]). *Capitalism, Socialism and Democracy*. New York: Harper.

Schybergson, O. (2014). The generation raised on touchscreens will forever alter tech design. *Wired* (http://www.wired.com/2014/06/generation-moth/ accessed 30 June 2014).

Scotinform Ltd. (1991). *Edinburgh Festivals Study 1990–91: Visitor Survey and Economic Impact Assessment, Final Report*. Edinburgh: Scottish Tourist Board.

Scott, D. (1995). A comparison of visitors' motivations to attend three urban festivals. *Festival Management and Event Tourism*, 3 (3), 121–128.

Scott, J. (2000). *Social Network Analysis: A Handbook* (2nd edn). London: Sage.

Scott, W. (2001). *Institutions and Organizations*. Thousand Oaks, CA: Sage.

Seguin, B., Parent, M. M. and O'Reilly, N. (2010). Corporate support: A corporate social responsibility alternative to traditional event sponsorship. *International Journal of Sport Management and Marketing*, 7 (3), 202–222.

Selznick, P. (1957). *Leadership in Administration*. Evanston, IL: Row, Peterson.

Senge, P. (1990). *The Fifth Discipline: The Art and Practice of the Learning Organization*. New York: Doubleday.

Senge, P., Roberts, C., Ross, R., Smith, B. and Kleiner, A. (1994). *The Fifth Discipline Fieldbook: Strategies and Tools for Building a Learning Organization*. New York: Doubleday.

Severt, D., Wang, Y., Chen, P. and Breiter, D. (2007). Examining the motivation, perceived performance, and behavioural intentions of convention attendees: Evidence from a regional conference. *Tourism Management*, 28 (2), 399–408.

Severt, K., Fjelstul, J. and Breiter, D. (2013). Information communication technologies: Usages and preferences of generation Y students and meeting professionals. *Journal of Convention & Event Tourism*, 14 (2), 124–143.

Shackley, M. (2001). *Managing Sacred Sites: Service Provision and Visitor Experience*. London: Continuum.

Shaffer, M., Greer, A. and Mauboules, C. (2003). *Olympic Costs and Benefits*. Ottawa: Canadian Centre for Policy Alternatives Publication, February.

Sharpe, E. (2008). Festivals and social change: Intersections of pleasure and politics at a community music festival. *Leisure Sciences*, 30 (3), 217–234.

Shaw, G. and Williams, A. (2004). *Tourism and Tourism Spaces*. London: Sage.

Shedroff, N. (2001). *Experience Design*. Indianapolis, IN: New Riders.

Sheehan, A., Hubbard, S. and Popovich, P. (2000). Profiling the hotel and conference center meeting planner: A preliminary study. *Journal of Convention and Exhibition Management*, 2 (2/3), 11–25.

Sherwood, P. (2007). *A Triple Bottom Line Evaluation of the Impact of Special Events: The Development of Indicators*. Unpublished Ph.D. thesis, Victoria University, Melbourne.

Shibli, S. and the Sport Industry Research Centre (2002). *The 2002 Embassy World Snooker Championship, An Evaluation of the Economic Impact, Place Marketing Effects, and Visitors' Perceptions of Sheffield*. For Sheffield City Council.

Shinde, K. (2010). Managing festivals in pilgrimage sites: Emerging trends, opportunities, and challenges. *Event Management*, 14 (1), 53–67.

Shipway, R. and Fyall, A. (eds) (2012). *International Sports Events: Impacts, Experiences and Identities*. Abingdon: Routledge.

Shipway, R. and Jones, I. (2007). Running away from home: Understanding visitor experiences and behaviour at sport tourism events. *International Journal of Tourism Research*, 9 (5), 373–383.

Shipway, R. and Jones, I. (2008). The great suburban Everest: An 'Insiders' perspective on experiences at the 2007 Flora London Marathon. *Journal of Sport and Tourism*, 13 (1), 61–77.

Shone, A. and Parry, B. (2004). *Successful Event Management: A Practical Handbook* (2nd edn). London: Continuum.

Silvers, J. (2004). *Professional Event Coordination*. Hoboken, NJ: Wiley.

Silvers, J. (2008). *Risk Management for Meetings and Events*. Oxford: Butterworth-Heinemann.

Silvers, J., Bowdin, G., O'Toole, W. and Nelson, K. (2006). Towards an international event management body of knowledge (EMBOK). *Event Management*, 9 (4), 185–198.

Simon, L. (2014). *The Greatest Shows on Earth: A History of the Circus*. London: Reaktion Books, distributed by University of Chicago Press.

Simons, I. (2015). How to slay a dragon slowly: Applying slow principles to event design. In G. W. Richards, L. Marques and K. Mein (eds), *Event Design: Social Perspectives and Practices*, pp. 78–91. Abingdon: Routledge.

Singh, N., Racherla, P. and Hu, C. (2008). Knowledge mapping for safe festivals and events: An ontological approach. *Event Management*, 11 (1/2), 71–80.

Singh, R. (2006). Pilgrimage in Hinduism: Historical context and modern perspectives. In D. Timothy and D. Olsen (eds), *Tourism, Religion and Spiritual Journeys*, pp. 220–236. London and New York: Routledge.

Sit, J. K. and Birch, D. (2014). Entertainment events in shopping malls-profiling passive and active participation behaviors. *Journal of Consumer Behaviour*, 13 (6), 383–392.

Skinner, B. (1938). *The Behavior of Organisms*. New York: Appleton-Century-Crofts.

Skinner, B. and Rukavina, V. (2003). *Event Sponsorship*. New York: Wiley.

Slack, T. and Thurston, A. (2014). The social and commercial impact of sport, the role of sport management. *European Sport Management Quarterly*, 14 (5), 454–463.

Slater, L. (2010). 'Calling our spirits home': Indigenous cultural festivals and the making of a good life. *Cultural Studies Review*, 16 (1), 143–154.

Smidt-Jensen, S., Skytt, C. B. and Winther, L. (2009). The geography of the experience economy in Denmark: Employment change and location dynamics in attendance-based experience industries. *European Planning Studies*, 17 (6), 847–862.

Smith, A. (2008). Using major events to promote peripheral urban areas: Deptford and the 2007 Tour de France. In J. Ali-Knight, M. Robertson, A. Fyall and A. Ladkin (eds), *International Perspectives of Festivals and Events: Paradigms of Analysis*, pp. 3–19. Oxford: Butterworth-Heinemann.

Smith, A. (2009). Spreading the positive effects of major events to peripheral areas. *Journal of Policy Research in Tourism, Leisure and Events*, 1 (3), 231–246.

Smith, A. (2012). *Events and Urban Regeneration: The Strategic Use of Events to Revitalise Cities*. Abingdon: Routledge.

Smith, A. (2014). 'Borrowing' public space to stage major events: The Greenwich Park controversy. *Urban Studies*, 51 (2), 247–263.

Smith, A. (Forthcoming). *Events in the City: Using Public Spaces as Event Venues*. Abingdon: Routledge.

Smith, D. M. (1977). *Human Geography: A Welfare Approach*. Oxford: Edward Arnold.

Smith, D. M. (1979). *Where the Grass is Greener: Geographical Perspectives on Inequality*. London: Taylor & Francis.

Smith, E. and Mackie, D. (2000). *Social Psychology* (2nd edn). New York: Worth Publishers.

Smith, K., Lockstone-Binney, L., Holmes, K. and Baum, T. (eds) (2014). *Event Volunteering: International Perspectives on the Event Volunteering Experience*. Abingdon: Routledge.

Smith, M. (2005). Spotlight events, media relations, and place promotion: A case study. *Journal of Hospitality and Leisure Marketing*, 12 (1/2), 115–134.

Smith, M. (2006). Entertainment and new leisure tourism. In D. Buhalis and C. Costa (eds), *Tourism Business Frontiers: Consumers, Products and Industry*, pp. 220–227. Oxford: Elsevier.

Smith, S. and Costello, C. (2009). Culinary tourism: Satisfaction with a culinary event utilizing importance-performance grid analysis. *Journal of Vacation Marketing*, 15 (2), 99–110.

Smith, S. and Godbey, G. (1991). Leisure, recreation and tourism. *Annals of Tourism Research*, 18 (1), 85–100.

Snaith, T. and Haley, A. (1999). Residents' opinions of tourism development in the historic city of York, England. *Tourism Management*, 20 (5), 595–603.

Sociology (www.sociology.org.uk, accessed 25 August 2015).

Sofield, T. (1991). Sustainable ethnic tourism in the South Pacific: Some principles. *Journal of Tourism Studies*, 1 (3), 56–72.

Sofield, T. and Li, F. (1998). Historical methodology and sustainability: An 800-year-old festival from China. *Journal of Sustainable Tourism*, 6 (4), 267–292.

Sofield, T. and Sivan, A. (2003). From cultural festival to international sport – the Hong Kong Dragon Boat Races. *Journal of Sport Tourism*, 8 (1), 9–20.

Solberg, H. and Preuss, H. (2007). Major sport events and long-term tourism impacts. *Journal of Sport Management*, 21 (2), 213–234.

Solberg, H., Andersson, T. and Shibli, S. (2002). An exploration of the direct economic impacts from business travelers at world championships. *Event Management*, 7 (3), 151–164.

Solis, B. (2013). *What's The Future of Business: Changing the Way Businesses Create Experiences*. Hoboken, NJ: John Wiley & Sons.

Solomon, J. (2002). *An Insider's Guide to Managing Sporting Events*. Champaign, IL: Human Kinetics.

Sonder, M. (2003). *Event Entertainment and Production*. New York: Wiley.

Song, H. J., Ahn, Y. J. and Lee, C. K. (2014). Examining relationships among Expo experiences, service quality, satisfaction, and the effect of the Expo: The case of the Expo 2012 Yeosu Korea. *Asia Pacific Journal of Tourism Research*, 1–20.

Sousa-Mast, F. R., Reis, A. C., Gurgel, L. A. and Duarte, A. F. P. (2013). Are cariocas getting ready for the Games? Sport participation and the Rio de Janeiro 2016 Olympic Games. *Managing Leisure*, 18 (4), 331–335.

Soutar, G. and Mcleod, B. (1993). Residents' perceptions on impact of the America's Cup. *Annals of Tourism Research*, 20 (3), 571–582.

Spaaij, R. (2009). Personal and social change in and through sport: Cross-cutting themes. *Sport in Society*, 12 (9), 1265–1268.

Spencer, D. M. and Holecek, D. F. (2007). Basic characteristics of the fall tourism market. *Tourism Management*, 28 (2), 491–504.

Spiller, J. (2002). History of convention tourism. In K. Weber and K. Chon (eds), *Convention Tourism: International Research and Industry Perspectives*, pp. 3–20. Binghampton, NY: Haworth.

Spilling, O. (1998). Beyond intermezzo? On the long-term industrial impacts of mega-events: The case of Lillehammer 1994. *Festival Management and Event Tourism*, 5 (3), 101–122.

Spiropoulos, S., Gargalianos, D. and Sotiriadou, K. (2006). The 20th Greek festival of Sydney: A stakeholder analysis. *Event Management*, 9 (4), 169–183.

Sport Business (www.sportbusiness.com, accessed 25 August 2015).

Sports Business Market Research Inc. (2000–2006). *Sports Business Market Research Handbook*. New York: EPM Communications Inc.

Spracklen, K. (2014). Leisure studies education: Historical trends and pedagogical futures in the United Kingdom and beyond. *Journal of Hospitality, Leisure, Sport and Tourism Education*, 15 (1), 20–23.

Stadler, R. (2013). Power relations and the production of new knowledge within a Queensland Music Festival community cultural development project. *Annals of Leisure Research*, 16 (1), 87–102.

Stadler, R., Reid, S. and Fullagar, S. (2013). An ethnographic exploration of knowledge practices within the Queensland Music Festival. *International Journal of Event and Festival Management*, 4 (2), 90–106.

Stallworth, H., Harris, L. and Wise, G. (n.d.). *The Economics of Sustainability*. Watershed Academy Web, US EPA. (http://cfpub.epa.gov/watertrain/pdf/economics_of_sustainability.pdf, accessed 25 August 2015).

Stebbins, R. (1982). Serious leisure: A conceptual statement. *Pacific Sociological Review*, 25 (2), 251–272.

Stebbins, R. (1992). *Amateurs, Professionals, and Serious Leisure*. Montreal, QC: McGill-Queen's University Press.

Stebbins, R. (2001). *New Directions in the Theory and Research of Serious Leisure*. Lewiston, NY: Edwin Mellen.

Stebbins, R. (2006). *Serious Leisure: A Perspective for Our Time*. Somerset, NJ: Aldine Transaction Publications.

Stebbins, R. A. and Graham, M. (eds) (2004). *Volunteering as Leisure/Leisure as Volunteering: An International Assessment*. Wallingford: CABI.

Stein, A. and Evans, B. (2009). *An Introduction to the Entertainment Industry*. New York: Peter Lang.

Stevens, Q. and Shin, H. R. (2014). Urban festivals and local social space. *Planning Practice and Research*, 29 (1), 1–20.

Stockdale, J. E. (1985). *What is Leisure? An Empirical Analysis of the Concept of Leisure and the Role of Leisure in People's Lives*. London: Sports Council and Economic and Social Research Council.

Stokes, R. (2004). A framework for the analysis of events-tourism knowledge networks. *Journal of Hospitality and Tourism Management*, 11 (2), 108–123.

Stokes, R. (2008). Tourism strategy making: Insights to the events tourism domain. *Tourism Management*, 29 (2), 252–262.

Stokes, R. (2014). The private sector and events. In S. J. Page and J. Connell (eds), *Routledge Handbook of Events*, pp. 215–233. Abingdon: Routledge.

Stone, C. (2008). The British pop music festival phenomenon. In J. Ali-Knight, M. Robertson, A. Fyall and A. Ladkin (eds), *International Perspectives of Festivals and Events: Paradigms of Analysis*, pp. 205–224. Oxford: Butterworth-Heinemann.

Stott, C., Hutchison, P. and Drury, J. (2001). 'Hooligans' abroad? Inter-group dynamics, social identity and participation in collective 'disorder' at the 1998 World Cup Finals. *British Journal of Social Psychology*, 40 (3), 359–384.

Strigas, A. and Newton-Jackson, E. (2003). Motivating volunteers to serve and succeed: Design and results of a pilot study that explores demographics and motivational factors in sport volunteerism. *International Sports Journal*, 7 (1), 111–123.

Suarez-Villa, L. (2009). *Technocapitalism: A Critical Perspective on Technological Innovation and Corporatism*. Philadelphia: Temple University Press.

Sundbo, J. and Bærenholdt, J.O. (2007). Indledning: Den mangfoldige oplevelsesøkonomi. In J.O. Bærenholdt and J. Sundbo (eds), *Oplevelsesøkonomi: Produktion, forbrug, kultur*, pp. 9–25. Frederiksberg: Samfundslitteratur.

Supovitz, F. and Goldblatt, J. (2004). *The Sports Event Management and Marketing Handbook*. New York: Wiley.

Swart, K. (2005). Strategic planning – implications for the bidding of sport events in South Africa. *Journal of Sport & Tourism*, 10 (1), 37–46.

Syme, G., Shaw, B., Fenton, D. and Mueller, W. (eds) (1989). *The Planning and Evaluation of Hallmark Events*. Aldershot: Avebury.

Tapp, A. (2004). The loyalty of football fans – we'll support you evermore? *Journal of Database Marketing and Customer Strategy Management*, 11 (3), 203–215.

Tarlow, P. (2002). *Event Risk Management and Safety*. New York: Wiley.

Tassiopoulos, D. (ed.) (2000). *Event Management: A Professional and Developmental Approach*. Lansdowne: Juta Education.

Tassiopoulos, D. (2011). *New Tourism Ventures: An Entrepreneurial and Managerial Approach* (2nd edn). Claremont, South Africa: Juta and Company Ltd.

Taylor, P. and Gratton, C. (1988). The Olympic Games: An economic analysis. *Leisure Management*, 8 (3), 32–34.

Taylor, R. and Shanka, T. (2002). Attributes for staging successful wine festivals. *Event Management*, 7 (3), 165–175.

Taylor, R. and Shanka, T. (2008). Cause for event: Not-for-profit marketing through participant sports events. *Journal of Marketing Management*, 24 (9–10), 945–958.

Taylor, T. and Toohey, K. (2011). Ensuring safety at Australian sport event precincts: Creating securitised, sanitised and stifling spaces? *Urban Studies*, 48 (15), 3259–3275.

Teigland, J. (1996). *Impacts on Tourism from Mega-Events: The Case of Winter Olympic Games*. Sogndal: Western Norway Research Institute.

Tellstrom, R., Gustafsson, I. and Mossberg, L. (2006). Consuming heritage: The use of local food culture in branding. *Place Branding*, 2 (2), 130–143.

Testa, A. (2014). Rethinking the festival: Power and politics. *Method and Theory in the Study of Religion*, 26 (1), 44–73.

Theilmann, J. (1987). Medieval pilgrims and the origins of tourism. *Journal of Popular Culture*, 20 (4), 93–102.

Theodoraki, E. (2007). *Olympic Event Organization*. Oxford: Butterworth-Heinemann.

Theodoraki, E. (2009). Organisational communication on the intended and achieved impacts of the Athens 2004 Olympic Games. *Journal of Policy Research in Tourism, Hospitality and Events*, 1 (2), 141–155.

Thrane, C. (2002). Music quality, satisfaction, and behavioral intentions within a jazz festival context. *Event Management*, 7 (3), 143–150.

Thrift, N. (1977). *An Introduction to Time Geography*. Norwich: Catmog.

Tilden, F. (1957). *Interpreting our Heritage*. Chapel Hill, NC: University of North Carolina Press.

Timothy, D. and Boyd, S. (2006). Heritage tourism in the 21st century: Valued traditions and new perspectives. *Journal of Heritage Tourism*, 1 (1), 1–16.

Timothy, D. and Olsen, D. (eds) (2006). *Tourism, Religion and Spiritual Journeys*. London and New York: Routledge.

Tkaczynski, A. (2013). A stakeholder approach to attendee segmentation: A case study of an Australian Christian music festival. *Event Management*, 17 (3), 283–298.

Tkaczynski, A. and Rundle-Thiele, S. (2013). Understanding what really motivates attendance: A music festival segmentation study. *Journal of Travel & Tourism Marketing*, 30(6), 610–623.

Tkaczynski, A. and Stokes, R. (2010). FESTPERF: A service quality measurement scale for festivals. *Event Management*, 14 (1), 69–82.

Tohmo, T. (2005). Economic impacts of cultural events on local economies: An input-output analysis of the Kaustinen Folk Music Festival. *Tourism Economics*, 11 (3), 431–451.

Tomlinson, A. (2014). Olympic legacies: Recurrent rhetoric and harsh realities. *Contemporary Social Science*, 9 (2), 137–158.

Tomlinson, G. (1986). The staging of rural food festivals: Some problems with the concept of liminoid performances. Paper presented to the Qualitative Research Conference on Ethnographic Research, University of Waterloo.

Toohey, K. (2008). Terrorism, sport and public policy in the risk society. *Sport in Society*, 11 (4), 429–442.

Toohey, K. and Veal, T. (2007). *The Olympic Games: A Social Science Perspective*. Wallingford: CABI.

Trail, G. and James, J. (2001). The motivation scale for sport consumption: Assessment of the scale's psychometric properties. *Journal of Sport Behavior*, 24 (1), 109–127.

Traugott, M. (editor and translator) (1978). *Emile Durkheim on Institutional Analysis*. Chicago, IL: University of Chicago Press.

Travel Industry Association of America (1999). *Profile of Travelers Who Attend Sports Events*. Washington DC: TIAA.

Travel Industry Association of America and Smithsonian Magazine (2003). *The Historic/Cultural Traveler*, Washington, DC.

Travel and Tourism Research Association Canada Chapter (1986). *Conference Proceedings of the Canada Chapter*, Travel and Tourism Research Association, Edmonton.

Treuren, G. (2014). Enthusiasts, conscripts or instrumentalists? The motivational profiles of event volunteers. *Managing Leisure*, 19 (1), 51–70.

Tribe, J. (1997). The indiscipline of tourism. *Annals of Tourism Research*, 24 (3), 638–657.

Tribe, J. (2002). The philosophic practitioner. *Annals of Tourism Research*, 29 (2), 338–357.

Tribe, J. (2004). Knowing about tourism – epistemological issues. In L. Goodson and J. Phillimore (eds), *Qualitative Research in Tourism: Ontologies, Epistemologies and Methodologies*, pp. 46–62. London: Routledge.

Tribe, J. (2005). *The Economics of Recreation, Leisure and Tourism* (3rd edn). Oxford: Elsevier.

Tribe, J. (2006). The truth about tourism. *Annals of Tourism Research*, 33 (2), 360–381.

Tribe, J. (2008). Tourism: A critical business. *Journal of Travel Research*, 46 (3), 245–255.

Tribe, J. (ed.) (2009). *Philosophical Issues in Tourism*. Bristol: Channel View.

Tribe, J. (2014). The curriculum: A philosophic practice? In D. Dredge, D. Airey and M. Gross (eds), *The Routledge Handbook of Tourism and Hospitality Education*. Abingdon: Routledge.

Tsouros, A. and Efstathiou, P. (eds) (2007). *Mass Gatherings and Public Health: The Experience of the Athens 2004 Olympics*. Copenhagen: World Health Organization, Europe.

Tum, J. (2014). Managing uncertainty: (Re)conceptualising aspects for operations for events. In S. J. Page and J. Connell (eds), *Routledge Handbook of Events*, pp. 212–312. Abingdon: Routledge.

Tum, J., Norton, P. and Wright, J. (2006). *Management of Event Operations*. Oxford: Butterworth-Heinemann/Elsevier.

Turco, D. (1995). Measuring the tax impacts of an international festival: Justification for government sponsorship. *Festival Management and Event Tourism*, 2 (3/4), 191–195.

Turco, D., Riley, R. and Swart, K. (2002). *Sport Tourism*. Morgantown, WV: Fitness Information Technology Inc.

Turner, E. (2012). *Communitas: The Anthropology of Collective Joy*. Basingstoke: Palgrave Macmillan.

Turner, J. (1997). The policy process. In B. Axford, G. Browning, R. Huggins, B. Rosamond and J. Turner (eds), *Politics: An Introduction*, pp. 409–439. London: Routledge.

Turner, V. (1969). *The Ritual Process: Structure and Anti-Structure*. New York: Aldine de Gruyter.

Turner, V. (1974). Liminal to liminoid, in play, flow and ritual: An essay in comparative symbology. In E. Norbeck (ed.), *The Anthropological Study of Human Play*. Rice University Studies, 60 (3), 53–92.

Turner, V. (1979). *Process, Performance, and Pilgrimage: A Study in Comparative Symbology*. New Delhi: Concept.

Turner, V. (ed.) (1982). *Celebration: Studies in Festivity and Ritual*. Washington DC: Smithsonian Institution Press.

Turner, V. and Turner, E. (1978). *Image and Pilgrimage in Christian Culture*. New York: Columbia University Press.

Turney, M. (www.nku.edu/~turney/, accessed on 25 August 2015).

Tyrrell, T. and Johnston, R. (2001). A framework for assessing direct economic impacts of tourist events: Distinguishing origins, destinations, and causes of expenditures. *Journal of Travel Research*, 40 (1), 94–100.

Tyrrell, T. and Johnston, R. (2014). A spatial extension to a framework for assessing direct economic impacts of tourist events. In S. J. Page and J. Connell (eds), *The Routledge Handbook of Events*, pp. 329–346. Abingdon: Routledge.

Tzelepi, M. and Quick, S. (2002). The Sydney organizing committee for the Olympic Games (SOCOG) 'Event Leadership' training course – an effectiveness evaluation. *Event Management*, 7 (4), 245–257.

UK Health and Safety Executive (1999). *The Event Safety Guide* (www.hsebooks.com, accessed 25 August 2015).

UK Institute for Volunteering (www.ivr.org.uk, accessed 25 August 2015).

UK National Outdoor Events Association (www.noea.org.uk, accessed 25 August 2015).

University of Toronto (www.mcluhan.utoronto, accessed 25 August 2015).

Unruh, D. (1980). The nature of social worlds. *Pacific Sociological Review*, 23 (3), 271–296.

Urry, J. (1990). *The Tourist Gaze: Leisure and Travel in Contemporary Societies*. London: Sage.

Urry, J. (1995). *Consuming Places*. London: Routledge.

Urry, J. (2002). *The Tourist Gaze: Leisure and Travel in Contemporary Societies* (2nd edn). London: Sage.

US Department of Labor (2005). *Volunteering in the United States, 2005* (www.bls.gov/news.release/volun. nr0.htm, accessed 25 August 2015).

Uysal, M. and Li, X. (2008). Trends and critical issues in festival and event motivation. In A. Aktas, M. Kesgin, E. Cengiz and E. Yenidip (eds.), *International Cultural and Event Tourism: Issues and Debates*, pp. 10–20. Ankara, Turkey: Detay Yayincilik.

Uysal, M., Gahan, L. and Martin, B. (1993). An examination of event motivations: A case study. *Festival Management and Event Tourism*, 1 (1), 510.

Van der Auwera, S. and Schramme, A. (2014). Commemoration of the Great War: A global phenomenon or a national agenda? *Journal of Conflict Archaeology*, 9 (1), 3–15.

Van der Wagen, L. (2006). *Human Resource Management for Events: Managing the Event Workforce*. Oxford: Butterworth-Heinemann.

Van der Wagen, L. (2008). *Event Management for Tourism, Cultural, Business and Sporting Events* (3rd edn). Frenchs Forest, NSW: Pearson Education Australia.

Van der Wagen, L. and White, L. (2014). *Human Resource Management for the Event Industry*. Abingdon: Routledge.

Vanhamme, J. and Snelders, D. (2001). The role of surprise in satisfaction judgments. *Journal of Consumer Satisfaction, Dissatisfaction and Complaining Behavior*, 14, 27–45.

Vanhove, D. and Witt, S. (1987). Report of the English-speaking group on the conference theme. *Revue de Tourisme*, 4, 10–12.

Vanwynsberghe, R., Surborg, B. and Wyly, E. (2013). When the games come to town: Neoliberalism, mega-events and social inclusion in the Vancouver 2010 Winter Olympic Games. *International Journal of Urban and Regional Research*, 37 (6), 2074–2093.

Van Winkle, C. and Backman, K. (2009). Examining visitor mindfulness at a cultural event. *Event Management*, 12 (3/4), 163–169.

Vargo, S. L. and Lusch, R. F. (2004). Evolving to a new dominant logic for marketing. *Journal of Marketing*, 68 (1), 1–17.

Vargo, S. L. and Lusch, R. F. (2006). Service-dominant logic: What it is, what it is not, what it might be. In S. L. Vargo and R. F. Lusch (eds), *The Service-Dominant Logic of Marketing: Dialog, Debate, and Directions*, pp. 43–56. Armonk, NY: M. E. Sharpe.

Vargo, S. L. and Lusch, R. F. (2008). Service-dominant logic: Continuing the evolution. *Journal of the Academy of Marketing Science*, 36 (1), 1–10.

Vaughan, R. (1979). *Does a Festival Pay? A Case Study of the Edinburgh Festival in 1976*. Tourism Recreation Research Unit, Working Paper 5, University of Edinburgh.

Veal, A. (2006). *Research Methods for Leisure and Tourism: A Practical Guide* (3rd edn). Harlow: Prentice Hall.

Veal, A. (2010). *Leisure, Sport and Tourism: Politics, Policy and Planning* (3rd edn). Wallingford: CABI.

Veal, A. (2011). *Research Methods for Leisure and Tourism: A Practical Guide* (4th edn). Harlow: Prentice Hall.

Veal, A. and Burton, C. (2014). *Research Methods for Arts and Event Management*. Harlow: Pearson.

Veal, A. and Darcy, S. (2014). *Research Methods in Sport Studies and Sport Management, A Practical Guide*. Abingdon: Routledge.

Veblen, T. (1899). *The Theory of the Leisure Class* (Penguin twentieth-century classics, 1994). New York: Penguin Books.

Verhoven, P., Wall, D. and Cottrell, S. (1998). Application of desktop mapping as a marketing tool for special events planning and evaluation: A case study of the Newport News Celebration in Lights. *Festival Management and Event Tourism*, 5 (3), 123–130.

Victorian Auditor General (2007). *State Investment in Major Events*. Victorian Government Printer, Victoria, Australia, May.

Voss, T. (2001). Institutions. In *International Encyclopedia of the Social and Behavioral Sciences*, pp. 7561–7566. Oxford: Elsevier.

Vroom, V. (1964). *Work and Motivation*. New York: Wiley.

Waitt, G. (2004). A critical examination of Sydney's 2000 Olympic Games. In I. Yeoman, M. Robertson, J. Ali-Knight, S. Drummond and U. McMahon-Beattie (eds), *Festivals and Events Management*, pp. 391–408. Oxford: Elsevier.

Waitt, G. and Stapel, C. (2011). 'Fornicating on floats'? The cultural politics of the Sydney Mardi Gras Parade beyond the metropolis. *Leisure Studies*, 30 (2), 197–216.

Walker, G. and Virden, R. (2005). Constraints on outdoor recreation. In E. Jackson (ed.), *Constraints to Leisure*, pp. 201–219. State College, PA: Venture Publishing.

Walker, G., Deng, J. and Dieser, R. (2005). Culture, self-construal, and leisure theory and practice. *Journal of Leisure Research*, 37 (1), 77–99.

Walker, R. A. (2013). Fill/flash/memory: A history of flash mobs. *Text and Performance Quarterly*, 33 (2), 115–132.

Walle, A. (1994). The festival life cycle and tourism strategies: The case of the Cowboy Poetry Gathering. *Festival Management and Event Tourism*, 2 (2), 85–94.

Walmsley, D. J., Boskovic, R. M. and Pigram, J. J. (1983). Tourism and crime: An Australian perspective. *Journal of Leisure Research*, 15 (2), 136–155.

Wang, N. (1999). Rethinking authenticity in tourism experience. *Annals of Tourism Research*, 26 (2), 349–370.

Wang, P. and Gitelson, R. (1988). Economic limitations of festivals and other hallmark events. *Leisure Industry Report*, August: 4–5.

Wanhill, S. (2006). Some economics of staging festivals: The case of opera festivals. *Tourism, Culture and Communication*, 6 (2), 137–149.

Wann, D. (1995). Preliminary validation of the sport fan motivation scale. *Journal of Sport and Social Issues*, 19 (4), 377–396.

Wann, D. (1997). *Sport Psychology*. Upper Saddle River, NJ: Prentice Hall.

Wann, D. and Branscombe, N. (1993). Sport fans: Measuring degree of identification with their team. *International Journal of Sport Psychology*, 24 (1), 1–17.

Wann, D., Grieve, F., Zapalac, R. and Pease, D. (2008). Motivational profiles of sport fans of different sports. *Sport Marketing Quarterly*, 17 (1), 6–19.

Wann, D., Royalty, J. and Rochelle, A. (2002). Using motivation and team identification to predict sport fans' emotional responses to team performance. *Journal of Sport Behavior*, 25 (2), 207–216.

Wann, D., Schrader, M. and Wilson, A. (1999). Sport fan motivation: Questionnaire validation, comparisons by sport, and relationship to athletic motivation. *Journal of Sport Behaviour*, 22 (1), 114–139.

Warf, B. (2008). *Time–Space Compression: Historical Geographies*. Abingdon: Routledge.

Waterman, S. (1998). Carnivals for elites? The cultural politics of arts festivals. *Progress in Human Geography*, 22 (1), 54–74.

Waters, H. (1939). *History of Fairs and Expositions*. London, ON: Reid Brothers.

Watson, R. and Yip, P. (2011). How many were there when it mattered? *Significance*, 8 (3), 104–107.

Watson, R., Tucker, L. and Drury, S. (2013). Can we make a difference? Examining the transformative potential of sport and active recreation. *Sport in Society*, 16 (10), 1233–1247.

Watt, J. (2014). Brazil 2014: World Cup where politics and social media invaded the pitch. *The Guardian* (http://www.theguardian.com/football/world-cup-2014 accessed 15 September 2014).

Weber, K. and Chon, K. (2002). *Convention Tourism: International Research and Industry Perspectives*. Binghampton, NY: Haworth.

Weber, K. and Ladkin, A. (2005). Trends affecting the convention industry in the 21st century. *Journal of Convention and Event Tourism*, 6 (4), 47–63.

Weed, M. (2008). *Olympic Tourism*. Oxford: Butterworth-Heinemann.

Weed, M. (2012). *Olympic Tourism* (2nd edn). Oxford: Butterworth-Heinemann.

Weed, M. and Bull, C. (2004). *Sports Tourism: Participants, Policy and Providers*. Oxford: Elsevier.

Weed, M. and Dowse, S. (2009). A missed opportunity waiting to happen? The social legacy potential of the London 2012 Paralympic Games. *Journal of Policy Research in Tourism, Hospitality and Events*, 1 (2), 170–174.

Weidenfeld, A., Butler, R. and Williams, A. (eds) (2015). *Visitor Attrations and Events: Locations and Linkages*. Abingdon: Routledge.

Weller, S. (2013). Consuming the city: Public fashion festivals and the participatory economies of urban spaces in Melbourne. *Urban Studies*, 50 (14), 2853–2868.

Weppler, K. and McCarville, R. (1995). Understanding organizational buying behaviour to secure sponsorship. *Festival Management and Event Tourism*, 2 (3/4), 139–148.

Westerbeek, H., Turner, P. and Ingerson, L. (2002). Key success factors in bidding for hallmark sporting events. *International Marketing Review*, 19 (3), 303–322.

White, L. (2011). The Sydney 2000 Olympic Games bid: Marketing indigenous Australia for the millennium games. *International Journal of the History of Sport*, 28 (10), 1447–1462.

White, L. (2013). Cathy Freeman and Australia's indigenous heritage: A new beginning for an old nation at the Sydney 2000 Olympic Games. *International Journal of Heritage Studies*, 19 (2), 153–170.

Whitfield, J. (2009). Why and how UK visitor attractions diversify their product to offer conference and event facilities. *Journal of Convention and Event Tourism*, 10, 72–88.

Whitfield, J. and Dioko, L. (2011). Discretionary corporate social responsibility: Introducing the 'Greener Venue'. *International Journal of Event and Festival Management*, 2 (2), 170–183.

Whitford, M. (2004a). Regional development through domestic and tourist event policies: Gold Coast and Brisbane, 1974–2003. *UNLV Journal of Hospitality, Tourism and Leisure Science*, 2, 1–24.

Whitford, M. (2004b). Event public policy development in the Northern Sub-Regional Organisation of Councils, Queensland Australia: Rhetoric or realisation? *Journal of Convention and Event Tourism*, 6 (3), 81–99.

Whitford, M. and Dickson, C. (eds), *Global Events Congress Proceedings*, pp. 268–285. Brisbane: University of Queensland.

Whitford, M. and Ruhanen, L. (2013). Indigenous festivals and community development: A sociocultural analysis of an Australian indigenous festival. *Event Management*, 17 (1), 49–61.

Whitson, D. and Macintosh, D. (1996). The global circus: International sport, tourism, and the marketing of cities. *Journal of Sport and Social Issues*, 20 (3), 275–295.

Wickham, T. and Kerstetter, D. (2000). The relationship between place attachment and crowding in an event setting. *Event Management*, 6 (3), 167–174.

Wicks, B. (1995). The business sector's reaction to a community special event in a small town: A case study of the Autumn on Parade Festival. *Festival Management and Event Tourism*, 2 (3/4), 177–183.

Wicks, B. and Fesenmaier, D. (1993). A comparison of visitor and vendor perceptions of service quality at a special event. *Festival Management and Event Tourism*, 1 (1), 1926.

Wicks, B. and Fesenmaier, D. (1995). Market potential for special events: A midwestern case study. *Festival Management and Event Tourism*, 3 (1), 25–31.

Wikipedia, The Free Encyclopedia (2010) G-20 Toronto Summit Protests (www.wikipedia.org, accessed 25 August 2015).

Wikipedia, The Free Encyclopedia (2010) Performance Studies (www.wikipedia.org, accessed 25 August 2015).

Williams, K., Laing, J. and Frost, W. (2013). *Fashion, Design and Events*. Abingdon: Routledge.

Williams, P. and Harrison, L. (1988). *A Framework for Marketing Ethnocultural Communities and Festivals*. Unpublished report to the Secretary of State Multiculturalism, Ottawa.

Williams, P., Dossa, K. and Tompkins, L. (1995). Volunteerism and special event management: A case study of Whistler's Men's World Cup of Skiing. *Festival Management and Event Tourism*, 3 (2), 83–95.

Williams, P. W. and Elkhashab, A. (2012). Leveraging tourism social capital: The case of the 2010 Olympic tourism consortium. *International Journal of Event and Festival Management*, 3 (3), 317–334.

Wilson, J. and Udall, L. (1982). *Folk Festivals: A Handbook for Organization and Management*. Knoxville, TN: The University of Tennessee Press.

Wood, D. and Gray, B. (1991). Toward a comprehensive theory of collaboration. *Journal of Applied Behavioural Science*, 27 (1), 3–22.

Wood, E. (2004). Marketing information for the events industry. In I. Yeoman, M. Robertson, J. Ali-Knight, S. Drummond and U. McMahon-Beattie (eds), *Festival and Events Management: An International Arts and Culture Perspective*, pp. 130–157. Oxford: Elsevier.

Wooten, M. and Norman, W. (2008a). Interpreting and managing special events and festivals. In A. Woodside and D. Martin (eds), *Managing Tourism: Analysis, Behavior and Strategy*, pp. 197–217. Wallingford: CABI.

Wooten, M. and Norman, W. (2008b). Differences in arts festival visitors based on level of past experience. *Event Management*, 11 (3), 109–120.

Word Spy (www.wordspy.com, accessed 25 August 2015).

World Future Society (2014). *Outlook 2015*. (www.wfs.org, accessed 25 August 2015).

Wuensch, U. (2008). *Facets of Contemporary Event Communication – Theory and Practice for Event Success*. Bad Honnef, Germany: K. H. Bock.

Xiao, H. and Smith, S. (2004). Residents' perceptions of Kitchener-Waterloo Oktoberfest: An inductive analysis. *Event Management*, 8 (3), 161–175.

Xie, P. (2003). The bamboo-beating dance in Hainan, China. Authenticity and commodification. *Journal of Sustainable Tourism*, 11 (1), 5–16.

Xie, P. (2004). Visitors' perceptions of authenticity at a rural heritage festival: A case study. *Event Management*, 8 (3), 151–160.

Xie, P. and Smith, S. (2000). Improving forecasts for world's fair attendance: Incorporating income effects. *Event Management*, 6 (1), 15–23.

Xue, K., Chen, X. and Yu, M. (2012). Can the World Expo change a city's image through foreign media reports? *Public Relations Review*, 38 (5), 746–754.

Yang, J., Zeng, X. and Gu, Y. (2010). Local residents' perceptions of the impact of 2010 Expo. *Journal of Convention and Event Tourism*, 11 (3), 161–175.

Yeoman, I., Robertson, M., Ali-Knight, J., Drummond, S. and McMahon-Beattie, U. (eds) (2004). *Festival and Events Management: An International Arts and Culture Perspective*. Oxford: Elsevier.

Yeoman, I., Robertson, M., McMahon-Beattie, U., Backer, E. and Smith, K. (eds) (2014). *The Future of Events and Festivals*. Abingdon: Routledge.

Yin, R. (2014). *Case study Research: Design and Methods* (5th edn). Beverly Hills, CA: Sage.

Yolal, M., Cetinel, F. and Uysal, M. (2009). An examination of festival motivation and perceived benefits relationship: Eskisehir International Festival. *Journal of Convention and Event Tourism*, 10 (4), 276–291.

Yoon, S., Spencer, D., Holecek, D. and Kim, D. (2000). A profile of Michigan's festival and special event tourism market. *Event Management*, 6 (1), 33–44.

Young, B., Bennett, A. and Seguin, B. (2015). Masters sport perspectives. In M. Parent and J.-L. Chappelet (eds), *Routledge Handbook of Sports Event Management*, pp. 139–162. Abingdon: Routledge.

Young, H. (1998). *Individual Strategy and Social Structure*. Princeton, NJ: Princeton University Press.

Yu, Y. and Turco, D. (2000). Issues in tourism event economic impact studies: The case of Albuquerque International Balloon Fiesta. *Current Issues in Tourism*, 3 (2), 138–149.

Zaichkowsky, J. (1985). Measuring the involvement construct. *Journal of Consumer Research*, 12 (3), 341–352.

Zelinsky, W. (1994). Conventionland USA: The geography of a latterday phenomenon. *Annals of the Association of American Geographers*, 84 (1), 68–86.

Zeppel, H. (1999). *Aboriginal tourism in Australia: A research bibliography*. Queensland, Australia: CRC for Sustainable Tourism.

Ziakis, V. (2010). Understanding an event portfolio: The uncovering of interrelationships, synergies, and leveraging opportunities. *Journal of Policy Research in Tourism, Leisure and Events*, 2 (2), 144–164.

Ziakas, V. (2013). *Event Portfolio Planning and Management: A Holistic Approach*. Abingdon: Routledge.

Ziakas, V. (2014). Planning and leveraging event portfolios: Towards a holistic theory. *Journal of Hospitality Marketing and Management*, 23 (3), 327–356.

Ziakas, V. and Boukas, N. (2013). Extracting meanings of event tourist experiences: A phenomenological exploration of Limassol carnival. *Journal of Destination Marketing and Management*, 2 (2), 94–107.

Ziakas, V. and Boukas, N. (2014). Contextualizing phenomenology in event management research: Deciphering the meaning of event experiences. *International Journal of Event and Festival Management*, 5 (1), 56–73.

Ziakas, V. and Costa, C. (2010a). 'Between theatre and sport' in a rural event: Evolving unity and community development from the inside-out. *Journal of Sport and Tourism*, 15 (1), 7–26.

Ziakas, V. and Costa, C. (2010b). Explicating inter-organizational linkages of a host community's events network. *International Journal of Event and Festival Management*, 1 (2), 132–147.

Zuckerman, M. (1979). *Sensation Seeking: Beyond the Optimal Level of Arousal*. Hillsdale, NJ: LEA.

Zuzanek, J., Robinson, J. P. and Iwasaki, Y. (1998). The relationships between stress, health, and physically active leisure as a function of life-cycle. *Leisure Sciences*, 20 (4), 253–275.

Index